Hospitality Management Accounting

Revised Printing

Hospitality Management Accounting

SEVENTH EDITION
REVISED PRINTING

Michael M. Coltman
Martin G. Jagels

JOHN WILEY & SONS, INC.
New York • Chichester • Weinheim • Brisbane • Singapore • Toronto

Copyright © 2001 by John Wiley & Sons, Inc. All rights reserved.

Published simultaneously in Canada.

This publication is designed to provide accurate and authoritative information in regard to the subject matter covered. It is sold with the understanding that the publisher is not engaged in rendering professional services. If professional advice or other expert assistance is required, the services of a competent professional person should be sought.

Library of Congress Cataloging-in-Publication Data

Coltman, Michael M., 1930-
    Hospitality management accounting / by Michael Coltman and Martin Jagels.—7th ed.
        p.   cm.
    Includes index.
    ISBN 0-471-20953-8 (alk.paper)
        1. Hotels—Accounting. 2. Taverns (Inns)—Accounting. 3. Food service—Accounting.
    4. Managerial accounting. I. Jagels, Martin. II. Title.

HF5686.H75 C53 2000
657'.837—dc21
                                                                                    00-043453

Printed in the United States of America

10 9 8 7 6 5 4 3 2 1

Contents

v

Preface

Welcome to the seventh edition of *Hospitality Management Accounting*! Your studies of the hospitality, tourism, and service industries are taking place during a time of amazing growth and success. Around the world, new operations are being created, while established companies continue to expand their products and services, which in turn enhances competition. This increasing growth and competition affects not only hospitality operators, but also the potential customers they seek to serve.

Across the industry, hospitality operators and managers are relying on managerial accounting techniques to help them succeed and thrive in this expanding environment. The industry as a whole is becoming more cost and profit conscious, while potential customers are placing increased importance on price, quality, and the level of services they receive. Hospitality industry providers have begun focusing greater attention on increasing their revenue, minimizing costs, and maximizing profit levels, without affecting the quality of service they can provide, relative to the cost of providing those services.

Hospitality Management Accounting continues to evolve with the industry, to give students a solid understanding of how they can use managerial accounting skills in their future careers. This text makes no attempt to cover the detailed concepts and mechanics of financial accounting, or the detailed procedures of bookkeeping. The scope and content is designed for the student who is taking courses that are related to the managerial aspects of the hospitality industry and are by their nature accounting oriented. Although most of the chapters are quite complete, they are not, nor are they meant to be, exhaustive. This book is introductory in nature and it is hoped that the reader will be prompted to independently explore some of the topics in other books where they are discussed in greater detail.

The book is designed to give students both a conceptual understanding and a practical use of internal accounting information by using structured analysis techniques. The structure and sequence of topics in the book was carefully planned to serve as a basis for developing managerial accounting procedures, quantitative analysis techniques, and reporting concepts. For the seventh edition, all information has been updated and several chapters have been revised significantly.

Chapter 1, "Accounting Review" has been revised to provide a condensed view of basic accounting concepts. Coverage of the fundamental accounting equation has been expanded to improve student understanding, and emphasize the equation's purpose, how changes to the equation are developed, recorded, and implemented, and how those changes affect the basic accounting equation. Straight-line depreciation is discussed in general terms. A detailed discussion of depreciation methods appears in Chapter 2. The concept of adjusting entries has been expanded, as well as the discussion of the accounting cycle of a profit-oriented business operation.

In Chapter 2, "Understanding Financial Statements," greater emphasis is given to creating an income statement, statement of ownership equity, and balance sheet. The section on inventory control methods has been revised to improve conceptual understanding, with greater emphasis placed on perpetual inventory. The section on the Statement of Cash Flows has been removed from Chapter 2 and incorporated into Chapter 10.

In Chapter 3, "Analysis and Interpretation of Financial Statements," the discussion and illustrations of comparative balance sheets and comparative income statements has been improved and expanded. Several supporting illustrations have also been revised.

The discussion of liquidity ratios in Chapter 4, "Ratio Analysis," has been supplemented with enhanced illustrations showing how changes in the current accounts affect the current ratio as well as working capital. The illustrations have been expanded to support the discussion of quick ratio and receivable ratios. Since trends in credit sales are rapidly changing towards credit card sales from accounts receivable or house accounts, a new current ratio covering credit card receivables has been added and discussed in detail in conjunction with accounts receivable.

The text and illustrations in Chapter 6, "The Bottom Up Approach to Pricing" have been revised considerably to better explain the nature and purpose of this pricing method, and how it can be compared to a completed income statement. Greater emphasis has been placed on the techniques to determine operating income (income before tax) and net income (after tax).

In Chapter 8, "The CVP Approach to Decisions," more emphasis has been placed on the relationship between breakeven sales volume and breakeven unit sales. Breakeven is discussed in detail to ensure that students have a clear understanding of this concept before going on to learn how added cost functions are brought in to complete a profit volume analysis.

Chapter 10, "Statement of Cash Flows and Working Capital Analysis" contains a new, detailed discussion of the statement of cash flows, indirect method, with supporting illustrations. By covering the statement of cash flows and working capital sequentially, students can follow a clear progression through the chapter and see how key operating, financial, and equity accounts are used to develop a statement of cash flows and a working capital analysis. The discussion of working capital analysis has been revised considerably, and more attention has been given to the link between the statement of cash flows and the working capital analysis.

While they are not essential components of a managerial accounting course, Chapter 13 "Feasibility Studies—An Introduction" and Chapter 14 "Financial Goals and Information Systems" can be used in class as supplemental chapters at the discretion of the professor.

Wherever new material has been incorporated within the text, exercises and problems have been added to test student assimilation of the new material. The book contains several pedagogical features in every chapter to help students grasp the concepts and techniques presented:

The *Introductions* introduce the key topics that will be presented in the chapter.

Chapter objectives list the specific skills, procedures, and techniques that students are expected to master after reading the material.

Key terms are repeated in the margin of the text, so that students can easily familiarize themselves with the language of managerial accounting and develop a working vocabulary.

Most chapters end with a paragraph called *Computer Applications* that explains how managers and accountants are using computers to process accounting information and improve managerial decision making.

The *Summary* concisely pulls together the many different points covered in the chapter to help trigger students' memories.

Discussion Questions ask students to summarize or explain important concepts, procedures, and terminology.

Each chapter contains an *Ethics Situation* that challenges students' decision-making abilities and teaches them to look beyond the numbers and consider how accounting information can be used to impact other areas of a hospitality operation.

A new collection of *Exercises* ties together concepts from each chapter.

Problems test students' basic accounting skills and the application of concepts. Each chapter has been upgraded to contain short exercises and problems.

The *Case* at the end of each chapter combines accounting applications and conceptual analysis using a business example. The case is ongoing throughout the book and builds on the concepts learned in previous chapters. Thus, each chapter's case will build on or rely on information a student derived in a preceding chapter's case as a starting point or as a source of supplemental information.

The appendix "Computers in Hospitality Management" has been revised and updated.

The *Glossary* summarizes the key terms presented in the text.

A **Student Workbook** (0-471-40031-9) is available to accompany this text. It contains an outline summary of the key topics in each chapter, a short series of word completion, true/false, and multiple-choice questions, short exercises, and comprehensive problems. The word completion, true/false, and multiple-choice questions are oriented towards a conceptual understanding of the chapter material, while the short exercises and comprehensive are practical and application oriented. Solutions to these questions and problems are included after each chapter. Following a three-chapter sequential block, the workbook contains a 3-chapter self-review test, with answers included, so students can gauge their progress through the course.

An **Instructor's Manual** (0-471-36929-2) is also available. It contains detailed solutions to each chapter's exercises, problems, and cases. Alternative math solutions are shown where possible. Course instructors may select the print version of the Instructor's Manual or go to www.wiley.com/college/coltman for an electronic version of the Instructor's Manual and an electronic test bank.

A number of professors and instructors have given suggestions and advice, which aided in the development of the Seventh Edition. We thank them for taking the time and effort to share their thoughts with us. They are:

Herbert F. Brown, III, University of South Carolina
Ronald F. Cox, New Mexico State University
Robert A. McMullin, East Stroudsburg University
Susan Reeves, University of South Carolina

We also want to thank the professors and instructors who in the past have provided us with input, and hope that they will continue to do so in the future.

Martin G. Jagels

I

Accounting Review

INTRODUCTION

Every profit-oriented business entity requires a reliable internal system of accountability. A business accounting system provides this accountability by recording all activities regarding the creation of monetary inflows of revenue and monetary outflows of expenses resulting from profit-directed operations. The accounting system provides the financial information needed to evaluate the effectiveness of current and past operations. In addition, the accounting system maintains data required to present reports showing the status of resources, creditors, and ownership equities of the business entity.

In the past, much of the work required to maintain an effective accounting system required extensive individual manual effort that was tedious, aggravating, and time-consuming. Such systems relied on individual effort to continually record transactions, to add, subtract, summarize, and check for errors.

The rapid advancement of computer technology has increased operating speed, memory storage, and reliability accompanied by a significant cost reduction. Inexpensive microcomputers and accounting software programs have advanced to the point where all of the records posting, calculations, error checking, and financial reports are *provided* quickly by the computerized system. The efficiency and cost-effectiveness of computerized supporting software allows management to maintain direct personal control of the accounting system.

To effectively understand concepts and analysis techniques discussed within this text, it is essential that the reader have a conceptual as well as a practical understanding of accounting fundamentals. This chapter reviews basic accounting principles, concepts, conventions, and practices. This review should be of particular benefit to the reader who has taken an introductory accounting course or who has not continued accounting training for some period of time.

CHAPTER OBJECTIVES

After studying this chapter and completing the assigned exercises and problems, the reader should be able to:

1. Define and explain the accounting principles, concepts, and the conceptual difference between the "cash" and "accrual" methods of accounting.

2. Explain the rules of debits and credits as applied to double entry accrual accounting by increasing or decreasing an account balance of the five basic accounts; Assets, Liabilities, Ownership Equity, Revenue, and Expenses.

3. Explain the basic balance sheet equation: "Assets = Liabilities + Owners Equity."

4. Explain the income statement and its major elements as discussed and applied to the hospitality industry.

5. Explain and demonstrate the difference between journalizing and posting of an accounting transaction.

6. Complete an unadjusted trial balance, balance sheet, and an income statement.

7. Explain and demonstrate the end-of-period adjusting entries required by the matching principle.

8. Complete an analysis to convert a business entity from cash to an accrual accounting basis.

CAREERS IN HOSPITALITY ACCOUNTING

The student interested in accounting has a variety of career opportunities available in the hospitality industry. First, there is general accounting, which includes the recording and production of accounting information and/or specialization in a particular area such as food service and beverage cost control. Second, larger organizations may offer careers in the design (or revision) and implementation of accounting systems. A larger organization may also offer careers in budgeting, tax accounting, and auditing—which verifies accounting records and reports of individual properties in the chain.

HOSPITALITY ACCOUNTING OVERVIEW

Cyclical revenue cycles

Hospitality business operations, as well as others, are generally identified as having a number of different cyclical revenue cycles. First, there is the daily operating cycle, which applies particularly to restaurant operations where daily revenue typically depends on meal periods. Second, there is a weekly cycle, in which business travelers normally use hotels, motels, and other hospitality operations during the week and generally provide little weekend hospitality business. On the other hand, local people most often frequent restaurants on Friday through Sunday more than they do during the week. Third, there is a seasonal cycle that depends on vacationers to provide revenue for hospitality operations during vacation months. Fourth, a generalized business period will exist during a recession cycle and hospitality operations typically experience a major decline in sales revenue.

The various repetitive operations cycles encountered in hospitality operations create unique difficulties in forecasting revenue and operating costs. In particular, variable costs such as cost of sales and labor costs require unique planning and procedures that assist in budget forecasting. Since hospitality operations are people-oriented and people-driven, it is more difficult to effectively automate and control costs as easily as businesses in other sectors such as manufacturing.

DIRECT VERSUS INDIRECT COSTS IN HOSPITALITY ACCOUNTING

Unfortunately, most accounting textbooks and generalized accounting courses emphasize accounting systems using procedures and applications applicable to services, retailing, and manufacturing businesses. These types of businesses do not normally require the use of the unique accounting procedures and techniques required by hospitality operations. In manufacturing operations, all

All costs are generally assigned to products or product lines

costs are generally assigned to products or product lines and identified as "direct costs" and "indirect costs." Direct costs include all materials and labor costs that are directly traceable to the product manufactured. Indirect costs generally refer to manufacturing or factory overhead, and include such items as factory supporting costs such as administrative overhead, salaries, wages, utilities, interest, taxes, and depreciation. The basic nature of indirect costs presents difficulties isolating specific costs since they are not directly traceable. A portion of supporting indirect costs are assigned by allocation techniques to each product or product line.

On the other hand, a hospitality operation tends to be highly departmentalized through separate operating divisions that provide rooms, food, beverage, banquet, and gift shop services. A hospitality accounting system must

Departmental accounting

allow an independent evaluation of each operating department and its operating divisions. Costs directly traceable to a department or division are identified as "direct costs." Typically the major direct costs include cost of sales (cost of goods sold), salary and wage labor, and specific operating supplies. After direct costs are determined, they are deducted from revenue to isolate "contributory income," which represents the department's or division's contribution to support undistributed "indirect costs" of the operation as a whole. Indirect costs are those costs not easily traceable to a department or division. Generally, no attempt is made at this stage of the evaluation to allocate indirect costs to the department or divisions. Management reviews operating results to insure that "contributory income" from all departments (or divisions) is sufficient to cover total indirect costs for the overall hospitality operation and provide excess funds to meet the desired level of profit.

General Accounting Knowledge Required

The objective of this text is to provide managers within the hospitality industry a working knowledge of how an accounting system develops, maintains, and provides financial information. Managerial analysis is enhanced with an understanding of the information provided by an accounting system. Without management's understanding of information being provided, management effectiveness will be greatly reduced.

Management effectiveness

Accounting is a common language developed by accountants over time to define the principles, concepts, procedures, and broad rules necessary for management's use in a viable accounting system in making decisions and maintaining an efficient, effective, and profitable business. An accounting system shows detailed information regarding assets, debts, ownership equity, revenue, and operating expenses, and governs recording, reporting, and preparation of financial statements that show the financial health of a business entity.

Accounting is not a static system; rather, it is a dynamic process that incorporates concepts and principles that evolve to suit the needs of financial statement readers, such as business management, equity owners, creditors, and governmental agencies with meaningful, dependable information. Such concepts and principles include the business entity concept, the money concept, the going concern principle, the cost principle, the periodicity concept, the full disclosure principle, the consistency principle, the conservatism principle, the materiality concept, the *objectivity* concept, and the matching principle. Each of these will be discussed in turn.

Business Entity Concept

From an accounting—if not from a legal—point of view, the transactions of a business entity operating as a proprietorship, partnership, or corporation are considered to be separate and distinct from all personal transactions of its ownership. The separation of personal transactions of the ownership from the business entity must be maintained, even if the ownership works in or for the business entity. Only the assets, liabilities, ownership equity, and other transactions of the business entity are entered in the organization's accounting records. The ownership's personal assets, debts, and expenses are not part of the business entity.

Personal assets, debts, and expenses are not part of the business entity

Money Concept

The assumption of the money concept is that the primary national monetary unit is used for recording numerical values of business exchanges and operating transactions. Obviously, the U.S. monetary unit is the dollar. Thus, the accounting function in our case records dollar value of inflows and outflows of the business entity during its operations. The money unit of the dollar also expresses financial information within the financial statements, and reports, and records of information provided and maintained in the accounting system.

Monetary unit is the dollar

Going Concern Concept

Under normal circumstances, the assumption is made that a business entity will remain in operation indefinitely. This continuity of existence assumes that the cost of business assets will be recovered over time by way of profits that are generated by successful operations. The balance sheet values for long-lived assets such as land, building, and equipment are shown at their actual acquisition cost. Since there is no intention to sell such assets, there is no reason to value them at market value. The original cost of a long-lived asset (other than land) is recovered over its useful life through a depreciation expense function. If a depreciable asset is disposed of, the total of the depreciation charges over its life are deducted from its original cost to find its "book value." When a long-lived asset is sold, traded, or otherwise disposed of, the book value of the asset is matched against the value received (not original-historical cost) to determine gain or loss recognition at disposal.

Balance sheet values at their actual acquisition cost

Cost Principle

The assumption made by the money concept is tied directly to the cost principle, which requires the value of business transaction to be recorded at the actual or equivalent cash cost. During extended periods of inflation or deflation, comparing income statements for different years becomes difficult, if not meaningless, under the stable dollar assumption. However, we find that some exceptions are made with respect to valuation of inventories for resale, and to express certain balance sheet and income statement items in terms of current, rather than historic, dollars.

True value may differ from historic cost

Periodicity Concept

This concept requires a business entity to complete an analysis to report financial condition and profitability of its business operation over a specific operating time period. An ongoing business operates continuously. Electrical power

Monthly financial
statements

in reality flows continuously to the user, yet in theory the flow stops when the service meter data is recorded. The billing statement gives the current date service technically ended although service continued without interruption. This example relates to a monthly period; however, the theory applies to any time period—monthly, quarterly, semiannually, or annually. Generally, the minimum period is once per calendar or fiscal year. A calendar year is a 12-month period beginning on January 1 and ending on December 31 of the same year. A fiscal year is any 12-month period beginning on any day other than January 1 and ending on any day other than December 31. In the hospitality business, statements are frequently prepared on a monthly and in some cases a weekly basis.

Full Disclosure Principle

Disclosures are most
frequently made by
footnotes

Financial statements are primarily concerned with a past period. The full disclosure principle states that any future event that may or will occur, and will have a material economic impact on the financial position of the business, should be disclosed to probable and potential readers of the statements. Such disclosures are most frequently made by footnotes.

For example, if a hotel is having a new wing built, or is planning to acquire another property, this should be reported. A restaurant facing a lawsuit from a customer who was injured by tripping over a frayed carpet edge should disclose the contingency of the lawsuit. Similarly, if accounting practices of the current financial statements were changed and differ from those previously reported, the changes should be disclosed. Changes from one period to the next that affect current and future business operations should be reported if possible. Changes of this nature will occur if made to the depreciation method used to determine depreciation expense or to the inventory valuation method, which, if changed, will increase or decrease the value of ending inventory, cost of sales, and the gross margin. All changes disclosed should indicate the dollar effects such disclosures have on financial statements.

Consistency Concept

Use same accounting
basis consistently

The consistency concept was established to ensure comparability and consistency of the procedures and techniques used in the preparation of financial statements from one accounting period to the next. For example, changing back and forth between the cash and accrual basis of accounting would not be consistent, nor would changing the methods of inventory valuation from one period to the next. When changes made are not consistent with the last accounting period, the disclosure principle indicates the disclosure of such changes to probable and potential readers of the statements. The disclosure should show the economic effects of the changes on financial results of the current period and the probable economic impact on future periods.

Conservatism Concept

It is apparent that a business should never prepare financial statements that will cause balance sheet items such as assets to be overstated or liabilities to be understated, sales revenues to be overstated, and expenses to be understated. Situations may exist where estimates are necessary to determine the inventory values or to decide an appropriate depreciation rate. An inventory valuation should be lower rather than higher. Conservatism in this situation increases cost of sales and decreases gross margin.

The costs of long-lived assets (other than land) are systematically recovered through depreciation expense, and should be higher rather than lower. Conservatism in this case will increase expense and lower reported operating income; the intent is to avoid overstating income. However, caution must be exercised to ensure conservatism is not taken to the extreme, which may cause misleading results. For example, restaurant equipment with an estimated five-year life could be fully depreciated in its first year of use. This procedure is certainly conservative, but hardly realistic.

Materiality Concept

In the previous discussion of conservatism, an item of restaurant equipment with a five-year life could be fully depreciated in its first year. This technique would be considered overly conservative, particularly if a material effect to operating income occurs. Consider the alternatives. First, the equipment costing $10,000 (no residual value) could be fully depreciated the first year to maximize depreciation expense, thus reducing operating income. Second, the equipment could be systematically depreciated over each year of estimated life, to allocate depreciation expense charges against sales revenue each year of serviceable life. Evaluate each alternative as shown in the following:

	First Alternative Fully depreciate $10,000 first year	Second Alternative Depreciate $2,000 per year, 5 years
Sales revenue	$100,000	$100,000
Operating expenses	< 90,000>	< 90,000>
Income before depreciation	$ 10,000	$ 10,000
Depreciation expense	< 10,000>	< 2,000>
Operating income	$ -0-	$ 8,000

Depreciating equipment systematically each year over the life of the asset provides the most realistic alternative. This technique recovers the cost of the asset by allocating depreciation expense based on the consumption of the benefits received from the asset over time periods of use. On the other hand, a restaurant might have purchased a supply of letterhead stationery for use over the next five years at a cost of $200. The restaurant could show the total amount of $200 as an expense in the year purchased, opting not to expense the stationery at $40 per year over five years. Operating income would not be materially affected by complete expensing of the purchase in year one.

Objectivity Concept

This concept requires a transaction to have a basis in fact. Some form of objective evidence or documentation must exist to support a transaction before it can be entered into the accounting system. Such evidence is the receipt of cash payment of a guest check or the acceptance of a credit card, or billing a house account that supports earned sales revenue. The accrual basis of accounting recognizes revenue when earned, not necessarily when received. Sales revenue is earned when cash is received or when credit is given, thereby creating accounts receivable; payment that is expected to be received in the near future. Expenses are incurred when cash is paid or when credit is received, creating an accounts payable on which payment is to be made in the near future.

If payment of a receivable becomes uncollectable, it may be written off as bad debt expense (income statement–tax method). An uncollectable account may also be written off through the creation of an allowance for uncollectable accounts (balance sheet method—for financial reporting purposes). The allowance for uncollectable accounts may be established to provide for future bad debts. However, the creation of an allowance account for bad debts (balance sheet method) is an example of an exception to the objectivity concept. The allowance account has no absolute basis in fact since it relates to future events that may or may not occur. However, the allowance account for bad debts is normally based on past historical experience regarding the percentage of receivables not collected. Evidence of past receivables, which were not collected, is considered supporting evidence within the bounds of the objectivity concept and the conservatism concept.

Matching Principle

The matching principle reinforces the "accrual basis" of accounting. Assets are consumed to generate sales revenue inflows; outflows of assets are identified as operating expenses. The matching principle mandates for each accounting period the recognition of all sales revenues earned, whether payment is received or not. This principle also mandates recognition of all operating expenses incurred, whether paid or not paid during the period. As previously discussed, sales revenue is recognized when earned and operating expenses are recognized when incurred, regardless of when cash is received or paid.

The matching principle also conforms to the revenue principle regarding the timing of the recognition of sales revenue inflows and expense outflows that allow matching of revenue to expenses for an accounting period. When a profit-directed operation ends its operating period, it seeks to determine the best estimate of operating results—net income or net loss. The financial statement that discloses financial results for an accounting period is the income statement. If all sales revenues earned and operating expenses incurred at the end of an operating period are not recognized, the resulting net income or net loss will not provide the most accurate estimate of profit or loss.

Cash versus Accrual Accounting

The cash and accrual basis are the two methods of accounting. The difference between the two methods is how and when sales revenues and expenses are recognized. The cash basis of accounting recognizes sales revenue inflows when cash is received, and expense outflows to generate revenue when cash is paid. Simply put, the cash basis recognizes revenue and expenses only when cash changes hands. The accrual basis of accounting recognizes inflows of sales revenues when earned, and expense outflows to produce sales revenues when incurred; it does not matter when cash is received or paid. Many small operations use the cash basis of accounting when appropriate for their type of business; no requirement to prepare and report their financial position to external users exists. To illustrate cash accounting, we will assume that a new restaurant purchased and sold inventory on a cash basis for two months of operation. A partial income statement prepared on a cash basis for the first two months of operation, assuming sales revenue of $10,000 and $8,000 of inventories for resale, would show the following:

Many small operations use the cash basis of accounting

	Month 1	Month 2
Cash sales	$10,000	$10,000
Cash purchases	< 8,000>	0
Gross margin (before other expenses)	$ 2,000	$10,000

This method gives a distorted view of the operations over two months. The combined two-month gross profit would be $12,000; however, the accrual method will give a more accurate picture of the real situation, which is gross margin (before other expenses) of $6,000 each month. In the following "accrual" example, "cost of sales" is estimated at 50% of sales revenue. Cost of sales is used to refer to cost of goods sold.

	Month 1	Month 2
Cash sales	$10,000	$10,000
Cost of sales	< 4,000>	< 4,000>
Gross margin	$ 6,000	$ 6,000

The examples given are not meant to suggest that the cash basis of accounting is never used. As indicated in the previous discussions, many small businesses may find the cash basis appropriate. However, the cash basis is not considered adequate for medium and larger business organizations, which normally use the accrual basis of accounting. The accrual method is used throughout this text, except in cases where the cash concept supplements the decision-making process. Exceptions to the accrual method to a cash concept will be discussed in Chapter 10, Statement of Cash Flows, indirect method, Chapter 11, Cash Management, and Chapter 12, The Investment Decision.

Medium and larger business organizations normally use the accrual basis of accounting

The necessity of creating and maintaining accounting records for a business entity to record inflows and outflows of assets is easily understood. Analysis of transactions—their recording, posting, adjusting, and reporting economic results and financial condition of a business entity—is the heart of double-accrual entry accounting. Without a basic knowledge of the system and the information provided, it will be difficult to produce or understand financial reports. The two major financial reports are the balance sheet and income statement.

The balance sheet reveals the financial condition of a business entity by showing the status of its assets, liabilities, and ownership equities on the specific ending date of an operating period. The income statement reports the economic results of the business entity by showing sales revenue inflows, and matches expense outflows to show the results of operations—net income or net loss. The income statement is generally considered the most important of the two major ending financial reports. Since it reports not only the results of operations, it clearly identifies sales revenue inflows and the cost outflows to produce revenue. The balance sheet equation is extended to include the income statement functions showing the effects of profit or loss operations.

$$Assets = Liabilities + Ownership\ Equity\ (Revenue - Expenses)$$

The balance sheet provides an easier basis for understanding double entry accounting and so will be discussed first. The balance sheet equation, as it is known, consists of three key elements, and defines the basic format of the balance sheet. (The basics of a balance sheet and income statement discussed in this chapter are expanded in Chapter 2.)

The balance sheet equation is A = L + OE; the equality point indicates the absolute necessity of maintaining equality on both sides of the equation. The sum total of the left side of the equation, total assets, must be equal to the total sum of the right side of the equation, liabilities plus ownership equity. When a transaction affects both sides of the equation, equality of the equation must be maintained. One side of the equation cannot increase or decrease without the other side increasing or decreasing in the same amount. If a transaction exists that affects only one side of the equation, total increases must equal total decreases.

Equality of the equation must be maintained

The assets consumed produce sales revenue to become cost of sales and operating expenses. The liabilities + ownership equity elements of the equation represent the claims against assets by creditors (liabilities) and claims against the assets by the ownership (OE). The following describes balance sheet elements:

$$\text{ASSETS} \quad = \quad \text{LIABILITIES} \quad + \quad \text{OWNERSHIP EQUITY}$$

$$\Updownarrow \qquad\qquad \Updownarrow \qquad\qquad\qquad \Updownarrow$$

Resources   Creditors' Equity   Ownership Equity

Assets (A) — Resources of value used by a business entity to create revenue, which in turn increases assets.

Liabilities (L) — Debt obligations owed to creditors as a result of operations to generate sales revenue; to be paid in the near future with assets. Liabilities represent creditor equity or claim against the assets of the business entity.

Ownership (OE) — Ownership equity represents claims to assets of a business entity. Three basic forms of ownership equity are:

a. Proprietorship—entity financing provided by a sole owner.

b. Partnership—entity financing provided by two or more owners (partners).

c. Corporation—entity financing provided by stockholders, where ownership is represented by stock shares; each share of stock represents one ownership claim.

The balance sheet equation is a simple linear equation with an equality point showing that one side requires equality to the opposite side. Knowing dollar values of two of the three basic elements allows the value of a missing element to be identified. The following balance sheet equation has values given for all three elements. Each of the three examples has the value of one element omitted from the equation, and shows how to find the value of the missing element:

$$\text{ASSETS} \;=\; \text{LIABILITIES} \;+\; \text{OWNERSHIP EQUITY}$$

$$\Updownarrow \qquad\qquad \Updownarrow \qquad\qquad\qquad \Updownarrow$$

$$\$100{,}000 \qquad \$25{,}000 \qquad\qquad \$75{,}000$$

$$[A - L = OE] = \$100{,}000 - \$25{,}000 = \underline{\$75{,}000}$$

$$[A - OE = L] = \$100{,}000 - \$75{,}000 = \underline{\$25{,}000}$$

$$[L + OE = A] = \;\; \$25{,}000 + \$75{,}000 = \underline{\underline{\$100{,}000}}$$

Double-Accrual Entry Accounting

For an accounting transaction to exist, at least one element of the balance sheet equation or the income statement function is being created or changed. An exchange between the business entity and an external entity, such as selling goods for cash or on credit, creates a transaction. A requirement to adjust the business entity accounts at the end of a period, adjusting deferrals and accruals creates an internal transaction. (Adjusting entries will be discussed in detail later in this chapter.) All transactions are analyzed and in a manual accounting system are "journalized." A journal entry records the amount and accounts affected by the transaction by name. The journal entry is then "posted" to the appropriate account in the accounts ledger.

No transaction can affect only one account

As we know, no transaction can affect only one account. In this way, the balance sheet equation is kept in balance and maintains the equality between both sides of the equation, $A = L + OE$. Each transaction directs the change to be made to each account involved in the transaction. Each directed change will cause an increase or decrease to a specified account. It is important to understand how a journal entry directs an increase or decrease to a specific account. This is accomplished through the use of two account columns to receive numerical values that follow the rules of debit and credit entries.

Rules of debit-credit functions and their effect on balance sheet accounts. Assets are debit-balanced accounts; debits increase debit-balanced accounts. Liabilities and ownership equity are credit-balanced accounts; credits increase credit-balanced accounts. The debit-credit rules as applied to balance sheet accounts are summarized as follows:

Assets (Debit-balanced Accounts)	=	Liabilities	+	Ownership Equity
		(Credit-balanced Accounts)		
Increased by Debits	= Increased by Credits	+ Increased by Credits
Decreased by Credits	= Decreased by Debits	+ Decreased by Debits

Rules of debit-credit functions and their effect on income statement accounts. Revenue accounts are credit-balanced; credits increase a credit-balanced account. Expense accounts are debit-balanced; debits increase a debit-balanced account. The debit-credit rules for income statement accounts are summarized below:

SALES REVENUES   and   EXPENSES

$\updownarrow$ $\updownarrow$

(Credit-balanced accounts)   (Debit-balanced accounts)

THE JOURNAL AND JOURNAL ENTRY

A journal is the historical record for a business entity

A journal includes all accounting transactions and is considered the historical record for a business entity. All transactions must be recorded through a journal entry before the accounts can be posted. Consider the following transaction where a proprietor, Gram Disk, begins a business entity called the Texana Restaurant on May 1, 2000. An initial investment of $100,000 cash is made to begin operations. The transaction creates the following balance sheet equation:

$$\underline{\text{ASSETS} \quad = \quad \text{LIABILITIES} \quad + \quad \text{OWNERSHIP EQUITY}}$$
$$\$100,000 \quad = \qquad \text{-0-} \qquad\qquad \$100,000$$

The equation shown above comes into existence only after a journal entry is written; it will be posted to the appropriate ledger account. Before a journal entry is posted, the journal entry must, as a minimum, insure the following:

a. The journal entry must cause at least two accounts to be changed.

b. The journal entry must show at least one debit and one credit entry.

c. Last but not least, the sum of the debits and credits must be equal.

A detailed journal entry to establish the $100,000 initial investment is shown in Exhibit 1.1.

Exhibit 1.1   Journal Entry to Initiate Accounting System

Date	Account Titles, Explanation	P/R	Debit	Credit
05-01-2000	Cash	100	$100,000	
	Capital, Gram Disk	500		$100,000

P/R: the posting reference identifying the number of the account posted.

The Ledger Accounts

In a manual accounting system, the "general ledger" maintains a separate account identified by name and account number using a standardized format. Ledger accounts are created as necessary to record transactional effects on all items reported on the financial statements. The ledger account records each dollar value posted and reports the account balance after each entry is posted. The journal entry made in the general journal is the source of instructions that identifies a specific account by name, the dollar value, and the debit or credit column to be entered. The effect of the debit or credit entry will increase or decrease the balance of the account posted, dependent on whether the normal balance of the account is debit- or credit-balanced. A ledger account page generally uses the following format:

Account Name:				Account No.	
Date	Explanation	Ref.	Debit	Credit	Balance

Ref: Identifies journal page of the entry that directs posting by name and amount.

A modified "T" account is a simpler format to understanding account posting. This technique allows a continuous balance that eliminates the necessity of totaling both the debit and credit columns to find correct balance of an account. The same principle of left-column debit, right-column credit applies whether a manual or computerized system is being used. A modified "T" format shows the key elements of a ledger account. The use of this format is more than adequate for academic understanding.

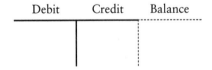

A journal entry names specific accounts and the debit or credit column to receive the directed dollar value. Posting a journal entry is made line by line until each line of the journal has been posted. Journalizing the owners' initial cash investment of $100,000 is posted here:

Debit	Credit	Balance		Debit	Credit	Balance
$100,000		$100,000			$100,000	$100,000

It is incorrect to view debits as increases and to view credits as decreases in the balance of all ledger accounts. The normal account balances for each of the five types of accounts and their debit–credit relationship is summarized as follows:

Account Category	Normal Balance	Balance Increased by	Balance Decreased by
Assets	*Debit*	*Debits*	*Credits*
Liabilities	Credit	Credits	Debits
Ownership Equity	Credit	Credits	Debits
Sales Revenue	Credit	Credits	Debits
Expenses	*Debit*	*Debits*	*Credits*

A simple journal entry using only two accounts was previously discussed, journalized, and posted to begin the accounting records for Texana Restaurant. To continue, on May 5, 2000, the restaurant owner, Gram Disk, purchased a former restaurant building for $150,000, paying $50,00 in cash and assuming a note payable for $100,000 balance owed. In addition, $8,000 of food inventory and $2,000 of beverage inventory were purchased for cash. Equipment was purchased for $12,000 on account (payable). These transactions were journalized in a compound entry, which uses more than two accounts and then posted to modified "T" ledger accounts, as shown in Exhibit 1.2.

Exhibit 1.2 Operating Journal Entry 2

Account Titles	Debit	Credit
FOOD INVENTORY	$ 8,000	
BEVERAGE INVENTORY	2,000	
BUILDING	150,000	
EQUIPMENT	12,000	
ACCOUNTS PAYABLE		$ 12,000
NOTES PAYABLE		100,000
CASH		60,000

As can be seen, a number of ledger accounts were created to post the journal entry:

CASH				FOOD INVENTORY				BEVERAGE INVENTORY		
Debit	Credit	Balance		Debit	Credit	Balance		Debit	Credit	Balance
$100,000		$100,000		$ 8,000		$ 8,000		$ 2,000		$ 2,000
	$ 60,000	$ 40,000								

BUILDING				EQUIPMENT				Accounts Payable		
Debit	Credit	Balance		Debit	Credit	Balance		Debit	Credit	Balance
$150,000		$150,000		$ 12,000		$ 12,000			$ 12,000	$ 12,000

Notes Payable				Gram Disk, Capital		
Debit	Credit	Balance		Debit	Credit	Balance
	$100,000	$100,000			$100,000	$100,000

After posting the compound journal entry, the balance sheet equation and a balance sheet become:

Assets	=	Liabilities	+	Ownership Equity
$212,000	=	$112,000	+	$100,000

Texana Restaurant
Balance Sheet (Interim)
May 5, 2000

Assets		Liabilities and Ownership Equity	
Cash	$ 40,000	Accounts Payable	$ 12,000
Food Inventory	8,000	Notes Payable	100,000
Beverage Inventory	2,000	Total Liabilities	$112,000
Building	150,000	Ownership Equity:	
Equipment	12,000	Capital, Gram Disk	$100,000
Total Assets	$212,000	Total Liabilities & OE	$212,000

THE INCOME STATEMENT

The income statement equation, as it is known, consists of three basic elements that produce three possible outcomes from for-profit operations. First, when total sales revenue equals the total cost of producing the revenue, "breakeven" is achieved; no profit or loss exists. Second, if total sales revenue exceeds total cost of producing the revenue, profit exists. Third, if total sales revenue is less than the total cost of producing the revenue, a loss exists. The income statement shows the ending results of operations as of a specific date for a specific time period. The following possible outcomes and a brief description of the major income statement elements are shown below.

The income statement shows the ending results of operations as of a specific date for a specific time period

Sales Revenue – Cost of Sales – Expenses = Breakeven, Net Income, or Net Loss

Sales Revenue (R)	Sales revenue produced from the sale of goods and/or services.
Cost of Sales (CS)	Cost of sales reflects the cost of inventories purchased for resale that were sold.
Expenses (E)	Cost of assets consumed during operations to produce sales revenue.
Breakeven (BE)	An economic result of operations when total sales revenue equals total costs; no profit (operating income) or loss will exist.
Operating Income (OI)	Income before taxes.
Net Income (NI)	An economic result of operations when total revenue is greater than total costs after taxes.
Net Loss (NL)	An economic result of operations when total sales revenue is less than total costs.

Sales revenue is earned when cash is received or when credit is extended, creating a receivable. Credit card sales represent the major source of total sales made on credit in the hospitality industry today. Accounts receivables (or house accounts) continue to be used but represent a small portion of total sales made on credit. Credit card sales create "credit card receivables" on which payment is expected to be received, ranging generally from one to five operating days, depending on the type of credit card accepted.

Continuing from the preceding May 1 and 5 Texana Restaurant transactions, we will look at typical operating transactions regarding sales revenue and operating expenses. Assume during the period May 6 to May 31, the following additional transactions occurred.

Paid two-year premium on liability and casualty insurance	$ 3,600
Purchased food inventory on account	4,200
Paid employee wages	3,400
Purchased beverage inventory; cash	1,400
Paid employee salaries	1,800
Received and paid May utilities expense	282
Sales revenue for May; $24,280 cash, $620 on credit cards	24,900
Paid miscellaneous expenses for the month	818

To maintain continuity and simplicity, no date or posting reference columns are shown in Exhibit 1.3, and each transaction is journalized separately.

Exhibit 1.3   Operating Journal Entry 3

Account Titles	Debit	Credit
Prepaid Insurance	$ 3,600	
Cash		$ 3,600
Food Inventory	$ 4,200	
Accounts payable		$ 4,200
Wages Expense	$ 3,400	
Cash		$ 3,400
Beverage Inventory	$ 1,400	
Cash		$ 1,400
Salaries Expense	$ 1,800	
Cash		$ 1,800
Utilities Expense	$ 282	
Cash		$ 282
Cash	$24,280	
Credit Card Receivables	620	
Revenue		$24,900
Miscellaneous Expense	$ 818	
Cash		$ 818

The above journal entries are posted for Texana Restaurant as follows:

General Ledger

Cash *(Asset)*

Debit	Credit	Balance
$100,000		$100,000
	$ 60,000	40,000
	3,600	36,400
	3,400	33,000
	1,400	31,600
	1,800	29,800
	282	29,518
24,280		53,798
	818	52,980

Credit Card Receivables *(Asset)*

Debit	Credit	Balance
$ 620		$ 620

Prepaid Insurance *(Asset)*

Debit	Credit	Balance
$ 3,600		$ 3,600

Food Inventory *(Asset)*

Debit	Credit	Balance
$ 8,000		$ 8,000
4,200		12,200

Beverage Inventory *(Asset)*

Debit	Credit	Balance
$ 2,000		$ 2,000
1,400		3,400

Building *(Asset)*

Debit	Credit	Balance
$150,000		$150,000

Equipment *(Asset)*

Debit	Credit	Balance
$ 12,000		$ 12,000

Accounts Payable *(Liab.)*

Debit	Credit	Balance
	$ 12,000	$ 12,000
	4,200	16,200

Notes Payable *(Liab.)*

Debit	Credit	Balance
	$100,000	$100,000

Sales Revenue *(Rev.)*

Debit	Credit	Balance
	$ 24,900	$ 24,900

Wages Expenses *(Exp.)*

Debit	Credit	Balance
$ 3,400		$ 3,400

Salaries Expense *(Exp.)*

Debit	Credit	Balance
$ 1,800		$ 1,800

Utilities Expense *(Exp.)*

Debit	Credit	Balance
$ 282		$ 282

Miscellaneous Expense *(Exp.)*

Debit	Credit	Balance
$ 818		$ 818

Gram Disk, Capital *(OE)*

Debit	Credit	Balance
	$100,000	$100,000

Match the total of all debit-balanced accounts to the total of all credit-balanced accounts

At this point in the cycle, it is advantageous to prepare an "unadjusted trial balance." All accounts with balances are listed. The objective is to match the total of all debit-balanced accounts to the total of all credit-balanced accounts. As you will see from the following unadjusted trial balance, the totals of the debit- and credit-balanced accounts are equal. However, it should not be assumed that everything is necessarily correct. For example, an entry may have been made for the correct amount but posted to the wrong account. Two accounts could be correctly identified with the wrong amount shown in both cases, or a transaction may have been entirely omitted and not journalized.

Such errors are not uncommon in a manual or computerized system, and normally show up in later stages in the accounting process. When a journal entry or posting error is identified, it is corrected by an adjusting journal entry.

The unadjusted trial balance based on the ledger accounts are shown in Exhibit 1.4.

End-of-Period Adjusting Entries

May 31, 2000, marks the end of the first month of operations for the Texana Restaurant. At the end of an accounting cycle, certain period ending adjustments are needed to insure financial statements are based on accurate data. The income statement, balance sheet, and statement of ownership equity must conform to the principle of matching revenues to expenses. Such end-of-period adjustments may be numerous or few, but necessary to recognize accruals and deferrals. Accruals represent end-of-period adjustments recognizing sales revenue earned and

Accruals represent end-of-period adjustments recognizing sales revenue earned and expenses incurred

Exhibit 1.4   Unadjusted Trial Balance, May 31, 2000

Accounts	Debit	Credit
Cash	$ 52,980	
Credit Card Receivables	620	
Prepaid Insurance	3,600	
Food Inventory	12,200	
Beverage Inventory	3,400	
Building	150,000	
Equipment	12,000	
Accounts Payable		$ 16,200
Notes Payable		100,000
Capital, Gram Disk		100,000
Sales Revenue		24,900
Wages Expense	3,400	
Salaries Expense	1,800	
Utilities Expense	282	
Miscellaneous Expense	818	
Accounts Totals	$241,100	$241,100

expenses incurred, with the receipt of payment or the making of payment expected to occur in the next accounting period. Deferrals represent end-of-period adjustments to revenues and expenses, and also include adjustments to assets and liabilities to reflect revenue earned and expenses incurred. In our continuing example, we will discuss six adjustments: cost of sales, inventory, prepaid expenses, depreciation, wages, and salaries expense.

Cost of sales and inventory adjustment. Any business maintaining inventory purchased or produced for resale will not expect to sell all items available during an accounting period. A restaurant operation will always maintain a minimum food and beverage inventory to take care of current daily and near-future business operations. At the end of an accounting period, the cost of inventory sold is identified as an expense described as "cost of sales." Ending inventory not sold will continue to be classified as an asset and not expensed. Cost of sales describes cost of goods sold. It is determined easily: know the beginning inventory, add inventory purchases, deduct inventory not sold, to find the cost of sales. Using previously discussed information for Texana Restaurant, cost of sales is calculated, assuming the May 31, 2000, ending food inventory is $3,200, and the ending beverage inventory is $1,175. The Cost of Sales for both inventory accounts is $11,225.

Beginning Inventory + Purchases − Ending Inventory = Cost of Sales

Food: Beginning Inventory + Purchases − Ending Inventory = Cost of Sales

-0- + $12,200 − $3,200 = $ 9,000

Beverage: Beginning Inventory + Purchases − Ending Inventory = Cost of Sales

-0- + $3,400 − $1,175 = $ 2,225

Total Net Cost of Sales is $9,000 + $2,225 = $11,225

Several different methods may be used to adjust the inventory accounts (for resale) and find cost of inventory sold. The cost of sales method will be used in this discussion. Normally, the first of two adjustments requires that cost of sales be debited in the amount equal to the balance of the inventory account, followed by credit to the inventory account equal to its balance. Posting of the entry brings the inventory to a zero balance, and in effect transfers the inventory account balance to the cost of sales account. The next adjustment requires the value of ending inventory to be debited to the inventory account and credited to the cost of sales account. Adjusting entries for food and beverage inventory accounts are written and posted as shown in Exhibit 1.5.

Exhibit 1.5   Cost of Sales and Food Inventory Adjustment

Account Titles: Explanation	Debit	Credit
Cost of Sales	$12,200	
Food Inventory		$12,200
Food Inventory	3,200	
Cost of Sales		3,200

Posting the adjusting entry will create the cost of sales account, thereby adjusting the food inventory account to the correct ending balance. Study the posting effects below:

Food Inventory				Cost of Sales		
Debit	Credit	Balance		Debit	Credit	Balance
$ 8,000		$ 8,000				-0-
4,200		12,200		$12,200		$12,200dr
	$12,200	-0-			$ 3,200	9,000dr
3,200		3,200				

Following the same procedures as shown above, the journal entry adjusts beverage inventory and cost of sales to the correct ending balances when posted, as shown in Exhibit 1.6.

Exhibit 1.6   Cost of Sales and Beverage Inventory Adjustment

Account Titles: Explanation	Debit	Credit
Cost of Sales	$ 3,400	
Beverage Inventory		$ 3,400
Beverage Inventory	1,175	
Cost of Sales		1,175

Posting the journal entry adjusts cost of sales and adjusts beverage inventory to the correct ending balance. Study the posting effects below:

Beverage Inventory				Cost of Sales		
Debit	Credit	Balance		Debit	Credit	Balance
$ 2,000		$ 2,000				-0-
1,400		3,400		$12,200		$12,200dr
	3,400	-0-			$ 3,200	9,000dr
1,175		1,175		$ 3,400		12,400dr
					1,175	11,225dr

Periodic and perpetual inventory control are commonly used in hospitality operations

Periodic and perpetual inventory control are the two methods discussed in this text that are commonly used in hospitality operations. The periodic method is used to continue the discussion of end-of-period adjustments for Texana Restaurant. The periodic method relies on an actual physical count and costing of the inventory over a specific time period to determine the cost of sales. Generally a physical count and costing is normally completed on a monthly basis. During a given time period, there is no record of inventory available for sale on any particular day. The periodic method is usually preferred for inventory control when many low-cost items are involved, which is often the case in food service operations.

The perpetual method requires a greater number of records to achieve continuous updating, showing the receipt and sale of each inventory item, and maintaining a running balance of inventory available. Perpetual inventory control is discussed in Chapter 2.

When expenses are paid in advance for future time periods, a prepaid asset account is created

Prepaid expense adjustments. When expenses are paid in advance for future time periods, normally exceeding a month, for such items as rent and/or insurance, a prepaid asset account is created. The prepaid names the benefit to be received and consumed as an expense over a specified number of time periods—months, quarters, or years (see Exhibit 1.7). The basic concept of expensing a prepaid can be expressed as prepaid cost ÷ life of prepaid. In our example, Texana Restaurant paid a two-year insurance policy in advance for $3,600 on May 6. If we expense the prepaid insurance on a monthly basis, the amount expensed for the month of May will be $3,600/24 = $150 per month. The prepaid insurance account will be reduced $150 and the insurance expense account will be increased $150 when the journal entry is posted.

Prepaid cost / months = $3,600 / 24 = $150 per month

Alternative:

Prepaid cost / years = $3,600 / 2 = $1,800 per year; or

$1,800 per year / 12 months = $150 per month

Exhibit 1.7   Prepaid Expense Adjustment

Account Titles: Explanation	Debit	Credit
Insurance Expense	$ 150	
Prepaid Insurance		$ 150

Posting of the adjusting journal entry creates the insurance expense account and adjusts the asset account prepaid insurance.

Insurance Expense *(Asset)*			Prepaid Insurance *(Exp.)*		
Debit	Credit	Balance	Debit	Credit	Balance
$ 150		$ 150	$ 3,600		$ 3,600
				$ 150	3,450

Depreciation is the systematic expensing of long-lived physical assets

Depreciation adjustment. Depreciation is the systematic expensing of long-lived physical assets that provide economic benefits (in excess of one year) over their useful lives. Although there are other depreciation methods, only the straight-line method is discussed in this chapter since it uses the easiest concept to understand depreciation. (Other methods will be discussed in Chapter 2.) In previous transactions of Texana Restaurant, equipment was purchased for $12,000. The equipment had a serviceable life estimated to be eight years with no residual value. Residual value refers to the estimated trade-in, salvage, or any estimated value to be recovered at the end of the asset's serviceable life. The straight-line method breaks the amount to be recovered through depreciation expense into equal time periods; months, quarters, and years are commonly used. Straight-line depreciation calculations will be described on yearly and monthly time periods.

Monthly Depreciation Calculation

Cost – Residual/life = Depreciation expense $12,000/96 months = $125 per month

Cost – Residual/life = Depreciation expense $12,000/8 years = $1,500 per year

In addition to the equipment, the building purchased must also be depreciated for the month of May. The building cost $150,000, its estimated life is 25 years, and it has a residual value of $30,000, as shown below:

Monthly Depreciation Calculation

Cost – Residual/life = Depreciation Expense $150,000 – 30,000/300 months = $400 per month

Yearly Depreciation Calculation

Cost – Residual/life = Depreciation Expense $150,000 – 30,000/25 years = $4,800 per year

The adjusting journal entry to recognize depreciation expense on the equipment and the building at May 31 is shown in Exhibit 1.8, followed by its posting to ledger the accounts.

Exhibit 1.8   Depreciation Expense Adjustment

Account Titles: Explanation	Debit	Credit
Depreciation Expense	$ 525	
Accumulated Depreciation: Equipment		$ 125
Accumulated Depreciation: Building		400

Depreciation Expense *(Exp.)*			Accumulated Depr: Equip.			Accumulated Depr: Bldg.		
Debit	Credit	Balance	Debit	Credit	Balance	Debit	Credit	Balance
$ 525		$ 525		$ 125	$ 125		$ 400	$ 400

The original cost of the long-lived asset equipment is not reduced. The going concern concept and cost principle require the original cost of a long-lived asset to be maintained in the accounting records. To maintain depreciation expense charges on each depreciable asset over its serviceable life, a contra-asset, credit-balanced account called "accumulated depreciation" is created. Each depreciable asset has its own separate accumulated depreciation account identified by name and account number. At disposal of a depreciable asset, a gain or loss can be determined by comparing the value received to the "book value" of the asset. Book value is the original cost minus accumulated depreciation. If the value received is greater than book value, the excess of book value is a gain; a loss on disposal exists if the value received is less than the book value.

Book value is the original cost minus accumulated depreciation

Wages and salaries adjustments. Unfortunately for employees, payday seldom falls on the last day of the month. It is not unusual for wages and salaries to be earned but not paid by the end of the month. An accrual adjusting entry is made to record payroll expense belonging to the current month just ended. This adjustment insures that the income statement and balance sheet reflect the correct expense and payroll payable. Continuing the Texana Restaurant discussion, we will assume that two days of wages and salaries were earned but not paid by May 31. The payroll owed consists of wages, $400, and salaries, $480. The adjusting entry is shown in Exhibit 1.9.

Exhibit 1.9   **Accrued Expense Adjustment**

Account Titles: Explanation	Debit	Credit
Wages Expense	$ 400	
Salaries Expense	$ 480	
Payroll Payable		$ 880

An additional account, payroll payable, is created for this transaction. The previous entry is posted as follows:

Wages Expense *(Exp.)*

Debit	Credit	Balance
$ 3,400		$ 3,400
400		3,800

Salaries Expense *(Exp.)*

Debit	Credit	Balance
$ 1,800		$ 1,800
480		2,280

Payroll Payable *(Liab.)*

Debit	Credit	Balance
	$ 880	$ 880

The general ledger showing the posted operating and adjusting journal entries is shown next, for review. The general ledger is the source used to prepare an adjusted trial balance that confirms the ledger accounts remain in balance.

Cash *(Asset)*

Debit	Credit	Balance
$100,000		$100,000
	$ 60,000	40,000
	3,600	36,400
	3,400	33,000
	1,400	31,600
	1,800	28,900
	282	29,518
24,280		53,798
	818	52,980

Credit Card Receivables *(Asset)*

Debit	Credit	Balance
$ 620		$ 620

Prepaid Insurance *(Asset)*

Debit	Credit	Balance
$ 3,600		$ 3,600
	$ 150	3,450

Food Inventory *(Asset)*

Debit	Credit	Balance
$ 8,000		$ 8,000
4,200		12,200
	$ 12,000	-0-
3,200		3,200

Beverage Inventory *(Asset)*

Debit	Credit	Balance
$ 2,000		$ 2,000
1,400		3,400
	$ 3,400	-0-
1,175		1,175

Building *(Asset)*

Debit	Credit	Balance
$150,000		$150,000

Accumulated Depr. Bldg. *(Contra)*

Debit	Credit	Balance
	$ 400	$ 400

Equipment *(Asset)*

Debit	Credit	Balance
$ 12,000		$ 12,000

Accumulated Depr. Equip *(Contra)*

Debit	Credit	Balance
	$ 125	$ 125

Accounts Payable *(Liab.)*

Debit	Credit	Balance
	$ 12,000	$ 12,000
	4,200	16,200

Payroll Payable *(Liab.)*

Debit	Credit	Balance
	$ 880	$ 880

Notes Payable *(Liab.)*

Debit	Credit	Balance
	$100,000	$100,000

Sales Revenue *(Rev.)*

Debit	Credit	Balance
	$ 24,900	$ 24,900

Wages Expense *(Exp.)*

Debit	Credit	Balance
$ 3,400		$ 3,400
400		3,800

Salaries Expense *(Exp.)*

Debit	Credit	Balance
$ 1,800		$ 1,800
480		2,280

Utilities Expense *(Exp.)*

Debit	Credit	Balance
$ 282		$ 282

Miscellaneous Expense *(Exp.)*

Debit	Credit	Balance
$ 818		$ 818

Insurance Expense *(Exp.)*

Debit	Credit	Balance
$ 150		$ 150

Depreciation Expense *(Exp.)*

Debit	Credit	Balance
$ 525		$ 525

Cost of Sales *(Debit Bal.)*

Debit	Credit	Balance
$ 12,200		$ 12,200
	$ 3,200	9,000
3,400		12,400
	1,175	11,225

Gram Disk, Capital *(OE)*

Debit	Credit	Balance
	$100,000	$100,000

Before determining operating income or loss, an "adjusted trial balance" is prepared by extracting each ledger account by name and balance, after adjustments are posted see Exhibit 1.10. The purpose is to verify the Texana Restaurant ledger is in balance.

Exhibit 1.10   Adjusted Trial Balance May 31, 2000

Accounts	Debit	Credit
Cash	$ 52,980	
Credit Card Receivables	620	
Prepaid Insurance	3,450	
Food Inventory	3,200	
Beverage Inventory	1,175	
Building	150,000	
Accumulated Depreciation: Bldg.		$ 400
Equipment	12,000	
Accumulated Depreciation: Equip.		125
Accounts Payable		16,200
Payroll Payable		880
Notes Payable		100,000
Capital, Gram Disk		100,000
Sales Revenue		24,900
Cost of Sales	11,225	
Wages Expense	3,800	
Salaries Expense	2,280	
Utilities Expense	282	
Miscellaneous Expense	818	
Insurance Expense	150	
Depreciation Expense	525	
Accounts Totals	$242,505	$242,505

The income statement in Exhibit 1.11 is prepared for Texana Restaurant from information given in the adjusted trial balance using the following format:

Sales Revenue − Cost of Sales = Gross Margin − Expenses = Net Operating Income

Exhibit 1.11   Income Statement for Texana Restaurant
Month Ended May 31, 2000

Sales Revenue		$ 24,900
Less: Cost of Sales		<11,225>
Gross Margin		$ 13,675
Expenses:		
Wages Expense	$ 3,800	
Salaries Expense	2,280	
Utilities Expense	282	
Miscellaneous Expense	818	
Insurance Expense	150	
Depreciation Expense	525	
Total Expenses		< 7,855>
Net Operating Income		$ 5,820

Closing journal entries. The last step in moving through the accounting cycle example for Texana Restaurant is to create closing entries, bringing the temporary accounts balances to zero. Closing the temporary accounts will transfer operating income or operating loss to the capital account. Operating income exists when total sales revenue is greater than the cost of sales and the total operating expenses. An operating loss exists when the cost of sales and total operating expenses are greater than the sales revenue. Operating income is the income before tax, and will become net income after tax is applied. Consider the possibilities shown in Exhibit 1.12 that may exist after closing the temporary income statement accounts:

Exhibit 1.12   Closing Journal Entries

Account Titles: Explanation	Debit	Credit
Sales Revenue	$ 24,900	
Cost of Sales		$ 11,225
Wages Expense		3,800
Salaries Expense		2,280
Utilities Expense		282
Miscellaneous Expense		818
Insurance Expense		150
Depreciation Expense		525
Capital, Gram Disk		5,820
"To close temporary accounts to OE Capital"		

After closing entries are posted from the closing journal entry to the ledger, only real, permanent balance sheet accounts remain in the Texana Restaurant ledger (See Exhibit 1.13). The post closing trial balance is the source of information needed to prepare a final balance sheet.

Exhibit 1.13   Post Closing Trial Balance
Month Ended May 31, 2000

Cash	$ 52,980	
Credit Card Receivables	620	
Prepaid Insurance	3,450	
Food Inventory	3,200	
Beverage Inventory	1,175	

(continued next page)

Exhibit 1.13   Post Closing Trial Balance
(Continued from previous page)

Building	$150,000	
Accumulated Depreciation: Building		$ 400
Equipment	12,000	
Accumulated Depreciation: Equipment		125
Accounts Payable		16,200
Payroll Payable		880
Notes Payable		100,000
Capital, Gram Disk		105,820
Post Closing Trial Balance Totals	$223,425	$223,425

From the post closing trial balance, a final post closing balance sheet is prepared for Texana Restaurant for the month of May (Exhibit 1.14).

Exhibit 1.14   Balance Sheet, May 31, 2000

Assets		Liabilities and Owners' Equity	
		Liabilities	
Cash	$ 52,980	Accounts Payable	$ 16,200
Credit Card Receivables	620	Payroll Payable	880
Prepaid Insurance	3,450	Notes Payable	100,000
Food Inventory	3,200	Total Liabilities	$117,080
Beverage Inventory	1,175		
Building	150,000	**Owners' Equity**	
Accumulated Depr: Bldg.	<400>	Gram Disk, Capital	$100,000
Equipment	12,000	Operating Income, May 2000	5,820
Accumulated Depr. Equip.	<125>	Total Owners' Equity	$105,820
Total Assets	$222,900	Total Liabilities and OE	$222,900

WORKSHEET

A worksheet (optional) is prepared at the end of an accounting period to insure that all of the accounts are in balance and to show all information needed to journalize adjusting and closing entries, and to prepare major financial statements. The sequence of completion of the worksheet begins with an unadjusted trial balance. End-of-period adjustments are made in the adjustment columns, then extended to the adjusted trial balance columns. Each account shown in the adjusted trial balance columns belongs to the income statement or balance sheet columns. Sales revenue, cost of sales, and expense accounts are extended to the income statement. Asset, liability, and ownership equity accounts are extended to the balance sheet. The debit–credit balances of each of the five two-column sets must be equal. If any total debit and credit balances of the five two-column sets are not equal, an error has been made requiring correction before continuing completion of the worksheet. If all column sets are balanced correctly, the worksheet is completed if no errors are noted.

All information is shown in the worksheet to journalize adjusting and closing entries, and to prepare the income statement and balance sheet. A worksheet is shown in Exhibit 1.15, to illustrate all operating transactions, adjusting, and closing journal entries, including the income statement and balance sheet for Texana Restaurant.

The following describes the column contents in Exhibit 1.15:

Debit–credit column sets 1, 2, and 3: Unadjusted trial balance, adjustments, and adjusted trial balance column sets verify that total debits are equal to total credits.

Debit–credit column set 4: The income statement columns shows a subtotal for total operating expense outflows and total sales revenue inflows. Unless total expenses are equal to total sales revenue (breakeven), the debit–credit subtotals will not be equal. If sales revenue is greater than expenses, the amount of the difference represents "operating income." If total expenses exceed total sales revenue, the amount of the difference represents "operating loss." The amount of the difference, debit, or credit is used to bring the balance of the total debit–credit columns showing equality.

Debit–credit column set 5: The balance sheet columns show the ending balance of total assets, liabilities, and ownership equity. "Operating income" increases ownership equity, whereas an "operating loss" decreases ownership equity. The worksheet shows all information needed to prepare an end-of-period balance sheet.

The accounting cycle can be summarized in these steps:

1. **Perform transactional analysis:** Verifying documentation or information such as invoices, sales, and checks indicate that a journal entry is required.
2. **Journalize:** Record of a business transaction in the journal.
3. **Post a journal entry:** Transfer journal instructions to a specific account and in the amount directed.
4. **Prepare an unadjusted trial balance:** List all accounts in the ledger with balances to confirm the debit-balanced accounts are equal to the credit-balanced accounts.
5. **Prepare a worksheet** (optional): Record the unadjusted trial balance; record end-of-period adjusting entries; develop adjusted trial balance; and

Exhibit 1.15 Texana Restaurant Worksheet
Month Ended May 31, 2000

Account Titles	1 Unadjusted Trial Debit	Credit	2 Adjustments Debit	Credit	3 Adjusted Trial Debit	Credit	4 Income Statement Debit	Credit	5 Balance Sheet Debit	Credit
Cash	$ 52,980				$ 52,980				$ 52,980	
Credit Card Receivables	620				620				620	
Prepaid Insurance	3,600			(c)$ 150	3,450				3,450	
Food Inventory	12,200		(a)$ 3,200	(a) 12,200	3,200				3,200	
Beverage Inventory	3,400		(b) 1,175	(b) 3,400	1,175				1,175	
Building	150,000				150,000				150,000	
Equipment	12,000				12,000				12,000	
Accounts Payable		$ 16,200				$ 16,200				$ 16,200
Notes Payable		100,000				100,000				100,000
Capital, Gram Disk		100,000				100,000				100,000
Sales Revenue		24,900				24,900		$ 24,900		
Wages Expense	3,400		(e) 400		3,800		$ 3,800			
Salaries Expense	1,800		(e) 480		2,280		2,280			
Utilities Expense	282				282		282			
Miscellaneous Expense	818				818		818			
Unadjusted Trial Balance Totals	$241,100	$241,100								
Cost of Sales			(a) 12,200	(a) 3,200	11,225		11,225			
			(b) 3,400	(b) 1,175						
Insurance Expense			(c) 150		150		150			
Depreciation Expense			(d) 525		525		525			
Accumulated Depreciation: Equip.				(d) 125		125				125
Accumulated Depreciation: Bldg.				(d) 400		400				400
Payroll Payable				(e) 880		880				880
Totals			$ 21,530	$ 21,530	$242,505	$242,505	19,080	24,900	$223,425	5,820
Operating Income, Increases Capital							5,820			5,820
							$ 24,900	$ 24,900	$223,425	$223,425

Adjustments: (a) and (b) adjusts Cost of Sales and Food and Beverage Inventories.
(d) Adjusts Depreciation Expense and Accumulated Depreciation.

(c) Adjusts Prepaid Insurance and Insurance Expense.
(e) Adjusts Wages and Salaries Expense and Accounts Payable.

extend appropriate accounts to the income statement and balance sheet columns.

6. **Adjust the ledger accounts:** Journalize and post end-of-period adjustments to the specified accounts. An unadjusted trial balance or a completed worksheet will provide needed information.

7. **Close the temporary accounts:** Journalize and post closing entries to bring the temporary accounts to a zero balance. An adjusted trial balance or a completed worksheet shows needed information.

8. **Prepare a post closing trial balance:** Take information from the ledger accounts or a post closing trial balance, or complete a worksheet to show needed information. The post closing trial balance verifies the accuracy of the adjusting and closing procedures and confirms all temporary accounts have been closed to a zero balance.

9. **Prepare the income statement:** Take information from the income statement ledger accounts or from a completed worksheet and prepare an income statement in proper format.

10. **Prepare the balance sheet:** Take information from the balance sheet ledger accounts or a post closing trial balance, or complete a worksheet, and prepare a balance sheet in proper format.

SUMMARY

In this chapter we discussed, outlined, described, and used basic accounting principles, concepts, rules, and procedures common to a manual system. It is interesting to note that a computerized system incorporates all of the fundamental accounting principles of the manual system. Accounting has been developed to accumulate, maintain, and provide financial information regarding internal business transactions. A common language has developed around the practice with its own set of rules or assumptions, commonly called principles and concepts. These assumptions include the following:

- Business entity concept
- Going concern concept
- Money concept
- Cost principle
- Periodicity concept
- Matching principle
- Full disclosure principle
- Consistency concept
- Conservatism concept
- Materiality concept
- Objectivity concept

It is important to have a good understanding of each of these principles and concepts to be able to interpret financial information correctly.

Depreciation is a method of systematically writing off the cost of major physical long-lived assets (building, furniture, and equipment) over the life of the asset. Only a portion of the cost is shown as a depreciation expense deduction from income on each period's income statement. There are various methods of depreciation, such as straight-line which was discussed in this chapter, and declining balance, sum-of-the-year digits, and units of production which are discussed in the next chapter.

The two main documents in a set of financial statements are the income statement and the balance sheet. The net income (or loss) from the income statement is transferred at the end of each accounting period to the ownership equity section of the balance sheet. The nature of double-entry accounting requires a balance sheet must always balance. The balance sheet equation is expressed as:

$$\text{Assets} = \text{Liabilities} + \text{Ownership Equity}$$

The income statement equation describes the economic results of profit operations: net income, net loss, or breakeven. The income statement format is expressed as:

$$\text{Revenue} - \text{Cost of Sales} - \text{Expenses} = \text{Breakeven, Net Income, or Net Loss}$$

Each ledger account is identified by name and account number. Each account is described as having a normal balance of either debit- or credit-balanced based on the type of account it is; assets, expenses, contra-assets, and contra-equity accounts are expected to be debit-balanced. Liabilities, ownership equity, and sales revenue accounts are expected to be credit-balanced. Each ledger account has two specific columns that are identified to receive numerical values. The left column is identified to receive only debit entries, and the right column receives only credit entries. Only by knowing the category of an account can you determine if an entry in the left or right column will increase or decrease the balance of the account. The debit–credit rules of whether entries increase or decrease the balance for each type of account are as follows:

Account Category	Normal Balance	Balance Increased by	Balance Decreased by
Assets	*Debit*	*Debits*	*Credits*
Liabilities	Credit	Credits	Debits
Ownership Equity	Credit	Credits	Debits
Sales Revenue	Credit	Credits	Debits
Expenses	*Debit*	*Debits*	*Credits*

DISCUSSION QUESTIONS

1. Explain the major difference between cash and accrual accounting.
2. In what way can a business manager use accounting information?
3. List and, in your own words, give a short description of five accounting principles or concepts.
4. Explain why a ledger account has only a debit and credit column to receive dollar value entries.
5. A hotel shows office supplies (such as stationery) on its balance sheet at a $500 cost, even though to any other hotel these supplies might have a value only as scrap paper. Which accounting principle or concept justifies this?
6. Describe depreciation and explain the straight-line method of depreciation.
7. A restaurant has purchased a new electronic point-of-sale register. With adequate maintenance the machine could last ten years; however, with the rapid advance of technological improvements it is expected that a newer register will be purchased within five years to replace the unit recently purchased. For depreciation purposes, what would be the useful life of the present new machine? Explain why.
8. What is the balance sheet equation? Is it possible for a transaction to affect an asset account without also affecting some other asset? Liability or owners'/ equity account?
9. Why is the rule for debit and credit entries the same for liability and owners' equity accounts?
10. Why are adjusting entries necessary at the end of each operating period before the end-of-period financial statements are prepared?
11. Discuss periodic inventory control and explain why an accumulated depreciation contra-asset account is needed to accumulate depreciation expense charges.
12. Under what circumstances might the individual account balances not be correct even though a trial balance is in balance?

ETHICS SITUATION

A restaurant manager has a contract with the restaurant's owner that he is entitled to eat meals in the restaurant without charge when on duty. The manager lives in a rented apartment above the restaurant with his wife and two children. Generally, the family members eat their meals in the restaurant every day of the week. No sales checks or other records make note of any consumed meals. Discuss the ethics of this situation based on the accounting principles and concepts discussed in this chapter.

EXERCISES

1.1 A number of accounting principles and concepts (such as the matching principle) were discussed in this chapter. For each of the following situations, state
which principle or concept is involved.

   a. A case of food poisoning occurred in a restaurant. The restaurant is being
       sued by a number of its customers who were hospitalized. The estimated
       cost of the loss the restaurant is likely to suffer from this lawsuit is recorded
       now as an expense because of the _____ principle.

   b. A hotel has traditionally depreciated its furniture and equipment using the
       straight-line method. This year a different depreciation method was used
       without advising its financial statement readers of this change. As a result,
       it is violating both the _____ and _____ concepts.

   c. A motel's normal payday for employees is every Friday. The year-end occurs
       on a Monday. The pay earned by employees for those three days is recorded
       in the motel's accounts because of the _____ principle.

   d. Last year a remote fishing resort purchased a floatplane to fly guests to the
       resort. The aircraft cost at that time was $150,000. This year, the plane is
       worth $160,000. However, it continues to be recorded on the books
       at $150,000 because of the going concern and the _____
       principles.

   e. If a restaurant operator takes home food from the restaurant and uses these
       products for his or her personal use, this act violates the _____
       concept.

   f. If a hotel estimated expenses to be higher than they actually might be, this
       reduces the hotel's profit and conforms to the _____ concept.

   g. A hotel purchased a box of 100 pencils for office use. At the end of the
       month, 90 pencils remain, with a total value of $4.50. The remaining
       pencils are not included as inventory on the balance sheet because of the
       _____ concept.

1.2 Write a short explanation of the following terms:
   a. Operating income
   b. Net income
   c. Net loss
   d. Breakeven

1.3 Identify the normal balance as debit or credit for each of the following categories of accounts:

Account:	Assets	Liabilities	Ownership Equity	Sales Revenue	Expenses
Balance:	_____	_____	_____	_____	_____

1.4   Complete the following sentences by filling in the missing words.

    a. Asset accounts are _____ by debits and _____ by credits.

    b. Liability accounts are _____ by debits and _____ by credits.

    c. Revenue accounts are _____ by debits and _____ by credits.

    d. Expense accounts are _____ by debits and _____ by credits.

1.5   Write the abbreviated linear equation for the balance sheet and income statement.

    Balance sheet equation is: _____

    Income statement equation is: _____

1.6   Equipment was purchased for $98,000. The equipment was estimated to have a serviceable life of 10 years and a residual trade-in value of $2,000. Using straight-line depreciation, answer the following:

    a. Depreciation expense per year $_____ per month $_____

    b. Give the journal entry to record depreciation expense for one year.

Account Title	Debit	Credit

1.7   Describe an accounting transaction that will:

    a. increase an asset and increase owners' equity.

    b. increase an asset and increase a liability.

    c. decrease an asset and decrease a liability.

    d. increase one asset and decrease another.

    e. decrease an asset and decrease owners' equity.

1.8   A restaurant paid $9,600 in advance for liability and casualty insurance for two years of coverage. Answer the following:

    a. Journalize the payment for the prepaid.

Account Title	Debit	Credit

    b. Insurance expense per year $_____ per month? $_____

c. Record the journal entry for insurance expense for six months.

Account Title	Debit	Credit

1.9 Referring to the journal entries you completed for exercises 1.8 (a) and (c) above, complete the modified "T" accounts below naming the accounts and posting both.

Acct. Name: _____			Acct. Name: _____			Acct. Name: _____		
Debit	Credit	Balance	Debit	Credit	Balance	Debit	Credit	Balance
(Begin. Bal.)		$ 18,400						

1.10 A business using the cash basis of accounting cannot locate all of its records for one month of operations. Beginning and ending cash balances of $14,840 and $11,320, respectively, are known. Cash payments made in the amount of $148,000 were determined by asking vendors for copies of receipts representing cash purchases. The amount of *cash* sales is not known. *Find the unknown cash sales revenue:*

Beginning Cash + Cash Sales Revenue? – Cash Payments = Ending Cash
$14,840   + $_____ – $148,000   = $11,320

PROBLEMS

1.1 Study each of the following restaurant transactions and make the necessary journal entries, skipping a line between each entry. Journal entries and ledger accounts can be prepared easily on lined paper. Journal entries and modified "T" accounts should follow examples shown in the text. To further simplify the problem, prepare modified "T" accounts for the following account titles shown by category. Balance sheet accounts: *Assets:* Cash, Credit Cards Receivable, Accounts Receivable, Food Inventory, Beverage Inventory, Prepaid Rent, Prepaid Insurance, Restaurant Supplies, Equipment, and Furnishings. *Liabilities:* Accounts Payable, Note Payable. *Capital (OE) Income Statement Accounts:* Sales Revenue, Salaries Expense, Wages Expense, Rent Expense, and Interest Expense.

a. Owner deposited $65,000 cash in the bank as an investment in a new restaurant.

b. Borrowed and deposited $20,000 on a note payable to the bank.

c. Paid one year of rent in advance on the restaurant space, $14,400 cash.

d. Purchased equipment for $44,000, paying $15,000 in cash and owing balance on account.

e. Purchased restaurant furnishings for $28,400 cash.

f. Purchased $3,000 of food inventory on account and $4,000 of beverage inventory for cash.

g. Purchased restaurant supplies for $2,650 cash.

h. Purchased $3,800 of food inventory on account.

i. Paid $2,400 for a one-year liability and casualty insurance policy.

j. Paid employee wages of $12,800 and salaries of $2,400.

k. Revenue for the first month was $32,800: 92% cash, 6% on credit cards, and 2% on accounts receivable.

l. Paid $12,000 on accounts payable.

m. Paid $2,000 on notes payable, plus interest of $200.

When all journal entries have been posted, prepare an unadjusted trial balance for the month ended March 31, 2000.

1.2 A friend has asked you to look at the accounts of his small restaurant and recommend the end-of-period adjusting entries. After viewing the accounts, it was apparent the following adjusting entries were required:

a. A total of $2,040 of prepaid insurance must be expensed.

b. A total of $5,000 of prepaid rent has been consumed.

c. Kitchen equipment depreciation in the amount of $3,500 must be recognized.

d. Wages earned and due employees but not paid total $692.

e. Restaurant supplies; $874 have been used.

f. Interest on a note payable in the amount of $290 must be accrued.

You are to record the adjusting journal entries to record the adjustments shown above.

1.3 The following transactions occurred for a new motor lodge owner prior to and during the first month of business operations.

a. Owner invested $160,000 cash deposited in the business bank account.

b. Paid $28,000 cash for land.

c. Paid cash for building $100,200.

d. Borrowed $75,000 on a mortgage payable.

e. Purchased equipment for $62,000, paying $22,000 cash and balance on a note payable.

f. Purchased furnishings for $28,000 cash.

g. Purchased linen inventory for $6,474 on account.

h. Purchased supplies for $2,800 on account.

i. Purchased vending inventory, $380 cash.

j. Room revenue during month, $44,000 cash.

k. Vending revenue from vending machines, $800 cash.

l. Paid wages $1,900 cash.

m. Paid $2,200 on accounts payable.

n. Paid $2,800 on annual liability and casualty insurance policy.

o. Paid $300 cash on the mortgage payable, plus $600 interest.

Journalize the above transactions, skipping a line between each journal entry, and post them to modified "T" accounts. Journal entries and modified T" accounts should follow examples shown in the text. Prepare modified "T" accounts for the following account titles shown by category: *Assets:* Cash, Prepaid Insurance, Vending Inventory, Supplies, Linen Inventory, Land, Building, Equipment, and Furnishings. *Liabilities:* Accounts Payable, Note Payable, Mortgage Payable. *Owners' Equity Account:* Capital. *Income Statement Accounts:* Room Revenue, Vending Revenue, Wages Expense, Supplies Expense, and Interest Expense.

After journalizing and posting the operating transactions, journalize the following adjusting entries:

a. Estimated closing value of the linen inventory, $5,700.

b. Wages earned by employees but unpaid, $400.

c. One-twelfth of the prepaid insurance has been consumed.

d. Interest owing, but not yet paid, on the equipment notes payable account is 1% of the balance owing at month-end.

e. Equipment depreciation is based on a life of 12 years with a $5,000 residual value, straight-line depreciation.

f. Furnishings depreciation is based on an 8-year life with a $400 residual (salvage) value, straight-line depreciation.

g. Building has a 40-year life with a residual (salvage) value of $18,000, straight-line.

h. Supplies used during the first month, $600.

1.4   Joe Fast started a mobile snack food service on January 2, 2000, investing $10,000 cash deposited in a bank account in the name of "Fast Snacks." He paid $8,000 for a second-hand, fully equipped truck and started operating on January 4, 2000, using the cash basis, keeping no formal accounting records. At year's end, he asks you to help him find his income or loss for the first year of operation. You have determined the following:

a. He operated on a cash basis and began operating on January 4, 2000.

b. He purchased a truck for $8,000 cash; depreciable at 20% per year.

c. He started the operation with $2,000 cash available.

d. He has $24 cash on hand and $555 cash in the bank.

e. His receipts for cash purchases of inventory for resale total $12,648.

f. The value of his ending inventory for resale is $275.

g. He paid cash for all truck operating costs; receipts total $914. In addition he has an invoice he has not paid for a recent truck repair in the amount of $27.

h. He also informed you that he took $1,500 a month for 12 months to use for living and other personal expenses.

   You discover Joe kept no record of the cash sales he made during the year. Cash sales revenue must be determined from the information already noted. Show Joe how cash sales were determined and prepare an income statement on the accrual basis showing his operating income for the year.

1.5   Art Angel operates a small seasonal lake marina, renting boats and selling snacks. He rents marina space for the mid-May to mid-September season each year for $800 per month. He started the current season with $5,000 in the bank and paid the marina seasonal rent in advance. In May, he bought three new boats for cash at $500 each. The new boats were estimated to have a four-year, depreciable straight-line life and a trade-in value of $100 each. Purchase invoices show he paid $7,458 cash for food and beverage inventory. There remains one unpaid invoice for food in the amount of $73. No food or beverage inventory remained at season end. Other costs incurred during the season were boat maintenance, $211, casual labor costs, $254. In addition, Art said he withdrew $1,000 per month during the season. The season ending cash balance in the bank is $4,697. No records exist regarding the amount of cash sales. He is confused as to why he has less cash now than when he started the season.

   Cash sales revenue must be determined using only the information already noted. Show him how you determine cash sales and prepare an income statement on the accrual basis showing his operating income before tax for the year. Discuss his concern regarding his remaining cash.

CASE 1

This is the first part of an ongoing case that will appear at the end of most subsequent chapters. It is recommended that you keep case solutions, notes, and other case-oriented information in a separate file or binder for quick reference.

Charlie Driver has $20,000 saved and has decided to attend college, taking courses in marketing and retailing. To help pay his tuition and living expenses, he contracted with a mobile catering company as an independent driver. Charlie will run his mobile catering business on a cash basis; he has named his business Charlie's Convenient Catering, or the 3C company for short. He opened a company bank account with $20,000. He bought a used, fully equipped mobile catering truck for $16,000, and operated from January 4 to December 31. Charlie had $11,110 in the bank and $48 in a cash drawer. Invoices show he purchased food, beverages, and supplies inventories from the company for $25,296; ending inventory remaining on the truck was $350. His invoices for truck operating expenses total $1,828 paid and he has one unpaid truck repair invoice for $254. Charlie withdrew $2,000 a month for personal expenses. The truck has a five-year life and no residual value; the depreciation method is straight-line.

Charlie asks you to help him put together his business information and reconstruct his cash sales. He recorded his daily cash sales in a notebook that cannot be found. Calculate 3C company's revenue and prepare an accrual income statement. Charlie is concerned he has less cash now then he had when he started. Explain why.

2

Understanding
Financial Statements

INTRODUCTION

This chapter discusses the two major financial statements—the balance sheet and the income statement. In hospitality operations, balance sheets are normally prepared for an overall operation, and income statements are prepared by each of the subordinate operating departments (or divisions). Two basic classifications of costs, direct and indirect, will be incurred in a hospitality operation.

Departmental income statements will identify operating costs as "direct costs," which are directly traceable to the department. "Indirect costs" are costs that are not easily traceable to a specific department, and are classified as "undistributed costs." Undistributed costs are normally incurred in support of the overall facility and will normally appear on a summary income statement. All costs shown in a generic income statement will be shown as "cost of sales," and named "expenses."

Cost of sales was discussed in a proprietary example in Chapter 1; however, cost of sales apply to partnerships and incorporated business operations as well and will be expanded in this chapter. Discussion will reference three perpetual inventory control methods and will explain how the cost of food and beverages may need to be adjusted to arrive at net cost of sales. Adjustments may be needed for interdepartmental transfers and for employee and promotion meals.

We will expand straight-line depreciation with discussion and examples of three other methods of depreciation—sum of the years digits, double declining balance, and units of production. Responsibility accounting will be introduced and discussed for "profit" and "cost" centers. Allocation methods used to distribute indirect costs to departments will be discussed, as will the effect a change to sales mix among departments would have on overall profit.

A balance sheet, when illustrated, will show each account by category appearing in the illustration. An account called "retained earnings" is demonstrated as the link between the income statement and balance sheet in a corporate business entity. This section will also discuss the difference between the equity section of a balance sheet for proprietary, partnership, and incorporated business entities.

CHAPTER OBJECTIVES

After studying this chapter and completing the assigned exercises and problems, the reader should be able to:

1. Explain the main purpose of the two financial statements discussed and the value of a uniform system of accounts.

2. Define and explain the difference between a balance sheet and the income statement.

3. Using examples, describe the difference between a direct cost, indirect cost, and undistributed costs (expenses).

4. Calculate the value of ending inventory using each method discussed, and demonstrate possible adjustments to find net cost of sales.

5. Demonstrate the use of each of the three additional depreciation methods discussed.

6. Prepare income statements in proper format and discuss the concept of responsibility accounting.

7. Explain the effect a specific change in interdepartmental revenue mix will have on overall operating income (income before tax).

8. List and give an example of each of the six major categories (classifications) of accounts that may appear on a balance sheet.

9. Define, calculate, and explain the purpose of retained earnings.

10. Prepare a balance sheet in proper format and state the two forms of balance sheet presentations. Discuss the importance and limitations of a balance sheet.

UNDERSTANDING FINANCIAL STATEMENTS

Being able to understand financial statements does not necessarily mean you must be able to prepare them. However, if you are able to prepare a set of statements, primarily a balance sheet and income statement, then you have the advantage of being able to analyze and use the resulting information to enhance the results of a business operation.

Users of financial statements

Although there are many internal and external users of financial statements from upper levels of management, owners, employees, stockholders, creditors, county, and local and national regulatory agencies, the primary emphasis of this text is keyed for use of internal management, from the department head up to general management. Managers at all levels need financial information if they are expected to make rational decisions for the immediate or near future. Rational decisions require relevant information.

THE UNIFORM SYSTEM OF ACCOUNTS

Most organizations in the hospitality industry (hotels, motels, resorts, restaurants, clubs) use the Uniform System of Accounts appropriate to their particular segment of the industry. The original Uniform System of Accounts for Hotels (USAH) was initiated in 1925 by the Hotel Association of New York. The system was designed for classifying, organizing, and presenting financial information so that uniformity prevailed and comparison of financial data among hotels was possible.

Comparison with averages

One of the advantages of accounting uniformity is that information can be collected on a regional or national basis from similar organizations within the hospitality industry. This information can then be reproduced in the form of average figures or statistics. In this way, each individual organization can compare its results with the averages. This does not mean that the individual hotel operator, for example, should be using national hotel average results as a goal for his own organization. Average results are only a standard of comparison, and there are many reasons why the individual organization's results may differ from industry averages. But, by making the comparison, determining where differences exist, and subsequently analyzing the causes, the individual operator at least has information from which he can then decide whether or not corrective action is required within his own organization.

INCOME STATEMENT AND BALANCE SHEET

Statements to be read jointly

Although the balance sheet and the income statement are treated separately in this chapter, they should, in practice, be read and analyzed jointly. The relationship between the two financial statements must always be kept in mind.

This relationship becomes extremely clear when one compares the definition and objective of each statement.

- The purpose of the balance sheet is to provide a picture of the financial condition of a business entity at a particular point in time. By category, each individual account, by name and its numerical balance, is shown at the end of a specific date in the operating period.
- The purpose of the income statement is to show economic results of profit-motivated operations of a business over a specific period of time.
- The ending date of an operating time period indicated in the income statement is normally the date of the balance sheet.

Operating time periods may be on a calendar year beginning on January 1 and ending on December 31, or a fiscal year beginning on any date other than January 1, and ending on any date other than December 31. In addition, a business entity may use an interim reporting period such as monthly, quarterly, or semiannually.

INCOME STATEMENT

While the balance sheet presentations for most hospitality operations differ little from one type of hospitality business to another (and indeed are also similar in presentation to most nonhospitality operations), that is not true of the income statement.

Operations are departmentalized

Most hospitality operations are departmentalized, and the income statement needs to show the operating results department by department as well as for the operation as a whole. Exactly how such an income statement is prepared and presented is dictated by the management needs of each individual establishment. As a result, the income statement for one hotel may be completely different from another, and income statements for other branches of the industry (resorts, chain hotels, small hotels, motels, restaurants, and clubs) will likely be very different from each other because each has to be prepared to reflect operating results that will allow management to make rational decisions about the business's future.

Discussion of the income statement in the chapter will be in general terms only and not limited to any one branch of the hospitality industry. A long-form income statement is recommended for larger hotels (USAH) developed by the Hotel Association of New York City, and used (though not mandatory) and approved by the American Motel and Hotel Association.

REVENUE

Revenue defined

Revenue is defined as an inflow of assets received in exchange for goods or services provided. In a hotel, revenue is derived from renting guest rooms, and in a restaurant from the sale of food and beverages. Revenue is also derived from many other sources such as catering, entertainment, casinos, space rentals, vending machines, and gift shop operations, located on or immediately adjacent to the property. It is not unusual for revenue to be received from interest income, investment dividends, and franchise or management fees.

The accrual accounting method will recognize revenue when earned, not necessarily when received. Revenue is created and recorded to a revenue account by receipt of cash or the extension (giving) of credit. Although the recognition of revenue will in theory increase ownership equity, in reality ownership equity will increase or decrease after expenses incurred are matched to revenues (matching principle) earned at the end of an operating period. Ownership equity increases if revenues exceed expenses (R > E); likewise if revenue is less than expenses (R < E), ownership equity will decrease.

As discussed in Chapter 1, the cash basis of accounting requires that cash change hands for the recognition of revenues or expenses; in theory, the capital account increases by a sale of goods or services and decreases as expense items are paid.

EXPENSES

Expenses defined

Expenses are defined as an outflow of assets consumed to generate revenue. The accrual method requires that expenses be recorded when incurred, not necessarily when payment is made. Although the recognition of expenses in theory increases ownership equity, in reality ownership equity will increase or decrease only after expenses incurred are matched to revenues earned at the end of an operating period.

The determination of ownership equity increasing or decreasing follows the same "R–E" functions noted in the preceding revenue discussion. For example, in a restaurant, food inventory is purchased for resale and recorded as an asset; the cost of sales for a food operation is not recognized until it has been determined how much food inventory was sold.

DEPARTMENTAL CONTRIBUTORY INCOME

Contributory income represents income before tax

Contributory income is also known as departmental income, which represents income before tax. The term departmental contributory income is used in this text since it clarifies its origin; contributory income is department revenue minus its direct costs.

By matching direct expenses (costs) with the various revenue-producing activities of a department, a useful evaluation tool is created. The departmental income statement provides the basis for an effective evaluation of the department's performance over an operating period. The general format, in condensed form, for a departmentalized operation is given below, using random numbers:

Departmental Revenue	$580,000
Less: Departmental Expenses (Direct Costs)	<464,000>
Departmental Contributory Income	$116,000

Provide maximum detail

It is most important that the contributory income statement provide maximum detail by showing each revenue and expense account to provide the information needed by management to conduct an effective and efficient evaluation.

If departmental managers are to be given authority and responsibility for their departmental operations, they need to be provided with more accounting information than revenue less total expenses. In other words, expenses need to be listed item by item, otherwise department heads will have no knowledge about which expenses are out of line and where additional controls may need to be implemented to curb those expenditures:

ANSWERS TO QUESTIONS

The income statement can provide answers to some important questions, such as:

Typical questions

- What were the sales last month? How does that compare with the month before and with the same month last year?
- Did last month's sales keep pace with the increased cost of food, beverages, labor, and other expenses?
- What were the sales, by department, for the operating period?
- Which department is operating most effectively?
- Is there a limit to maximum potential sales? Have we reached that limit? If so, can we increase sales in the short run by increasing room rates and menu prices and/or in the long run by expanding the premises?
- What were the food and beverage cost and gross profit percentages? Did these meet our objectives?
- Were operating costs (such as for labor and supplies) in line with what they should be for the sales level achieved?
- How did the operating results for the period compare with budget forecasts?

The income statement shows the operating results of a business for a period of time (week, month, quarter, half-year, or year). The amount of detail concerning revenue and expenses to be shown on the income statement depends on the type and size of the hospitality establishment and the needs of management for more or less information.

For example, a typical hotel would prepare departmental income statements for each of its operating departments. Exhibit 2.1 illustrates one for the food department. Similar ones would be prepared for the beverage department and the rooms department. Others would be prepared for any other operating departments large enough to warrant it. Alternatively, all the other, smaller departments could be grouped together into a single income statement (this would include operating areas such as newsstands, gift shops, laundry, telephone, parking, and so on).

It should be noted that in many establishments, it is not possible to show the food department as a separate entity from the beverage department. The reason is that, since these two departments work very closely together, they have many common costs that cannot accurately be identified as belonging to one or the other. Because of this, there is only one income statement produced for the food and beverage department. Wherever possible, it is suggested that the revenue and expenses for food be kept separate from the revenue and expenses for beverages because in this way the income statements are more meaningful. In this text, therefore, food and beverage are shown as separate operating departments, even though it is recognized that, in practice, this may not always be possible. If it is possible, the two separate sets of figures can always be added together later to give a combined food and beverage income statement for comparison with other establishments or with industry averages.

As you review the sample departmental income statement in Exhibit 2.1, take particular note of the following: (1) Each individual revenue division is identified. (2) The cost of employee meals is deducted from food service cost of sales. The cost of employee meals is actual cost, and no revenue that consists of cost plus profit markup was generated. The term *net food cost* implies that all necessary adjustments to cost of sales food have been made, and represent the actual cost incurred to produce revenue. Cost of employee meals became a part of the employee benefits reported as a departmental expense.

Each department's income statement will have allocated to it its share of the expenses directly attributable to it, which are the responsibility of the department head to control. These direct costs are directly traceable and would include cost of sales (food cost, beverage cost); salaries, wages, and related payroll costs of the employees working in the department; and linen, laundry, and all the various other categories of supplies required to operate the department. The resulting departmental incomes (revenue less direct expenses) are sometimes referred to as contributory incomes because they contribute to the indirect, undistributed expenses not charged to the operating departments. The individual departmental (contributory) incomes are added together to give a combined, total departmental income (see Exhibit 2.2). As mentioned earlier,

Departmental income statements

Direct expenses charged to departments

Exhibit 2.1   Sample Departmental Income Statement
Hotel Theoretical Departmental Income Statement—Food Department
(Year Ending December 31, 0006)

Revenue

Dining room	$201,600	
Coffee shop	195,900	
Banquets	261,200	
Room service	81,700	
Bar	111,200	
Total revenue		$851,600
Cost of sales		
Cost of food used	$352,500	
Less: employee meals	(30,100)	
Net food cost		322,400
Gross profit		$529,200
Departmental expenses		
Salaries and wages	$277,400	
Employee benefits	34,500	
Total payroll and related expenses	$311,900	
China, glassware	7,100	
Cleaning supplies	6,400	
Decorations	2,200	
Guest supplies	6,500	
Laundry	15,500	
Licenses	3,400	
Linen	3,700	
Menus	2,000	
Miscellaneous	800	
Paper supplies	4,900	
Printing, stationery	4,700	
Silver	2,300	
Uniforms	3,100	
Utensils	1,700	
Total operating expenses		(376,200)
Departmental contributory income (loss)		$153,000

each departmental income figure would be supported by a departmental income statement similar to Exhibit 2.1.

From the total departmental income figure are deducted what are sometimes referred to as *indirect expenses*. Indirect expenses are those that are not directly related to the revenue-producing activities of the operation. Indirect expenses are broken down into two separate categories: the undistributed operating expenses and the fixed charges. Undistributed operating expenses include costs such as administrative and general, marketing, property operation and maintenance, and energy costs. Other expenses that might be included in this category, in certain establishments, are management fees, franchise fees, and guest entertainment. All these undistributed operating expenses are considered controllable, but not by the operating department heads or managers. They are controllable by and are the responsibility of the general manager. Note that these undistributed operating expenses include the cost of salaries and wages of employees involved.

Income before fixed charges is an important line on an income statement because it measures the overall efficiency of the operation's management. At this point, the fixed charges are not considered in this evaluation because they are capital costs resulting from owning the property (that is, from the investment in land and building) and are thus not controllable by the establishment's operating management.

The final level of expenses, generally referred to as *fixed charges,* are then deducted. In this category are such expenses as property taxes, insurance, interest, and depreciation. Income tax is then deducted to arrive at the final net income.

This net income figure is transferred to the statement of retained earnings and eventually appears on the balance sheet. This will be illustrated later in the chapter.

Each of the expenses listed in Exhibit 2.2 would have, if the size of the establishment warranted it, a separate schedule listing all the detailed costs making up the total expense. For example, the administrative and general expense schedule could show separate cost figures for such items as:

- Salary of general manager and other administrative employees
- Secretarial and general office salaries/wages
- Accountant and accounting office personnel salaries/wages
- Data processing and/or credit office employees' salaries/wages
- Postage and fax expense
- Printing and stationery expense
- Legal expense
- Bad debts and/or collection expenses
- Dues and subscriptions expense
- Travel expense

Exhibit 2.2   Sample Summary Income Statement
Hotel Theoretical Income Statement
(Year Ending December 31, 0006)

Departmental income (loss)		
Rooms		$ 782,900
Food		153,000
Beverage		119,100
Other income		18,600
Total departmental income		$1,073,600
Undistributed operating expenses		
Administrative and general	$238,000	
Marketing	66,900	
Property operation and maintenance	102,000	
Energy costs	71,000	477,900
Income before fixed charges		$ 595,700
Fixed charges		
Property taxes	$ 98,800	
Insurance	22,400	
Interest	82,400	
Depreciation	160,900	364,500
Income before income tax		$ 231,200
Income tax		114,700
Net income		$ 116,500

Exhibit 2.3 shows another method of income statement presentation. Accompanying this income statement should be separate departmental income statements for each operating department, similar to the one for the food department illustrated in Exhibit 2.1. Also, where necessary, the income statement should be accompanied by schedules giving more detail of the unallocated expenses. Exhibit 2.4 illustrates income statements for a major hotel company (Marriott International, Inc.): Exhibit 2.5 shows income statements for a large restaurant chain (Shoney's Inc.).

Exhibit 2.3 Alternative Summary Income Statement
Hotel Theoretical Income Statement
(Year Ending December 31, 0006)

	Net Revenue	Cost of Sales	Payroll and Other Expense	Expenses	Operating Income
Departmental income (loss)					
Rooms	$1,150,200		$251,400	$115,900	$ 782,900
Food	851,600	$322,400	311,900	64,300	153,000
Beverage	327,400	106,800	86,300	15,200	119,100
Other income	38,200	10,600	8,700	300	18,600
Operating department totals	$2,367,400	$439,800	$658,300	$195,700	$1,073,600
Undistributed operating expenses					
Administrative and general			$115,600	$122,400	
Marketing			35,100	31,800	
Property operation and maintenance			52,900	49,100	
Energy costs			15,800	55,200	
			$219,400	$258,500	(477,900)
Income before fixed charges					$ 595,700
Fixed charges					
Property taxes				$ 98,800	
Insurance				22,400	
Interest				82,400	
Depreciation				160,900	(364,500)
Income before income tax					$ 231,200
Income tax					(114,700)
Net income					$ 116,500

Cost of Sales

With reference to Exhibit 2.1, note that net food cost has been deducted from revenue to arrive at gross profit before deducting other departmental expenses. To arrive at net food cost (and net beverage cost), some calculations are necessary to match up food and beverage sales with cost of the inventory sold for food and beverages, or to find the cost of sales incurred to generate those sales. In the first chapter we discussed the "cost of sales" method to isolate the cost

Exhibit 2.4   Income Statements Marriott International, Inc.
(Courtesy of Marriott International, Inc.)

Marriott International, Inc. and Subsidiaries

Fiscal years ended December 29,1995, December 20, 1994 and December 31, 1993	1995	1994	1993
	(in millions, except per share amounts)		
Sales			
Lodging			
Rooms	$3,273	$3,036	$2,529
Food and beverage	1,289	1,210	1,102
Other	765	703	583
	5,327	4,949	4,214
Contract Services	3,634	3,466	3,216
	8,961	8,415	7,430
Operating Costs and Expenses			
Lodging			
Departmental direct costs			
Rooms	772	727	595
Food and beverage	973	922	844
Other operating expenses, including remittances to hotel owners	3,222	2,998	2,520
	4,967	4,647	3,959
Contract Services	3,504	3,355	3,115
	8,471	8,002	7,074
Operating Profit			
Lodging	360	302	255
Contract Services	130	111	101
Operating profit before corporate expenses and interest	490	413	356
Corporate expenses	(64)	(68)	(63)
Interest expense	(53)	(32)	(27)
Interest income	39	29	9
Income Before Income Taxes and Cumulative Effect of a Change in Accounting Principle	412	342	275
Provision for income taxes	165	142	116
Income Before Cumulative Effect of a Change in Accounting Principle	247	200	159
Cumulative effect of a change in accounting for income taxes	—	—	(33)
Net Income	$ 247	$ 200	$ 126

Exhibit 2.5   Income Statements Shoney's Inc.

	Years Ended		
	October 29 1995	October 30 1994	October 31 1993
Revenues			
Net sales	$1,029,314,432	$1,035,832,226	$1,022,413,791
Franchise fees	23,886,704	25,793,886	25,872,439
Other income	131,284	10,833,006	3,460,506
Total revenues	1,053,332,420	1,072,459,118	1,051,746,736
Costs and expenses			
Cost of sales			
Food and supplies	430,990,408	447,959,750	442,045,520
Restaurant labor	251,196,828	234,547,471	229,860,922
Operating expenses	240,357,620	213,385,949	205,674,912
	922,544,856	895,893,170	877,581,354
General and administrative expenses	63,904,769	55,397,496	54,440,288
Interest expense	39,815,887	41,236,895	44,465,636
Litigation settlement		(1,700,000)	
Restructuring expense	7,991,539		
Total costs and expenses	1,034,257,051	990,827,561	976,487,278
Income from continuing operations before income taxes, extraordinary charge and cumulative effect of change in accounting principle	19,075,369	81,631,557	75,259,458
Provision for income taxes			
Current	9,087,000	19,940,000	22,720,000
Deferred	(1,214,000)	9,374,000	5,736,000
Total income taxes	7,873,000	29,314,000	28,456,000
Income from continuing operations before extraordinary charge and cumulative effect of change in accounting principle	11,202,369	52,317,557	46,803,458
Discontinued operations, net of income taxes	8,136,588	10,276,649	11,206,520
Gain on sale of discontinued operations, net of income taxes	5,532,748		
Extraordinary charge on early extinguishment of debt, net of income tax benefit		(1,037,808)	
Cumulative effect of change in accounting for income taxes		4,468,386	
Net income	$ 24,871,705	$ 66,024,784	$ 58,009,978

of sales on a monthly basis using the periodic inventory control method. The periodic method relies on a physical count and costing of the inventory over a specific time period to determine the cost of sales. Using the periodic method normally will not provide a record of inventory available for sale on any particular day. The calculation of cost of sales using the periodic method used this procedure, which was introduced in Chapter 1 and is shown below:

Beginning Inventory + Purchases − Ending Inventory = <u>Cost of Sales</u>

The control of inventory for sale is important for a number of reasons, such as:

- If inventories are not known, the possibility exists that inventory may run out and sales will stop. This situation will certainly create customer dissatisfaction.
- If inventories are in excess of projected needs, spoilage may occur, creating an additional cost that could be avoided.
- If inventories are maintained in excess of the amount needed, holding excess inventories will create an additional cost.
- The cost and control of inventories on hand, including items held in storerooms, in the kitchen, in preparation, or available on a customer self-service basis, should be held accountable.

Perpetual method allows continuous updating

On the other hand, even though the perpetual inventory method requires a number of records, it will provide the daily information needed to achieve excellent inventory control (see Exhibit 2.6). The perpetual method allows continuous updating, showing the receipt and sale of each inventory item, and allows maintenance of a daily running balance of inventory available. There are a number of different inventory valuation methods of which we will discuss four.

1. Specific Item Cost
2. First-in, First-out
3. Last-in, First-out
4. Weighted Average Cost

To illustrate the four control methods, consider the specific identification, perpetual inventory record shown in Exhibit 2.6. This method records the actual cost of each item. Assume 10 items remain in stock at month end—3 from the purchase of June 2, and 7 from the purchase of June 15. The value of ending inventory (EI) on June 30 would be:

3 @ $20 = $60 + 7 @ $22 = $154 = <u>$214 Total EI</u>

Exhibit 2.6   Specific Identification, Perpetual Control Record

| Item Description: *Chateau Dupont* | | | Balance Available | |
Date	Received Purchased	Issued-Sales	Units	Cost
June 01			2	$ 18.00
02	6		8	$ 20.00
08		3	5	
12		3	2	
15	10		12	$ 22.00
20		3	9	
24		3	6	
28	6		12	
30		2	10	$ 19.00

This method of inventory valuation is normally used only for high-cost items, such as high-cost wines.

First-in, First-out Method

Commonly referred to as FIFO, the inventory control procedure is as the name implies—the first items received are assumed to be the first items sold. Simply put, the oldest items are assumed to be sold first, leaving the newest items remaining in inventory. This method, when practiced, is based on the concept of stock rotation. Stock rotation is essential with perishable stock, and will help insure stock is sold before it becomes spoiled. Using FIFO, ending inventory is valued at $202 dollars. Study Exhibit 2.6-A.

Concept of stock rotation

FIFO creates tiers of inventory available. The first tier is the oldest, the second tier the next oldest, and so on; thus, the oldest units are always sold first. The sales flow is from top to bottom of the inventory tiers. Any tier is split to account for the number of units sold. Cost of sales is determined at any point in time by adding the issued-sales column. The value of ending inventory is the total cost shown in the final tier of the balance available column. FIFO uses the earliest costs, and in a period of inflationary costs, lowers cost of sales and increases the value of EI.

Exhibit 2.6-A   FIFO Perpetual Inventory Control Record

Item Description: *Chateau Dupont*			Balance Available
Date	Purchase-Received	Issued-Sales	Units × cost = Tot. Cost
06-01-20	Bal. Fwd.		2 @ $18.00 = $ 36.00
06-02-20	6 @ $20.00 = $120.00		2 @ $18.00 = $ 36.00 6 @ $20.00 = $120.00
06-08-20		2 @ $18.00 = $ 36.00 1 @ $20.00 = $ 20.00	5 @ $20.00 = $100.00
06-12-20		3 @ $20.00 = $ 60.00	2 @ $20.00 = $ 40.00
06-15-20	10 @ $22.00 = $220.00		2 @ $20.00 = $ 40.00 10 @ $22.00 = $220.00
06-20-20		2 @ $20.00 = $ 40.00 1 @ $22.00 = $ 22.00	9 @ $22.00 = $198.00
06-24-20		3 @ $22.00 = $ 66.00	6 @ $22.00 = $132.00
06-28-20	6 @ $19.00 = $114.00		6 @ $22.00 = $132.00 6 @ $19.00 = $114.00
06-30-20		2 @ $22.00 = $ 44.00	4 @ $22.00 = $ 88.00 6 @ $19.00 = $114.00
Ending		Cost of sales = $288.00	Ending Inv. = $202.00

Last-in, First-out Method

Commonly referred to as LIFO, the inventory control procedure is as the name implies—the newest or last items received are assumed to be the first items sold, leaving the oldest items remaining in inventory. Simply put, the newest items are assumed to be sold first. LIFO uses the same concept as FIFO, of creating tiers of inventory available; however, the newest units are assumed to be sold first. Using LIFO, ending inventory is valued at $200.00. Study Exhibit 2.6-B.

Sales flow is from bottom to top of the inventory tiers with the LIFO method. Any tier will be split to account for the number of units sold. Cost of sales is determined at any point in time by adding the issued-sales column. The value of ending inventory is the total cost shown in the final tier of the balance available column.

LIFO reduces profit

Use of the LIFO method during inflationary periods will cause an increase to cost of sales and will reduce gross margin. This effect is true since newer inventory purchases will cost more than older inventory purchases. In some cases, this method is favored based on the following logic: If inventory cost is

Exhibit 2.6-B   LIFO Perpetual Inventory Control Record

Item Description: *Chateau Dupont*			Balance Available
Date	Purchase-Received	Issued-Sales	Units × cost = Tot. Cost
06-01-20	Bal. Fwd.		2 @ $18.00 = $ 36.00
06-02-20	6 @ $20.00 = $120.00		6 @ $20.00 = $120.00
06-08-20		3 @ $20.00 = $ 60.00	2 @ $18.00 = $ 36.00 3 @ $20.00 = $ 60.00
06-12-20		3 @ $20.00 = $ 60.00	2 @ $18.00 = $ 36.00
06-15-20	10 @ $22.00 = $220.00		2 @ $20.00 = $ 40.00 10 @ $22.00 = $220.00
06-20-20		3 @ $22.00 = $ 66.00	2 @ $18.00 = $ 36.00 7 @ $22.00 = $154.00
06-24-20		3 @ $22.00 = $ 66.00	2 @ $18.00 = $ 36.00 4 @ $22.00 = $ 88.00
06-28-20	6 @ $19.00 = $114.00		2 @ $18.00 = $ 36.00 4 @ $22.00 = $ 88.00 6 @ $19.00 = $114.00
06-30-20		2 @ $19.00 = $ 38.00	2 @ $18.00 = $ 36.00 4 @ $22.00 = $ 88.00 4 @ $19.00 = $ 76.00
Ending		Cost of sales = $290.00	Ending Inv. = $200.00

increasing, then generally revenues are expected to increase since cost increases are passed on through higher selling prices. Higher costs will be matched to higher revenues resulting in a lower taxable operating income and lower taxes. LIFO will also reduce the value of inventory for resale and will be lower than if FIFO was used.

This logic can be seen in some respects by viewing the difference in the value of ending inventories when the FIFO and LIFO exhibits, 2.6-A and 2.6-B, are reviewed.

Weighted Average Cost Method

This method calculates a "weighted average" cost for each category of inventory available for sale. Each time additional inventory is received into stock, a new "weighted average" cost is calculated. All items of a specific category of inventory will be reported at its weighted average cost per unit. With reference to Exhibit 2.6-C, there were two items on hand at $18 each at a total value of $36. On June 2, six additional items at $20 each with a total value of $120

Cost calculation

were added into stock. The new cost of the total eight items at "weighted average" is $19.50 each. The calculation made was:

$$\text{Total cost units available} \div \text{Total units available} = \text{Weighted Average cost}$$

$$\underline{\$156.00} \qquad \div \qquad 8 \text{ units} \qquad = \qquad \underline{\$19.50 \text{ each}}$$

or, as abbreviated:

$$\text{T.C. / T.U.} = \$156/8 = \underline{\$19.50}$$

Similar calculations are required each time inventory is added on June 15 and June 28. Review Exhibit 2.6-C and confirm the weighted average calculations.

The weighted average inventory evaluation method can generally reduce effects of price-cost increases or decreases during a month or for longer operating periods.

Having discussed the four different inventory evaluation methods, we will now compare the results:

Specific Identification	$214.00
First-in, First-out	$202.00
Last-in, First-out	$200.00
Weighted Average Cost	$205.00

Although the differences among the four inventory valuation methods do not appear to be significant, one must remember that only one single item of inventory in stock was evaluated. If a full inventory were evaluated, the differences

Exhibit 2.6-C   Weighted Average Perpetual Inventory Control Record

06-01-20	Bal. Fwd.		2 @ $18.00 = $ 36.00
06-02-20	6 @ $20.00 = $120.00	*[$156 ÷ 8 = $ 19.50]*	8 @ $19.50 = $156.00
06-08-20		3 @ $19.50 = $ 58.50	5 @ $19.50 = $ 97.50
06-12-20		3 @ $19.50 = $ 58.50	2 @ $19.50 = $ 39.00
06-15-20	10 @ $22.50 = $225.00	*[$264 ÷ 12 = $ 22.00]*	12 @ $22.00 = $264.00
06-20-20		3 @ $22.00 = $ 66.00	9 @ $22.00 = $198.00
06-24-20		3 @ $22.00 = $ 66.00	6 @ $22.00 = $132.00
06-28-20	6 @$19.00 = $114.00	*[$246.00 ÷ 12 = $ 20.50]*	12 @ $20.50 = $246.00
06-30-20		2 @ $20.50 = $ 41.00	10 @ $20.50 = $205.00
Ending	**Adjusted Cost of sales**	Cost of sales = $290.00	Ending Inv. = $205.00

may well become significant, and have an effect on the value of the entire inventory, cost of sales, operating income, and taxes. However, if each single inventory method is consistently followed, the effect on inventory valuation, cost of sales, and operating income will be relatively minor over time.

Finally, note that the FIFO method generally produces a higher net income when cost prices are increasing and a lower net income when cost prices are declining. It is generally the easiest method to use, particularly when the inventory records are manually maintained. For this reason, it is often the preferred method used for food inventories.

When each item has been counted and costed, total inventory value can be calculated. The costing of items sounds like a simple process, and is for most items. In the case of other items, however, the process can be more difficult. For example, what is the value of a gallon of soup that is being prepared in a kitchen at the time inventory is taken? In such a case, that value (because the soup has many different ingredients in it) may have to be estimated. The accuracy of the final inventory is, therefore, a question of the time taken to value it. There is a trade-off between accuracy and time required. If inventory is not as accurate as it could be, then neither food (and beverage) cost nor net income will be accurate. Normally, however, relatively minor inventory-taking inaccuracies tend to even out over time. Inventory figures for food should be calculated separately from those for alcoholic beverages.

Compared to costing inventory, the cost of purchases can be calculated relatively easily because it is the total amount of food and beverages delivered during the month (less any products returned to suppliers for such reasons as unacceptable quality). Invoices recorded in the purchases account during the month can readily provide this figure. In order to calculate food cost separately from beverage cost, purchase cost for these two areas must also be recorded in separate purchase accounts.

Adjustments to cost of sales

To date, we have only discussed the calculation of the cost of food used. Why is this figure called "cost of food used" rather than "net food cost," "cost of food sold," or "food cost"? In many small restaurants, cost of food used may be the same as net food cost, but in most food and beverage operations it may be necessary to adjust cost of food used before it can be accurately labeled net food cost. Some of these adjustments might be

- Interdepartmental transfers: For example, in a restaurant with a separate bar operation there might be items purchased and received in the kitchen (and recorded as food purchases) that are later transferred to the bar for use there (for example, fresh cream, eggs, or fruit used in certain cocktails). In the same way, there may be purchases received by the bar (and recorded as beverage purchases) that are later transferred to the kitchen (for example, wine used in cooking). A record of transfers should be maintained so that at the end of each month, both food cost and beverage cost can be adjusted to ensure they are as accurate as possible.

- Employee meals: Most food operations allow certain employees, while on duty, to have meals at little or no cost. In such cases, the cost of that food has no relation to sales revenue generated in the normal course of business. Therefore, the cost of employee meals should be deducted from cost of food used. Employee meal cost is then transferred to another expense account (for example, it could be added to payroll cost as an employee benefit). Note that if employees pay cash for meals but receive a discount from normal menu prices, this revenue should be excluded from regular food revenue (because otherwise it will distort the food cost percentage calculation) and be transferred to a separate revenue account, such as "other income."

Employee meals as benefit

- Promotional expense: Restaurants sometimes provide customers with complimentary (free) food and/or beverages. This is a beneficial practice if it is done for good customers who are likely to continue to provide the operation with business. The cost of promotional meals should be handled in the same way as the cost of employee meals. The cost should not be included in food cost of sales and/or beverage cost of sales because, again, the food and/or beverage cost will be distorted. The cost should be removed from food cost and/or beverage cost and be recorded as advertising or promotion expense. Employees who are authorized to offer promotional items to customers should be instructed always to make out a sales check to record the item's sales value. Some restaurants, for promotional purposes, issue coupons that allow two meals for the price of one. In this case, the value of both meals should still be recorded on the sales check, even though the customer pays for only one meal. From sales checks, the cost of promotional meals can be calculated by using the operation's normal food cost and/or beverage cost percentage.

Use of coupons

DEPRECIATION METHODS

Straight-line depreciation was discussed in Chapter 1; however, to maintain continuity in our study of depreciation, several essential concepts of depreciation will be visited again during the review of the straight-line method. The review will set the stage for the introduction of the three additional methods of depreciation. The additional methods are units of production, sum-of-the-years-digits, and double declining balance.

Systematic expensing of depreciable assets

Depreciation is the systematic expensing of depreciable assets over a time period in excess of one year. Any estimated value recovered at the end of the assets serviceable life, such as trade-in value, salvage, or scrap value, is referred to as residual value. Straight-line breaks depreciation expense to be recovered into equal time periods, such as months, quarters, or years. We will assume equipment was purchased for $34,200 that has 14 years of serviceable life and a $600 residual value. Straight-line calculations are described for yearly and monthly periods:

Depreciation Calculation

Cost – Residual/life = Depreciation expense $34,200 – 600/14 yrs. = $2,400 per yr.

Cost – Residual/life = Depreciation expense $34,200 – 600/168 mo. = $200 per mo.

or

$2,400 / 12 months = $200 per month

All long-lived depreciable assets must remain in the accounting records at their historical cost. This requirement precludes the reduction of the depreciable asset when depreciation expense is recognized and necessitates the creation of a special account to record and accumulate depreciation expense charges. The account is named so as to indicate its purpose and is called accumulated depreciation. Each depreciable asset has a specific credit-balanced, accumulated depreciation account assigned. Thus, a journal entry to record one year of depreciation expense on the equipment is shown as follows:

Account Titles: Explanation	Debit	Credit
Depreciation Expense	$ 2,400	
Accumulated Depreciation: Equipment		$ 2,400

The same two accounts, depreciation expense and accumulated depreciation, are used to record an individual depreciation entry regardless of the depreciation method used.

UNITS OF PRODUCTION METHOD

Units of production depreciation share some elements with the straight-line method. Cost minus residual remains the numerator and life of the asset remains the denominator, but life is expressed in units, such as miles, gallons, hours, and so on. As an example, assume a van is purchased for $18,500 to provide delivery services. It is estimated that the van has a life of 100,000 miles and a residual value of $500. Calculated based on miles, depreciation is:

$$\frac{\text{Cost} \quad - \quad \text{Residual} \quad \div \quad \text{Life (units)} \quad = \quad \text{Depreciation rate per unit}}{\$18,500 \quad - \quad \$500 \quad \div \quad 100,000 \quad = \quad \$0.18 \ \{\text{or 18 cents per mile}\}}$$

$$24,400 \text{ miles} \times \$0.18 = \$4,392 = \text{Depreciation Expense}$$

Subsequent years' depreciation would be calculated in the same manner—miles driven times the depreciation rate per mile. In a generic sense, both the units of production and straight-line expense the cost of a long-lived asset equally, straight-line based on a life of time periods and units of production based on a life of use. The production method has a few disadvantages: It does not allow an advance calculation of depreciation, which is useful for budgeting; nor does it provide the ability to accelerate depreciation charges in the early years of an asset's life.

SUM-OF-THE-YEARS DIGITS METHOD

Greater amounts of depreciation

Sum-of-the-years is an accelerated depreciation method that is commonly called the SYD. An accelerated method allows greater amounts of depreciation to be expensed in the early years of the life of a depreciable asset. To accomplish this, SYD determines the amount to be depreciated using a fraction—using the maximum year of life as the numerator in the first year and then reducing the numerator by one in each subsequent year of the asset's life. The denominator is determined using the additive function of summing the years of an asset's life, such as:

$$1 + 2 + 3 + 4 + 5 = 15 \text{ tenths}$$

which represents 100% of the amount to be depreciated in denominator elements. We will assume equipment is bought for $34,200, with a residual value of $600, and an estimated life of five years. The equation to calculate SYD depreciation is:

$$\text{SYD fraction} \times \text{Cost} - \text{residual} = \text{Depreciation expense}$$

The additive function can be used; or an equation in which the letter "n" stands for the number of years in the asset's life can be used.

$$\frac{n(n + 1)}{2} = \frac{5(5 + 1)}{2} = \frac{5 \times 6}{2} = \frac{30}{2} = 15: \text{ is the denominator.}$$

The numerator of the fraction will begin with maximum years of the asset's life in the first year, minus one each subsequent year. A five-year depreciation schedule is:

Year	SYD fraction	×	Cost – residual	=	Depreciation
1	5/15	×	$33,600	=	$11,200
2	4/15	×	$33,600	=	$ 8,960
3	3/15	×	$33,600	=	$ 6,720
4	2/15	×	$33,600	=	$ 4,480
5	1/15	×	$33,600	=	$ 2,240
	Σ = 15/15 or 1		Total depreciation		$33,600

Reviewing the SYD depreciation schedule, it is apparent that depreciation is accelerated by expensing larger amounts in the earlier years. An accelerated method presumes an asset becomes less and less efficient over its life; thus, it allows the matching of depreciation to the efficiency loss of the asset over time.

DOUBLE DECLINING BALANCE METHOD

Double declining balance, also called DDB depreciation, is the second accelerated method. This method doubles the straight-line depreciation rate (1/years) to find a DDB%. This method, unlike straight-line, units of production, and SYD, ignores any type of residual value. The DDB% is multiplied by "book value" to determine the amount of depreciation expense. Assume equipment that had a five-year life and a residual value of $1,000 was purchased for $16,000. The DDB% is calculated as 100% or 1, divided by years of life: 1/5 = 20% × 2 = 40% or 0.4; in other words, the straight-line rate is doubled. For example, year one depreciation is 40% × $16,000 (cost of the asset) = $6,400, and the book value becomes $16,000 – $6,400 = $9,600 after the first-year depreciation expense is recorded. Each element of the DDB calculation is shown below, followed by a five-year DDB depreciation schedule:

- DDB % = 1/years of life = 20% straight-line rate × 2 = 0.40 (or 40%)
- Since we are doubling the straight-line rate, we can express the numerator as 200% or 2. DDB% = 2/years of life = 2/5 = 0.4 (or 40%)
- *Book Value* = Cost – Accumulated Depreciation
- *Depreciation Expense* = DDB% × Book Value = Depreciation Expense

Ignores any type of residual value

Depreciation Schedule

Year	DDB%	×	Book Value	=	Depr. Expense	Net Book Value
0						$16,000
1	40%	×	$16,000	=	$6,400	9,600
2	40%	×	9,600	=	3,840	5,760
3	40%	×	5,760	=	2,304	3,456
4	40%	×	3,456	=	1,382	2,074
5	40%	×	2,074	=	830	1,244
Balance, Accumulated Depreciation:				=	$14,756	BV = $1,244

Although the double declining method ignores residual values, the book value of an asset that is fully depreciated may be more, but not be less, than cost minus residual. Using the same equipment discussed in the previous example of DDB; cost $16,000 with a five-year life, had its residual value changed from $1,000 to $1,500. The DDB depreciation schedule previously discussed will remain the same, except for the calculation of year five; study the following:

Year	DDB%	×	Book Value	=	Depr. Expense	Net Book Value
4	40%	×	$ 3,456	=	$ 1,382	$ 2,074
5	40%	×	2,074	=	* 574	* 1,500
Balance, Accumulated Depreciation:				=	*$14,500	**BV = $1,500

It is apparent the total depreciation changed from $14,756 to $14,500. Depreciation expense for year 5 was $830 in the first example and has changed to $574 to insure the correct net book value. Changes are calculated and made in the year necessary to insure depreciation expense recorded will bring net book value to cost minus residual.

RESPONSIBILITY ACCOUNTING

A hospitality business with several departments, each with the responsibility for controlling its own costs and with its department head accountable for the departmental profit achieved, is practicing what is known as *responsibility accounting*. Responsibility accounting is based on the principle that department heads or managers should be held accountable for their performance and the performance of the employees in their department.

There are two objectives for establishing responsibility centers:

1. To allow top-level management to delegate responsibility and authority to department heads so they can achieve departmental operating goals compatible with the overall establishment's goals.

2. To provide top-level management with information (generally of an accounting nature) to measure the performance of each department in achieving its operating goals.

Cost centers or profit centers

Within a single organization practicing responsibility accounting, departments can be identified as either cost centers or profit centers. A cost center is one that generates no direct revenue (such as the maintenance department). In such a situation, the department manager is held responsible only for the costs incurred. A profit center is one that has costs but also generates revenue that is directly related to that department (such as the rooms department's generating revenue from guest room sales). The manager of a profit center should have some control over the revenue it can generate. In both cost and profit centers where responsibility accounting is practiced, a key question is what costs should be assigned to each center. Generally, only those costs that are directly controllable by that center's department head or manager are assigned. Common direct costs should be allocated to each center in some logical way.

Profit centers are responsible for both maximizing revenue and minimizing expenses, which in turn maximizes departmental profit. Each profit center manager or department head can then be measured on how well profit was maximized while continuing to maintain customer service levels established by top-level management.

Some establishments also have revenue centers. These are departments that receive revenue, but have little or no direct costs associated with their operation. For example, a major resort hotel might lease out a large part of its floor space to retail stores. The rent income provides revenue for the department, all of which is profit.

Another form of responsibility accounting occurs in a large or chain organization with units located in several different towns or cities. Each unit in the organization is given full authority over how it operates and is held responsible for the results of its decisions. In a large organization such as this, each unit is said to be decentralized and units are sometimes referred to as *investment centers.*

Investment centers

Investment centers are measured by the rate of return achieved by their general managers on the investment in that center.

In some chain organizations, products are transferred from one unit to another. For example, in a multiunit food organization, raw food ingredients might

Problems of cost
transfers

be purchased and processed in a central commissary before distribution to each individual unit. A question arises about the cost to be transferred to each unit for the partially or fully processed products. Many different pricing methods are available. It is important that an appropriate pricing method be decided so that each unit can be properly measured on its performance through responsibility accounting.

For example, the transfer price could be the commissary's cost plus a fixed percentage markup to cover its operating costs. Another method might be to base the transfer price on the market price of the products. The market price would be what the unit would have paid if it had purchased the products from an external supplier. In some cases, the market price might be reduced by a fixed percentage to reflect the commissary's lower marketing and distribution costs. Obviously, each user unit would prefer to have the transfer price as low as possible so that its costs are lower, and the commissary would prefer to have the transfer price as high as possible to enhance its performance.

DISTRIBUTION OF INDIRECT EXPENSES

Prorating expenses
among departments

One controversial issue concerning the income statement is whether or not the indirect expenses should be distributed to the departments in the same way the direct expenses are. The problem arises in selecting a rational basis on which to allocate these costs to the operating departments. Some direct expenses may also have to be prorated between two operating departments on some logical basis. For example, an employee in the food department serving food to customers may also be serving them alcoholic beverages. The food department will receive the credit for the food revenue, the beverage department for the beverage revenue. However, it would be unfair for either of these two departments to have to bear the full cost of that employee's wages. That cost should be split between the two departments, possibly prorating it on the basis of the revenue dollars. Such interdepartmental cost transfers are easily made; they are necessary in order to have a reasonably correct profit or loss for each operating department for which the appropriate department head is accountable.

One of the arguments in favor of allocating indirect expenses to departments is that, although departmental managers are not responsible for controlling those costs, they should be aware of what portion of them is related to their department since this could have an impact on departmental decision making, such as establishing selling prices at a level that covers all costs and not just direct costs.

When this type of full-cost accounting is implemented in a responsibility accounting system, it allows a manager to know the total minimum revenue that must be generated to cover all costs, even though the control of some of those costs is not their responsibility.

Some of the normally undistributed expenses can perhaps be allocated easily and logically. For example, marketing could be distributed on a revenue ratio basis (although, if a particular advertising campaign had been made specifically for one department, and it was thought that little, if any, benefit would accrue to other departments, then the full cost of that campaign could reasonably be charged to that one department).

With reference to Exhibit 2.3, note that the total marketing expense is $66,900. If management wished to charge (allocate) that expense to the operating departments on a revenue ratio basis, the first step is to convert each department's revenue to a percentage of total revenue as follows (percentage figures are rounded to the nearest whole number):

Department	Revenue	Percentage
Rooms	$1,150,200	49%
Food	851,600	36
Beverage	327,400	14
Other	21,200	1
Total	$2,350,400	100

The marketing cost can then be allocated as follows:

Department	Share of Cost		
Rooms	$66,900 × 49%	=	$32,800
Food	66,900 × 36	=	24,000
Beverage	66,900 × 14	=	9,400
Other	66,900 × 1	=	700
Total			$66,900

The other indirect costs could be distributed by using the same procedure, but on a different basis. For example, total department payroll and related expenses might be an appropriate basis on which to allocate the administrative and general expense. The square foot (or cubic foot) area could be used for allocating property operation and maintenance, and energy costs. Alternatively, property operation and maintenance expenses could be charged directly to the department(s) concerned at the time of invoicing. Property (real estate) taxes may similarly be charged to a specific department. Alternatively, square footage or revenue basis could be appropriate. Insurance could be charged on the basis of each department's insurable value relative to the total insurable value. Depreciation on a building might be apportioned on the basis of each department's property value relative to total property value, or, if this is difficult to determine, square footage might be appropriate. Depreciation on equipment and furniture could probably easily be prorated on the basis of each department's equipment and furniture cost, or value, relative to total cost or value. Finally, with respect to interest expense, the only logical basis would be on each department's share of the asset value to total asset value at the time the obligation (mortgage, bond, debenture, loan) was incurred. If a department does not have any assets covered by the obligation, then it should bear none of the interest expense.

Consistent basis to be used

Once a method of allocating any, or all, of these indirect costs to the operating departments is selected, it should be adhered to consistently so that comparison of income statements of future periods is meaningful. However, remember that comparison with other, similar organizations' income statements may not be meaningful if that organization had not selected the same allocation basis. The resulting departmental income or loss may or may not be more revealing to the individual manager than the more traditional approach, which takes the departmental income statement to the departmental operating income (contributory income) level only. If indirect expenses are allocated, the department head should still be made responsible only for the income (or loss) before deduction of indirect expenses, since indirect expenses are not normally

Advantages of indirect cost allocating

controllable by the department head. By allocating indirect expenses, top management will be able to determine if each department is making an income after all expenses. If any are not, it may be that the allocation of indirect costs is not fair. Alternatively, analysis of such costs may indicate ways in which the costs could be reduced to eliminate any individual departmental losses and increase overall total net income.

Finally, whether or not indirect expenses are allocated to the various operating departments, the resulting net income (bottom line) figure for the entire operation will not differ.

REVENUE MIX EFFECT ON NET INCOME

Change in revenue volume among departments

Even though the allocation of the indirect expenses to the departments does not affect the operation's total net income (because total indirect expenses are the same), there is one factor that will affect net income even though there is no change in total indirect expenses or in total revenue. That factor is a change in the revenue mix. In this particular instance, a change in the revenue mix is understood to be a change in the revenue volume of the various operating departments.

Consider Exhibit 2.7, where the contributory income percentage figures have been rounded to the nearest whole number. It can be seen that, since the rooms department has the lowest total of direct costs in relation to its revenue, its departmental income is the highest, at 68 percent of revenue. Expressed differently, this means that, for every dollar increase in room revenue, $0.68 will be available as a contribution to the total indirect costs.

Contributory income percent will stay constant

This is important if there is a change in the revenue mix. In Exhibit 2.8 there has been a change. Room revenue has been increased by $100,000, and food and beverage have each been decreased by $50,000. There is, therefore, no change in total revenue. It is assumed that the contributory income percentage for each department will stay constant, despite a change in revenue volume. This may, or may not, be the case in practice. Given this assumption, Exhibit 2.8 shows that, even with no change in total revenue or total indirect expenses, because of a revenue transfer from food and beverage into the rooms department, there has been an increase in total contributory income and net income of $39,200. An awareness by management of the influence each department has on total departmental (contributory) income and thus on net income could be important for decision making. For example, it could indicate how the marketing budget should best be spent to emphasize the various departments within the organization. Alternatively, if a limited budget were available for building expansion to handle increased business, a study of each department's relative contributory income would help in deciding how to allocate the available funds.

Exhibit 2.7   Contributory Income Schedule

	Revenue	Direct Expenses	Departmental (Contributory) Income	Contributory Income Percentage
Rooms	$1,150,200	$ 367,300	$ 782,900	68%
Food	851,600	698,600	153,000	18
Beverage	327,400	208,300	119,100	36
Other	21,200	19,600	1,600	8
Totals	$2,350,400	$1,293,800	$1,056,000	
Total indirect expenses			(825,400)	
Operating Income (before income tax)			$ 230,600	

Exhibit 2.8   Contributory Income Schedule

	Revenue	Direct Expenses	Departmental (Contributory) Income	Contributory Income Percentage
Rooms	$1,250,200	$ 400,100	$ 850,100	68%
Food	801,600	657,300	144,300	18
Beverage	277,400	177,500	99,900	36
Other	21,200	19,600	1,600	8
Totals	$2,350,400	$1,254,500	$1,095,900	
Total indirect expenses			(825,400)	
Income before income tax			$ 270,500	

BALANCE SHEET

Balance sheet equation

The balance sheet provides a picture of the financial condition of a business at a specific point in time. As indicated earlier, the balance sheet can be presented in a horizontal account format or in a vertical report format. Regardless of the format used, total assets must always equal total liabilities and ownership equity. A balance sheet in report format is shown in Exhibit 2.9.

CURRENT ASSETS

Current assets defined

Current assets represent cash items or other assets expected to be converted to cash within a short period, less than one year.

Cash on Hand

Most business operations should deposit in the bank the total cash receipts from the preceding day. The amount of cash on hand reported in the balance sheet will normally be equivalent to approximately one day's cash receipts, plus any point-of-sale cash drawer or service-staff-operating cash banks.

Cash in Bank

Excess cash to be invested

Cash in the bank should normally be sufficient to pay current debt liabilities as they come due for payment in each operating period. Cash in excess of amounts needed for payment of current debt should be invested in short-term interest bearing instruments.

Exhibit 2.9 Sample Balance Sheet

Balance Sheet

(as of December 31, 0006)

Assets					Liabilities and Stockholders' Equity			
Current assets					*Current liabilities*			
Cash					Accounts payable—trade			$ 19,200
on hand		$ 8,100			Accrued expenses			3,500
in bank		19,800	$ 27,900		Income tax payable			12,300
Marketable securities, at cost			10,000		Deposits and credit balances			500
(market value $10,500)								
					Current portion of long-term			27,200
					mortgage			
Accounts receivable		$ 24,600						
Less: allowance for uncollectible accounts		1,500	23,100					
Inventories					Total current liabilities			$ 62,700
food		$ 8,200			*Long-term liabilities*			
beverages		9,600			Mortgage on building		$840,100	
supplies		2,100	19,900		Less: current portion		27,200	812,900
Prepaid expenses			5,200		Total liabilities			$ 875,600
Total current assets			$ 86,100					
Fixed assets					*Stockholders' equity*			
Land, at cost		$ 161,800			Capital stock:			
Building, at cost	$1,432,800							
Less: accumulated depreciation	356,900	1,075,900			authorized 5,000 common			
Furniture and equipment, at cost	$ 374,700				shares @ $100 par value; issued			
Less: accumulated depreciation	275,300	99,400			and outstanding 3,000 shares		$300,000	
China, glass, silver, linen, and		25,600			Retained earnings		279,000	579,000
uniforms								
Total fixed assets			1,362,700					
Other assets								
Organization expense			5,800					
Total assets			$1,454,600		Total liabilities and stockholders' equity			$1,454,600

73

Marketable Securities

Cash that is in excess of operating requirements can be invested in a number of different interest bearing instruments. One way is to invest excess funds in short-term securities until the cash is needed in the future. Normally this type of current asset is shown at cost. When the market value of such securities is different from their cost on the balance sheet date, the securities market value should be reported in the balance sheet by a disclosure footnote. If the securities qualify as "trading securities," an unrealized gain or loss can be recognized for accounting purposes by comparing their cost to the present market value.

Credit Card Receivables

These represent credit receivables not yet reimbursed by the credit card company at the end of an operating period. This amount will normally equate to card credit extended from one to four days prior to the balance sheet date. Reimbursement will vary based on the type of card and the issuing credit card company.

Accounts Receivable

Bad debts as
contra-account

Generally, the use of accounts receivable are being replaced by credit cards. When accounts receivable are used as a current asset, they represent the extension of credit for rooms, food and beverages to individuals, or companies for which payment was not immediately received. If an account receivable is not paid, and it appears it will not be paid, the account is normally written off as a bad debt expense.

Inventories

Two different categories of inventories exist. For inventories to be considered as a current asset, they must have been purchased for resale; food, beverage and supplies inventories. Inventories of glassware, tableware, china, linen and uniforms are classified as "other assets" and are normally reported following property, plant, and equipment, which is also called simply fixed assets.

Prepaid Expenses

Prepaid items represent the use of cash to obtain benefits that will be consumed with the passage of a period of time. Prepaid insurance premiums, prepaid rent or lease costs, prepaid advertising, prepaid license fees, prepaid taxes and other such items are classified as current assets. Although prepaid items are not expected to be converted to cash, they replace cash as a current asset until the benefits are received and recognized as expenses.

FIXED ASSETS (LONG-LIVED ASSETS)

Fixed assets defined

Fixed assets are also known as property, plant, and equipment and are commonly referred to as capital assets. These assets are long lived and of a more permanent and physical nature. These assets are used by a business in its operations and are not intended to be sold.

Land, Building, and Furniture and Equipment

Assets recorded at cost

These are three major and common fixed assets used in the hospitality industry. They are generally shown at their cost, or cost plus any expenditures to put the asset in condition for use (such as freight and installation charges for an item of equipment). If any part of the land or a building is not used for the ordinary purposes of the business (such as a parcel of land held for investment purposes), it should be shown separately on the balance sheet. On some balance sheets this section is entitled Property, Plant, and Equipment.

Accumulated Depreciation

The costs of building, plus furniture and equipment (not land), are reduced by accumulated depreciation. Accumulated depreciation reflects the decline in value of the related asset due to wear and tear, the passage of time, changed economic conditions, or other factors. This traditional method of accounting, which shows the net book value (cost less accumulated depreciation) of the asset, does not necessarily reflect the market value or the replacement value of the asset or assets in question.

Net book value

China, Glass, Silver, Linen, and Uniforms

This amount is made up from two figures. The estimated value of items in use is added to the cost of those items still new and in storage.

OTHER ASSETS

There are other assets a company may have that do not fit into either current assets or fixed assets. Some of the more common ones are discussed here.

Deposits

Refundable deposits are an asset

If the deposit is refundable at some future time it can be considered an asset. An example of this would be a deposit with a public utility company.

Investments

Long-term investments (as opposed to short-term investments in marketable securities) in other companies or in property or plant not connected with the day-to-day running of the business (such as a separate building that is owned but is rented out to another organization) are shown as a separate category of asset.

Leasehold Costs or Leasehold Improvements

Amortization of costs

It is not uncommon for land to be leased. Where a long-term lease is paid for in advance, the unexpired portion of this cost should be shown as an asset. Similarly, if improvements are made to a leased building, these improvements are of benefit during the life of the business or the remaining life of the lease. The costs should be spread (amortized) over this life. Any unamortized cost should be shown as an asset. The term amortization is similar in concept to the term "depreciation," discussed in Chapter 1. Depreciation is generally used in conjunction with tangible assets, such as buildings and furniture and equipment. Amortization is generally used with reference to intangible assets, such as goodwill or deferred expenses.

Deferred Expenses

Mortgage discount

Deferred expenses are similar to prepaid expenses (a current asset item) except that the deferred expense is of a long-term nature and is to be amortized over future years. An example of this might be the discount (prepaid interest) on a mortgage. This discount is amortized annually over the life of the mortgage. This discount is amortized annually over the life of the mortgage. Preopening expenses (for example, for advertising, the benefit of which may be earned in future periods) would also fit into this category.

TOTAL ASSETS

All of the various assets discussed, when added together, represent the total assets of a company, or the total resources available to it. This information appears on the left-hand side of the balance sheet. The right-hand side is composed of two major sections: liabilities and stockholders' equity. The liabilities are further broken down into short-term and long-term. The stockholders' equity section is generally made up of capital stock and retained earnings.

CURRENT LIABILITIES

Current liabilities defined

Current liabilities are those debts that must be paid, or are expected to be paid, within a year.

Accounts Payable—Trade

Included here are the amounts owing to suppliers of food, beverages, and other supplies and services purchased on account or contracted for in the normal day-to-day operation of a hospitality business.

Accrued Expenses

This item includes those current debts that are not part of accounts payable. This would include unpaid wages or salaries, payroll tax and related deductions, interest owing but not yet paid, rent payable, and other similar expenses.

Income Tax Payable

This is the income tax owed to the government on the company's taxable income.

Deposits and Credit Balances

Unearned income

Money is often given in advance by prospective guests as a deposit on room reservations and banquet bookings. The accounts of guests staying in a hotel may have credit balances on them. The total of all these items should be shown as a liability because the money is due to the guest until it has been earned.

Current Portion of Long-Term Mortgage

Since, by definition, current liabilities are debts due within one year, the amount of any portion of a long-term liability payable within a year should be deducted from the long-term obligation and shown under current liabilities.

Dividends Payable

If any dividends had been declared but not yet paid at the balance sheet date, they would be recorded under current liabilities.

LONG-TERM LIABILITIES

Long-term liabilities defined

Long-term liabilities are those due beyond one year after the balance sheet date. Included in this category would be mortgages, bonds, debentures, and notes payable. If there are any long-term loans from stockholders, they also would appear in that section.

STOCKHOLDERS' EQUITY

In general terms, the stockholders' equity section of the balance sheet can be stated to be the difference between total assets and total liabilities. It represents the equity, or the interest, of the owners in the enterprise. It comprises two main items, capital stock and retained earnings, although other items, such as capital surplus, may appear.

Capital Stock

Authorized shares

Any incorporated company is limited by law to a maximum number of shares it can issue. This limit is known as the authorized number of shares. Shares generally have a par, or stated, value, and this par value, multiplied by the number of shares actually issued up to the authorized quantity, gives the total value of capital stock. Most companies issue shares in the form of common stock. However, it is not uncommon to see balance sheets with another type of share, known as preferred stock. Preferred stock ranks ahead of common stock, up to certain limits, as far as dividends are concerned. Preferred stockholders may have special voting rights, and they rank ahead of common stockholders in the event of company liquidation.

Paid-in Capital, Excess of Par

Stock sold for more than its par value

The term was formally referred to as capital surplus and represents the amount received by incorporated companies when their stock sold for more than its par value. This term also applies to companies who sold stock at a price exceeding its stated value. The excess amounts received from selling stock for more than its par or stated value appears in the stockholders' equity section of the balance sheet.

Retained Earnings

Records and accumulates income and net losses

Retained earnings is the account that records and accumulates all net income and net losses of an incorporated business. In addition, retained earnings is charged (reduced) by the value of all cash or stock dividends declared to be paid or issued by the company. A historical record of the success or failure (profit or loss) of a company and dividends given to stockholders is shown in this account. Retained earnings can only be used to offset dividends, extraordinary losses, prior period adjustments, or retained earnings can be retained for capital expansion to provide for the growth of the company. A retained earnings does represent not cash, although it is a critical link to the income statement and balance sheet. Details regarding changes to retained earnings over an accounting period is shown in a statement of retained earnings, as shown in Exhibit 2.10.

Exhibit 2.10   Sample Retained Earnings Statement
Statement of Retained Earnings
(For the Year Ending December 31, 0006)

Retained earnings January 1, 0006	$192,500
Add: Net income for year 0006	116,500
	$309,000
Less: Dividends paid	(30,000)
Retained earnings December 31, 0006	$279,000

Exhibit 2.11   Link Between Balance Sheets, Income Statement, and Statement of Retained Earnings

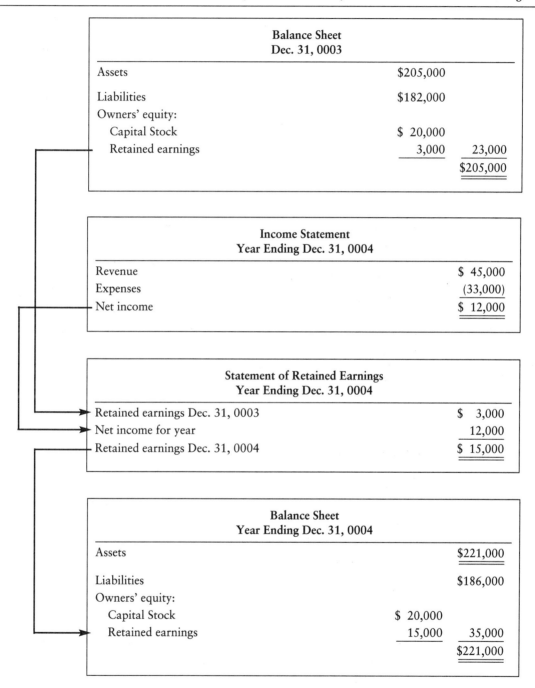

Balance Sheet
Dec. 31, 0003

Assets	$205,000	
Liabilities	$182,000	
Owners' equity:		
Capital Stock	$ 20,000	
Retained earnings	3,000	23,000
		$205,000

Income Statement
Year Ending Dec. 31, 0004

Revenue	$ 45,000
Expenses	(33,000)
Net income	$ 12,000

Statement of Retained Earnings
Year Ending Dec. 31, 0004

Retained earnings Dec. 31, 0003	$ 3,000
Net income for year	12,000
Retained earnings Dec. 31, 0004	$ 15,000

Balance Sheet
Year Ending Dec. 31, 0004

Assets	$221,000	
Liabilities	$186,000	
Owners' equity:		
Capital Stock	$ 20,000	
Retained earnings	15,000	35,000
		$221,000

The detail shown in the statement of retained earnings shown in Exhibit 2.10 can and has been incorporated into the retained earnings section of stockholders' equity rather than simply showing its ending balance at the end of a period of operations. Exhibit 2.11 illustrates the link between the income statement and balance sheet over two successive accounting periods.

PROPRIETORSHIP AND PARTNERSHIPS

Authorized shares

Capital stock is issued only in incorporated business entities. The sole owner of a business is the proprietor and a partnership consists of two or more owners. The equity, or "statement of capital," is shown as follows:

Beginning Capital + Net Income (or – Net Loss) – Owner withdrawals = Ending Capital

This format of a statement of capital will follow the format shown in Exhibit 2.12.

The difference between a statement of capital and a "statement of partnership capital" is the use of a separate capital and withdrawal account for each partner. Distribution of net income or net loss in a partnership is based on the partnership agreement. Detail in the statement will follow the basic format shown in Exhibit 2.13.

TOTAL LIABILITIES AND STOCKHOLDERS' EQUITY

The total of all the liabilities and stockholders' equity, or capital, accounts should agree with the total asset accounts on the left-hand side of the balance sheet. These liability and equity, or capital, accounts show how the company's resources (assets) are currently financed.

Exhibit 2.12   Sample Proprietor's Capital Statement
Statement of Proprietor's Capital
(For the Year Ending December 31, 0006)

Investment January 1, 0006	$492,500
Add: Net income for year 0006	116,500
	$609,000
Less: Withdrawals during year	(30,000)
Balance December 31, 0006	$579,000

Exhibit 2.13   Sample Partners' Capital Statement
Statement of Partners' Capital
(Year Ending December 31, 0006)

	Partner A	Partner B
Investment January 1, 0006	$246,250	$246,250
Add: Net income for year 0006	58,250	58,250
	$304,500	$304,500
Less: Withdrawals during year	(15,000)	(15,000)
Balance December 31, 0006	$289,500	$289,500

BALANCE SHEET DETAIL

The amount of detail shown on a balance sheet depends on the amount of information desired, the operation's size and complexity, and whether it is a proprietorship, partnership, or incorporated company. For example, one business's balance sheet might show each type of cash account as a separate item, and another business's balance sheet might combine all the various cash accounts into a single figure.

Some operators want their balance sheets simplified as much as possible because this makes them easier to "read" at first glance. Where more detail about an account is needed, this might then be shown as an addendum or footnote on an adjoining page. For example, the inventories might be shown in total only on the balance sheet and be supported by a separate schedule that shows them broken down into separate figures for food, beverages, supplies, and others.

BALANCE SHEET PRESENTATION

Account form versus report form

The balance sheet in Exhibit 2.9 is indicative of the way many balance sheets are presented, with assets on the left and liabilities and capital on the right. This presentation is known as the account form, or method, and is the one most commonly used.

Another common method is the report form. This method is vertical rather than horizontal as in the account form. In the report form, the balance sheet is considered to have a top half and a bottom half. The top half is for the assets and the bottom half is for liabilities and owners' equity. Exhibit 2.14 illustrates report-form balance sheets for a large hotel (Rio Hotel & Casino, Inc.), and Exhibit 2.15 represents report-form balance sheets for a large restaurant chain (Wendy's International, Inc.).

Exhibit 2.14   Balance Sheets Rio Hotel & Casino, Inc.

	December 31,	
	1995	1994

ASSETS

Current assets:		
Cash and cash equivalents	$ 19,992,695	$ 76,426,258
Accounts receivable, net	4,313,442	3,204,416
Federal income taxes receivable	190,914	139,329
Inventories	1,794,850	1,378,598
Prepaid expenses and other current assets	4,638,090	4,716,701
Total current assets	30,929,991	85,865,302
Property and equipment:		
Land and improvements	37,509,960	24,666,679
Building and improvements	192,818,896	137,005,432
Equipment, furniture and improvements	68,500,267	43,108,873
Less: accumulated depreciation	(46,707,850)	(32,826,276)
	252,121,273	171,954,708
Construction in progress	17,173,483	38,521,773
Net property and equipment	269,294,756	210,476,481
Other assets:		
Other, net	8,566,847	4,823,489
	$308,791,594	$301,165,272

LIABILITIES AND STOCKHOLDERS' EQUITY

Current liabilities:		
Current maturities of long-term debt	$ 25,252	$ 15,032,534
Accounts payable	4,562,132	2,425,645
Accrued expenses	9,136,226	7,830,706
Accounts payable-related party	6,641,506	10,026,210
Accrued interest	4,726,915	351,864
Total current liabilities	25,092,031	35,666,959
Noncurrent liabilities:		
Long-term debt, less current maturities	110,176,765	110,146,869
Deferred income taxes	10,634,898	7,512,277
Total noncurrent liabilities	120,811,663	117,659,146
Total liabilities	145,903,694	153,326,105
Commitments and contingencies		
Stockholders' equity:		
Common stock, $0.01 par value; 100,000,000 shares authorized; 21,139,146 (1995) and 21,371,346 (1994) shares issued and outstanding	211,392	213,714
Additional paid-in capital	113,520,158	117,214,582
Retained earnings	49,156,350	30,410,871
Total stockholders' equity	162,887,900	147,839,167
	$308,791,594	$301,165,272

Exhibit 2.15 Balance Sheets Wendy's International, Inc.*
December 31, 1995, and January 1, 1995

(Dollars in thousands)	1995	1994
Assets		
Current assets		
Cash and cash equivalents	$ 206,127	$ 119,639
Short-term investments, at market	7,682	23,235
Accounts receivable, net	49,555	41,568
Notes receivable, net	12,272	10,457
Deferred income taxes	18,389	10,807
Inventories and other	27,254	26,941
	321,279	232,647
Property and equipment, at cost		
Land	288,029	251,515
Buildings	471,599	407,408
Leasehold improvements	251,176	214,974
Restaurant equipment	383,701	349,195
Other equipment	65,643	64,929
Capital leases	67,420	63,531
	1,527,568	1,351,552
Accumulated depreciation and amortization	(520,824)	(486,399)
	1,006,744	865,153
Cost in excess of net assets acquired, net	42,927	30,780
Deferred income taxes	19,233	16,142
Other assets	118,978	70,083
	$1,509,161	$1,214,805
Liabilities and Shareholders' Equity		
Current liabilities		
Accounts and drafts payable	$ 108,182	$ 100,708
Accrued expenses		
Salaries and wages	23,158	22,473
Taxes	20,828	17,480
Insurance	29,320	26,037
Other	24,207	20,063
Income taxes	(2,516)	1,683
Due to officer	63,221	39,992
Current portion of long-term obligations	29,469	57,674
	295,869	286,110
Long-term obligations		
Term debt	297,029	104,842
Capital leases	40,200	40,018
	337,229	144,860
Deferred income taxes	47,853	39,799
Other long-term liabilities	9,431	13,823
Due to officer		28,286
Commitments and contingencies		
Shareholders' equity		
Preferred stock, authorized: 250,000 shares		
Common stock, $.10 stated value, authorized: 200,000,000 shares		
Issued: 103,993,000 and 101,787,000 shares, respectively	10,399	10,179
Capital in excess of stated value	199,804	171,888
Retained earnings	614,799	529,294
Unrealized loss on investments	(1,504)	(723)
Translation adjustments	(3,007)	(3,787)
Pension liability adjustment		(3,212)
	820,491	703,639
Treasury stock at cost: 129,000 shares	(1,712)	(1,712)
	818,779	701,927
	$1,509,161	$1,214,805

*Courtesy of Wendy's International Inc.

Importance of Balance Sheet

The balance sheet is important because it can provide information about matters such as

- A business's liquidity, or ability to pay its debts when they have to be paid.
- How much of the operation's profits have been retained in the business to help it expand and/or reduce the amount of outside money (debt) that has to be borrowed.
- The breakdown of assets into current, fixed, and other, with details about the amount of assets within each of these broad categories.
- The business's debt (liabilities) relative to owners' equity. In general, the greater the amount of debt relative to equity, the higher is the operation's financial risk.

Balance Sheet Limitations

There are some aspects of a business that the balance sheet may not disclose. For example:

- Because transactions are recorded in the value of the dollar at the time the transaction occurred, the true value of some assets on the balance sheet may not be apparent. Suppose a hotel owned the land on which the building sits and that land had been purchased several years ago. Because of inflation and demand for limited land, it is likely that the land is today worth far more than was paid for it. This may also be true of some other assets. The balance sheet normally does not show this market value.
- If the operation was purchased from a previous owner who had built up a successful business, and if an amount for that business above the actual market value of the purchased assets had been paid, that amount would have been recorded on the balance sheet at the time of purchase as "goodwill." Goodwill that a business has is only normally recorded at the time a business is transferred from seller to buyer. Therefore, if a business was started from scratch, and has a good location compared to its competitors, and/or a good reputation and faithful clientele, and/or a superior work force with a good morale, it is probably worth far more than the balance sheet assets show, simply because the goodwill built up is not reflected on the balance sheet.
- Another value similar to goodwill that is not shown on a business's balance sheet is the investment in its employees. This investment takes the form of time and money spent on recruiting, training, evaluating, and promoting motivated individuals. Obviously, it is difficult to assign a value to these human resources, but they are, nevertheless, an asset to any hospitality business.

- Many items recorded on balance sheets are a matter of judgment or estimate. For example, what is the best depreciation method and rate to use, and what is the best of several available methods for valuing inventories? There are no absolute answers to these questions. For this reason, a balance sheet may not reflect the correct value for all assets. If the judgments or estimates used are wrong, then the balance sheet is incorrect.
- Balance sheets also reflect the financial position of a business at only one moment in time, subsequent to which the balance sheet is constantly changing. These changes will not be shown until another balance sheet is produced a month or more later. If a balance sheet showed a healthy cash position at one time, and a week later most of that cash was spent on new furniture, the balance sheet will reveal nothing about the impending use of most of the cash available.

COMPUTER APPLICATIONS

By using a general ledger software package in which only journal entries have to be entered in the computer, an operation's balance sheet and income statement can be automatically prepared and printed at the end of each accounting period.

Inventory control software can be used to maintain a perpetual inventory, as well as to calculate total inventory value at each period end.

SUMMARY

Financial statements provide information management needs for rational decision making. Most hotel and food service operations pattern their financial statements along the lines of one of the various types of Uniform System of Accounts available to the industry.

The two main statements in a set of financial statements are the income statement and the balance sheet. The income statement shows the operating results of a business over a period of time, ending on the balance sheet date, whereas the balance sheet gives a picture of the financial position of a business at a particular point in time.

Income statements in the hospitality industry are, wherever possible, departmentalized. In other words, each operating department prepares an income statement. Revenue and direct costs are controllable by and the responsibility of that department.

There are a number of different methods of inventory valuation and four were discussed in this chapter: specific identification, FIFO, LIFO, and weighted average.

For most food service operations, it is necessary to adjust cost of food used to arrive at a net food cost figure for an income statement. Such adjustments cover such items as interdepartmental transfers, employee meals, and promotion items.

Many hospitality businesses also use income statements to evaluate responsibility accounting, which is based on the principle that department heads or managers should be held accountable for their performance and the performance of their employees.

Summarized departmental incomes are brought together in a general income statement and all remaining fixed costs and undistributed (indirect) expenses are deducted to arrive at operating income (income before tax). Although it is possible to allocate and distribute all fixed and undistributed costs to operating departments, the difficulty lies in finding a realistic and practical method of prorating them to the departments.

An important point to remember regarding an income statement reporting on two or more operating departments is the effect a change in revenue may have across the departments. A given change in the revenue in one department may have a completely different effect on operating income than the same amount of revenue change in another department. Since different departments normally have different contributory income percentages, management needs to be alert to possible changes in revenue mix, which can result in changes in operating income potential.

The net income (or net loss) is transferred to the balance by way of a statement of retained earnings, described as follows:

$$\text{Beginning Retained Earnings} + \text{NI (or} - \text{NL)} - \text{Dividends}$$
$$= \text{Ending Retained Earnings}$$

The statement of retained earnings will show all items that affect ending retained earnings, or ending retained earnings may be shown alone as a consolidated summarized value. The income statement is the source of information regarding net income or net loss.

In account format, the balance sheet is composed of assets on one side and liabilities and stockholders' equity on the other. In a report format shown below, assets are reported and followed by liabilities and stockholders' equity.

ASSETS
Current assets: Cash
                                                                      Credit Card Receivables
                                                                      Accounts Receivable (net)
                                                                      Marketable Securities
                                                                      Inventories
                                                                      Supplies
                                                                      Prepaid Expenses

        Total Current Assets:

Fixed assets: Land (also called Property plant &
                                                                          equipment)
                                                                      Building
                                                                      Furnishings
                                                                      Equipment
                                                                      Less: Accumulated Depreciation

        Total Fixed Assets:

Other assets: Deferred expenses
                                                                      China, Glassware, Silverware, Linen,
                                                                          and Uniforms

        Total Assets:

LIABILITIES AND OWNERS' EQUITY:
Current liabilities: Accounts Payable
                                                                      Accrued Expenses
                                                                      Income Taxes Payable
                                                                      Deposits and Credit Balances
                                                                      Current Portion of Mortgage Payable
Long-term liabilities: Mortgage (or other Long-Term Debt
                                                                          Payable Deferred Taxes

        Total Liabilities:

Stockholders' equity: Capital Stock
                                                                      Paid in Capital, Excess of Par
                                                                      Retained Earnings

        Total Stockholders' Equity:
Total Liabilities & Stockholders' Equity:

Note that the amount of detail appearing in a balance sheet is a managerial decision. Balance sheets may be shown in a horizontal account format A = L + SHE or in vertical format as shown in the preceding example. Finally, it is important to remember that a balance sheet has a great number of uses, but it also has a number of limitations.

DISCUSSION QUESTIONS

1. Why does management of a motel or food service operation need financial statements?

2. Of what value is a uniform system of accounts?

3. What is the difference between a balance sheet and an income statement?

4. What is departmental contributory income?

5. In a departmental organization, what is the difference between direct expenses and undistributed (or indirect) expenses?

6. State the equation for calculating cost of sales.

7. What is the difference between FIFO and LIFO as inventory valuation methods?

8. Briefly discuss three types of adjustments that may be necessary to convert cost of sales food, to net cost of sales.

9. Discuss some specific types of indirect expenses and an appropriate method or methods by which to allocate them to individual operating departments.

10. Why should a change in the revenue mix among departments have any effect on net income, even if there is no change in total revenue?

11. For each of the following balance sheet categories, list three accounts by name and briefly discuss each one:

   a. Current Assets

   b. Current Liabilities

   c. Fixed Asset (Long-lived)

11. How do current assets differ from fixed assets (property plant and equipment)?

13. Define retained earnings, and explain how ending retained earnings is determined.

14. Why are deposits and credit balances on accounts shown as a current liability?

15. Define the concept of depreciation.

16. How is the book value of a long-lived asset determined?

17. What is the purpose of the accumulated depreciation account?

18. Name the two methods of accelerated depreciation discussed in this chapter.

19. What is the difference between periodic and perpetual inventory control?

20. What is the double declining balance percentage equation?

21. Explain the straight-line depreciation method.

ETHICS SITUATION

The assistant night manager of a mid-size motor hotel has a number of duties, one of which is to assist in the preparation of the income statement each month. A new nearby competitive motor hotel is due to open in about six weeks. The assistant manager has applied for the assistant day managers' position. He was told by the new motor hotel's owner that he has the job if he provides the owner with income statements of the motor hotel for which he has worked for the past three years. Discuss the ethics of this situation.

EXERCISES

2.1 A hospitality operation may maintain a number of different inventory accounts. Some of these accounts hold direct costs and others hold period costs. What determines if an inventory is classified as a "current asset" or an "other asset"?

2.2 Is there a key word that defines the difference between a direct cost and an indirect cost?

2.3 A new restaurant during the first month of operations purchased the following the wines:

March 2: Purchased 12 each 750ml of M & B wine @ $12.00 each.

March 16: Purchased 12 each 750ml of M & B wine @ $13.00 each

March 31: Sold 18 units during March @ $26 each.

Determine the value of M & B ending inventory and cost of sales for March using:

a. First-in, First-out method.

b. Last-in, First-out method.

c. Weighted average method.

2.4 Identify the missing dollar amounts in the equation shown below:

Beginning Inventory	+	Purchases	–	Ending Inventory	=	Cost of Sales
$40,000	+	?	–	$20,000	=	$100,000

2.5 A hospitality operation began with retained earnings of $126,000. During the year, cash dividends of $55,200 were paid to the owners. Net income for the year was $228,000. Answer the following:

a. What is the ending balance of retained earnings?

b. What would be the ending balance of retained earnings if a net loss of $22,200 is reported rather than net income?

2.6 A new van cost $46,000 with an estimated residual value of $6,000 and a serviceable life of four years, or 100,000 miles. What is the first year of depreciation expense under each of the following separate assumptions? *first 3 years*

    a. Straight-line

    a. Sum-of-the-years-digits

    a. Double declining balance

2.7 Referring to the information regarding the van purchased in Exercise 2.6, find the depreciation expense if 28,000 miles were driven in the first year. *UOP*

2.8 Match each of the terms in the left column with the account categories given in the right column.

a. Total assets—Total liabilities	1. Fixed asset
b. Revenue—Expenses	2. Liabilities
c. Depreciable asset	3. Contributory income
d. Debt owed to creditors	4. Net assets, Owners' Equity
e. Revenue—Direct costs	5. Operating income

2.9 Indirect, undistributed cost of $8,000 is to be allocated to a specific department. Two different allocation bases are being considered. The department contributes 40% of overall revenue and occupies 52% of the square footage available. Calculate the amount to be allocated based on revenue and square footage.

2.10 A department with three operation divisions reported the revenues for each division. Determine the percentage of revenue provided by each division from the following.

Rooms division	$1,269,008
Food service division	878,544
Beverage division	292,848
Total revenue	$2,440,400

PROBLEMS

2.1 Prepare a food department income statement in proper format from the following information:

Revenue:

Grill room	$153,100
Coffee garden	78,900
Banquets	298,400
Net food costs	$211,700
Salaries & wages expense	$174,400
Employee meals expense	17,200
Supplies expense	10,300
Glass & tableware expense	4,300
Laundry and linen expense	13,000
License expense	1,900
Printing expense	4,900
Miscellaneous expense	6,200
Other Income	600

2.2 A restaurant has the following food cost information for a given month. Calculate cost of sales, food and net cost of sales, food. The following information is provided.

Food inventory, March 1	$2,428
Food inventory, March 31	1,611
Food purchases, March	8,907
Employee meals cost	209
Promotional meals cost	278

2.3 A restaurant has separate food and bar operations. Calculate cost of sales, food and net cost of sales, food for a given month. The following information is provided:

Food inventory, August 1	$14,753
Food inventory, August 31	12,811
Food purchases, August	48,798
Employee meals cost	1,208
Transfers kitchen to the bar	107
Transfers bar to the kitchen	48
Promotional meals cost	278
Complimentary meals cost	132

2.4   The following information is taken from a perpetual inventory record.

Perpetual Inventory Control Record

Description: *M & B Supreme*

Date	Purchase-Received	Issued-Sales	Units	Unit Cost
June 1	Balance forward		3	$10.00
4		2		
6	8		9	$10.50
9		3	6	
12		3	3	
15	6		9	$11.00
18		2	7	
20		3	4	
22	6		10	$ 9.50
25		2	8	
28		3	5	

For each of the following inventory valuation methods, calculate the value of ending inventory on September 30. Use formats of Exhibits 2.6-A, B, and C.

a. First-in, First-out method

b. Last-in, First-out method

c. Weighted Average method

2.5   A restaurant has three revenue divisions with direct costs and average monthly figures given in the information shown below.

	Dining Room	Banquet Room	Beverages
Revenue	$208,000	$112,000	$80,000
Cost of sales	83,200	33,600	28,000
Wages and salaries cost	66,560	24,640	12,000
Other direct costs	16,640	8,960	1,600

The restaurant also has the following indirect, undistributed costs.

Administrative and general expenses	$13,000
Marketing expenses	9,000
Utilities expense	6,000
Property operation & maintenance	12,000
Depreciation expense	14,000
Insurance expense	2,000

a. Prepare a consolidated contributory income statement. Showing each division side by side for comparison, allocate no indirect costs.

b. Allocate indirect costs to the divisions and prepare an income statement for each division. Administrative & general and marketing costs are allocated "based on revenue." The remaining indirect costs are allocated based on square footage being used by each division: Dining 2,400 sq. ft., Banquet 3,000, sq. ft., and Beverage 600 sq. ft.

c. After allocating the direct costs, would you consider closing any of the divisions? If so, state why? If not, state why not?

2.6 Using the adjusted trial balance shown below, prepare a "balance sheet" in vertical report format. Identify each account using specific categories and classifications (current assets, current liabilities, etc.). After completing the balance sheet, prepare a "trial balance" to verify that the balance sheet is in balance.

Adjusted Trial Balance

Accounts	Debit Balanced	Credit Balanced
Cash	$ 4,100	
Credit Card Receivables	7,560	
Accounts Receivable	1,940	
Inventories	8,200	
Prepaid Expenses	1,900	
Land	80,000	
Building	712,800	
Accumulated Depreciation: (Building)		$ 186,400
Equipment	119,080	
Accumulated Depreciation: (Equipment)		35,625
Furnishings	64,120	
Accumulated Depreciation: (Furnishings)		11,875
China and Tableware	9,680	
Glassware	2,420	
Accounts Payable		8,600
Accrued Expenses Payable		2,700
Income Taxes Payable		6,100
Current Portion, Mortgage Payable		13,100
Mortgage Payable		406,900
Capital Stock		151,000
Retained Earnings		189,500
Trial Balance Totals	$1,011,800	$1,011,800

CASE 2

Charlie Driver was greatly pleased with the results of his "3C" Company's first year of operation, especially since he only operated on a par time basis. In fact, he found the catering business to be not only profitable but also an enjoyable challenge. He decided to continue the 3C Company for another year, finish his hospitality and marketing education, and search for a suitable restaurant to acquire and operate.

Near the end of the following year, Charlie found an 84-seat restaurant that had been closed for several months and was the type of facility he had been looking for. After locating the owner, he reached an agreement to lease the restaurant for five years. The lease set the first year's rental cost at $24,000 and stipulated a 10% yearly rental increase in each of the remaining four years of the five-year lease. In addition, the owner agreed to allow Charlie to trade in the old equipment and furnishings for whatever he can get to purchase new equipment and furnishings. The equipment and furnishings were traded on new equipment with a net cost of $171,524 and new furnishings with a net cost of $53,596. The new equipment was estimated to have a 12-year life with a residual value of $6,500. The new furnishings had an estimated 8-year life and a residual value of $2,620.

Charlie realized that for tax purposes and other considerations, he should incorporate a new company as "Charlie's Classic Cuisine Corporation." We will simplify this name to the "4C Company." With cash he had saved from operating the 3C Company and from the sale of the truck, Charlie purchased $50,000 of 4C Company's $2.00 par value common stock. Charlie used his reputation and good business record over the past two years to obtain a corporate loan from his bank in the amount of $250,000. The loan was to be repaid over the next five years in monthly installments of principle and interest.

Although Charlie hired a bookkeeper, he has asked you, a personal friend, to prepare the 4C Company's year-end financial statements and discuss the results of his first year of operations with him. You agreed to prepare the year-end statements from a year-ending unadjusted trial balance of accounts provided to you. To make the necessary adjustments you are given the following information: Inventory figures in the unadjusted trial are for the beginning of year one. December 31 year-end inventories are $5,915 for food and $2,211 for beverages. In addition, accrued payroll of $2,215, and depreciation on equipment and furnishings using the straight-line method, must recognized. The bank loan principle to be paid in year two is $38,260.

Using the unadjusted trial and additional information, prepare an income statement and balance sheet in good form for the 4C Company for the year ended December 31, 0001. Use an income tax rate of 22% of operating income (income before tax).

The following unadjusted trial balance is provided:

4C Company
Unadjusted Trial Balance
December 31, 0001

Accounts	Debit	Credit
Cash	$ 36,218	
Credit card receivables	13,683	
Accounts receivable	3,421	
Inventories, food	6,128	
Inventories, beverages	3,207	
Prepaid insurance	2,136	
Equipment	171,524	
Furnishings	53,596	
Accounts payable		$ 8,819
Bank loan payable		163,518
Common stock		50,000
Revenue, food operations		458,602
Revenue, beverage operations		180,509
Purchases, food (net)	181,110	
Purchases, beverages (net)	38,307	
Salaries and wages expense	221,328	
Laundry expense	16,609	
Kitchen fuel expense	7,007	
China and tableware expense	12,214	
Glassware expense	1,605	
Contract cleaning expense	5,906	
Licenses expense	3,205	
Misc. operating expenses	4,101	
Administrative—general expenses	15,432	
Marketing expenses	6,917	
Utilities expense	7,918	
Insurance expense	1,895	
Rental expense	24,000	
Interest expense	23,981	
Unadjusted trial balance totals	$861,448	$861,448

3

Analysis and Interpretation of Financial Statements

INTRODUCTION

The first part of this chapter introduces the reader to the various groups of people who might be interested in analyzing a company's financial statements. However, the rest of the chapter concentrates on the types of techniques useful for internal management.

Two types of balance sheet analyses are illustrated: comparative and comparative common-size. Income statement analysis is illustrated using the same two methods. A further method of income statement analysis is explored using average check, average cost, and average income per guest.

Trend results (operating results over a period of time) are discussed, as is the use of an index trend to obtain more meaningful figures.

The implications of price and cost level changes (inflation or deflation) on the operating results of a business are covered in some detail. The reader is shown how to use a readily available index, or compile his or her own index for a specific business, and how to convert historic sales figures to current dollar amounts.

CHAPTER OBJECTIVES

After studying this chapter, the reader should be able to:

1. Explain some of the ways in which different readers of financial statements are interested in different aspects of those statements.

2. Describe comparative analysis and use it for balance sheet and income statement analysis.

3. Describe comparative common-size analysis and use it for balance sheet and income statement analysis.

4. Calculate average sale, average cost, and average income, per guest.

5. Prepare trend results.

6. Prepare an index trend.

7. Use index numbers to convert historic dollars to current dollars.

ANALYSIS AND INTERPRETATION OF FINANCIAL STATEMENTS

Analysis and interpretation of financial statements means looking at the various parts of the financial statements, relating the parts to each other and to the picture as a whole, and determining if any meaningful and useful interpretation can be made out of this analysis.

All of the various readers of financial statements (managers, owners, investors, and creditors) have an interest in analyzing and interpreting the financial statements. However, what is of interest to one may be of less interest to another. For example, managers are very concerned about the internal operating efficiency of the organization and will look for indications that things are running smoothly, that operating goals are being met, and that the various departments are being managed as profitably as possible. Stockholders, on the other hand, are more interested in the net income picture and about future earnings and dividend prospects. In many cases, they would not be concerned about or be familiar with internal departmental results.

Management concerned about operating efficiency

Investors other than stockholders and creditors may be interested in the net income picture but are even more interested in the debt-paying ability of the company. A company may have good earnings but, because of a shortage of cash, may not be able to meet its debt obligations.

An exhaustive coverage of analysis and interpretation of financial statements is beyond the scope of this text. Therefore, discussion will be confined to some of the more fundamental analysis techniques that lend themselves well to the hospitality industry. Also, comment will be confined to the two major financial statements: the balance sheet and the income statement. The analysis techniques illustrated are those that normally would be used by the operation's management.

COMPARATIVE BALANCE SHEETS

A basic set of financial statements includes a balance sheet at a specific date and an income statement for the accounting period ended on that date. Some sets of financial statements may include a balance sheet and income statement for both the previous and current accounting periods. When prior and current period statements are provided, the changes occurring over the current operating period can easily be seen by a trained individual. However, to an average reader of financial statements, these changes may not be as obvious. It is not easy to mentally compare the differences between two sets of figures, and it is extremely useful to have additional information available to supplement an analysis.

Completion of a comparative (horizontal) analysis of a balance sheet or an income statement requires two consecutive periods of information. The objective is to find and identify changes that have occurred over an accounting period. The dollar value reported in each line item, subtotal, or total of the statement being compared is identified as a positive or negative dollar value change. The change, positive or negative, is divided by the prior period amount to determine the percentage of change. For example, assume the ending balance of the cash account in year 0001 was $22,900 and in year 0002, the ending balance was $35,400; assume that the ending balance of prepaid expenses in year 0001 was $5,200 and the year 0002 ending balance was $4,900. We can easily see the difference between the beginning and ending cash balance is $12,500 positive, and the difference between the beginning and ending prepaid expense account is $300 negative.

Cash Account Analysis

Period 1	Period 2	$ Change	÷ Period 1	=	% Change
$22,900	$35,400	+$12,500	÷ $22,900	=	.546 or 54.6%

*Note: From a calculator you will read 0.54585→; always multiply by 100 and round the first position right of the decimal for all text calculations to produce an answer stated as a percentage.

Prepaid Expense Account Analysis

Period 1	Period 2	$ Change	÷ Period 1	=	% Change
$5,200	$4,900	–$ 300	÷ $5,200	=	–.058 or –5.8%

*Note: From a calculator you will read 0.05769→; always multiply by 100 and round the first position right of the decimal for all text calculations to produce an answer stated as a percentage.

Completing comparative (horizontal) analysis of any item, subtotal, or total appearing in a financial statement is not the difficult part of a comparative analysis. The difficult part is understanding what the analysis is telling you.

Exhibit 3.1 shows balance sheet information for two successive years. The identity of each line item, subtotals, and totals for all assets, liabilities, and stockholders' equity is shown. In addition, two extra columns are added for comparative analysis, one to show the dollar value change and the other to express the percentage of change for each line item reported.

These latter two columns are most helpful in pinpointing large changes that have occurred, either dollar amount changes or percentage changes. Consider the cash account. The change from year 0001 to year 0002 is $12,500. This may or may not be a large change in dollar amount, depending on the size of the hotel. The change becomes obvious when expressed in percentage terms: 54.6% ($12,500 divided by $22,900 and multiplied by 100). Why has the cash account more than doubled in the past year? With reference to the marketable securities account, which has declined by $13,000 (86.7%), it looks as if most of the securities held have been cashed in during the year. Is this conversion for a specific purpose? If not, perhaps we should use some of it to reduce accounts payable, which have gone up by $7,300 (or 38%).

Notice also that the amount of money tied up in inventories has gone up by $4,800. This may not be much in dollars, but it is an increase of 24.1% over the previous year. Has our volume of sales increased sufficiently to justify this increase in inventories? An analysis of change in inventory turnover rates might answer this question. (See Chapter 11 for a discussion of inventory turnover.)

Note that the deposits and credit balances account has gone up by 260%. Has there been a change in the policy concerning deposits required for future bookings or reservations, or is this change indicative of a big increase in guaranteed future business compared to a year ago?

Absolute versus Relative Changes

In comparative analysis, the terms "absolute" and "relative change" are sometimes used. An absolute change shows the dollar change from one period to the next. A relative change is the absolute change expressed as a percentage.

An absolute change may sometimes appear large (for example, $10,000) but when compared to its base figure (for example, $1,000,000) represents a relative change of only 1%. By the same token, a relative change may seem high (for example, 50%) but when compared to its base figure is quite small in absolute terms (for example, a $50 base figure increasing to $75). In terms of the total income statement, this $25 change (even though it shows a relative increase of 50%) is insignificant. Therefore, when analyzing comparative statements, both the absolute and the relative changes should be looked at, and only those that exceed both acceptable norms should be of concern.

For example, absolute changes of concern might be established at $10,000 and relative changes at 5%, and only those changes that exceeded both $10,000

Exhibit 3.1 Comparative Balance Sheets

	Year Ending December 31		Increase (+) or Decrease (–) from
	0001	0002	Year 0001 to Year 0002
ASSETS			5-4.
Current assets			
Cash	$ 22,900	$ 35,400	+ $12,500 o\ + 54.6%
Accounts receivable	23,100	25,200	+ 2,100 + 9.1
Marketable securities	15,000	2,000	– 13,000 – 86.7
Inventories	19,900	24,700	+ 4,800 + 24.1
Prepaid expenses	5,200	4,900	– 300 – 5.8
Total current assets	$ 86,100	$ 92,200	+ $ 6,100 + 7.1%
Fixed assets			
Land	$ 161,800	$ 161,800	0 0
Building	1,432,800	1,432,800	0 0
Furniture and equipment	374,700	415,600	+ $40,900 + 10.9%
China, glass, etc.	25,600	28,400	+ 2,800 + 10.9
	$1,994,900	$2,038,600	+ $43,700 + 2.2%
Less: accumulated depreciation	(632,200)	(722,000)	+ (89,800) + (14.2)
Total fixed assets	$1,362,700	$1,316,600	– $46,100 – 3.4%
Total assets	$1,448,800	$1,408,800	– $40,000 – 2.8%
LIABILITIES AND STOCKHOLDERS' EQUITY			
Current liabilities			
Accounts payable	$ 19,200	$ 26,500	+ $ 7,300 + 38.0%
Accrued expenses	3,500	4,100	+ 600 + 17.1
Income taxes payable	12,300	10,900	– 1,400 – 11.4
Deposits and credit balances	500	1,800	+ 1,300 +260.0
Current portion of mortgage	27,200	25,100	– 2,100 – 7.7
Total current liabilities	$ 62,700	$ 68,400	+ $ 5,700 + 9.1%
Long-term liability			
Mortgage payable	$ 812,900	$ 787,800	– $25,100 – 3.1%
Stockholders' equity			
Common shares	$ 300,000	$ 300,000	0 0
Retained earnings	273,200	252,600	– $20,600 – 7.5%
Total stockholders' equity	$ 573,200	$ 552,600	– $20,600 – 3.6%
Total liabilities and stockholders' equity	$1,448,800	$1,408,800	– $40,000 – 2.8%

and 5% would be investigated. In this situation, the following changes would not be investigated:

- Above $10,000 but below 5%.
- Above 5% but below $10,000.
- Below $10,000 and below 5%.

COMPARATIVE COMMON-SIZE BALANCE SHEETS

Another technique used to analyze balance sheet information is to convert the statement to a common-size (vertical) analysis format. This method requires only one period of balance sheet financial data. Common size means that every numerical item of a financial statement is a part of the numerical total of the items being evaluated. In a conversion of a balance sheet to common-size format, total assets have a value of 100% and the numerical value of each item being converted represents a fractional part of total assets. Every item in a balance sheet, subtotals, and totals, can be expressed as a percentage of total assets since assets = liabilities and stockholders' equity and each side of the equation shares the same total numerical value. Exhibit 3.2 shows the common-size (vertical) conversion of the comparative balance sheet shown in Exhibit 3.1. The common-size statement shows that the cash account in year 0001 is 1.6 % of total assets, which was calculated by dividing the cash balance by total assets; $22,900 ÷ $1,448,800. Accounts payable in year 0001 is 1.3% of total assets, $19,200 ÷ $1,448,800. In Exhibit 3.2, we can see clearly that each balance sheet item shown for year 0001 is divided by total assets. The addition of each item percentage shown for year 0001 will equal 100%, which is the product of total assets divided by total assets.

> Common size means that every numerical item of a financial statement is a part of the numerical total of the items being evaluated

Any subset of a balance sheet such as current assets, fixed assets, current liabilities, long-term liabilities, or stockholders' equity can be converted vertically to a common-size format and analyzed separately. Since each current liability is a part of total current liabilities, a vertical common-size analysis will express each individual current liability as a percentage of total current liabilities. As an example, we will demonstrate how each of three assumed current liability accounts is converted to express each as a percentage of total current liabilities.

Accounts payable	+	Payroll payable	+	Interest payable	=	Current Liabilities
$8,184 = n1	+	$4,488 = n2	+	$528 = n3	=	$13,200 = Σn

The vertical analysis equation: n1 + n2 + n3 + etc., = Σn. Each element, n1, n2, and n3, can be divided by the sum of "Σn" to find its percentage relationship; n1 ÷ Σn identifies what percentage n1 is of the Σn.

Exhibit 3.2 Comparative Common-Size Balance Sheets

	Year Ending December 31		Common Size	
	0001	0002	0001	0002
ASSETS				
Current assets				
Cash	$ 22,900	$ 35,400	1.6%	2.5%
Accounts receivable	23,100	25,200	1.6	1.8
Marketable securities	15,000	2,000	1.0	0.1←
Inventories	19,900	24,700	1.4	1.8
Prepaid expenses	5,200	4,900	0.4	0.3
Total current assets	$ 86,100	$ 92,200	6.0%	6.5%
Fixed assets				
Land	$ 161,800	$ 161,800	11.2%	11.5%
Building	1,432,800	1,432,800	98.7	101.7←
Furniture and equipment	374,700	415,600	25.9	29.5←
China, glass, etc.	25,600	28,400	1.8	2.0
	$1,994,900	$2,038,600	137.6%	144.7%
Less: accumulated depreciation	(632,200)	(722,000)	(43.6)	(51.2)
Total fixed assets	$1,362,700	$1,316,600	94.0%	93.5%
Total assets	$1,448,800	$1,408,800	100.0%	100.0%
LIABILITIES AND STOCKHOLDERS' EQUITY				
Current liabilities				
Accounts payable	$ 19,200	$ 26,500	1.3%	1.9%
Accrued expenses	3,500	4,100	0.2	0.3
Income taxes payable	12,300	10,900	0.8	0.8
Deposits and credit balances	500	1,800	0.1	0.1
Current portion of mortgage	27,200	25,100	1.9	1.8
Total current liabilities	$ 62,700	$ 68,400	4.3%	4.9%
Long-term liability				
Mortgage payable	$ 812,900	$ 787,800	56.1%	55.9%
Stockholders' equity				
Common shares	$ 300,000	$ 300,000	20.7%	21.3%
Retained earnings	273,200	252,600	18.9	17.9
Total stockholders' equity	$ 573,200	$ 552,600	39.6%	39.2%
Total liabilities and stockholders' equity	$1,448,800	$1,408,800	100.0%	100.0%

Thus,

$$[n1 \div \Sigma n] = \$8,184 \div \$13,200 = .62 \text{ or } (62\%) \text{ of current liabilities}$$

$$[n2 \div \Sigma n] = \$4,488 \div \$13,200 = .34 \text{ or } (34\%) \text{ of current liabilities}$$

$$[n3 \div \Sigma n] = \$ \;\; 528 \div \$13,200 = .04 \text{ or } (4\%) \text{ of current liabilities}$$

Using the same three current liabilities, we can also use a math equation that may be more familiar: X = $13,200 total current liabilities [A + B + C = X].

$$A \div X = \$8,184 \div \$13,200 = .62 \text{ or } (62\%)$$

$$B \div X = \$4,488 \div \$13,200 = .34 \text{ or } (34\%)$$

$$C \div X = \$ \;\; 528 \div \$13,200 = .04 \text{ or } (4\%)$$

Regardless of whether you are converting a balance sheet or a subset of assets, liabilities, or stockholders' equity, the conversion procedure is the same.

Advantage of comparative common-size statements   The advantage of comparative common-size statements is that they show changes in proportion of individual accounts from one period to the next. For example, the cash account in year 0001 was 1.6% of total assets. In year 0002 it was 2.5% of total assets. This change in proportion would normally attract a reader's attention and raise questions. Attention might also be drawn to other accounts where large changes have occurred. The comparative, common-size technique is particularly useful when comparing two companies whose size and/or level of business is so different that other techniques of analysis are not appropriate.

Answers to questions improve effectiveness   Whether a hotel or food service operation uses comparative balance sheets or comparative common-size balance sheets is a matter of choice. Normally only one or the other would be wanted since both draw the attention of the reader to the relevant accounts where changes have occurred. These changes, in turn, should provoke questions, the answers to which may be helpful in running the business more effectively. Attention should be focused on the balance sheet because of the need for effective control or management of a company's assets. However, as a management technique for controlling internal day-to-day operations, comparative income statements are often more useful than comparative balance sheets.

COMPARATIVE INCOME STATEMENTS

Exhibit 3.3 shows two consecutive annual income statements for a food department of a hotel operation. Comparative (horizontal) analysis techniques discussed and described for balance sheets are applicable to the analysis of an

Exhibit 3.3   Comparative Departmental Income Statement—Food Department

	Year Ending December 31		Increase or Decrease from Year	
	0001	0002	0001 to 0002	
Revenue				
Dining room	$201,600	$221,900	+$20,300	+10.1%
Coffee shop	195,900	201,700	+ 5,800	+ 3.0
Banquets	261,200	241,100	− 20,100	− 7.7
Room service	81,700	82,600	+ 900	+ 1.1
Bar	111,200	121,800	+ 10,600	+ 9.5
Total sales revenue	$851,600	$869,100	+ $17,500	+ 2.1%
Cost of sales				
Cost of food used	$352,500	$373,700	+$21,200	+ 6.0%
Less: employee meals	(30,100)	(32,500)	+(2,400)	+ 8.0
Net food cost	(322,400)	(341,200)	+ 18,800	+ 5.8%
Gross profit	$529,200	$527,900	− $ 1,300	− 2.5%
Departmental expenses				
Salaries and wages	$277,400	$304,500	+$27,100	+ 9.8%
Employee benefits	34,500	37,800	+ 3,300	+ 9.6
China, glassware	7,100	7,800	+ 700	+ 9.9
Cleaning supplies	6,400	6,800	+ 400	+ 6.3
Decorations	2,200	1,800	− 400	−18.2
Guest supplies	6,500	7,000	+ 500	+ 7.7
Laundry	15,500	18,400	+ 2,900	+18.7
Licenses	3,400	3,500	+ 100	+ 2.9
Linen	3,700	4,200	+ 500	+13.5
Menus	2,000	2,500	+ 500	+25.0
Miscellaneous	800	1,100	+ 300	+37.5
Paper supplies	4,900	5,700	+ 800	+16.3
Printing, stationery	4,700	4,600	− 100	− 2.1
Silver	2,300	2,100	− 200	− 8.7
Uniforms	3,100	2,400	− 700	−22.6
Utensils	1,700	1,800	+ 100	+ 5.9
Total expenses	(376,200)	(412,000)	+ 35,800	+ 9.5%
Departmental income	$153,000	$115,900	− $37,100	−24.2%

Find the percentage
of change

income statement. Line by line, find the numerical value change and divide the change by the prior year to find the percentage of change. For example, revenue increased by 10.1% from year 0001 to year 0002. The calculation to identify the percentage of change is:

Rev. 0002	−	Rev. 0001	=	Change	÷	Rev. 0001	=	Change %
$221,900	−	$201,600	=	$20,300	÷	$201,600	=	.1006 or (10.1%)

As we can see, comparative (horizontal) analysis follows the same procedures to calculate the numerical change of each line item and the percentage the change represents. It matters not what financial information is being compared, as long as two consecutive operating periods of information are provided. The concept remains:

Item: Period 1 − Period 2 = Dollar Change ÷ Period 1 = % of Change

The other percentage change figures are calculated in the same way. Note that within each revenue area, except banquets, the revenue has increased, but total revenue has gone up only 2.1%. The reason for this relatively small increase in total revenue is that banquet revenue was down 7.7% over the year. Can the reasons be determined? (Is the sales department not doing an effective job? Is there a new, competitive operation close by? Are prices too high?)

Income should increase
with revenue increase

Even with the total revenue increase, small as it is, income has declined $37,100, or 24.2%. This is a drastic change. With revenue up, all other factors being equal, income should also be up, not down.

All other things are, obviously, not equal, because analysis of costs shows that the majority of them have increased at a greater rate than the revenue increase. To select only one example, the laundry cost has gone up $2,900 over the year, or 18.7%. Are we using more linen than before? Has our supplier increased the cost to us by this percentage? Whatever the reason, corrective action can be taken once the cause is known. Each expense can be analyzed in its own way. In this particular illustration, assuming the increased costs were inevitable, perhaps the increased costs have not yet been adjusted for in-menu selling prices.

Exhibit 3.4 shows comparative income statements for a major restaurant chain (McDonald's Corporation).

COMPARATIVE COMMON-SIZE INCOME STATEMENTS

Total revenue equals
100%

Income statements can also be converted to a comparative common-size (vertical) analysis format. With the conversion of the income statement, total sales revenue takes the value of 100% and all other items on the income statement

Exhibit 3.4   Comparative Statements for McDonald's Corporation
Consolidated Operating Results
Increases (Decreases) in Operating Results Over Prior Year

(Dollars rounded to millions, except per common share data)	1994		1993	
	Amount	%	Amount	%
Systemwide sales	$2,401	10	$1,702	8
Revenues				
Sales by company-operated restaurants	$ 636	12	$ 55	1
Revenues from franchised restaurants	277	12	220	11
Total revenues	913	12	275	4
Operating costs and expenses				
Company-operated restaurants	481	12	38	1
Franchised restaurants	55	14	32	9
General, administrative, and selling expenses	142	15	81	9
Other operating (income) expense—net	(22)	35	2	(3)
Total operating costs and expenses	656	12	153	3
Operating income	257	13	122	7
Interest expense	(10)	(3)	(58)	(15)
Nonoperating income (expense)—net	(56)	NM	48	NM
Income before provision for income taxes	211	13	228	16
Provision for income taxes	69	12	104	21
Net income	$ 142	13	$ 124	13
Net income per common share*	$ .23	16	$ 16	12

NM - Not Meaningful
*Restated for two-for-one common stock split in June 1994.

are expressed as a fraction of total sales revenue. A comparative common-size income statement is illustrated in Exhibit 3.5. For example, in year 0001 dining room revenue was 23.7% of total sales revenue, calculated as follows:

Dining revenue	÷	Total sales revenue	=	% of Total sales revenue
$201,600	÷	$851,600	=	.2367 or (23.7%)

All items on the example comparative income statement in Exhibit 3.5 are calculated the same way, using $851,600 as the denominator and the individual item as the numerator. Note that the percentage given for gross margin cannot be included to arrive at a 100%, the total sum of the item percentages. Gross margin is a derived subtotal representing sales revenue minus cost of sales and in fact does not represent an operating cost, nor does it represent a resulting profit or loss from operations.

Expense items also use $851,600 as the denominator for year 0001. Net food cost, for example, is calculated as follows:

$$\frac{\$322,400}{\$851,600} \times 100 = 37.9\%$$

Separate food and beverage cost percentages

If this were a combined food and beverage operation, food cost should still be calculated as a percentage of food revenue and beverage cost as a percentage of beverage revenue, even if all other costs are expressed as a percentage of combined food and beverage revenue.

One way of interpreting the common-size income statement information in year 0001 is to say that, out of every $1.00 of revenue, 37.9 cents was for food, 32.6 cents was for salaries and wages, 4.0 cents for employee benefits, and 7.5 cents for all other operating expenses, leaving only 18 cents for income. In year 0002 this income was down to 13.3 cents out of every $1.00 of revenue. Comparative, common-size income statements show which items, as a proportion of revenue, have changed enough to require investigation.

Food cost increase causes income decline

For example, one of the causes for the decline to 13.3 cents profit from each dollar of revenue in year 0002 is that the amount spent on food (net food cost) has risen from 37.9 cents to 39.3 cents out of each dollar of revenue. This 1.4-cent increase may seem insignificant, but if it had not occurred we would have made $12,167.00 more income, calculated as follows:

$$\$869,100 \times 1.4\% = \$12,167.00$$

In the interest of brevity in Exhibit 3.5, a number of expenses have been added together under "all other operating expenses." In year 0001, this figure is 7.5% of revenue, and in year 0002, 8.1% of revenue. This is a relatively small change and might normally be unnoticed. It is small only because many of the individual expense item increases are offset by several that decreased, thus burying the facts. In practice it would be best to detail each individual expense and express it as a percentage of revenue to have full disclosure.

The income statement illustrated for the food operation was both comparative (Exhibit 3.3) and comparative common-size (Exhibit 3.5). Normally, only one

Exhibit 3.5   Comparative Common-Size Income Statement—Food Department

	Year Ending December 31		Year Ending December 31	
	0001	0002	0001	0002
Revenue				
Dining room	$201,600	$221,900	23.7%	25.5%
Coffee shop	195,900	201,700	23.0	23.2
Banquets	261,200	241,100	30.7	27.7
Room service	81,700	82,600	9.6	9.5
Bar	111,200	121,800	13.0	14.1
Total sales revenue	$851,600	$869,100	100.0%	100.0%
Cost of sales				
Cost of food used	$352,500	$373,700	41.4%	43.0%
Less: employee meals	(30,100)	(32,500)	(3.5)	(3.7)
Net food cost	(322,400)	(341,200)	(37.9%)	(39.3%)
Gross profit	$529,200	$527,900	62.1%	60.7%
Departmental expenses				
Salaries and wages	$277,400	$304,500	32.6%	35.0%
Employee benefits	34,500	37,800	4.0	4.3
All other operating expenses	64,300	69,700	7.5	8.1
Total expenses	($376,200)	($412,000)	(44.1%)	(47.4%)
Departmental income	$153,000	$115,900	18.0%	13.3%

Attention to problem areas

or the other would be used. They each draw attention, albeit in a different way, to problem areas requiring investigation and if necessary corrective action.

Note again that the comparative common-size method is the more appropriate one to use when comparing two companies whose size or scale of operation is quite different.

The statement of cash flows is not normally analyzed in the same way that income statements and balance sheets are using comparative and comparative common-size methods. However, some ratios can be prepared from this statement. Those ratios will be illustrated and discussed in the next chapter.

There is one other method of comparative analysis particularly suited to the food operation, and that is to calculate and compare average sales revenue per guest, average cost per guest, and average income per guest information.

Average Check, Cost, and Income Per Guest

Find the "per guest average"

It is always wise for management to have averages for sales revenue and cost functions. Any time we concern ourselves with averages, understanding the basic concept of how to calculate averages is essential. The question is to find the "per guest average" of what? "What" must be identified in this situation as total sales revenue, revenue by division, total cost, or cost by category. We can determine a "per guest" average using the following concept: revenue ÷ guests, cost ÷ guests, or operating income ÷ guests. Exhibit 3.6 shows two consecutive years of income statement revenue, associated operating costs, and operating income (income before taxes). Two columns have been added: column one to identify the number of guests served by each revenue division and the costs incurred by each major cost category, and column two to show the average check and average cost per guest. The averages for several different items in year 0006 are:

Total sales revenue	÷	Total guests	=	Avg. check per guest
$2,554,800	÷	215,560	=	$11.85

Dining revenue	÷	Total guests	=	Avg. check dining guest
$604,800	÷	35,130	=	$17.22

Net food cost	÷	Total guests	=	Avg. food cost per guest
$967,200	÷	215,560	=	$4.49

Total cost	÷	Total guests	=	Avg. cost per guest
$2,095,800	÷	215,560	=	$9.72

Operating income	÷	Total guests	=	Avg. operating income per guest
$459,000	÷	215,560	=	$2.13

Typical questions raised

Some of the facts that come to light are that the number of guests served in all revenue areas increased, except in banquets where there was a decrease of 9,410 (60,190 less 50,780). This is a decrease of 15.6% (9,410 divided by 60,190, then multiplied by 100). At the same time, in the banquet area the average spending per guest increased from $13.02 to $14.24. This is an increase of $1.22 per guest, or 9.4% ($1.22 divided by $13.02, then multiplied by 100). The combination of higher average check (average revenue) but reduced numbers of guests meant that our banquet revenue was $60,300 lower in year 0007 than in year 0006. Is this a desirable trend? Is our banquet selling policy causing us to sell higher priced banquets but not allowing us to sell to as

Exhibit 3.6 Comparative Average Check, Cost, and Income per Guest—Food Department

	Year Ending December 31, 0006			Year Ending December 31, 0007		
	Revenue	Guests	Average Check	Revenue	Guests	Average Check
Department						
Dining room	$ 604,800	35,130	$17.22	$ 665,700	36,210	$18.38
Coffee shop	587,700	71,200	8.25	605,100	78,200	7.74
Banquets	783,600	60,190	13.02	723,300	50,780	14.24
Room service	245,100	16,870	14.53	247,800	17,110	14.48
Bar	333,600	32,170	10.37	365,400	35,490	10.30
Totals	$2,554,800	215,560	$11.85	$2,607,300	217,790	$11.97
	Cost	Guests	Average Cost	Cost	Guests	Average Cost
Operating Costs						
Net food cost	$ 967,200	215,560	$ 4.49	$1,023,600	217,790	$ 4.70
Salaries and wages	832,200	same	3.86	913,500	same	4.19
Employee benefits	103,500	same	0.48	113,400	same	0.52
Other expenses	192,900	same	0.89	209,100	same	0.96
Totals	$2,095,800	215,560	$ 9.72	$2,259,600	217,790	$10.37
Income	$ 459,000	215,560	$ 2.13	$ 347,700	217,790	$ 1.60

many customers? Has an increase in selling prices driven away a considerable amount of business?

In terms of total average revenue per guest for the food operation in year 0007, we took in 12 cents more per guest ($11.97 – $11.85) but we spent 65 cents more per guest ($10.37 – $9.72), and thus our income per guest declined 53 cents ($2.13 – $1.60). Obviously our costs per guest have risen much faster than our revenue per guest. The individual items of expense, on a per guest basis, have all increased, some more than others. They need to be investigated to see whether the trend cannot be reversed. Alternatively, sales prices may need to be increased to compensate for uncontrollable, increasing costs.

Although Exhibit 3.6 illustrated a food operation, a beverage department could be analyzed equally as well using the same approach. Similarly, a hotel rooms department could be analyzed using number of guests or number of rooms as the unit figure to be divided into sales revenue, costs, or income.

TREND RESULTS

The balance sheet and income statement illustrations discussed so far have only taken into consideration comparisons and analysis between two successive periods. Limiting an analysis to only two periods (weeks, months, or years) can be misleading if an unusual occurrence or factor distorted the results for either of the two periods. Looking at results over a greater number of periods of time can often be more useful in indicating the direction in which a business is heading. For example, the following shows trend results for a cocktail lounge for six successive months:

Month	Revenue	Change in Revenue	Percentage Change
1	$25,000		
2	30,000	+$5,000	+20
3	33,000	+ 3,000	+10
4	35,000	+ 2,000	+ 6
5	36,000	+ 1,000	+ 3
6	36,000	0	0

To determine a trend percentage, year 1 is always set to 0. For subsequent years the trend percentage is determined as follows:

$$\frac{\text{Period 3} - \text{Period 2}}{\$33,000 - \$30,000} = \frac{\text{Sales revenue change}}{\$3,000} \div \frac{\text{Prior year}}{\$30,000} = \frac{\text{Trend \%}}{.1 \text{ or } (10\%)}$$

Calculation of change in sales revenue

In the above, the change in revenue dollar amount for each period is calculated by subtracting from each period's sales revenue the sales revenue of the preceding period. For example, in period 3:

$$\$33,000 - \$30,000 = \$3,000 \text{ change in sales revenue}$$

Calculation of percentage change

The percentage change figures are calculated by dividing each period's change in sales revenue dollar amounts by the sales revenue of the previous period and multiplying by 100. For example, in period 3:

$$\frac{\$3,000}{\$30,000} \times 100 = 10\%$$

Over a long enough period of time, trend results show the direction in which a business is going. In our particular case, the trend results indicate that, although business has been increasing over the past few periods, it now seems to have leveled off. Has the business reached its maximum potential in sales revenue? Trend information may be found useful in such areas as forecasting or budgeting, or in decision making. (Is it time we spent money on advertising to increase volume?)

The particular trend result just illustrated was for a specific item (sales revenue in a bar), but comparison of trends of related items (sales revenue and expenses) can be indicative of problems. For example, the cost of sales (liquor cost) figures for our lounge for the same six periods are:

Period	Liquor Cost
1	$ 7,500
2	9,200
3	10,300
4	10,800
5	11,100
6	11,200

This basic information regarding the liquor costs for six periods can also be converted.

Month	Liquor Costs	Cost Change	% Change
1	$ 7,500		
2	9,200	$1,700	+22.7%
3	10,300	1,100	+12.0%
4	10,800	500	+ 4.9%
5	11,100	300	+ 2.8%
6	11,200	100	+ 0.9%

As can be seen, these relationships are calculated very quickly and provide a great deal of information regarding cost increases and decreases for specific time periods.

This technique can be expanded into a more useful approach in which an index trend is calculated.

$$\frac{\text{Sales revenue last period } - \text{ Sales revenue current period}}{\text{Sales revenue last period}} \times 100 = \frac{\text{Index}}{\text{Trend Percentage}}$$

Or

$$\frac{\text{Cost last period} - \text{Cost current period}}{\text{Sales revenue last period}} \times 100 = \frac{\text{Index}}{\text{Trend Percentage}}$$

INDEX TREND

Year one equals 100

An index trend is calculated by assigning a value of 100 (or 100%) in period one for each item being tabulated as follows:

Period	Revenue	Liquor Cost	Revenue Index	Liquor Cost Index
1	$25,000	$ 7,500	100	100
2	30,000	9,200	120	123
3	ͺ33,000	10,300	132	137
4	35,000	10,800	140	144
5	36,000	11,100	144	148
6	36,000	11,200	144	149

Calculation of index number

The index figure for each succeeding period is calculated by dividing the dollar amount for that period by the base period dollar amount and multiplying by 100. For example, in period 2, the revenue index is:

$$\frac{\$30,000}{\$25,000} \times 100 = 120$$

In period 5, the liquor cost index is:

$$\frac{\$11,100}{\$7,500} \times 100 = 148$$

Our completed index trend results show us that the liquor cost has been increasing faster than liquor revenue. Expressed another way, sales revenue is up 44% (144 − 100) and liquor cost is up 49% (149 − 100). This is normally an undesirable trend that needs investigation and possibly correction.

PRICE AND COST LEVEL CHANGES
(INFLATION OR DEFLATION)

Consider implications of
price and cost changes

When comparing operating results, and in particular when analyzing trend figures, the reader must be aware of the effect changing dollar values have on the results. One hundred pounds of vegetables a few years ago weighed exactly the same as one hundred pounds of vegetables today; but the amount of money required to buy one hundred pounds today is probably quite different from the amount of money needed a few years ago. Prices change over time. In the same way that prices change to us, so too do the prices we charge our customers for rooms, food, beverages, and other services. When comparing income and expense items over a fairly long period of time, it is necessary to consider the implications of upward changing prices or costs (inflation), or the reverse (deflation).

Consider a restaurant with the following sales revenue in two successive years:

Year 1 $100,000

Year 2 $105,000

Dollars of unequal
value

This is a $5,000 or 5% increase in volume. But if restaurant menu prices had been increased over the year by 10% due to inflation, then our year 2 revenue should have been at least $110,000 just to stay even with year 1 volume. In other words, when we try to compare sales revenue for successive periods in inflationary or deflationary times, as in this case, we are comparing unequal values. Last year's dollar does not have the same value as this year's. What a dollar would buy last year may now require $1.10. Is there a method that will allow us to convert a previous period's dollars into current period dollars so trends can be analyzed more meaningfully? The answer is yes, with the use of index numbers.

Use of index to adjust
revenue

The consumer price index is probably one of the most commonly used and widely understood indexes available. But many other indexes are produced by the government and other organizations. By selecting an appropriate index, conversion of the previous period's dollars into current year dollars is simple. Consider the following figures showing trend results for a restaurant's sales revenue for the past five years.

Year	Sales Revenue	Change in Sales Revenue	Percentage Change
1	$420,000	$ 0	0.0%
2	450,000	30,000	7.1
3	465,000	15,000	3.3
4	485,000	20,000	4.3
5	510,000	25,000	5.2

The trend shows increasing sales revenue each year, generally a favorable trend. But is it reasonable to compare $420,000 of sales revenue in year 1 with $510,000 of sales revenue in year 5? By adjusting all sales revenue to comparable year 5 dollars, a more realistic picture of our restaurant revenue may emerge. The index used to do this would be based on restaurant revenue, and we would need to use the index numbers for the same five-year period for which we wish to adjust our restaurant revenue. Let us suppose the index numbers were as follows:

Year	Index Number
1	105
2	112
3	119
4	128
5	142

Equation for conversion to current dollars

The equation for converting past periods' (historic) dollars to current (real) dollars is as follows:

$$\text{Historic dollars} \times \frac{\text{Index number for current period}}{\text{Index number for historic period}} = \text{Current dollars}$$

The following tabulation shows the index numbers used to convert the earlier sales revenue figures into terms of today's current dollars.

Year	Index	Historic Sales Revenue	×	Conversion Equation	=	Current Dollars
1	105	$420,000	×	142 / 105	=	$568,000
2	112	450,000	×	142 / 112	=	571,000
3	119	465,000	×	142 / 119	=	555,000
4	128	485,000	×	142 / 128	=	538,000
→ 5	142	510,000	×	142 / 142	=	510,000

The resulting picture is quite different from the unadjusted sales revenue figures. In fact, in terms of current dollars, our annual sales revenue has generally declined from year 1 to year 5, and this would not normally be a desirable trend.

Using own in-house index

If a restaurant sales revenue index were not readily available, an operator could easily compile one by converting the annual average check figure for each of a number of years to an index, giving year 1 the value of 100. This is illustrated as follows:

Year	Check	Average Index
1	$10.20	100
2	11.01	108
3	12.06	118
4	12.63	124
5	13.68	134

The index numbers for each year, other than year 1, are calculated by dividing the average check for that year by the average check for year 1 and multiplying by 100. For example, the year 3 index number is:

$$\frac{\$12.06}{\$10.20} \times 100 = \underline{\underline{118}}$$

Care in use of an index

A restaurant creating its own index in this way might find it much more accurate since it reflects only what has happened to prices within that restaurant. A national average restaurant index might have factors built into it that have no bearing on any one individual operation. Preferably, such an individual index should be used only if the size and nature of the operation have not changed during the period under review; otherwise the results could be misleading.

Once the index has been prepared, it can be applied using the equation already demonstrated to convert historic revenue to current dollars. A bar could use the same type of homemade index using average customer spending. For its rooms revenue, a hotel or motel could use average room rates converted to an index.

Converting complete income statements

Costs can be converted in the same way, using an appropriate index for the particular cost or expense under review (for example, a wage index would probably be appropriate for adjusting labor costs). Alternatively, an individual establishment might be able to construct its own index for each individual expense, as was just demonstrated for prices, basing the indexes on a cost per guest or cost per room occupied. In fact, complete income statements for past periods can be reconstructed by converting them in their entirety to current period, or current year, dollars.

Such wholesale conversions would probably go beyond the needs of most hotel, or food service, management needs; but, whether or not such a major accounting conversion is used, the implications of price and cost level changes should not be ignored. Balance sheets are also implicated. A balance sheet showing a cash balance on hand of $100,000 in each of two successive years may seem to indicate no change in the cash position. But will $100,000 now buy as much as $100,000 a year ago? Similarly, the historic cost prices of land, buildings, and equipment on balance sheets may also be misleading. However, a complete and comprehensive discussion of inflation accounting or current dollar accounting is far beyond the scope of this book.

COMPUTER APPLICATIONS

With a spreadsheet program, a computer can prepare and print out both comparative and comparative common-size balance sheets and income statements including the relevant dollar and percentage changes. In addition, many spreadsheets have a graphics capability that can provide management with more easily interpreted information about the trend of specific items. These graphs can be presented in various forms, such as bar graphs or pie charts.

SUMMARY

Financial statement analysis is a matter of relating the various parts of the statements to each other and to the whole, then interpreting the results. Different users of financial statements have different sections and specific items they are interested in and most likely will have different interpretations of the information being viewed. It is most likely that different readers of financial statements may arrive at different conclusions based on the results of their analysis.

Comparative (horizontal) analysis as demonstrated in this chapter is one of the techniques used. This involves putting two consecutive balance sheets or two consecutive income statements side by side and showing the numerical value changes and the percentage the change represents for each line item, subtotals, and totals. The analysis will conclude with an interpretation of the results.

$$\text{Period 1} - \text{Period 2} = \$\text{Change} \div \text{Period 1} = \%\ \text{Change}$$

Comparative (vertical) common-size analysis of financial statements requires only one balance sheet or one income statement. A common-size analysis of a balance sheet will express each item, subtotal, and total as a percentage of total assets. Total assets are used as the 100% total of the balance sheet and has the same numerical value as total liabilities and stockholders' equity (A = L + SHE). A common-size analysis of an income statement will divide each item, subtotal, and total appearing in the income statement by total sales revenue, which expresses the percentage of each element as a percentage of 100% of total sales revenue.

$$\text{Revenue Item} \div \text{Total sales revenue} = \% \text{ of total sales revenue}$$

Or

$$\text{Cost Item} \div \text{Total sales revenue} = \% \text{ of total sales revenue}$$

Another useful approach in the evaluation of an income statement is to express the items of sales revenue and costs on an average per guest basis.

$$\text{Sales revenue or cost item} \div \text{Item guests} = \text{Avg. item per guest}$$

Trend results are similar to comparative statements, except that they show figures for several successive periods, showing the change in dollars and the percentage change from each period to the next. A refinement of the raw trend figures is an index trend. An index trend begins with the assignment of a 100 (or 100%) for the first time period, monthly, quarterly, or yearly. Subsequent periods of revenue and/or cost figures are expressed as a percentage of the revenue or cost figures used in the first time period.

$$\frac{\text{Sales revenue last period} - \text{Sales revenue current period}}{\text{Sales revenue last period}} \times 100 = \text{Index Trend \%}$$

Or

$$\frac{\text{Cost last period} - \text{Cost current period}}{\text{Cost last period}} \times 100 = \text{Index Trend \%}$$

One major factor to be considered when analyzing financial results for two or more successive years is that the figures must be interpreted with price/cost (inflation) level implications in mind. To convert previous historical period dollars into current period dollars, an appropriate index scale can be used. The equation is:

$$\text{Historic Dollars} \times \frac{\text{Index number Current Period}}{\text{Index number Historic Period}} = \text{Current dollars}$$

DISCUSSION QUESTIONS

1. Explain in what way a stockholder reading a financial statement might be interested in items different from the manager of the enterprise.

2. What is comparative (horizontal) balance sheet analysis?

3. Discuss absolute and relative changes with reference to comparative (horizontal) financial statement analysis.

4. Why are differences between two comparative statements frequently better shown in percentages rather than only in dollars?

5. What is the objective of comparative (vertical) common-size income?

6. How is average sales revenue per guest calculated?

7. Why are trend results often more meaningful than a comparison limited to two successive accounting periods?

8. How is an index trend calculated?

9. In inflationary times, why is comparative analysis and an index trend misleading?

10. What is the equation for converting past historic period dollars to current period dollars?

ETHICS SITUATION

A restaurant manager has received a bonus for each of the past five years based on increases in sales revenue that have averaged about 5% over the previous year. The restaurant owner asked to have the sales revenue figures for the last five years adjusted for inflation and the manager has an accountant adjust the figures. On reviewing the results, the manager notices that sales revenues have remained virtually flat and in one year, sales revenues actually declined slightly. Before submitting the adjusted figures to the owner, the manager decides to change them to show that sales revenue increases averaged approximately 3% a year. By changing the adjusted figures, the manager hopes to show the owner the annual bonuses were justified. Discuss the ethics of this situation.

EXERCISES

3.1 A restaurant owner expressed concern regarding the changes in cash, credit card receivables, food and beverage inventories accounts in the months of July and August of the current year. He wants you to show him the dollar changes and the percentage of change for each of these accounts using comparative analysis.

	July	August
Cash	$ 8,880	$ 7,104
Credit card receivables	1,240	1,984
Food inventories	4,480	6,272
Beverage inventories	2,220	1,887
Total current assets	$16,820	$17,247

3.2 After being shown the comparative analysis (exercise 3.1), the owner now wants to see a common-size (vertical) analysis. Using the same data from exercise 3.1, prepare a common-size analysis for July and August.

3.3 Complete a common-size vertical analysis on the condensed income statement presented below.

Condensed Income Statement

Sales revenue	$480,000
Cost of sales	201,600
Gross margin	$278,400
Operating expenses	206,400
Operating income	$ 72,000

3.4 A rooms operation had an average room rate of $48.00 in the first year, $44.00 in year two, and $53.00 in year three. You are to establish an index trend starting with the average room rate for first year and determine the index trend numbers for year two and year three.

3.5 Based on the following, determine the average check per guest.

	Sales Revenue	Guests
Dining Room	$128,880	9,206
Bar-Lounge	$ 66,586	5,202

3.6 Based on the following, determine the average cost of sales revenue per guest.

	Cost of Sales Revenue	Guests
Dining Room	$51,552	9,206
Bar-Lounge	$25,386	5,202

3.7   The following data from a restaurant operation show a partially completed comparative income statement analysis for two consecutive years. Determine and fill in the missing values and percentages.

	Year 0001	Year 0002	Changes	
			▲ Dollars	▲ %
Sales revenue	$23,502	$	+1,110	+
Cost of sales revenue	– 9,208	– 9,438	+	+ 2.5%
Gross margin	$	$	+	+
Direct costs	–10,202	–	+ 1,420	+
Contributory Income	$	$ 3,552	–	–
Indirect costs	– 2,477	–	–	–3.0%
Operating Income	$	$ 1,149	–	–

3.8   Sales revenue for a restaurant operation is given for the months of March, April, and May of year 0002. The index numbers are stated for each month. Convert the months of March, April, and May to current dollars. Round answers to the highest dollar.

Year 0002	Sales Revenue	Index Number
March	$38,000	110
April	$40,000	112
March	$44,000	115

PROBLEMS

3.1   Present in the proper form a comparative (horizontal) analysis of the balance sheet shown below with two consecutive years—0004 and 0005. Comment on any items of difference that you consider significant.

ASSETS	Year 0004	Year 0005
Current Assets		
Cash	$ 11,300	$ 15,400
Credit card receivables	3,900	6,300
Accounts receivable	11,700	18,900
Vending inventories	7,800	8,400
Prepaid expenses	3,900	4,100
Total Current Assets	**$ 38,600**	**$ 53,100**

Property Plant and Equipment

Land	$ 81,200	$ 81,200
Building	758,100	795,300
Furnishings	83,712	93,412
Equipment	90,688	90,688
Accumulated depreciation	(315,500)	(335,800)
Glassware, linen inventories	12,200	15,300
Total Property & Equipment (net)	$710,400	$740,100
Total Assets	$749,000	$793,200

Liabilities & Stockholders' Equity

Current Liabilities

Accounts Payable	$ 9,100	$ 12,200
Accrued Expenses Payable	4,200	4,900
Taxes Payable	12,400	15,500
Current Portion, Mortgage Payable	13,600	11,200
Total Current Liabilities	$ 39,300	$ 43,800

Long-Term Liabilities

Mortgage Payable	$423,500	$412,300
Total Liabilities	$462,800	$456,100

Stockholders' Equity

Capital Stock	$125,200	$145,200
Retained Earnings	161,000	191,900
Total Stockholders' Equity	$286,200	$337,100
Total Liabilities & Stockholders' Equity	$749,000	$793,200

3.2 Using the information shown in problem 3.1, present in proper form a comparative (vertical) common-size balance sheet analysis for year 0004 and year 0005. Comment on any changes you consider significant.

3.3 The following information has been extracted from a hotel's food department for the months of August and September.

	Month of August		Month of September	
Departmental Divisions	**Revenue**	**Guests**	**Revenue**	**Guests**
Room Service	$ 11,300	927	$ 9,000	756
Dining Room	75,900	4,628	63,700	3,765
Bar-Lounge	5,500	846	4,100	637
Coffee Shop	53,400	9,709	48,700	8,604
Banquets	66,200	6,687	70,500	6,805
Totals	$212,300	22,797	$196,000	20,567

Departmental Operating Income August: $34,000; September: $28,900

	Month of August	Month of September
Cost of Sales	$68,100	$63,900
Wage-Salaries Costs	75,800	71,100
Benefits Costs	11,400	10,700
Linen Costs	3,200	3,000
China Costs	5,300	4,900
Supplies Costs	4,900	4,700
Other Costs	9,600	8,800

a. Prepare average sales revenue figures (average check) per guest for each sales revenue division for each month.

b. Determine the departmental average sales revenue (average check) per guest for each month.

c. Determine the departmental average cost per guest for each month.

d. Determine the departmental operating income per guest for each month.

3.4 A company owns two restaurants in the same town. Operating results for the first three months of the current year for both restaurants "A" and "B" are:

	"Restaurant A"		"Restaurant B"	
Sales Revenue		$154,300		$206,100
Cost of Sales		− 60,200		− 78,900
Gross margin		$ 94,100		$127,200
Direct Costs				
Wages Expense	$45,600		$70,400	
Supplies Expense	12,700		16,800	
Other Direct Costs	4,500	− 62,800	6,100	− 93,300
Contributory Income		$ 31,300		$ 33,900
Indirect Costs				
Rent Expense	$ 6,500		$ 9,000	
Insurance Expense	2,000		3,000	
Other Indirect Expenses	3,200	− 11,700	3,600	− 15,600
Operating Income		$ 19,600		$ 18,300

The owners of the restaurant are concerned that restaurant "B" reports a higher sales revenue yet produces a lower operating income than restaurant "A." Convert the information shown above into a comparative (vertical) common-size income statement for each restaurant to analyze the situation, and comment on the results.

3.5 The sales revenue, food cost of sales, and guests served for a small fast food carryout division of a restaurant for the past six months are given below.

Month	Sales Revenue	Cost of Sales, Food	Guests Served
1	$ 31,800	$12,200	10,200
2	32,600	12,600	10,400
3	34,300	13,400	10,300
4	33,900	13,800	10,100
5	34,700	14,500	10,400
6	36,200	14,700	10,500
Totals	$203,500	$81,200	61,900

For each of the six months calculate average check, average costs of sales food, and an index number rounded to the nearest whole figure. Set the index for month one at 100 and complete index trend numbers for the remaining five months. With the index numbers identified, convert sales revenue and cost of sales food from historic to current dollars.

3.6 A motel had the following annual sales revenue and average room rate figures for the last five years. During this five-year period there were no changes in the number or type of rooms available and the clientele remained basically the same.

Year	Annual Sales Revenue	Average Room Rate
1	$654,000	$35.00
2	$710,000	$37.90
3	$746,000	$39.10
4	$802,000	$41.40
5	$830,000	$42.70

Prepare index trend numbers from the average room rates using 100 as the base index number for year one. Use the index numbers identified to convert the reported yearly sales revenue to current dollars. After completing the conversion, comment on the results after your analysis.

3.7 Two successive monthly income statements for the food department of a motor lodge are shown below. Present the income statements in a comparative (horizontal) analysis format.

Sales Revenue	August	September
Room Service	$11,300	$ 9,000
Dining Room	75,900	63,700
Bar-Lounge	5,500	4,100
Coffee Shop	53,400	48,700
Banquets	66,200	70,500
Total Sales Revenue	$212,300	$196,000
Cost of Sales	(68,100)	(63,900)
Gross Margin	$144,200	$132,100
Operating Expenses		
Wages and Salaries	$75,800	$71,100
Employee Benefits	11,400	10,700
Linen and Laundry	3,200	3,000
China, Glassware, & Tableware	5,300	4,900
Miscellaneous Operating Costs	4,900	4,700
Operating Supplies	9,600	8,800
Total Operating Expenses	(110,200)	(103,200)
Departmental Operating Income	$ 34,000	$ 28,900

3.8   Using the information presented in problem 3.7, present in proper format a comparative (vertical) common-size a income statements analysis and comment on any significant results noted.

CASE 3

a. With reference to the financial statements prepared for the "4C" Company for year 0001 (see case 2), prepare a comparative (vertical) common-size statement. Use total sales revenue as the 100% figure. The local restaurant association provided Charlie with statistical data that are applicable for a table service, family-oriented, lunch and dinner restaurant similar to his. The data provide percentage ranges if typical elements of an income statement. Comment on how the operating income (income before tax) of the "4C" restaurant compares to similar restaurants. Is this a valid comparison? Explain.

	Low (%)	High (%)
Sales Revenue		
Food Operations	70.0	80.0
Beverage Operations	20.0	30.0
Total Sales Revenue	100%	
Cost of Sales	35	44.0
Gross Margin	56	65.0
Operating Expenses		
Wages Expense	26.0	31.0
Salaries Expense	2.0	6.0
Employee Benefits Expense	3.0	5.0
Employee Meals Expense	1.0	2.0
Laundry, Linen, Uniforms Expense	1.5	2.0
Replacements Expense	0.5	1.0
Services Supplies Expense	1.0	2.0
Menus, Printing Expense	0.3	0.5
Miscellaneous Expense	0.3	0.5
Entertainment Expense	0.5	2.0
Advertising, Promotion Expense	0.7	2.5
Utilities Expense	2.0	4.0
Administrative Expense	3.0	6.0
Repairs, Maintenance Expense	1.0	2.0
Rent Expense	4.5	7.0
Property Taxes Expense	0.5	1.5
Insurance Expense	0.8	1.0
Interest Expense	0.3	1.0
Depreciation Expense	2.0	2.8
Franchise Expense (if applicable)	3.0	8.0
Total Operating Expenses	51.5%	62.5%
Operating Income (before tax)	1.5%	12.0%

b. The guest count (covers) for the "4C" restaurant for the year was 75,428. Determine the average check (revenue) for food and beverages. In your opinion, does the average check for food and beverages appear reasonable for a budget-conscious, family-type table service restaurant?

c. Calculate the cost percentages for food cost and beverage cost, the total cost of sales as a percentage of sales revenue. How do the cost of sales for food and beverages and the total cost of sales compare to the ranges provided for a restaurant of this type?

d. Given the choice, would it be better to have a higher or lower percentage of beverage sales revenue compared to food sales revenue?

4

Ratio Analysis

INTRODUCTION

The preceding chapters concentrated on developing a general but solid understanding of accounting principles and concepts and their applications to business transactions. Knowing how an accounting system works internally creates an understanding of the source and specific nature of information needed for the preparation of financial statements. This chapter continues financial statement analysis by discussing various ratio and percentage analysis techniques used to identify proportional relationships between different values and quantities reported in financial statements. To effectively analyze different values and quantities, one must know where to look for the information needed to conduct a ratio or percentage analysis.

To express the relationship between two values or quantities, various commonly used ratios and at least four general methods of finding and evaluating a ratio or percentage will be discussed: industry figures, external competitive figures, the results of operations from a previous period, or predetermined budgetary standards. Typical ratios and percentage analysis techniques used by a company to express the status of its operations are broken into five major categories: current liquidity ratios, profitability ratios, long-term solvency ratios, and operating ratios.

Types of ratios

Liquidity Ratios: The primary purpose of liquidity ratios is to identify the relationship between current assets to current liabilities; thus, liquidity ratios provide the basis for an evaluation of the ability of a company to meet its current liabilities. Liquidity ratios that provide a direct analysis of current and quick assets in relation to current liabilities are the current ratio (or the working capital ratio) and the quick ratio (or acid test ratio). The analysis of credit sales provides an analysis of the average time that lapses between the creation and collection of current receivables. Typical ratios concerning receivables are the credit card receivables turnover; credit card receivables as a percentage of net credit sales; credit cards average collection period; accounts receivable turnover; accounts receivable as a percentage of net credit sales; and accounts receivable average collection period. Inventory turnover ratios reflect liquidity based on consumption of all inventories held for resale and the relationship between inventories for resale to the cost of sales over an operating period. In addition, the average days of inventory for resale on hand can be determined.

Profitability Ratios: Resources and assets are made available to management to conduct sales revenue generating operations, and the profitability ratios show management's effectiveness in using the resources (assets) during operations periods. Profitability ratios to be discussed are return on assets, profit to sales ratio, return on ownership equity, return on total investment, and earnings per share.

Long-Term Solvency Ratios: These ratios are also called net worth ratios, and they measure a company's ability to meet its long-term debt repayment responsibilities. Included are ratios that describe total assets to total liabilities, total liabilities to total assets, total liabilities to total ownership equity, cash flow from operating activities to total liabilities, cash flow from operating activities to interest, and the number of times interest is earned.

Operating Ratios: The final category to be discussed includes statistical analysis of items that are oriented primarily to food, beverage, and rooms operations. Operating ratios are generally summarized on the manager's daily or weekly report. This chapter concludes with a discussion on financial leverage, or simply put, the use of debt to obtain capital. Basically, there are two sources of obtaining operating capital: assuming long-term debt or increasing ownership equity by selling additional ownership rights. Leverage is the term used to describe the use of debt, rather than equity financing to increase the return on ownership equity.

CHAPTER OBJECTIVES

After studying this chapter, the reader should be able to:

1. Determine why creditors are normally concerned with specific areas of financial statements.

2. Define leverage and explain why is it used.

3. List and briefly explain each of the liquidity ratios discussed and illustrated.

4. List and briefly describe each of the profitability ratios.
5. Explain the difference between operating income and net income.
6. Explain the purpose of an analysis of credit card receivables.
7. Explain the meaning of gross margin.
8. List and describe at least five of the food and beverage operating ratios.
9. List and describe at least five of the rooms operating ratios.
10. Discuss the importance of inventory turnover ratios.

RATIO ANALYSIS

Types of ratio analysis

Ratio analysis in the simplest terms is the comparison of two figures, numerical dollar values or quantity values. Ratio analysis allows an evaluation of balance sheet items in conjunction with some income statement information to determine various relationships between selected items. We have already discussed two basic types of ratio analysis in Chapter 2—comparative (horizontal) and common-size (vertical) analysis of a balance sheet and income statement. Comparative analysis finds the numerical change and expresses the numerical change as a percentage. Common-size analysis expresses each item as a percentage of a series of items.

Types of ratios

Ratios can express relationships as a percentage, a numerical value, a quantity, or per unit basis. Ratios use a fractional format where the numerator is expressed in a form that shows its relationship to the denominator. For example, assume sales revenue for a given month was $48,000, cost of sales was $19,200. If we want to know what *cost of sales is as a percentage of sales revenue,* the calculation is:

$$\text{Cost of sales} \div \text{Sales revenue} = \$19,200/\$48,000 = 0.4 \text{ or } \underline{40\%}$$

If we know total current assets is $5,000 and total current liabilities is $2,000 and we want to find the relationship of *total current assets to total current liabilities* as of a specific date, two calculations can be made based on the same information:

$$\text{Total current assets} \div \text{Total current liabilities} = \$5,000/\$2,000 = 2.5 \text{ to } 1 \text{ or } \underline{2.5{:}1}$$

or

$$\text{Total current liabilities} \div \text{Total current assets} = \$2,000/\$5,000 = 0.4 \text{ or } \underline{40\%}$$

The first ratio tells us total current assets are 2.5 times greater than total current liabilities, or in essence there is $2.50 in current assets for each $1.00

of current liabilities. The second ratio expresses total current liabilities as 40% of total current assets. The way a ratio is expressed is dependent on a ratio format that will best describe the relationship between two figures and information available.

Realistic relationship

It is important to remember that when two figures are converted to a ratio, the relationship between the two figures must be realistic, meaningful, and understandable. If we compare food cost of sales to the sales revenue produced, the ratio analysis would be realistic, meaningful, and understandable. Certainly this would not be the case if food cost of sales were compared to management salaries, as no useful information is provided.

Ratio Comparisons

Comparison with standard

Ratios are used to help a business entity evaluate financial and economic results of profit-oriented operations over a given accounting period. A ratio standing alone is simply a number and appears to have little value in that the ratio does not directly show favorable or unfavorable results. For example, a restaurant's food inventory turnover of four times per month may appear good, but until the turnover ratio is compared with some standard, such as the average turnover ratio in the restaurant industry for that type of restaurant, its true value can't be determined.

A ratio must be comparable to a standard

For a ratio to have meaning, it must be comparable to a standard or an established base ratio. A standard ratio would of course be an industry average, but such a standard ratio may be the least valuable. Industry standards are generally developed by including hospitality organizations of the same type; however, those establishments may be spread over a large geographic area. Different operating conditions prevail in different locations within the geographical area, such as average family income, salaries, hourly pay rates, and cost of living levels to name a few. As a result of such economic variances across a geographical area, there may not be one operation that is just like the "average operation" from which the standard ratios are determined.

Another method of ratio comparison could use comparable ratios from competitive operations; however, locating the competitive ratios may prove difficult. If competitive ratios are known and they differ from the ratios of your operation, which is better? There are many reasons that may explain individual ratios between competitors.

A better technique is to compare current operating period ratios with previous operating period ratios. For example, how does current room occupancy or seat turnover ratio compare with the same ratio from the previous month, or the previous ratio from the previous ratio last operating year? What is the trend? Is room occupancy or seat turnover increasing (good), or is room occupancy or seat turnover decreasing (bad). Depending on the ratio to be evaluated, how do you determine if the difference in the ratio is good or bad? Even with limited exposure, one soon discovers that a hospitality business operates in a dynamic and rapidly changing environment, and that comparison of current period ratios to past period ratios may be like comparing copper to gold.

Best method

The best method of ratio comparison is to evaluate current period ratios to predetermined standards for that operating period. The predetermined standard should consider both internal and external factors affecting the operation. Internal factors might include the composition of sales revenue (cash versus credit sales), fixed costs and variable costs, internal operating policies, changes in operating procedures, and many other similar operating variables. External factors may include the general economic conditions in the area of operations and what the competition is doing.

Periodic predetermined operating standards can establish operating plans in an annual operating budget (income statement). The operating budget can be broken down into monthly or quarterly operating periods, which are adjusted for seasonal variations. Operating budgets should project future operations based not only on past operating results but also on current operating results. Budgeting is an important and time-sensitive management skill which is discussed in depth in Chapter 9, Operations Budgeting.

USERS OF RATIOS

Managers, creditors, owners

Generally three broad groups of people are interested in the evaluation of ratios: internal operating managers, current and potential creditors, and the organization's owners. A proprietorship has one owner, a partnership two or more owners, and a corporation normally has a number of owners called stockholders (or shareholders).

Management has the responsibility of safeguarding the assets, controlling costs, and maximizing profit for the business operation. Ratio evaluation is a major technique used by management to monitor the operation's performance against predetermined standards to determine if the operating budget objectives are being achieved. Certain ratios are used to evaluate the effectiveness of day-to-day operations, its liquidity position, and other economic positions, which define certain objectives to satisfy ownership as well as creditors. A number of different ratios used by management to evaluate whether the performance objectives are being achieved are discussed in this chapter.

Creditors of a business operation have an equity claim to assets of the operation which is shown as the liabilities element of the basic equation $A = L + OE$. Creditors advance funds or extend trade credit to the business operation. As such, creditors are normally interested in certain ratios of a business operation, which may indicate the level of safety of their loan of funds or trade credit. In addition, existing and potential creditors use certain ratios to estimate their potential risk regarding future loans the business operation may need. In some cases a creditor, during negotiations, may require the borrower to maintain a specified level of working capital, a specific level of current assets greater than current liabilities.

Exhibit 4.1   Comparative, Consecutive Annual Balance Sheets

	Year Ending December 31	
	Year 0001	Year 0002
Assets		
Current Assets		
Cash	$ 18,500	$ 29,400
Credit card receivables	9,807	11,208
Accounts receivable	5,983	6,882
Marketable securities	15,400	2,000
Inventories	12,880	14,700
Prepaid expenses	10,800	14,900
Total Current Assets	$ 73,370	$ 79,090
Property Plant & Equipment		
Land	$ 60,500	$ 60,500
Building	828,400	884,400
Equipment	114,900	157,900
Furnishings	75,730	81,110
Net: Accumulated depreciation	(330,100)	(422,000)
China, glass, silver, & linen	16,600	18,300
Total Property Plant & Equipment	$766,030	$780,210
Total Assets	$839,400	$859,300
Liabilities & Stockholders' Equity		
Current Liabilities		
Accounts Payable	$ 19,200	$ 16,500
Accrued expenses payable	4,200	5,000
Taxes payable	12,400	20,900
Current mortgage payable	26,900	26,000
Total Current Liabilities	$ 62,700	$ 68,400
Long-Term Liabilities		
Mortgage payable	$512,800	$486,800
Total Liabilities	$575,500	$555,200
Stockholders' Equity		
Common stock	$200,000	$200,000
Retained earnings	63,900	104,100
Total Stockholders' Equity	$263,900	$304,100
Total Liabilities & Stockholders' Equity	$839,400	$859,300

Last but not least, the ownership of a business operation can use certain ratios to measure such items as their return on investment or the risk level of their investment or to estimate the probability of success in future operations.

In many cases, members of the three groups may not agree on what a particular ratio means. This is not unusual since each group interprets the ratio from a different perspective.

RATIO CATEGORIES

Ratio analysis will be discussed in the following five major categories using information from Exhibit 4.1, Comparative balance sheets for two successive years, and Exhibit 4.2, for the year 0002:

Exhibit 4.2   Condensed Annual Income Statement
(Year Ended December 31, 0002)

Revenue		
Sales revenue (see footnote)		$1,175,200
Cost of Sales		(219,400)
Gross Margin		*$ 955,800*
Direct Operating Expenses		
Payroll expenses	$319,200	
Other expenses	201,400	
Total Direct Operating Expenses		*(560,600)*
Operating Income		*$ 435,200*
Undistributed Operating Expenses		
Administrative and general expenses	$ 67,900	
Marketing expenses	20,700	
Property operation and maintenance	35,400	
Energy expenses	25,100	
Total Undistributed Operating Expense		*(149,100)*
Income before fixed expenses		$ 286,100
Property taxes	$ 48,800	
Insurance expense	13,100	
Depreciation expense	91,900	
Total Fixed Expenses		*(153,800)*
Income Before Interest and Income Tax		*$ 132,300*
Interest expense		*(51,900)*
Income before Income Tax		*$ 80,400*
Income Tax		(40,200)
Net Income		*$ 40,200*

Footnote: Total sales revenue on average consisted of: cash sales at 28%, credit card sales at 62%, and accounts receivable at 10%.

- Current liquidity ratios
- Long-term solvency ratios
- Profitability ratios
- Turnover ratios
- Operation ratios

Ratios are categorized only for purposes of convenience. For example, some people may classify working capital turnover as a current liquidity ratio, whereas in this chapter it is included among the turnover ratios. It is important to understand the ratio's meaning and how a ratio can be interpreted rather than its category. This often requires an analysis of the causes that led to a ratio not being what was expected. Individual ratios normally provide information about one aspect of a business operation, whereas the analysis and interpretation of several ratios jointly will yield a more comprehensive view of a business operation than financial statements alone.

CURRENT LIQUIDITY RATIOS

Net income but
no cash

Current liquidity ratios indicate the ability of an operation to meet its short-term obligations for the repayment of debt without difficulty. A business's operating income statement may show operating income (before taxes) or a net income (after taxes) without the business operation having the ability to pay its current liabilities, let alone its long-term debt obligations. This situation is discussed and demonstrated in Chapter 11, which discusses cash management. In particular, the reader is referred to the section on cash conservation and working capital management discussed in that chapter. At this point, we will turn our attention to some of the current liquidity ratios that indicate the effectiveness of working capital management.

CURRENT RATIO

The most commonly used ratio to express current liquidity is the current ratio. This ratio shows the ability of an operation to pay its short-term debts, which are classified as current liabilities. The current ratio is:

$$\text{Current assets} \div \text{Current liabilities}$$

Current ratio equation

$$\text{The calculation, year 0001: } \frac{\text{Current assets}}{\text{Current liabilities}} = \frac{\$73,370}{\$62,700} = \underline{1.17}$$

$$\text{The calculation, year 0002: } \frac{\text{Current assets}}{\text{Current liabilities}} = \frac{\$79,090}{\$68,400} = \underline{1.16}$$

Rule of thumb

The ratio for year 0002 from Exhibit 4.1 shows $1.16 of current assets are available for every $1.00 of current short-term debt (current liabilities). In general, a rule of thumb exists that current assets should exceed current liabilities on a ratio of two to one, which implies $2.00 of current assets exist for each $1.00 of current liabilities. However, this general rule was set to provide a safety margin for operations, which normally have a large amount of current assets tied up in inventories such as manufacturing and other processing operations. Looking at the hospitality industry, the largest inventories held by a hotel and motel operation is in the form of guest rooms available for sale and these are included under building, which is a part of fixed assets, or property plant and equipment. The only current inventories (inventories for resale) held for resale by hotel–motel operations are for food and beverage services, and these current inventories represent a rather small portion of current assets.

Current ratio balance

Hotels can operate with a current ratio of 1.5 or less; motels and restaurants have shown they can operate on a current ratio of less than 1 to 1. For each individual hospitality operation, a minimum ratio must be determined. The minimum ratio will be one, which does not create a short-term liquidity problem, or sacrifice profitability for safety's sake. Money tied up in working capital (current assets minus current liabilities) is money that is not being put to use earning income.

Creditors prefer
high ratio

Creditors and potential creditors prefer to see a high ratio of current assets to liabilities, since it provides a positive indicator of a business operation's capability to repay its debt obligations. Many creditors require a minimum current ratio before funds are loaned or credit is extended. Once a loan or credit is extended, the creditor may require that a minimum current ratio be maintained. If a minimum current ratio is required and the current ratio falls below the required level, the creditor may have the right to demand payment in full on any balance outstanding.

The opposite is true for owners, who normally prefer a low ratio of current assets to current liabilities, since a high ratio may indicate more money is tied up in working capital and not being used efficiently. Inventories for resale may be excessive to the anticipated needs and, as such, increase the cost of holding inventory or receivables not being collected as quickly as they should be. Management of the operation must try to maintain a current ratio that is acceptable to both ownership and creditors—a task not easily achieved.

Improving ratio

It is possible to change the current ratio to make it appear better than it really is. Exhibit 4.3 presents the current asset and current liability sections for year 0001 of the balance sheet shown in Exhibit 4.1. If $15,000 of marketable securities was sold just prior to the end of an accounting period and the cash to reduce accounts payable by $15,000, the adjustment will reflect a higher current ratio as shown in Exhibit 4.4.

Exhibit 4.3   **Current Section of Period Balance Sheet**

Current Assets		Current Liabilities	
Cash	$18,500		
Credit card receivables	9,807		
Accounts receivable	5,983	Accounts payable	$19,200
Marketable securities	15,400	Accrued expenses	4,200
Inventories	12,880	Taxes payable	12,400
Prepaid expenses	10,800	Current mortgage payable	26,900
	$73,370		$62,700

Working Capital: CA − CL = $73,370 − $62,700 = $10,670

Exhibit 4.4   **Current Section of Period Balance Sheet**

Current Assets		Current Liabilities	
Cash	$18,500		
Credit card receivables	9,807		
Accounts receivable	5,983	Accounts payable	$ 4,200
Marketable securities	400	Accrued expenses	4,200
Inventories	12,880	Taxes payable	12,400
Prepaid expenses	10,800	Current mortgage payable	26,900
	$58,370		$47,700

Working Capital: CA − CL = $58,370 − $47,700 = $10,670

The comparable current ratios would be:

Exhibit 4.3   CA / CL = $73,370 / $62,700 = 1.17 or <u>1.17:1</u>

Exhibit 4.4   CA / CL = $58,370 / $47,700 = 1.22 or <u>1.22:1</u>

Window dressing

When the current ratio is changed in this manner, the working capital does not change. This form of manipulation is referred to as *window dressing*. However, if accounts payable of $15,000 were due, there would be no harm in paying them off in the manner illustrated. Reducing the payables to improve the current ratio makes good sense if the business anticipates the need for short-term financing in the immediate future. Other reasonable methods of window dressing include borrowing on a long-term payable, or obtaining additional ownership contributions. Physical property, plant and equipment assets no longer needed can be sold and converted to cash.

COMPOSITION OF CURRENT ASSETS

Assessing current assets

Assessing the change in the liquidity of current assets is accomplished by converting each current asset to a common-size (vertical) analysis percentage using the same techniques discussed in Chapter 2 for the conversion of a balance sheet or income statement to a common-size format. Any subset of a financial statement such as total current assets can be analyzed to show the percentage relationship of each item within the subset. The value of each item in a subset is divided by the total of the subset. Total current assets represent the 100% sum of all individual current asset values, as seen in Exhibit 4.5.

The current asset sections of Exhibit 4.1, for years 0001 and 0002, are shown in Exhibit 4.5 in a common-size (vertical) analysis format. The illustration shows the change in the liquidity of all current assets over a two-year period. Each current asset of year 0001 is divided by total current assets of $73,370; cash $18,500 ÷ $73,370 = 0.252 or 25.2%. The same types of calculations are made to find percentages for year 0002.

Liquid current assets decreased

This exhibit shows that cash as a percentage of total current assets changed from 25.2% in year 0001 to 37.2% in year 0002. However, the most liquid current assets of cash, the receivables, and marketable securities have decreased in total from 67.7% (25.2% + 13.4% + 8.1% + 21%) in year 0001, to 62.6% (37.2% + 14.2% + 8.7% + 2.5%) in year 0002. The cash position has improved, but the total of the four most liquid assets has declined. The major item causing the decline was the selling of marketable securities in year 0001 to reduce current liabilities and increase the current ratio. The most liquid current

Quick assets

assets are often classified as quick assets.

Exhibit 4.5   Change in Liquidity of Current Assets

Current Assets	Year 0001		Year 0002	
	Amt.	%	Amt.	%
Cash	$18,500	25.2%	$29,400	37.2%
Credit card receivables	9,807	13.4%	11,208	14.2%
Accounts receivable	5,983	8.1%	6,882	8.7%
Marketable securities	15,400	21%	2,000	2.5%
Inventories	12,880	17.6%	14,700	18.6%
Prepaid expenses	10,800	14.7%	14,900	18.8%
	$73,370	100%	$79,090	100%

QUICK RATIO (ACID TEST RATIO)

Quick ratio equation

The quick ratio, also called the acid test ratio, uses an extreme view of liquidity, using only current assets that can be readily converted to cash if the need should arise. Current assets that are considered readily convertible to cash are called quick assets and will not include current assets such as inventories, prepaid expenses, and other nonliquid assets. The quick ratio is calculated using the current asset and current liability information shown in Exhibit 4.1.

The quick ratio for year 0001:

$$\frac{\text{Cash + Credit card receivables + Accounts receivable + Marketable securities}}{\text{Total current liabilities}}$$

$$\frac{\$18,500 + \$9,807 + \$5,983 + \$15,400}{\$62,700} = \frac{\$49,690}{\$62,700} = \underline{0.79:1}$$

The quick ratio for year 0002:

$$\frac{\$29,400 + \$11,208 + \$6,882 + \$2,000}{\$68,400} = \frac{\$49,490}{\$68,400} = \underline{0.72:1}$$

An alternative method to find the quick ratio is expressed as:

$$\frac{\text{Total current assets – Inventories – Prepaid expenses}}{\text{Current liabilities}}$$

Quick ratio, year 0002: $79,090 – $14,700 – $14,900 = $49,490 / $68,400 = $\underline{0.72:1}$

High inventory
turnover

The quick ratio for year 0001 is 0.79:1, showing there is $0.79 of quick assets for every $1.00 of current liabilities. In year 0002, the quick ratio has fallen to 0.72:1, showing only $0.72 of quick assets to every $1.00 of current liabilities. This tells us the most liquid current assets are below a $1.00 to $1.00 ratio, which is generally considered as a low-end safety range for the quick ratio. These low quick ratios indicate a larger value of current assets considered to be the least liquid (or nonliquid) of the current assets, and normally consist of inventories for resale and prepaid expenses. Certainly prepaid expenses are nonliquid since prepaid items are consumed over the period of time they provide benefits. However, the removal of inventories for resale in the hotel, food and beverage industry may be questionable since inventories of food and beverages turn over rapidly in periods measured in days rather than months. If this is generally the case, inventories for resale are being converted to sales revenue that is recognized as cash and quick turnover receivables, which will be collected in cash within days, or at the most within a week or so.

Certainly, the exception of inventories may be valid in some industries, where the nature of their business requires inventory availability for periods of months or more. Since the major difference in the current and quick ratios is inventory, some hospitality operations such as a motel without a food or beverage operation may see little variance between the two ratios.

Creditors, owners, and managers analyze and interpret the quick ratio the same way they analyze and interpret the current ratio. Creditors still prefer to see a high ratio, owners prefer a low ratio, and management must continue to maintain a balance between the creditors' and owners' viewpoints.

RECEIVABLE RATIOS

To provide the most accurate evaluation on an annual, monthly, quarterly, or semiannual basis, total sales revenue should be broken into three components: cash, credit card, and accounts receivable sales revenue.

Method of determining
a receivable ratio

The most accurate method of determining a receivable ratio is one that evaluates each individual receivable in relation to the type of credit sales produced. If credit card and accounts receivable are not maintained by subsidiary accounts within the total sales revenue figure, the second best alternative is to maintain total sales that are shown to consist of cash plus credit sales. This alternative will skew receivable ratios since reported credit sales will consist of two different components—credit cards and accounts receivable. The next alternative is to simply use total sales revenue to evaluate receivable ratios; however, the skewing of the ratios will increase because total sales revenue will not show any consideration of credit sales by any category. The last but worst alternative is to rely on past historical percentages of credit sales by category to evaluate receivable ratios. The ever-present danger in using historical information is that the current cash to credit sales ratio may have changed.

Credit card sales represent the major portion of sales revenue in the hospitality industry today and should not be ignored as a current receivable to be evaluated. Major large hospitality organizations are normally computerized with fully automated accounting systems, which are capable of immediately accessing ratios they choose to review whenever they wish to do so. However, this is not particularly true for smaller operations, which may not have the computerized on-line resources of a larger organization. Credit card sales revenue is a near cash transaction due to quick reimbursement by the credit card company of the receivable. Collections of credit card receivables normally range from one to five operating days. Larger hospitality operations that are tied electronically online with a card-clearing center are reimbursed at the time of sale or on the same day a credit card sale is made. A discount rate is charged by credit card companies, which can range from 1.5 to 5%. The variances in the discount rate may depend on volume of credit card sales, the size and type of organization, and/or a negotiated rate. The variance in discount rates charged and the average credit card collection period are two major items affecting cash flows.

Variances in the discount rate

A debit card is an exception to the general line credit card. Normally, a local financial banking company issues a debit card and the customer's account is charged in essence at the time of sale. The nature and speed of the reimbursement classifies the use of a debit card as a cash sale.

Debit card as a cash sale

Although credit card use continues to increase in relation to use of accounts receivable (trade credit), they will continue to service private clubs, corporate organizations, special food and beverage functions (banquets), and other hospitality areas where the use of credit in the form of an accounts receivable is considered appropriate.

The traditional use of ratios as applied to accounts receivable based on total sales revenue produces a ratio that is skewed because total sales revenue is used rather than credit sales revenue. The skewing effect has continued through failure to recognize the increase of credit card sales revenue, which has added a second credit sales revenue component to total revenue. This skewing effect, if unnoticed, may increase steadily for years.

As the percentage of credit card sales increases beyond 50–60% of total credit sales, it may become prudent to integrate credit card sales under the general classification of accounts receivable. In general credit card receivables can be integrated into the accounts receivable classification through the use of subsidiary accounts receivables which identify each credit card accepted by name—Visa, MasterCard, etc. The same technique of using subsidiary accounts to identify a person or company extended trade credit should be in place.

Credit card receivables

Discussion and illustrations of the basic methods used (except of historical data) to determine various ratios applicable to credit receivables begin with credit card receivables followed by accounts receivable. The illustrations and discussion of credit card receivables as a separate classification of credit sales is designed to impress the importance and effect of this classification of credit sales. The potential skewing effects of an operating receivable ratio will become apparent, as each receivable ratio is illustrated for credit card sales, accounts receivable credit sales, total credit sales, and total sales revenue. Although receivable ratios may be evaluated on an annual, semi-annual, quarterly, or monthly basis, only the annual basis is discussed and illustrated.

Credit Card Receivables Ratios

Credit card receivables ratios will be discussed as a percentage of total credit card revenue, total credit revenue, and total sales revenue. The ratios will be discussed in the following sequence:

- Credit card receivables ratios based on different sales revenues
- Credit card receivables turnover ratios
- Credit card receivables average collection periods

The information used to calculate each of the following ratios is extracted from Exhibit 4.1 and Exhibit 4.2. Total sales revenue: $1,175,200 with cash sales of 20%, credit card sales of 62%, and accounts receivable sales of 10%.

Credit Card Receivables as a Percentage of Credit Card Revenue

This ratio will show the relationship of credit card receivables to credit card revenue, which is the most accurate method. The equation based on annual data is:

$$\text{Average credit card receivables} \div \text{Total credit card revenue}$$

$$\text{The calculation:} \quad \frac{\text{Average credit card receivables}}{\text{Total credit card revenue}} = \frac{\$10,508}{\$728,624} = \underline{1.44\%}$$

This ratio clearly defines credit card receivables remaining uncollected on a given day of operations; it averages only 1.44% of total credit card sales. In addition, this low percentage of average credit card receivables indicates an apparent short collection period for credit card receivables. In our example, credit card sales represent 62% of total credit revenue, thus, $0.62 of each dollar of revenue is generated through credit card sales. In a seasonal operation where revenue fluctuates, it may be best to add each month's credit card revenue and divide by 12. This method also allows the determination of monthly average credit card receivables for a seasonal operation.

An annual skewing effect occurs when credit card receivables are combined with accounts receivable to express total credit revenue. The resulting ratio will omit any reference to the type of receivables created by credit sales. The equation to show only the relationship of total credit card receivables as a percentage of total sales revenue is:

$$\text{Average credit card receivables} \div \text{Total credit revenue}$$

$$\text{The calculation:} \quad \frac{\text{Average credit card receivables}}{\text{Total credit revenue}} = \frac{\$10,508}{\$846,144} = \underline{1.24\%}$$

By combining all credit sales regardless of category into a single sum of total credit revenue, we see the original estimate of credit card receivables has decreased from 1.44% of total credit card sales to 1.24% of total credit sales, which is due to the inclusion of accounts receivable. The example showing credit card receivables evaluated as a percentage of total credit sales fails to recognize that credit card sales are $0.62 per dollar of sales revenue. Using unclassified total credit revenue will now show a credit revenue figure that includes $117,520 of accounts receivable.

By not discriminating differences between credit card revenue and accounts receivable revenue, a skewing effect is further amplified that prevents the determination of an accurate estimate of all categories of receivables created by credit sales. The ultimate skewing of credit card receivables occurs when any reference to credit sales of any category is omitted. The ratio to express credit card receivables as a percentage of total revenue, which excludes both forms of credit revenue, is:

$$\text{Average credit card receivables} \div \text{Total sales revenue}$$

$$\text{The calculation:} \quad \frac{\text{Average credit card receivables}}{\text{Total sales revenue}} = \frac{\$10,508}{\$1,175,200} = \underline{0.89\%}$$

With the failure to classify the sources of credit revenue totaling 72% of revenue (62% credit card and 10% accounts receivable) has been eliminated. The average collection period for credit card receivables and accounts receivable based on total credit revenue or total revenue is less accurate and less meaningful. Use of average credit card receivables as a percentage of credit card revenue rather than total credit revenue or total sales revenue provides the most accurate and meaningful results.

Credit Card Receivables Turnover

Turnover ratio

The turnover ratio expresses the relationship of credit card revenue to average credit card receivables that is the reverse of the previous ratio. The credit card receivables turnover ratio describes the average number of times during an annual operating period the repetitive cycle of credit card sales and their reimbursement occurred. As with the ratio previously discussed, changing the operating period to monthly or quarterly can also calculate this ratio. The equation using an annual period is:

$$\text{Total credit card revenue} \div \text{Average credit card receivables}$$

$$\text{The calculation:} \quad \frac{\text{Total credit card revenue}}{\text{Average credit card receivables}} = \frac{\$728,624}{\$10,508} = \underline{69.3 \text{ times}}$$

If only total credit revenue is available, the equation is modified to:

Total credit revenue ÷ Average credit card receivables

The calculation: $\dfrac{\text{Total credit revenue}}{\text{Average credit card receivables}} = \dfrac{\$846,144}{\$10,508} = \underline{80.5 \text{ times}}$

If only total revenue is available, the equation is modified to:

Total sales revenue ÷ Average credit card receivables

The calculation: $\dfrac{\text{Total sales revenue}}{\text{Average credit card receivables}} = \dfrac{\$1,175,200}{\$10,508} = \underline{111.8 \text{ times}}$

The skewing continues and is easily apparent. The correct turnover ratio for credit card receivables is 69.3 times per year; however, if total credit revenue or total revenue were used initially, the turnover ratio increases to 80.5 times per year and 111.8 times per year respectively. In no way can a turnover of 80.5 or 111.8 times per year realistically apply to credit card receivables based on the information shown in Exhibit 4.1 and Exhibit 4.2.

Depending on the volume of credit card sales and the efficiency of credit card companies' payment of credit card receivables, the turnover rate showing the repetitive credit revenue cycle on average may vary from 73 to 243 times per annual operating period. This states turnover relative to times per year and may prove difficult to correlate, but it is essential in helping calculate the credit card receivables average collection period which expresses the turnover in days. The average credit card collection period will convert the annual turnover ratio from times per year to a day cycle of the average collection of credit card receivables.

Average Credit Cards Collection Period

This ratio uses the credit card turnover ratio to show an understandable correlation to the repetitive cycle of credit card sales and the collection of credit card receivables over an annual operating period in days. In essence, this collection ratio tells us the average number of days it is taking to collect on credit card receivables. The equation to calculate the average credit card collection period, when credit sales revenue is used, is:

365 days ÷ Credit card receivables turnover ratio

The calculation: $\dfrac{365 \text{ days}}{\text{Credit card turnover ratio}} = \dfrac{365}{69.3} = \underline{5.3 \text{ days}}$

Continuing with the discussion on skewing credit card ratios, the average collection period is shown based on credit revenue and total revenue comparisons in the previous examples.

Based on credit revenue:

$$\text{The calculation:} \quad \frac{365 \text{ days}}{\text{Credit card turnover ratio}} = \frac{365}{80.5} = \underline{4.5 \text{ days}}$$

Based on total revenue:

$$\text{The calculation:} \quad \frac{365 \text{ days}}{\text{Credit card turnover ratio}} = \frac{365}{111.8} = \underline{3.3 \text{ days}}$$

Credit card receivables collection period

Another method to calculate the credit card receivables collection period is:

$$\text{Credit card receivables \% of Total credit card revenue} \times 365 \text{ days}$$

The calculation: $10,508 / $728,624 = 0.014421704 \times 365 = 5.3 days

$$\text{The calculation:} \quad \frac{365 \text{ days}}{\text{Credit card turnover ratio}} = \frac{365}{69.3} = \underline{5.3 \text{ days}}$$

The credit card collection period indicates the average number of days to collect credit card receivables from credit card companies. As discussed earlier, the collection period generally ranges from one to five days and should average 2.5 days. It is wise to set up subsidiary accounts for each card company that will identify which companies are not paying within the average of two to three days. The need to determine the average days taken by each credit card accepted would appear valid in our example, which used the best and most accurate method, and shows a 5.3-day collection period. It would not be unusual to find that at least one credit card company is taking from eight to ten days to reimburse.

ACCOUNTS RECEIVABLE RATIOS

Although accounts receivable are decreasing in their use due to increasing use of credit cards, they will continue in use. Our discussion of accounts receivable ratios will follow the same approach used for credit card ratios. The skewing effect shown and illustrated for credit card receivables will also apply to accounts receivable; however, they will not be illustrated in depth again for accounts receivable.

The three basic approaches used to analyze accounts receivable will use average accounts receivable and accounts receivable revenue.

- Accounts receivable as a percentage of accounts receivable credit revenue
- Accounts receivable turnover
- Accounts receivable average collection period

Accounts Receivable as a Percentage of Accounts Receivable Credit Revenue

This ratio is best expressed as accounts receivable as a percentage of accounts receivable credit revenue. Normally this ratio provides information on an annual operating period, but can also be used for monthly, quarterly, and semi-annual periods to evaluate accounts receivable. If cash and credit card and accounts receivable credit sales are not maintained within the total sales revenue figure, a historical percentage of credit sales to total sales revenue may be used. However, use of historical information is a last alternative since historical information may easily produce inaccurate results that the relationship between cash, credit card and accounts receivable revenue may have changed. Thus, the ratios used will produce the best and most accurate evaluation of average accounts receivable in relation to account receivable credit revenue.

Exhibit 4.1 and Exhibit 4.2 are used again to find the values used in the discussion of accounts receivable ratios. The equation to find accounts receivable as a percentage of accounts receivable credit revenue is:

$$\text{Average accounts receivable} \div \text{Accounts receivable credit revenue}$$

$$\text{The calculation:} \quad \frac{\text{Average accounts receivable}}{\text{Accounts receivable credit revenue}} = \frac{\$6,433}{\$117,520} = \underline{5.47\%}$$

The ratio tells us that over the year an average of 5.47% of accounts receivable credit revenue was in the form of accounts receivable during any given day of operations. In a drive-in cash-only operation this ratio would obviously be 0%. If a private club permits only charge transactions with members being
billed monthly, accounts receivable as a percentage of revenue could range from 10% to 20%. In a typical hotel or restaurant operation, some customers will pay cash, the majority will pay by credit card, and a few customers may have access to a house account or accounts receivable. Credit card use may easily represent a total of 40–70% of total revenue and house accounts or accounts receivable could represent from 4–10% of total revenue. These figures represent adjusted industry averages, but an organization should be most concerned with information regarding existing trends within its own operation, not a comparison with industry averages.

Accounts receivable as a percentage of revenue

The procedure discussed on an annual basis uses the beginning accounts receivable plus the ending accounts receivable divided by 2. Earlier, we discussed the best method for a seasonal operation with highly fluctuating revenue. Average accounts receivable may best be calculated by adding each month's accounts receivable and dividing by 12 months. This method also allows a best estimate of average accounts receivable on a monthly basis. Though far from being the best methods, an annual ratio could be calculated using total credit revenue or total sales revenue rather than accounts receivable credit revenue. If one of these methods is used, the ratios will be skewed and not produce the best results, as shown below. Use of total credit revenue or total revenue should be avoided if at all possible.

Average accounts receivable ÷ Total credit revenue

$$\text{The calculation:} \quad \frac{\text{Average accounts receivable}}{\text{Total credit revenue}} = \frac{\$6,433}{\$846,144} = \underline{0.76\%}$$

Average accounts receivable ÷ Total sales revenue

$$\text{The equation:} \quad \frac{\text{Average accounts receivable}}{\text{Total revenue}} = \frac{\$6,433}{\$1,175,200} = \underline{0.55\%}$$

In a cash-only operation, it is obvious that accounts receivable would not exist relative to sales revenue. On the other hand, for a private club that permits only credit charge transactions, billing each member at the month-end, the accounts receivable as a percentage of sales revenue may be as high as 10 to 12%. Updated industry averages exist, but what is most important is the trend of the figures within hospitality operations. Either the use of total credit sales revenue or total sales revenue will show the percentage of credit card receivables relative to any given day of operations over the operating year; however, the use of credit sales rather than total sales provides the best and most accurate results.

Note the calculation of average accounts receivable uses the same method used to find average credit card receivables; beginning accounts receivable plus ending accounts receivable divided by 2.

Accounts Receivable Turnover

The accounts receivable turnover ratio equation reverses the previous equation. The equation is:

Accounts receivable
turnover ratio equation

Total credit revenue ÷ Average accounts receivable

The calculation: $\dfrac{\text{Accounts receivable credit revenue}}{\text{Average accounts receivable}} = \dfrac{\$117,520}{\$6,433} = \underline{18.3 \text{ times}}$

Depending on the volume of accounts receivable, credit sales, and the efficiency of accounts receivable collections, this turnover ratio could vary from 10 to 30 times per year. If this ratio used total credit sales or total sales, the ratio would be highly skewed as demonstrated earlier. Although it may be difficult to conceptualize the meaning of times per year, this ratio is necessary to calculate an average collection period in days.

Accounts Receivable Average Collection Period

Average collection
period equation

The equation to calculate the accounts receivable average collection period is:

365 days ÷ Accounts receivable turnover ratio

The calculation: $\dfrac{365 \text{ days}}{\text{Accounts receivable turnover ratio}} = \dfrac{365}{18.3} = \underline{19.9 \text{ days}}$

The lower the collection period, the more efficient the ability to collect accounts receivable within the business operation. An operation that extends 30-day accounts receivable credit could expect to see an average collection period of 30 to 35 days. An operation extending 15-day accounts receivable credit could see an average collection period of 15 to 20 days. However, if the collection period exceeds 10 days or more beyond the number of days credit is granted, the operation should become concerned and should review their credit collection procedures and reevaluate their credit policies.

To reiterate, the discussion of credit receivables emphasized the use of accounts receivable credit revenue rather than total credit or total revenue to produce the best and most accurate results. Examples were shown where total credit revenue and total revenue replaced credit card and accounts receivable revenues. This resulted in skewed ratios and the skewing was very obvious.

In general, owners and creditors prefer to see a low average collection period or a high turnover ratio on all credit receivables. On the other hand, management prefers a higher average collection period and a lower turnover period as long as they are within or close to the number of days allowed.

CASH FLOW FROM OPERATING ACTIVITIES TO CURRENT LIABILITIES

The cash flow from operating activities to current liabilities ratio is calculated as follows:

Equation

$$\frac{\text{Cash flow from operating activities}}{\text{Average current liabilities}}$$

We will use a cash flow from operating activities of $131,580. The result is

$$\frac{\$131,580}{(\$62,700 + \$68,400)/2}$$

or

$$\frac{\$131,580}{\$65,550}$$

$$= 2.0 \text{ times or } 200\%$$

This ratio has advantages over the current and acid test ratios.

Those ratios are calculated at a single point in time—the balance sheet date. If, on the balance sheet date, the amounts used in the calculations are considerably higher or lower than normal, then distorted ratios will result. The cash flow from operations to current liabilities ratio overcomes this problem since the cash flow is for a period of time and average current liabilities from two successive balance sheets are used. It is suggested that a minimum of 40% is desirable, and the more the ratio exceeds that minimum figure, the better will be the operation's liquidity. Our result of 200% is considerably higher than the suggested minimum.

The use of this ratio does not mean that the traditional current and acid test ratios should be discontinued. They still have a value and, indeed, many lenders require that a minimum level of these ratios be maintained.

LONG-TERM SOLVENCY RATIOS

Solvency ratios are sometimes referred to as net worth ratios. Net worth is defined as total tangible assets (that is, total assets excluding nontangible items such as goodwill) less total liabilities. In other words, net worth is usually the same as total stockholders' equity (assuming no intangible assets). Total assets in any business can be financed primarily by either debt (liabilities) or equity

Debt or equity
financing

(shares and retained earnings). Solvency ratios show the balance between these two methods of financing. There are three main solvency ratios, each showing this balance in a different way. These three ratios are total assets to total liabilities ratio, total liabilities to total assets ratio, and total liabilities to total stockholders' equity ratio. We need three figures from each year's balance sheet to calculate these ratios. These figures are

	Year 0001	Year 0002
Total assets	$839,400	$859,300
Total liabilities	575,500	555,200
Total equity	263,900	304,100

TOTAL ASSETS TO TOTAL LIABILITIES RATIO

The total assets to total liabilities ratio is:

Assets to liabilities
equation

$$\text{Ratio} = \frac{\text{Total assets}}{\text{Total liabilities}}$$

$$\text{Year 0001} = \frac{\$839,400}{\$575,500} = 1.46$$

$$\text{Year 0002} = \frac{\$859,300}{\$555,200} = 1.55$$

High ratio equals high
lender security

This ratio tells us that in year 0001 there were $1.46 in assets for each $1.00 in liabilities (debt). Creditors (people to whom we owe money or with whom we have a debt) prefer to see this ratio as high as possible, that is, as high as 2:1 or more. The higher the ratio, the more security they have. They want to be assured that they will recover the full amount owed them in the event of bankruptcy or liquidation of the business. If the ratio sinks below 1:1, it could mean that if bankruptcy occurred, they might not recover the full amount owed them. In bankruptcy cases, the value of assets decreases rapidly. This is known as "asset shrinkage"; it occurs because the value of many of the productive assets declines when those assets are not employed in a going concern. In the situation illustrated, note that in year 0002 the ratio improves (from the point of view of the creditors) to 1.55:1.00.

Appreciation of assets
over time

The total assets to total liabilities ratio is traditionally based on assets at their book value. If a hotel or food service operation includes land and building (which it owns) at book value in this calculation, the ratio could be misleading.

Land and buildings frequently appreciate (increase in value) over time. There-fore, a total assets to total liabilities ratio based on book value of assets figures showing a result as low as 1:1 may not be as bad as it seems from the creditors' point of view. If assets were used at fair market or replacement value, the ratio would probably improve and then show a comfortable cushion of safety.

TOTAL LIABILITIES TO TOTAL ASSETS RATIO

The total liabilities to total assets ratio is the reverse of the total assets to total liabilities ratio:

Liabilities to assets
equation

$$\text{Ratio} = \frac{\text{Total liabilities}}{\text{Total assets}}$$

$$\text{Year 0001} = \frac{\$575,500}{\$839,400} = 0.69$$

$$\text{Year 0002} = \frac{\$555,200}{\$859,300} = 0.65$$

Traditional debt to
equity financing ratio

The ratio tells us that in year 0001 each $1.00 of assets was financed $0.69 by debt (the balance of $0.31 was by equity). In year 0002 each $1.00 of assets was financed $0.65 by debt (and $0.35 by equity). Traditionally, the hospitality industry has been financed with between $0.60 to $0.90 of debt and $0.10 to $0.40 of equity. As debt financing reaches the higher number ($0.90 out of each $1.00), it becomes more and more difficult to raise money by debt. The risk is higher for the lender, and therefore potential lenders of money are more difficult to find. Again, this ratio is based on assets at book value. If fair market or replacement value of assets were used (assuming that this value is higher than book value), then the ratio would decline and perhaps more realistically present the true situation.

TOTAL LIABILITIES TO TOTAL EQUITY RATIO

Sometimes known as the debt to equity ratio, the total liabilities to total equity ratio is calculated as follows:

Debt to equity equation

$$\text{Ratio} = \frac{\text{Total liabilities}}{\text{Total stockholders' equity}}$$

$$\text{Year 0001} = \frac{\$575,500}{\$263,900} = 2.18$$

$$\text{Year 0002} = \frac{\$555,200}{\$304,100} = 1.83$$

High debt to equity ratio
equals high risk to
lender

This ratio tells us that in year 0001 for each $1.00 the stockholders have invested, the creditors have invested $2.18. In year 0002 the comparable figures are stockholders $1.00 and creditors $1.83. The higher the creditors' investment for each $1.00 of stockholders' investment, the higher is the risk for the creditor. In such circumstances, if a hotel or food service operation wished to expand, debt financing would be more difficult to obtain and interest rates would be higher.

The risk situation can perhaps be explained with some simple figures. Total assets equal total liabilities plus stockholders' equity. Assume total assets are $100,000, total liabilities are $50,000, and stockholders' equity $50,000. The debt to equity ratio will be:

$$\frac{\$50,000}{\$50,000} = 1 \ (or \ \$1.00 \ to \ \$1.00)$$

Under these circumstances total assets of $100,000 could decline by 50%, to $50,000, before the creditors would be running a serious risk.

Assume, with the same total assets of $100,000, total liabilities are $65,000 and stockholders' equity $35,000. The debt to equity ratio will be:

$$\frac{\$65,000}{\$35,000} = 1.86 \ (or \ \$1.86 \ to \ \$1.00)$$

With this debt to equity ratio (higher than the earlier one, therefore riskier from the creditors' point of view), the assets could only decline 35% (as opposed to 50%) in value (from $100,000 down to $65,000) before the creditors would be facing a difficult situation.

Use of leverage

Therefore, although the creditors prefer not to have the debt to equity ratio too high, the hotel or food service operator often finds it more profitable to have it as high as possible. A high debt to equity ratio is known as having high leverage or trading on the equity. Using leverage will be discussed in a later section of this chapter.

CASH FLOW FROM OPERATING ACTIVITIES TO TOTAL LIABILITIES

The cash flow from operating activities to total liabilities ratio is calculated as follows:

Equation

$$\frac{Cash \ flow \ from \ operating \ activities}{Average \ total \ liabilities}$$

In our situation, given the cash flow amount of $144,200 and using figures from Exhibit 4.1, the calculation is:

$$\frac{\$131,580}{(\$575,500 + \$555,200)/2}$$

or

$$\frac{\$131,580}{\$565,350}$$

$$= 0.2327 \text{ or } 23.3\%$$

The often-used solvency ratio of total assets to total liabilities is calculated at a single point in time (the balance sheet date) whereas the cash flow from operations to average total liabilities ratio covers a period of time and is thus considered more useful.

Uses period of time

Further, the total assets to total liabilities ratio does not take into account the different liquidity of the various assets used in the equation and the cash flow from operations to average total liabilities ratio overcomes that problem and is more indicative of the operation's ability to pay its various types of debt. It is suggested that a minimum ratio of 20% is acceptable, and the higher this ratio is the better is the operation's ability to pay off its debts with cash. Our result of 23.3% is comfortably above the suggested minimum.

NUMBER OF TIMES INTEREST EARNED

Another way of looking at the margin of safety in meeting debt interest payments is to calculate the number of times per year interest is earned.

Times interest earned equation

$$\text{Times interest earned} = \frac{\text{Income before interest and income tax}}{\text{Interest expense}}$$

$$= \frac{\$132,300}{\$51,900} = 2.55 \text{ times in year 002}$$

It is considered good if interest is earned two or more times a year.

Creditors, owners, and management all like to see this ratio as high as possible. To creditors, a high number indicates a reduction of their risk and shows that the establishment will be able to meet its regular loan interest payments when due. To owners, a high number is also desirable (particularly if the establishment has a high debt to equity ratio). Therefore, management also prefers a high ratio because it pleases each of the other two groups. Note, however, that if this ratio is extremely high it may indicate that leverage is not being maximized.

CASH FLOW FROM OPERATING ACTIVITIES TO INTEREST

The cash flow from operating activities to interest ratio is calculated as follows:

Equation

$$\frac{\text{Cash flow from operating activities} + \text{Interest expense}}{\text{Interest expense}}$$

In our case, given the cash flow amount of $131,580, and with reference to Exhibit 4.2, the calculation is:

$$\frac{\$131,580 + \$51,900}{\$51,900}$$

or

$$\frac{\$183,480}{\$51,900}$$

$$= 3.5 \text{ times or } 350\%$$

This ratio is a more realistic one than the number of times interest earned ratio just discussed because interest has to be paid with cash and not with net income. This ratio can provide a more obvious warning that an inability to pay interest may be on the horizon than does the traditional interest coverage ratio. The higher this ratio is the more comfortable will be the operation's creditors.

PROFITABILITY RATIOS

The main objective of most hospitality operations is to generate a profit. In a partnership or proprietorship, the profit can be withdrawn by the owners to increase their personal net worth. In an incorporated company, the profit can be paid out in dividends or be retained in the business to expand it, increase the profits further, and improve the value of the owners' equity investment in the company. Creditors of a company also like to see increases in the business's profit, because the higher the profits the less is the risk to them as lenders. Therefore, one of the main tasks of management is to ensure continued profitability of the enterprise. It is with profitability ratios that management's effectiveness in achieving this is most often measured.

Profit versus profitability

Caution needs to be exercised in the use of the word "profitability." A company may have a net income on its income statement, and this net income, expressed as a percentage of revenue, may seem acceptable; however, the relationship between this net income and other items (for example, the amount of money invested by stockholders) may not be acceptable or profitable.

RETURN ON ASSETS

The return on assets ratio (also known as gross return on assets) measures the effectiveness of management's use of the organization's assets. The equation is:

Return on assets equation

$$\frac{\text{Income before interest and income tax}}{\text{Total average assets}} \times 100 = \frac{\$132,300}{(\$839,400 + \$859,300) \div 2} \times 100$$

$$= \frac{\$132,300}{(\$1,698,700 \div 2)} \times 100$$

$$= \frac{\$132,300}{\$849,350} \times 100 = 15.6\%$$

Average based on monthly figures

In this illustration, total average assets are calculated by adding the beginning of year and the end of year figures and dividing by 2. If the figures fluctuated widely during the year because of such factors as purchase and sale of long-term assets, and if monthly figures were available, the average should be calculated by adding each of the monthly figures and dividing by 12.

Interest is added back to net income (as is income tax) in the equation in order to compare the resulting percentage (in our case 15.6%) to the current market interest rate. For instance, if, in our example, an expansion of the building were contemplated and the money were to borrowed at a 10% interest rate, one could assume that the new building asset would earn a rate of return of 15.6% and would have no difficulty in meeting the 10% interest expense. This would leave the expanded part of the business 5.6% on assets before income tax.

NET RETURN ON ASSETS

The gross return on assets calculation measures management's effectiveness in its use of assets and is also useful in assessing the likelihood of obtaining more debt financing for expansion. The net return on assets, on the other hand, evaluates the advisability of seeking equity (as opposed to debt) financing. The equation is:

Net return on assets equation

$$\frac{\text{Net income after tax}}{\text{Total average assets}} \times 100 = \frac{\$40,200}{(\$839,400 + \$859,300) \div 2} \times 100$$

$$= \frac{\$40,200}{(\$1,698,700 \div 2)} \times 100$$

$$= \frac{\$40,200}{\$849,350} \times 100 = 4.73\%$$

Assets at replacement or market value

Since dividends are payable out of earnings after income tax, if we used equity (stockholder) financing for a building, the stockholders would not be able to anticipate a very good dividend yield. On the basis of current results, assets are only yielding a 4.7% return, and stockholders would probably assume that the new assets would earn the same rate of return as the old assets. This may be a poor assumption, since the old assets are at book (depreciated) value. If the calculation were made on assets at their replacement or market value, the rate could well drop below the present 4.73%. Under these circumstances, management would have to improve its performance considerably in order to convince stockholders to part with more money for expansion.

NET INCOME TO REVENUE RATIO

The net income to revenue ratio (also known as the profit margin) measures management's overall effectiveness in generating sales and controlling expenses. It is calculated as follows:

Net income to revenue equation

$$\text{Net income to revenue ratio} = \frac{\text{Net income after income tax}}{\text{Sales revenue}} \times 100$$

$$= \frac{\$40,200}{\$1,175,200} \times 100 = \underline{3.4\%}$$

This means that, out of each $1.00 of revenue, we had 3.4 cents net income. In absolute terms, this may not be very meaningful, because it does not truly reflect the profitability of the firm. Consider the following two cases:

	Case A	Case B
Revenue	$100,000	$100,000
Net income	5,000	10,000
Net income to revenue ratio	5%	10%

Effectiveness of management

With the same revenue it seems that Case B is better. In Case B, the organization is making twice as much net income, in absolute terms, as is organization A ($10,000 to $5,000). This doubling of net income is supported by the net income to revenue ratio (10% to 5%). If these were two similar firms, or two branches of the same firm, these figures would indicate the relative effectiveness of the management of each in controlling costs and generating a satisfactory level of net income. However, in order to determine the profitability of A to B, we need to relate the net income to the investment:

	Case A	Case B
Revenue	$100,000	$100,000
Net income	5,000	10,000
Net income to revenue ratio	5%	10%
Investment	$40,000	$80,000
Profitability (return on investment)	$\dfrac{\$5,000}{\$40,000} \times 100$ $= \underline{12.5\%}$	$\dfrac{\$10,000}{\$80,000} \times 100$ $= \underline{12.5\%}$

Comparable profitability

As can now be seen, despite the wide difference in net income and net income to revenue ratio, there is no difference between the two organizations as far as profitability is concerned: they are both equally good, returning 12.5% on the investment.

CASH FLOW FROM OPERATING ACTIVITIES MARGIN

The cash flow from operating activities margin ratio is calculated as follows:

Equation

$$\frac{\text{Cash flow from operating activities}}{\text{Sales revenue}}$$

In our case, given the cash flow amount of $131,580 and with reference to Exhibit 4.2, the calculation is:

$$\frac{\$131,580}{\$1,175,200}$$

$$= 0.1119 \text{ or } 11.2\%$$

The ratio compares the amount of cash generated per dollar of sales. Although this ratio is similar to the profit margin ratio discussed earlier, it is again considered to be a more realistic one since it compares sales revenues with cash rather than net income.

In our case, because the cash flow amount of $131,580 is higher than the net income amount of $40,200, we know the cash flow from operating activities margin ratio will be higher than the profit margin ratio because both ratios use the same denominator.

RETURN ON STOCKHOLDERS' EQUITY

Various definitions

There are many equations and definitions for return on investment. For example, should we use (1) income before income tax, (2) income before interest and income tax, or (3) net income after tax? Is the investment (1) the book value of assets, (2) the replacement or market value of the assets, (3) the total investment of debt and equity, or (4) only the stockholders' equity? Perhaps the most useful definition of return on investment is to use net income after income tax (because dividends can only be paid out of after-tax profits) and relate that net income to the stockholders' investment. It is to this group of people, the stockholders or owners, that operating management is primarily responsible. The equation for this calculation is:

Return on equity equation

Return on stockholder's equity =

$$\frac{\text{Net income after income tax}}{\text{Average stockholder's equity}} \times 100 = \frac{\$40,200}{(\$263,900 + \$304,100) \div 2} \times 100$$

$$= \frac{\$40,200}{(\$568,000 \div 2)} \times 100$$

$$= \frac{\$40,200}{\$284,000} \times 100 = 14.2\%$$

Matter of opinion

This percentage shows the effectiveness of management's use of equity funds. How high should it be? This is a matter of personal opinion. If an investor could put money either into the bank at a 10% interest rate or into a hotel investment at only 8% with more risk involved, the bank might seem the better choice of the two.

Note that, if the business has issued both preferred and common stock, the return on stockholders' equity equation can be modified, with the numerator becoming net income less preferred dividends and the denominator becoming average common stockholders' equity. To the common stockholders, preferred stock is a form of "debt" on which a fixed dividend rate must be paid. To the extent that profits are enhanced by borrowing from preferred stockholders and the added profits exceed the fixed rate of dividends paid to preferred stockholders, the additional earnings accruing to the common stockholders will be improved.

OTHER PROFITABILITY RATIOS

Publicly traded stocks

Other measures of profitability include annual earnings per share, dividend rate per share, and book value per share. Such ratios are of most concern to those buying and selling publicly traded stock on the open market and are of less concern to the internal management of the firm. However, management is held accountable by stockholders for producing a net income satisfactory to them. This net income is frequently measured by earnings per share. The earnings per share are important also because they tend to dictate the value of the shares in the market or indicate the desirability of purchasing stock in the company to a potential purchaser. The equation is:

Earnings per share equation

$$\text{Earnings per share} = \frac{\text{Net income after tax}}{\text{Average number of shares outstanding}}$$

Assuming that the average number of shares outstanding (beginning of the year number plus end of the year number dividend by 2) was 40,000, our earnings per share would be:

$$\frac{\$40,200}{\$40,000} = \$1.005 \text{ or } \$1.01 \text{ per share}$$

Deduct preferred dividends

If both common and preferred stock have been issued, this equation has to be modified. The numerator will be net income (after tax) less preferred dividends. The denominator will be average number of common shares outstanding.

Note that earnings per share can be increased over time by not paying out all earnings in dividends to shareholders. By retaining some or all potential dividends and reinvesting them in expanding the business, future profits (earnings) will be increased while the number of shares outstanding is held constant.

CREDITORS, OWNERS, AND MANAGEMENT

In general, all three groups (creditors, owners, and management) interested in financial ratios prefer to see profitability ratios high and growing rather than low and stable. Creditors will be interested in a ratio such as return on assets, particularly if it is increasing, because this indicates management's effectiveness in its use of all assets and reduces the creditors' risk.

Comparison with alternatives

On the other hand, the ratio of most interest to owners is return on their equity investment because they can easily compare this ratio with the return they might receive from alternative investments. In public companies, if equity investors are not satisfied with their return they can remove their investment by selling their shares in the stock market and purchasing shares in more "profitable" companies. If many equity investors with large shareholdings do this, it will depress the market price of the shares. In turn, this will make it more difficult for the company to raise money when needed in the future because there will be a reluctance by potential investors to buy the new shares. Stock market investors often measure the value of a share by its price earnings ratio calculated as follows:

Price earnings equation

$$\frac{\text{Market price per share}}{\text{Earnings per share}}$$

If the market price of the shares were \$10.00, our price earnings ratio would be:

$$\frac{\$10.00}{\$1.01} = 9.90 \text{ times}$$

The price earnings ratio for any specific hospitality company's shares is affected by how purchasers and sellers of those shares perceive the stability and/or trend of earnings, the potential growth of earnings, and the risk of investing in those shares.

Management's task is to maintain all profitability ratios at as high a level as possible so that both creditors and owners (investors) are satisfied. Management's effectiveness in this regard will be measured by the level of that satisfaction.

TURNOVER RATIOS

Turnover ratios (sometimes known as activity or efficiency ratios) are calculated to determine the activity of certain classes of assets, such as inventories, working capital, and long-term assets. The ratios express the number of times that an activity (turnover) is occurring during a certain period and can help in measuring management's effectiveness in using and controlling these assets.

INVENTORY TURNOVER RATIOS

Inventory turnover ratios are discussed in some detail in the section on cash conservation and working capital management in Chapter 11. For our purpose, only the basic equation is included in this chapter:

Inventory turnover equation

$$\text{Inventory turnover} = \frac{\text{Cost of sales for the period}}{\text{Average inventory during the period}}$$

Food inventory turnover normally varies between two and four times a month. Beverage turnover varies from one-half to one time a month. An individual operator should determine, in each case, the turnover rate appropriate to that establishment (since there are major exceptions to these guidelines) and then watch for deviations from those rates.

WORKING CAPITAL TURNOVER

The working capital turnover ratio is a measure of the effectiveness of the use of working capital. Working capital is current assets less current liabilities. Our balance sheet (Exhibit 4.1) gives us the following:

	Year 0001	Year 0002
Current assets	$73,370	$79,090
Current liabilities	(62,700)	(68,400)
Working capital	$10,670	$10,690

The equation for working capital turnover is

Working capital turnover equation

$$\text{Working capital turnover} = \frac{\text{Total sales revenue}}{\text{Average working capital}}$$

$$= \frac{\$1,175,200}{(\$10,670 + \$10,690) \div 2}$$

$$= \frac{\$1,175,200}{(\$21,360 \div 2)}$$

$$= \frac{\$1,175,200}{\$10,680} = 110 \text{ times (which is high)}$$

Appropriate level of
working capital

This ratio can vary widely, from as low as ten times per year (for a restaurant) to as high as 50 times or more a year (for a hotel).

A hospitality operation should probably try to find its most appropriate level of working capital and then compare future performance with this optimum level. Too much working capital (that is, too low a turnover ratio) means ineffective use of funds. Too little working capital (indicated by too high a turnover ratio) may lead to cash difficulties if revenue begins to decline.

Note also that, all other factors being equal, the higher the working capital turnover ratio the lower will be the current ratio. This means that if an establishment has little or no credit sales and a very low level of inventory (for example, a motel doing cash-only business), it will have both a low current ratio and a high working capital turnover. Thus, with reference to the earlier section on the current ratio, creditors prefer a low working capital turnover, owners prefer a high turnover, and management tries to maintain a reasonable balance between the two extremes in order to maximize profits by reducing the amount of money tied up in current assets, while maintaining sufficient liquidity to take care of unanticipated emergencies requiring cash.

FIXED ASSET TURNOVER

The fixed asset turnover ratio assesses the effectiveness of the use of fixed assets in generating revenue. The equation is:

Fixed asset turnover
equation

$$\text{Fixed asset turnover} = \frac{\text{Total sales revenue}}{\text{Total average fixed assets}}$$

$$= \frac{\$1,175,200}{(\$766,030 + \$780,210) \div 2}$$

$$= \frac{\$1,175,200}{(\$1,546,240 \div 2)}$$

$$= \frac{\$1,175,200}{\$773,120} = 1.52 \text{ times}$$

In the hotel industry, this turnover rate could vary from as low as one-half to as high as two or more times per year. In the food service industry, a restaurant could find it has a turnover of four or five times a year (assuming it is in rented premises). The reason the turnover rate is lower for a hotel is that it has, relatively speaking, a much higher investment in public space (lobbies, corridors) and in guest rooms (the capacity of which cannot be changed in the short run) than does a restaurant. A restaurant can increase its fixed asset turnover rate by increasing the number of seats or, if the demand is there, serve more customers during individual meal periods.

A high fixed asset turnover ratio indicates management's effectiveness in its use of fixed assets, whereas a low ratio either indicates that management is not effective or that some of those assets should be disposed of in order to increase the ratio. All groups (creditors, owners, and management) like to see the ratio as high as possible. One of the problems with this ratio, however, is that the older the assets are (and the more accumulated depreciation there is) the lower is their net book value. This automatically tends to increase the fixed asset turnover ratio. In addition, the use of an accelerated depreciation method hastens this process. Thus, management should resist the temptation to continue to use old and inefficient fixed assets and/or to use an accelerated depreciation method only in order to have a high fixed asset turnover.

Use of fixed asset turnover ratio

One of the uses of this ratio is in evaluating new projects. If the current turnover is four in a restaurant, and a new project costing $250,000 is going to generate $750,000 in revenue, giving a turnover of only three ($750,000 divided by $250,000), the new project may not seem as profitable.

OPERATING RATIOS

Selection of appropriate tool

There are many other revenue and cost analysis techniques and tools available apart from those already mentioned. Some of the more common ones are discussed briefly in the next section. Caution must be exercised in their use. It is important to select the appropriate analysis tool. It is also important to remember that the information provided from the use of these techniques may only indicate that a problem exists. The solution to the problem is entirely in the hands of management.

FOOD AND BEVERAGE OPERATIONS

Food and/or Beverage Cost Percentage

This is expressed as a percentage of the related revenue as illustrated and discussed in the previous chapter with reference to Exhibit 3.5. The percentage can be compared with a standard or predetermined percentage established as a goal. Wide deviations from standard should be investigated.

Labor Cost Percentage

Labor cost calculation

Labor cost includes employee benefits and is expressed as a percentage of related revenue. With reference to Exhibit 3.5, in year 0001 it is:

$$\frac{\$277,400 + \$34,500}{\$851,600} \times 100 = \frac{\$311,900}{\$851,600} = 36.6\%$$

and in year 0002:

$$\frac{\$304,500 + \$37,800}{\$869,100} \times 100 = \frac{\$342,300}{\$869,100} = 39.4\%$$

As with food and beverage cost percentages, labor cost percentage can be compared with an established standard. Again, large differences should be investigated.

Dollars of Revenue

This may be in terms of per employee per meal period or per day, week, or month or number of guests served per employee per meal period or per day, week, or month. For example, if a restaurant had revenue for a meal period of $1,200, 100 guests were served, and eight employees were on duty, the dollars of revenue per employee for that meal period would be:

$$\frac{\$1,200}{8} = \underline{\$150}$$

and the number of guests served per employee would be:

$$\frac{100}{8} = \underline{12.5}$$

These ratios are used primarily to assess employee productivity against a standard or to determine any upward or downward trend in productivity.

Average Food and/or Beverage Check by Meal Period and by Revenue Area

Change of menu item on average check

The method of calculating the average check was explained in Chapter 3. The trend of this figure is important, but it can also be used to determine, for example, the effect that a change in menu item(s) may have an average customer spending.

Seat Turnover by Meal Period or by Day

Calculated by dividing total guests served during a meal period or a day by the number of seats the restaurant has. For example, if a restaurant had 40 seats and 100 guests were served during a meal period, the turnover for that meal period would be:

$$\frac{100}{40} = \underline{2.5}$$

A high turnover is generally preferable to a low one, as long as the customers are receiving good service and not being rushed. The trend of turnovers should be analyzed. A declining trend may indicate a lowering of service or may indicate that high prices or low-quality food are keeping customers away.

Daily, Weekly, Monthly, or Annual Revenue Dollars per Available Seat

Revenue per seat available

Calculated by dividing revenue for the period by the number of seats the restaurant has. For example, if a 125-seat restaurant had monthly sales of $250,000, monthly revenue per seat is:

$$\frac{\$250,000}{125} = \$2,000$$

The trend of this figure can be revealing. It might also be useful to compare it with the results for similar types of establishments.

Percentage of Beverage Revenue to Food Revenue

For example, a restaurant had total monthly revenue of $85,160, of which food was $68,950 and beverages were $16,210. Beverages are 23.5% of food revenue, calculated as follows:

$$\frac{\$16,210}{\$68,950} \times 100 = 23.5\%$$

Since beverage revenue is generally more profitable than food revenue, sales efforts should be directed toward promoting beverage revenue (wine with meals, for example) to increase the ratio.

Percentage of Beverage Revenue and/or Food Revenue to Rooms Revenue

This would apply to a hotel. The calculation is similar to that in item 7 above, except that room revenue becomes the denominator and the numerator is either food revenue or beverage revenue. A change in the revenue mix among departments (such as a change in the percentages) can be important since some departments are more profitable than others. Advertising dollars are often more beneficially spent, from a cost/benefit point of view, on departments or areas with the highest profitability.

ROOMS DEPARTMENT IN A HOTEL OR MOTEL

Average Rate per Occupied Room

Average room rates

Calculated daily by dividing rooms occupied into revenue from rooms. For example, if a hotel had total revenue for a night of $7,200 from 80 occupied rooms, its average rate per occupied room is:

$$\frac{\$7,200}{80} = \$90$$

If it is to be calculated on a monthly basis, it is derived from dividing total rooms occupied during the month into total revenue for the month. The method is similar for an annual occupancy, except that annual figures are used. The trend of this figure is important. It can be influenced upward by directing sales efforts into selling higher priced rooms rather than lower priced ones, by increasing the rate of double occupancy (see the next item), or by altering other factors.

Revenue per Available Room

REVPAR

A hotel's occupancy percentage and average room rate have traditionally been the tools used to measure the rooms department's performance. By themselves, each of these tools has limited value. For example, Hotel A with 200 rooms might have an occupancy of 80% and an average daily rate of $70, while Hotel B also with 200 rooms has an occupancy of 70% and an average daily rate of $85. All other things being equal, which is the better performing hotel? It is difficult to determine without knowing the revenue per available room (often abbreviated to REVPAR), calculated as follows:

$$\text{Revpar} = \frac{\text{Total room revenue}}{\text{Available rooms}}$$

or it can be more simply calculated as follows:

$$\text{Revpar} = \text{Occupancy percentage} \times \text{Average room rate}$$

Using these figures, the relative performance of the two hotels measured in terms of revpar is as follows:

Hotel A	Hotel B
80% × $70 = $56	70% × $85 = $59.50

For measuring performance, revpar is thus an improvement over either occupancy percentage or average room rate.

Occupancy Percentage and/or Double Occupancy

Occupancy percentages

This may be on a daily, weekly, monthly, or annual basis. Occupancy is calculated by dividing the rooms used during a period (a night, a week) by the rooms available during that period (rooms in the establishment times days in the period) and multiplying by 100. For example, with reference to item 1, if this hotel had 100 rooms, occupancy for that night is:

$$\frac{80}{100} \times 100 = 80\%$$

Double occupancy percentage is the percentage of rooms occupied that are occupied by more than one person. For example, if 20 of the 80 occupied rooms on that night were occupied by more than one person, the double occupancy is:

$$\frac{20}{80} \times 100 = 25\%$$

Double occupancy is sometimes expressed by calculating the average number of people per room occupied (total number of guests for a period divided by total rooms occupied during that period). For example, if our 80 occupied rooms were occupied by 100 guests, the double occupancy would be:

$$\frac{100}{80} = 1.25$$

Resort hotels

Double occupancy is usually higher for resort hotels (catering to the family trade) than for transient hotels (catering primarily to the business person traveling alone).

Obviously, a high occupancy and a high double occupancy are both desirable because this indicates greater use of the rooms facilities and also potentially greater usage of food and beverage facilities by guest room occupants. Therefore, the trend of this information is important.

Note that, when an occupancy percentage is calculated for a period of time (such as a week), this does not mean that was the occupancy every night of the week. For example, a hotel could have an average occupancy of 70% for a week, with an occupancy of over 90% per night from Monday to Friday and a very low occupancy percentage at the weekend.

Labor Cost Percentage

This is expressed as a percentage of room revenue (in the same way as was illustrated in item 2 for food and beverage operations) and compared with an established standard.

Number of Rooms Cleaned

Productivity measures

This may be based on per maid per day and/or dollars of room revenue per front desk clerk per day, week, or month. These are both productivity measures calculated in a similar way to the productivity measures illustrated in item 3 for food and beverage operations. These productivity measures can be compared against a standard or used to detect undesirable trends.

Annual Revenue per Available Room

This figure is obtained by dividing annual revenue by rooms in the establishment. The trend of this figure is important, but it is also useful to compare it with results from similar types of hotel or motel.

Undistributed Cost Dollars per Available Room per Year

Undistributed costs include such expenses as administrative and general, marketing, property operation and maintenance, and energy costs. The total cost of each for the year is divided by rooms in the establishment. Trends are again important, and comparison with similar establishments' results can be revealing.

MANAGER'S DAILY REPORT

Detection of trends important

Many of the operating statistics that are useful for analyzing the ongoing progress of an establishment can be calculated on a day-to-day basis. In this way the success level of the establishment can be monitored on a daily basis. Trends, favorable or unfavorable, can be detected while they are occurring, rather than too late for effective action to be taken. A sample of a manager's daily report that would be useful in a small hotel operation is illustrated in Exhibit 4.6. A food operation's operating statistics might be summarized as shown in Exhibit 4.7. Each establishment's management should decide which operating statistics are most useful for getting a daily overview and, subsequently, prepare a form that will allow these statistics to be summarized quickly each day.

INTERNAL AND EXTERNAL COMPARISONS

Do not ignore external trends

Up to this point only internal comparisons and trends of selected information have been emphasized. An internal change of selected information over time is probably the most meaningful method of seeking out problem areas so that any necessary corrective action can be taken. Nevertheless, external comparisons and trends should not be ignored. Many industrywide external trends are available that could be useful for comparison with internal results. However, trying to change internal results so they match external industry averages should be done with caution. Industry averages are only that—averages. An average industry figure may not be typical of any specific hotel or food service operation.

Exhibit 4.6   Manager's Daily Report

	TODAY	MONTH TO DATE	FORECAST MONTH TO DATE	LAST MONTH TO DATE	LAST YEAR MONTH TO DATE
ROOMS					
FOOD					
BEVERAGE					
TELEPHONE / TELEGRAM					
VALET					
LAUNDRY					
OTHER					
TOTAL REVENUE					

STATISTICS

	TODAY	MONTH TO DATE	FORECAST MONTH TO DATE	LAST MONTH TO DATE	LAST YEAR MONTH TO DATE	BANK REPORT	
TOTAL ROOMS OCC.						BALANCE YESTERDAY	
COMP. & HOUSE USE						RECEIPTS	
VACANT ROOMS						DISBURSEMENTS	
TOTAL ROOMS AVAIL.						BALANCE TODAY	
AVERAGE ROOM RATE						ACCOUNTS RECEIVABLE	
% OF OCCUPANCY							
NO. OF DOUBLES						BALANCE YESTERDAY	
% OF DOUBLE OCC.						CHARGES	
% OF FOOD COST						CREDITS	
% OF BEVERAGE COST						BALANCE TODAY	

PAYROLL AND RELATED EXPENSES

	TODAY		FORECAST MONTH TO DATE		LAST MONTH MONTH TO DATE		LAST YEAR TO DATE		MONTH TO DATE	
	AMOUNT	%	AMOUNT	%	AMOUNT	%	AMOUNT	%	AMOUNT	%
ROOM										
FOOD & BEVERAGE										
OVERHEAD DEPTS.										

Date _____

Day _____

Weather _____

Exhibit 4.7   Daily Report

Day _____ Date _____ Weather _____

MEALS SERVED:	Number of Covers					Average Check	
	Breakfast	Lunch	Dinner	Total Today	Total to Date	Average Today	Check to Date
Dining Room							
Coffee Shop							
Room Service							
Banquet							
TOTAL							

CONCLUDING COMMENTS ON RATIO ANALYSIS

To summarize this discussion of ratios, note these points:

- Financial ratios are generally produced from historical accounting information. As a result, some accounting numbers reflect historic costs rather than present values. An example is a building's cost recorded on the balance sheet at its original purchase price and offset by accumulated depreciation to produce net book value. A ratio based on total assets (such as return on assets) may show a result that is more than acceptable. If it were based on the current replacement cost of those assets, however, it would produce a much more realistic ratio that can then be compared with alternative investments. For this same reason, this type of ratio cannot be readily compared with the ratio for other hospitality companies because they may have purchased their assets at different times, at different costs, and may have used different depreciation methods.

Leasing of assets

- Many of the guidelines or rules of thumb given in this chapter on ratio analysis have assumed ownership of all assets. If assets (particularly land and building, and furniture and equipment) are leased rather than owned, then these industry quoted guidelines must be used with caution. Indeed, rules of thumb should always be used with great care, because every organization that is part of the hospitality industry has its own unique features. This leads to the next comment.

Trends of ratios over time

- Ratios are only of value when two related numbers are compared. For example, the current ratio compares current assets with current liabilities. This is a meaningful comparison. On the other hand, if current assets are compared to owner equity, this ratio has little value because there is no direct relationship between the two numbers.

Selectivity of ratios

- Although external comparisons of ratios (that is, comparison of your ratios with industry averages or other similar hotels or food operations) are interesting, what is probably of more value is comparing the trend of your own ratios over time. If the working capital turnover ratio is constantly increasing over the years, with little change in sales revenue, this may be more indicative of a problem than the fact that the ratio is below the industry average.

Ratios—a means to an end

- This chapter has tried to include all the ratios that could be useful to a hospitality enterprise. There is no suggestion that a particular operator should use all of them. Selectivity is important. One should use those that are of benefit in evaluating the results of a business in relation to its objectives.

- Ratios should not be an end in themselves. An objective of a company might be to have the happiest stockholders in the world. Emphasis might then be placed solely on increasing net income to the point where the stockholders will see an incredibly large return on their investment. The end result might be that, to achieve this, selling prices have been set so high, and expenses cut so low, that the business collapses.

- Finally, ratios by themselves cure no problems but only indicate possible problems. For example, the trend of the accounts receivable ratio may show that the time that it is taking to collect the average accounts receivable is becoming longer. That is all the ratio shows. It is only management analysis of this problem to discover the causes that can correct this deteriorating situation.

LEVERAGE

Equity versus debt financing

Earlier in this chapter, the concept of leverage, or trading on the equity, was introduced. To illustrate this, consider the case of a new restaurant that is to be opened at a cost of $250,000 (for furnishings, equipment, and working capital). The owners have the cash available but they are considering not using all their own money. Instead, they wish to compare their relative return on equity on the basis of using either all their own money (100% equity financing) or using 50% equity and borrowing the other 50% (debt financing) at a 10% interest rate. Regardless of which method they use, revenue will be the same, as will all operating costs. With either choice, they will have $50,000 income before interest and taxes. There is no interest expense under 100% equity financing. With some debt financing there will be interest to be paid. However, interest expense is tax deductible. Assuming a tax rate of 50% on taxable income, Exhibit 4.8 shows

Exhibit 4.8   Effect of Leverage on ROI

	Option A	Option B
Investment required	$250,000	$250,000
Equity financing	$250,000	$125,000
Debt financing	0	$125,000 @ 10%
Income before interest and income tax	$ 50,000	$ 50,000
Interest expense	0	(12,500)
Income before income tax	$ 50,000	$ 37,500
Income tax (50%)	(25,000)	(18,750)
Net income	$ 25,000	$ 18,750
Return on equity		

$$\frac{25,000}{250,000} \times 100 \qquad\qquad \frac{18,750}{125,000} \times 100$$

$$= 10\% \qquad\qquad\qquad = 15\%$$

the comparative operating results and the return on investment (ROI) based on initial equity investment.

Increasing debt ratio

In Exhibit 4.8, not only do the owners make a better return on their initial investment under option B (15% versus 10%), but they still have $125,000 in cash they can invest in a second venture. In this case, if a 50/50 debt to equity ratio is more profitable than 100% equity financing, would not an 80/20 debt to equity ratio be even more profitable? In other words, what would be the return on initial investment if the owners used only $50,000 of their own money and borrowed the remaining $200,000 required at 10%? Exhibit 4.9 shows the result of this more highly leveraged situation.

Advantage of leverage

Under Option C, Exhibit 4.9, our return on initial investment has now increased to 30%, and we have $200,000 cash still on hand, enough for four more similar restaurant ventures. The advantages of leverage are obvious: the higher the debt to equity ratio, the higher will be the owners' return on equity. However, this only holds true if income (before interest) as a percentage of debt is greater than the interest rate to be paid on the debt. For example, if the debt interest rate is 10%, the income to debt ratio must be greater than 10% for leverage to be profitable. With high debt (high leverage) there is a risk.

Risk involved

If income declines, the more highly leveraged a company is, the sooner it will be in financial difficulty. In Option B (relatively low leverage) income before interest and income tax could decline from $50,000 to $12,500 before net income would be zero. In Option C (relatively high leverage) income before interest and income tax could decline from $50,000 to only $20,000.

Exhibit 4.9   Effect of High Leverage on ROI

	Option C
Investment required	$250,000
Equity financing	$ 50,000
Debt financing	$200,000 @ 10%
Income before interest and income tax	$ 50,000
Interest expense	(20,000)
Income before income tax	$ 30,000
Income tax (50%)	(15,000)
Net income	$ 15,000

Return on equity $\dfrac{\$15,000}{\$50,000} \times 100 = 30\%$

COMPUTER APPLICATIONS

Because most of the ratios discussed in this chapter result from an operation's income statement and balance sheet, if a computer is used to produce those statements, then the ratios can also be automatically produced.

In addition to the period-end ratios, if information about the operation's daily operations is stored in the computer, then even the daily operating ratios desired can be calculated and printed out on the daily report. For example, if a hotel's night audit is computerized, ratios such as occupancy, double occupancy, average room rate, and revenue per available room can also be automatically calculated.

For a restaurant there are also programs available that keep track of daily purchases, usage, and sales of food, from which a daily and accumulated food cost is automatically calculated.

Further, if an operation's payroll is computerized and linked to a computerized time clock, each employee's pay rate can be applied to daily hours worked, and total daily labor cost can be calculated by department. If each day's sales are entered for a department, a daily labor cost percentage can be calculated for cost control purposes.

SUMMARY

A number of different ways of expressing ratios were detailed in this chapter, as were four methods of evaluating a ratio: industry averages, competitors' figures, the operation's results from a previous period, and a predetermined standard for the operation. Current liquidity ratios measure a company's ability to meet its short-term obligations. Some of the more common liquidity ratios are:

1. Current ratio:

$$\frac{\text{Current assets}}{\text{Current liabilities}}$$

2. Quick (acid test) ratio:

$$\frac{\text{Cash + Credit card receivables + Accounts receivable + Marketable securities}}{\text{Total current liabilities}}$$

or

$$\frac{\text{Total current assets} - \text{Inventories for resale} - \text{Prepaid expenses}}{\text{Current liabilities}}$$

3. Credit card receivables as a percentage of credit card revenue:

$$\frac{\text{Average credit card receivables}}{\text{Credit card revenue}}$$

4. Credit card receivables turnover:

$$\frac{\text{Credit card revenue}}{\text{Average credit card receivables}}$$

5. Average credit cards collection period:

$$\frac{365 \text{ days}}{\text{Credit card turnover ratio}}$$

6. Accounts receivable as a percentage of accounts receivable credit revenue:

$$\frac{\text{Average accounts receivable}}{\text{Accounts receivable credit revenue}}$$

7. Accounts receivable turnover:

$$\frac{\text{Accounts receivable credit revenue}}{\text{Average accounts receivable}}$$

8. Accounts receivable average collection period:

$$\frac{365}{\text{Accounts receivable turnover ratio}}$$

Another useful technique is to make a comparative analysis of current assets. Total current assets are 100%, and each item of current asset is expressed as a proportion of 100%. Such an analysis can indicate a change in liquidity of current assets due to a change in the proportions of each current asset relative to total current assets.

Long-term solvency ratios, sometimes called *net worth ratios*, measure a company's ability to meet its long-term credit obligations. Some of the ratios are:

$$1. \quad \text{Total assets to total liabilities ratio} \ = \ \frac{\text{Total assets}}{\text{Total liabilities}}$$

$$2. \quad \text{Total liabilities to total assets ratio} \ = \ \frac{\text{Total liabilities}}{\text{Total assets}}$$

$$3. \quad \text{Total liabilities to total equity ratio} \ = \ \frac{\text{Total liabilities}}{\text{Total stockholder's equity}}$$

4. Cash flow from operating activities to Total liabilities ratio

$$\frac{\text{Cash flow from operating activities}}{\text{Total liabilities ratio}} \qquad$$

$$5. \quad \text{Times interest earned ratio} \ = \ \frac{\text{Income before interest and income tax}}{\text{Interest expense}}$$

6. Cash flow from operating activities to interest earned ratio:

$$\frac{\text{Cash flow from operating activities} + \text{Interest expense}}{\text{Interest expense}}$$

Profitability ratios provide information that can be used to measure the effectiveness of management's use of the assets (resources) available to conduct operations. Some of the ratios are:

$$1. \quad \text{Return on assets} \ = \ \frac{\text{Income before interest and income tax}}{\text{Total average assets}}$$

$$2. \quad \text{Net return on assets} \ = \ \frac{\text{Net income after tax}}{\text{Total average assets}}$$

3.   Net income to sales revenue ratio $= \dfrac{\text{Net income after income tax}}{\text{Sales revenue}}$

4. Cash flow from operating activities margin ratio:

$$\dfrac{\text{Cash flow from operating activities}}{\text{Total sales revenue}}$$

5.   Return on stockholders' equity $= \dfrac{\text{Net income after income tax}}{\text{Average stockholders' equity}}$

6.   Earnings per share $= \dfrac{\text{Net income after income tax}}{\text{Average number of shares outstanding}}$

7.   Price/earnings ratio $= \dfrac{\text{Market price per share}}{\text{Earnings per share}}$

Turnover ratios include the following:

1.   Inventory turnover ratio $= \dfrac{\text{Cost of sales for the period}}{\text{Average inventory for the period}}$

2.   Working capital turnover ratio $= \dfrac{\text{Revenue}}{\text{Average working capital}}$

3.   Fixed asset turnover ratio $= \dfrac{\text{Revenue}}{\text{Total average fixed assets}}$

    Many individual operating ratios are available for food and beverage operations, as well as for the rooms operations in a motel or hotel. Ratios should be selected for use which are most appropriate for the operation being analyzed and evaluated. A daily manager's report is normally prepared to record information and statistics that management requires.

    Although internal comparisons and analysis are most useful, there are a great many industrywide statistics published for different hospitality organizations. External data and information should not be overlooked to assist in comparison of internal results. Comparison of appropriate external statistics to a completed internal analysis can provide greater insight into the effectiveness of the internal analysis.

The reader is cautioned to use ratio analysis with care and not to use "general rules of thumb" as necessarily being the norm for all businesses. What is most valuable is not how an individual operation's ratios differ from similar external operation, but how the internal results are changing over time. Selection and discretion in using the right ratio for the right occasion should be exercised. Ratios should not become an end in themselves.

Finally, ratios cannot solve problems, they only identify possible problems that only management's evaluation and corrective action can resolve.

This chapter concluded with some comments on the concept of leverage, or trading on the equity to increase capital. Leverage is obtained by increasing debt rather than equity investment in structuring the financing of an enterprise. As long as operating income before interest is greater than interest expense, the owners' return on equity will be higher. However, a too highly leveraged company may quickly be in financial trouble if operating income before interest begins declining.

DISCUSSION QUESTIONS

1. Describe the three ways in which a ratio can be expressed.
2. List and briefly discuss the four bases on which a ratio can be compared.
3. Which three groups are the main users of financial ratios?
4. What is the value in calculating a current ratio? Contrast how creditors and owners view this ratio.
5. Why can a hotel, motel, or restaurant usually operate with a current ratio considerably lower than for other types of businesses, such as manufacturing companies?
6. Why is maintaining a current ratio that is too high not a good business practice?
7. Explain why the calculation of a credit card receivables average collection period is a meaningful statistic.
8. What is the advantage that the ratio of cash flow from operating activities to average current liabilities has over the current or acid test ratios?
9. Define the term profitability.
10. Why is a high total asset to total liabilities ratio desired by creditors?
11. Why can the book values of assets be misleading when used in the total assets to total liabilities ratio, or the total liabilities to total assets ratio?
12. State the equation for the credit card turnover ratio.

13. Explain the return on assets ratio measure; what value is it to a potential creditor?

14. How does the net return on assets ratio differ from the return on assets ratio, and why is its calculation valuable?

15. Discuss the purpose of a quick ratio.

16. What does the return on stockholders' equity measure?

17. State how revenue per available room is calculated.

18. Discuss the term leverage or trading on the equity.

19. List four possible operating ratios that could be used in a food operation.

20. List and discuss three operating ratios that could be used in a rooms operation.

ETHICS SITUATION

A hotel manager wishes to borrow additional funds from his bank early in the next year. He knows the bank manager uses the hotel's current ratio as a major factor in his loan decision making. He also knows that the bank manager likes to see a current ratio that is considerably higher than that for a typical hotel. On December 31, he instructs his accountant to make up journal entries on that date to record the sale of all of the hotel's marketable securities and the use of the cash proceeds to reduce accounts payable (even though none were actually sold). In this way, the December 31 balance sheet will show a current ratio much higher than it actually is. The accountant was also instructed to reverse the journal entries on January 1. Discuss the ethics of this situation.

EXERCISES

4.1 A restaurant reported the following current assets: cash $12,000, credit card receivables $1,800, accounts receivable $180, food inventory $4,400, and prepaid expenses, $1,120. Current liabilities total $7,800. Answer the following:

a. Calculate the current ratio.

b. Calculate the quick ratio (acid test ratio).

4.2 Referring to information in Exercise 4.1, calculate working capital and describe what it means.

4.3 On March 31, a restaurant reported credit card revenues of $56,280. Credit card receivables began with a balance of $2,884 and ended the month with a balance of $3,120. Answer the following:

a. What is the average of credit card receivables?

b. What does credit card receivables represent as a percentage of total credit card revenue?

4.4   The following is an extract of restaurant and beverage operation for two months of operations:

	Month 1	Month 2
Cash	$11,270	$13,524
Credit card receivables	2,890	2,933
Accounts receivable	289	301
Total Quick Assets	$14,449	$16,758

Complete a common-size vertical analysis of quick assets for both months and comment on the changes to quick assets liquidity. Round answers to the nearest tenth of a percentage.

4.5   A restaurant operation shows a cash flow from operations for the operating year of $40,400. The beginning total current liabilities were $58,200 and ending total current liabilities were $60,800. Answer the following:

a.   What is the average of current liabilities for the year?

b.   What is the cash flow from operating activities to current liabilities?

c.   Does this cash flow from operations to current liabilities meet or exceed the recommended percentage?

4.6   Total current assets reported for an operation were $86,100 and total current liabilities were $62,400. Determine working capital for the period and define its structure and purpose.

4.7   A restaurant and beverage operation reported the following for the operating month of March. March has 23 operating days.

	1 March	March 31	Cost of Sales
Food service inventory:	$8,868	$5,740	$36,520

For the month of March, calculate the food inventory turnover ratio and average period in days it takes for food inventory to turn over.

4.8   Information showing total assets and total liabilities for two consecutive operating years is given below:

	Year 0003	Year 0004
Total assets	$486,400	$512,240
Total liabilities	$330,752	$347,290

Calculate the total assets to total liabilities ratio for both years and comment on the change.

4.9 Assume you were given information regarding current ratios for three consecutive years. Can you determine the general condition of working capital without an actual calculation? If the following ratios apply to a restaurant, would the ratio for year 3 be considered adequate?

	Year 1	Year 2	Year 3
Current ratio	1.44:1	1.35:1	1.20:1

State your answer to the questions.

4.10 Conduct a comparative, horizontal analysis of the change in each current asset account from year 1 to year 2. Express each change in dollars and the percentage each change represents. Comment on each change that exceeds 10%.

Current Assets	Year 1	Year 2
Cash	$12,800	$14,720
Credit card receivables	2,800	3,360
Accounts receivable	420	100
Food inventories	4,280	4,366
Beverage inventories	1,850	1,702
Prepaid expenses	1,400	1,610
Total Current Assets	$23,550	$25,858

PROBLEMS

4.1 A hotel provided the following information for year 0006: The cash flow from operating activities was $143,200, average current liabilities were $68,300, average long-term liabilities were $823,300, and total revenue for the year was $2,406,800. Calculate the following ratios:

a. The cash flow from operating activities to current liabilities ratio.

b. The cash flow for operating activities to long-term liabilities ratio.

c. The cash flow from operating activities margin.

4.2 You have the following information regarding current assets and current liabilities of a restaurant operation for two successive years:

Current Assets	Year 0003	Year 0004
Cash	$11,500	$15,700
Credit card receivables	3,720	4,880
Accounts receivable	480	220
Marketable securities	12,500	15,500
Inventories	5,600	8,100
Prepaid expenses	2,100	2,800
Total Current Assets	$35,900	$47,200

Current Liabilities	Year 0003	Year 0004
Accounts payable	$ 9,600	$13,100
Accrued expenses payable	4,700	6,200
Taxes payable	6,800	7,400
Interest payable	500	600
Current mortgage payable	11,200	9,900
Total Current Liabilities	$32,800	$37,200

Calculate the following for years 0003 and 0004:

a. Working capital

b. Current ratio

c. Quick ratio

Revenue for year 0004 is $544,800. The composition of revenue is cash 34%, credit card revenue 63.5%, and accounts receivable credit revenue 2.5%. For year 0004, calculate the following:

d. Credit card receivables as a percentage of credit card revenue

e. Credit card receivables turnover ratio

f. Credit card average collection period

g. Accounts receivable as a percentage of accounts receivable credit revenue

h. Accounts receivable turnover ratio

i. Accounts receivable average collection period

j. Cost of sales was $212,472; calculate cost of sales as a percentage of sales revenue

k. Comment on what these ratios tell you about the restaurant?

4.3 With reference to the information in problem 4.2, use a common-size vertical analysis to determine the composition of current assets and current liabilities for years 0003 and 0004. Discuss the results.

4.4 A fire occurred in a friend's restaurant overnight on December 31, year 0005 and the friend has asked for your help. Although many accounting records were lost, some were recovered. With the recovered records and information obtained from outside sources, you believe a balance sheet can be reconstructed for the period ending on the date of the fire. The information provided by the friend is:

- The forecasted current ratio as of December 31, year 0005 was 1.25 to 1.
- Balance sheets for the previous three years indicated that current assets on average represented 25% of total assets.
- The bank reported the year-end bank balance was $763. It was estimated that $1,000 in the restaurant's safe was destroyed during the fire.
- The bank also indicated that it is owed $23,000 on a long-term note and the current amount due in year 0006 is $3,414.
- The value of ending inventories was $4,915.
- Restaurant suppliers indicated that in total they were owed $3,210 at the close of business on December 31, year 0005.
- All employees were paid up to and including the night of the fire.

Calculate the following:

a. Calculate total current assets.

b. Calculate credit card receivables assuming current assets consisted only of cash, credit card receivables, and inventories.

c. Calculate total assets.

d. Prepare a balance sheet as of December 31, year 0005 to give to your friend.

4.5 You have the following information taken from balance sheet for two successive years for a hotel operation.

	Year 0002	Year 0003
Total assets	$411,200	$395,700
Total liabilities	302,400	315,500
Total stockholders' equity	108,800	80,200

For each year calculate:

a. Total assets to total liabilities ratio.

b. Total liabilities to total assets ratio.

c. Total liabilities to total ownership equity.

Discuss the changes that have taken place over the two-year period from the viewpoint of an investor who has been asked to loan the hotel money for expansion.

4.6   In addition to the information given in problem 4.5, an income statement for the hotel for year 0003 is shown below:

Sales revenue	$851,800
Operating costs	(798,900)
Operating income, before interest and tax	$ 52,900
Less: Interest	(26,100)
Income before tax	$ 26,800
Less: Income tax	(6,700)
Net Income	$ 20,100

For year 0003, calculate the following:

a. Return on assets

b. Net return on assets

c. Number of times interest is earned

d. Net income to revenue ratio and discuss hotel profitability

e. Return on stockholders' equity and discuss hotel profitability

4.7   You have the following information from a restaurant operation:

Balance Sheets, December 31st

Assets	Year 0007	Year 0008
Cash	$ 6,100	$ 11,200
Credit card receivables	7,920	9,240
Accounts receivable	5,280	6,160
Food inventory	14,600	13,900
Prepaid expenses	3,800	4,500
Land	32,000	32,000
Building	315,800	323,200
Equipment	66,640	73,200
Furnishings	16,660	18,300
Accumulated depreciation	(113,700)	(124,500)
Total assets	$355,100	$367,200

Balance Sheets, December 31st

Liabilities & Stockholders' Equity	Year 0007	Year 0008
Accounts payable	$ 16,700	$ 12,500
Bank note payable	4,900	3,600
Income tax payable	12,500	12,600
Accrued expenses payable	7,100	7,500
Mortgage payable (current)	10,400	12,100
Long-term mortgage payable	192,000	180,900
Common stock	10,000	10,000
Retained earnings	101,500	128,000
Liabilities & Stockholders' Equity	$355,100	$367,200

Income Statement, Condensed
For the Year Ending December 31, 0008

Sales revenue		$742,600
Cost of sales	$301,900	
Operating expenses	381,200	
Total Operating Costs		(683,100)
Operating income, before interest and tax		$ 59,500
Interest expense		(19,400)
Income before tax		$ 40,100
Income tax		(12,600)
Net Income		$ 27,500

Note: Sales revenue consisted of: 22% cash, 64% credit cards, and 14% on accounts receivable.

From the information given, calculate the following:

a. Working capital for years 0007 and 0008.

b. Current ratio for years 0007 and 0008.

c. Credit card receivables as a percentage of credit card revenue for year 0008.

d. Credit card receivables turnover ratio based on credit card revenue for year 0008.

e. Credit card receivables average collection period ratio based on credit card revenue for year 0008.

f. Accounts receivable as a percentage of accounts receivable credit revenue for year 0008.

g. Accounts receivable turnover ratio based on accounts receivable credit revenue for year 0008.

h. Accounts receivable average collection period based on accounts receivable credit revenue for year 0008.

i. Total assets to total liabilities for years 0007 and 0008.

j. Total liabilities to total assets for years 0007 and 0008.

k. Total liabilities to stockholders' equity for years 0007 and 0008.

l. Return on total assets for year 0008.

m. Number of times interest is earned for year 0008.

n. Net income to total revenue ratio for year 0008.

o. Return on stockholders' equity for year 0008.

p. Food inventory turnover ratio for year 0008.

q. Property plant and equipment (fixed assets) turnover ratio for year 0008.

Comment on any of the calculated ratios that appear unusually high or low or totally out of range of what is considered acceptable.

4.8 The owners of a cocktail bar have the following annual income statement information:

Annual sales revenue	$210,000
Cost of sales (30% of revenue)	60,000
Payroll expense	50,000
Other operating expenses	20,000
Direct expenses (charges including depreciation)	40,000

The owners are considering new furnishings for the bar at an estimated cost of $20,000 using their own funds. They anticipate the new furnishings will bring in additional customers and their revenue will increase by 10% above their current level. The new furnishings are estimated to have a five-year life with no residual value. The new furnishings will be depreciated using straight-line depreciation.

To provide service to the additional customers, more staff would be hired at an additional cost of $125 per week. Other operating costs will increase by $1,400 per year. There will be no increase to direct (fixed) charges other than depreciation expense. The income tax rate will remain at 25%. The owners will go ahead with the project only if the return on their $20,000 investment is 15% per year or more in the first year.

a. Should they make the $20,000 investment in new furnishings?

b. If they had the alternative of using only $10,000 of their own funds and borrowing the other $10,000 at 10% interest, would the decision change?

4.9 A restaurant has the following statistical information calculated from its financial statements for the past three years:

	Year 0007	Year 0008	Year 0009
Current ratio	1.04:1	1.25:1	1.40:1
Credit card turnover ratio	70 times	64 times	61 times
Accounts receivable turnover	18 times	24 times	31 times
Food inventory turnover ratio	37 times	28 times	22 times
Total liabilities to total equity	2.75:1	2.4:1	1.95:
Return on stockholders' equity	9.72%	9.51%	8.74%
Annual revenue	$875,400	$881,900	$879,300

Using this information, answer each of the following questions and explain your answer. A simple, yes, no, more, less, or maybe won't do!

a. Are current assets in relation to current liabilities increasing or decreasing?

b. Is the restaurant becoming more or less efficient in the collection of its credit card receivables?

c. Is the restaurant becoming more or less efficient in the collection of its accounts receivable?

d. Over the three-year period, has more or less money been tied up in food inventory?

e. With the stockholders' viewpoint in mind, is the profitability improving or not improving?

f. If the restaurant needed to borrow capital through long-term debt, would it be easier to find a lender now than three years ago?

g. Has the restaurant been using leverage to the advantage of the stockholders over the three-year period?

4.10 A restaurant has the following statistical information calculated from its financial statements for the past three years:

	Year 0001	Year 0002	Year 0003
Current ratio	1.24:1	1.18:1	1.05:1
Credit card turnover ratio	91 times	93 times	98 times
Accounts receivable turnover	14 times	24 times	31 times
Food inventory turnover ratio	38 times	44 times	48 times
Total liabilities to total equity	1.94:1	2.52:1	2.95:1

Return on stockholders' equity	7.72%	9.58%	9.88%
Annual revenue	$880,000	$882,500	$872,300

Using this information, answer each of the following questions and explain your answer. A simple, yes, no, more, less, or maybe won't do!

a. Are current assets in relation to current liabilities increasing or decreasing?

b. Is the restaurant becoming more or less efficient in the collection of its credit card receivables?

c. Is the restaurant becoming more or less efficient in the collection of its accounts receivable?

d. Over the three-year period, has more or less money been tied up in food inventory?

e. With the stockholders' viewpoint in mind, is the profitability improving or not improving?

f. If the restaurant needed to borrow capital through long-term debt, would it be easier to find a lender now than three years ago?

g. Has the restaurant been using leverage to the advantage of the stockholders over the three-year period?

4.11 A Resort Hotel has 75 guest rooms and a small dining room with 40 seats. The hotel recorded the following information for the month of March.

1. Room revenue was $91,108.

2. A total of 1,798 rooms were occupied.

3. A total of 3,417 guests are using the 1,798 rooms occupied.

4. Dining room food revenue was $45,209.

5. Dining room beverage revenue was $14,810.

6. The dining room serviced a total of 3,720 guests.

7. Cost of sales food was $18,904.

8. Cost of sales beverage was $4,805.

9. Guest rooms labor costs were $30,020.

10. Dining room labor costs were $15,011.

Calculate the following for the Resort Hotel:

a. Average rate per room occupied

b. Rooms occupancy percentage

c. Room double occupancy percentage

d. Food cost percentage

e. Beverage cost percentage

f. Rooms labor cost percentage

g. Dining room labor cost percentage

h. Average check, dining room

i. Dining room average seat turnover

j. Average monthly revenue per dining room seat

k. Beverage revenue to food revenue percentage

l. Beverage revenue to room revenue percentage

m. Dining revenue to rooms revenue percentage

4.12 Owners of a catering company also own a number of relatively small restaurants, one of which shows excellent potential to increase its revenue. Selected annual operating figures are:

Annual sales revenue	$120,000
Cost of sales (40% of revenue)	48,000
Payroll expense	33,600
Other operating expenses	24,000

Based on the potential of increasing revenue, the owners are seriously considering a ten-year lease on an adjoining property, which requires a full ten-year up front payment of $25,000. New equipment at a cost of $10,000 would have to be purchased. The equipment is estimated to have a ten-year life and no residual value. An additional investment in food inventory of $400 would be required.

Revenue is estimated to increase by 20% above the present level and the cost of sales is expected to remain at the current cost of sales percentage. Payroll costs are expected to increase by $75 per week and other costs by $40 per week. A minimum 15%, pretax return on the investment is wanted by the owners.

a. Should the investment be made?

b. As an alternative, the owners are considering borrowing $20,000 of the required investment at a 10% interest rate. Would the decision change if debt financing were obtained rather than the owners using their funds?

CASE 4

With reference to the 4C Company's balance sheet and income statement (Case 2) for the year ending December 31, 0001, calculate each of the following. (If two values are not given to calculate an average when needed, use the number shown as the average.)

a. Working capital

b. Current ratio

c. Quick ratio

d. Credit card receivables average collection period (assume credit card revenue is 60% of total revenue)

e. Accounts receivable average collection period (assume accounts receivable is 10% of total revenue)

f. Net return on assets (use December 31, 0001 total assets as average assets)

g. Net income to total sales revenue ratio

h. Return on stockholders' equity

i. Food inventory turnover ratio

j. Beverage inventory turnover ratio

k. Cost of sales percentage, food

l. Cost of sales percentage, beverages

   (1) In order to conserve cash during the first year of operation, Mr. Driver has limited his salary to $1,500 per month. Are the funds being withdrawn as a salary considered as a deductible operating expense to the "4C" Company?

   (2) Prepare a short discussion of each calculated ratio, which you believe may be unsatisfactory, and explain why.

   (3) It appears "4C" has a good liquid cash position and Mr. Driver is considering using $20,000 of "4C" cash to redeem some of his shares of common stock before the final financial statements of the current year are prepared, and he asks for your opinion. Review any of the preceding ratios that will be effected by the repurchase of the stock and discuss the effects if the stock repurchase is made.

5

Internal Control

This chapter explains the objectives of internal control and discusses some of the reasons why internal control for hospitality operations is more difficult than for some other businesses.

The chapter continues by discussing some of the principles of internal control, such as implementing controls as preventative procedures, management's having an effective philosophy of control, monitoring the control system, selecting and training employees, establishing responsibilities and preparing written control procedures, maintaining adequate records, separating record keeping and asset control, limiting access to assets, conducting surprise checks, dividing the responsibility for related transactions, rotating jobs, using machines for control, establishing standards and evaluating results, using forms and reports, bonding employees, requiring mandatory vacations, using external audits, providing audit trails, numbering all control documents, and ensuring continuous system review.

Control of purchases is discussed. The documents that aid in this are illustrated and explained, and the proper procedures for product storage and inventory control are outlined.

Specific controls required for cash receipts and cash disbursements, including the use of a voucher system, are also discussed. A monthly bank reconciliation, as an aspect of control of disbursements, is illustrated.

The setting of performance standards and evaluating actual results with those standards is demonstrated with reference to control over food cost.

The chapter concludes with listings of various methods of loss or fraud that could occur in such areas as delivery and receipt of merchandise, cash funds, accounts payable and payroll, food and beverage sales, and in the front office of a hotel or motel.

CHAPTER OBJECTIVES

After studying this chapter, the reader should be able to:

1. Define the purpose of internal control.
2. Briefly describe the two basic requirements for good internal control.
3. Briefly discuss some of the basic principles of good internal control, such as defining job responsibilities, separating record keeping from control of assets, and dividing responsibilities for related tasks.
4. Explain how "lapping" can be used for fraudulent purposes.
5. List and briefly discuss each of the five control documents used to control purchases.
6. List and discuss the proper procedures for product storage and inventory control.
7. Describe how a petty cash fund operates.
8. Explain briefly how control can be established over cash receipts and cash disbursements.
9. List the procedures necessary to control payroll disbursements.
10. Complete a bank reconciliation.
11. Calculate a standard food or beverage cost from given information.

INTERNAL CONTROL

This text discusses management accounting and management control systems. It is the understanding and effective use of information provided by management accounting that management uses, makes, and implements decisions to safeguard the assets, control costs, increase sales revenue, and maximize profitability. The information provided must be accurate and current to assist to managers in carrying out their responsibilities. Effective and efficient internal control policies and procedures apply to all facets of an establishment's operations, from purchases through sales, control, and accountability of cash receipts, cash disbursements, and the many other assets an organization has to conduct operations.

Internal control objectives

In a small, owner-operated business, such as an independent restaurant or small motel, very few internal controls are required since the control is carried out by the owner who handles all the cash coming in and payments going out and, by his or her presence, ensures the smooth and efficient operation of the business.

Organizational charts

In larger establishments, one-person control is no longer feasible. In fact, in larger organizations it is necessary to organize operations into various departments and to draw up a plan of the organization, or an organization chart. Indeed, the organization chart itself is the foundation of a good internal control system since it establishes lines of communication and levels of authority and responsibility.

Organization charts for various types and sizes of hospitality establishments are illustrated in Exhibits 5.1, 5.2, 5.3, 5.4, and 5.5. In large establishments, as the organization charts show, lines of authority, responsibility, and communication become more complex. Therefore, the internal control system in a large establishment will also be more complex.

Exhibit 5.1   Organization Chart for 50-room Motel

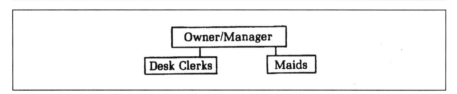

Source: M. Coltman, 1989. *Cost Control for the Hospitality Industry.* New York: Van Nostrand Reinhold.

Exhibit 5.2   Organization Chart for 120-seat Coffee Shop

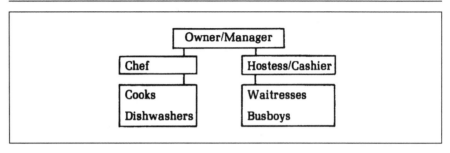

Source: M. Coltman, 1989. *Cost Control for the Hospitality Industry.* New York: Van Nostrand Reinhold.

Exhibit 5.3   Organization Chart for 150-room Motor Hotel with 100-seat Dining Room and 80-seat Cocktail Lounge

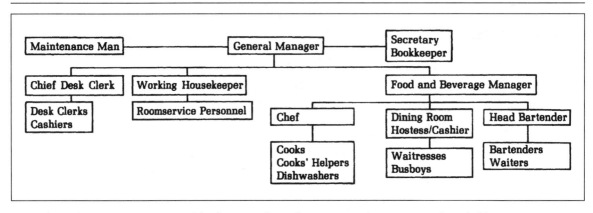

Source: M. Coltman, 1989. *Cost Control for the Hospitality Industry.* New York: Van Nostrand Reinhold.

Exhibit 5.4   Organization Chart for Restaurant Complex

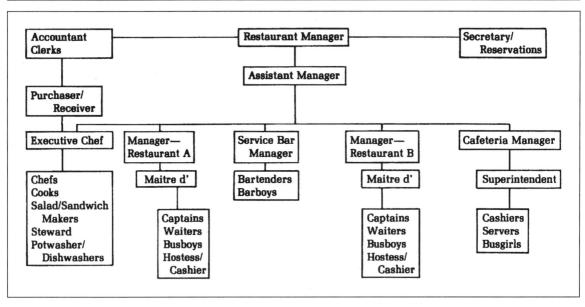

Source: M. Coltman, 1989. *Cost Control for the Hospitality Industry.* New York: Van Nostrand Reinhold.

Exhibit 5.5   Organization Chart for a Very Large Hotel with Full Facilities

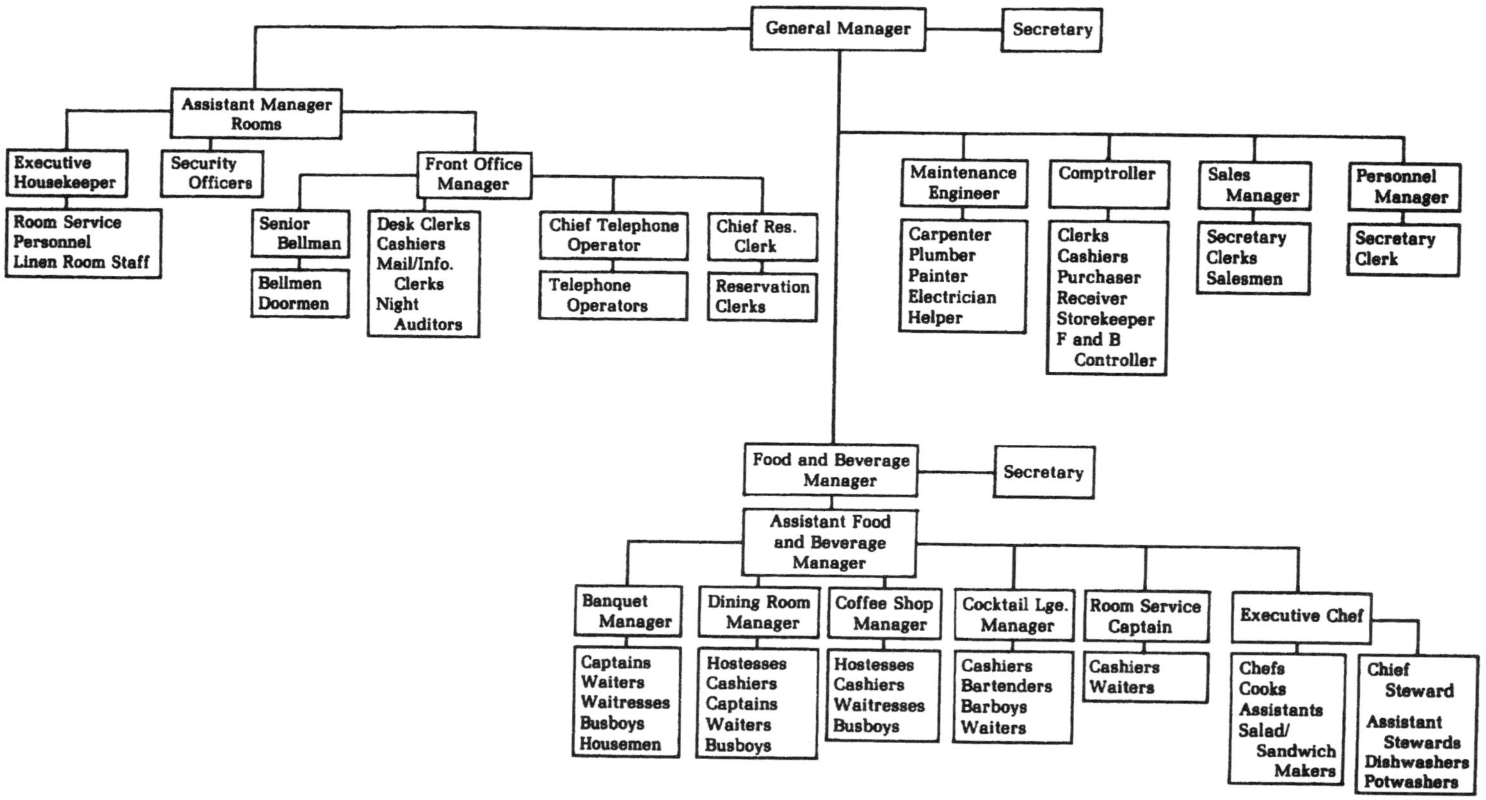

Source: M. Coltman, 1989. *Cost Control for the Hospitality Industry.* New York: Van Nostrand Reinhold.

195

A system of internal control encompasses the following two broad requirements:

Requriements of system

- Methods and procedures for the employees in the various job categories to follow in order to ensure that they follow management policies, achieve operational efficiency, and protect assets from waste, theft, or fraud. Assets are defined as cash, accounts receivable, inventory, equipment, buildings, and land. The types of safeguards needed include the use of safes for holding large sums of cash, use of locked storerooms for inventories of food and beverage, access restrictions to locations where cash and products are stored, and maintenance of all equipment in efficient working order.
- Reliable forms and reports that will measure the efficiency and effectiveness of the employees and provide information, usually of an accounting or financial nature, that, when analyzed, will identify problem area. This information must be accurate and timely if it is to be useful. It must also be cost effective; in other words, the benefits (cost savings) of an internal control system must be greater than the cost of its implementation and continuation. Information produced must also be useful. If the information is invalid and cannot be used, then effort and money have been wasted.

Requirements in conflict

It may seem that these two major requirements are in conflict. For example, the procedures used to store and safeguard food products and the paperwork requirements to obtain those products from storage may be so cumbersome that employees in departments (such as the dining room) that need those products do not bother to replenish depleted stocks. As a result, the operation's efficiency is reduced and sales may be lost. Alternatively, if employees complete all paperwork requirements to ensure they always have sufficient products on hand, the added labor cost may exceed potential losses of products from theft or waste.

Although in this chapter we shall be viewing internal control primarily from an accounting point of view, control is not limited to financial matters. For example, an establishment's personnel policies are part of the system of internal control. A company's policies on such matters as employee skill upgrading and education are important since they are eventually reflected in the company's financial results.

SPECIAL PROBLEMS

Although most businesses have many shared problems relating to internal control, the hospitality business has some unique problems that often complicate and make more difficult the implementation of total control. Some of these characteristics are discussed.

BUSINESS SIZE

Just about every hospitality operation (even if the individual property is part of a large international chain) can be described as a small business, and it is generally more difficult for a small business to have as comprehensive a control system as a large business.

CASH TRANSACTIONS

Use of cash

Even though many hospitality industry customers today use credit cards to pay for their transactions, there are still many others who continue to pay cash (particularly in restaurants and beverage outlets). This means that there is a great deal of cash accumulating in sales departments each day, making it easy for some of this cash to "disappear." To further complicate cash handling and its control, many hospitality operations have some departments operating on a three-shift basis around the clock.

INVENTORY PRODUCTS

Even though the assets in inventory for most hospitality operations are only a small proportion of total assets, many individual products forming those inventories (such as bottles of quality wine and expensive containers of food products) are valuable to dishonest employees, who may be tempted to remove them from the establishment for personal consumption or even to sell them for personal gain.

HIGH EMPLOYEE TURNOVER

Lack of training

Finally, the industry is characterized by a much higher employee turnover rate than most other businesses. This means that employees often do not receive the length of training time that many of them need (because they are often unskilled), nor do they have the same loyalty to the operation that long-time employees often develop.

PRINCIPLES OF INTERNAL CONTROL

Some of the basic principles that provide a solid foundation for a good internal control system are discussed in the following sections.

Establish Preventative Procedures

Internal control procedures need to be preventative. In other words, they should be established so that they minimize and/or prevent theft. This is much more effective than suffering losses from theft or fraud and having a system that detects the culprits only after the event.

Enterprise Management Supervision

The majority of employees are honest by nature, but, because of a poor internal control system, or, worse still, complete absence of any controls, employees become dishonest because temptation is put in their way. If management does not care, why should the employees?

Management
supervision required

Control systems, by themselves, do not solve all problems. The implementation of a control system does not remove from management the necessity to observe constantly the effectiveness of the system by supervision. A control system does not *prevent* fraud or theft; but the system may point out that it is happening. Also, some forms of fraud or theft may never be discovered even with an excellent control system. Collusion (two or more employees working together for dishonest purposes) may go undetected for long periods of time. The important fact to remember is that no system of control can be perfect. An effective manager will always be alert to this fact.

Monitor Systems

System redundancy

Any system of control must also be monitored to ensure that it is continuing to provide the desired information. The system must therefore be flexible enough to be changed to suit different needs. If a reporting form needs to be changed, then it should be changed. If a form becomes redundant, then it should be scrapped entirely or replaced by one that is more suitable. To have employees complete forms that no one subsequently looks at is a costly exercise, and employees quickly become disillusioned when there seems to be no purpose to what they are asked to do.

Institute Employee Selection and Training System

Important aspects of effective internal control are employee competence, trustworthiness, and training. This means having a good system of screening job applicants, selecting employees and providing employee orientation, on-the-job training, and periodic evaluation. Obviously, supervisory personnel must also be competent, with skills in maintaining the operation's standards, motivating employees they supervise, preparing staffing schedules, maintaining employee morale (to reduce the cost of employee turnover), and implementing procedures to control labor and other costs. A poor supervisor will fail to extract the full potential from employees and will thus add to the operation's cost.

ESTABLISH RESPONSIBILITIES

Who does it?

One of the prerequisites for good internal control is to clearly define the responsibilities for tasks. This goes beyond designing an organization chart. For example, in the case of deliveries of food to a hotel, who will do the receiving? Will it be the chef, the storekeeper, a person whose sole function is to be receiver, or anybody who happens to be close to the receiving door when a delivery is made? Once the designated person is established, that person must be given a list of receiving procedures, preferably in writing, so that if errors or discrepancies arise, that person can be held accountable.

PREPARE WRITTEN PROCEDURES

Document policy and procedures

As mentioned, once procedures have been established for each area and for each job category where control is needed, these procedures should be put into writing. In this way employees will know what the policy and procedures are. Written procedures are particularly important in the hospitality industry where turnover of employees is relatively high and continuous employee training to support the system of internal control is necessary.

It is impossible in this chapter to establish procedures that will fit every possible situation in the hospitality industry because of the wide variety of types, sizes, and styles of operation. Even in two establishments of similar nature and size, the procedures for any specific control area may differ due to management policy, type of customer, layout of the establishment, or numerous other reasons. However, for illustrative purposes only, the following might be the way a written set of procedures could be prepared for the receiver in a food operation:

Typical steps in food receiving

1. Count each item that can be counted (number of cases or number of individual items).
2. Weigh each item that is delivered by weight (such as meat).
3. Check the count or weight figure against the count or weight figure on the invoice accompanying the delivery.
4. Check that the items are of the quality desired.
5. If specifications were prepared and sent to the supplier, check the quality against these specifications.
6. Spot check case goods to ensure that they are full and that all items in the case are of the same quality.

7. Check prices on invoice against prices quoted on the market quotation sheet.

8. If goods were delivered without an invoice, prepare a memorandum invoice listing name of supplier, date of delivery, count or weight of items, and, from the market quotation sheet, price of the items.

9. If goods are short-shipped or if quality is not acceptable, prepare a credit memorandum invoice listing items returned and obtaining delivery driver's signature acknowledging he has taken the items back or that they were short-shipped. Staple this credit memorandum to the original invoice.

10. Store all items in proper storage locations as soon after delivery as possible.

11. Send all invoices and credit memoranda to the accounting office so that extensions and totals can be checked and then be recorded.

As another example, the following could be a set of procedures for front office staff of a hotel or motel for the handling of credit cards:

Typical procedures for credit card verification

1. When the guest checks in: Ask whether payment will be by credit card or some other method.

2. If it is to be by credit card, ask to see the card.

3. Verify that the card is one acceptable to this hotel (such as American Express, Diners Club, Carte Blanc, Visa, or MasterCard).

4. If acceptable, check date on card to make sure it has not expired.

5. Copy credit card number and name as it appears on the card in the space provided on the guest's folio (account).

6. As you return the card, remind the guest to see the front office cashier before departing to verify the accuracy of the account and sign the credit card voucher for the charge.

7. Before filing the folio with the cashier, check the credit card number to make sure it is not on the credit card company's cancellation list. If it is, advise the front office manager of the situation.

8. Initial the credit card number on the folio to show that the card has been checked against the cancellation list and is not listed.

Credit card checkout procedures

When the guest checks out:

9. Check the guest account to ensure the credit card number has been initialed.

10. If it has not been, check the cancellation list and advise the front office manager if it is listed. Do not return the card to the guest.

11. If not listed, complete the appropriate credit card company voucher, using the imprinter.

12. Have the guest sign the voucher. Check the voucher signature against the credit card signature.

13. Return the credit card to the guest with his/her copy of the voucher.

MAINTAIN ADEQUATE RECORDS

Written records required

Another important consideration for good internal control is to have good written records. For example, for food deliveries there should be, at the very least, a written record on a daily order sheet of what is to be delivered, from which suppliers, and at what prices. In this way the designated receiver can check invoices (which accompany the delivered goods) both against the actual goods and against the order form. The larger the establishment, the more written records might be necessary, such as a market quotation sheet so that some responsible person can be designated to obtain quotes from two or more suppliers before any orders are placed. Without good records employees will be less concerned about doing a good job. The forms, reports, and other records that are part of the internal control system will depend entirely on the size and type of establishment.

SEPARATE RECORD KEEPING AND CONTROL OF ASSETS

City ledger (accounts receivable) control

One of the most important principles of good internal control is to separate the functions of recording information about assets and the actual control of the assets. Consider the accounts of the guests who have left a hotel and have charged their accounts to a credit card or company. Such accounts are an asset—accounts receivable—and in some hotels are left in the front office until payment is made. These accounts are known as city ledger accounts. Checks received in payment are given to the front office cashier, who then records the payments on the accounts. These checks, along with other cash and checks received from departing guests, are turned in as part of the total remittance at the end of the cashier's shift. There is nothing wrong with this procedure as long as the cashier is honest!

Lapping

A dishonest cashier could, however, practice a procedure known as lapping. Mr. X left the hotel and his account for $175 is one of the accounts receivable. When he receives his statement at the month-end, he sends in his check for $175. The cashier does not record the payment on Mr. X's account. Instead, the check is simply put in the cash drawer and $175 in cash is removed for personal use by the cashier. The cashier's remittance at the end of the shift will balance, but Mr. X's account will still show an outstanding balance of

$175. When Mr. Y, who has an account in the city ledger for $285, sends in his payment, the cashier records $175 as a payment on Mr. X's account, puts the $285 check in the cash drawer and removes a further $110 in cash for personal use. A few days later Mr. Z's payment of $350 on his city ledger account is received. The cashier records $285 on Mr. Y's account, puts the $350 check in the cash drawer and takes out $65 more in cash. This lapping of accounts will eventually snowball to the point where the cashier can no longer cover a particular account and the fraud will be discovered. However, the outstanding account may be so large that the misappropriated cash cannot be recovered from the dishonest cashier.

Procedures to prevent lapping

To aid in preventing this type of loss, the separation of cash receiving and recording on accounts should be instituted. Checks or cash received in the mail in payment for city ledger accounts could be kept in the accounting office for direct deposit to the bank. The front office cashier is simply given a list of account names and amounts received, and the appropriate accounts can be credited without the cashier handling any money. This procedure may not, however, prevent collusion between the person in the accounting office and the cashier.

The separation of asset control and asset recording does not pertain only to cash. For example, inventories of food and beverage in a storeroom may be controlled (received and issued) by a storekeeper, but it is often a good idea to have the records of what is in the storeroom (for example, perpetual inventory cards) maintained by some other person.

Limit Access to Assets

The number of employees who have access to assets such as cash and inventory should be limited because the larger the number of employees with access, the greater is the potential for loss from theft or fraud. In the same way, the amount of cash and inventory should be kept to a minimum. This requires a

Balancing act

balancing act, because cashiers need to have enough cash to make change and the stores departments need sufficient inventory so that they are not continually running out of products and unable to satisfy customer demand. Also, control procedures for access to those assets should not be so cumbersome that they severely restrict access.

Conduct Surprise Checks

Surprise checks (such as counting cash or taking inventory) should be carried out at unusual times. Two principles are involved here. First, these checks should be performed by an employee independent of that part of the operation. In other words, the person who normally takes the month-end storeroom inventory should not be the person who takes the surprise check. Second, such checks should be carried out frequently enough that they become routine, but without following a predictable pattern.

Divide the Responsibility for Related Transactions

One person verifies the work of another

The reason for suggesting that the responsibility for related transactions should be separated is to have the work of one person verified by the work of another. This is not to suggest duplication of work—that would be costly—but to have two tasks that must be carried out for control reasons done by two separate employees.

Cash register possibilities of error

For example, many restaurants record items sold and their prices on hand-written sales checks. These checks, when the customers pay, are then inserted in a cash register that prints the total amount paid on the sales check and on a continuous audit tape. At the end of the shift or the day the machine is cleared, that is, the total sales are printed on the audit tape and the audit tape is removed by the accounting department. The total cash turned in should agree with the total sales on the audit tape. But even if there is agreement, there is no guarantee that the audit tape figure is correct. Overrings or underrings could occur, or a sales check may have been rung up more than once or not rung up at all or may have been rung up without being inserted in the register.

Audit of sales checks

Because of all these possibilities, further control over sales checks is needed. First, the prices, extensions, and additions of all sales checks should be verified (if time does not allow this daily, then it should be done on a spot-check basis). Then the sequence of numbers of sales checks turned in should be verified to make sure there are no missing sales checks. Finally, an adding machine listing of sales checks should be made. Assuming no errors on this adding machine listing, it will be the total on this listing against which cash turned in should be reconciled. If no errors were made by the cashier, the register audit tape will also agree with the adding machine listing.

The job of verifying sales checks for prices, extensions, and additions; of ensuring there are no missing sales checks; and of preparing the adding machine tape should be carried out by a person other than the cashier. In this way the responsibility for sales control is divided, and one person's work is verified by another. The cost of the second person's time will probably be more than recovered in increased net income as a result of reduction of losses from undiscovered errors.

Explain the Reasons

Sales check losses

Employees who carry out internal control functions should have the reasons they are asked to perform these tasks explained to them. For example, in the previous section it was suggested a second person verify the work of the cashier. The losses that can occur from servers making errors in pricing items on sales checks, in multiplying prices by quantities, and in totaling sales checks could add up to many dollars. So could losses from missing sales checks where the cash was paid by the customer, but a dishonest server or cashier kept the cash and destroyed the sales check. The importance of ensuring the minimization of these losses should be explained to the employee doing the task.

ROTATE JOBS

Job rotation reduces collusion possibilities

Wherever possible, jobs should be rotated. Obviously this cannot be easily done in a small establishment with few employees. In a larger operation, cashiers could be moved from one department to another from time to time, or accounting office employees could have their jobs rotated every few months. Employees knowing they are not going to be doing the same job for a long length of time will be less likely to be dishonest. The possibilities of collusion are also reduced. Job rotation also has another advantage in that it prevents employees from becoming bored from constantly carrying out the same tasks. It also builds flexibility into job assignments and will give the employees a better understanding of how the various jobs relate to each other.

USE MACHINES

Machines aid in control

Whenever possible, machines should be used. Although machines cannot prevent all possibilities of theft or fraud, they can vastly reduce these possibilities. The installation of a machine may also reduce labor cost if an employee is no longer required to perform a task manually. Such machines include front office billing/audit equipment, restaurant and bar cash registers and/or precheck machines, and mechanical or electronic drink dispensing bar equipment. For example, an electronic, preset, precheck restaurant register will eliminate many of the losses from the types of errors mentioned earlier. Also, the saving in labor (because the manual verifications will no longer be required) will contribute toward the cost of the equipment.

SET STANDARDS AND EVALUATE RESULTS

One of the requirements of a good internal control system is not only to control the obvious visible items, such as cash or inventory, but also to have a reporting system that indicates whether or not all aspects of the business are operating properly.

Food cost percentage standard

For example, one of the many benchmarks used in the food industry to measure the effectiveness of the business is the food cost percentage. Management needs to know whether the food cost percentage actually achieved is close to the standard desired.

Later in this chapter we shall see how cost control standards can be established and actual results evaluated.

Design Forms and Reports

Once procedures have been definitely established and the various employees given detailed written guidelines about how to perform tasks, standards of performance should be established and results evaluated. This will require designing forms and reports to provide information about all aspects of the business. Properly designed forms or reports will provide management with the information it needs to determine whether standards are being met and to make decisions that will improve the standards, increase performance, and ultimately produce higher profits. The manager's daily report, shown earlier in Exhibit 4.6, is one type of form.

Another set of standards derives from budgets and budget reports that allow actual results to be compared with those budgeted. Budgets are discussed in Chapter 9.

Bond Employees

Fidelity bonds

Consideration should be given to bonding employees. For example, fidelity bonds protect the operation from losses incurred by employee dishonesty because the establishment is reimbursed (up to the face value of the insurance policy) for the amount of loss suffered.

Insist on Mandatory Vacations

Make vacations mandatory, particularly for employees who have control of assets. Employees inclined to be dishonest may be discouraged from theft or fraud if they know that during their vacation time some other person will have control of those assets and that, if theft or fraud has occurred, it may be discovered during this vacation time. Even if theft or fraud has not occurred, the new person doing the job may be able to discover weaknesses in the control system that were not previously apparent. Additional preventative controls can then be implemented.

Conduct External Audits

No guarantee

Use audits conducted by an outside firm. External audits do not guarantee that fraud or theft has not occurred, but if they have occurred they are more likely to be discovered by an objective outside firm of auditors.

MAKE AN AUDIT TRAIL

Most good internal control systems are based on having an audit trail that documents each transaction from the time that it was initiated through source documents (such as purchase orders or sales checks) and defined procedures through to the final recording of the transaction in the operation's general ledger. A good audit trail allows each transaction, where necessary, to be tracked again from its starting to its finishing points.

CONTROL DOCUMENTS

Sequential numbering

Wherever possible, all documents (such as sales checks, requisitions, and purchase orders) should be sequentially preprinted with a number. In this way, individual documents can be tracked and accounted for. Numbering is particularly important for revenue control forms, such as sales checks.

When numbered documents are issued, they should be signed for by the individual who receives them so that that person can be held responsible and accountable for them.

All control documents should be controlled by the accounting department even though they are actually used by employees in other departments. In other words, they should be designed, ordered, stored, issued, and have their usage controlled by the accounting office. It is also the accounting office's responsibility to periodically account for documents by checking the sequence of all numbered and used ones to ensure that none are missing.

SUPERVISE THE SYSTEM AND CONDUCT REVIEWS

Missing sales checks

One of the management's major responsibilities in internal control is constant supervision and review of the system. This supervision and review is necessary because the system becomes obsolete as business conditions change. Also, without continuous supervision the control system can collapse. For example, one of the important control techniques in a food service operation is to ensure each day that there are no missing, prenumbered checks on which sales are recorded. If an employee (after having served food and beverages, presented the sales check and collected the cash) retains both the sales check and the cash and is subsequently not questioned about this, he or she will realize that the control system is not working effectively. The employee is then free to continue to hold back sales checks and pocket cash.

Internal audit

In small operations, the supervision and review of the internal control system is the responsibility of the general manager. In larger establishments, with accounting departments, the supervision and review responsibility is turned over to the employees in that department. In the largest of companies, internal auditing teams will be established. They will be responsible for appraising the effectiveness of the operating and accounting controls, and verifying the reliability of forms, records, reports, and other supporting documentation to ensure that internal control policies and procedures are being followed and assets adequately safeguarded.

CONTROL OF PURCHASES

To understand the necessity for control of purchases, assume that, in a restaurant operation, every employee had the authority to buy food for resale and that there were no control procedures or forms in use. In such a situation there would be absolute confusion concerning what had been ordered and received. In addition there would be duplications, mistakes, over- and short shipments, payments for items not received, and constant opportunities for dishonest employees to commit theft or fraud.

In order to have control over purchasing, it is necessary to divide the responsibilities among several individuals or departments. Coordination over the various purchasing tasks is achieved using five basic documents:

Five control documents
- Purchase requisition
- Purchase order
- Invoice
- Receiving report
- Invoice approval form or stamp

Each of these is discussed in turn in the following sections.

Purchase Requisition

Centralized purchasing

In making purchases, those responsible for purchasing, whether it be employees of a purchasing department or an individual, cannot constantly be fully aware of the supply and service needs of the various operating departments. Generally, the responsibility for having an adequate supply of items in each department is delegated to each department manager. However, the department managers should not be allowed to deal directly with suppliers since control of purchasing could not then be coordinated. In order to have this control over purchases and the liabilities (accounts payable) that result, purchasing must be centralized. The purchaser, or the purchasing department, must be advised by each department manager of that department's supply requirements. This advice is made by means of a purchase requisition, prepared in triplicate. The original and duplicate are sent to the purchaser or purchasing department, the third copy is retained by the department head for later checking. A sample requisition is illustrated in Exhibit 5.6.

Exhibit 5.6   Sample Purchase Requisition

Date _____	Requested by _____	4964
Department _____	Department head checked _____	
Date required _____	Purchasing manager approved _____	

Note: Please use a separate purchase requisition
for each item or group of related items.

Description	Quantity	Purchase order number	Suggested supplier

Purchasing department's role

The purchasing department's role is to make sure that supplies, equipment, and services are available to the operation in quantities appropriate to predetermined standards, at the right price, and at a minimum cost to meet desired standards. Generally, those responsible for purchasing have the authority to commit the establishment's funds to buying required goods or services. Sometimes a maximum dollar amount for any individual purchase may be established beyond which a higher level of authority is required before proceeding with the purchase. Those responsible for purchasing may have authority to question individual purchase requisitions with reference to the particular need or the stipulated specifications.

Purchase Order

Four copies

A purchase order is a form prepared by the purchasing department authorizing a supplier to deliver needed goods and services to the establishment. A sample purchase order is illustrated in Exhibit 5.7. Generally, four copies are prepared—one for the supplier, one for the department initiating the purchase requisition (this advises them that the required items have been ordered), one that remains with the purchasing department, and the fourth, with a copy of the purchase requisition attached, is sent for control purposes to the accounting department. For control purposes it is also a good idea to cross reference the purchase order number to the requisition number, and vice versa.

In many cases in the hospitality industry, particularly where it involves day-to-day food and supplies ordering, a system of purchase orders is just not practical since most orders are placed at short notice and by telephone. In such cases special procedures and forms will prevail.

Exhibit 5.7   Sample Purchase Order

FRANKLYN HOTEL
1260 South St., Manchester
Telephone: (261)434-5734

PURCHASE ORDER   663
(The purchase order number must appear on all
invoices, bills of lading, or correspondence
relating to this purchase. Invoice must
accompany shipment).

Department _____   Purchase requisition #_____
Purchase order date _____   Delivery date _____
To supplier:

Description	Quantity	Price

Purchasing manager's signature _____

INVOICE

Invoices with goods

The third document in the system of purchasing control is the invoice. An invoice is simply an itemized listing of the goods or services. Generally in the hospitality industry suppliers are asked to have the priced and totaled invoice accompany the shipped goods, since this aids the receiving department in the receiving process. However, for control purposes it is a good idea to have the supplier also send a copy of the invoice directly to the establishment accounting office.

RECEIVING REPORT

The person or persons responsible for receiving should record each shipment received on a receiving report. A sample receiving report for food and beverages is illustrated in Exhibit 5.8. A report such as this should be completed on a daily basis and sent at the end of each day with accompanying invoices to the accounting office.

INVOICE APPROVAL FORM OR STAMP

Checking invoices

When the accounting department receives the receiving report, it can match with it a copy of the original purchase requisition, a copy of the purchase

Exhibit 5.8   Sample Receiving Report

Daily Record of Purchases and Issues

Hotel _____

Dept. _____   Date _____ 19 _____   Day of Week _____

Purchases			Stock to Storeroom				Bar				
1	2	3	4	5	6	7	8	9	10	11	12
Name of Item	Amount of Invoice	Direct Issues to Kitchen	Meat, Fish and Poultry	Staples	Fruits & Vegetables	Dairy Products	Liquor	Beer	Wine	Mixes Ingred	Cartage

A Today's Purchases											
B Balance Forward from Yesterday											
C Total to Date This Month											

13	14	15	16	17	18	19	20	21	22	23	24	25
				Direct Issues								
	Meat	Fish	Poultry	Fruits	Veget.	Dairy Products	Bakery Products	Staples	Coffee	Butter	Eggs	Food Cost 14 to 24
Direct Iss.												
Stores Iss.												
Total Iss.												
Fwd. Bal.												
Total M D												
I Beginning Inventory Last Month End												
J Stock to Store Room C4 to 7									5c			
K Store Room Issues E 14 to 24									21 to 25			
L (I + J=K) Balance on Hand												
M Physical Inventory												
N (L + or -M) Adjustment $												
O (N%to M) Adjustment %												
P (Sales/M) Inventory Turnover												

order, and the related invoice(s). All the relevant information can be compared and verified. The items on the invoice should be compared to the purchase requisition and the purchase order and to the receiving report. The invoice prices should be compared to the prices quoted and recorded on the purchase order. Finally, the invoice should be checked for arithmetical errors. If everything is in order, the accounting department can approve the invoice for payment. This can be done by stamping it or attaching a form to it. An outline of this stamp or form is illustrated in Exhibit 5.9. Initials or signatures should be put in the appropriate places to indicate that all the proper checks have been completed.

STORAGE

Recommended practices

The following practices should be used for product storage:

- Immediately after goods have been delivered and all receiving checks performed, they should be moved to storage areas or sent directly to the departments that requested them. Proper storage facilities (such as refrigerated areas for perishable food products) should be used.
- Storage areas should be locked when the storekeeper is not present. Access to storerooms should be limited to the storekeeper and other authorized employees.
- Storekeepers should not maintain or have access to formal inventory records, nor should accounting department employees who maintain those records have access to storeroom locations except to take inventories.

Perpetual inventory cards

- Inventory counts of stored products should be taken periodically by accounting office employees and compared to perpetual inventory cards

Exhibit 5.9   Sample Invoice Approval Form

Purchase order number	_____
Requisition checked	_____
Purchase order checked	_____
Receiving report checked	_____
Invoice prices checked	_____
Invoice calculations checked	_____
Approved for payment	_____

(if used), completed by the storekeeper. A perpetual inventory card is maintained for each separate item in stock. It has recorded on it, for each item, quantities received in and quantities issued from the storeroom to provide a running balance of what should be in inventory.

A sample perpetual inventory card is illustrated in Exhibit 5.10. The *In* column figures are taken from the invoices delivered with the goods. The figures in the *Out* column are recorded from the requisitions completed by departments requiring items from storage. A sample requisition is illustrated in Exhibit 5.11.

Blank requisitions should only be made available, preferably in duplicate, to those authorized to sign them. The original, listing items and quantities required, is delivered to the storekeeper. Duplicates are kept by the person ordering so that quantities received from the storeroom

Exhibit 5.10   Sample Perpetual Inventory Card

| Item _____ Supplier _____ Tel. # ____ |
| Minimum _____ Supplier _____ Tel. # ____ |
| Maximum _____ Supplier _____ Tel. # ____ |

Date	In	Out	Balance	Requisition Cost Information

Exhibit 5.11   Sample Requisition

| Department _____ Date __6329____ |

Quantity	Item description	Item cost	Total

| Authorized signature _____ |

can be checked. Issuing each department with blank requisitions of a different color aids in department identification.

The best procedure for taking inventory is to make two accounting office employees responsible. One completes the actual physical count; the other compares this with the perpetual inventory card figure and then records the actual count on an inventory sheet.

- If there are any significant differences that cannot be reconciled between the inventory count and what should be in inventory according to perpetual inventory cards, the differences should be investigated to determine the cause. In this way, new procedures to help prevent future differences can be implemented.
- To aid in inventory count, preprinted inventory sheets that list items in the same order as they are located on storeroom shelves should be used.

CASH RECEIPTS

Good cash handling and control procedures are not only important to the business owner or manager but also to the employees involved, because a good system will allow them to prove that they have handled their responsibilities correctly and honestly.

Proper receipt and deposit of cash

In hotels and restaurants, cash is received in payment for food, beverages, and services at any number of points. For each cash handling position (restaurants and/or bar cashiers, front office cashiers, general cashier in the accounting office) definite procedures need to be established to ensure that all cash due to the business is properly received, recorded, and deposited in the bank. The procedures vary from one operation to another because of differences in use of equipment, number of employees involved, whether or not credit is extended to customers or guests, and for numerous other possible reasons.

Cash removal precluded

In restaurants, bars, and other revenue outlets, each cash sale should be rung up on a cash register at the time of sale. Each cash register should have a locked-in tape on which is printed the amount of each sale. Those ringing up sales should not have access to this tape (another example of separation of assets and the recording thereof). The tape should be removed each day by a person from the accounting office. In the accounting office the recording of the daily sales register readings should be made by someone other than the person who collects and handles the cash. In this way, the tape forms the basis for the entry in the accounting records and that entry can be verified against the records of the person who handles cash remittances. This precludes the possibility of the person handling the cash removing cash and changing the accounting records.

Control over cash received by mail in payment for accounts receivable was discussed earlier in this chapter. When checks are received in payment for those accounts, they should immediately be endorsed by a stamp with a statement such as "For deposit only to the ABC Hotel's account number 3459."

An important aspect to controlling losses from uncollectible accounts is to age them periodically. This should be done monthly. (Aging of accounts is discussed in Chapter 11.)

If any account receivable is to be written off as uncollectible, this should only be authorized by the general manager or a delegated responsible person who does not handle cash or have any access to recording amounts on accounts receivable. When it is apparent that someone is delinquent in paying an account, all collection efforts should be carefully documented before the final decision to write off the uncollectible amount is made.

Receipts deposited intact daily

All cash receipts should be deposited intact each day in the bank. A deposit slip stamped by the bank should be kept by the business. This is a form of receipt showing how much was deposited each day. If all cash received that day is deposited daily, no one who handles the cash will be tempted to "borrow" cash for a few days for personal use. It also ensures that no payments are made in cash on invoices (if this were allowed, a dishonest employee could make out a false invoice and collect cash for it).

Employees who handle cash (and other assets, such as inventories) should be bonded. In this way losses are less likely to occur since the employee knows he or she will have to answer to the insurance company.

CASH DISBURSEMENTS

Petty cash fund

To handle minor disbursements requiring cash, a petty cash fund should be established. Initially, the fund should be established with sufficient cash to handle approximately one month's transactions. The responsibility of accountability and administration of the fund should be under the control of one person. The amount of cash placed into the fund is called the fund limit and is accounted for at least monthly. A receipt, invoice, voucher, or a memorandum explaining the purpose of each disbursement must support payments from the fund. The receipt, invoice, voucher, or memoranda should be noted as "paid" in such a manner as to preclude reuse.

Accountability of the fund is summarized as:

Fund limit = Cash (coin and currency on hand) + Receipts

Random spot checks of the fund should be made to insure the amount of cash on hand in the fund, plus the receipts, invoices, and so on, equals the limit of the fund. No IOUs or post-dated checks should be allowed. The fund is replenished as required to bring the fund back to its limit by exchanging cash for the receipts, invoices, and so on.

Payment by check

All other disbursements should be made by check and should be supported by an approved invoice. All checks should be prenumbered sequentially and be used in sequence. The person who prepared checks in payment of invoices should not be the person who has authority to sign checks. Preferably, two authorized signatures should be required on checks, and invoices should be canceled in some way when paid so they cannot be paid twice. Those authorized to sign checks should not be allowed to prepare them or control the supply of unused (blank) checks. Only those who prepare (but do not sign) checks should have access to blank checks. Any checks spoiled in preparation should be voided in some way so that they cannot be reused.

It is advisable to use a check protector to print amounts on checks, because this generally prevents anyone from altering the amounts.

If a mechanical check-signing machine is used, the key that allows this machine to operate should be in the hands of the employee authorized to use it. If the machine keeps a sequential count of the number of checks processed through it, someone in authority should maintain a separate count of the number of blank checks used and reconcile this periodically with the machine count. Once checks have been signed (either manually or mechanically), they should not subsequently be available to the person who prepared them. They should immediately be mailed to suppliers, or distributed to employees in the case of payroll checks.

Voucher system

Some larger hotels and restaurants control check disbursements by means of a voucher system. With a voucher system, the procedures for control by purchases outlined earlier in this chapter are assumed to be in effect. When the invoice receives approval for payment (see Exhibit 5.9), a final document called a voucher is prepared. Vouchers are numbered in sequence and summarize some of the information from the other documents. There is also space on the voucher for recording the date of payment and number of the check made in payment of the voucher. The supporting documents are attached to the voucher. When the voucher is to be paid, it is given to the person who prepares the checks. The person (or persons) who eventually signs the checks then knows the transaction is an authentic one since the check is accompanied by a voucher and the voucher has attached to it the purchase requisition and purchase order, the receiving report showing goods received, and the invoice, which has been checked for accuracy. There is little likelihood of fraud, unless all the documents were stolen and authorized signatures forged, or unless there is collusion.

Reduced possibility of fraud

PAYROLL

The procedures for cash disbursements discussed so far are intended to control purchases made externally. But since labor cost is such a high proportion of operating costs, equal care must be taken to ensure that proper control is exercised in this internal cost. Payroll checks should be written on a different bank account than that used for general disbursement checks, and the preparation and signing of payroll checks should be supported by a sound internal control system so that only properly authorized labor is paid for.

Control procedures

In addition, the following internal control procedures should be in effect for payroll:

- Only the general manager, a department head, or the personal department (in a large hotel) should authorize the hiring or replacement of an employee and approve a salary or wage rate. The person or persons with this authority should have nothing to do with payroll check preparation.
- After an employee is hired, any subsequent pay rate increase should be authorized and approved on a change in rate of pay form, such as that illustrated in Exhibit 5.12.
- Procedures should be implemented for recording hours worked for hourly paid employees and reporting them to the person who prepares payroll checks. In some establishments, hours worked are recorded by time clock. Time clock cards should be approved by the employee's department head before they are forwarded to the payroll department.
- Alternatively, the department head should not refer to the time cards, but instead record on a separate form each employee's starting and finishing

Exhibit 5.12   Authorization for Change in Rate of Pay

Employee   _____

Position   _____

Present pay rate   _____

New pay rate   _____

Effect date   _____

Signatures:

Department head   _____

Manager   _____

hours for each day of the pay period. In such a case, the payroll department should then compare the department head's record with each employee's time card and investigate any serious differences by discussing the situation with the employee and the department head.

- No overtime hours should be paid for without approval by the employee's department head. An overtime approval form is illustrated in Exhibit 5.13.
- From time to time an authorized accounting office employee should spot-check all payroll sheets to verify that hours worked, pay rates, and gross and net pay calculations are accurate.
- All payments for work performed should be made by check. Check usage control procedures should be the same as outlined earlier, in the section on cash disbursements.
- A separate payroll bank account should be maintained with sufficient funds transferred to it each payday to cover payroll checks issued.
- Payroll check preparation and check distribution should be handled by employees independent of each other.
- Any paychecks that cannot be distributed to employees should be turned over to the chief accountant or to some other delegated person who has no responsibility for payroll check preparation. These checks should be held by that person until collected by the employees.
- In small hospitality operations, paychecks are generally picked up by each employee from the payroll office. In larger establishments, department heads often receive, sign for, and distribute checks to their department's employees. In such cases, employees are often known either to the payroll office employee(s) or to the department heads.

Exhibit 5.13 Overtime Authorization Form

Date _____ Department _____

Employee _____

Position   _____

Overtime hours _____ Overtime rate _____

Reason   _____

Department head signature _____

- For further control in some large establishments, an employee of the accounting or audit office is delegated to ensure that an employee actually exists for each check prepared and issued. Because that employee might not be able to identify that each person receiving a paycheck is actually an employee, each person receiving a check is required to sign for it on a form that lists all current employees according to personnel office records. Some operations take this control one step further by ensuring that the employee's signature for the check compares with the one on that employee's initial job application form.
- Wherever possible, avoid paying wages in cash because cash wage forms can be easily forged by a dishonest department head. Alternatively, department heads may get around full-time staffing restrictions by employing part-time employees and authorizing cash payments to them.

However, it is recognized that sometimes payment of cash wages cannot be avoided. For example, banquet employees are often hired as needed for each separate function, and it would be unfair to make an employee (who has worked for only a handful of hours during a pay period) wait until the end of the pay period before being paid by check. Indeed, in many hospitality operations these employees are paid at the end of each function by check or, more often, by cash. In the latter case, each employee should be required to sign a banquet cash-payment form, indicating that the pay (less any necessary deductions) has been received.

Similarly, cash wage advances should be avoided unless a real hardship case is evident. Employees given wage advances often find that it makes their situation more difficult (because they will receive less than the normal pay amount on the regular pay day). Most requests for wage advances are made by employees who have a track record of advance-pay requests.

BANK RECONCILIATION

Monthly bank statement required

An essential control procedure in an effective internal control system is a monthly bank reconciliation. Bank reconciliation is a most effective tool for the management of money. The check register (checkbook) is an important tool providing indicators of sales, potential profit, period and fixed costs, employee benefits costs, deposits of excess cash into marketable securities, and many other little bits of important information. Each month, courtesy of an organization's bank, you should receive a bank statement providing essential items of information, which at a minimum should include the following:

- Deposits made, amount, and date.
- The amount and date of each check paid, by check number.

- Amounts added to the bank account and why they were added.
- Amounts deducted by the bank from your account and why each was deducted.
- Checks paid and cancelled should be returned for your records and information.

The essence of the bank statement reconciliation is to bring the reported bank statement balance into equality with the check register balance. Adjustments are made to the reported bank balance by adding or deducting information shown in the check register but not yet handled by the bank. Typically, bank omissions will be deposits made but not shown and checks issued but not cashed by the bank. The bank statement will inform the business of additions and deductions made from the business checking account that are not known until shown on the bank statement.

To insure control of cash, the person who controls cash should not control the reconciliation. The steps in the bank reconciliation are:

Steps in bank reconciliation

1. Review information in the bank statement, noting date and balance reported by the bank, which will be reconciled to the check register (checkbook).

2. Review the check register (checkbook) and compare bank deposits made to those shown as received by the bank. Deposits made but not shown on the bank statement are deposits to be added to the bank statement balance.

3. Review the checks cashed and returned by the bank to the checks written per the check register. All checks issued but not cashed by the bank are noted and classified as "outstanding" and deducted from the reported bank statement balance. Any errors made by the bank should be reported to the bank for correction.

4. Note the balance of the check register and use information regarding additions and/or deductions to the company bank account that are not known until receipt of the bank statement. Adjust the check register (checkbook).

To illustrate how the bank reconciliation is carried out, the following hypothetical information is used:

Reported bank statement balance	$4,442
Check register (checkbook) balance	$5,012
Deposits in transit	$1,206
Outstanding checks: #2820 @ $284	
#2828 @ $138	
#2832 @ $332	$ 754

Interest earned on checking account	$ 42
NSF* check	$125
NSF check charges	$ 15
Bank service charges	$ 20

*NSF refers to a deposited check that was not cashed due to insufficient funds.

Example reconciliation is shown as follows:

Bank Statement Reconciliation

Bank Statement Balance	$4,442	Check Register Balance	$5,012
Add: Deposits in transit	1,206	Add: Account Interest	42
Subtotal	$5,648	Subtotal	$5,054
Deduct: Outstanding checks		Deductions:	
#2820 @ $284		NSF check $125	
#2828 @ 138		NSF check charge 15	
#2832 @ 332	(754)	Service charges 20	(160)
Reconciled Balance	$4,894	Reconciled Balance	$4,894

A separate reconciliation should be conducted on each separate bank account maintained by a business.

CASHIER'S DEPARTMENT

To reduce the possibility of fraud, the head cashier and other employees in that department should not have the responsibility nor be allowed to:

- Prepare or mail invoices or month-end statements to customers who owe the establishment money.
- Record any amounts in or have any access to accounts receivable records.
- Authorize rebates, allowances, or any other reductions to any accounts receivable.
- Write off any account as "uncollectible."
- Prepare checks or other forms of cash disbursement.
- Reconcile bank accounts.

ESTABLISHING COST STANDARDS

One of the requirements of a good internal control system is not only to control the obvious visible items, such as cash or inventory, but also to have a reporting system that indicates whether or not all aspects of the business are operating properly and according to desired standards.

For example, one of the benchmarks used in the food industry to measure the effectiveness of the business is the food cost percentage. Management needs to know if the food cost percentage actually achieved is close to the standard desired.

Establishing procedures

If proper procedures are established for receiving, storing, issuing, and producing menu items, this is useful for good internal control. To improve the situation further, standard recipes for all menu items should be established, standard portion sizes determined, and menu items individually costed. The individual menu item standard costs would be revised, when necessary, to reflect changes in prices of ingredients used in recipes or changes in recipes or portion sizes. Therefore, these costs should be current ones and should not be estimated or based on some past situation that no longer reflects the current situation. Selling prices can then be determined to give a fair markup over cost and to offer the customer a competitive price.

A form, such as that illustrated in Exhibit 5.14, can then be used to record information about the individual menu item cost and selling prices. The quantity sold figures are the quantities actually sold of each particular menu item during the past week. This information can be obtained by taking a tally from all the sales checks used that week. Alternatively, it can be obtained from electronic sales register records. The total standard cost column is a multiplication of the menu item cost and quantity sold figures. The total standard sales is a multiplication of the menu item selling price and quantity sold figures.

Menu item cost percentage

The far-right column shows the individual standard cost percentage for each menu item. It is obtained by dividing menu item cost by menu item selling price and multiplying by 100. This information is useful when analyzing the food cost results. For example, a change in the sales mix (that is, a change in what the customers are choosing from the menu) can affect the food cost percentage. The individual menu item standard cost percentage information might also be useful when deciding which items to add to or delete from a menu or to promote.

The overall standard cost percentage can be calculated using information from the total standard cost and total standard sales columns, as illustrated in Exhibit 5.15. Finally, the actual cost percentage should be calculated, as illustrated in Exhibit 5.15. The information for actual cost is taken from the accounting records and from actual physical inventories using the general equation: beginning of the period inventory + purchases – end of the period inventory = cost of goods sold (actual food cost). Note that this actual food cost figure may have to be adjusted for interdepartmental transfers during the period and for employee meals. Actual sales would normally be the same as standard sales. A difference between the two might occur if sales prices were recorded incorrectly on the sales checks or on the sales register.

The difference between the standard and actual food cost percentages can then be recorded. A difference is to be expected because the standard is based

Exhibit 5.14   Partially Completed Standard vs. Actual Cost Form—Week 1

Menu Item	Menu Item		Quantity Sold	Total Standard Cost	Total Standard Revenue	Cost Percentage
	Cost	Selling Price				
1	$4.00	$6.50	486	$ 1,944.00	$ 3,159.00	61.5%
2	2.10	6.00	1,997	4,193.70	11,982.00	35.0
3	1.25	2.75	1,810	2,262.50	4,977.50	45.5
4	1.50	5.50	939	1,408.50	5,164.50	27.3
5	0.75	2.00	602	451.50	1,204.00	37.5
TOTALS				$10,260.20	$26,487.00	

$$Standard\ Cost\ Percentage = \frac{Total\ Standard\ Cost}{Total\ Standard\ Revenue} = \frac{10,260.20}{26,487.00} \times 100 = 38.7\%$$

$$Actual\ Cost\ Percentage = \frac{Total\ Actual\ Cost}{Total\ Actual\ Revenue} = \frac{\quad}{\quad} \times 100 \quad = \underline{\quad}$$

Difference

Exhibit 5.15   Completed Standard vs. Actual Cost Form—Week 1

Menu Item	Menu Item		Quantity Sold	Total Standard Cost	Total Standard Revenue	Cost Percentage
	Cost	Selling Price				
1	$4.00	$6.50	486	$ 1,944.00	$ 3,159.00	61.5%
2	2.10	6.00	1,997	4,193.70	11,982.00	35.0
3	1.25	2.75	1,810	2,262.50	4,977.50	45.5
4	1.50	5.50	939	1,408.50	5,164.50	27.3
5	0.75	2.00	602	451.50	1,204.00	37.5
TOTALS				$10,260.20	$26,487.00	

$$Standard\ Cost\ Percentage = \frac{Total\ Standard\ Cost}{Total\ Standard\ Revenue} = \frac{10,260.20}{26,487.00} \times 100 = 38.7\%$$

$$Actual\ Cost\ Percentage = \frac{Total\ Actual\ Cost}{Total\ Actual\ Revenue} = \frac{10,281.40}{26,487.00} \times 100 \quad = 38.8\%$$

Difference   0.1%

on what the cost should be if everything goes perfectly. Such perfection seldom exists. Management must decide what difference will be tolerated before an investigation is carried out to determine the cause.

Standard and actual percentages change

Exhibit 5.16 shows the completed form for the following week. Note that the figures for both the standard and actual percentages have changed. The reason is that different quantities of the various menu items offered have been sold and the ratio of what has been sold among the various menu items has changed (that is, there has been a change in the sales mix).

Therefore, it is to be expected that the total standard cost and sales figures as well as actual cost and sales figures (and the related percentages) will change. But with this analysis technique, management can now monitor the situation in an ongoing way. However, note that there has been absolutely no change in the cost percentage of any individual menu item.

Even though calculating a weekly standard cost seems like a lot of work, it can be readily computerized. As long as menu item cost and selling prices do not change, the only information that has to be entered each week is the quantity figure for each item sold, and in most operations today these figures are

Exhibit 5.16   Completed Standard vs. Actual Cost Form—Week 2

Menu Item	Menu Item		Quantity Sold	Total Standard Cost	Total Standard Revenue	Cost Percentage
	Cost	Selling Price				
1	$4.00	$6.50	502	$2,008.00	$ 3,263.00	61.5%
2	2.10	6.00	1,724	3,620.40	10,344.00	35.0
3	1.25	2.75	1,828	2,285.00	5,027.00	45.5
4	1.50	5.50	759	1,138.50	4,174.50	27.3
5	0.75	2.00	742	556.50	1,484.00	37.5
TOTALS				$9,608.40	$24,292.50	

$$\text{Standard Cost Percentage} = \frac{\text{Total Standard Cost}}{\text{Total Standard Revenue}} = \frac{9,608.40}{24,292.50} \times 100 = 39.6\%$$

$$\text{Actual Cost Percentage} = \frac{\text{Total Actual Cost}}{\text{Total Actual Revenue}} = \frac{9,816.70}{24,292.50} \times 100 = 40.4\%$$

$$\text{Difference} \quad \underline{0.8\%}$$

readily available from point-of-sale terminals. Any computer (even one as small as a laptop or notebook) can be programmed to carry out all of the remaining calculations.

Alcoholic beverage sales

Although the discussion and illustrations in this section have been related to food, the same technique can be used equally as well for alcoholic beverage sales.

There are many other techniques applicable for control for food cost and also for beverage cost, labor cost, labor productivity, and so on. Because of the complex nature of complete internal control, it is impossible in this chapter to describe and illustrate all of them. Furthermore, most of these techniques have to be developed for or adapted to each specific establishment with its unique operating problems. Suffice to say that good internal control would not be complete without some such monitoring techniques.

METHODS OF THEFT OR FRAUD

Collusion always difficult to control

The remainder of this chapter will be devoted to the ways in which theft or fraud has occurred in hospitality industry enterprises. These lists are not exhaustive; they include the more common ways in which misappropriations of assets have occurred. The lists can never be complete because, regardless of the improvements that are made to internal control systems, there is always a method of circumventing the control system, particularly if there is collusion between employees.

DELIVERIES

There are various methods that suppliers or delivery drivers can use to defraud a hotel or restaurant when they observe that the internal control procedures for receiving are not being used.

Many ways to lose on deliveries

- Invoice for high-quality merchandise when poor quality has been delivered.
- Put correct-quality items on the top of a box or case with subquality items underneath.
- Open boxes or cases, remove some of the items, reseal the boxes or cases, and charge for full ones.
- Deliver less than the invoiced weight of meat and other such items.
- Use padding or excess moisture in items priced by weight.
- Put delivered items directly into storage areas and charge for more than was actually delivered.

- Take back unacceptable merchandise without issuing an appropriate credit invoice.

RECEIVING AND INVENTORY

The people working in and around receiving and storage areas, if these are not properly controlled, could defraud by:

Control required over receiving area and storeroom

- Working with a delivery driver approving invoices for deliveries not actually made to the establishment.
- Working with a supplier approving invoices for high-quality merchandise when poor-quality merchandise has been delivered.
- Pocketing items and walking out with them at the end of the shift.
- Using garbage cans to smuggle items out the back door.
- Removing items from a controlled storeroom and changing inventory records to hide the fact.

CASH FUNDS

Under cash funds are included general reserve cash under the control of the head cashier, the petty cash fund, and banks or change funds established for front office or food and beverage cashiers for making change. Persons handling cash can cheat by:

Watch for cash removals and cover-ups

- Removing cash and showing it as a shortage.
- Using personal expenditure receipts and recording them as paidouts for business purposes.
- Removing cash for personal use and covering it with an IOU or post-dated check.
- Underadding cash sheet columns and removing cash.
- Selling combinations to safes.
- Failing to record cash income from sundry sales, such as vending machines, empty returnable bottles, and old grease from the kitchen.

ACCOUNTS PAYABLE AND PAYROLL

The person(s) handling accounts payable and/or payroll can practice fraud by:

But don't forget noncash areas

- Setting up a dummy company and making out checks on false invoices in the name of this company.
- Working in collusion with a supplier and having the supplier send padded or dummy invoices directly to the accounts payable clerk.
- Making out checks for invoices already paid.

- Padding payroll with fictitious employees.
- Padding gross pay amount on employee(s) checks in collusion with the employee(s).
- Carrying employees on the payroll beyond termination date.

FOOD AND BEVERAGE REVENUE

For good revenue control, a system of sales checks and duplicates should be established (although there are exceptions, for example, a cafeteria). Even with sales checks, servers or cashiers could practice the following:

Good sales check control imperative to minimize losses

- Obtain food and beverages from kitchen or bar without recording items on original sales check; these items would be for personal consumption.
- Collect cash from the customer without a sales check and not record the sale.
- Collect cash from the customer with a sales check already presented to another customer and not record the sale.
- Collect cash from the customer with a correct sales check, destroy the check, and not record the sale.
- Overadd the sales check, collect from the customer, then change the total of the check to correct amount.
- Purposely underadd the sales check or neglect to include an item on it to influence a bigger tip.
- Collect cash with the correct sales check and record the sales check as canceled or void.
- Collect cash with the correct sales check and record it as a charge, with a false signature, to a room number or credit card number.
- Use sales checks obtained elsewhere to collect from customers and not record the sale.

Credit cards also a vehicle for fraud

- Not return a customer's credit card after sale is complete, and subsequently use this stolen card to convert cash sales to charge sales using a false signature.
- Since the customer in the preceding situation will eventually discover his or her card is missing and report it to the credit card company, exchange this stolen card after a few days with one from another customer (since customers seldom check to see if they are getting the correct card back); this can prolong this fraud for a long time.
- Collect the credit card from the customer for an authentic charge transaction, but before returning the card to the customer, run off additional blank charge vouchers with this card through the imprinter and subsequently using the vouchers to convert cash sales to charge ones.

- Collect cash but record sale as a "customer walkout." One should always be alert to actual walkouts (both intentional and unintentional) in all revenue areas.

BAR REVENUE

In bars where the bartender also handles cash, one needs to be even more alert to the possibilities for fraud. In particular, watch for collections of toothpicks, or matches, or coins the bartender is using to keep track of drinks sold but not recorded so that he knows how much cash to remove when the bar is closed. Watch also for:

Bar area requires some special precautions

- Underpouring drinks (assume by one-eighth ounce on a one-ounce drink), not recording the sale, and pocketing the cash on every eighth drink sold. Using measuring devices brought in personally that are smaller than the establishment's standard ones is one way to hide this.
- Overpouring drinks (and underpouring others to compensate) to influence a bigger tip.
- Bringing in personally purchased bottles, selling their contents, and not recording sales.
- Not recording sales from individual drinks until sufficient to add up to a full bottle, then recording the sale as a full-bottle sale (which usually has a lower markup) and keeping the difference in cash.
- Selling drinks, keeping the cash, and recording drinks as spilled or complimentary.
- Diluting liquor and pocketing the cash from extra sales.
- Substituting a low-quality brand for a high-quality brand requested and paid for by customer, pocketing the difference in cash.

FRONT OFFICE

Hotel/motel front office losses

The front office area can also be a source of extra income for dishonest employees. A dishonest desk clerk could practice fraud by:

- Registering a late-arriving guest who is also checking out early, collecting in advance, destroying the registration card, and failing to record the revenue on a guest account or folio. This may require collusion between the desk clerk and the maid who cleans the room.
- Keeping cash from day-rate guests under circumstances similar to those in the previous situation.
- Registering the guest, collecting the advance, and subsequently canceling the registration card and blank guest folio as a "did not stay." Again this may require collusion between the desk clerk and maid.

- Charging a high rate on the guest's copy of the account and recording a lower rate on the hotel's copy where the accounting system is a manual one.
- Changing the hotel's copy of the account to a lower amount after the guest has paid and gone.
- Making a false allowance/rebate voucher with a forged signature after a guest has paid and gone and using this voucher to authenticate a reduction of the hotel's copy of the guest folio.
- Creating false paidouts for fictitious purchases for the hotel or using personal expenditure receipts to justify the payout.
- Charging cash-paid guest accounts to fictitious companies.
- Using credit cards from authentic charge sales to convert a cash sale to a charge sale subsequently (see tenth, eleventh, and twelfth situations under Food and Beverage Revenue).
- Lapping payments received on city ledger accounts (see earlier section in this chapter where this was discussed).
- Collecting cash from a city ledger account previously considered to be a bad debt and not recording the cash credit to the account.
- Recording the guest account as a "skip" (a guest who intentionally leaves without paying) after the guest has actually paid the account.
- Receiving deposits for room reservations in advance of the guest's arrival and failing to set up a folio in advance with the deposit credited.
- In collusion with the guest, not charging for an extra person in the room in order to receive a tip.
- Selling deposit box or room keys to thieves or burglars.
- Collecting cash from a city ledger account thought to be uncollectible, pocketing the cash, and writing the account off as a bad debt.

Here is what a major hotel company (Doubletree Corporation) had to say in a recent annual report about its internal control system:

The Company maintains a system of internal control over financial reporting, which is designed to provide reasonable assurance to the Company's management and board of directors regarding the preparation of reliable financial statements. The system includes a documented organizational structure and division of responsibility, established policies and procedures which are communicated throughout the Company, and the selection, training, and development of employees. Internal auditors monitor the operation of the internal control system and report findings and recommendations to management and the board of directors, and corrective actions are taken to control deficiencies and other opportunities for improving the system if and as they are identified.

There are inherent limitations in the effectiveness of any system of internal control, including the possibility of human error and the circumvention or overriding of controls. Accordingly, even an effective internal control system can provide only reasonable assurance with respect to financial statement preparation.

Furthermore, the effectiveness of an internal control system can change with circumstances.

COMPUTER APPLICATIONS

With reference to internal control, a computerized word processing software program allows management to easily produce a policies and procedures manual for each new employee. When policies and/or procedures change, manuals can be revised and new copies distributed to all affected employees.

Computers can also be used for many aspects of internal control, such as preparing and issuing purchase orders, inventory, cash, and payroll preparation. Security can also be enhanced. For example, the person recording cash payments received in the mail can access the cash account to make the necessary entries but will not be able to access the accounts receivable account and vice versa.

In particular, a spreadsheet program can be used for producing the daily receiving report and completing all the calculations necessary for preparation of a standard versus actual cost form, as illustrated in Exhibits 5.14, 5.15, and 5.16.

SUMMARY

An important aspect of any business is the safeguarding of assets. A good internal control system will accomplish this and will provide management with information on which to base business decisions. The internal control system should include methods and procedures for the employees to follow and reliable forms and reports to provide the required information. With any internal control system, it is important to realize that the system may not prevent all forms of loss or dishonesty. For example, collusion is sometimes difficult to detect.

Once established, the control system needs to be monitored from time to time to insure it is working well and continuing to provide valid and timely information. It is important to establish clear responsibilities for the various jobs to be performed so that a specific employee can be held accountable in the event of errors or losses. Employees who are given responsibility should also be provided with detailed written procedures about how to perform their functions.

Written records (forms or reports) should be established to help the employees carry out their jobs and to document information. A major principle of good internal control is to separate, whenever possible, record keeping and the actual control of the assets. For example, the person who handles cash should not be the same person who makes entries in the accounting records; otherwise it would be too easy to remove cash and alter the accounting records to hide the fact. By separating the two functions, collusion would then be required to hide theft. Similarly, wherever possible, the responsibility for related transactions should be divided so that the work of one employee will also check on the work of another. This does not mean to suggest that another person should duplicate the work of one person.

Employees should have their work explained to them so that they understand why they are doing specific tasks. In this way, the job should have more meaning to them. Job rotation is also a good idea. One way to reduce the possibilities of fraud is to employ machines to do certain tasks that improve internal control; this may also lead to a labor cost-saving. Other principles of internal control are to limit access to assets, to carry out surprise checks at unusual times, to bond employees, to make vacations mandatory, to use external audits and provide audit trails, and to number all control documents.

Finally, any system of internal control requires constant supervision and review by management to guard against the system becoming obsolete. A major area requiring a good system of internal control is purchasing. This can be accomplished using five basic documents: a purchase requisition, a purchase order, an invoice, a receiving report, and an invoice approval stamp or form. Special procedures must be established for those handling cash, such as the cashiers at the various sales outlets, the front office cashier in a hotel, and the general cashier in the accounting office. Cash is the most liquid of assets and without complete control can disappear too easily if employees are dishonest. Employees who are handling cash should be bonded.

Precautionary procedures for the handling of checks must be instituted and a bank reconciliation should be performed once a month. Standards of performance should be established and results evaluated so that management can determine if standards are being met and so that decisions can be made that will improve standards, increase performance, and ultimately produce higher profits.

DISCUSSION QUESTIONS

1. What are the two basic requirements for an internal control system?
2. Define collusion and explain why you think it is difficult to detect.
3. Why is it necessary to define responsibility for particular jobs?

4. Explain what is meant by separation of record keeping from control of assets.
5. Explain how lapping works.
6. What is meant by the term division of responsibilities?
7. List the five documents or forms used for control of purchases. Briefly explain the use of any two of these documents.
8. List and briefly discuss appropriate procedures for control over product storage and explain how perpetual inventory cards can be used in inventory control.
9. Why should all cash receipts be deposited each day intact in the bank?
10. Describe how a petty cash fund is established.
11. In paying invoices by check, how can control be established?
12. List the special procedures that are necessary for control of payroll and distribution of paychecks.
13. Explain the reasons why payment of cash wages should be avoided.
14. The balance of a company's check register normally will not agree with the bank statement balance prior to reconciliation. Why?
15. List the steps to reconcile the bank statement balance to the check register balance.

ETHICS SITUATION

A restaurant manager recently decided to change wine suppliers and switch to a supplier whose owner is a good friend. The first purchase order was for 15 cases (each containing 12 bottles) of various wines. When the manager arrived home that night, she found an unsolicited case of wine at the house provided free by the supplier. She decided not to tell the restaurant's owner and not take the free case to the restaurant for sale. Discuss the ethics of this situation.

EXERCISES

5.1 Define the major objective of internal control.

5.2 Define the purpose of a petty cash fund.

5.3 A petty cash fund with a $150 limit had receipts of $112 and cash (coin and currency) of $36. Explain the status of the fund.

5.4 Explain the purpose of bank reconciliation.

5.5 Explain the purpose of standard cost control.

5.6 Identify to what a standard food cost percentage is compared.

5.7 Assume a situation existed in which the same person handled all cash and checks received in payment of an account. Explain how lapping works and, using the following information showing the day in July each payment was received, determine the amount "lapped."

Customer Name	Amount of Check	Payment Received
Arnold	$ 51.40	2
Sayers	62.11	4
Carter	101.10	7
Tuney	110.90	12
Lossie	141.20	14
Martie	162.75	17
Buddy	172.83	22
Smithe	185.22	27
Brown	202.90	30

5.8 Define the difference between a purchase order and a purchase requisition.

PROBLEMS

5.1 A motel has established a petty cash fund in the amount of $100. The fund is under the control of the day shift desk clerk. During the month of October, the following disbursements supported by receipts or memoranda were made from the fund. Calculate the amount of the reimbursement check to the fund at the end of October.

October 2	$13.51	plants for lobby
2	4.30	postage stamps
5	15.28	cleaning supplies
7	7.11	freight on delivery of linen
8	1.58	office supplies
15	11.50	postage stamps
16	5.00	refund to guest
20	12.00	cash wages for casual help
22	0.48	postage due
28	3.75	cutting new keys
31	6.45	flowers for VIP guest

In the same establishment, the following disbursements were made out of the petty cash fund in November:

November	1	$ 3.07	office supplies
	4	14.20	flowers for lobby
	7	1.30	office supplies
	7	12.00	casual wages
	10	0.32	postage due
	13	11.50	postage stamps
	14	4.60	COD parcel for owner
	18	11.00	taxi cost for owner
	21	3.26	collect telegram
	24	4.02	freight on linen delivery
	24	1.16	office supplies
	29	10.50	postage stamps (note there was no receipt for this)
	30	1.16	stamps

The desk clerk has added these items and requests a refund check in the amount of $88.09. A count of the cash by the manager shows there is $1.91 still in the fund plus an IOU from the clerk in the amount of $10.00. What comments do you have about the petty cash fund for the month of November?

5.2 Tavara's Tavern carries out a monthly bank reconciliation. At the beginning of July, it found the following concerning the June reconciliation: The bank balance on the bank statement was $4,810, and the bank balance according to the tavern's records was $5,112. Checks #306 in the amount of $27, #309 in the amount of $108, and #311 in the amount of $87 were still unpaid by the bank at June 30. At the end of June, the bank had added to the tavern's bank account an amount of $38 for interest earned on a separate savings account it has at the bank and had deducted $8 for a service charge. A deposit made by the tavern on June 30 in the amount of $554 did not appear on the bank's statement. Prepare Tavara's bank reconciliation for June 30.

5.3 A hotel company carries out a monthly bank reconciliation. At the beginning of November, it found the following concerning the October reconciliation: The bank balance on the bank statement was $3,506, and the bank balance according to the company records was $4,740. Checks #3581 and #3650 in the amounts of $298 and $402, respectively, were still unpaid by the bank. The bank had credited (added) to the company's bank statement an amount of $356, which the company had earned from a separate savings account it has at the bank. The bank had also debited the bank statement wrongly with a check in the amount of $20 that had not been drawn by the hotel company. There was a $4 service charge on the bank statement. The company's deposit on October 31 in the amount of $2,266 had not been recorded by the bank on the statement. Prepare the company's bank reconciliation for October.

5.4 A restaurant carries out a monthly bank reconciliation. The August 31 reconciliation showed the following: Restaurant bank balance $4,112. Bank statement balance $2,760. Deposits in transit August 30, $456 and August 31, $1,212 not yet recorded by the bank. Checks #167 for $61, #169 for $30, and #175 for $172 were still outstanding. The bank statement showed a service charge of $6 and an interest credit amount of $61. A check received by the restaurant in payment of a customer's meal in the amount of $11, and deposited in the bank on August 25, was debited back to the bank statement on August 31 with the notation that there was not sufficient money in the customer's bank account to pay the check. In verifying the bank's record of daily deposits against the restaurant's records, it is discovered that the bank statement deposit of August 11 shows $1,321 while the company records show $1,312. Further checking shows the bank statement figure is the correct one. Prepare a bank reconciliation.

5.5 The bookkeeper who has been working for more than 30 years for a small hotel is retiring. Because he was such a reliable employee, he was given more and more responsibility over the years and did virtually all of the work, such as keeping all the accounting records, approving invoices for payment, preparing checks, and in the absence of the hotel's owner, signing checks that needed to be sent to suppliers. His daily duties included collecting the cash at the end of the day from the front office and restaurant, cleaning the machine tapes, counting and verifying cash against tapes, depositing the cash in the bank, and making the necessary entries in the hotel's bookkeeping records. At month-end he would do the bank reconciliation. The hotel's owner realizes that she cannot hire and train someone to take over all the responsibilities of the retiring bookkeeper and that it would not be desirable for internal control purposes to do so. She knows that she will have to assume some of the retiring employee's duties. She is busy already, since, as well as generally managing the hotel she does all the ordering of food supplies for the restaurant and all the ordering and receiving of bar supplies. From an internal control point of view, discuss which of the retiring bookkeeper's responsibilities the owner should take over while, at the same time, minimizing the amount of time this would require.

5.6 The owner of Charlene's restaurant believes that her food cost is higher than it should be. Charlene thinks that the problem might be in the receiving area and/or the dining area since she says she has good control over fod in storage and production. She has asked you to see what you can determine. By observation, you notice that when drivers make deliveries they obtain a signature from any restaurant employee who happens to be near the receiving dock in the absence of the receiver/storekeeper. Deliveries are then left at the receiving dock until the receiver can move the goods to storage areas. Sometimes invoices are left with food containers; at other times no documentation is left, and it is assumed invoices are then mailed by the suppliers to Charlene's office.

In the dining area you notice that servers do not use printed sales checks to record customer's orders but simply note orders on scratch pads. They then tell cooks what they need and pick up and deliver food to customers. When the customers wish to pay, servers jot down the total amount due on the scratch pad page, present the page to the customer, collect the cash, and put it into a cash drawer. No sales are recorded in a cash register. "Used" scratch pad pages are placed in a box beside the cash drawer.

In both receiving and dining areas, outline the possible problems that present procedures create and suggest to Charlene practices that would probably solve the problems.

5.7 A restaurant has been in operation for the past five years and has successfully increased its revenue each year. One of the reasons is that in the third year the owner began extending credit to local businesspeople who regularly used the restaurant. They were allowed to sign their sales checks and were then sent an invoice at each month-end. The owner is concerned that this credit policy may have led to increases in losses from bad debts (uncollectible accounts receivable) that were not justified by increases in revenue. The restaurant operates at a 60 percent gross profit ratio, and other operating expenses (not including bad debts) are 50 percent of revenue. Following are the credit revenue and bad debt figures for the past five years:

Year	Credit Revenue	Bad Debts
1	$160,000	$ 960
2	180,000	900
3	240,000	3,840
4	300,000	4,500
5	360,000	5,400

In a columnar schedule for each year, record the credit revenue, cost of sales, gross profit, operating expenses, income before bad debts, bad debts, and net income. In addition, for each year, calculate the bad debts as a percentage of charge or credit revenue. Write a brief report to the owner with particular reference to control over bad debt losses and the restaurant's credit policy.

5.8   A small hotel has an outside accountant prepare an income statement after the end of each month. For the last three months the amount shown as bad debts had increased considerably over any previous month. The owner asked the accountant to verify the authenticity of all accounts receivable written off as bad debts over the last three months. The accountant discovered that a number of accounts in large amounts had in fact been paid and the persons contacted had canceled checks endorsed with the hotel's stamp to prove this. About three months ago a new hotel bookkeeper had been hired to carry out all record keeping and also act as cashier, receiving and depositing the cash from the front office cashier and handling and depositing payments on accounts receivable received by mail. As the hotel's outside accountant, explain to the owner what you think has been happening and suggest how the problem can be resolved so that the same situation does not occur again.

5.9   At some of the banquets held in a hotel, the bar is operated on a cash basis. All drinks are the same price. Banquet customers buy drink tickets from a cashier at the door. The customers then present the tickets to the bartender to obtain drinks. The bartender will not serve any drink without a ticket. As each ticket is presented, it is torn in half by the bartender to prevent its reuse. Torn tickets are subsequently discarded. At the end of the function the amount of drinks sold, calculated by taking an inventory of liquor still in bottles and deducting from the opening inventory, is compared with the cash taken in by the cashier and with the number of tickets sold.

     In order to cut costs the hotel is considering eliminating the cashier's position and the sale of tickets. The customers will pay the bartender directly for the drinks. From an internal control point of view, what comments do you have about this proposal?

5.10   A fast-food restaurant features only three entree items on its menu with the following cost and selling prices:

Item	Cost	Selling Price
1	$1.00	$3.30
2	2.20	4.40
3	2.70	6.75

a. For each item calculate the food cost percentage.

b. If 50 of each item are sold each day, what will the standard food cost percentage be?

c. If only 25 each of items one and three were sold and 100 of item two, what effect will this have on the standard cost percentage?

5.11 The sales records for a coffee shop that has only six items on its menu show the following quantities sold during the month of January. Item standard cost and selling prices are also indicated.

Item	Cost	Selling Price	Quantity Sold
1	$2.00	$6.00	654
2	1.10	4.50	2,196
3	2.25	7.00	1,110
4	1.75	5.00	990
5	2.25	5.00	295
6	2.00	7.95	259

Actual cost for the month of January was $9,201. Actual revenue for the month of January was $30,060.05.

a. Calculate the standard cost percentage and the actual cost percentage for January. Round all dollar amounts to the nearest dollar.

b. Compare the results. If you were the dining room manager, explain why you would or would not be satisfied with the results.

5.12 A fast-food restaurant uses a standard cost approach to aid in controlling its food cost. The following are the standard cost, sales prices, and quantities sold of each of the five items featured on the menu during a particular week:

Item	Standard Cost	Sales Price	Quantity Sold
1	$1.80	$3.95	$260
2	2.10	4.95	411
3	4.20	8.95	174
4	3.05	6.95	319
5	1.40	3.95	522

Total actual cost for the week was $3,804.10 and total actual revenue $8,873.40.

a. Calculate actual and standard food cost percentages and comment on the results.

b. The following week, with no change in menu or standard cost and selling prices, there was a change in the sales mix. Although quantities sold of items two, three, and five were virtually the same, many more of item four and many less of item one were sold. As a result of this, would you expect the overall standard cost percentage to increase or decrease? Explain your answer.

CASE 5

a. The 4C Company's restaurant, with 84 seats, is not large. For this reason it does not have a large number of people on the payroll. Charlie has been handling the general manager's responsibilities and has a good friend working half a day, five days a week, to take care of such matters as bank deposits, preparing accounts payable and payroll checks, and all other routine office and bookkeeping work.

  Charlie is not concerned about the honesty of the person, but he has learned from courses that he has taken that there is a need for any company, however small, to have some internal controls. Write a short report to Charlie pointing out three specific areas where you feel controls might need to be implemented. For each of the three areas, advise Charlie what might happen if a dishonest bookkeeper were hired and how internal control can be implemented to prevent dishonesty.

b. From his experience in the mobile catering company, Charlie had learned the value of standard cost control. In that business he purchased most of his food items preportioned and wrapped. Portion sizes were always the same. Food cost was easy to control since, each day, an inventory count of each item he carried, plus the quantity purchased of that item that day, less the quantity still in inventory at the day's end, gave him a figure that, when multiplied by the selling price of the item, produced the standard sales revenue that he should have. When this was done for all food items, he could then compare his total standard food revenue each day with the actual revenue to make sure there were no differences. In this situation he was in complete control of the entire operation.

  In the 4C Company's restaurant, because food dishes are produced in the restaurant's own kitchen, it is not feasible to operate and control costs and revenue as with the 3C Company. The restaurant basically operates with eight main entree items on its menu, with three soups and four desserts. These are changed seasonally. Coffee is free if an entree is ordered; otherwise there is a charge. Explain as briefly as possible to Charlie the steps that could be implemented to have a system of standard food cost and revenue control. What about the problem that some people have free coffee while others pay, and the fact that customers have to pay for items such as milk and soft drinks?

6

The "Bottom Up" Approach to Pricing

INTRODUCTION

This chapter introduces various pricing methods that have been used in the hospitality industry and points out the need for current, tactical, and long-range pricing methods. The concept of considering net income after tax as a typical cost function in the process of determining product-selling prices is introduced and discussed in detail. Treating net income after tax as a cost function is illustrated for a restaurant operation as an average check is forecasted, which will cover all costs of the operation including net income after tax. The illustration continues by showing how an average check per meal period is determined.

The subject of pricing individual menu items is discussed, as are the possible difficulties that may be encountered. The relationship that exists between the sales mix, the average check, and gross margin is discussed, as well as the topics of seat turnover and integrated pricing.

Menu engineering is discussed, using a technique of menu analysis that focuses on the contribution margin (gross margin) of each separate menu item, combined with its popularity, which is measured by customer demand.

The chapter continues with a discussion of the use of net income after tax as a cost function for a rooms operation. The same techniques used to determine the required average check in a restaurant operation would apply to calculating the required average room rate for a hotel or motel operation.

The approach used to convert an overall average room rate into an average single and double room rate is discussed and illustrated. A different method of determining average room rates, based on the square footage of each type of room, is shown. The relationship between room rates and room occupancy is also discussed.

Room-rate discounting and the use of an equation is illustrated to calculate the equivalent occupancy necessary to maintain total revenue (less marginal costs) constant if the rack rate is discounted. The use of a potential average room rate and its use as a measuring device, and the establishment of discounted room rates for various market segments, is discussed. Other pricing considerations such as an organization's objectives, elasticity of demand, cost structure, and competition are also discussed.

This chapter concludes with a section on yield management that matches customers' purchase patterns with their demand for guest rooms. This technique allows ownership to derive a future occupancy forecast with greater accuracy to meet the objective of maximizing room revenues.

CHAPTER OBJECTIVES

After studying this chapter, the reader should be able to:

1. Discuss the advantages and disadvantages of various traditional pricing methods used in the hospitality industry and understand the difference between long-range and tactical pricing.

2. Explain the concept of using net income after tax as a cost function.

3. Calculate total annual revenue required for a restaurant operation to cover all forecasted costs including net income after tax and convert the annual revenue to an average check amount.

4. Use existing information to calculate an average check per meal period and explain the effect sales mix of a menu item will have on an average check.

5. Discuss the considerations to be kept in mind when pricing a menu item, calculating seat turnover figures. Also discuss integrated pricing for a restaurant.

6. Discuss the structure of a menu engineering worksheet.

7. Calculate an average room rate to cover all forecasted costs including net income after tax and convert the average rate to an average single and average double rate.

8. Calculate room rates based on the basis of room square footage.

9. Discuss room rate discounting and calculate occupancy percentage for a discount grid, and calculate a potential average room rate and discounted rates for various market segments.

10. Discuss some of the important considerations in pricing such as objectives of an organization, elasticity of demand, cost structure, competition, and use of yield management techniques.

THE BOTTOM-UP APPROACH TO PRICING

Generally, pricing theory suggests that a hospitality operation should price its rooms and its food and beverage menu items to control costs and maximize profit, while at the same time offering guests an appropriate value for their money. The reasoning behind the pricing theory is that ownership equity should be provided a satisfactory return on their investment if the products being sold are properly priced.

The method used to price products will to a degree dictate whether or not financial goals will be achieved. If prices are too high, customers will come to believe they are not receiving an adequate value for their money and seek other sources to provide the product and services. On the other hand, if prices are too low, sales potential is not maximized. In either event, profits can be expected to be lower than they should be.

Different methods

As will be seen, hospitality operators establish price structures using a number of different methods, each with their advantages and disadvantages.

INTUITIVE METHOD

The intuitive method requires no real knowledge of the business or research into costs, profits, prices, competition, or the market. The operator just assumes that the prices established are the right ones because customers are willing to pay them. This method has no advantages. Its main disadvantage is that the prices charged are unrelated to profits.

RULE-OF-THUMB METHOD

Rule-of-thumb methods (such as that a restaurant should price its menu items at 2.5 times food cost to achieve a 40% cost of sales) may have had validity at one time but should not be relied on in today's highly competitive environment because they pay no attention to the marketplace (competition, value for money, and so forth).

TRIAL-AND-ERROR METHOD

With the trial-and-error method, prices are changed up and down to see what effect they have on sales and profits. When profit is apparently maximized, prices are established at that level. However, this method ignores the fact that there are many other variables (such as general economic conditions, seasonality of demand, and competition) that affect sales and profits apart from prices, and what appears to be the optimum pricing level may later be affected by these other factors. This method can also be confusing to customers during the price-testing period.

Variables affect sales and profits

PRICE-CUTTING METHOD

Price cutting occurs when prices are reduced below those of the competition. This can be a risky method if it ignores costs, because if variable costs are higher than prices, profits will be eroded. Some restaurant operators set their food menu prices below costs on the risky assumption they will more than make up the losses by profits on alcoholic beverage sales. To use this method, the reduction in prices must be more than compensated by selling additional products. If the extra business gained is simply taken away from competitors, they will also be forced to reduce their prices and a price war may result.

HIGH PRICE METHOD

Another pricing method is to deliberately charge more than competitors and use product differentiation, emphasizing such factors as quality, which many customers equate with price. If this strategy is not used carefully, however, it can encourage customers to move elsewhere when they realize that high price and high quality are not synonymous.

Product differentiation

COMPETITIVE METHOD

Competitive pricing means matching prices to those of the competition and then differentiating in such areas as location, atmosphere, and other nonprice factors. When there is one dominant operator in the market that generally takes the lead in establishing prices, with its close competitors matching increases and decreases, this method is then referred to as the follow-the-leader method. Competitive pricing tends to ensure there is no price cutting and resulting reduction in profits. In other words, there is market price stability. This may be a useful method in the short run. However, if competitive pricing is used without knowledge of the differences that exist (in such matters as product and costs) between one establishment and another, then this method can be risky.

Market price stability

MARKUP METHOD

The markup method is used, for example, when a restaurant's traditional food cost percentage (as it appears on past income statements) is applied to determine the price of any new menu items offered. For example, if traditionally the restaurant has been operating at a 40% food cost, any new menu items offered will be priced so that they also result in a 40% food cost. The major problem with this method is that it assumes that 40% is the correct food cost for the restaurant to achieve its desired profit.

USING THE RIGHT METHOD

Many of the pricing methods just reviewed are commonly used because operators understand them and find them easy to implement. Unfortunately, if the establishment is not operating as efficiently as it should, these methods simply tend to perpetuate the situation and sales and profits will not be maximized. Owners or managers who use these methods are not fully in control of their operations and are probably failing to use their income statements and other financial accounting information to guide them in improving their operating results.

Pricing is a tool
Pricing is a tool that can be used effectively to improve profitability. The dilemma is often a matter of finding the balance between prices and profits. In other words, prices should only be established after considering their effect on profits. For example, a restaurant can lower its prices to attract more customers, but if those prices are lowered to the point that they do not cover the costs of serving those extra customers, profits will decline rather than increase.

LONG-RUN OR STRATEGIC PRICING

Over the long run, price is determined in the marketplace as a result of supply and demand. When prices are established to compete in that marketplace, they must be set with the establishment's overall long-term financial objectives in mind. A typical objective could be any one of the following to maximize sales revenue, to maximize return on owners' investment, to maximize profitability, to maximize business growth (in a new operation), or to maintain or increase

Strategic objectives
market share (for an established operation). A clearly thought out pricing strategy will stem from the financial objective or objectives of the business, as well as recognize that these objectives may change over the long run.

TACTICAL PRICING

In addition to a long-run pricing strategy, a hospitality operation also needs short-run, or tactical, pricing policies to take advantage of situations that arise from day to day. Some of these situations might be

Typical situations
- Reacting to short-run changes in price made by competitors.
- Adjusting prices because of a new competitor.
- Knowing how large a discount to offer group business while still making a profit.
- Knowing how much to increase prices to compensate for an increase in costs.

- Knowing how much price increases can be justified to compensate for renovations made to premises.
- Adjusting prices to reach a new market segment.
- Knowing how to discount prices in the off-season to attract business.
- Offering special promotional prices.

Many of the remaining chapters in this book are concerned with using accounting-oriented approaches to controlling various kinds of costs in order to minimize them and thus maximize net income and return on investment. However, it is equally important to control sales revenue, that is to say, to control the prices that are established for the goods and services offered. Since there is a relationship between prices charged and total sales revenue, prices must therefore affect the general financial results, such as the ability to cover all operating costs and provide a net income that yields an acceptable return on investment. Price levels also affect such matters as budgeting, working capital, cash management, and capital investment decisions—all of which will be discussed in later chapters.

The traditional method of looking at an income statement is from the top down, that is, by calculating sales revenue and the costs associated with that revenue in order to determine if there is a net income. A different approach might be to start with the net income that is required, calculate costs, and determine what sales revenue is required and what prices are to be charged in order to achieve the desired net income. This "bottom up" approach assumes that net income is a cost of doing business, which indeed it is. If a mortgage company lends money at a particular interest rate to a hotel or food service operation, the interest expense is considered to be a cost. The mortgage company is an investor. Another group of investors are the owners of the company (either stockholders or unincorporated individuals). They also expect interest on their investment of money and/or time, except that their interest is called net income. Therefore, net income is just another type of cost. This concept, and the bottom up approach to calculating revenue, can be useful in deciding prices.

Net income is also a cost

RESTAURANT PRICING

In general, we could view the relationship of income statement components being expressed as a variable percentage of total sales revenue or as identifiable (known) dollar values. We know that a common-size vertical analysis will allow us to express every element of an income statement as a percentage of total sales revenue set as 100%. Known dollar values will consist of costs that are considered fixed or repetitive costs that can be estimated with sufficient accuracy to treat them as semi-fixed by their nature. The following illustrates how total sales required covering the variable costs and estimated known dollar value costs to provide operating income (before tax) at the breakeven total sales revenue point with no profit or loss. The example uses typical restaurant variable cost percentages and a selected few of the typical cost classifications which are fixed or can be estimated with a great deal of accuracy:

Sales revenue	@ 100%
Cost of sales, food (a variable % of total sales revenue)	@ (38%)
Cost of sales, beverage (a variable % of total sales revenue)	@ (15%)
Labor costs (a variable % of total sales revenue)	@ (25%)
Other operating costs (a variable % of total sales revenue)	@ (2%)
Gross Margin	@ (80%)

Known Operating Costs

Management salaries	$38,000	
Administrative expenses	18,000	
Depreciation expense	24,000	= 20%
Utilities expense	6,500	
Property taxes expense	4,500	
Total known costs		$91,000
Operating income		$ -0-

Knowing that the known dollar values totaling $91,000 is 20% of the unknown total sales revenue figure (100% − 80% = 20%) and is found as follows:

Total sales revenue equals $91,000/.20 = <u>$455,000</u>

Sales revenue	$455,000
Cost of sales, food (38% × $455,000)	(172,900)
Cost of sales, beverage (15% × $455,000)	(68,250)
Labor costs (25% × $455,000)	(113,750)
Other operating costs (2% × $455,000)	(9,100)
Gross Margin	$ 91,000

Known operating costs

Management salaries	$38,000	
Administrative expenses	18,000	
Depreciation expense	24,000	= 20%
Utilities expense	6,500	
Property taxes expense	4,500	
Total known costs		(91,000)
Operating income		$ -0-

Calculation of an
average check

Building on the techniques of the previous example, the concept of treating net income after tax as a cost can be easier understood. Let us now consider a situation regarding a 100-seat restaurant whose owner wants to know what sales revenue must be in the coming year. Knowing total sales revenue will allow the calculation of an average check necessary to meet the revenue objective for the next year of operation. Information àbout costs and cost percentages shown in Exhibit 6.1 will be evaluated and incorporated into an income statement using the preceding discussion format in Exhibit 6.2.

An alternative calculation of income tax is to apply the tax rate to operating income before tax as follows:

$$\text{Operating income (before tax)} \times \text{tax rate} = \text{tax: } \$68,750 \times 36\% = \underline{\$24,750}$$

Exhibit 6.1   Projected Restaurant Costs for Next Year

Net income after tax:	A 20% after-tax return on a $220,000 investment in furnishings and equipment is wanted.
Income tax rate:	36% of operating income (before tax).
Depreciation rate:	10% of $220,000, the book value of furnishings and equipment.

Annual costs

Rent expense	$42,000
Insurance and license expense	5,400
Utilities and maintenance expense	6,800
Administration, office and phone expenses	12,200
Management salary	25,600

Variable costs

Cost of sales food, averages 38% of total revenue.
Labor cost percentage averages 27% of total revenue.
Other variable operating costs averages 15% of total revenue.

Return on owner investment:

$$\text{Net Income after tax} = \text{Investment of } \$220,000 \times 0.2 = \$44,000$$

Calculation of operating income and tax:

$$\frac{\text{NI after tax}}{1 - \text{Tax rate}} = \text{Operating income before tax} - \text{NI after tax} = \underline{\underline{\text{Tax}}}$$

$$\frac{\text{NI after tax}}{1 - \text{Tax rate}} = \frac{\$44,000}{1 - .36} = \frac{\$44,000}{.64} = \$68,750 - \$44,000 = \underline{\underline{\$24,750}}$$

Exhibit 6.2 Projected Restaurant Income Statement for Next Year (Incomplete)

Sales revenue	$Unknown	100%
Cost of sales, food		(38%)
Labor cost		(27%)
Other operating costs		(15%)
Management salary	$ 25,600	
Administration and office expenses	12,200	
Utilities and maintenance expenses	6,800	
Insurance and license expense	5,400	
Rent expense	42,000	
Depreciation expense ($220,000 × 10%)	22,000	
Income tax	24,750	
Net income	44,000	
Total	$182,750	= 20%

Exhibit 6.3 Condensed Restaurant Income Statement for Next Year (Complete)

Sales revenue ($182,750/0.2)		$913,750
Cost of sales food, labor and other variable costs ($913,750 × .8)		(731,000)
	Contributory income	$182,750
Total operating costs		(114,000)
	Operating income (before tax)	$ 68,750
	Income tax	(24,750)
	Net income	$ 44,000

Assuming cost projections are accurate, total annual sales revenue of $913,750 is required to yield a 20% after-tax return on the owner's investment next year. Now we can look at the relationship to the individual customer to total sales revenue of $913,750. The relationship to total sales revenue is the average check.

The average check will tell us the average amount each customer will spend in the restaurant over the next year to meet our required total sales revenue objective. Assuming the restaurant is open 6 days per week for 52 weeks, operations will be conducted for 312 days (6 × 52) with an average seat turnover of 2 times per day during the next annual operating period. The equation to calculate the average check is:

Average seat turnover

$$\text{Average check} = \frac{\text{Total annual sales revenue}}{\text{Seats} \times \text{Seat turnover} \times \text{Operating days}}$$

$$= \frac{\$913,750}{100 \times 2 \times 312} = \frac{\$913,750}{62,400} = \underline{\underline{\$14.64}}$$

If we believe faster service can be implemented, it is possible to increase seat turnover from 2 to 2.5 times per day, which in turn would decrease the average check from $14.64 to $11.71.

$$\text{Average check} = \frac{\$913,750}{100 \times 2.5 \times 312} = \frac{\$913,750}{78,000} = \underline{\underline{\$11.71}}$$

Regardless what the average check is, it does not tell us what each menu item should be priced at. The average check indicates what each customer on average is expected to spend. The average check does give us an idea of what the pricing structure of the menu should be with a balance of prices, on average some higher and some lower.

The average check also provides a barometer that allows an evaluation of whether or not we are achieving the net income objective as the year progresses. If actual spending per customer is less than the level required and all other items such as seat turnover, operating costs, and other costs have not changed, then we know something must be done to correct the potential net income shortfall.

If seat turnover must be improved, selling prices may have to be raised, costs may have to be decreased, or a combination of these variables may be required. The average check discussed to this point represents an average for all meal periods combined. The next section will discuss average check per meal period.

AVERAGE CHECK BY MEAL PERIOD

Calculation of average check by meal period

Most restaurants serving more than one meal period per day will have an average check that is different for each meal period. As a general rule, the average check will increase from breakfast to lunch and increase again from lunch to dinner. Since there is a variance in the average check per meal period, it would be extremely useful to determine the average check for each meal period served to supplement the total daily average check.

To determine the average check per meal period, it is necessary to know what percentage of total sales revenue and the seat turnover each meal period is generating. In an ongoing operation, historical records can provide the necessary information; however, a new restaurant will be dependent on management forecasting to obtain the information needed. As an example, we will assume a restaurant has 80 seats and serves lunch and dinner over an operating period of 6 days per week or 312 days annually. Records indicate that 40%

of total revenue is from the lunch period with a 1.25 seat turnover, and 60% of total revenue is from the dinner period with a 1.0 seat turnover. To determine the average check per meal period we will use $825,000 as total sales revenue using the same concept of the previously shown equation to find the average check, modified to finding the average check per meal period:

$$\text{Average check meal period} = \frac{\text{Meal period revenue (\%)} \times \text{Total sales revenue}}{\text{Seats} \times \text{Meal period seat turnover} \times \text{Operating days}}$$

The calculation of the average lunch check is:

$$\frac{40\% \times \$825,000 = \$330,000}{80 \times 1.25 \times 312 = 31,200} = \underline{\$10.58}$$

The calculation of the average dinner check is:

$$\frac{60\% \times \$825,000 = \$495,000}{80 \times 1.0 \times 312 = 24,960} = \underline{\$19.83}$$

Accuracy of average checks

The accuracy of the average checks determined for both meal periods is verified as:

Lunch: 80 seats × 1.25 turnover × $10.58 average check × 312 days =	$330,096
Dinner: 80 seats × 1.0 turnover × $19.83 average check × 312 days =	$494,957
Total sales revenue	$825,053

Our original estimated annual sales revenue was $825,000 and the estimated annual sales revenue using the calculated average meal period checks is $53 greater, due to rounding of the average checks to the closest cent.

PRICING MENU ITEMS

Use of a cost percentage

One of the more common methods used to determine the selling prices of menu items is based on the use of a cost percentage. The cost percentage is derived from costing the specific ingredients of each menu item to identify a "standard cost" (what the cost should be) for each menu item. This pricing method can be calculated two different ways to find a selling price based on a cost percentage. As an example, we know from Exhibit 6.2 that 40% was the variable food cost of sales as a percentage of sales revenue. To illustrate the use of a 40% cost percentage, both methods will be used to set a selling price on a menu item with a cost of $ 4.00 as follows:

$$\frac{\text{Menu item cost}}{\text{Cost \%}} = \frac{\$4.00}{.40} = \underline{\$10.00} \text{ selling price}$$

or

$$\text{Menu item cost} \times (1 \div 40\%) = \$4.00 \times 2.5\% = \underline{\$10.00} \text{ Selling price}$$

Although the use of a cost percentage is easy to understand and use, it may not be practical to apply the division or multiplication factors across the board for all menu items. When determining selling prices, the market being serviced must be considered as well as what potential customers are willing to pay for certain menu items, and what other competitive operations are charging for the same menu item must be evaluated. Setting menu selling prices that are influenced by customers and competitive prices can become a juggling act, causing some selling prices to be set at a cost percentage higher and others lower than the average cost of sales percentage.

It is also important to remember individual food cost percentages share the stage with the resulting gross margin realized from the sale of a menu item. To illustrate, compare the analysis of the following two menu items:

Item	Cost	Selling Price	Cost %	Gross Margin
1	$5.00	$10.00	50%	$5.00
2	$1.00	$ 4.00	25%	$3.00

Higher gross profit items

All other considerations being equal, it would be more profitable to sell menu item 1, which has a higher cost percentage but also gives a higher gross margin of $5.00 per unit. Menu item 2 has a lower cost percentage and a lower gross margin. Certainly, it appears that selling more of menu item 1 will increase sales revenue, gross margin and result in a higher average check regardless of the 50% food cost.

What people choose from a variety of menu selections is known as the sales mix. In menu pricing it is a good idea to keep the likely sales mix in mind since the average check, and ultimately net income, can be influenced by a change in the sales mix. To illustrate this refer to the following, which shows a sales mix for a fast food restaurant giving an average check of $4.66:

The sales mix

Menu Item	Quantity Sold	Selling Price	Total Revenue
1	25	$3.00	$ 75.00
2	75	4.00	300.00
3	50	5.00	250.00
4	60	5.00	300.00
5	40	6.00	240.00
Totals	250		$1,165.00

$$\text{Average check } \frac{\$1,165.00}{250} = \$4.66$$

Changing sales mix

Let us assume that, by promotion or other means, the sales mix was changed, with 25 people no longer selecting menu item 2: 5 will switch to menu item 1, and the other 20 will choose menu item 4. The new sales mix is shown below with a new higher average check of $4.72. The higher average check would normally result in a higher gross margin and net income, in addition to higher revenue.

Menu Item	Quantity Sold	Selling Price	Total Revenue
1	30	$3.00	$ 90.00
2	50	4.00	200.00
3	50	5.00	250.00
4	80	5.00	400.00
5	40	6.00	240.00
Totals	250		$1,180.00

$$\text{Average check } \frac{\$1,180.00}{250} = \$4.72$$

However, it may be more meaningful to see how a changed sales mix affects gross profit rather than average check. Consider the previous two menus, but with three new columns added—food cost of each menu item, gross profit for each item, and total gross profit for each item and in total.

Menu Item	Quantity Sold	Food Cost	Selling Price	Gross Profit	Total Gross Profit
1	25	$1.50	$3.00	$1.50	$ 37.50
2	75	1.75	4.00	2.25	168.75
3	50	2.00	5.00	3.00	150.00
4	60	2.00	5.00	3.00	180.00
5	40	2.50	6.00	3.50	140.00
Total gross profit					$676.25
1	30	1.50	3.00	1.50	$ 45.00
2	50	1.75	4.00	2.25	112.50
3	50	2.00	5.00	3.00	150.00
4	80	2.00	5.00	3.00	240.00
5	40	2.50	6.00	3.50	140.00
Total gross profit					$687.50

Changed sales mix

In the second situation the changed sales mix has resulted in an additional gross profit of $11.25, and, all other things being equal (labor and other direct costs), this will result in the same increase in profit (operating income).

Menu Engineering

Another method of menu analysis is known as menu engineering. The term and concept of menu engineering were first introduced in a book by Michael L. Kasavana and Donald J. Smith called *Menu Engineering—A Practical Guide to Menu Analysis* (Lansing, MI: Hospitality Publications, 1982).

Separate meal periods

To use menu engineering, a worksheet such as that illustrated in Exhibit 6.4 is used. A separate worksheet needs to be used for each meal period, and for each meal period a separate worksheet has to be used for each menu category, such as appetizers, entrees, and desserts. The reason for this is that menu engineering uses each menu item's contribution margin (or gross profit, that is, selling price less food cost) in the analysis. Wide variations in contribution margin can arise between, for example, appetizers and entree items, and if those contribution margins were compared, no meaningful analysis will be arrived at.

Menu engineering focuses on the contribution margin (gross profit) of each menu item and ratio analysis combined with customer popularity and demand. The variable cost nature of cost of sales items should never be ignored in menu engineering. The contribution margin should be looked at closely even though contribution margins are generally defined as high or low when compared to the average contribution margin for all items sold. For example, an average contribution of $6.50 for all items becomes the center point and if a item has a contribution margin of $5.50 it is considered low, whereas an item with a contribution margin of $7.00 is considered to high.

Item popularity

Similarly, each item's popularity is also defined as either high or low by comparing its sales mix percentage to the average sales mix percentage, that is, the quantity sold of each menu item as a percentage of the total quantity sold of all menu items.

A completed menu engineering worksheet is shown in Exhibit 6.5. The following is a summary of each column or box on this exhibit:

> *Column A—Menu item name:*   Lists all the items in the menu category being analyzed.
>
> *Column B—Number sold (MM):*   MM stands for menu mix (sales mix). This column records the quantity of each menu item sold for the period being analyzed, with the total of all items sold recorded at the bottom of the column in Box N.
>
> *Column C—Menu mix %:*   Converts the number sold of each menu item from column B into a percentage of all items sold. The quantity sold of

Exhibit 6.4   Blank Menu Engineering Worksheet

Restaurant: _____

Date: _____

Meal Period: _____

(A) Menu Item Name	(B) Number Sold (MM)	(C) Menu Mix %	(D) Item Food Cost	(E) Item Selling Price	(F) Item CM (E-D)	(G) Menu Costs (D*B)	(H) Menu Revenues (E*B)	(L) Menu CM (F*B)	(P) CM Category	(R) MM% Category	(S) Menu Item Classification	(T) Profit Factor
Column Totals:	N					I	J	M				

Additional Computations:

$K = I/J$ $O = M/N$ $Q = (100/Items) (70\%)$

253

each item is divided by the total of all items sold then multiplied by 100. For example, for the first item on the menu the calculation is:

$$\frac{331}{2873} \times 100 = 11.5\%$$

Column D—Item food cost: Lists the food cost for each menu item.

Column E—Item selling price: Lists the selling price of each menu item.

Column F—Item CM (E–D):   Records the CM (contribution margin) of each menu item by deducting its food cost (column D) from its selling price (column E). The contribution margin is the amount of money obtained from each item sold to cover all other costs and the profit desired by the operation.

Column G—Menu costs (D*B):   Lists the total cost for each menu item sold. It is calculated by multiplying the number sold of each menu item (column B) by its food cost (column D). The dollar amounts in this column of the worksheet have been rounded to the nearest dollar for the sake of simplicity.

Column H—Menu revenues (E*B):   Lists the total sales or revenue for each menu item sold. It is calculated by multiplying the number sold of each menu item (column B) by its selling price (column E). The dollar amounts in this column have also been rounded to the nearest dollar for the sake of simplicity.

Box I: Records the total cost of all menu items sold and is the total of column G.

Box J: Records the total sales or revenue generated from all menu items sold and is the total of column H.

Box K = I/J: Used if an overall food cost percentage for the period is desired. It is calculated by dividing the box I total by the box J total and multiplying by 100.

Column L—Menu CM (F*B):   Records the total contribution margin (gross profit) for each menu item. It is obtained by multiplying the quantity sold figure (column B) by the contribution margin figure (column F). Alternatively, it can be calculated by deducting the total food cost for each item (column G) from its total revenue (column H). Again, the dollar amounts in this column have been rounded to the nearest dollar for the sake of simplicity.

Box M: Records the total of column L.

Box N: As previously stated, box N records the total of column B.

Box O = M/N: Records the average contribution margin for all items sold. It is obtained by dividing the total contribution margin (box M) by the total number of items sold (box N). It is the resulting figure in this box to which the contribution margin of each individual menu item is compared to determine if its contribution margin is higher or lower than the average contribution margin.

Column P—CM category: Records either an H (for high) or an L (for low) after that item's individual contribution margin is compared with the average contribution margin in box O. If it is higher than the average, an H is recorded; if lower than the average, an L is recorded. For example, the first menu item has a contribution margin of $7.45 in column F, which is lower than the average of $7.78 in box O, so an L is recorded in column P.

Box Q = (100/items) (70%):   Records the average popularity of all menu items. In Exhibit 6.5 there are 10 items on the menu, so average popularity is 100% divided by 10 = 10%. (Note: If there were only 5 items on the menu, average popularity would be 100% divided by 5 = 20%, and if there were 20 items on the menu, average popularity would be 100% divided by 20 = 5%).

In our case, the average popularity of each item should be 10% of all items sold. However, Kasavana and Smith state that it is unreasonable in practice to expect that every menu item will achieve this minimum level of sales and suggest, based on their experience, that the minimum popularity of each menu item should be only 70% of the average popularity number In our situation this would be 7% (70% times 10%).

Column R—MM% category: Records either an H (for high) or an L (for low). These definitions are made by comparing each menu item's menu mix percentage (from column C) with the average percentage of 7 from box Q. If the figure from column C is higher than the average, an H is recorded; and if it is less than average, an L is recorded. For example, the first menu item shows 11.5% in column C, and this is higher than 7% in box Q, so an H is shown in column R.

Column S—menu item classification: Lists each menu item in one of four categories. There are four possible combinations of letters in columns P and R: HH, HL, LH, and LL. Using the terminology of Kasavana and Smith, the categories are stars, plowhorses, puzzles, and dogs:

Exhibit 6.5   Completed Menu Engineering Worksheet

Restaurant: __Pavilion__

Date: ____July 1, 0003__

Meal Period: ____Dinner__

(A) Menu Item Name	(B) Number Sold (MM)	(C) Menu Mix %	(D) Item Food Cost	(E) Item Selling Price	(F) Item CM (E-D)	(G) Menu Costs (D*B)	(H) Menu Revenues (E*B)	(L) Menu CM (F*B)	(P) CM Category	(R) MM% Category	(S) Menu Item Classification	(T) Profit Factor
Steak 8 oz.	331	11.5	5.50	12.95	7.45	1,821	4,286	2,466	L	H	plowhorse	1.10%
Steak 10 oz.	295	10.3	6.80	15.95	9.15	2,006	4,705	2,699	H	H	star	1.21%
Chicken breast	320	11.1	3.25	7.95	4.70	1,040	2,544	1,504	L	H	plowhorse	0.67%
Veal neptune	175	6.1	5.75	12.45	6.70	1,006	2,179	1,173	L	L	dog	0.52%
Prime rib	452	15.7	5.95	16.95	11.00	2,689	7,661	4,972	H	H	star	2.22%
Lamb chops	307	10.7	5.70	12.95	7.25	1,750	3,976	2,226	L	H	plowhorse	0.99%
Fried shrimp	254	8.9	4.20	10.95	6.75	1,067	2,782	1,715	L	H	plowhorse	0.77%
Sole filet	314	10.9	5.05	12.45	7.40	1,586	3,909	2,324	L	H	plowhorse	1.04%
Crab legs	246	8.6	6.10	13.95	7.85	1,501	3,432	1,931	H	H	star	0.86%
Salmon steak	179	6.2	4.95	12.45	7.50	886	2,229	1,343	L	L	dog	0.60%
	N					I	J	M				
Column Totals:	2,873					15,352	37,703	22,353				

Additional Computations:

K = I/J	O = M/N	Q = (100/Items) (70%)
40.7%	7.78%	100 / 10 x 70% = 70%

256

- Stars are items with both higher than average contribution margin and higher than average popularity, that is, HH items.
- Plowhorses have lower than average contribution margin but higher than average popularity, that is, LH items.
- Puzzles have higher than average contribution margin but lower than average popularity, that is, HL items.
- Dogs have both lower than average contribution margin and lower than average popularity, that is, LL items.

These four categories will be discussed in more detail later in the chapter.

Column T—profit factor: Shows each item's share of the total menu contribution margin. The profit factor is calculated in two steps:

Two steps

1. Divide the menu's total contribution margin by the number of items on the menu to obtain the average contribution margin per menu item. In our case, the total contribution margin of $22,353 from box M is divided by 10 menu items for an average contribution margin of $2,235.
2. Divide each item's total contribution margin by the average contribution margin to arrive at the profit factor. For example, in Exhibit 6.5, the first menu item shows a total contribution margin of $2,466 in column L. This figure divided by the average of $2,235 from step 1 results in a profit factor of 1.10, which is recorded in column T.

It is wrong to assume that if an item has a very high profit factor this is good. Because of the way in which profit factors are calculated, the average of all profit factors is 1.0. This means that any profit factors higher than 1.0 have to be balanced by other profit factors lower than one. In other words, the higher some items' profit factors are, the lower others will be.

Unbalanced menu

Thus, the menu will not be a balanced menu, which it would be if all menu items differ only slightly from the average of 1.0. If some items that have a vary high profit factor are offset by items with very low profit factors, the operating expenditures for the very low menu items are generally considered as being wasted. Such expenditures are for purchasing, receiving, storing, issuing, preparation, and service. However, this point of view is far from correct from a marketing point of view. It is important not to lose sight of this, and the consideration of the variance and availability of a balanced menu from the viewpoint of customers and their anticipated demands for specific menu items.

Stars

Stars are menu items that the restaurant manager would prefer to sell whenever possible. These items should be left on the menu unless there is a good reason to remove them. However, do not be misled by the profitability of the stars if the menu is unbalanced as indicated by the profit factors showing that too much of the total contribution margin is derived from too few of the menu items. The total contribution margin should be spread more equitably over all menu items or maximized even further by eliminating the low contribution margin items.

Stars should also be located in the most favorable position on the menu so they continue to remain stars. Also, because of their relative popularity, the prices of such items can often be raised without affecting that popularity, thus increasing profits. Generally, stars are the least price sensitive (inelastic) items on the menu. Prices of these items should never be reduced because the quantity sold will likely not be affected but total contribution margin will be reduced. On the other hand, if star prices are increased, demand will not be affected and total contribution margin will increase. However, if the demand for stars is elastic, a price reduction might considerably increase sales (and profits) for these items.

Finally, since stars are the most popular and profitable items on the menu, quality control in their preparation and service is extremely important.

One could question whether stars should always be retained. For example, consider the following three menu items:

Menu Item	Classification	Item Contribution Margin	Quantity Sold	Total Contribution Margin
1	Plowhorse	$4.95	500	$2,475
2	Puzzle	$5.45	400	$2,180
3	Star	$7.05	300	$2,115

Menu item 1's total contribution margin is $2,475, and number 2's is $2,180. Both of these are higher than the star's total contribution margin of $2,115, which means that, from a profit point of view, it is a less desirable menu item than either the plowhorse or the puzzle items. Therefore, a critical factor in menu engineering analysis is not to ignore total contribution margin for each item.

Plowhorses

Plowhorses are items that, though popular with customers, provide a low contribution margin. They should generally be kept on the menu, but the restaurant manager should try to increase their contribution margin without affecting demand. Raising their prices is one way to do this. Another way is to review the recipes and purchase specifications with the objective of decreasing the cost of ingredients or reducing the portion size. Alternatively, contribution margin can be increased by repackaging the item with a side item and repricing the package upwards. If contribution margin cannot be increased, plowhorses should be relegated to a less favorable position on the menu. Because plowhorses have a low contribution margin, lowering their prices is not a good idea because this will reduce the overall total contribution margin. Favoring these items through improved menu location or server suggestion is also not a good idea because that will simply take business away from more profitable menu items.

Profit factors are
important
The profit factors (from column T of the worksheet) are very important with plowhorses. Some items can, by the high quantity sold, account for significant total contribution margin and, thus, profits. They must be analyzed very carefully.

Puzzles

Puzzles have higher than average contribution margin but lower than average popularity. They are profitable items but do not sell well. Possible reasons for not selling well are that their prices are too high, that their quality is not satisfactory, or that they are just not suited to the restaurant's customers. They should not generally be removed from the menu, but the restaurant manager should try to increase demand for them by renaming them, making their menu descriptions more appealing, or relocating them to a more favorable position on the menu. Another alternative is to reduce the price, particularly if the item has a relatively high contribution margin and an elastic demand. In other words, sales should be encouraged because such items may be facing price resistance from customers. However, do not reduce the price too much since this can take business away from the stars.

Increase price
In some cases the price of a puzzle item can be raised, if it is very popular only with a few customers whose demand is inelastic. Increased prices will not affect the demand from these customers, but total contribution margin will increase.

If a puzzle item remains truly unpopular, it should be removed from the menu and replaced by one that a customer survey shows would be much more popular.

Dogs

Dogs have both lower than average contribution margin and lower than average popularity. From the restaurant operator's point of view, these are generally the least desirable items to have on the menu. If their contribution margin and/or popularity cannot be increased, these items should generally be replaced on the menu with new and more popular items that also have a higher contribution margin.

Retain some dogs

However, sometimes there may be a good reason to retain a dog on the menu. If a dog is popular with a few regular customers it might be a mistake to take it off the menu. In this case a price increase should be considered so that it moves into the puzzle category. Alternatively, over time its popularity might increase and move it into the plowhorse category.

Summary

Menu engineering concentrates on three variables: customer demand (that is, how many customers eat in the restaurant), analysis of the menu items' sales mix to determine the profitability of individual menu items, and item contribution margin (the difference between an item's selling price and its food cost). A menu that provides the highest overall contribution margin is considered the most desirable and overall food cost percent is not a consideration.

Note that any changes made to a menu as a result of menu engineering should be reviewed after a suitable period of time. If a revised menu produces no more total contribution margin than before, then nothing has been achieved. Total contribution margin can be generally improved by emphasizing the stars to customers, reducing the number of puzzles, and eliminating the dogs.

Finally, a problem with menu engineering is that it is oriented toward maximizing item contribution margin. The high contribution margin items are usually those that have not only the highest prices but also the highest food cost percentage. Higher prices can also decrease customer demand and profit. However, menu engineering works well when sales revenues are increasing at a good pace, although that is often not the case for many restaurants. Also, below a certain volume of sales, a particular menu item may provide a contribution margin that seems satisfactory but does not cover its total cost.

Variables make menu
pricing a complex task

Because of all the variables (that different menu items must be offered with different prices and different markups, that gross profit dollars will vary from menu item to menu item, that food cost percentage by itself may not be a meaningful guide to determining selling prices, and that the sales mix must be kept in mind), menu pricing can be a complex task for management.

The comments made in this section on setting food menu selling prices are equally as valid for establishing beer, wine, and liquor prices in a beverage operation.

Integrated Pricing

In pricing food and alcoholic beverages, the manager should also keep integrated pricing in mind. This simply means that products should not be priced independently of each other. This is particularly true if the beverage operation is closely integrated with the food operation: that is, the customers eating in the dining area are the ones who provide most of the business for the beverage operation. In such cases, both food and beverage prices should complement each other to achieve profit objectives. Generally, in such a situation, the more food that is sold, the higher beverage sales will be (a concept known as derived demand) and vice versa.

SEAT TURNOVER

Increasing seat turnover

Earlier in this chapter, it was stated that one way to offset a declining average check, or average customer spending, is to increase customer counts or seat turnover. Let us have a look at a case concerning two different restaurants, each with 200 seats.

	Restaurant A		Restaurant B	
	Customers	**Seat Turnover**	**Customers**	**Seat Turnover**
Sunday	200	1.0	350	1.75
Monday	250	1.25	350	1.75
Tuesday	350	1.75	350	1.75
Wednesday	350	1.75	350	1.75
Thursday	450	2.25	350	1.75
Friday	550	2.75	450	2.25
Saturday	650	3.25	600	3.0
	2,800	14.00	2,800	14.00

Average number
of customers

Average seat turnover

$$\frac{2,800}{7} = 400 \qquad\qquad \frac{2,800}{7} = 400$$

$$\frac{14}{7} = 2 \qquad\qquad \frac{14}{7} = 2$$

Weekly distribution
of customers

Daily seat turnover is calculated by dividing the number of customers each day by the number of seats available (200 in this case). Average turnover for the week can be calculated by dividing total turnover for the week (14 in our case) by 7. Even though the average results in both restaurants are the same—an average of 400 customers per day, or an average seat turnover of 2 per day—the distribution of customers throughout the week is quite different. Such an analysis can be helpful in decisions concerning staffing and advertising, as well as seeing where a declining average check might be compensated for by increasing seat turnover to maintain total sales revenue and protect net income.

ROOM RATES

Room supply fixed

The approach illustrated earlier in this chapter for determining a required average restaurant check can also be used for calculating room rates. Hotel or motel rooms are, however, a different type of commodity from restaurant seats. Restaurant seats can be increased in the short run by squeezing in some extra tables to take care of high demand.

Alternatively, service can be speeded up and seat turnover increased to accommodate peak demand periods. The same cannot be done with guest rooms in a hotel or motel. Supply cannot be increased in the short run. The number of rooms is fixed. Neither can turnover be increased. Apart from selling rooms during the day for meetings or similar uses, the normal turnover rate of a room is only once per 24-hour period at a maximum. One hundred single beds in a hotel can only be occupied by 100 persons each 24 hours. One hundred seats in a restaurant can be occupied by 100, 200, or even 300 persons or more, if the demand is there, during a meal period or day.

Room revenue lost forever

One other factor to be considered is that if revenue for a room on a particular night is not obtained, that revenue is gone forever. The room revenue and the cost of providing that unsold space cannot be recovered directly. This differs from food and beverages. If these items are purchased by the restaurant and not sold on a particular day, they can be stored for short periods and sold at a later date. The cost is still recoverable. The importance of having a room rate that will permit costs of providing the space to be recovered and the importance of as high a utilization of the rooms as possible is thus emphasized.

THE $1 PER $1,000 METHOD

Relationship between building cost and room rate

One of the methods developed many years ago for setting an appropriate room rate is the so-called $1 per $1,000 approach. Since the greatest cost in a hotel or motel property is the investment in building (from 60 to 70% of total investment), it was argued that there should be a fairly direct relationship between the cost of the building and the room rate to be charged. From this developed the rule of thumb that for each $1,000 in building cost, $1 of room rate should be charged in order for the investment to be profitable. In other words, if a 100-room hotel had a building cost of $4,000,000, its average cost of construction is:

$$\frac{\$4,000,000}{100} = \underline{\$40,000} \text{ per room}$$

The $1 per thousand calculation

Then, for each $1,000 of construction cost per room, there should be $1 of room rate. The average room rate would then be:

$$\frac{\$40,000}{\$1,000} = 40 \times \$1 = \underline{\underline{\$40.00}}$$

This rule of thumb worked under certain circumstances and assumptions. Some of these assumptions were that the hotel was a relatively large one (several hundred rooms), that there was sufficient rent from shops and stores in the building to pay for interest and real estate taxes, that other departments (food, beverages, and so on) were contributing income to the overall hotel operation, and that the average year-round occupancy was 70%. These assumptions are all quite specific. Consider the following two small hotel operations: Hotel A, which has no public facilities, and Hotel B, with more spacious lobbies and a dining room/coffee shop and banquet rooms.

	Hotel A	Hotel B
Building cost	$2,000,000	$2,600,000
Number of rooms	50	50
Cost per room	$40,000	$52,000
Room rate at $1 per $1,000	$40	$52

If the $1 per $1,000 rule of thumb were used, Hotel B would find itself at a distinct disadvantage to Hotel A, assuming the two properties were in the same competitive market. These two competitive properties are of course not in fact in the same competitive market since Hotel A has no public facilities.

The $1 per $1,000 rule also leaves room rates tied to historical construction costs and ignores current costs, including current financing costs. The bottom-up approach to room rates overcomes the pitfalls inherent in the $1 per $1,000 method. This bottom-up approach to room pricing is frequently referred to as the Hubbart formula, which was developed some years ago for the American Hotel and Motel Association.

The Bottom-Up Approach

The bottom-up approach to room rates is quite similar to that discussed earlier with reference to determining the average check required in a restaurant. We will use the facts illustrated in Exhibit 6.6. The motel has 50 rooms. Note that the cost projections, even though based on past information from income statements, have been projected to take care of anticipated increases for next year. Our total cost of operating next year is, therefore, as in Exhibit 6.7.

Assuming the motel is going to continue to operate at a 70% occupancy, it will sell the following number of rooms per year.

Exhibit 6.6   Motel Cost Projections Next Year

Net income required	10% after-tax on present investment of $550,000 = $55,000
Income tax	50% rate
Depreciation	present book value of building $1,200,000—depreciation rate 5% = $60,000
	present book value of furniture and equipment $150,000—depreciation rate 20% = $30,000
Interest	present mortgage payable $750,000 @ 10% = $75,000
Property taxes and insurance	$30,000
Administrative and general	$47,000
Marketing	$25,000
Utilities	$17,000
Repairs and maintenance	$32,000
	Total $121,000
Rooms department operating costs	$137,000 a year for wages, linen, laundry, and supplies. This is based on past income statements at a 70% occupancy.
Coffee shop contributory income	$15,500 a year at 70% rooms occupancy

Rooms available × Occupancy % × 365

50   ×   70%   ×   365 = $\underline{12,775}$

Its average room rate will therefore have to be:

Calculation of required average rate

$$\frac{\text{Sales revenue required}}{\text{Rooms to be sold}} = \frac{\$547,500}{12,775} = \$42.86, \text{ rounded to } \underline{\$43.00}$$

Note that this figure, $43, is only an average room rate and is not necessarily the rate for any specific room. Most large hotels have a variety of sizes and types of rooms, each type having a rate for single occupancy and a higher rate for double occupancy. Motels, even if they have only one size and type of room, have a single rate and a double rate for it.

Where there are multiple types of rooms and multiple rates, the calculated average rate can only be a guide to what the actual rate for each specific type of room will be. Size of room, decor, and view will be some of the factors to consider in arriving at a balance of rates that will both be fair and allow the resulting average rate to work out to the required figure.

Exhibit 6.7   Motel Total Cost of Operating Next Year

Rooms department operating costs		$137,000
Total overhead costs		121,000
Property taxes and insurance		30,000
Interest		75,000
Depreciation		
building	$60,000	
furniture and equipment	30,000	90,000
Income tax		55,000
Net income required		55,000
Total costs		$563,000
Less coffee shop contributory income		(15,500)
Total net costs to be covered by revenue in rooms department		$547,500

Effect of double occupancy

    Another factor to consider is the rate of double occupancy of rooms. A room that is occupied by two persons has a higher rate than the same room occupied by one person. The higher the proportion of double occupancies, the higher will be the resulting average rates. In our example, a safe way to assure that we achieve at least a $43 average would be to make that the minimum single rate for any room. Any rooms we then sell that have a higher single rate, or any rooms sold at the double occupancy rate, would guarantee that our average rate will end up higher than $43. Unfortunately, competition and customer resistance may preclude this approach.

    In a simple motel situation, with only one standard type of room and all rooms having the same single or double rate, is there a method of calculating what these rates should be? The answer is yes—as long as we decide what the spread will be between the single rate and the double, and as long as we have a good idea of the double occupancy percentage.

CALCULATING SINGLE AND DOUBLE RATES

To illustrate this we will use the information about our 50-room motel. We know that $43 is the average rate required to cover all costs and give us the return on investment we want. Present average occupancy is 70%. We know from past experience that our double occupancy rate is 40% and that we want a $10 difference between the single and the double rates. The double occupancy rate is calculated as follows:

Calculation of double occupancy percentage

Total number of guests during year	17,885
Less number of rooms occupied	(12,775)
Equals number of rooms double occupied	5,110

$$\text{Double occupancy rate} = \frac{5,110}{12,775} \times 100 = \underline{\underline{40\%}}$$

A double occupancy rate of 40% in our operation tells us that 50% of all rooms sold were occupied by two people. In our motel of 50 rooms, with 70% occupancy rate on a typical night, we would have:

$$70\% \times 50 = 35 \text{ rooms occupied}$$

of which

$$40\% \times 35 = 14 \text{ will be double occupied}$$

and

$$35 - 14 = 21 \text{ will be single occupied}$$

Also, in our operation, on a typical night, our total revenue will be:

Total nightly revenue

$$35 \text{ rooms} \times \$43.00 \text{ average rate} = \underline{\underline{\$1,505}}$$

The question now is, at what rates can we sell 21 single rooms and 14 double rooms (at a price $10 higher than the singles) so that total day revenue is $1,505? Expressed arithmetically, this becomes (with x the unknown single rate):

Calculation of average single rate

$$21x + 14(x + \$10) = \underline{\underline{\$1,505}}$$

$$21x + 14x + \$140 = \$1,505$$

$$35x = \$1,505 - \$140$$

$$35x = \$1,365$$

$$x = \frac{\$1,365}{35}$$

$$x = \underline{\underline{\$39.00}}$$

Proof of correctness

Therefore, our single rate is $39 and our double rate is $39 + $10 = $49. Let us prove the correctness of these rates.

$$
\begin{array}{llr}
21 \text{ singles} & \times \$39.00 = & \$819.00 \\
14 \text{ doubles} & \times \$49.00 = & \underline{686.00} \\
35 \text{ rooms} & \times \$43.00 = & \underline{\underline{\$1,505.00}}
\end{array}
$$

These, then, would be the rates under the given circumstances. They are the rates that, given the correctness of our assumptions about next year, we should be charging. They may not be the rates we do charge. Competition, customer resistance, or age of the property may oblige us to reduce them, in which case we will end up with a smaller return on investment than desired. On the other hand, newer establishments in the area with higher construction and operating costs and higher rates, and with a customer willingness to pay them, may allow us to increase our rates above our calculated required ones. In this case we will have a higher return on investment than required.

In trying to determine appropriate room rates, influencing factors tending to decrease the average rate include:

Room rate influencing
factors

- Family rates
- Commercial discounts
- Travel agent commissions (unless accounted for separately)
- Convention or group rates
- Special company or government rates
- Weekly or monthly special rates

On the other hand, extra charges for three or more person in a room would influence the average in an upward direction.

ROOM RATES BASED ON ROOM SIZE

One other possible way of determining average rates for different size rooms is to work on square foot of area basis.

Let us suppose our motel had two different sizes of rooms: 25 of them are 220 square feet (including room entranceway, bathroom, and closet areas) and the other 25 are 180 square feet. The demand for each size of room is about equal. Total square footage available for rental is:

Calculation of available
square footage

$$25 \times 220 \text{ sq. ft.} = 5,500$$
$$25 \times 180 \text{ sq. ft.} = \underline{4,500}$$
$$\text{Total} \qquad \underline{10,000}$$

Even though there is a total of 10,000 square feet available, we are running at a 70% average occupancy. Therefore, on average, each night we are selling:

$$70\% = 10,000 = 7,000 \text{ square feet}$$

Since we must take in $1,505 a night, on average, to give us the required net income, each square foot sold should produce in revenue:

Calcualtion of rate per
square foot

$$\frac{\$1,505}{7,000} = \$0.215$$

Therefore, the average rate that should be charged for our small and large rooms is:

Average rates based on
square footage of room

Small room 180 sq. ft. × $0.215 = $38.70

Large room 220 sq. ft. × $0.215 = $47.30

We can check the accuracy of these figures. Since the two room sizes are in equal demand, we will sell, on average, 17.5 of each per night (25 rooms × 70% occupancy).

17.5 small × $38.70	=	$ 677.25
17.5 large × $47.30	=	827.75
Total revenue per night	=	$1,505.00

Convert to single and
double rates

Note that these average rates for the small and the large size of room must still be converted, using the method illustrated earlier in this chapter, into single and double rates for each size.

AVERAGE OCCUPANCY

Earlier in this chapter, it was demonstrated how an analysis of restaurant seat turnover might indicate where the turnover could be increased to compensate for a declining average check. A parallel situation could exist with reference to average room rates and occupancies. Refer to the following:

	Hotel A	Hotel B
Saturday	40%	60%
Sunday	40	60
Monday	70	70
Tuesday	90	70
Wednesday	90	80
Thursday	90	80
Friday	70	70
	490%	490%
Average	$\frac{490}{7} = 70\%$	$\frac{490}{7} = 70\%$

Analysis of occupancy
by days of week

Both hotels have the same average occupancies, but the analysis by day shows a different picture for each. Hotel A has very low occupancy during weekends and very high occupancy during the week. An advertising campaign directed toward bringing in weekend guests would benefit the rooms department and, no doubt, other departments in the hotel. On the other hand, Hotel B has a relatively high weekend business and good, but not high, occupancy during the week. Its advertising should be geared not just toward weekend promotions but also toward improving midweek occupancy.

ROOM RATE DISCOUNTING

Rack rate defined

Room rate discounting is the practice of reducing prices below the rack rate. The rack rate is defined as the maximum rate that will be quoted for a room. When rates are discounted for some rooms on any night, this prevents the hotel from achieving its maximum potential average room rate and maximum potential total revenue for that night. Rooms are typically discounted for groups, such as convention delegates and corporate and government travelers who are regular customers of the hotel. The discounts given are a normal cost of business to maintain occupancy levels, and the reduced room revenue is often compensated for by extra profits achieved from those room guests patronizing the hotel's food and beverage facilities.

Because a hotel's variable costs for each occupied room are relatively low compared to the room rate, a considerable increase in net income results from selling each additional room. For example, if the rack rate for a room is $99, and variable cost is $19, $80 of additional net income is obtained from selling each extra room that would otherwise stay unoccupied. Theoretically, this hotel could reduce the rate to $20 (let us say) and still make $1 of additional net income. This does not imply that selling all rooms for $20 would be a good long-term decision. In the long term, only those rooms that would otherwise not be sold should have their rates discounted. Before doing any discounting, a hotel should sell all the rooms it can at its highest rate to those customers who are the least price sensitive. When this is achieved, rates should be discounted to obtain business from those who are more price sensitive and then discounted further to those who are most price sensitive.

Traditionally, this is not the way hotels have operated, particularly with reference to city hotels catering to the business traveller whose demand for rooms is primarily during the week, with little or no demand for rooms on weekends. Hotels have reasoned that by offering companies a discounted rate, they would obtain more of that company's business, increase market share, and increase profits. As competitive hotels do the same thing to retain their market share, corporate rates are further reduced by all hotels, and nobody wins. Further, these discounted rates are being offered to the market segment that is the least price sensitive since the corporate guest is not very concerned about the price of the room since the company pays the bill.

The negative effect of this strategy of discounting the corporate rate is often combined with the policy of selling as many rooms as possible to that market segment (in order to retain that business) even when those rooms could be sold at higher rates to other market segments.

DISCOUNT GRID

In reviewing room rates and deciding on the discounts to be offered, it is useful to prepare a discount grid. This grid shown in Exhibit 6.8 shows the impact of various room rate discounts on total room revenue.

Marginal costs

To prepare the grid, the marginal (variable) costs of selling each additional room must be known. Normally, marginal costs occur only in the housekeeping department because no extra costs are incurred in the reservations or front office departments to sell an extra room. Housekeeping costs include such items as employee time to clean the room, cost of linen laundering, cost of guest supplies (soap, shampoo, and similar items), and additional utility costs for lighting and heating or air conditioning. For most hotels, marginal costs are easy to determine.

Let us assume that a 100-room hotel's marginal cost for renting each additional room was $10. The following equation can be used to calculate the equivalent occupancy needed to hold total sales revenue less marginal costs constant if the rack rate is discounted.

Equivalent occupancy equation

$$\text{Equivalent occupancy} = \frac{\text{Rack rate} - \text{Marginal cost}}{[\text{Rack rate} \times (1 - \text{Discount percentage})] - \text{Marginal cost}}$$

Assume that all the hotel's rooms have the same rack rate of $80 and that the hotel currently operates at a 70% occupancy. If rates are discounted by 10%, the equivalent occupancy required (using the equation) would be:

$$70\% \times \frac{\$80 - \$10}{[\$80 \times (1 - 0.10)] - \$10}$$

$$= 70\% \times \frac{\$70}{(\$80 \times 0.9) - \$10}$$

$$= 70\% \times \frac{\$70}{\$72 - \$10}$$

$$= 70\% \times \frac{\$70}{\$62}$$

$$= 70\% \times 1.13 = 79.1\%$$

Proof of calculation

This can be proved. Nightly room revenue before discounting is:

$$70\% \text{ occupancy} \times 100 \text{ rooms} \times \$80 \text{ rack rate} = \$5,600$$

and total marginal costs are:

$$70\% \text{ occupancy} \times 100 \text{ rooms} \times \$10 = \$700$$

Net revenue is therefore:

$$\$5,600 - \$700 = \$4,900$$

After discounting, nightly revenue at 79% occupancy will be:

$$79\% \text{ occupancy} \times 100 \text{ rooms} \times \$72 \text{ rate} = \$5,688$$

and total marginal costs will be:

$$79\% \text{ occupancy} \times 100 \text{ rooms} \times \$10 = \$790$$

Net revenue is therefore $5,688 – $790 = $4,898. In other words, net revenue (total sales revenue less marginal costs) is the same as before. (The small difference is due to rounding out the required occupancy level to 79% from 79.1%).

Tabulating results

Similar calculations can be made for various occupancy levels and discount percentages and the results tabulated in a grid such as that in Exhibit 6.8. Once this has been done, the grid shows the equivalent occupancy that must be achieved to maintain room revenue (less marginal costs) at a stipulated level as discounts are increased or decreased. Thus the grid allows management to make sensible pricing decisions.

For example, the grid shows that if the hotel discounts room rates by 15% and its current occupancy is 70%, the equivalent occupancy after discounting would have to be 84.7%. In our 100-room hotel, this means an additional 15 rooms would have to be sold per night. If there is an advertising cost to sell 15 extra rooms this must be considered, as would additional revenue that the additional guests might provide in the food and beverage departments. In other words, the grid should be used only as an aid in decision making and not be the only criterion.

POTENTIAL AVERAGE ROOM RATE

The potential average room rate is defined as the average rate that would result if all rooms occupied overnight were sold at the rack rate without a discount.

Exhibit 6.8   Discount Grid

	New Occupancy Level Necessary to Maintain the Same Current Profitability if an $80 Rack Rate Is Discounted by:			
Occupancy	5%	10%	15%	20%
70%	74.2%	79.1%	84.7%	91.0%
65	68.9	73.5	78.7	84.5
60	63.6	67.8	72.6	78.0
55	58.3	62.2	66.6	71.5
50	53.0	56.5	60.5	65.0

This potential average rate can be used to monitor the actual average room rate.

Multiple rack rates

To this point, we have stated that the rack rate is the maximum rate that will be charged for a room. But in fact, most hotels have two or more rack rates for each room. There may be a rack rate for single occupancy, a rack rate for double occupancy, and even a rack rate for occupancy by three or more. How can a potential average room rate be determined in such a situation?

If a hotel sold all its rooms at single occupancy, its potential average rack rate would be the average rate if all rooms were single occupied. If the hotel sold all its rooms at double occupancy, its potential average rate would be the average rate if all rooms were double occupied. For most hotels, neither of these extremes is likely. For most properties on a typical night, some rooms will be single occupied and others will be double occupied. A further complication is that there may be different types of rooms, whose single or double rack rates are different. Thus, the potential average rate must be calculated by taking the hotel's normal sales mix into consideration.

Consider sales mix

To illustrate, assume that if all of a 100-room hotel's various rooms were each occupied by one person (single occupancy) at the maximum single occupancy rack rate, total sales revenue would be $7,500. Potential minimum average rate is therefore:

$$\frac{\$7,500}{100} = \underline{\underline{\$75}}$$

On the other hand, if all 100 rooms were double-occupied at the maximum double occupancy rack rate, total sales revenue would be $8,500. Potential maximum average rate is therefore:

$$\frac{\$8,500}{100} = \underline{\underline{\$85}}$$

(Note that if the hotel has suites or special rooms at higher rates, these can be included in the maximum potential double rate.)

Rate spread

The difference between $85 and $75 is known as the rate spread. If this hotel's percentage of double occupancy were 40% (that is, 40% of all rooms occupied are occupied by two people), the potential average room rate can be calculated as follows:

Potential average single rate + (Percentage of double occupancy × Rate spread)

In our case, this results in a potential average room rate of:

$$\$75 + (40\% \times \$10.00)$$
$$= \$75 + \$4 = \$79$$

COMPARING ACTUAL AVERAGE TO POTENTIAL AVERAGE

Once the potential average room rate has been calculated, the hotel can compare its actual rate to this potential each day or each period. There may be occasions when the actual rate will be higher than the potential. This could occur when the double occupancy rate exceeds the normal 40% and/or if additional charges are made for a third person in a room and/or if front desk employees are doing a good job of selling the most expensive rooms first.

Average rate ratio

In other cases, the actual average rate will be below the potential rate and can be measured by dividing it by the potential rate and converting to a percentage to arrive at the average rate ratio. For example, if the actual rate achieved during a particular week were $72, the percentage would be:

$$\frac{\$72}{\$79} \times 100 = \underline{\underline{91\%}}$$

This means the hotel achieved only 91% of its potential average rate. This could occur because the double occupancy ratio fell below normal and/or because the front desk employees did a poor job and sold the lower-priced rooms first. Alternatively, all other factors being equal, it could mean that rack rates had been discounted 9% on average.

ROOM RATES FOR EACH MARKET SEGMENT

With reference to the $79 potential average room rate calculated earlier, it is possible to calculate the room rate for each type of market (market segment) with which the hotel deals. Suppose we have the following information for each of three segments:

Market Segment	Annual Room Nights	Percentage	Rack Rate (%)
Business travellers	5,110	40	100%
Conference groups	4,471	35	90
Tour groups	3,194	25	80
	12,775	100	

Information for calculations

The percentage column figures show how much of total business each segment produces. For example, business travellers constitute $5,110/12,775 \times 100 = 40\%$ of total room nights. The rack rate column tells us the percentage of the rack rate that we are going to charge customers in that market segment. For example, business travellers are going to pay 100% of the rack rate (and receive no discount), whereas conference groups will be charged 90% of the rack rate (or receive a 10% discount), and tour groups 80% of the rack rate (or receive a 20% discount). What must those rates be to ensure that we continue to achieve a $79 average room rate?

New potential average rack rate

We must first calculate what the new potential average rack rate is going to be for the business travellers who receive no discount. We know that it will be higher than before because some segments are going to receive a discounted rate, and thus the new rack rate must increase to compensate for these discounts. The calculation is made by weighting the discount percentage for each market segment and, at the same time, taking into account the percentage of business that each market segment generates as follows:

$$\frac{\$79.00}{(40\% \times 100\%) + (35\% \times 90\%) + (25\% \times 80\%)}$$

Note that, in each set of parentheses in the denominator, the first figure represents the portion of the business provided by that segment and the second represents the rack rate percentage for that segment. For example, in the first set of figures the business travellers provide 40% of the business at the full rack rate. Following through on the calculations, we have:

$$\frac{\$79.00}{40\% + 31.5\% + 20\%} = \frac{\$79.00}{91.5\%} = \$86.34$$

The discounted rates for the other segments are:

Conference groups	$86.34 \times 90\% = \$77.70$
Tour groups	$86.34 \times 80\% = \$69.07$

Proof of calculations

We can prove that these rates will generate the sales required to yield our desired potential average room rate:

Market Segment	Room Nights		Average Rate		Total Sales
Business travellers	5,110	×	$86.34	=	$ 441,197
Conference groups	4,471	×	$77.70	=	347,397
Tour groups	3,194	×	$69.07	=	220,610
Totals	12,775				$1,009,204

and

$$\frac{\$1,009,204}{12,775} = \underline{\underline{\$79.00}}$$

OTHER PRICING CONSIDERATIONS

Simplicity ignores other factors

The method demonstrated in this chapter for determining meal selling prices and room rates to ensure an adequate return on investments has its shortcomings. So does the cost plus method used in conjunction with establishing food and beverage prices relative to the cost of food and beverage ingredients. Both the return on investment and cost plus methods are simple and easy to use, but, because of their simplicity, they ignore many other factors that must be taken into consideration in establishing prices. For that reason, return on investment and cost plus pricing should be used as reference points only and should not be the only determinants in setting final prices.

In addition, assumptions are made about rooms occupancy (in a hotel situation) and seat turnover (in a restaurant situation), although adjustments can be made to prices during the actual period when it is seen that rooms occupancy and/or seat turnovers differ from those used in the initial calculations.

Unfortunately, the revised decisions turn out to be the reverse of those that should be made in the circumstances. To illustrate, consider the situation of a hotel that had based its average room rate of $xx.xx for next year on a predicted occupancy of 70%. During the year, it is seen that actual occupancy is closer to 65%, and the average room rate is revised upward to compensate so that the desired profit (operating income) will still be achieved.

Typical situation

However, when you consider a typical business situation, a price increase will often result in a further decrease in demand for rooms, reducing occupancy still further. In normal economic situations, that is, when all other things are equal, the correct thing to do is to lower prices (to stimulate demand) as demand decreases.

If wrong decisions are made as a result of blindly using a "bottom up" pricing approach, empty hotel rooms and empty restaurant seats (and thus reduced profit) will probably result. Similarly, there may be missed profit opportunities because prices could be raised above those calculated using cost-plus when market conditions are such that customers are prepared to pay those higher prices.

Cost-plus pricing can work during periods of low inflation (as long as economic activity is not declining at the same time) and when there is not an oversupply of hotel rooms or restaurant seats (that is, when there is not a particularly acute competitive situation). However, it is rare for this situation to prevail, and for that reason many hotels have begun to employ more sophisticated methods that systematically take into consideration all the relevant factors that should be considered in the pricing decision. One of these less simplistic approaches is yield management (to be discussed later in the chapter).

Rare situation

Some of the other considerations in pricing are discussed in the following sections.

ELASTICITY OF DEMAND

Elasticity of demand is related to the responsiveness of demand for a product or service when prices are changed. A large change in demand resulting from a small change in prices is referred to as elastic demand. A small change in demand following a large change in prices is referred to as inelastic demand. The following is an equation for calculating the elasticity of demand:

Demand versus prices

$$\frac{\text{Change in quantity demanded / Base quantity demanded}}{\text{Change in price / Base price}}$$

For example, suppose a hotel sold 2,000 rooms during the past month at an average rate of $70. For the following month the room rate was increased by $7 to $77. As a result, during the next month 1,900 rooms were sold—a decrease of 100. Placing these numbers in the equation we have:

$$\frac{100 / 2,000}{7 / 70}$$

$$= .05 / .10$$

$$= \underline{0.5}$$

If the calculations show that the elasticity of demand is less than 1, then the demand is said to be inelastic. If the result is more than 1, then demand is elastic. In our case, demand is inelastic because even though the price increase caused fewer rooms to be demanded, total revenue nevertheless increased.

Month 1: 2,000 rooms × $70 = $140,000
Month 2: 1,900 rooms × $77 = $146,300

Thus, the easiest way to test whether demand is elastic or inelastic is to note what happens to total sales revenue when prices are changed. If demand is elastic, a decline in price will result in an increase in total sales revenue because, even though a lower price is being received per unit, enough additional units are now being sold to more than compensate for a lower price.

Example of elastic demand

A generalization is that, if demand is elastic, a change in price will cause total sales revenue to change in the opposite direction. If demand is inelastic, a price decline will cause total sales revenue to fall. The small increase in sales revenue that occurs will not be sufficient to offset the decline in sales revenue per unit. Again, one can generalize and say that, if demand is inelastic, a change in price will cause total sales revenue to change in the same direction.

Availability of substitutes

One of the factors that influences elasticity of demand is the availability of substitutes. Generally, hospitality businesses that charge the highest prices are able to do so since there is little substitution possible. An elite hotel with little competition can charge higher room rates, since its customers expect to pay higher rates, can afford to do so, and generally would not move to a lower-priced, less luxurious hotel if room rates were increased. Demand is inelastic.

On the other hand, a restaurant that is one of many in a particular neighborhood catering to the family trade would probably lose considerable business if it raised its menu prices out of line with its competitors. Its trade is very elastic. Its price-conscious customers would simply take their business to another restaurant. Alternatively, a high-average-check restaurant will probably find less customer resistance to an increase in menu prices. In general, one can say, therefore, that the lower the income of a business's customers, the more elastic is their demand, and vice versa.

Customer habits and loyalty

Closely related to income levels are the habits of a business's customers. The more habit prone the customers are, the less likely are they to resist some upward change in prices, since customers tend to have "brand" loyalties to hotels and restaurants, just as they have with other products they buy. Enterprises that need to count on repeat business must be very conscious of the effect that price changes may have on that loyalty. Note also that the demand for a product or service tends to be more elastic as the time period under consideration increases. Even though customers are creatures of habit and do develop loyalties, those habits and loyalties can change over time.

Each separate hospitality enterprise must therefore be aware of the elasticity of demand of the market in which it operates and of the loyalty of its customers. In other words, it must have a market-oriented approach to pricing. This market orientation is particularly important in short-run decision making, such as offering reduced weekend and off-season room rates to help increase occupancy or special food and beverage prices during slow periods. These reduced rates or prices are particularly appropriate where demand is highly elastic.

Cost Structure

Fixed and variable costs

The specific cost structure of a business is also a major factor influencing pricing decisions. Cost structure in this context means the breakdown of costs into fixed and variable ones. Fixed costs are those that normally do not change in the short run, such as a manager's salary or insurance expense. Variable costs are those that increase or decrease depending on sales volume. An example is food cost.

A business with high fixed costs relative to variable ones will likely have less stable profits as the volume of sales revenue increases or decreases. In such a situation, having the right prices for the market becomes increasingly important. In the short run, any price in excess of the variable cost will produce a contribution to fixed costs and net income, and the lower the variable costs, the wider is the range of possible prices. For example, if the variable, or marginal, costs (such as housekeeping wages, and linen and laundry expense) to sell an extra room are $10, and that room normally sells for $40, any price between $10 and $40 will contribute to fixed costs and net income. In such a situation those who establish prices have at their discretion a wide range of possibilities for imaginative marketing and pricing to bring in extra business and maximize sales revenue and profits (operating income).

Imaginative pricing possibilities

Note that this concept of variable or marginal costing is only valid in the short run. Over the long run prices must be established so that all costs (both fixed and variable) are covered in order to produce a long-run net income.

The subject of fixed and variable costs is covered in some depth in Chapter 7, Cost Management, and Chapter 8, The CVP (Cost-Volume-Profit) Approach to Decisions. In particular, in Chapter 8, the use of the break-even equation is demonstrated in conjunction with the effect a change in room rates has on volume and profits.

The Competition

A hospitality enterprise's competitive situation is also critical in pricing. Very few hospitality businesses are in a monopolistic situation (although some are, such as a restaurant operator who has the only concession at an isolated airport).

Monopolistic pricing

Where there is a monopolistic, or near monopolistic, situation, the operator has greater flexibility in determining prices and may indeed tend to charge more than is reasonably fair. However, in these situations the customer still has the freedom to buy or not buy a meal or drink, or to stay fewer nights in that accommodation. Also, in a monopolistic situation where high prices prevail, other new entrepreneurs are soon attracted to offer competition.

Oligopolistic pricing

In a more competitive, but not completely competitive, situation there often exists an oligopoly. In an oligopoly there tends to be one major or dominant business and several smaller, competitive businesses. In an oligopoly the dominant business is often the price leader. When the price leader's prices are raised or lowered, the prices of the other businesses are raised or lowered in tandem. An oligopolistic situation could arise in a resort area where there is one major resort hotel, surrounded by several other motels catering to a slightly lower income level of customer.

Competitive pricing

However, most hospitality enterprises are in a purely competitive situation, where the demand for the goods and services of any one establishment is highly sensitive to the prices charged. In such situations there is little difference, from a price point of view, between one establishment and the next. Where there is close competition, competitive pricing will often prevail without thought to other considerations. For example, an operator practicing competitive pricing may fail to recognize that his or her particular product or service is superior in some ways to that of competitors and could command a higher price without reducing demand.

Product differentiation

In a highly competitive situation an astute operator will look at the strengths and weaknesses of his or her own situation, as well as those of competitors. In analyzing strengths and weaknesses, operators should try to differentiate themselves and their products and services from their competitors'. The establishments that are most successful in differentiating then have more freedom in establishing their prices. This differentiation can be in such matters as ambience and atmosphere, decor, location, view, and similar factors. Indeed, with differentiation, psychological pricing may be practiced. With psychological pricing the prices are established according to what the customer expects to pay for the "different" goods or services offered. The greater the differentiation, the higher prices can be set. For example, this situation prevails in fashionable restaurants and exclusive resorts, where a particular market niche has been created. At this point, a monopolistic or near monopolistic situation may again prevail.

In summary then, there is no one method of establishing prices for all hospitality enterprises. Each establishment will have somewhat different long-run pricing strategies related to its overall objectives and will adopt appropriate short-run pricing policies depending on its cost structure and market situation.

YIELD MANAGEMENT

The main goal of the rooms department in many hotels is to sell hotel rooms to increase the occupancy percentage. Management's objective is to maximize the sales revenue (or yield) from the rooms available. Unfortunately, many of the methods presently used to measure a hotel's marketing effort do not generate sales decisions that maximize revenue. Marketing effort has been traditionally judged in terms of either the occupancy percentage or the average room rate achieved.

Occupancy percentage misleading

The problem with occupancy percentage is that it does not show whether sales revenue is being maximized. For example, a hotel may be 100% occupied, but many of those guest room occupants may be paying less than the maximum (rack) rate for the room. In other words, managers whose performance is measured by room occupancy are tempted to increase occupancy at the expense of room rate.

Other managers are judged by the average room rate. Again, the average room rate can be increased by refusing to sell any rooms at less than the rack rate, turning away potential customers who are unwilling to pay this rate. Average room rate will be maximized at the expense of occupancy. Average room rate can be slightly more meaningful if it is expressed as a ratio of the maximum potential average rate, as discussed in an earlier section of this chapter, but by itself it does not provide a complete picture.

Instead of focusing on a high occupancy or a high average rate, a better measure of a manager's performance is the yield statistic. Yield is defined as:

Yield statistic equation

$$\frac{\text{Actual revenue}}{\text{Potential revenue}} \times 100$$

Potential revenue is defined as the room sales that would be generated if 100% occupancy was achieved and each room was sold at its maximum rack rate. For example, if a hotel has 150 rooms, each of which has a maximum rack rate of $100, potential sales revenue is:

$$150 \times \$100 = \underline{\underline{\$15,000}}$$

and if actual sales revenue on a particular night is $10,000, then yield is:

$$\frac{\$10,000}{\$15,000} \times 100 = \underline{\underline{66.7\%}}$$

Two factors involved

Yield thus combines two factors: the number of rooms available (inventory) and rooms pricing. Rooms inventory management is concerned with how many rooms are made available to each market segment and its demand for rooms. Pricing management is concerned with the room rate quoted to each of these market segments.

Note that there can be different combinations of room rates and occupancies that achieve the same yield percentage. For example, consider the following three situations that each show various combinations that generate the same actual revenue, and thus the same yield percentage:

Case A 100 rooms occupied × $100.00 average rate = $10,000
Case B 120 rooms occupied × $ 83.33 average rate = $10,000
Case C 140 rooms occupied × $ 71.43 average rate = $10,000

Same yield percentages

In each of these three situations, if potential sales revenue was $15,000, the yield will be the same: 66.7%. However, even though each of these situations is equal insofar as total sales revenue and yield percentage are concerned, they may not be equal in terms of other factors. For example, in Cases B and C there are more rooms occupied than in Case A; thus there will be additional housekeeping and energy costs. On the other hand, Cases B and C also mean more guests in the hotel who are likely to patronize and increase sales revenue in food and beverage areas. Further, if those additional customers are first-time guests of the hotel and leave with a favorable impression, they are likely to be repeat customers and will provide positive word-of-mouth advertising, thus increasing future sales revenue.

Finally, note that because the yield statistic is a combination of occupancy percentage and average room rate, it can be calculated by multiplying the actual occupancy percentage by the average rate ratio. The average rate ratio is the actual average rate expressed as a percentage of the average maximum potential rate. In our 150-room hotel, the maximum average potential rate is $100 ($15,000 potential maximum revenue divided by 150 rooms). In Case A, with 100 rooms occupied (66.7% occupancy) and an average rate ratio of 1.0 or 100% (because the actual average rate is the same as the maximum potential rate), the yield can be calculated as:

Average rate ratio
defined

$$66.7\% \times 1.0 = \underline{\underline{66.7\%}}$$

In Case B it would be:

$$\frac{120}{150} \times \frac{\$83.33}{\$100}$$

= 80% occupancy × 0.8333 average rate ratio = 66.7% yield

and in Case C it would be:

$$\frac{140}{150} \times \frac{\$71.43}{\$100}$$

= 93.33% occupancy × 0.1743 average rate ratio = 66.7% yield

Integrated statistic

Even though the occupancy percentage and the average rate ratio by themselves do not provide complete information, by multiplying them together to provide the yield percentage, a single integrated statistic is produced that is much more meaningful and a more consistent measure of a hotel's performance.

In order to improve this statistic, a practice known as yield management has recently been adopted by some hotels.

The objective of yield management is to maximize hotel room revenue by using basic economic principles to allocate the right type of room to the right type of guest at a price the guest is prepared to pay. The concept of maximizing sales revenue is not new. Indeed, hotel managers have always known that during slow periods they can increase the demand for rooms by looking at the number of reservations they already have for future periods and then reducing the prices of still-available rooms to stimulate further demand. Conversely, during high-demand periods when occupancy will be at or near 100%, they can increase room rates, knowing that customers are prepared to pay higher rates in order to guarantee a reservation. Most hotel operators have traditionally used this concept of supply and demand in their pricing.

When a hotel's sales manager contracts with a conference group at a room rate lower than that for transient guests, she is practicing a form of yield management. Similarly, offering lower transient rates on weekends than during the week is another form of yield management, as is refusing to discount any rates below the rack rate during the peak vacation period. However, it is important for management to go beyond these ad hoc room rate pricing methods to obtain the full benefits of yield management. For example, it has been a common practice for hotels to stop accepting reservations for those days when reservations have reached a certain level. As a result of subsequent cancellations and no shows, empty rooms result. These "spoiled" rooms could have been filled if extra reservations had been taken. A good yield management system can track the level of these spoiled rooms and indicate when extra reservations should be accepted, thus increasing room revenue and increasing guest satisfaction because customers who would otherwise have their reservations declined are able to stay at their hotel of choice. A computerized yield management system can also indicate how much additional sales revenue was produced as a result of management decisions based on yield management.

Traditionally, many hotels have quoted a rate (usually the highest, or rack rate) to inquiring customers and have then reduced this quoted rate (sometimes several times) as the customer shows resistance. Hotels that practice this will end up with a declining average rate because of the high number of rooms sold at a discount. This strategy has little to do with rational yield management. In addition, there will be increasing customer dissatisfaction as guests realize that by offering further resistance they could have obtained an even lower rate.

Airline Practices

Other branches of the tourism industry also use yield management to stimulate demand. For example, the airlines have many different fares for the same aircraft

Supply and demand pricing

Use of computer
programs

seat and either directly or through a travel agency quote a price for that seat, depending on who the customer is and what he or she is prepared to pay to fly. Over the years, the airlines have developed sophisticated computer programs to help them determine how many seats on each aircraft can be allocated in advance for each type of discounted fare in order to fill all seats and maximize their sales revenue on each flight.

What makes airline yield management different from traditional hospitality industry discount pricing is that the airlines constantly update the price decision making process. The computer systems allow discounted prices to change daily to match each day's demand from the various market segments with whom the airlines deal. In other words, airlines constantly adjust the number of seats available at any one price to maximize their revenue or yield.

SIMILARITY OF HOTELS AND AIRLINES

Guest rooms and airline
seats

In many ways, hotel guest rooms are similar to aircraft seats. For example:

- There is a fixed supply in the short run. The objective is thus to use this fixed availability in the most profitable way possible to maximize revenue.
- In many cases, a known proportion of aircraft seats and hotel rooms is reserved some time ahead of their actual usage.
- A guest room not sold (just like an aircraft seat unsold) is lost revenue that can never be recovered. In other words, the inventory is extremely perishable.
- Demand for both airline seats and hotel rooms can fluctuate a great deal, particularly on a seasonal basis. However, it can also vary monthly, and even daily by day of the week. Management must know how and when each market segment makes reservations (by time of year and day of week), must have an overbooking policy for each market segment, and must know the elasticity of demand for each market segment. Computers can easily provide this information by analyzing past experience so that it can be used in forecasting. Indeed, demand forecasting is the basis of effective yield management.

Low marginal costs

- Marginal costs (the cost to sell an extra aircraft seat or hotel room) are relatively low compared to marginal sales revenue. For example, to sell an extra hotel room does not require any more labor in the reservations or front office area. The only additional costs are for housekeeping labor, guest room laundry and supplies expense, and energy.
- Customer characteristics (that is, the market segments with which airlines and hotels deal) are similar. These segments can be easily identified from past demand.

- There is a certain amount of price and time sensitivity for some market segments for both airline seats and hotel rooms. For example, vacation travellers usually reserve both airline seats and hotel rooms well ahead of travel time. These customers reserve primarily on the basis of price. Thus, to reach this market, prices must be reduced and made known to potential customers well in advance. Last-minute price reductions to fill airline seats or hotel rooms are unlikely to generate additional volume from the vacation market.

COMPLICATIONS FOR HOTELS

Note, however, that the yield management practices of the airline industry become somewhat more complicated when applied to the hotel industry. For example, when a customer makes a hotel reservation, that reservation can be for one night, for one night that the guest, after arriving, extends for two or more nights, or for more than one night with the guest subsequently staying for a shorter period than originally reserved. This creates questions, such as the following:

- Will a guest making a low-demand day reservation at a discounted price be allowed, subsequently, to extend that stay at the same price through one or more high-demand days that follow?
- In a situation where a guest inquires about a rate for a stay starting on a low-demand day but extending into high-demand days, should a high-demand price be quoted for the entire period? If so, will the potential customer decide to shop around for a better price at a competitive hotel? The yield management system must consider this type of trade-off possibility.

In addition, when guests make reservations, the derived demand they provide other departments must be considered, along with the market segment that the guest is in. Guests of one market segment might be more likely to use the hotel's food and beverage areas (thus increasing revenue in those areas) than guests of another market segment. Thus, the yield management system must be programmed to consider sales revenue and profitability from more than the rooms department.

Finally, airlines have many different prices for the same seat on an aircraft, and customers know that the earlier they make a reservation for a flight the lower the price is likely to be. This has not traditionally been the way hotels operate, and a hotel converting to a yield management pricing system must consider the effect this will have on its potential customers. For example, in North America the major airlines presently operate in an oligopolistic environment, and the airline customer often has little choice about using a particular airline to fly from point A to point B. Hotels, on the other hand, generally operate in a highly competitive environment, and the potential customer (except in extremely high-demand periods) can shop around for a room rate appropriate to his or her budget.

Note that on a national basis and in the general market area where a hotel is located, total demand for hotel rooms is relatively inelastic. At the local level, however, demand for any particular hotel's rooms (and thus the elasticity of demand for its rooms) can be affected by its pricing decisions. It is thus

Elasticity of demand

important for any individual hotel's management to know what its market segments are and to determine how elastic the demand for each market segment is so that it can adjust its prices to obtain a larger share of each segment.

IMPLEMENTING YIELD MANAGEMENT

Many hotels have adopted yield management and abandoned the practice of pricing rooms according to traditional methods, such as room type and season of the year. By using computers to forecast room demand, they have eliminated a great deal of guesswork from the room rate decision making process. This process involves the number of rooms that should be sold at various room rates.

Wider range of rates

Currently, hotels do not generally have as wide a variety of rates as airlines. Hotels implementing yield management might find it appropriate to parallel the airlines in this regard by having a much wider range of rates than they have traditionally had in order to maximize the benefits that yield management can offer. By having more room rates, the yield management system is better able to influence demand and even length of stay to improve profits. In other words, yield management controls rooms inventory availability.

Customer education

Potential hotel customers may initially consider it unfair (because they are not used to this) to be quoted a different room rate depending on how far in advance they make a reservation. What is therefore required when yield management is implemented are a customer-education program and flexibility in the system to allow reservation department employees to use their judgment when they feel that potential customers are resisting quoted high prices.

Customer education may not be as difficult a process as it seems because, to a degree and depending on who they are, hotel customers are used to paying different rates for the same room. Most hotel guests know that convention delegates are quoted lower rates than transient travellers who might use the same type of room. Large corporations whose representatives stay at a particular hotel when travelling can also generally negotiate a lower rate for rooms. Vacation travellers with a group tour also have a lower room rate negotiated for them by the tour wholesaler. The last-minute walk-in guest normally pays the highest (rack) rate and has little basis for negotiating a lower rate.

Need for compromises

Clearly, yield management involves compromises. For example, the preferred situation would be to have 100% room occupancy with all rooms sold at the rack rate. For most hotels, however, this is unrealistic on a year-round basis and would likely lead to empty rooms and lost sales revenue because the demand for rooms at the maximum rate is not there. An alternative might be to lower all rates to ensure that there is 100% occupancy year round. Again, however, this will lead to lost sales revenue because some of the customers paying low rates would have been prepared to pay higher rates. Thus, in both of these situations, yield (revenue) is not maximized. The objective of yield management is to decide what the trade-off will be between maximizing room rates and maximizing occupancy and how many rooms at rack rates and how many at discounted rates will be offered during each period to each different market segment.

IDENTIFYING MARKET SEGMENTS

A critical aspect for implementing yield management is that the hotel must be able to group its demand for rooms by market segment. This is the most important aspect of yield management and is often the most difficult to achieve, but by producing a market segment analysis, each segment can then be charged an appropriate room rate based on its needs and behavior.

Market segmentation requires a detailed analysis of past customer practices to identify the characteristics of each different market group. Among the questions that need to be asked are the following:

- What types of guests are demanding our rooms?
- What value and benefits do they see in our rooms?
- How do the demands and needs of each market segment differ?

The objective of this analysis is to determine the quantitative demand for each group, preferably over a year's period, broken down into at least seasonal periods. It is necessary to include in this analysis more than occupied rooms, because this does not show how many customers were not able to be provided with rooms, how many cancelled their reservations, and how much "no show" business occurred. This additional information will likely show a different demand pattern than if only occupied rooms were analyzed. With the full information analyzed, forecasts can be made about the number of rooms that should be made available for each different market segment. If total demand exceeds the amount of rooms available, the forecast will ensure that high-room-rate business is not replaced by low-room-rate business.

Although in some cases the market segment analysis could be done manually, it is best handled by computer. Special yield management software programs are now available to the hotel industry that not only will analyze demand, turned-away business, cancellations, and no-shows, but will also:

- Indicate when to restrict the sale of discounted rooms.
- Show the revenue lost when potential high-price-room customers are displaced by group business accepted at a lower room rate.
- Control reservations based on a potential customer's room rate and length of stay.

Two major segments

Generally, two major market segments for hotels can be identified: the business traveller and the vacationer. However, each of these broad market segments can be broken down into subsegments. For example, the business travel segment can be subsegmented into regular business travellers, government travellers, and convention/conference delegate travellers. For each market segment or subsegment, the hotel will apply a different marketing plan in order to sell each segment an appropriate number of rooms at a price that segment is prepared to pay.

Different marketing plans

Typically, the marketing plan for the business traveller is to allocate a fixed number of rooms at the rack rate available for last-minute reservations. For the business traveller reserving in advance, the plan might be to make available a block of rooms with a small discount from the rack rate. For group business (such as conventions), a large number of rooms might be allocated and held (sometimes years in advance for large conventions) at a heavily discounted rate, and those not reserved by individual convention delegates by a stipulated period (for example, three months prior to the actual convention) will be released to other market segments. For the vacationers, the plan might be to allocate a limited number of highly discounted rooms that must be reserved well in advance and cannot be reserved at the last minute.

All these situations contain uncertainties that must be decided in advance. For example:

- How many rooms at the very lowest rate should be set aside for the budget-conscious vacation traveller? What is the likelihood of there being customers in a different market segment prepared to pay a higher rate for those rooms?
- Should the business from a small conference group that is prepared to pay only a low rate for rooms be accepted, or should the rooms be held open until later when they might be sold at higher rates to regular business travellers?

Analyzing historic data

An effective yield management system can, of course, answer this type of question for the hotel manager by analyzing historic room reservation data.

RESTRICTIONS

Airlines control the demand for seats by applying restrictions, such as advance reservation requirements, prepayment of tickets, nonavailability of full refund in case of cancellation, and Saturday night stayovers. Airline customers know that they will receive a particular benefit (a lower price) if they accept the restrictions. In other words, they understand that they are buying a different product. Hotels must learn to differentiate their product in the same way, so that a potential guest knows that if he or she pays $99 for a room it is not the same product that will be received if he or she is willing to pay $129. But, if product differentiation is not perceived by the hotel's customers, they will consider the hotel's pricing policies as unfair and lower total sales revenues may result.

Hotels can differentiate their product in a number of different ways, such as reducing prices, if the customer

- Makes a reservation a minimum number of days in advance.
- Agrees to make a nonrefundable deposit at the time of making the reservation.
- Stays for a minimum number of days.
- Stays for a weekend.
- Pays a penalty for changing a reservation date.

Hotels must question how large the restriction will be or how many restrictions will apply for each discounted rate class. If the restrictions are too large and too numerous, the potential customers may perceive this as unjust and take their business elsewhere. Hotels must make sure that the restrictions are reasonable to both parties and that the customer is aware of all restrictions at each rate class level.

In addition, hotels can often differentiate their product by offering package prices. A package price might include one or more meals during a stay or a free ticket to the theatre or a sporting event. The actual discount on the room is thus buried in the package price and may indeed not be very much. In addition, a hotel may make an additional profit from the "breakage," that is the parts of the package that the guests do not in fact use. Package prices must be planned in such a way that they are of little interest to the rate-insensitive market segments, but offer great appeal to the price-sensitive markets whose extra business can considerably increase profits. Package prices can also include one or more of the restrictions listed.

Discounted and package prices should only be offered if the hotel will not be filled with rack rate customers and be oriented to those who would generally never consider staying at the hotel at full rack rate.

Group Sales

Yield management can be a problem in group bookings. Employees responsible for booking group sales often have their job performance measured by the volume of sales (number of room nights) that they make. The group booking department's objective is to sell rooms. To make those sales they usually have the authority to reduce room rates. Yield management, however, may show that some low-rate group sales do not maximize sales revenue at certain times of the year when those rooms could be sold to transient (business) travellers at a higher rate. Thus, yield management may prevent a sales employee from making a group sale. This obviously reduces that person's incentive to sell.

Transient displacement   Another consideration is that a group booking often creates a situation where transient travellers who would otherwise stay at the hotel at higher rates are displaced. Those displaced transients will then reserve rooms at a competitor hotel. They may also be encouraged to stay at that competitor hotel on future visits. Obviously, this reduces future revenue of the hotel accepting the group booking.

It is also argued that group room sales should be separated from other room sales under yield management and that the group sales department's effectiveness should not be measured on number of room nights booked over a period (such as a month) but on a combination of room nights times average rate to arrive at total revenue.

Employee Training

Employees must be trained in the use of the computer's yield management system. For example, consider the following situation. A potential customer inquires about the availability of rooms and their rates for a forthcoming three-day stay starting on a Monday. The reservation agent checks with the computer and determines that four rate classifications are open for that arrival date: $89, $99, $109, and $119. If the customer is quoted the $89 rate, the hotel would lose $60 if the only rooms available for the Tuesday and Wednesday were at the maximum $119 rate. In another situation, a potential customer might wish to arrive on the Tuesday for three days and would be quoted the $119 rate for all three nights, despite the fact that on Thursday rooms were again available at the $89 rate. In this case the potential customer might shop around at competitive hotels for a lower rate for all three nights and again the hotel would lose money. Obviously, to avoid these situations, the yield management system must be designed to show rooms and rates available for a guest's entire stay.

Evaluate System

The yield management system, once in place, needs to be evaluated from time to time to ensure it is working as intended. Some questions that could be asked could include the following:

- Are the actual demands for rooms by each market segment close to those forecast?
- Were there any events (such as a new competitor) overlooked and not included in the forecast?

Did any other events occur that were not included in the forecasts but affected market sector demand?

Summary

In summary, yield management is an attempt to match customers' purchase patterns and their demand for guest rooms with future occupancy forecasts. It is a method of measuring a hotel's marketing performance. It attempts to balance the demand of each market segment the hotel deals with and the supply of rooms made available to this segment by adjusting the major variable that the hotel can most effectively control: the room rate. The yield management system should match room rates to market demand, indicate how many rooms should be held for last-minute high-rate customers, and indicate when room rates should be discounted to increase occupancy. Yield management should not be viewed as a method of forcing customers to pay the highest rate, but rather as an attempt to bring room rates into line with normal economic forces. The foundations of a good yield management system are the accuracy and availability of the information that a hotel has about its customers' historic reservation patterns.

Balancing supply and demand

Hotels that practice yield management must also be careful not to concentrate on short-term maximization of yield. In other words, they must not ignore the long-term benefits that would accrue from other alternatives, such as improving service. By ignoring service there could be dissatisfied customers who transfer their patronage to competitor hotels, thus causing a decline in net income.

Note, however, that yield management does not make decisions. It is only a tool that provides information on which management can base decisions. For example, the system might indicate that a rate of $89 for a conference group during a certain period is not high enough. But that does not mean that those employees responsible for the final decision cannot stay with the $89 rate if they so choose. While yield management indicates how many rooms to sell in each rate class and when to open and close each rate class, the actual raising or lowering of room rates at any time is a management decision, and it is up to management to subsequently determine whether that decision was a good or bad one. The yield management system can also indicate to management when its room rates need to be adjusted upward or downward, but it is management's task to decide when to make the changes, how to make those changes, and how large they will be.

Use in other
departments

Even though the material in this section has concentrated on the rooms department of a hotel, the principles can be applied equally well to other departments. For example, most hotels have function or banquet rooms of different capacities available for group meal and/or meeting business. The banquet department can sell these rooms in various ways (for example, for meetings only, for meals only, for meetings and meals, and so forth). How these rooms are made available to different market segments, how they are priced for meetings, and how meals are priced can all affect the yield of those function rooms and indicate whether revenue is being maximized.

OTHER OPTIONS

While yield management is often a suitable tool to use in the short run, in the long run this market-demand pricing strategy can result in excessive discounting in a highly competitive situation. As a result, profits can be reduced and even seriously eroded because, in the long run, an operation must obtain an average room rate (in a hotel situation) or average check (in a restaurant situation) that covers both variable and fixed costs. For this reason, many hospitality operations today are looking at other solutions, such as sales revenue management and market segment profit analysis.

SALES REVENUE MANAGEMENT

Sales revenue management differs from yield management in that yield management's objective is to manage rooms inventory by offering a certain quantity of rooms at a certain price to a particular market segment to maximize yield. Sales revenue management goes a step beyond by offering an even more flexible pricing policy that quickly and continuously adjusts to supply and demand. Its objective is to sell all rooms at all times and reduce empty rooms to zero. Sales revenue management (and maximization) is a valuable tool because it increases the funds derived from existing demand.

MARKET SEGMENT PROFIT ANALYSIS

Another method is to use market segment profit analysis (MSPA). Traditionally, hospitality operations record and analyze sales revenue and direct expenses in terms of each department. It is not common in the industry to allocate indirect expenses to those departments

Nevertheless, the objective of MSPA is to analyze both sales revenue and expenses (including indirect expenses) by market segment. This method aids management in deciding to compete in any individual market segment on the basis of price or to use some other competitive strategy. As a result, management can base operating decisions with profit maximization (rather than revenue maximization) as the goal.

MSPA provides a method for considering various alternatives, including (in a hotel) markets such as local banquet business, that are not potential guest room users. In summary, it allows an analysis of all sales revenues and all expenses by market segment in order to evaluate the contribution of each to overall profits.

Both sales revenue management and MSPA are advanced techniques beyond the scope of this book.

COMPUTER APPLICATIONS

Computerized spreadsheet programs can be extremely useful in making pricing decisions because they can so rapidly perform the calculations in "what if" situations that would take hours to produce if done manually.

For example, a variety of room rates can be entered in the computer along with an assumed occupancy percentage for each separate room rate. For each room rate and occupancy percentage, the expected level of variable expenses can also be entered. The computer can then calculate the total sales revenue and anticipated departmental profit (operating income) for each possible situation to provide management with information about which average room rate is the most profitable. More sophisticated programs can also predict what effect each room rate and occupancy level will have on other departments, such as food and beverage.

A spreadsheet program can also easily handle the calculations necessary for such things as average checks, seat turnovers, menu gross profit, the Hubbart formula, and a discount grid as illustrated in Exhibit 6.8.

There are also special menu engineering software packages available that can be used to eliminate the extensive time necessary to produce the worksheets manually. Only each item's cost, selling price, and menu mix have to be entered, and all of the remaining calculations are automatically performed and printed out.

Finally, as mentioned earlier in this chapter, there are special yield management software packages on the market today that can be used to implement a yield management system.

SUMMARY

This chapter introduced the reader to various pricing methods that have been used in the hospitality industry. It pointed out the need for both long-range and tactical pricing approaches. The usual way of looking at an income statement is to deduct costs from sales revenue, and call any excess of sales revenue over costs operating income (before tax) rather than net income (after tax). However, if net income (after tax) is considered as a cost, it can then be budgeted for like any other cost; and the required revenue that must be realized to cover all costs, including net income after tax, can be calculated in advance each month, quarter, or year.

Once it has been calculated for a restaurant, this figure permits us to calculate an average check or average customer spending. This is calculated as follows:

$$\text{Average check} = \frac{\text{Total sales revenue}}{\text{Seats} \times \text{Seat turnover} \times \text{Operating days}}$$

The overall average check can be further broken down by meal period by using the following equation:

$$\text{Meal period average check} = \frac{\text{Meal period revenue}}{\text{Seats} \times \text{Seat turnover} \times \text{Operating days}}$$

The average check is only an average and not of the price of every item on the menu. Menu pricing of individual items can be a complex problem for management, requiring consideration of a great number of factors. Factors considered include the menu price ranges needed to accommodate clientele catered to; gross margin of different menu items; and pricing of the competition. It is important to evaluate the influence the menu sales mix can have on the average check as well as the effect on gross margin.

The effect that seat turnovers can have on total sales revenue should never be ignored and seat turnover management can compensate for a declining average check. Menu engineering is a method of menu analysis that combines each menu item's contribution margin (gross profit) with its popularity or the demand for that item by the restaurant's customers. Menu items are then classified into one of four categories: stars, plowhorses, puzzles, and dogs.

The average room rate required for a hotel or motel to cover all costs, including net income, can be calculated in a way similar to the calculation of average check for a restaurant. The equation is:

$$\text{Average room rate} = \frac{\text{Total sales revenue}}{\text{Rooms} \times \text{Occupancy (\%)} \times \text{Operating days}}$$

The average room rate, like the average check, is only an average and not necessarily the rate for all classifications of rooms. Normally, the average room rate is broken down into an average rate for single rooms and average rate for double rooms. Room rates are also calculated on the basis of the square footage for rooms with different sizes. Total room revenue is a combination of average room rate and actual room occupancy. Therefore, one should keep in mind the occupancy of rooms by day of the week since a declining room rate can be compensated for by increasing room occupancy, and vice versa.

In room rate discounting, an equation can be used to calculate the equivalent occupancy needed to hold total sales revenue less marginal costs constant if the rack rate is discounted. The equation is:

$$\text{Equivalent occupancy} \times \frac{\text{Rack rate} - \text{Marginal cost}}{[\text{Rack rate} \times (1 - \text{Discount } \%)] - \text{Marginal cost}}$$

A potential average room rate can be compared with the actual average. Once a potential average rate has been calculated, it can be used to establish discounted room rates for various market segments.

Note that both the return on investment method and the cost-plus method of establishing prices should be used primarily as reference points in establishing actual prices. There are several other considerations to be kept in mind. For example, prices must be established to meet the organization's long-run objective or objectives. In addition, factors such as the elasticity of demand, the business's cost structure (breakdown between fixed and variable costs), and the competitive environment in which it operates are all very important factors.

Most hotels measure their rooms department's effectiveness by using either occupancy percentage or average rate, both of which have shortcomings. An alternative is to use the yield statistic, which is a combination of occupancy percentage and average rate. The chapter concluded with a section on yield management, a method of matching customers' purchase patterns and their demand for guest rooms to derive more precise occupancy forecasts with the objective of maximizing room's revenue.

DISCUSSION QUESTIONS

1. Discuss the advantages and disadvantages of the three traditional pricing methods used by the hospitality industry.
2. Differentiate long-run from tactical pricing and list four events that might necessitate tactical pricing.
3. Explain why net income (after tax) can be treated as just another cost of running a business operation.

4. Explain how forecasted (budgeted) revenue for a hospitality operation can be used to determine an average check and an average room.

5. If an average check was established to support a specific level of total sales revenue in a restaurant and the seat turnover rate becomes too low to support the desired total revenue, explain how the seat turnover needs to be changed.

6. Define the term sales mix and explain what influence sales mix can have on an average check.

7. What factors would a restaurant manager need to consider when establishing individual menu item prices?

8. Explain why you do or do not think that the food cost percentage figure is important in menu pricing.

9. In menu engineering, which are the two main factors about each menu item that are to be considered?

10. In menu engineering, state what menu items defined as dogs are.

11. Why is loss of sales revenue from hotel rooms not occupied on a given day more of a problem than loss of sales revenue from customers who did not show up in a restaurant on a given day?

12. Explain briefly how a motel's average room rate can be calculated or projected by using the bottom up approach.

13. If a hotel has an average room rate of $75, explain why every customer staying in the hotel will not pay this average rate.

14. Describe how a double occupancy percentage for rooms is calculated.

15. Of what value might it be to calculate hotel room occupancy by day of the week, or seat turnover in a restaurant by day of the week, rather than using an average weekly figure?

16. Define the terms rack rate and potential average room rate.

17. Define elasticity of demand and, using figures of your own choosing, show how a reduction in a hotel's average room rate and the resulting change in total sales revenue would indicate an inelastic demand situation.

18. State the equation for calculating elasticity of demand.

19. What implications does the breakdown of a business's costs into fixed and variable ones have on the pricing decision?

20. Discuss the concept of product and/or service differentiation in a restaurant situation.

ETHICS SITUATION

A hotel manager has set a rack rate for all rooms in the hotel of $149 for next year. Corporations, conventions, and conference groups were advised that early next year the rack rate charged could be reduced to a lower rate of $99 and the potential reduction will depend on the volume of business they provide. Travel agencies, which book a good number of hotel reservations for independent travellers, were advised that room rate discounts are available for $139, $129, and $119 with restrictions. The travel agencies were also advised that rooms booked at the $149 rate would increase their commission to 15% rather than the normal 10% for a discounted rate reservation. Individuals that telephone the hotel directly for a reservation are first quoted the $149 rate; however, reservation booking employees have been trained to lower this rate to $139, $129, and $119, but never lower than $119. In addition, room-booking employees are required to advise potential guests of the restrictions that apply at each rate level. Discuss the ethics of this situation.

EXERCISES

6.1   Determine the amount of operating income necessary to yield a net income after tax of $28,000 using a current tax rate of 20%.

6.2   Using information given in exercise 6.1, identify the amount of income tax to be paid.

6.3   If the total fixed and other identified operating costs are estimated to be $145,000 and all variable costs total 84% of total sales revenue, what is estimated total sales revenue?

6.4   Average revenue of a restaurant with 88 seats for a month with 26 operating days and a seat turnover of 2.5 is $46,800. Determine the average check for the month.

6.5   Using information from exercise 6.4, determine the effect on the average check if seat turnover decreases from 2.5 to 2 times per day.

6.6   A restaurant with 108 seats, serving both lunch and dinner 6 days per week, reported total annual sales revenue of $988,000. Dinner generates 65% of total sales revenue with a seat turnover of 1.75. What is the average check for dinner?

6.7   A rooms operation reported a total of 8,760 rooms sold with a total of 10,512 guests in the previous year. What was the double occupancy rate?

6.8   A small motel operation with 40 rooms has an average occupancy rate of 70%. The forecasted sales revenue for the coming year is $388,360. What is the average room rate expected to be?

6.9   Assume a rooms operation had 40 each, 240-square-foot rooms and 20 each, 180-square-foot rooms. The average occupancy for both types of rooms is 74%. An average of least $2,220 of sales revenue is required per day. What is the rate per square foot to be charged per square footage of each type room?

6.10 Using the following information, determine the average single and double room rates:

Average rooms sold per day: 40
Average rooms double occupied: 15
Spread wanted between single and double room rate: $8.00
Average daily revenue: $1,880

PROBLEMS

6.1 You have the following projections about the costs in a family restaurant for next year:

Net income required	15% after income tax on the owners' present investment of $80,000, income tax rate is 25%.
Depreciation	Present book value (consolidated) of furniture and equipment is $75,500, depreciation rate is 20%.
Interest	Interest on a loan outstanding of $35,000 is 8%.

Break even

Known Costs		*Variable Costs*
Insurance	$ 3,000	Food cost, 36% of sales revenue
License	2,500	Wage cost, 34% of sales revenue
Utilities	8,400	Other costs, 12% of sales revenue
Maintenance	3,600	
Administration	9,800	
Salaries	32,400	

a. What sales revenue would the restaurant have to achieve next year in order to acquire the desired net income after tax?

b. What is the required average check needed to the annual revenue objective if the restaurant is open 365 days had 60 seats and an average seat turnover of 2.5 times per day?

6.2 A 25-room budget motel expects its occupancy next year to be 80%. The owner's present investment is $200,800. They want an after-tax return on their investment of 10%. Tax rate is 50%.

- Interest on a long-term mortgage is 10%. Present balance outstanding is $403,200.
- Depreciation rate on the building is 10% of the present book value of $350,100. Depreciation on the furnishings and equipment is at 20% of the consolidated present book value of $75,200.
- Other known fixed costs total $70,900 a year.

- At 80% occupancy rate, the motel's operating expenses, wages, supplies, laundry, etc. are calculated to be $27,700 a year.
- The motel has other income from vending machines of $2,600 a year.

a. To cover all costs and produce the required net income after tax, what should the motel's average room rate be next year?

b. Round your average room rate answer to a. to the nearest dollar. If the motel operates at 30% double occupancy and has an $8.00 spread between its single and double rates, what will the single and double room rates be? Assume only one common room size, all with the same rates.

6.3   A restaurant has 90 seats. Total annual sales revenue for next year is projected to be $ 975,000. The restaurant is open 52 weeks a year and serves breakfast and lunch 6 days a week. Dinner is served 7 days a week. Seat turnover per day is anticipated to be 2.0 times for breakfast, 1.5 times for lunch, and 1.25 times for dinner. Sales revenue is derived at 20% from breakfast, 30% from lunch, and 50% from dinner. Calculate the restaurant's average check by meal period.

6.4   A 140-seat dining room had a weekly customer count by meal period and day:

	Lunch	**Dinner**
Sunday	Closed	180
Monday	160	110
Tuesday	170	112
Wednesday	175	108
Thursday	160	120
Friday	180	210
Saturday	50	250

a. For each meal period and for each day of the week calculate the seat turnover.

b. Calculate the average number of customers per day and the average seat turnover for the week for each meal period.

c. List some of the ways in which the information in parts a and b would be useful to the restaurant manager or owner.

6.5   You have the following information about a menu with 10 items:

Menu Item	Number Sold (MM)	Menu Item Food Cost	Menu Item Selling Price
1	197	$ 3.30	$ 9.95
2	206	3.95	9.95

3	294	2.80	7.95
4	301	4.40	10.95
5	188	5.10	12.95
6	215	3.70	8.95
7	260	4.40	10.45
8	155	4.45	10.75
9	199	5.05	12.95
10	230	4.95	12.75

Prepare a blank menu engineering worksheet and complete it using the information given above. Exhibit 6.4 and 6.5 can be used as a format and guide.

6.6 An owner invested $90,000 in a new family-style restaurant, of which $80,000 was immediately used to purchase equipment and $10,000 was retained for working cash. Estimates for the first year of business are as follows:

- Menu selling prices to be established to give a markup of 150% over cost of food sold
- Variable wages, 28% of revenue
- Fixed wages, $25,800
- Other variable costs, 7% of revenue
- Rent, $16,000
- Insurance, $2,400
- Depreciation on equipment, 20%
- Return on investment desired, 12%
- Income tax rate, 25%

The restaurant has 60 seats and is open five days a week for lunch and dinner only. Lunch revenue is expected to be 40% of total volume with two seat turnovers. Dinner revenue will be 60% of total volume with one turnover.

Calculate the average check per meal period that will cover all costs, including desired return on investment.

6.7 You have been given the following information about a hotel for the next year. The hotel has 40 rooms and expected occupancy rate of 70%. Rooms department operating expenses wages, supplies, laundry, and so on is 27% of room's sales revenue.

Administrative and general	$	38,300 ;
Marketing		28,900
Energy costs		35,100 -
Repairs and maintenance		28,800 .
Property taxes		17,600 .

Insurance	4,800 ‹
Telephone department operating loss	(9,700)
Contributory income, food and beverage departments	103,200
First mortgage, at 8% interest, present balance	601,000
Second mortgage, at 12% interest, present balance	402,000
Ownership equity (after-tax return of 15% is expected)	280,000
Book value of fixed assets before depreciation charge:	
Land	250,000
Building	1,860,000
Furniture and equipment (combined)	382,000
Depreciation rate on building	5%
Depreciation rate on furniture and equipment (combined)	20%
Income tax rate	25%

a. Calculate the hotel's average room rate for next year.

b. What would the hotel's average rate per guest be with a 30% double occupancy?

c. If the hotel did operate at 30% double occupancy and management wanted a $15 spread between the single and double room rates, what would these rates be?

6.8 A motel has 30 rooms and expects a 70% occupancy next year. The owners' investment is presently $520,000 and they expect a 12% after-tax annual return on their investment. The motel is in a 50% tax bracket. The motel is carrying two mortgages: the first mortgage in the amount of $359,000 at a 10% interest rate and the second mortgage in the amount of $140,000 at a 14% interest rate. Present book value of building is $632,000, and depreciation rate is 5%. Present combined book value of furniture and equipment is $117,000, and the combined depreciation rate is 20%. Indirect costs are $44,800 and direct costs are $59,300. The motel also receives an additional $12,000 a year leasing out its restaurant.

a. Calculate the motel's required average room rate to cover all expenses and provide the owners with their desired return on investment.

b. Round this rate to the nearest dollar and then calculate the average single and double rates, assuming a 60% double occupancy and a $12 difference between singles and doubles.

6.9 A 45-room resort hotel has three sizes of rooms, as follows:

- 15 singles at 150 square feet each
- 15 doubles at 220 square feet each
- 15 suites at 380 square feet each

Occupancy is 80%. Demand for each type of room is about equal. The projected total sales revenue from rooms next year is $912,500. If average room rate were to be based solely on room size, what would the average room rate for each type of room be next year?

6.10   The Resolute Resort hotel currently operates at a 75% occupancy, using a rack rate for all rooms of $60 and a marginal cost per room sold of $8. Calculate the occupancy figures for discount grid using discount percentages of 5, 10, 15, and 20%.

6.11   Motley Motel's potential average room rate is calculated to be $31.00. Assume that this motel had three market segments. Vacation travellers comprise 75% of the room nights and are charged 100% of the rack rate. Business travellers comprise 15% of the room nights and are charged 90% of the rack rate. Sports teams account for 10% of the room nights and are charged 80% of the rack rate.

a. Calculate the room rate by market segment.

b. Prove that your calculations are correct, assuming that total annual room nights are 7,300.

6.12   The Inviting Inn has 500 available guest rooms. For a certain week next month, the anticipated transient demand for rooms is:

Monday	200
Tuesday	200
Wednesday	200
Thursday	200
Friday	100
Saturday	50
Sunday	50

The Inn also has committed the following number of rooms for group sales during the same week:

Monday	200
Tuesday	200
Wednesday	300
Thursday	300
Friday	100
Saturday	100
Sunday	100

The Inn has the possibility of booking another group of 100 rooms for the nights of Tuesday, Wednesday, Thursday, and Friday of that week at a discounted rate of $60 per room. The Inn's rack rate for transient guests is $80, and its marginal cost per room sold is $15.

a. Assuming the new group is booked, calculate the additional net sales revenue (gross sales revenue less marginal costs) to the Inn.

b. What factors, other than net sales revenue, might you consider before committing to this new group sale?

CASE 6

In the case at the end of Chapter 3, you calculated the average food and beverage check for the 4C Company's restaurant for year 0001. The restaurant was open for 52 weeks, 6 days a week for lunch, and 5 days a week for dinner. An analysis of sales checks indicated that the average lunch turnover was 1.5 times and 1.25 times for dinner. Lunch contributes about 40% of total sales revenue and dinner, 60%.

a. Calculate the average lunch and average dinner checks. Beverage revenue is about 10% of total sales revenue at lunchtime and about 30% at dinnertime. Break down lunch and dinner average check figures into their food and beverage components. This information will be used in a later case to prepare the 4C Company's budget for year 0002.

b. Suggest to Charlie a number of ways in which he could attempt to raise the average check and the total food and beverage revenue for year 0002.

c. In part a, one of the ways might be to substitute, on the food menu, items with a low selling price for items with a high selling price. Write a short report to Charlie about the effect this might have on the restaurant's guests, its food cost percentage, and its gross profit and net income.

7

Cost Management

INTRODUCTION

This chapter introduces and illustrates various costs that exist in a business operation, including direct costs, indirect costs, controllable costs, joint costs, discretionary costs, relevant and nonrelevant costs, sunk costs, opportunity costs, fixed costs, variable costs, standard costs, and semifixed, semivariable costs.

The allocation of indirect costs continues with an allocation method for the distribution of indirect costs to departments; the potential difficulties encountered are discussed and illustrated.

The analysis of using relevant costs to assist in determining which item of equipment to buy is addressed and illustrated.

Fixed and variable costs are discussed in relation to their use in the management decision process; that is, whether to accept or reject an offered price for services to be rendered. The evaluation of fixed and variable costs is illustrated in three additional problems: to close or not close during an off-season period; deciding which business to buy; and deciding whether to accept a fixed or variable lease on a facility.

Having discussed and illustrated the importance of understanding fixed and variable cost relationships as applied to the decision process, the chapter concludes with an illustration of how semifixed or semivariable costs can be separated into their fixed and variable elements.

CHAPTER OBJECTIVES

After studying this chapter, the reader should be able to:

1. Briefly define and give examples of some of the major types of cost, such as direct and indirect costs, fixed and variable costs, and discretionary costs.

2. Prorate indirect costs to revenue departments and make decisions based on the results.

3. Use relevant costs to help determine which piece of equipment to buy.

4. Use knowledge about fixed and variable costs for a variety of different business decisions, such as whether or not to close during the off-season.

5. Define the term "high operating leverage" and explain its advantages and disadvantages.

6. Explain and use each of the following three methods to separate semifixed or semivariable costs into their fixed and variable elements: maximum/minimum calculation, multipoint graph, and regression analysis.

COST MANAGEMENT

Most of the sales revenue in a hotel or food service enterprise is eaten up by costs: as much as 90 cents or more of each revenue dollar may be used to pay for costs. Therefore, cost management is important. Budgeting costs and cost analysis is one way to control (manage) costs to improve net income. Another way to improve net income is to cut costs, without regard to the consequences. The latter course of action may not always be wise. Perhaps a better way is to look at each cost (expense) and see how it contributes toward net income. If advertising (a cost) leads to higher net income than would be the case if we did not advertise, then it would not pay to cut the advertising expense.

Understand type of cost

One of the ways to better manage costs is to understand that there are many types of cost. If one can recognize the type of cost that is being considered, then better decisions can be made. Some of the most common types of cost are defined in the following sections.

TYPES OF COST

DIRECT COST

A direct cost is one that is directly traceable and considered the responsibility of a particular department or department manager. Most direct costs will go up or down, to a greater or lesser degree, as sales revenue goes up and down. For this reason they are considered to be controllable by, and thus the responsibility of, the department to which they are charged. Examples of this type of cost are food, beverages, wages and salaries, operating supplies and services, and linen and laundry.

INDIRECT COST

Responsibility for indirect costs

An indirect cost is one that is not easily traceable and identified with a particular department or area and thus cannot be charged to any specific department. General building maintenance could only be charged to various departments (such as rooms, food, or beverage) with difficulty. Even if this difficulty could be overcome, it must still be recognized that indirect costs cannot normally be made the responsibility of an operating department manager. Indirect costs are frequently referred to as undistributed costs.

CONTROLLABLE COST

The mistake is often made of calling direct costs controllable costs and indirect costs noncontrollable costs. It is true that direct costs are generally more easily controlled then indirect costs, but in the long run all costs are controllable by someone.

JOINT COST

Difficulty of allocation

A joint cost is one that is shared by, and thus the responsibility of, two or more departments or areas. A dining room waiter who serves both food and beverage is an example. His labor is a joint cast and should be charged (in proportion to revenue, or by some other appropriate method) partly to the food department and the remainder to the beverage department. Most indirect costs are also joint costs. The problem is to find a rational basis for separating the cost and charging part of it to each department.

DISCRETIONARY COST

This is a cost that may or may not be incurred at the sole discretion of a particular person, usually the general manager. Nonemergency maintenance is an example of a discretionary cost. The building exterior could be painted this year, or the painting could be postponed until next year. Either way sales revenue should not be affected. The general manager has the choice, thus it is a discretionary cost. Note that a discretionary cost is only discretionary in the short run. For example, the building will have to be painted at some time in order to maintain its appearance.

Relevant Cost

A relevant cost is one that affects a decision. For example, a restaurant is considering replacing its mechanical sales register with an electronic one. The relevant costs would be the cost of the new register (less any trade-in of the old one), the cost of training employees on the new equipment, and any change in maintenance and material supply costs on the new machine. As long as no change is necessary in number of servers required, the restaurant's labor cost would not be a relevant one. It would make no difference to the decision.

Sunk Cost

No effect on future decisions

A sunk cost is a cost already incurred and about which nothing can be done. It cannot affect any future decisions. For example, if the same restaurant had spent $250 for an employee to study the relative merits of using mechanical or electronic registers, the $250 is a sunk cost. It cannot make any difference to the decision.

Opportunity Cost

An opportunity cost is the cost of not doing something. An organization can invest its surplus cash in marketable securities at 10%, or leave the money in the bank at 6%. If it buys marketable securities its opportunity cost is 6%. Another way to look at it is to say that it is making 10% on the investment, less the opportunity cost of 6%; therefore, the net gain is a 4% interest rate.

Fixed Cost

Fixed costs are those that, over the short run (a year or less), do not vary with sales revenue. Examples are management salaries, fire insurance expense, rent paid on a square foot basis, or the committed cost of an advertising campaign. Over the long run all these costs can, of course, change. But in the short run they would normally change, if at all, only by a specific top management decision.

Variable Cost

Linearity of variable costs

A variable cost is one that varies on a linear basis with sales or sales revenue. Very few costs are strictly linear, but two that are (with only a slight possibility that they will not always fit this strict definition) are the costs of food and beverages. The more food and beverages sold, the more have to be purchased. If sales are zero, then purchases will also be zero.

SEMIFIXED OR SEMIVARIABLE COST

Most costs do not fit neatly into the fixed or the variable category. Most have an element of fixed expense and an element of variable—and then not always variable directly to sales on a straight-line basis. Such costs would include payroll, maintenance, utilities, and most of the direct operating costs. In order to make some useful decisions, it is advantageous to break down these semifixed or semivariable costs into their two elements: fixed or variable. Ways of doing this will be discussed later in this chapter.

STANDARD COST

Standard costs differ in each establishment

A standard cost is what the cost should be for a given volume or level of sales. We saw some uses of such standards in Chapter 5. Other uses would be in budgeting (see Chapter 8), in pricing decisions, and in expansion planning. Standard costs need to be developed individually by each establishment since there are many factors that influence standard costs and that differ from one establishment to another.

Let us look at some of the ways in which an analysis of the type(s) of cost(s) with which we are dealing would help us make a better decision.

ALLOCATING INDIRECT COSTS TO REVENUE AREAS

One of the difficulties in allocating indirect costs to sales is in determining the correct basis on which to apportion the cost to each department. Some of the methods that could be used are discussed in Chapter 2. If an allocation of indirect costs is made on an incorrect basis, then wrong decisions could be made. If the correct allocation is made, then presumably the wrong decisions would not be made.

Consider the following restaurant complex that has two main sales outlets, a dining room, and a snack bar. Sales revenue and direct costs for each sales area and indirect costs for the entire operation are shown below for a typical month with an average monthly operating income of $8,000.

	Dining Room	Snack Bar	Total
Sales revenue	$70,000	$30,000	$100,000
Direct costs	(50,000)	(26,000)	(76,000)
Contributory income	$20,000	$ 4,000	$ 24,000
Indirect costs			(16,000)
Operating income			$ 8,000

Management feels that the indirect costs should be charged to each of the two operating departments and that the $16,000 total indirect cost should be prorated and allocated according to revenue. In other words, 70% should be allocated to the dining room and 30% to the snack bar. The following is the new monthly income statement:

	Dining Room	Snack Bar	Total
Sales revenue	$70,000	$30,000	$100,000
Direct costs	(50,000)	(26,000)	(76,000)
Contributory income	$20,000	$ 4,000	$ 24,000
Indirect costs	(11,200)	(4,800)	(16,000)
Operating income (loss)	$ 8,800	($ 800)	$ 8,000

This shows that, by distributing indirect costs on a basis of sales revenue, the snack bar is losing $800 a month. Management of the restaurant complex has an opportunity to lease out the snack bar, as is, for $500 a month rent. The new operator will pay for his own indirect costs (such as administration, advertising, utilities, maintenance). This seems to be a good offer. A $500 profit appears better than an $800 loss. After a few months, the dining room monthly income statement is as follows:

Sales revenue	$70,000
Direct costs	(50,000)
Contributory income	$20,000
Indirect costs	(12,900)
Income before rent	$ 7,100
Rent income	500
Operating income	$ 7,600

These figures indicate that the dining room's net income including rent is only $7,600. Earlier it was calculated to have been $8,800 without any rent income. Overall, net income is now worse than it was before ($7,600 versus $8,000). Obviously, the mistake was made in allocating indirect costs to the dining room and the snack bar on the basis of sales revenue and then making a decision based on this allocation. A more careful assessment of indirect costs should have been made, with allocation made on a more logical basis. If this had been done (with the information we now have about the dining room's indirect costs) the real situation would have been as follows, which shows that both sales departments were, in fact, making a net income:

	Dining Room	Snack Bar	Total
Sales revenue	$70,000	$30,000	$100,000
Direct costs	(50,000)	(26,000)	(76,000)
Contributory income	$20,000	$ 4,000	$ 24,000
Indirect costs	(12,900)	(3,100)	(16,000)
Operating income	$ 7,100	$ 900	$ 8,000

This shows that renting out the snack bar, which is making $900 a month profit, for $500 a month would not be profitable. To look at it another way, the $500 is the opportunity cost of not renting out, but since it is less than the $900 we are presently making we can comfortably ignore it.

WHICH PIECE OF EQUIPMENT SHOULD WE BUY?

Choosing among
alternatives

One of the ongoing decisions all managers face is that of choosing between alternatives. Which items to offer on a menu, which employee to hire, how to spend the advertising budget? One area of such decision making where a knowledge of costs is helpful is that of selecting a piece of equipment. The following might be a typical situation.

A motel owner has asked his public accountant to research the front office guest accounting equipment available and to recommend the two best pieces of equipment on the market. A decision will then be made by the motel owner about which of the two to use. The accountant's fee for this research was $500. The accountant, in her report, produced the following information:

	Equipment A	Equipment B
Initial cost, including installation	$10,000	$ 8,000
Economic life	10 years	10 years
Scrap value at end of economic life	0	0
Initial training cost	$ 500	$ 1,000
Annual maintenance	$ 400	$ 300
Annual cost of forms	$ 750	$ 850
Annual wage cost	$22,500	$22,500

Note that the $500 fee is a sunk cost: It has to be paid regardless of the decision and, indeed, would have to be paid even if a decision to buy neither piece of equipment were made.

Determine relevant
information
In order to make a decision, the motel owner must sort out the relevant information, which is as follows for year 1:

	Equipment A	Equipment B
Depreciation	$1,000	$ 800
Initial training cost	500	1,000
Annual maintenance	400	300
Annual cost of forms	750	850
Total for year 1	$2,650	$2,950

Note that the initial cost of the equipment is not relevant, but the annual depreciation is. Staff wage cost is also irrelevant since it is the same in both cases.

The relevant cost information shows that in year 1 equipment A is cheaper
than equipment B by $300. However, this saving is in year 1 only. Perhaps the
motel owner should look ahead to see what the relevant costs are over the full
economic life of the equipment. The following shows the information concerning these costs for each of the years 2 to 10:

	Equipment A	Equipment B
Depreciation	$1,000	$ 800
Annual maintenance	400	300
Annual cost of forms	750	850
Total annual cost	$2,150	$1,950
Total cost for years 2 to 10	9 × $2,150 = $19,350	9 × $1,950 = $17,550

Training cost a sunk cost
Note in these calculations that the training cost of year 1 is now a sunk cost; it
is no longer relevant.

To finalize the decision, the motel manager must then add the total cost for
years 2 to 10 to the cost for year 1.

	Equipment A	Equipment B
Year 1 cost	$ 2,650	$ 2,950
Years 2 to 10 total cost	19,350	17,550
Total cost	$22,000	$20,500

This shows that, despite year 1, the total ten-year cost is less for Equipment B.
Certain assumptions have been made: that one can forecast costs for ten years

Factors other than cost

and that the costs as originally estimated are accurate. In the final decision, costs may not be the only factor to be considered. A more comprehensive look at the investment decision situation will be taken in Chapter 12.

CAN WE SELL BELOW COST?

Calculation of daily fixed cost

The obvious answer to a question of selling below cost is dependent on whether the person responding to the question understands the nature of fixed and variable costs. In general, the answer would be, "Not unless you plan to go broke." However, before the question can be answered intelligently, we should first answer which cost. The best answer would be: "If variable costs are covered and a contribution toward fixed costs is made, selling below cost can be considered."

Consider a catering company that rents its facilities for $80,000 per year and additional annual fixed costs for management salaries, insurance, depreciation charges on furnishings and equipment, and other fixed costs of $66,000. The total fixed costs would be $146,000, or an average of $400 per day:

$$\text{Fixed costs}/365 \text{ days} = \$146,000/365 = \underline{\$400}$$

Reduction of loss

The catering company and its facilities can handle only one function per day, and operates with a variable cost of 60% of total sales revenue. The company was approached by an organization wanting to sponsor a lunch for 60 people but can only pay of $10.00 per person. Normally, this catering company would not consider handling a group luncheon this small; however, on this occasion the catering company does not see any likelihood of booking a function in the next few days. If the catering company accepts this function, its income situation will be as follows:

Revenue (60 people × $10.00 each)	$600.00
Less: Variable costs (60% × $ 600)	(360.00)
Contribution margin	$240.00
Less: Fixed costs	(400.00)
Operating Loss	$(160.00)

On the surface, the net loss appears unfavorable; however, considering the $400 fixed cost we incur whether we accept the function or not, we see a different perspective of accepting the function. By selling below total cost of $760 ($360 + $400) we offset $240 of the $400 of fixed costs that would be incurred with or without the function.

In the short run, as long as sales revenue exceeds variable costs and contributes toward fixed costs, it is beneficial to accept the business.

SHOULD WE CLOSE DURING THE OFF-SEASON?

The same reasoning as in the previous case can be applied to a seasonal operation in answering the question of staying open or closing during the off-season. Consider the case of a motel that has the income statement shown below:

Sales revenue	$130,000
Expenses	(110,000)
Net income	$ 20,000

Off-season loss

The owner decided to make an analysis of his sales revenue and costs by the month and found that for ten months he was making money and for two months he was losing money. His variable costs were 20% of sales revenue; his total fixed costs were $84,000, or $7,000 a month. The following summarizes his findings:

	10 months	2 months	Total
Sales revenue	$125,000	$ 5,000	$130,000
Variable costs	$ 25,000	$ 1,000	$ 26,000
Fixed costs	70,000	14,000	84,000
Total costs	$ 95,000	$15,000	$110,000
Net income	$ 30,000	($10,000)	$ 20,000

His analysis seemed to indicate to him that he should close to eliminate the $10,000 loss during the two-month loss period. But if he does, the fixed costs for the two months ($14,000) will have to be paid out of the ten months' net income, and $30,000 (10 months' net income) less two months' fixed costs of $14,000 will reduce his annual net income to $16,000 from its present $20,000. If he does not want a reduction in annual net income, he should not close.

Close-down and start-up costs

In such a situation, there might be other factors that need to be considered and that would reinforce the decision to stay open. For example, there could be sizable additional close-down and start-up costs that would have to be included in the calculation of the cost of closing.

Also, would key employees return after an extended vacation? Is there a large enough pool of skilled labor available and willing to work on a seasonal basis only? Would there be recurring training time (and costs) at the start of each new season? These are some of the types of questions that would have to be answered before any final decision to close was made.

WHICH BUSINESS SHOULD WE BUY?

Just as a business manager has to make choices between alternatives on a day-to-day basis, so too does an entrepreneur going into business or expanding an existing business frequently have to choose between alternatives. Let us look at one such situation.

A restaurant chain is eager to expand. It has an opportunity to take over one of two similar existing restaurants. The two restaurants are close to each other, they have the same type of clientele and size of operation, and the asking price is the same for each. They are also similar in that each is presently taking in $1,000,000 in sales revenue a year, and each has a net income of $100,000 a year. With only this information it is difficult to make a decision as to which would be the more profitable investment. But a cost analysis as shown in Exhibit 7.1 reveals differences.

Different cost structures

Although the sales revenue and net income are the same for each restaurant, the structure of their costs is different, and this will affect the decision of which one could be more profitable. The restaurant chain that wishes to take over either A or B is optimistic about the future. It feels that, without any change in fixed costs, it can increase annual sales revenue by 10%. What effect will this have on the net income of A and B? Net income will not increase for each restaurant by the same amount. Restaurant A's variable cost is 50%. This means that, out of each dollar of additional sales revenue, it will have variable expenses of $0.50 and a net income of $0.50 (fixed costs do not increase). Restaurant B has variable costs of 30%, or $0.30 out of each revenue dollar, leaving a net income of $0.70 from each dollar of extra sales revenue (again, fixed costs do not change).

Exhibit 7.1   Statements Showing Differences in Cost Structure

	Restaurant A		Restaurant B	
Sales revenue	$1,000,000	100.0%	$1,000,000	100.0%
Variable costs	$ 500,000	50.0%	$ 300,000	30.0%
Fixed costs	400,000	40.0%	600,000	60.0%
Total costs	$ 900,000	90.0%	$ 900,000	90.0%
Net income	$ 100,000	10.0%	$ 100,000	10.0%

Exhibit 7.2   Effect of Increased Sales Revenue on Costs and Net Income

	Restaurant A		Restaurant B	
Sales revenue	$1,100,000	100.0%	$1,100,000	100.0%
Variable costs	$ 550,000	50.0%	$ 330,000	30.0%
Fixed costs	400,000	36.4%	600,000	54.5%
Total costs	$ 950,000	86.4%	$ 930,000	84.5%
Net income	$ 150,000	13.6%	$ 170,000	15.5%

Assuming a 10% increase in sales revenue and no new fixed costs, the income statements of the two restaurants have been recalculated in Exhibit 7.2. Note that Restaurant A's net income has gone up by $50,000 (to $150,000), but Restaurant B's has gone up by $70,000 (to $170,000). In this situation Restaurant B would be the better investment.

A company that has high fixed costs relative to variable costs is said to have high operating leverage. From a net income point of view, it will do better in times of rising sales revenue than will a company with low operating leverage (low fixed costs relative to variable costs). A company with low fixed costs, however will be better off when sales revenue starts to decline. Exhibit 7.3 illustrates this, under the assumptions that our two restaurants are going to have a decline in sales revenue of 10% from the present $1,000,000 level and that there will be no change in fixed costs. Exhibit 7.3 shows that, with declining sales revenue, Restaurant A's net income will be higher than Restaurant B's.

Break-even revenue level

In fact, if sales revenue declines far enough, Restaurant B will be in financial difficulty long before Restaurant A. If the break-even point were calculated (the break-even point is that level of sales revenue at which there will be neither net income nor loss), Restaurant A's sales revenue could go down to $800,000, while Restaurant B would be in difficulty at $857,000. This is illustrated in Exhibit 7.4.

Exhibit 7.3   Effect of Decreased Sales Revenue on Costs and Net Income

	Restaurant A		Restaurant B	
Sales revenue	$900,000	100.0%	$900,000	100.0%
Variable costs	$450,000	50.0%	$270,000	30.0%
Fixed costs	400,000	44.4%	600,000	66.7%
Total costs	$850,000	94.4%	$870,000	96.7%
Net income	$ 50,000	5.6%	$ 30,000	3.3%

Exhibit 7.4 Break-even Revenue Level Depends on Cost Structure

	Restaurant A		Restaurant B	
Sales revenue	$800,000	100.0%	$857,000	100.0%
Variable costs	$400,000	50.0%	$257,000	30.0%
Fixed costs	400,000	50.0%	600,000	70.0%
Total costs	$800,000	100.0%	$857,000	100.0%
Net income	0	0	0	0

One could determine the break-even level of sales revenue by trial and error, but there is a formula for quickly calculating this level. The formula, and a more in-depth discussion of fixed and variable costs and how an awareness of this structure can be of great value in many types of business decisions, is covered in Chapter 8.

PAYING A FIXED OR A VARIABLE LEASE

Another situation where fixed and variable cost knowledge can be very useful is in comparing the alternative of a fixed lease cost versus a variable lease based on a percentage of sales. For example, consider the case of a restaurant that has an opportunity to pay a fixed rent for its premises of $5,000 a month ($60,000 a year) or a variable rent of 6% of its revenue. Before making the decision, the restaurant's management needs to first determine the break-even point of sales at which the fixed rental payment for a year would be identical to the variable rent. The equation for this is:

Break-even equation

$$\text{Annual break - even revenue} = \frac{\text{Fixed lease cost}}{\text{Variable lease percentage}}$$

and inserting the figures we can to determine the sales revenue level as follows:

$$\frac{\$60,000}{0.06} = \underline{\underline{\$1,000,000}}$$

In other words, at $1,000,000 of sales it makes no difference whether the restaurant paid a fixed rent of $60,000 or a variable rent of 6% of sales. At this level of sales, management would be indifferent. For this reason the break-even revenue point is sometimes referred to as the indifference point.

If management expected revenue to exceed $1,000,000, it would select a fixed rental arrangement. If revenue were expected to be below $1,000,000, it would be better off selecting the percentage of sales arrangement.

SEPARATING COSTS INTO FIXED AND VARIABLE ELEMENTS

Methods of breaking
down semicosts

Once costs have been categorized into fixed or variable elements, valuable information is then available for use in decision making. Some costs are easy to identify as definitely fixed or definitely variable. The semifixed or semivariable types must be broken down into the two separate elements.

A number of different methods are available for breaking down these semicosts into fixed and variable, some more sophisticated (and thus usually more accurate) than others. Three will be discussed:

- Maximum/minimum calculation
- Multipoint graph
- Regression analysis

To set the stage, we will use the income statement of the Model Motel for a year's period (see Exhibit 7.5). The Model Motel is a no-frills, 70-unit budget operation without food or beverage facilities. It operates at a 60% occupancy and, as a result of good cost controls, is able to keep its average room rate down to $20.00. Last year it sold a total of 15,300 rooms ($306,000 total income divided by $20.00).

Previous accounting
records useful

The first step is to list the expenses by category (fixed, variable, semivariable). The owner's or manager's past experience about the costs of the Model Motel, or the past year's accounting records, will be helpful in this listing. The

Exhibit 7.5   Income Statement without Cost Breakdown

Sales revenue		$306,000
Expenses		
Employee wages	$120,800	
Management salary	20,000	
Laundry, linen, and guest supplies	38,700	
Advertising	7,500	
Maintenance	17,300	
Utilities	18,100	
Office/Telephone	4,000	
Insurance	4,600	
Interest	8,300	
Property taxes	20,100	
Depreciation	35,000	
Total expenses		(294,400)
Net income		$ 11,600

Exhibit 7.6   Costs Allocated as Fixed, Variables, and Semivariable

	Fixed	Variable	Semivariable
Employee wages			$120,800
Management salary	$20,000		
Laundry, linen, and guest supplies		$38,700	
Advertising	7,500		
Maintenance			17,300
Utilities			18,100
Office/Telephone			4,000
Insurance	4,600		
Interest	8,300		
Property taxes	20,100		
Depreciation	35,000		

figures in the fixed column (see Exhibit 7.6) are those that do not change during the year with a change in volume (number of rooms sold). In other words, even though a fixed cost may change from year to year (for example, insurance rates do change, the amount to be spent on advertising can be increased or decreased at management's discretion), such changes are not directly caused by the number of guests accommodated. The items in the variable column are the costs that are the direct result of guests using the facilities (if there are no customers, there will be no cost for laundry, linen, and guest supplies). The higher the occupancy, the higher this cost will be. The figures in the semi column are those we must analyze into their fixed and variable components.

Monthly analysis adequate

To demonstrate the three methods of breakdown of a semicost, we will use the wage amount of $120,800. Since much of the wage cost is related to number of rooms sold, we need a month-by-month breakdown of the sales revenue for each month and the related wage cost for each month. (This information could be broken down by week, but there should be sufficient accuracy for all practical purposes with a monthly analysis.) The sales and labor cost breakdown is given in Exhibit 7.7. Note that the sales column figures are in numbers of units sold. This column could have been expressed in dollars of sales revenue without it affecting our results (as long as the average room rate of $20.00 had been relatively consistent during the year).

MAXIMUM/MINIMUM METHOD

With reference to Exhibit 7.7, note that the month of January has the word minimum alongside it. In January, units sold and wage cost were at their low-

Exhibit 7.7   Analysis of Units Sold and Wages by Month

	Units (Rooms) Sold	Wage Cost
January (minimum)	500	$ 7,200
February	1,000	7,900
March	1,300	9,900
April	1,200	10,800
May	1,400	12,200
June	1,500	12,100
July	2,100	13,100
August (maximum)	2,100	13,200
September	1,500	11,800
October	1,000	7,600
November	1,000	7,400
December	700	7,600
Totals	15,300	$120,800

Three strps required

est for the year. In contrast, August was the maximum month. There are three steps in the maximum/minimum (also known as the high/low) method.

Step 1: Deduct the minimum from the maximum figures.

	Units (Rooms)Sold	Wage Cost
August (maximum)	2,100	$13,200
January (minimum)	500	7,200
Differences	1,600	$ 6,000

Step 2: Divide wage different by units sold difference,

$$\frac{\$6,000}{\$1,600} = \$3.75$$

which is the variable cost per unit sold.

Calculation of fixed cost amount

Step 3: Use the answer to step 2 to calculate the fixed cost element.

Total wages for August	$13,200
Variable cost, 2,100 units sold × $3.75 a unit =	7,875
Fixed cost	$ 5,325

Instead of units sold, dollars of sales revenue could equally well have been used, as follows:

Step 1:

	Units Sold		Average Rate		Total Sales Revenue	Wage Cost
August (maximum)	2,100	×	$20.00	=	$42,000	$13,200
January (minimum)	500	×	20.00	=	10,000	7,200
Differences					$32,000	$ 6,000

Step 2: $\dfrac{\$6,000}{\$32,000} = \underline{\$0.1875}$

which is the variable cost per dollar of sales revenue.

Step 3:

Total wages for August	$13,200
Variable cost $42,000 sales revenue × $0.1875 =	(7,875)
Fixed cost	$ 5,325

Use minimum or maxumum month

Also in this step, we could have used the minimum sales month (instead of the maximum) to calculate our fixed cost and still have obtained the same result, as shown:

Total wages for January	$7,200
Variable cost, 500 units sold × $3.75 a unit =	(1,875)
Fixed cost	$5,325

The calculated fixed cost is $5,325 a month, or:

$$12 \times \$5,325 = \underline{\$63,900} \text{ a year}$$

Breakdown of total cost

With reference to Exhibit 7.6, we can now separate our total annual wage cost into its fixed and variable elements.

Total annual wages	$120,800
Fixed cost	63,900
Variable cost	$ 56,900

The calculation of the monthly fixed cost figure has been illustrated by arithmetical means. The maximum/minimum figures could equally as well have been plotted on a graph, as illustrated in Exhibit 7.8, and the fixed cost read off where the dotted line intersects the vertical axis. If the graph is accurately drawn, the same monthly figure of approximately $5,300 is obtained.

Possible distortions

The maximum/minimum method is quick and simple. It uses only two sets of figures. Unfortunately, either one or both of these sets of figures may not be typical of the relationship between sales and costs for the year (for example, a one-time bonus may have been paid during one of the months selected). Other, perhaps less dramatic, distortions may be built into the figures.

These distortions can be eliminated, as long as one is aware of them, by adjusting the raw figures. Alternatively, standard costs (rather than actual costs) could be used for the minimum and for the maximum sales months.

Another way to improve the maximum/minimum method and remove possible distortions in individual month figures is to plot the cost and sales figures for each of the 12 months (or however many periods are involved) on a graph.

MULTIPOINT GRAPH

Dependent and independent variables

Exhibit 7.9 illustrates a multipoint graph for our sales in units and our wage cost for each of the 12 months. Sales and costs were taken from Exhibit 7.7. The graph illustrated is for two variables, sales and wages. In this case, wages are given the name dependent variable and are plotted on the vertical axis.

Exhibit 7.8

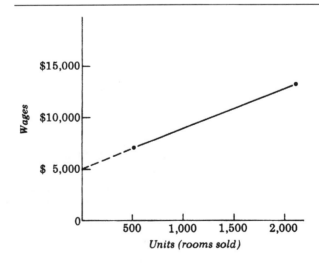

Exhibit 7.9

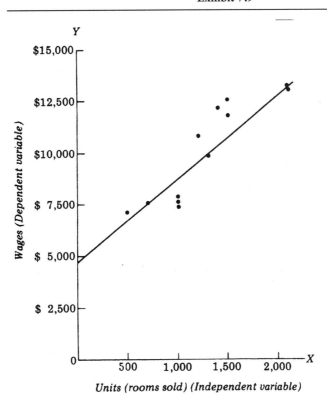

Units (rooms sold) (Independent variable)

Wages are dependent on sales: They vary with sales. Sales, therefore, are the independent variable. The independent variable is plotted on the horizontal axis. After plotting each of the 12 points, we have what is known as a scatter graph: a series of points scattered around a line that has been drawn through them. A straight line must be drawn.

There is no limit to how many straight lines could be drawn through the points. The line we want is the one that, to our eye, seems to fit best. Each individual doing this exercise would probably view the line in a slightly different position, but most people with a reasonably good eye would come up with a line that, for all practical purposes, is close enough. The line should be drawn so that it is continued to the left until it intersects the vertical axis (the dependent variable). The intersect point reading is our fixed cost (wages, in this case).

Fixed cost on vertical axis

Note that, in Exhibit 7.9, our fixed cost reading is $4,500 (approximately). This is the monthly cost. Converted to annual cost, it is:

$$\$4,500 \times 12 = \underline{\$54,000}$$

Our total annual wage cost would then be broken down into:

Fixed	$54,000
Variable	$66,800 ($120,800 less $54,000)

Note that, in drawing graphs for the purpose discussed, the point at which the vertical and horizontal axes meet should be given a reading of 0. The figures along each axis should then be plotted to scale from 0.

Line of best fit

The straight line on a scatter graph can be drawn by eye, and for most purposes will give us a fixed cost reading that is good enough. However, the question arises whether there is one best line that can be drawn that is the most accurate. The answer is yes. The method used to determine it is known as regression analysis.

REGRESSION ANALYSIS

Different equations

With regression analysis there is no need to draw a graph, plot points, and draw a line through them. The objective in drawing the line is to find out where the line intersects the vertical axis so we can read, at that intersection point, what the fixed costs are. Once we know the fixed costs, we can then easily calculate the variable costs (total costs – fixed costs = variable costs). From regression analysis, a number of equations have been developed for different purposes. One of the equations allows us to calculate the fixed costs directly, without a graph.

Before the equation is used, we have to take the units (rooms) sold and the wage cost information from Exhibit 7.7 and develop it a little further, as has been done in Exhibit 7.10. In Exhibit 7.10 the units (rooms) sold column has been given the symbol X (X is for the independent variable). The wage cost column (the dependent variable) has been given the symbol Y. Two new columns have been added: XY (which is X multiplied by Y) and X^2 (which is X multiplied by X). The equation is:

Equation for fixed costs

$$\text{Fixed costs} = \frac{(\Sigma Y)(\Sigma X^2) - (\Sigma X)(\Sigma XY)}{n(\Sigma X^2) - (\Sigma X^2)}$$

Two new symbols have been introduced in this equation: Σ means the sum of, or the column total figure, and n is the number of periods, in our case 12 (months).

Exhibit 7.10   Illustration of Calculation of Regression Analysis Data

Month	Units (Rooms) Sold X	Wage Cost Y	XY (X × Y)	X² (X × X)
1	500	$ 7,200	$ 3,600,000	250,000
2	1,000	7,900	7,900,000	1,000,000
3	1,300	9,900	12,870,000	1,690,000
4	1,200	10,800	12,960,000	1,440,000
5	1,400	12,200	17,080,000	1,960,000
6	1,500	12,100	18,150,000	2,250,000
7	2,100	13,100	27,510,000	4,410,000
8	2,100	13,200	27,720,000	4,410,000
9	1,500	11,800	17,700,000	2,250,000
10	1,000	7,600	7,600,000	1,000,000
11	1,000	7,400	7,400,000	1,000,000
12	700	7,600	5,320,000	490,000
Totals	15,300	$120,800	$165,810,000	22,150,000

Replacing the symbols in the above equation by the column totals from Exhibit 7.10, we have

$$\text{Fixed costs} = \frac{\$120,800(22,150,000) - (15,300)(165,810,000)}{12(22,150,000) - (15,300)(15,300)}$$

$$= \frac{\$2,675,720,000,000 - \$2,536,893,000,000}{265,800,000 - 234,090,000}$$

$$= \frac{\$138,827,000,000}{31,710,000}$$

$$= \$4,378.02 \text{ a month}$$

Total annual fixed cost

Our answer could be rounded to $4,400 a month, which gives us a total annual fixed cost of:

$$\$4,400 \times 12 = \$52,800$$

COMPARISON OF RESULTS

Let us compare the results of our fixed/variable breakdown of the Model Motel's annual wage cost using each of the three methods described. The results are tabulated as follows:

	Fixed	Variable	Total
Maximum/minimum	$63,900	$56,900	$120,800
Multipoint graph	54,000	66,800	120,800
Regression analysis	52,800	68,000	120,800

In practice, only one of the three methods would be used. We know that regression analysis is the most accurate; however, because it requires time to perform the necessary arithmetic, it should probably only be used by those who are mathematically adept or as a spot-check on the results of either of the other two methods. Alternatively, the figures can be fed into a programmed calculator that will carry out all the necessary calculations.

Graph can give good results

Multipoint graph results are fairly close to the regression analysis figures. which seems to imply that, if the graph is well drawn, we should have results accurate enough for all practical purposes. The maximum/minimum results are about 20% different from what regression analysis tells us the most correct result should be. Therefore, this method should be used with caution and only if the two periods selected are typical of all periods, which might be difficult to determine.

Once a method has been selected, it should be applied consistently to all semivariable expenses. With reference to our Model Motel's cost figures in Exhibit 7.6, so far we have analyzed the semivariable wage cost. We need to analyze similarly the three other semivariable costs: maintenance, utilities, and office/telephone. Let us assume we have done so; our completed cost analysis gives us the fixed and variable costs shown in Exhibit 7.11.

Exhibit 7.11   Final Cost Allocation by Fixed or Variable

	Fixed	Variable
Employee wages	$ 52,800	$ 68,000
Management salary	20,000	
Laundry, linen, and guest supplies		38,700
Advertising	7,500	
Maintenance	15,400	1,900
Utilities	14,200	3,900
Office	3,500	500
Insurance	4,600	
Interest	8,300	
Property taxes	20,100	
Depreciation	35,000	
Totals	$181,400	$113,000

ALTERNATIVE METHOD

As an alternative to separating semivariable costs by individual expense, the situation can be simplified by first adding together all semivariable costs, then applying one of the three methods outlined in this section to separate only the total into its fixed and variable elements. This considerably reduces the time and effort involved. On the other hand, it might reduce the accuracy of the results. In many cases, however, this reduced accuracy might still be satisfactory for decisions.

In Chapter 8 we shall see how we can use this cost breakdown information for decision making concerning many aspects of our motel operation. Even though a motel situation has been used, the same type of analysis can be carried out equally well for a restaurant or a department in a hotel. Regarding hotel departments, the difficulty may be in allocating the overhead costs in an equitable manner to the individual departments.

COMPUTER APPLICATIONS

A computerized spreadsheet program can be used to apply most of the concepts discussed in this chapter. The formula for each concept has to be entered into the program only once, and it will automatically calculate the results for each individual situation. A spreadsheet can also be used to carry out the calculations necessary to separate costs into their fixed and variable elements, using all three methods outlined in this chapter.

SUMMARY

One way of increasing net income in a business is to increase sales revenue. Another way is to control costs. In order to do this, one must understand that there are different types of costs.

A direct cost is one that is the responsibility of, and controllable by, a department head or department manager. An indirect cost, sometimes called an overhead cost, is not normally charged to an individual department. If such costs are broken down by department and shown on the departmental income statement, the resulting departmental profit or loss figure must be interpreted with great care.

All costs are controllable costs whether they are direct or indirect ones; it is only the level of responsibility for control of a cost that changes.

A joint cost is one that is shared by two or more departments, or by the organization as a whole. A joint cost could be a direct one (such as wages) or an indirect one (such as building maintenance). A discretionary cost is one that can be incurred only at the discretion of a particular person, generally the manager.

A relevant cost is one that needs to be considered when making a specific decision. If a cost makes no difference to the decision, then it is not relevant.

A sunk cost is an example of a cost that is not relevant to certain decisions. The initial expenditure on a piece of equipment bought five years ago and now to be traded in is a sunk cost insofar as the decision to buy a new machine today is concerned.

An opportunity cost is the income forgone by not doing something. A motel could run its own restaurant at a profit, or lease it out. If it runs it itself, the loss of rent income is an opportunity cost. However, the motel owner would happily endure this opportunity cost if net income from running the operation were greater than any potential rent income.

A standard cost is what a cost should be for a given level of revenue or volume of business.

The final three types of cost discussed in this chapter were fixed costs, variable costs, and semifixed or semivariable costs. Fixed costs are costs that do not change in the short run, regardless of the volume of sales (the general manager's annual salary is an example). Variable costs are those that do vary in the short run and do so in direct proportion to sales (food and liquor costs are two good examples of variable costs). Most costs, however, do not fall neatly into either the fixed or the variable category; they are the semifixed or semivariable category. In order to make useful decisions concerning fixed and variable costs and their effect on net income at various levels of sales, the semi costs must be analyzed into their fixed and variable elements. Three methods were used to illustrate how this can be done.

- The maximum/minimum method, which, although quick and easy to use, may give misleading results if the maximum and minimum sales periods selected are not truly representative of all periods.
- The multipoint graph eliminates the possible problem built into the maximum/minimum method. The graph is subject to some element of personal judgment, but in most cases will give results that are close enough for most decision making purposes.
- Regression analysis, which is the most accurate method, involves quite a number of calculations and can probably best be used as a spot-check on the results of using one of the other two methods.

DISCUSSION QUESTIONS

1. Differentiate between a direct cost and an indirect cost.
2. Define discretionary cost and give two examples (other than those given in the text) of such a cost.

3. Differentiate between a fixed cost and a variable cost and give an example of each.
4. Why are some costs known as semifixed or semivariable?
5. Why might it not be wise to allocate an indirect cost to various departments on the basis of each department's sales revenue to total sales revenue?
6. What do you think might be the relevant costs to be considered in deciding which one of a number of different vacuum cleaner models to buy for housekeeping purposes?
7. Explain why you think it sometimes makes sense to sell below cost.
8. Define the term high operating leverage and explain why, in times of increasing sales revenue, it is more profitable to have high rather than low operating leverage.
9. With figures of your own choosing, illustrate how the maximum/minimum calculation method can be used to separate the fixed and variable elements of a cost.
10. Explain why the maximum/minimum method may not be a good one to use to separate the fixed and variable portions of a cost.
11. Give a brief explanation of how to prepare a graph when using the multipoint graph method for separating the fixed and variable elements of a cost.

ETHICS SITUATION

A hotel owner decides that to control his costs he cannot offer employees any raise next year. However, they are not told that the hotel's manager has been offered a 10% increase in salary if he can convince the employees that the no-pay-raise policy is justified. He has agreed to do this and accept his raise. Discuss the ethics of this situation.

EXERCISES

7.1 If revenue from a sale was $4,800 and variable costs were $2,304, what is the variable cost percentage?

7.2 If sales revenue was $24,440 and variable costs were 42%, what is the contribution margin?

7.3 You were asked to cater a buffet for 40 people at $15 per person, your variable costs average 75% and fixed costs are $50 per day. Determine your contribution margin and operating income or loss and whether you will accept or reject the proposal.

7.4   You have decided to allocate $14,000 of indirect costs to your café and bar op-
erations based on square footage used. The café occupies 1,920 square feet and
the bar occupies 480 square feet. How much of the $14,000 will be allocated
to the cafe?

7.5   Using the maximum-minimum method, find *total fixed cost* and the *variable
cost per guest* if you had 14,000 guests and 10,000 guests and labor costs were
$15,500 and $12,000 respectively.

PROBLEMS

7.1   You are planning to purchase a new electronic register and have to make a
choice among the following three models:

	Model 1	**Model 2**	**Model 3**
Cash cost	$ 5,000	$ 5,500	$ 5,300
Estimate life	5 years	5 years	5 years
Trade-in value at end of life	$ 1,000	$ 1,200	$ 800
Cash from sale of old machine	$ 200	$ 200	$ 200
Installation of new machine	$ 75	$ 100	$ 100
Initial training cost in year 1 on new machine	$ 350	$ 300	$ 250
Annual maintenance contract	$ 300	$ 275	$ 200
Annual cost of supplies	$ 200	$ 200	$ 200
Annual wage cost of employees operating machine	$32,000	$32,000	$32,000

Strictly on the basis of lowest cash cost over the five-year period, which model
would be the best investment? (Note: In your calculations ignore any costs that
are not relevant.)

7.2   The fixed cost of the banqueting department of a hotel is $400 a day. A cus-
tomer has selected a menu for 100 persons that would have a food cost of
$6.00 per person, a variable wage cost of $1.75 per person, and other variable
costs of $0.25 per person.

a. Calculate the total cost per person if this banquet were booked.

b. What should be the total selling price (revenue) and the price per person if
a 20% net income on sales revenue is wanted?

c. The customer does not want to pay more than $11.25 per person for this
function. She is a good customer and has booked many functions in the
banquet room in the past and is expected to do so in the future. The function is for three days from now. There is no likelihood you will be able to

book the room for any other function. Explain why you would, or would not, accept the $11.25 per person price.

(Note: Assume that the hotel has only one banquet room.)

7.3 You have the following annual information about a restaurant complex comprising three departments:

	Dining Room	Coffee Shop	Lounge	Total
Sales revenue	$184,800	$135,600	$152,900	$473,300
Direct costs	154,600	129,000	127,600	411,200
Contributory Income	$ 30,200	$ 6,600	$ 25,300	$ 62,100
Indirect costs				(52,000)
Operating income				$ 10,100

The owner is thinking that, to get a better picture of how each department is doing, the indirect costs should be allocated to each department prorated according to area compared to total area. Square footage is as follows:

Dining room	1,200 sq. ft.
Coffee shop	840
Lounge	960

a. Allocate the indirect costs as indicated and advise the owner whether or not he should accept an offer from a souvenir store operator who is willing to take over the coffee shop space for a rental of $8,000 a year.

b. Before making a final choice, the operator of the restaurant decides to carry out more analysis about his indirect costs and what would happen to them if he rented out the coffee shop space. The information is:

	Present Cost	Cost if Coffee Shop Rented
Administrative and general	$14,100	$13,400
Advertising and promotion	9,800	9,200
Utilities	4,500	4,300
Repairs and maintenance	4,200	3,900
Insurance	3,600	3,300
Interest	5,400	5,400
Depreciation	10,400	7,100

One other factor to be considered is that, if the coffee shop is not operated, lounge revenue will decline by $13,600 a year and lounge direct costs will go down by $10,200. Dining room revenue and direct costs will not be affected. Should the owner accept the offer to rent out the coffee shop?

7.4   You have the following income statements for each of the four quarters of a restaurant operation:

	Quarter 1	Quarter 2	Quarter 3	Quarter 4
Sales revenue	$34,200	$44,800	$37,200	$20,300
Cost of sales	12,800	16,900	14,700	8,400
Gross profit	$21,400	$27,900	$22,500	$11,900
Expenses:				
Wages	$ 9,800	$11,600	$10,200	$ 7,400
Supplies	1,600	1,900	1,700	900
Advertising	600	800	700	400
Utilities	2,500	2,900	2,600	1,900
Maintenance	300	400	300	200
Insurance	500	500	500	500
Interest	600	600	600	600
Depreciation	400	400	400	400
Rent	3,000	3,000	3,000	3,000
Total expenses	$19,300	$22,100	$20,000	$15,300
Net income (loss)	$ 2,100	$ 5,800	$ 2,500	($ 3,400)

The owner is contemplating closing down the restaurant in Quarter 4 in order to eliminate the loss and take three months vacation. The owner has asked for your help and, after analysis of the expenses allocated to Quarter 4, you determine the following:

- *Wages.* $3,000 is a fixed cost of key personnel who would be kept on the payroll even if the operation were closed for three months.
- *Supplies.*   Cost varies directly with sales revenue, none fixed.
- *Advertising.*   Half of the cost is fixed, the rest is variable.
- *Utilities.*   Even if closed for three months, the restaurant will still require some heating; this is expected to cost $100 a month.
- *Maintenance.*   Some maintenance work could be done during the closed period; estimated cost $100.

- *Insurance.* There would be a $200 reduction in the insurance cost if closed for three months.

- *Interest.* Will still have to be paid, even if closed.

- *Depreciation.* With less customer traffic and reduced wear and tear on equipment, there would be a 75% reduction in this expense.

- *Rent.* This expense is an annual contract for $12,000 that must be paid regardless of whether the restaurant is open or closed.

What advice would you give the owner?

7.5 A company owns three motels in a ski resort area. Although there is some business during the summer months, the company finds it very difficult to staff the three operations during this period and is contemplating closing one of the three motels. The sales revenue and breakdown of costs during this period are as follows:

	Motel A	Motel B	Motel C
Sales revenue	$265,000	$325,000	$425,000
Variable costs	160,000	150,000	135,000
Fixed costs	110,000	167,000	260,000

a. Assuming one of the motels must be closed and that its closing will have no effect on the sales revenue of the other two, explain which motel should be closed and why.

b. Would your answer be the same if, with sales revenue as shown above, the costs were broken down as follows:

	Motel A	Motel B	Motel C
Variable costs	$100,000	$167,000	$250,000
Fixed costs	110,000	113,000	112,000

7.6 An entrepreneur is contemplating purchasing one of two similar, competitive motels and has asked for your advice. Present revenue of each motel is $450,000 per year. Jack's motel has annual variable costs of 50% of sales revenue and fixed costs of $200,000; Jock's motel has annual variable costs of 60% of sales revenue and fixed costs of $155,000. The entrepreneur thinks that, if he purchased Jack's motel, he could save $10,000 a year on interest expense (a fixed cost). Alternatively, if he purchased Jock's motel, he could improve staff scheduling to the point that the wage saving would reduce total variable cost to 55%. In the case of either purchase, he thinks that sales revenue can be increased by 20% a year. Calculate the present net income of each motel, then, given these assumptions, advise the entrepreneur which one he should buy, including any cautionary comments.

7.7   Stella's Steak House has been operating for the past ten years, and Stella has to negotiate her lease on the premises for the next five years. Her options are to pay a fixed monthly rent of $2,500 or to pay a variable monthly rent of 6% of her sales. Over the next five years she anticipates her sales to average $550,000 per year.

a. What is Stella's indifference point on an annual sales basis?

b. Which option should she choose? Explain.

7.8   A hotel wishes to analyze its electricity cost in its rooms department in terms of fixed and variable elements. Monthly income statements show that during its busiest and slowest months, cost and rooms occupied information is as follows:

	Rooms Cost	Rooms Sold
Busiest	$2,600	2,400
Slowest	2,000	1,200

Use the maximum/minimum method to calculate

a. The variable cost per room occupied.

b. The total variable cost for the busiest and for the slowest month.

c. The total fixed cost per month.

7.9   You have the following information from the records of a restaurant:

	Sales Revenue	Wages
January	$11,100	$5,500
February	13,100	5,900
March	14,900	6,100
April	19,100	7,100
May	22,000	9,000
June	24,200	9,600
July	26,300	9,700
August	27,000	9,900
September	23,900	8,500
October	20,100	7,600
November	18,200	8,000
December	16,000	7,100

Use the maximum/minimum method to calculate total fixed cost and total variable cost for a year.

7.10   Take the information concerning sales and wages in problem 7.9 and use regression analysis to calculate total fixed cost and total variable cost for a year. Compare the results with the results obtained in both parts of problem 7.9 and comment about the three sets of figures.

7.11   A restaurant has the following 12-month record of revenue and wages:

	Sales Revenue	Wages
January	$24,900	$11,300
February	24,200	11,100
March	25,600	11,200
April	24,200	11,400
May	34,000	13,200
June	46,200	18,600
July	53,300	21,600
August	44,000	16,100
September	34,200	15,100
October	30,400	12,800
November	28,200	11,200
December	27,000	13,000

Included in the July wages is a lump sum retroactive wage increase of $2,400, which would not normally be part of the July wage cost. Also, in December, the restaurant catered to a special Christmas function that brought in $3,200 in revenue and cost the restaurant an additional $900 in wages. The December wage figure also included $1,200 in Christmas bonuses to the staff. Use the maximum/minimum method to calculate the restaurant's fixed wage cost.

CASE 7

Charlie is thinking of spending $3,000 more next year on advertising (part of marketing expense). Because of his marketing courses he feels he can design appealing advertisements to be placed in local newspapers and aimed at the business luncheon trade. He estimates that if the ads are placed they will bring in 15 more people at lunch each day.

The average check for the additional lunch guests would be the same as that calculated in Case 6. Use a 52-week year. Assume that the food and beverage total cost of sales percentage will be the same as in year 0001. (This percentage was calculated in Case 3.)

To serve the extra guests, a new employee will have to be hired at lunch for four hours. Hourly rate of pay including fringe benefits (a free meal while on duty, vacation pay, and so on) will be $5.42 an hour. The following variable expenses will remain at the same percentage to sales revenue as they were in year 0001 (see Case 3):

- Laundry
- China, glass, etc.
- Other operating expenses

All other expenses are assumed to be fixed and unaffected by the increased volume of business.

Prepare calculations to show whether or not the $3,000 should be spent. Refer to the income statement for the 4C Company's restaurant for year 0001.

8

The Cost-Volume-Profit Approach to Decisions

INTRODUCTION

This chapter introduces the cost-volume-profit (CVP) method, which can assist management in choosing the decision process to evaluate current and potential future effects regarding sales revenue inflow and cost outflows. A number of basic questions will be identified and discussed through illustrations that can be answered using CVP analysis.

Before discussing and illustrating the CVP method, several specific key assumptions and limitations inherent in the CVP approach will be addressed. Break-even analysis will be discussed prior to an expansion of break-even to a cost-volume-profit mode that may incorporate changes in sales revenue, fixed and variable costs, and profit.

An illustration is presented to show the overall CVP analysis; it is followed by an explanation. The illustration is discussed relative to break-even sales revenue and the integration of CVP elements to determine profit levels for a particular volume of sales revenue.

To provide an analysis resulting in the most accurate information, the CVP equation is used rather than a graphical view. The CVP equation is used to determine the sales revenue level to break-even (sales revenue equals total cost) and the sales needed to give a stipulated level of profit. The CVP equation will determine the sales level necessary for a new fixed cost, to provide for a change in a variable cost and multiple changes in costs. These answers can be determined in sales revenue volume (dollars) or sales revenue quantity (units) such as rooms sold or guests served.

The chapter concludes with a discussion of how the CVP equation can be used to evaluate various situations concerning joint costs in multiple-department organizations.

CHAPTER OBJECTIVES

After studying this chapter, the reader should be able to:

1. Briefly discuss the assumptions and limitations inherent in CVP analysis.

2. Discuss and identify the various functions shown in a graph regarding sales levels, fixed and variable costs.

3. State the basic break-even equation used to determine sales revenue in dollars.

4. State the basic break-even equation used to determine sales revenue in units.

5. State the CVP equation used to determine the sales level in dollars and the equation used to determine the sales level in units.

6. Demonstrate by example how the break-even equations are used to determine break-even sales in dollars and in units.

7. Demonstrate by example how the CVP equations are used to determine sales volume in dollars and sales quantity in units.

8. Explain the term "contribution margin" and the format of a "contribution margin income statement."

9. Discuss how operating income before tax and net income (after tax) can be used in the CVP equation.

10. Discuss the use of CVP analysis to solve problems concerning joint fixed costs in a multiple-department organization.

THE CVP APPROACH TO DECISIONS

Managers of hotel, motel, restaurant, and beverage operations, as well as other hospitality operations providing general goods and services, ask questions such as:

- What will my operating income be at a specified level of sales revenue?
- What is the amount of additional sales revenue needed to cover the cost of expansion and still provide me the operating income I want?

- What effect will a change of selling prices have on my operating income?
- What effect will a change in the variable cost of sales have on my operating income?
- What increase in sales revenue is necessary to cover the cost of a wage increase and still provide the operating income level wanted?

These are but a few of many such questions, which cannot be answered simply from a traditional income statement. They are however, easily answered through the use of a cost-volume-profit (CVP) approach. The CVP method breaks income statement sales revenue and costs in variable and fixed elements, which are then analyzed and used to make an informed and rational decision. But, before the CVP approach can be used, the assumptions and limitations inherent in the CVP method must be clearly understood.

CVP ASSUMPTIONS AND LIMITATIONS

The following assumptions and limitations are built into CVP analysis:

Breakdown of costs into fixed and variable

- CVP analysis assumes costs associated for a specific level of sales revenue can be broken into variable and fixed elements with a reasonable level of accuracy.
- CVP assumes that identified fixed costs will remain fixed at the same level during the period affected by the decision being made.
- CVP assumes that variable costs will increase or decrease in a consistent linear relationship with sales revenue during the period being evaluated.
- CVP is limited to specific situations, operating divisions, or departments. Great caution should be used concerning decisions for the entire organization when multiple divisions and departments contribute to overall income. In such cases, it may be appropriate to evaluate sales revenue mix (discussed in Chapter 2).
- CVP assumes that economic and other conditions will remain relatively stable during the period being evaluated. During a highly inflationary period it would be rather difficult to forecast sales revenue, selling prices, and cost functions during a period exceeding more than a month. Certainly it would be dangerous rather than simply difficult to apply CVP analysis for the next year.

Analysis only guide to final decision

In conclusion, CVP analysis produces only best estimates to assist management in the decision process. CVP analysis relies on accounting information and mathematical computations, which may indicate a decision in a certain direction that does not consider customer and employee relations, social and potential environmental impact concerns.

The Break-even Analysis

CVP analysis a logical expansion of break-even analysis

Before we begin our discussion of CVP analysis, we must become familiar with the basic analysis method upon which it is based. CVP analysis is a logical expansion of the break-even analysis. The objective of using the break-even equation is to find the sales level in dollars or units necessary to cover all operating costs and produce operating income resulting in no profit or loss. However, begin with the following terms and the use of capital letters to designate their identity in each of the two basic break-even equations, break-even sales and break-even units:

The Break-even Sales Equation

$$\frac{\text{Fixed costs}}{1 - \text{Variable costs/sales}} = \frac{\text{Fixed costs}}{\text{Variable cost \%}} = \frac{\text{Fixed costs}}{\text{Contribution margin}} = \underline{\underline{\text{Break-even sales}}}$$

Abbreviations	Break-even Sales Equation
Break-even Sales = BES Fixed Costs = FC	$\text{Break-even sales} = \dfrac{FC}{1 - VC/Sales}$
Variable Cost = VC Variable Cost % = VC/Sales	$= \dfrac{FC}{VC\%}$
100% of Unknown Sales = 1 Contribution Margin = 1 – VC%	$= \dfrac{FC}{CM\%} = \underline{\underline{\text{Break-even sales revenue}}}$

Example A: FC is \$128,000, sales revenue is \$240,000, and VC is \$187,200. What is break-even sales revenue?

$$\frac{FC}{1 - VC/S} = \frac{FC}{1 - VC\%} = \frac{FC}{CM\%} = \underline{\underline{\text{Break-even sales revenue}}}$$

$$\frac{\$128,000}{1 - (\$187,200 \,/\, \$240,000)} = \frac{\$128,000}{1 - 78\%} = \frac{\$128,000}{22\%} = \$581,818.18 \cong \underline{\underline{\$581,818\,BE}}$$

Break-even Units Equation

$$\frac{\text{Fixed cost}}{SP - VC[u]} = \frac{\text{Fixed cost}}{\text{Contribution margin [u]}} = \underline{\underline{\text{Break-even units}}}$$

Abbreviations	Break-even Units Equation
Break-even Sales Units = BE [u] Fixed Costs = FC	$\text{Break-even units} = \dfrac{FC}{SP - VC[u]}$
Variable Cost per Unit = VC [u] Variable Cost % = VC [u]/SP	$= \dfrac{FC}{CM[u]}$
Sales Price per Unit = SP Contribution Margin = SP – VC [u]	$= \underline{\underline{BE[u]}}$

Example B: Let's assume FC = \$128,000, VC are \$187,200 on sales of \$240,000 and the average selling price of the units sold is \$20 each, find break-even sales in units.

$$\frac{\text{Fixed cost}}{SP - VC[u]} = \frac{\text{Fixed cost}}{\text{Contribution margin [u]}} = \underline{\underline{\text{Break-even units}}}$$

$$\frac{\$128,000}{\$20 - \$15.60} = \frac{\$128,000}{\$4.40} = 29,090.909 \cong \underline{\underline{29,091\,BE[u]}}$$

Four interesting relationships can be seen in these two equations. Referring to Examples A and B we can see that variable cost, sales revenue, and units of sales are neatly tied together with respect to break-even sales volume in dollars and break-even sales in units.

First, if we had known the average selling price per unit in Example A, where we found break-even sales revenue, we could have also found break-even units:

$$BES/SP = BE[u] = \$581,818.18/\$20 = \underline{\underline{29,091}}\ BE\ units$$

Note that any time sales in dollars and average selling price is being used to convert to sales in units, the entire decimal function must be used. The same requirement exists when sales in units are being used to convert to sales in dollars.

Second, the reverse is also true—having found break-even units and knowing the selling price, we can find break-even sales revenue.

$$29,090.909 \times \$20 = \underline{\underline{\$581,818}}\ BE\ sales\ revenue$$

Third, since the relationship between sales, units selling price, variable cost percentage of sales, and the variable cost per unit are based on one set of data, we could have found the break-even sales by using the base data shown in Example B.

$$\frac{\text{Fixed cost}}{1 - \text{VC[u]/SP}} = \frac{\$128,000}{1 - \$15.60/\$20} = \frac{\$128,000}{1 - 78\%} = \frac{\$128,000}{22\%} = \underline{\underline{\$581,818.18}}$$

Fourth, if you have the total variable costs, total sales revenue, and know the average unit selling price, the variable cost per unit can also be found:

$$\text{VC} = \$187,200, \ \text{Sales revenue} = \$240,000, \ \text{Average unit selling price is } \$20.$$

$$\$187,200/\$240,000 = 78\%, \ \text{thus}, \ \$20 \times 78\% = \underline{\$15.60} = \text{VC[u]}$$

It is important to note that final dollar answers are rounded to the dollar and final percentage answers are rounded to $\frac{1}{10}$ of a percent. Rounding of dollar or percentage answers cannot be made to the figure or percentage when moving from units to sales or sales to units. To preclude any difficulty in rounding a decimal, use the same technique referred to in Chapter 1.

As you will soon see, these elements as described in the calculation of break-even sales revenue or break-even units are used time and time again in completing a CVP analysis.

In this chapter, for the most part we will use information developed in Chapter 7 concerning the Model Motel's Sales, fixed costs, and variable costs. The information needed is summarized in Exhibit 8.1.

In many cases, CVP analysis is presented in the form of a contribution margin income statement to check the validity of the CVP calculations. The contribution margin income statement is also used to answer questions concerning operating income when actual operating data do not agree with the forecasted sales level. The contribution margin income statement shown below uses the income statement information from Exhibit 8.1.

Contribution Margin Income Statement	
Sales revenue	$306,000
Less: Variable cost	(113,000)
Contribution margin	$193,000
Less: Fixed costs	(181,400)
Operating income	$ 11,600

Exhibit 8.1   Information Required for a BE or CVP Analysis

Sales revenue	$306,000
Variable cost of sales	(113,000)
Contribution margin	$193,000
Fixed costs	(181,400)
Operating income [before tax]	$ 11,600

Other Information:

a.   70 Rooms [units]

b.   Average room rate = $20.00

c.   Occupancy rate = $\dfrac{15,300}{70 \times 365} = \dfrac{15,300}{25,550} = \underline{\underline{60\%}}$

d.   Average number of rooms occupied = 60% × 70 rooms (units) = $\underline{\underline{42}}$ rooms

e.   Variable cost per room occupied = $\dfrac{\$113,000}{15,300} = \underline{\underline{\$7.39}}$

f.   Variable cost as a % of sales revenue = $\dfrac{\$113,000}{\$306,000} = \underline{\underline{37\%}}$

Normally, details of variable and fixed costs, item by item, are shown directly on a statement or supporting schedule. The contribution to fixed costs is typically referred to as the contribution margin. The contribution margin is sales revenue minus the cost of sales, which can also be expressed as a percentage of sales revenue. There may be other costs which are classified as variable costs, but they will directly relate to expense items shown in the operating expense section of an income statement.

If an income statement were to be shown for a large organization with a number of departments, sales revenue and cost of sales would be shown for each department and a combined contribution margin for all departments would be shown. Total fixed costs of an organization are then to be deducted to arrive at operating income which describes income before tax. The contribution margin will be discussed further in this chapter.

Before we proceed further, let us look at a graphical presentation taken from the information shown in Exhibit 8.1, from the standpoint of break-even analysis. The same procedures are followed if a graphical presentation is made for a CVP analysis.

GRAPHICAL PRESENTATION

Generally, three steps are used in the preparation of a graph for break-even or CVP analysis and presentation using sales revenue in dollars and sales units. To prepare a graph, sales revenue is shown on the vertical axis and sales in units are shown on the horizontal axis, as shown in Exhibit 8.2.

> *Step 1.* Using information from Exhibit 8.1, the fixed costs are shown by inserting a horizontal line from the vertical axis across the graph. The fixed cost line will originate at a position on the vertical axis approximating $181,400 as shown in Exhibit 8.2

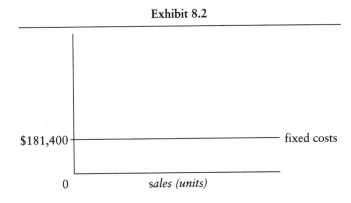

Exhibit 8.2

Steps in graph
presentation

> *Step 2.* Insert $294,000 in a relative position above fixed cost. Next, plot a point inserted on the graph horizontally opposite of the $294,000 point on the vertical axis. From the point on the vertical axis where fixed costs intersect, extend a line to intercept the point plotted opposite of the total cost, as shown in Exhibit 8.3.

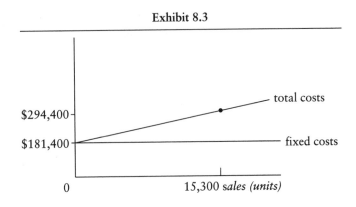

Exhibit 8.3

Step 3. Draw a sales revenue line horizontally from a $306,000 relative sales revenue point inserted on the vertical axis line and on the horizontal axis line to represent 15,300 sales units. Connect the intersect point of the vertical and horizontal line projecting at a 45-degree angle through the graph. The point where the total cost line intersects the 45-degree line is the break-even point. Any level below the break-even point shows a loss and any level above the break-even point shows operating income (profit before tax).

Exhibit 8.4 shows a completed break-even graph. (Exhibits 8.2, 8.3, and 8.4 are for basic illustration only, so they were not drawn to scale.) Exhibit 8.5 shows a completed graph drawn approximately to scale. This allows us to read certain information with better accuracy. The break-even is defined with greater accuracy at the point where sales revenue line intersects with the total cost line; dotted horizontal and vertical lines aid in defining the intersection point. The dotted lines also allow us to estimate the total sales revenue and sales units with reasonable accuracy. Using information from Exhibit 8.5, break-even is approximately $288,000 of sales revenue and 14,400 sales units.

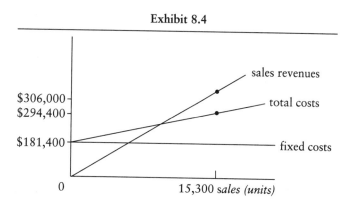

Exhibit 8.4

Graphs are accurate enough to give us an acceptable answer and lend themselves to being excellent tools to visually depict the information shown; however, as one can readily see, structuring a graph can be time consuming. This is true if a number of changes are needed to bring the graph up to date as a result of changing costs. Are graphs the best tool to estimate break-even or CVP sales in dollars or units? One can answer the question if knowledgeable of the break-even and CVP equations. Let us answer the question using a contribution margin income statement based on Exhibit 8.1.

Exhibit 8.5

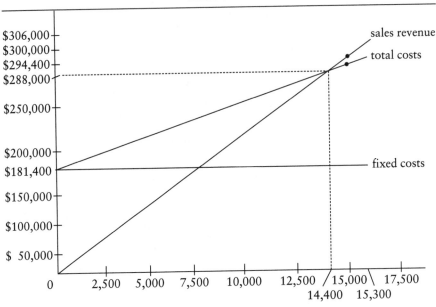

Sales revenue at break-even	$288,000
Cost of sales (37% × $288,000)	(106,560)
Contribution margin	$181,440
Less: Fixed costs	(181,400)
Operating income [before tax]	$ 40

Using the contribution margin method, a $40 operating income is shown. Using the break-even equation, the break-even sales revenue would be:

$$\frac{FC}{1-VC\%} = \frac{\$181,400}{1-37\%} = \frac{\$181,400}{.63} = \$287,936$$

In the final analysis, the break-even equation will provide the most accurate estimate of break-even. If sales revenue falls below $287,937, the Model Motel will begin losing money. Other questions that pertain to changing costs, sales revenue, or sales units can be answered more accurately and in less time by use of the break-even equation.

Before moving to a discussion of CVP analysis, a comment is required regarding other fixed income an operation may be receiving, and how it should be treated during CVP analysis. We will assume the Model Motel has a coffee

How to handle other income

shop that is being leased out for $10,000 per year. The $10,000 received is other income and should not be included with regular sales revenue since it is a fixed inflow. The easiest and most acceptable solution is to deduct the lease income from operating sales revenue. This method is based on a concept that to include other income would taint the actual sales revenue received from normal operations. The motel is not in business to lease property it owns, but to earn sales revenue by selling the rooms it maintains. The calculation after sales revenue is reduced by $10,000 of other revenue, using the established variable cost percentage from Exhibit 8.1:

Reduction from Sales Revenue

$$\text{Sales Revenue } [\$306,000 - \$10,000] = \underline{\underline{\$296,000}}$$

$$\text{Variable Cost } [\$296,000 \times 37\%] \quad = \underline{\underline{\$109,520}}$$

$$\frac{\text{FC}}{1 - \text{VC\%}} = \frac{\$181,400}{1 - 37\%} = \frac{\$181,400}{.63} = \frac{\$287,937}{\text{Break-even}}$$

Neither the variable cost percentage nor the contribution percentage changes and the calculation produces the same $287,937 break-even that was calculated following the discussion of Exhibits 8.2, 8.3, and 8.4.

THE CVP ANALYSIS

CVP analysis is a logical extension of the break-even analysis, which was discussed earlier in the chapter. Having an understanding of break-even analysis and the basic equations used has set the foundation for an understanding of the CVP equations and CVP analysis. The CVP considers additional costs being added to the numerator of the CVP equations in addition to the normal fixed cost. These additional costs are evaluated relative to the contribution margin to determine the sales revenue level necessary to cover the costs. As was the case with break-even analysis, CVP also uses two basic equations—CVP sales revenue and CVP sales units. The basic equations are:

$$\text{Sales revenue} = \frac{\text{Fixed cost + Added cost? + Added cost? + Etc.?}}{\text{Contribution margin \%}}$$

$$\text{Sales units} \quad = \frac{\text{Fixed cost + Added cost? + Added cost? + Etc.?}}{\text{Contribution margin[u]}}$$

It is necessary to identify a few terms to include potential added cost items.

Operating Income = OI: Identifies operating income before tax. This identification is used on income statements and contribution margin income statements and in general discussion to indicate income before tax.

Profit. Identifies income before tax, as does operating income. It is commonly used in the CVP equation rather than operating income since it is shorter and means the same thing as operating income.

Both operating income and profit defines income before tax. They are derived from:

[Sales revenue − Cost of sales = Gross margin − Operating expenses = Operating income]

$$\text{Net income} = \text{NI} = \text{Income after tax}$$

$$\text{Sales revenue} = \text{SR} \qquad \text{Sales units} = \text{SU}$$

In addition to using the identified terms, we will discuss changes that can be made to the elements of the CVP equation. Changes can effect variable cost percentages for sales revenue, sales units, variable costs sales and unit selling prices in response to a number of questions regarding: sales revenue, variable costs, variable cost percentages, unit cost, variable cost per unit, selling prices, and multiple changes of elements of the equation. Several more topics of interest will also be discussed.

We begin with CVP break-even analysis to using the same figures used earlier in discussions of graphs.

$$\frac{FC + 0}{1 - VC\%} = \frac{FC + 0}{CM\%} = \underline{\underline{CVP\ Break\text{-}even}}$$

$$\frac{\$181,400 + 0}{1 - 37\%} = \frac{\$181,400}{.63} = \underline{\underline{\$287,937}}$$

The source of information again is Exhibit 8.1, and the figures will continue to be used. As you have noticed by now, either a percentage or decimal figure can be used in the denominator, which has been illustrated in the solutions of earlier equations. It is important to remember that data being used to forecast break-even and CVP are in themselves generally estimates and break-even is in itself a best estimate.

AT WHAT LEVEL OF SALES REVENUE WILL WE MAKE AN OPERATING INCOME OF $39,000?

This CVP question is answered quickly using the CVP equation:

$$\text{Sales revenue} = \frac{\$181,400 + \$39,000}{1 - 37\%}$$

$$= \frac{\$220,400}{.63}$$

$$= \underline{\underline{\$349,841}}$$

How Much Must Revenue Increase to Cover a New Fixed Cost?

Higher revenue equals higher variable costs

Normally, if fixed costs increase and no change Is made in selling prices, profits can be expected to decline by the amount of the additional fixed cost. We can then ask the question: By how much must sales revenue increase to compensate for a fixed cost increase and not have a reduction in profit? A simple answer is that sales revenue has to go up by the same amount as the fixed cost increases. But this is not correct, because to increase sales revenue (with no increase in selling prices) we have to sell more units; if we sell more units, our variable costs (such as wages and guest supplies) are going to increase. By trial and error, we could arrive at a solution, but our equation will solve this kind of question for us quickly:

$$\text{Sales revenue} = \frac{\text{Old cost} + \text{New fixed cost} + \text{Operating income}}{1 - \text{Variable Cost \%}}$$

Suppose we wish to increase our advertising by \$5,000 per year. What is the additional sales revenue level we must generate to provide this \$5,000 added cost and maintain our present operating income at \$11,600?

$$\text{Sales revenue} = \frac{\$181,400 + \$5,000 + \$11,600}{1 - 37\%}$$

$$= \frac{\$198,000}{.63}$$

$$= \underline{\underline{\$314,286}}$$

We can verify the calculation by using a contribution margin income statement:

Verify calculation

Sales revenue	\$314,286
Variable costs [\$314,285 × 37%]	(116,286)
Contribution margin	\$198,000
Less: Fixed costs	(181,400)
Operating income [Before Tax]	\$ 16,600

The solution requires sales revenue to be $314,286 to provide for the fixed cost, added cost, and operating income. The sales level increased by $8,286 from the previous level of $306,000. To find the number of additional rooms that must be sold, we use the average room rate of $20 from Exhibit 8.1 and divide the increase by the average room rate:

Increase in sales revenue/Average room rate = Additional rooms

$8,286/$20 = 413.3 or <u>414</u> rooms per year

Since we can't sell a part of a room, it is suggested we round up rather than down from 413.3 to 414 rooms. If we divide the 414 additional rooms by 365 operating days, a little more than one room per day must be sold. If it is anticipated that more than 414 rooms can be sold, not only will the added cost of $5,000 be covered, but it is possible that the additional variable cost per room occupied will also be covered and there is a good probability operating income may also increase slightly.

Solutions in dollars or units

In the problem just discussed, we worked the solution by evaluating additional sales revenue required, which was then converted to rooms to be sold. As we will see later in this chapter, we could have answered the question working directly with room data. Variable cost per unit is $7.39 (see Exhibit 8.1) and average sale per unit (average room rate) is $20.

$$\text{Variable cost } \% = \frac{\$7.39}{\$20.00} \times 100 = 36.95\% \text{ or } \underline{37\%}$$

Increase in wage variable cost

Included in the $7.39 variable cost per unit is the cost of the wages of a maid to clean the unit. Suppose the hourly wage rate for maids (including all benefits) is $4.00 an hour, and a maid takes one-half hour to clean a room. Therefore, $2.00 of the $7.39 variable cost per room sold is for wages and benefits. Let us assume a 20 percent increase in maids' wages; our wage cost per unit will not be:

$$\$2.00 + (20\% \times \$2.00) = \$2.00 + \$0.40 = \underline{\$2.40}$$

Alternatively, we could say that our variable cost per unit is going to go up by $0.40 and will now be:

$$\$7.39 + \$0.40 = \underline{\$7.79}$$

But if our variable cost per unit is now $7.79 and there is no change in the average room rate, our variable cost percentage will no longer be the same as before. It will be:

New variable cost
percentage

$$\frac{\$7.79}{\$20.00} \times 100 = 38.95 \text{ or } \underline{39\%}$$

We can now use this to answer the question: What must my new level of revenue be if my fixed costs do not change, my profit must not drop, but my maids' wages are going to increase by 20 percent?

$$\text{Sales revenue} = \frac{\text{Fixed cost} + \text{Operating income}}{1 - \text{VC\%}}$$

$$= \frac{\$181,400 + \$11,600}{1 - 39\%}$$

$$= \frac{\$193,000}{.61}$$

$$= \$316,393 \text{ rounded to } \underline{\$316,400}$$

Again, we'll use the contribution margin income statement to verify the answer:

Proof of new revenue
level

Sales revenue	$316,400
Variable costs [$316,400 × 39%]*	(123,400)
Contribution margin	$193,000
Less: fixed costs	(181,400)
Operating income [Before Tax]	$ 11,600

* = Rounded

WHAT ABOUT MULTIPLE CHANGES?

Combined changes

So far, only single changes have been considered. Multiple changes can be handled in the same way with no difficulties. For example, let us assume we are going to spend $5,000 more on advertising, that our maids are to get a 20 percent wage increase and, in addition, we now want our profit to be $20,000 rather than $11,600. What must our revenue level be? Combining all these changes into one equation we have:

$$\text{Sales revenue} = \frac{\text{FC} + \text{NFC} + \text{OI}}{1 - \text{VC\%}} \text{ where NFC} = \text{New fixed costs}$$

$$\text{Sales revenue} = \frac{\$181,400 + \$5,000 + \$20,000}{1 - 39\%}$$

$$= \frac{\$206,400}{.61}$$

$$= 338,361 \text{ or } \underline{\$338,400}$$

And the verification is:

Sales revenue	$338,400
Variable costs [$338,400 × 39%]*	(132,000)
Contribution margin	$206,400
Less: fixed costs	(186,400)
Operating income [Before Tax]	$ 20,000

*=Rounded

How Can We Convert the Sales Revenue Level Directly into Units?

In the equation used so far, the denominator has been:

$$100\% - \text{Variables costs as a \% of sales revenue}$$

The resulting net figure in the denominator is referred to as the contribution margin. In other words, if sales revenues is 100% and variable costs are 39%, then 61% of revenue is available as the contribution toward fixed costs and profit. The 61% figure is the contribution margin.

Contribution margin in dollars

The contribution margin can be expressed as a dollar amount, rather than as a percentage figure. For example, the Model Motel's average room rate (average sale per room) is $20 and the variable costs (assuming an increase in maids' wages) total $7.79 per room; therefore, the contribution margin is $12.21. In fact, our general equation for the sales level (either revenue or units) can be simplified to:

$$\text{Sales revenue} = \frac{\text{Fixed costs} + \text{Operating income}}{\text{Contribution margin [u]}}$$
$$= \frac{FC + OI}{SP - VC[u]}$$

The denominator of this equation is sometimes referred to as the contribution margin ratio. This is an important figure for any hospitality operation's manager to know because it shows how much of each sales dollar is available to cover fixed costs and provide a profit.

If we use this equation and express our contribution margin in percentages (which we have been doing), then our sales level will be expressed in revenue dollars. If we use the equation and express the contribution margin in dollars, we shall have a sales level expressed in units. Let us test this using information from the problem in the preceding section.

Sales level result in units

$$\text{Sales revenue} = \frac{\text{FC} + \text{OI}}{\text{SP} - \text{VC[u]}} = \frac{\text{FC} + \text{OI}}{\text{CM[u]}}$$

$$\text{Sales revenue} = \frac{\$181,400 + \$5,000 + \$20,000}{\$20.00 - \$7.79}$$

$$= \frac{\$206,400}{\$12.21}$$

$$= 16,904 \text{ Rooms}$$

The reason we might want the solution in units is that in the case of a motel or hotel it might be useful to have the sales level required converted to an occupancy percentage. This can be quickly calculated if we know the sales level in units.

From Exhibit 8.1 we know that our present occupancy level for the 70-room Model Motel is 60%. This is calculated by dividing units used by units available, or:

$$\frac{15,300}{70 \times 365} \times 100 = 60\%$$

To cover our changed fixed and variable costs, we are now going to have to sell 16,904 units a year, which is an occupancy of:

New occupancy
percentage required

$$\frac{16,904}{70 \times 365} \times 100 = 66 + \%$$

IF WE CHANGE ROOM RATES, HOW WILL THIS AFFECT UNITS SOLD?

The contribution margin expressed in dollars is also used in answering questions concerning a change in selling prices. For example, assuming fixed costs are $186,400, profit required is $20,000, and variable costs are $7.79 per room used, what will our occupancy have to be to offset a 10% reduction in selling prices? In other words, our new average rate will be $18.00 instead of $20.

Effect of change in rates

$$\text{Sales level (in units)} = \frac{\$186,400 + \$20,000}{\$18.00 - \$7.79}$$

$$= \frac{\$206,400}{\$10.21}$$

$$= 20,216 \text{ units (rooms)}$$

Occupancy will therefore have to be:

$$\frac{20,216}{70 \times 365} \times 100 = \underline{79 + \%}$$

In other words, to compensate for a 10% cut in selling prices, our occupancy will have to jump from 66 + % to 79 + %. Expressed another way, we could say that we are going to have to sell nine more rooms per night on average (13% × 70 rooms available) to pay for a decrease in average rate of 10%.

We could have arrived at the same result using the contribution margin expressed in percentages. In fact, it is sometimes necessary to do it this way when we have sales figures or results that cannot be converted to a unit basis. The equation in this case is a little lengthier:

Equation for contribution margin in percentage

$$\text{Sales level} = \frac{\text{Fixed cost} + \text{Profit desired}}{100\% - \left(\dfrac{\text{Present variable cost \%}}{100\% \pm \text{Proposed percentage change in prices}} \right)}$$

We will use the same figures we have been using: fixed cost is \$186,400, profit desired \$20,000, present variable cost 39%, and a proposed rate decrease of 10%. Substituting in the equation, we have:

Illustration of use of equation

$$\text{Sales level} = \frac{\$186,400 + \$20,000}{100\% - \left(\dfrac{39\%}{100\% - 10\%} \right)}$$

$$= \frac{\$206,400}{100\% - \left(\dfrac{39\%}{90\%} \right)}$$

$$= \frac{\$206,400}{100\% - 43.3\%}$$

$$= \frac{\$206,400}{56.7\%}$$

$$= \underline{\$364,020}$$

In terms of number of units to be sold, this is:

$$\frac{\$364,020}{\$18 \text{ (new rate)}} = \underline{20,223}$$

Rounding figures

This answer of 20,223 differs slightly from the answer obtained by using the earlier method (20,216), but the difference is caused solely by some slight rounding out of certain figures in our calculations.

How Does the Equation Work If We Have a Loss?

So far we have looked at the CVP equation in break-even or profitable situations only. It can also be used to answer questions concerning a loss position. For example, suppose the Model Motel were in the following situation:

Sales revenue	$272,100	(13,605 units)
Variable costs [37% × $272,100]*	$100,700	($7.40/unit)
Fixed costs	181,400	
Total costs	$282,100	
Loss	($ 10,000)	

*=Rounded

Elimination of loss

The question is: How much do we have to do in extra sales to eliminate the loss? The answer is to divide the amount of the loss by the contribution margin (using percentage figures if we want the answer in dollars or using dollar figures if we want the answer in units).

$$\text{Extra sales required} = \frac{\$10,000}{100\% - 37\%} \text{ or } \frac{\$10,000}{\$20.00 - \$7.40}$$

$$= \frac{\$10,000}{63\%} \text{ or } \frac{\$10,000}{\$12.60}$$

$$= \underline{\$15,873} \text{ or } 794 \text{ units at } \$20$$

Eliminate loss and give profit

If we wanted to calculate the addition volume required to eliminate the loss and give a profit of $15,000, the numerator becomes the amount of the loss plus the profit desired.

$$\text{Sales level required} = \frac{\$10,000 + \$15,000}{100\% - 37\%} \text{ or } \frac{\$10,000 + \$15,000}{\$20.00 - \$7.40}$$

$$= \frac{\$25,000}{63\%} \text{ or } \frac{\$25,000}{\$12.60}$$

$$= \underline{\$39,683} \text{ or } 1,984 \text{ units at } \$20$$

Is our answer the correct one? This can be tested (rounding the additional revenue required to $39,700).

Proof of correctness

Previous revenue level	$272,100
Additional revenue required	39,700
Total revenue	$311,800
Variable costs [37% × $311,800]*	$115,400
Fixed costs	181,400
Total costs	$296,800
Profit (income)	$ 15,000

*=Rounded

WHAT ABOUT A NEW INVESTMENT?

Estimation of costs

The CVP equation has been used so far to illustrate how historical information from accounting records can be used to make decisions about the future. CVP analysis is equally as valid when we have no past accounting information to help us. In such a case the fixed and variable costs have to be estimated in the best possible way. Suppose our Model Motel were considering renting the adjacent premises and converting them to a 50-seat coffee shop to better serve the needs of its motel customers. The owner of the motel and the accountant have developed the cost projections shown in Exhibit 8.6. With this information we can answer the question: What must the minimum sales be to earn the return on investment desired? This can be answered by using the basic CVP equation.

$$\text{Sales level} = \frac{\text{Fixed expenses} + \text{Return on investment (profit)}}{100\% - \text{variable cost \%}}$$

$$= \frac{\$42,800 + \$15,100}{100\% - 55\%}$$

$$= \frac{\$57,900}{45\%}$$

$$= \$128,667, \text{ or rounded to } \$129,000$$

Feasibility of sales
volume forecast

Assuming the estimates of costs are reasonably accurate, the owner of the Model Motel would have to decide whether the projected required revenue of $129,000 could be attained from motel customers and other potential customers in the area. If the volume could be reached, then the new venture would be profitable.

Once in business with the new restaurant, decisions about the restaurant can then be made using CVP analysis in the same way as was demonstrated for the motel operation. Restaurant sales can also be handled on a unit basis. In this case the unit is the customer and the average check is the measure of the

Exhibit 8.6.   Investment and Cost Data for Proposed Coffee Shop

Investment required for remodeling and for equipment and furniture, table settings, inventories, and other pre-opening items	$100,500
Annual fixed costs are estimated to be	
Rent	$ 7,500
Depreciation of furniture and equipment	5,200
Basic labor cost for supervision, food preparation, and service	24,200
Insurance, telephone, utilities, advertising	5,900
Total	$ 42,800
Variable operating costs will be kept to these levels relative to revenue	
Food cost	35%
Labor cost	15%
Other items	5%
Total	55%
Return on investment required (15% on initial investment of $100,500) =	$ 15,100*

*=Rounded

amount of sale per unit, or customer. For example, at a restaurant sales level of $129,000 and with a $6.00 average check, the number of units (customers) is

$$\frac{\$129,000}{\$6.00} = 21,500$$

WHAT ABOUT THE PROBLEM OF JOINT COSTS?

Costs shared by departments

In the problems handled to date, the fixed costs have been identified with a single operation (a motel) or department (the restaurant), and this identification has been easy. What happens in the case of joint cost if, for example, a restaurant that has a food department and beverage department? Some of the costs involved will be joint costs shared by the entire operation. In such a case, as long as the variable costs can be identified for each department, CVPO analysis can still be useful. The fixed costs and the fixed portion of semifixed costs can still be handled in a joint manner.

Different effect on profits

Let us consider the restaurant situation in Exhibit 8.7. Because each of the two departments has a different percentage of variable costs, and therefore a different percent of contribution margin, a given revenue increase for one department will affect profit in a way different from the same given sales revenue increase in the other. Consider a $15,000 sales increase in each of the two departments in Exhibit 8.7. Assuming no fixed cost change, the effect on profit will be as follows:

	Food Department	Beverage Department
Revenue increase	$15,000	$15,000
Variable costs	7,500 (50%)	6,000 (40%)
Increase in profit	$ 7,500	$ 9,000

The problem of which department the additional sales revenue is to come from if a revenue increase is desired is one of revenue mix. The problem does not, however, prevent us from using our CVP analysis.

Different ways to increase revenue

Let us suppose the restaurant wanted a $5,000 increase in profits, with no change in the fixed costs or in the variable cost percentages. Under these circumstances, there are three ways to obtain the extra profit: an increase in food revenue only, an increase in beverage revenue only, and (what is more likely to happen in practice) a combined increase in food and beverage revenue.

Increase in Food Revenue Only

In the case of increasing food revenue only, the solution is arrived at with the basic CVP equation:

$$\text{Food revenue} = \frac{\text{Profit required}}{100\% - \text{Variable food \% to food revenue}}$$

$$= \frac{\text{Profit required}}{\text{Food contribution margin \%}}$$

$$= \frac{\$5,000}{50\%}$$

$$= \$10,000$$

Substitution of contribution margin

Increase in Beverage Revenue Only

The approach is exactly the same as for a food revenue increase only, except that we substitute the beverage contribution margin percentage for the food contribution margin percentage.

$$\text{Beverage revenue} = \frac{\$5,000}{60\%}$$

$$= \$8,333$$

Exhibit 8.7   Operation with Joint Fixed Costs

	Food Department		Beverage Department	
Sales revenue	$150,000	100%	$50,000	100%
Variable costs	75,000	50%	20,000	40%
Contribution margin	$ 75,000	50%	$30,000	60%
Total contribution margin		$105,000 ($75,000 + $30,000)		
Fixed costs		(85,000)		
Profit (income)		$ 20,000		

Combined Increase in Food and Beverage Revenue

Since food revenue increases have a different effect on profit than beverage revenue increases, to calculate how much we need in combined total revenue we have to specify the anticipated ratio of food revenue to total revenue and the ratio of beverage revenue to total revenue. Let us suppose that any revenue increases will be in the ratio of 75% food and 25% beverage. Our equation for solving this type of revenue mix problem is:

$$\begin{pmatrix} \text{Combined sales} \\ \text{revenue required} \end{pmatrix} = \frac{\text{Profit}}{\begin{array}{c}(\text{Food revenue to total revenue percentage} \times \text{Food contribution margin}) \\ + (\text{Beverage revenue to total revenue percentage} \\ \times \text{Beverage contribution margin})\end{array}}$$

$$= \frac{\$5,000}{(75\% \times 50\%) + (25\% \times 60\%)}$$

$$= \frac{\$5,000}{37\,1/2\% + 15\%}$$

$$= \frac{\$5,000}{52\,1/2\%}$$

$$= \$9,524$$

Weighted contribution margin

It should be noted that the 52½% contribution margin in this illustration is a weighted figure. It is weighted by the revenue mix. We can easily check the accuracy of the answer obtained.

	Food	Beverage
Sales revenue	75% × $9,524 = $7,143	25% × $9,524 = $2,381
Variable costs	50% × $7,143 = 3,572	40% × $2,381 = 952
Contribution to operating income	$3,571	$1,429
Combined operating income	$3,571 + $1,429 = $5,000	

Compound Changes

Compound changes can be made with no difficulty. With reference to Exhibit 8.7, let us ask the following question: What would the total revenue level be if we wanted a profit of $25,000, if fixed costs increased to $87,000, and if the revenue ratio changed to 70% for food and 30% for beverage? There is no change in the contribution margin percentages. The solution is

Illustration of multiple changes

$$\text{Total sales revenue} = \frac{\$87,000 + \$25,000}{(70\% \times 50\%) + (30\% \times 60\%)}$$

$$= \frac{\$112,000}{(35\% + 18\%)}$$

$$= \frac{\$112,000}{53\%}$$

$$= \$211,320$$

To confirm whether this is the correct answer, we can prepare a new income statement for the restaurant, as in Exhibit 8.8.

	Food Department	Beverage Department
Sales revenue	70% × $211,320 = $147,924	= 30% × $211,320 = $63,396
Less: Variable costs	50% × $147,924 = (73,962)	= 40% × $ 63,396 = (25,358)
Contribution margin	$ 73,962	$38,038
Combined contribution margins	$112,000	
Less: Fixed costs	87,000	
Operating Income	$ 25,000	

INCOME TAXES

To this point in the discussion of CVP analysis, the effect of income taxes has been ignored. Obviously, at the break-even level of sales there are no tax implications because there is no profit. Also, with a proprietorship or partnership the organization pays no income taxes. Any profits are deemed to be paid out to the owner(s), who then pay income tax on those profits at personal tax rates.

An incorporated company that has a taxable net income must, however, consider the tax implications when using CVP for decisions. Unfortunately, income tax is neither a fixed cost nor a variable cost dependent on sales. Taxes vary with income before tax and thus require special treatment in CVP analysis. This requires adjusting the CVP equation, substituting the term "profit desired" by "profit before tax."

Consider the figures used earlier in this chapter where the motel's net income desired was $39,000 and the sales required to achieve this were calculated to be $350,000. Assume now that the motel is in a 45% tax bracket. What sales are required to achieve a $39,000 after-tax profit? The $39,000 can be converted to a before-tax figure as follows:

Before tax equation

$$\text{Operating income} = \frac{\text{Net income [AT]}}{1 - \text{Tax rate}}$$

$$= \frac{\$39,000}{1 - 45\%}$$

$$= \frac{\$39,000}{55\%}$$

$$= \$70,909$$

$$\text{Tax} = \$70,909 - \$39,000 = \$31,909$$

Thus, if the motel with $181,400 of fixed cost and variable costs of 37% of sales revenue and a net income after of $39,000, one can see that the operating income would have to be $71,000, and the tax equation would be used as shown in the preceding.

$$\text{Sales Revenue} = \frac{\text{Fixed cost} + \left(\dfrac{\text{Net income [AT]}}{1 - \text{Tax rate}} \right)}{1 - \text{Variable cost \%}}$$

$$= \frac{\$181,400 + \left(\dfrac{\$39,000}{1 - 45\%} \right)}{1 - 37\%}$$

$$\text{Sales Revenue} = \frac{\$181,400 + \$70,909}{.63} = \$400,490$$

Summary:

$$\frac{\text{Fixed Costs} \ + \ \text{Operating income}}{1 - \text{VC\%}} = \text{Sales revenue}$$

$$= \frac{\$252,309}{1 - 37\%} = \frac{\$252,309}{.63} = \underline{\underline{\$400,490}}$$

CONCLUDING COMMENTS

We have seen only a few of the ways in which the CVP approach and the CVP equations can provide useful information for decision making However, the mathematical answers arrived at are only as accurate as the cost breakdowns used and the forecasts about changing costs and sales levels. The results of CVP analysis are not guaranteed because uncertainty about the future can never be eliminated. However, uncertainty is reduced using CVP analysis. Without it, decisions made might be nothing more than guesses. Finally, the reader is cautioned to refer again to the assumptions and limitations about CVP analysis listed at the beginning of this chapter.

Refer to assumptions
and limitations

COMPUTER APPLICATIONS

A computerized spreadsheet program lends itself extremely well to performing the calculations for each of the equations or formulas discussed in this chapter. For example, the break-even equation has to be entered only once into the program; for each given level of fixed and variable costs, the break-even sales level can then be calculated, as can the total revenue required to achieve a desired profit. The results of one department can also be combined with those of others to indicate the effect on the overall net income of the operation. For example, if each additional occupied room generated an extra $20 of food and beverage sales, this can be built into the spreadsheet program. Some spreadsheet programs also have a graphics capability which some managers often find more helpful than numbers alone.

SUMMARY

CVP analysis is a method of using knowledge about the level of fixed and variable costs in a business to help in making certain business decisions. The CVP approach must be used only with full knowledge about the assumptions and limitations inherent in it.

Information about sales, costs, and profits can be presented in a graphical form. Graphs are easy to prepare, and the information wanted can be read quickly. Graphs, however, are not very flexible when a variety of possible changes are to be introduced. In such cases, an arithmetical approach using the CVP formula is much handier. The basic equation is:

$$\text{Sales revenue} = \frac{\text{Fixed costs} + \text{Operating income}}{1 - \text{Variable cost \%}}$$

If we wanted a sales level expressed in number of units (for example, number of rooms or number of customers) the equation is:

$$\text{Sales units} = \frac{\text{Fixed costs} + \text{Operating income}}{\text{Selling price} - \text{Variable cost [u]}}$$

In both of these equations, the denominator is termed the "contribution margin." Depending on whether the sales level is wanted in dollars or units, the general CVP formula can be abbreviated to:

$$\text{Sales revenue} = \frac{\text{Fixed costs} + \text{Operating income}}{\text{Contribution margin \%}}$$

With the CVP equation, any of the variables (fixed costs, profit, variable costs) can be changed individually, or they can all be changed together, and the required sales level can be calculated. A special equation is required if unit selling prices are to be changed and variable costs are to be expressed as a percentage of revenue. It is:

$$\text{Sales units} = \frac{\text{Fixed costs} + \text{Operating income}}{\text{Contribution margin [u]}}$$

The CVP formula can also be used where there are two or more departments (even if they have joint fixed costs) as long as the variable costs can be identified for each department, and thus a contribution margin percentage calculated for each department. The equation is:

$$\text{Sales revenue} = \frac{\text{Fixed costs} + \text{Operating income}}{1 - \left[\dfrac{\text{Present variable cost \%}}{1 - \text{\% Change in price}} \right]}$$

Although the equation shown is for two departments, it can be extended for as many departments as an establishment may have.

Finally, the CVP analysis equation can be amended to take income tax rates into consideration. The equation for converting an after-tax profit to a before-tax profit is:

$$\text{Sales revenue} = \frac{\text{Fixed costs}\ +\ \text{Operating income}}{\left(\begin{array}{c}\text{Dept. ``A''}\%\ \text{of Total}\\ \text{Revenue}\ \times\ \text{Dept. CM}\%\end{array}\right) + \left(\begin{array}{c}\text{Dept. ``B''}\%\ \text{of Total}\\ \text{Revenue}\ \times\ \text{Dept. CM}\%\end{array}\right)}$$

$$\text{Operating income}\left(\text{increase}\right) = \frac{\text{Net income [AT]}}{1 - \text{Tax rate}}$$

$$\text{Operating income}\left(\text{increase}\right) - \text{Net income [AT]} = \underline{\text{Tax}}$$

$$\frac{\text{Fixed Costs} + \text{Operating income}}{1 - \text{VC}\%} = \text{Sales revenue}$$

DISCUSSION QUESTIONS

1. Discuss two of the assumptions built into CVP analysis.

2. Discuss two of the limitations built into CVP analysis.

3. Give a brief explanation of how to prepare a break-even graph or chart to be used in CVP analysis.

4. If one has used a break-even graph to determine the break-even level of revenue, how can one arithmetically test that the level selected is correct?

5. In an ongoing business, why is a graph not necessarily the best technique to use in CVP analysis?

6. What is the equation for calculating a particular revenue level in dollars using CVP analysis?

7. What is the equation for calculating a sales level in units using CVP analysis?

8. Define the term "contribution margin."

9. If an enterprise is operating at a low and management wants to know the sales level it would have to achieve in order to make a specific profit, how can sales level be calculated?

10. In studying the feasibility of a new operation, how can CVP analysis be used to determine the volume of sales required to give a desired return on investment?

11. A restaurant has a good department and a beverage department. Total revenue is made up of 80 percent food and 20 percent beverages. Food variable costs are 35 percent, beverage variable costs are 33 percent. What is the restaurant's combined contribution margin?

12. State the equation for converting an after-tax profit figure to a before-tax profit amount.

ETHICS SITUATION

A restaurant manager has decided to change the restaurant's contribution margin percentages by lowering it for food and increasing it for beverages. In this way he hopes to convince the restaurant's owner that a new investment in bar equipment will be rapidly paid for. Discuss the ethics of this situation.

EXERCISES

8.1 A restaurant has sales revenue of $240,000, fixed costs of $100,800, and variable costs of $96,000. What is break-even sales revenue?

8.2 Fixed costs are $145,000 and variable costs are 38%. What is break-even sales revenue?

8.3 Fixed costs are $240,000 and the contribution margin is 48%. What is break-even sales revenue?

8.4 A restaurant has fixed costs of $40,000 for the month of March 0002. The average check is $12.50 with an average variable cost of $7.50. What is break-even units of sales for the month of March?

8.5 A small pub serving specialty beer only has fixed costs of $50,400 per year. The average contribution margin on sales is $2.24. What is the number of units to be sold to reach break-even?

8.6 A restaurant has an average check-selling price of $12.95 with an average variable cost of $5.44. Fixed costs are $140,000. Calculate the following:

   a. What is the unit contribution margin?

   b. What is break-even units?

   c. What is the variable cost percentage?

   d. What is the unit contribution margin as a percentage?

   e. What is break-even sales revenue?

8.7 The owner of a restaurant and bar operation wants a 20% net income after-tax return on his investment of $180,000. The tax rate is 28%. What is the wanted net income after tax?

8.8 A hospitality operation has sales revenue of $444,000 with variable cost averaging 42%. Fixed costs are $188,482. The owner wants a net income after tax of $48,000 based on a tax rate of 28%. Answer the following questions:

   a. What is the total additional sales revenue needed to support the desired net income after tax?

b. What is the total sales revenue required to cover fixed costs, tax, and net income after tax?

8.9   An operation operates with a variable cost percentage of 74%. The owner wants to increase sales by an amount necessary to provide for an additional $500 a month or $6,000. What is the additional increase in sales revenue required?

8.10   Assume the following information is provided:

$$\frac{\text{Fixed cost} + \text{Added cost} + \text{Increase for NI [AT]}}{1 - \text{VC/SR}}$$

$$\frac{\$120,000 + \$12,000 + \$55,556}{1 - [\$151,200 / \$280,000]} = \underline{\$407,730}$$

Explain how each numerator item in the CVP equation is an individual item that can be calculated on its own to find the necessary sales revenue to cover that item. Calculate each element in the numerator individually item by item and total the individual calculations to confirm the $407,730 for total sales revenue required is correct.

PROBLEMS

8.1   A restaurant with an average check of $10.00 per guest has the following average monthly figures:

Sales revenue	$500,000
Variable costs	260,000
Fixed costs	160,000

a. What is break-even sales revenue?

b. If revenue were $440,000, what would the restaurant's operating income be?

c. Assuming that $440,000 was the restaurant's actual level of sales revenue, how many fewer customers per month would be served than at a level of $500,000 (assume average check remained at $10)?

8.2   A small inn has annual fixed costs of $86,000, variable costs of 70% of sales revenue, and a tax rate of 25%. The owner of the inn wants an after-tax net income of $30,000.

What sales revenue must the inn achieve to provide $30,000 net income after tax? Be prepared to discuss your answer.

8.3 A restaurant is being considered that will require an investment of $150,000 in equipment by the owner. The following represents a forecast of variable cost percentages, identifiable fixed and semi-fixed costs.

Variable costs will be:
Food, 40% of sales revenue
Wages, 25% of sales revenue
Other items, 10% of sales revenue

Other known costs will be:

Management salary and wages	$48,000
Insurance	2,800
Advertising and utilities	4,500
Utilities including phones	1,020
Rent	12,000
Equipment depreciation	20%

   a. What is the break-even level of sales revenue for the restaurant?

   b. What level of sales revenue will it have to be achieved if the owner wants a 20% return on his investment before tax?

8.4 A cocktail bar is presently doing $500,000 a year in sales. Liquor cost is 40% and other variable costs at this level of revenue total $150,000. Fixed costs are $120,000.

   a. What is the present annual operating income (income before taxes)?

   b. The owner wants to increase the manager's salary by $10,000 more a year. By how much will sales revenue have to increase to provide this additional salary and maintain the present level of operating income? (Any added revenue will come from increasing seat turnover by increasing customer service.)

   c. Rather than increasing sales revenue by increasing seat turnover and customer service, the owner decides to increase menu prices by 5%. The owner believes the price increase can be made without losing any present customers and without increasing cost of sales or other variable costs. The original variable cost functions and the manager salary increase still apply. What will the bar's operating income (before tax) be?

   d. With the new pricing structure as indicated in part c, how much can sales revenue decrease before operating income falls below $30,000 per year?

8.5 A motel has 70 rooms it usually rents out in the following proportions:

40% singles at:	$48.00 per night
40% doubles at:	$60.00 per night
20% triples at:	$72.00 per night

The motel has annual fixed costs of $345,000 and variable costs average $15.00 per room occupied.

a. Calculate the motel's break-even level of occupancy.

b. Calculate the occupancy that will give the owner an operating income before tax of $60,000 a year.

c. Calculate the occupancy necessary to provide an operating income (before tax) of $60,000, if the average room rate were decreased by 20%.

d. Calculate the occupancy necessary to provide an operating income (before tax) of $60,000, assuming the average room rate will increase by 10%. Variable costs per unit sold will increase to $16.20 and $30,000 per year will be spent on advertising.

8.6 A 90-room motel has a present average room rate of $65.60. Its fixed costs are $300,000 a year, and its variable costs total $476,000 at an average occupancy of 70%.

a. What is the motel's break-even level?

b. What level of sales revenue is required to give an operating income (before taxes) of $100,000 a year?

c. If the average room rate is increased by $8.00, and $100,000 a year is desired as operating income, how many fewer rooms per night would need to be sold than was the case in part b?

d. Wage rates for maids are to be increased by $4.00 an hour. It takes a maid one-half hour to clean a room. Other cost increases will cause an increase of $1.00 in the variable cost per room occupied. Fixed wages and other fixed costs are expected to go up by $4,000 per month. To compensate for the increase in room rate to $73.60 (see part c), $30,000 more per year is to be spent on advertising to bring in more guests. The owners want operating income (before tax) to increase by 20% over the present $100,000 per year. What level of sales revenue is required? What is the sales revenue in terms of an occupancy percentage?

8.7 The Relax Inn's rooms department has annual sales of $600,000 and variable costs of $180,000. The inn's food department has annual sales of $200,000 and variable costs of $180,000. The inn's fixed costs are $220,000. The total sales revenue of $80,000 is generated jointly by both departments.

a. Calculate the inn's break-even point assuming that the ratio of rooms sales to food sales remains constant at any level of total sales.

b. The owners want to increase their restaurant's sales revenue and they plan to spend $1,000 on brochures to be displayed in the inn's entry lobby and in the guest rooms. What level of incremental food sales must be achieved to cover the brochure cost? (Assume that room sales remain constant.)

c. If the inn's owners want to increase operating income by $40,000 by increasing room occupancy rate, what is the incremental room sales revenue required supporting the $40,000 increase to operating income? (Assume no effect on restaurant sales.)

8.8 A restaurant has a café and bar operation. The café provides 65% of total revenue with a 48% variable cost. The bar provides 35% of total revenue with a 38% variable cost. Answer the following questions.

a. What is the contribution margin of the café?

b. What is the contribution margin of the bar?

c. What is the combined contribution margin of the café and bar?

d. Assume the owner wants sales revenue to increase by $50,000 with the increase being provided jointly by the café and bar. What is the additional sales revenue required?

8.9 A motel has a rooms department and a dining room. The operation has fixed cost of $335,000. Annual revenue and cost figures are:

	Rooms	Food
Sales revenue	$440,000	$110,000
Variable costs	$13,2000	$ 66,000

a. What will be the increase in contributory income if there is a $20,000 increase in sales revenue only in the rooms department?

b. What will be the increase in contributory income if there is a $20,000 increase in sales revenue only in the food department?

c. If we want to double the present contributory income with direct costs remaining the same, what will room revenue have to be? What is the amount of the increase?

d. If we want to double the present contributory income with direct costs remaining the same, what will food revenue have to be? What is the amount of the increase?

e. If we want to double the present contributory income with direct costs remaining the same, what will revenue have to be if the increase is provided jointly by both departments combined? (Assume revenue ratios stay as at present.)

f. What would total revenue have to be to give us all of the following:

- A doubling of present profit.
- $5,000 more spent on advertising.

- The revenue ratio to change from its present 80%:20% (rooms: food) to 75%:25%.
- Food variable costs to be decreased by 50%.

8.10 A neighborhood restaurant opens for lunch only and has a menu limited to five meals. A history of each menu item relative to its percentage of total sales, selling price (SP), and variable costs (VC) are shown in the following:

Menu Item	% of Sales	Selling Price	Variable Cost
Food 1	16	$7.50	$3.90
Food 2	20	6.30	3.78
Food 3	22	5.50	2.75
Food 4	14	4.40	1.54
Food 5	8	4.80	3.36

Total variable cost of beverages averages 55%. The restaurant has fixed costs of $273,000 a year and wants an operating income (before tax) of at least $25,000 per year.

a. What level of revenue will give the desired operating income before tax?

b. Because of the low sales of menu item 5 and its relatively high variable cost percentage, management is considering removing this item from the menu. It is believed customers who formerly favored this item would then be split evenly over the remaining four menu items. Management also believes that improved cost control can reduce the beverage variable costs from 55% to 52%. Given these assumptions are valid, what level of revenue will be necessary to provide $25,000 of operating income before tax?

c. Assuming that the level of sales revenue shown in part a was achieved, what would be the restaurant's operating income before tax?

8.11 An owner has $100,000 to invest in a new restaurant. Equipment and furniture are to be purchased for $80,000, and $20,000 will be used for initial working capital. First-year estimates anticipate variable costs as a percentage of sales revenue and food cost at 35%, variable wage costs at 30%, and other variable costs of 15%. Other fixed and semi-fixed costs estimates are:

Management salaries	$24,600
Rent expense	16,000
Insurance expense	2,400
Depreciation, furniture, and equipment	20%

The owner wants a 20% before-tax (operating income) on his initial investment. The owner wants an alternative to using all of his capital by assuming debt. This alternative considers borrowing $30,000 from a bank at a 10% interest rate and rather than purchasing $20,000 of the needed equipment, it would be rented at a cost of $5,000 per year. For each alternative, (1) using his own capital or (2) assuming debt and renting some of the equipment, calculate the required annual sales revenue that will provide the desired return, operating income before tax of 20% of the initial investment.

8.12 A resort hotel has total annual sales revenue of $1,000,000, variable costs of $350,000, and fixed costs of $570,000. The fixed costs include $80,000 a year for land rental lease.

a. Calculate the hotel's break-even point.

b. If the owners had an equity investment in the hotel of $1,000,000, what level of sales revenue is required for a 12% return (operating income before tax) on their investment?

c. In a renegotiation of the land rental lease, the owner of the land has offered management an alternative to the current fixed lease that is currently being paid. The alternative is 10% of the resort's contribution margin.

  • If management accepts this proposal, what would be the resort hotel's new break-even point?

  • Should management accept this proposal if next year's total sales revenue is expected to be $1,200,000?

  • Should management accept this proposal if next year's total sales revenue is expected to be $1,400,000?

  • Calculate the indifference point.

CASE 8

An analysis of the 4C Company's restaurant costs for the year 0001 revealed the following:

• Food and beverage: Directly variable with total revenue.

• Salary and wages: $156,400 fixed, the remainder directly variable with total sales revenue.

• Laundry: Directly variable with total sales revenue.

• Kitchen fuel: $3,800 fixed, the remainder directly variable with total sales revenue.

• China, glass, etc.: Directly variable with total sales revenue.

• Contract cleaning: Fixed

• Licenses: Fixed.

- Other operating expenses: Directly variable with total sales revenue.
- Administrative and general: Fixed.
- Marketing: Fixed.
- Energy costs: $3,100 fixed, the remainder directly variable with total sales revenue.
- Insurance: Fixed.
- Rent: Fixed.
- Interest: Fixed
- Depreciation: Fixed.

    a. Refer to the income statements in Cases 2 and 3 and calculate the restaurant's total variable costs as a percentage of total sales revenue.

    b. Calculate the restaurant's total fixed costs.

    c. Calculate the restaurant's break-even level of sales revenue and express it in terms of number of guests.

    d. In year 0001 the restaurant's operating income before tax is 3% of total sales revenue. How many extra guests would be required to increase operating income before tax to 5%?

9

Operations Budgeting

INTRODUCTION

This chapter begins by defining budgeting and its purposes; then it describes various kinds of budgets, such as capital, operating, department, master, fixed, and flexible.

The responsibility for budget preparation is discussed. The advantages and disadvantages of budgeting are covered.

The reader is then taken through the five-step cycle of the budgeting process.

1. Establishing attainable goals or objectives.
2. Planning to achieve these goals or objectives.
3. Comparing actual results with those planned and analyzing the differences (variances).
4. As a result of step 3, taking any corrective action, if required.
5. Improving the effectiveness of budgeting.

The steps in the preparation of a departmental income budget are then detailed (since it is from these budgets that most of the other kinds of budgets are derived). Budgeting in a new operation, which has no information from the past on which to base budgets, is then discussed.

Zero-based budgeting (ZBB) is covered with reference to its value in controlling some types of undistributed cost. The two major aspects of ZBB (decision unit analysis and ranking) are discussed in some detail.

Variance analysis is discussed in this chapter, which concludes with a section on forecasting methods using techniques such as moving averages and regression analysis.

CHAPTER OBJECTIVES

After studying this chapter, the reader should be able to:

1. Explain the concept of budgeting.

2. Define the three purposes of budgeting.

3. Describe some of the types of budgets, such as departmental, capital, fixed, and flexible.

4. Briefly discuss some of the advantages and disadvantages of budgeting.

5. List and briefly discuss each of the five steps in the budget cycle.

6. Briefly explain some of the limiting factors to be kept in mind when budgeting.

7. Define the term "derived demand."

8. Explain what information is required to determine budgeted revenue in a restaurant operation and budgeted revenue in the rooms department of a hotel or motel.

9. Prepare budgeted (pro forma) income statements given appropriate information about estimated revenue and costs.

10. Discuss ZBB with reference to decision units and the ranking process.

11. Briefly discuss the pros and cons of ZBB.

12. Use variance analysis to compare budgeted figures with actual results.

13. Use mathematical techniques, such as moving averages and regression analysis, in forecasting.

BUDGETING

Forecasts up to
five years

Budgeting is planning. In order to make meaningful decisions about the future, a manager must look ahead. One way to look ahead is to prepare budgets or forecasts. A forecast may be very simple. For a restaurant owner/operator, the budget may be no more than looking ahead to tomorrow, estimating how many customers will eat in the restaurant, and purchasing food and supplies to accommodate this need. On the other hand, in a large organization a budget may entail forecasts up to five years (such as for furniture and equipment purchases), as well as requiring day-to-day budgets (such as staff scheduling). Budgets are not necessarily always expressed in monetary terms. They could involve numbers of customers to be served, number of rooms to be occupied, number of employees required, or some other unit, as opposed to dollars. The main purposes of budgeting can be summarized as follows:

1. To provide organized estimates of future revenues, expenses, manpower requirements, or equipment needs, broken down by time period and department.

2. To provide a coordinated management policy, both long-term and short-term, expressed primarily in accounting terms.

3. To provide a method of control so that actual results can be evaluated against budget plans and adjustment, if necessary, can be made.

KINDS OF BUDGETS

There are a number of different kinds of budgets. The following are some of these:

LONG-TERM VERSUS SHORT-TERM BUDGETS

Budgets can generally be considered to be either long-term or short-term. A long-term or strategic budget would be anywhere from one year to five years ahead. Such a budget concerns the major plans for the organization (expansion, creation of a new market, financing, and other related matters). From such long-term plans evolve the policies concerning the day-to-day operations of the business, and thus the short-term budgets.

Policies for long-term plans

Short-term budgets could be for a day, a week, a quarter, or a year. Such budgets involve middle management in using its resources to meet the objectives of the long-term plans.

CAPITAL BUDGET

A capital budget relates to items that appear on the balance sheet. A three-month cash budget for a restaurant is a capital budget. A five-year replacement schedule for hotel room furnishings is also a capital budget.

OPERATING BUDGET

Budget for ongoing revenue and expenses

An operating budget concerns the ongoing projections of revenue and expense items that affect the income statement. For example, a forecast of sales revenue for a restaurant for a month is an operating budget. Similarly, in a multidepartment hotel the forecast of total payroll expense for the year is an operating budget.

DEPARTMENT BUDGET

Periodic departmental budgets

A department budget would only be of concern to a restaurant complex (with, for example, dining room, bar, and banquet areas) where departmental income statements are prepared, or to a hotel that has a number of departments.

A department budget would therefore be for a specific department and show the forecast revenue less operating expenses for that department. Alternatively, if a department does not directly generate any revenue (for example, the maintenance department of a hotel), a department budget could be prepared showing anticipated expenses in detail for a period of time. Generally such department budgets are prepared annually, broken down month by month.

Difficulty with fixed budget

Master Budget

A master budget is the most comprehensive of all budgets. Generally, a master budget is prepared for a year's period and includes a balance sheet for a year hence and all the departmental income and expense statements for the next year's period.

Fixed versus Flexible Budgets

Management prepared for adjustment

A fixed budget is based on a certain level of activity or sales revenue. Expense estimates are based on this level of sales. No attempt is made to introduce greater or lesser levels of sales revenue, and thus, different expense amounts in the budget. The disadvantage of such a budget is that, if the actual sales level differs from budgeted sales level because there is no plan covering this possibility, expenses can only then be adjusted in the short run by guesswork. For example, suppose the rooms department budget in a hotel is based on an average year-round rooms occupancy of 70%. Operating costs (such as payroll, supplies, linen, and laundry) are based on this level of occupancy. If actual occupancy dropped to 60% because of unforeseen economic conditions, it might be difficult for the rooms department manager to know, in the short run, what the new payroll level should be. The same is true for all other expenses.

On the other hand, a flexible (or variable) budget is prepared based on several levels of activity. In our rooms department, sales revenue could be forecast for 60%, 70%, and 80% occupancy levels (or as many levels as are appropriate). As the actual year progresses, it can be determined at which level the operation is going to fit best, and the appropriate expense levels will have already been determined for this level. In other words adjustment is easier. The question could be raised, using the rooms department example, whether it is truly flexible (variable) budgeting or whether it is three (or more, if more occupancy levels are used) fixed budgets at three different occupancy levels. The question is valid, but the practical result is that management is prepared to adjust to the actual situation when adjustment is required.

Even with flexible budgeting it is possible for a particular expense to remain fixed. For example, a budget might be prepared for a restaurant based on a number of levels of sales revenue. Expenses are calculated based on each different revenue level. However, advertising expense might be left the same (that is, fixed) regardless of the actual level of sales revenue. In other words, regardless of the volume of sales, a definite, fixed amount is budgeted to be spent on this expense. A really flexible budget would show expenses that are truly variable, with sales revenue as a percentage of that sales revenue and fixed costs as a dollar amount.

BUDGET PREPARATION

In a small, owner-operated restaurant or motel, the owner would prepare the budget. If it were a formal budget, the help of an accountant might be useful. If the budget were an informal one, there might be no written supporting figures. The owner might just have a mental plan about where he or she wants to go and operating from day to day to achieve the objective, or come as close to it as possible.

Involve department heads

In a larger organization, a great many individuals might be involved in budget preparation. In such organizations budgets are prepared from the bottom up. At the very least, the department heads or managers must be involved. If their subsequent performance is to be evaluated on the plans included in the budget, then they should be involved in preparing their own departmental budgets. They in turn might well discuss the budget figures with employees in their own departments.

Above the department heads would be a budget committee. Department managers might be members of this committee. Such a committee is required for overall coordination of the budget to ensure that the final budget package is meaningful. For example, the rooms occupancy of a hotel determines, to a great extent, the breakfast revenue for the food department. The budget committee must ensure that the food breakfast sales are not based on an occupancy that differs from the rooms department figure.

Final budget submission

The formal preparation of the budget is a function of the accounting department. The organization's comptroller would probably be a member of the budget committee, and his or her task is to prepare final budget information for submission to the general manager for approval.

The worst form of budget preparation is to have budgets imposed from the top down through the accounting department to the operating and other departments. Coordination might be present, but the cooperation of the employees where the activity takes place will be minimal.

WHEN ARE BUDGETS PREPARED?

Long-range budgets for up to five years are generally prepared annually by top-level management. They may or may not involve department managers. Each

Revising monthly
budgets

year such budgets are revised for the next period (up to five years) forward. For coordination the budget committee would be involved.

Short-term budgets are prepared annually, for the most part, with monthly projections. Each month, budgets for the remaining months of the year should be revised to adjust for any changed circumstances. Department managers should be involved in such revisions, as should the budget committee for overall coordination.

Weekly or daily short-range budgets are usually handled internally by the department heads or other supervisory staff. For example, the housekeeper would arrange the maid staffing schedule (which affects the payroll budget) on a daily basis based on the anticipated rooms occupancy.

ADVANTAGES AND DISADVANTAGES OF BUDGETING

A number of advantages accrue to an organization that uses a budget planning process:

- Since the budgeting process involves department heads and possibly other staff within the department, it encourages their participation and thus improves communication and motivation. The operating personnel can better identify with the plans or objectives of the organization.

Alternative courses
of action

- In preparing the budget, those involved are required to consider alternative courses of action. For example, should the advertising budget be spent to promote the organization as a whole, or would better results be obtained if emphasis were placed more on a particular department? At the department level, a restaurant manager might need to consider increasing the number of customers to be served per meal period per waiter (increased productivity per waiter) against the possible effects of slower service, reduced seat turnover, and perhaps lower total sales revenue.

- Budgets outline in advance the sales revenues to be achieved and the cost involved in achieving these revenues. After each budget period the actual results can be compared with the budget. In other words, a standard for comparison is predetermined, and subsequent self-evaluation by all those involved in the operation is possible.

Adjustment of level of
activity

- In the case of flexible budgets, the organization as a whole and each department within it are prepared for adjustment to any level of activity between minimum and maximum sales, assuming that the departments have been involved in developing their budgets within these sales levels.

- Budgeting forces those involved to be forward-looking. This is not to suggest that what happened in the past is not important and not to be considered in budget preparation; but from now on only future sales revenue and future costs are important to future plans and profits. For example, do our menu item selling prices need to be changed to take care of anticipated future increases in food, labor, and other operating costs?

- Budgeting requires those involved to consider both internal and external factors. Internal factors include such matters as seating capacity, seat turnover, and menu prices in a restaurant and rooms available, rooms occupancy, and room rates in a hotel. External factors include such matters as the competition, the local economic environment in which the business operates, and the general inflation rate trend.

Obviously, just as there are advantages to budgeting, so too are there disadvantages. Some of these are:

- The time and cost to prepare budgets can be considerable. Usually, the larger the organization the larger is the amount of time, and thus the cost, of preparing budgets.
- Budgets are based on unknown factors (as well as some known factors) that can have a big bearing on what does actually happen. (It could be argued that this is not a disadvantage since it forces those involved to look ahead and prepare for the unknown.)
- Budget preparation may require that confidential information be included in the budget.
- The "spending to the budget" approach can be a problem. If an expense budget is overestimated, there can be a tendency to find ways to spend the money still in the budget as the end of the budget period arrives. This tendency can be provoked by a desire to demonstrate that the budget forecast was correct to begin with and to protect the budget from being cut for the next period.

Unpredictability of future

Spending "surplus" funds

However, despite these "disadvantages," in most cases the advantages far outweigh the disadvantages.

THE BUDGET CYCLE

The budget cycle is a five-part process that can be summarized as follows:

1. Establishing attainable goals or objectives.
2. Planning to achieve these goals or objectives.
3. Comparing actual results with those planned, and analyzing the differences (variances).
4. As a result of step 3, taking corrective action, if required.
5. Improving the effectiveness of budgeting.

Each of these five steps will be discussed in turn.

Establishing Attainable Goals or Objectives

Limitations on sales revenue

In setting goals, what would be the most desirable situation must be tempered with realism. In other words, if there are any factors present that limit sales revenue to a certain maximum level, these factors must be considered. An obvious example is that a hotel cannot achieve more than a 100% room occupancy. In the short run, room revenue (if a hotel were full every night) can only be increased by increasing room rates. But since very few hotels do run at 100% occupancy year-round, it would be unwise, desirable as it might be, to use 100% as the budgeted occupancy on an annual basis.

Similarly, a restaurant is limited to a specific number of seats. If it is running at capacity, sales revenue can only be increased, again in the short run, by increasing meal prices or increasing seat turnover (seat occupancy). But, again, there is a limit to increasing meal prices (customer resistance and competition often dictate upper pricing levels), and if seat turnover is increased by giving customers rushed service, the end result may be declining sales.

Training and supervision

Other limiting factors are a lack of skilled labor or skilled supervisory personnel. Increased productivity (serving more customers per waiter) would be desirable and would decrease our payroll cost per customer, but well-trained employees, or employees who could be trained, are often not available. Similarly, supervisory personnel who could train others are not always available.

Shortage of capital could limit expansion plans. If financing is not available to add guest rooms or expand dining areas, it would be a useless exercise to include expansion in our long-term budget.

Management's policy concerning the market in which the organization will operate may limit budgets. For example, a coffee shop department head may propose that catering to bus tour groups would help increase sales revenue. On the other hand, the general manager may feel that catering to such large transient groups is too disruptive to the regular clientele.

Another limiting factor might be in the area of increasing costs. An operation might find that it is restricted in its ability to pass on increasing costs by way of higher prices to its customers.

Supply and demand

Finally, customer demand and competition must always be kept in mind when budgeting. In the short run there is usually only so much business to go around. Adding more rooms to a hotel does not automatically increase the demand for rooms in the area. It takes time for demand to catch up with supply, and new hotels or an additional block of rooms to an existing hotel will usually operate at a lower occupancy than normal until demand increases. A new restaurant or additional facilities to an existing restaurant must compete for its share of business.

Planning to Achieve Goals or Objectives

Once objectives have been determined, plans must be laid to achieve them. At the departmental level, a restaurant manager must staff with employees skilled enough to handle the anticipated volume of business. A chef or purchaser must purchase food in the quantities required to take care of anticipated demand, and of a quality that meets the required standards expected by the customers and that allows the food operation to match as closely as possible its budgeted food cost. Over the long term, a budget expansion of facilities might require top management to make plans for financing and seek the best terms for repayment to achieve the budgeted additional profit required from expansion.

Comparing Actual Results with Those Planned, and Analyzing the Differences

Importance of comparison of results

This is probably the most important and advantageous step in the budget cycle. Comparing actual results with the budget allows one to ask questions such as:

- Our actual dining room revenue for the month of April was $30,000 instead of the budgeted $33,000. Was the $3,000 difference caused by a reduction in number of customers? If so, is there an explanation (for example, are higher prices keeping customers away or did a competitive restaurant open nearby)? Is the $3,000 difference a result of reduced seat turnover (is service slowing down)? Are customers spending less (a reduced average check, or customer spending, because of belt tightening by the customer)?
- Yesterday the housekeeper brought in two more maids than were required to handle the actual number of rooms occupied. Is there a communication problem between the front office and the housekeeper? Did the front office fail to notify the housekeeper of reservation cancellations, or did the housekeeper err in calculating the number of maids actually required?
- The annual cocktail lounge departmental income was greater than the previous year, but still fell short of budgeted income. Did the sales revenue increase reach budgeted level? Or did costs increase over the year more than in proportion to revenue? If so, which costs? Was there a change in what we sold (change in the sales mix)? in other words, are we now selling less profitable items (such as more beer and wine than liquor) in proportion to total sales revenue?

Variances may indicate problems

These are just a few examples of the types of questions that can be asked, and for which answers should be sought, in analyzing differences between budgeted performance and actual performance. Analysis of such differences will be commented upon further in a later section of this chapter on variance analysis. It should be noted that the variances themselves do not offer solutions to possible problems. They only point out the fact that problems may exist.

IF REQUIRED, TAKING CORRECTIVE ACTION

Action to take care of causes of variance

Step 3 in the budget process points to differences and possible causes of the differences. The next step in the budget cycle necessitates taking corrective action, if required. The cause of a difference could be the result of a circumstance that no one could foresee or predict (for example, weather, a sudden change in economic conditions, or a fire in part of the premises). On the other hand, a difference could be caused by the fact that selling prices were not increased sufficiently to compensate for an inflationary rate of cost increases; or that the budgeted forecast in occupancy of guest rooms was not sufficiently reduced to compensate for the construction of a new, nearby hotel; or that staff were not as productive in number of customers served or rooms cleaned as they should have been according to predetermined standards. Whatever the reason, it should be corrected if it can be so that future budgets can more realistically predict planned operations. The fact that there are variances between budget and actual figures should not be an argument in favor of not budgeting. For, without a budget, the fact that the operation is not running as effectively as it should and could be would not even be apparent. If the variance were a favorable one (for example, guest room occupancy was higher than budgeted), the cause should also be determined because that information could help in making future budgets more accurate.

IMPROVING THE EFFECTIVENESS OF BUDGETING

Improving budgeting process

This is the final step in the five-step budget cycle. All those involved in budgeting should be made aware of the constant need to improve the budgeting process. The information provided from past budgeting cycles and particularly the information provided from analyzing variances between actual and budgeted figures will be helpful. By improving accuracy in budgeting, the effectiveness of the entire organization is increased.

DEPARTMENTAL BUDGETS

The starting point in any complete budgeting process is the departmental income statement. The rest of the budgeting process hinges on the results of these operating departments. For example, a budgeted balance sheet cannot be made up without reference to the income statements; a cash budget cannot be prepared without knowledge of departmental revenue and expenses; long-term budgets for equipment and furniture replacement, for dividend payments, or for future financing arrangements cannot be prepared without a budget showing what income (or funds) is (are) going to be generated from the internal operation.

Budgeted income statements

The departmental budgets are probably the most difficult to prepare. However, once this has been done, the preparation of the rest of any budgets required is a relatively straightforward process. This chapter will therefore only deal with income statement budgets since they are the prime concern of day-to-day management of a hotel or restaurant. In summary, the procedure is as follows:

1. Estimate sales revenue levels by department.
2. Deduct estimated direct operating expenses for each department.
3. Combine estimated departmental operating incomes and deduct estimated undistributed expenses to arrive at net income.

ESTIMATE REVENUE LEVELS BY DEPARTMENT

Annual comparisons too infrequent

Even though departmental income statements are prepared for a year at a time, they should be initially prepared month by month (with revisions, if necessary, during the budget year in question). Monthly income statements are necessary so that comparisons with actual results can be made each month. If comparison between budget and actual were only made on a yearly basis, any required corrective action might already be 11 months too late. The following should be considered in monthly revenue projections:

- Past actual sales revenue figures and trends
- Current anticipated trends
- Economic factors
- Competitive factors
- Limiting factors

Information about how top management views these trends and factors must be communicated to those who prepare departmental budgets. This information must also be put into language that the department managers understand, that is, in specific numeric terms rather than in vague, general language. For example, if an anticipated competitor is due to open nearby during the budget period, top management must state in specific percentage terms how that may impact the operation's sales.

For example, the dining room revenue for the past three years for the month of January was:

$$
\begin{array}{ll}
0001 & \$30,000 \\
0002 & 35,000 \\
0003 & 37,000
\end{array}
$$

It is now December in year 0003, and we are finalizing our budget for year 0004, commencing with January. The increase in volume for year 0002 over 0001 was about 17% ($5,000 divided by $30,000). Year 0003 increase over year 0002 was approximately 6%. These increases were caused entirely by increases in number of customers. The size of the restaurant has not changed and no change in size will occur in year 0004. Because a new restaurant is opening a block away, we do not anticipate our customer count to increase in January, but neither do we expect to lose any of our current customers. Because of economic trends, we are going to be forced to meet rising costs by increasing our menu prices by 10% commencing in January 0004. Our budgeted sales revenue for January 0004 therefore would be:

Calculation of budgeted sales revenue

$$\$37,000 + (10\% \times \$37,000) = \$40,700$$

The same type of reasoning would be applied for each of the 11 other months of year 0004, and for each of the other operating departments. One other factor that in some situations might need to be considered in sales revenue projections is that of derived demand. In other words, what happens in one department may have an effect on what happens to the sales revenue of another. An example of this might be a cocktail bar that generates sales revenue from customers in the bar area as well as from customers in the dining room where drinks are served from the adjacent bar.

Interdependence of departments

In budgeting the bar total sales revenue, the sales revenue would have to be broken down into sales revenue within the lounge area and sales revenue derived from dining room customers. Similarly, in a hotel the occupancy of the guest rooms will affect the sales revenue in the food and beverage areas. The interdependence of departments must, therefore, be kept in mind in the budgeting process.

Deduct Estimated Direct Operating Expenses for Each Department

Since most departmental direct operating costs are specifically related to sales revenue levels, once the sales revenue has been calculated, the major part of the budget has been accomplished. Historic accounting records will generally show that each direct expense varies within very narrow limits as a percentage of sales revenue. The appropriate percentage of expense to sales revenue can

Direct expenses as
percentage of revenue

therefore be applied to the budgeted sales revenue in order to calculate the dollar amount of the expense. For example, if laundry expense for the rooms department of a hotel varies between 4½ and 5½% of sales revenue, and sales revenue in the rooms department for a particular month is expected to be $100,000, then the laundry expense for that same month would be:

$$5\% \times \$100,000 = \$5,000$$

The same is true for all other direct expenses for which cost to revenue percentages are obvious.

In certain cases, however, the problem may not be as simple because there may not be as direct a relationship between cost and sales revenue. A good example of this is labor, where much of the cost is fixed and does not vary as sales revenue goes up or down. In a restaurant the wages of the restaurant manager, the cashier, and the host are generally fixed. Such people receive a fixed salary regardless of volume of business. Only the wages of servers and bus help can be varied in the short run. In such cases, a month-by-month staffing schedule must be prepared listing the number of variable staff of each category required for the budgeted sales revenue level, calculating the total variable cost, and adding this to the fixed cost element to arrive at total labor cost for that month. It is true that this requires some detailed calculations, but without it the budget might not otherwise be as accurate as it could be for effective budgetary control.

Preparation of staffing
schedules

Staffing schedules for each department for various levels of sales could be developed. These schedules would be based on past experience and the standards of performance required by the establishment. Then when sales levels are forecast, the appropriate number of man-hours or staff required for each type of job can be read directly from the staffing schedule. The number of hours of staffing required or number of employees can then be multiplied by the appropriate rates of pay for each job category. A typical such staffing schedule is illustrated in Exhibit 9.1.

Alternatively, if labor (and other costs) have been broken down for use with CVP analysis (see Chapter 8) into their fixed and variable elements, then this information is already available for use in budgeting.

COMBINE ESTIMATED DEPARTMENTAL OPERATING INCOMES AND DEDUCT ESTIMATED UNDISTRIBUTED EXPENSES TO ARRIVE AT NET INCOME

Deduction of
unallocated expenses

The departmental operating incomes budgeted for in steps one and two can now be added together. At this point certain undistributed expenses must be calculated and deducted. These expenses are not distributed to the departments

Exhibit 9.1   Staffing Schedule—Coffee Shop

Monthly Volume in Covers	Waitress Hours	Bus Help Hours
Up to 5,500	970	485
5,550 to 6,500	1,040	485
6,500 to 7,500	1,210	485
21,500 to 22, 500	3,890	990
Over 22,500	4,160	1,040

because an appropriate allocation is difficult to arrive at. Nor are they, for the most part, controllable by or the responsibility of the department managers.

These unallocated expenses (including fixed charges) usually include:

- Administrative and general
- Marketing
- Property operation and maintenance
- Energy costs
- Property or municipal taxes
- Rent
- Insurance
- Interest
- Depreciation
- Income taxes

Since these expenses are usually primarily fixed, they vary little with sales revenue; historic records will generally indicate the narrow dollar range within which they vary.

Discretionary expenses

Sometimes these expenses will vary at the discretion of the general manager. For example, it may be decided that a special extra allocation will be added to the advertising and promotion budget during the coming year or that a particular item of expensive maintenance can be deferred for a year. In such cases the adjustment to the budget figures can be made at the general manager's level. Usually these undistributed expenses are calculated initially on an annual basis (unlike departmental sales revenue and direct operating expenses, which are initially calculated monthly). If an overall pro forma (projected or budgeted) income statement, including undistributed expenses, is to be prepared monthly, then the simplest method is to divide each undistributed expense by 12 and show one-twelfth of the expense for each month of the year. A three-month budget would show one-fourth of the total annual expense. (Note that it is only the undistributed expenses that are handled in this way. Sales revenue and allocated direct expenses should be calculated correctly month by month to take care of monthly or seasonal variations.)

Unallocated expenses as a ratio of revenue

For example, Exhibit 9.2 shows how the undistributed costs could be allocated in a budget prepared on a quarterly basis. Exhibit 9.2 also indicates a budgeted loss in two of the quarters. It is argued that such budgeted losses are misleading, because the quarters with low sales revenue are unfairly burdened with undistributed costs. A fairer way to distribute such costs would be in ratio to budgeted sales revenue. Such a distribution would be calculated as in Exhibit 9.3

The revised budget, prepared on the new allocation of undistributed expenses to the various quarters, would be as in Exhibit 9.4. The method illustrated in Exhibit 9.4 may, as it does in our case, ensure that no period has a budgeted loss. Over the year, however, there is no change in total net income.

Exhibit 9.2 Undistributed Costs Allocated on Time Basis

	Quarter 1	Quarter 2	Quarter 3	Quarter 4	Annual Total
Sales revenue	$300,000	$600,000	$800,000	$300,000	$2,000,000
Direct operating expenses	(250,000)	(450,000)	(550,000)	(250,000)	(1,500,000)
Operating income	$ 50,000	$150,000	$250,000	$ 50,000	$ 500,000
Undistributed costs	(75,000)	(75,000)	(75,000)	(75,000)	(300,000)
Net income (loss)	($ 25,000)	$ 75,000	$175,000	($ 25,000)	$ 200,000

Exhibit 9.3 Calculation of Undistributed Cost Breakdown by Sales by Volume

Quarter	Sales Revenue	Percentage to Total Revenue	Share of Undistributed Costs
1	$ 300,000	15	15% × $300,000 = $ 45,000
2	600,000	30	30 × $300,000 = 90,000
3	800,000	40	40 × $300,000 = 120,000
4	300,000	15	15 × $300,000 = 45,000
Totals	$2,000,000	100%	$300,000

Exhibit 9.4   Allocation of Undistributed Costs on Sales Volume Basis

	Quarter 1	Quarter 2	Quarter 3	Quarter 4	Annual Total
Sales revenue	$300,000	$600,000	$800,000	$300,000	$2,000,000
Direct operating expenses	(250,000)	(450,000)	(550,000)	(250,000)	(1,500,000)
Operating income	$ 50,000	$150,000	$250,000	$ 50,000	$ 500,000
Undistributed costs	(45,000)	(90,000)	(120,000)	(45,000)	(300,000)
Net income (loss)	$ 5,000	$ 60,000	$130,000	$ 5,000	$ 200,000

BUDGETING IN A NEW OPERATION

New hotels and restaurants will find it more difficult to budget in their early years because they have no internal historic information to serve as a base. If a feasibility study had been prepared prior to opening, it could serve as a base for budgeting. Alternatively, forecasts must be based on a combination of known facts and industry or market averages for the type and size of operation. For example, a restaurant could use the following equation for calculating its breakfast revenue:

Forecasting meal period revenue

$$\text{Number of seats} \times \text{Seat turnover rate} \times \text{Average check} \times \text{Days open in month} = \text{Breakfast total monthly sales revenue}$$

This same equation could be used for the luncheon period, for the dinner period, and even separately for coffee breaks. Meal periods should be separated because seat turnover rates and average check figures can vary considerably from period to period. The number of seats and days open in the month figures in this equation are known facts. The seat turnover rates and average check figures can be obtained by reference to published information or from observation at competitive restaurants.

Once monthly sales revenue figures have been calculated for each meal period, they can be added together to give total sales revenue. Direct operating expenses can then be deducted, applying industry average percentage figures for each expense to the calculated budgeted sales revenue.

In a rooms department a similar type of equation would be:

Forecasting room revenues

$$\text{Forecast occupancy percentage} \times \text{Average room rate} \times \text{Number of rooms available} \times \text{Days in month} = \text{Total sales revenue for month}$$

Again, direct operating expenses can then be budgeted for using industry percentages for the type of hotel. Note that, to arrive at the average room rate to be used in the equation, one must consider the rooms sales mix: that is, the rates for different rooms and for different market segments and for discounted rates for weekends and off-seasons. The reader is referred to Chapter 6 for a comprehensive discussion of room rate pricing.

Beverage figures are a little more difficult to calculate. There are some industry guidelines in that a coffee shop serving beer and wine generates alcoholic beverage revenue approximating 5 to 15% of food revenue. In a dining room the alcoholic beverage revenue (beer, wine, and liquor) approximates 25 to 30% of food revenue. For example, a dining room with $100,000 a month of food revenue could expect to have about $25,000 to $30,000 of total liquor revenue. These are only approximate figures, but they may be the only ones that can be used until the operation can refer to its own accounting records.

Refer to historic records

As for beverage figures in a cocktail lounge, there is no simple equation. An average check figure (such as average spending figure per customer) can be misleading. For example, one customer can occupy a seat and spend $4 on five drinks; average spending for that customer is $20. On the other hand, five different customers could occupy the same seat and each spend $4 over the same period of time: average spending, $4. Therefore, the equation used for calculating food revenue may be difficult to apply in a bar setting. One alternative is to use the current industry average revenue per seat per year in a cocktail bar.

Forecasting lounge revenue

$$\begin{array}{ccccc} \text{Average annual} & & \text{Number} & & \text{Total} \\ \text{sales revenue} & \times & \text{of} & = & \text{annual sales} \\ \text{per seat} & & \text{seats} & & \text{revenue} \end{array}$$

To convert to a monthly basis for budget purposes, this figure can then be divided by 12 and added to the already calculated beverage revenue by month generated from the food departments. Direct operating expenses can then be allocated by using industry average percentage guidelines.

Although these equations do not cover all possible approaches, they should give the reader some idea of the methods that can be used when budgeting for a new operation.

Break down past sales revenue into elements

However, the equations illustrated are not limited to a new operation. They could also be used in an ongoing organization. For example, instead of applying an estimated percentage of sales revenue increase to last year's figure for the current year's budget, it might be better to break down last year's sales revenue figure into its various equation elements and adjust each of them individually (where necessary) to develop the new budget amount. For example, last year rooms revenue was $100,200 for June. This year we expect a 5% increase, therefore budgeting sales revenue will be

$$\$100,200 \times (5\% \times \$100,200) = \$105,210$$

A more comprehensive approach would be to analyze last year's figure in the following way:

Actual occupancy percentage	×	Average room rate	×	Number of rooms available	×	Days in month	=	Total sales revenue for month
83.5%	×	$40.00	×	100	×	30	=	$100,200

We can then apply the budget year trends and information to lasts year's detailed figures. In the budget period, because of a new hotel in the area, we expect a slight drop in occupancy down to 80%. This will be compensated for by an increase in our average room rates of 12%. Our budgeted sales revenue is therefore:

Budgeted occupancy percentage	×	Budgeted average room rate	×	Number of rooms available	×	Days in month	=	Budgeted monthly sales revenue
80.0%	×	$44.80	×	100	×	30	=	$107,520

This approach to budgeting might require a little more work but will probably give budgeted figures that are more accurate and can be analyzed more meaningfully than would otherwise be the case.

SUMMARY OF RESULTS

As each period goes by (day, week, month, quarter), budgeted figures should be compared with actual figures. This can best be done by summarizing the figures on a report by department or by type of cost. For example, one of the major and most difficult costs to control in a hotel or food operation is labor, and an ongoing comparison of actual with budgeted labor cost is useful in controlling this cost. An illustration of a type of report summarizing payroll costs is shown in Exhibit 9.5. The variances each day would require explanation.

Variances require explanation

Exhibit 9.5 Sample Payroll Costs Summary and Analysis

	Number of Employees Today		Labor Cost Today		Date: September 3			
					Labor Cost to Date		Labor Cost Variance	
Department	Budget	Actual	Budget	Actual	Budget	Actual	Today	To Date
Rooms								
Front office	10	10	$ 440	$ 440	$1,320	$1,320		
Housekeeping	42	43	1,280	1,310	3,840	3,900	$+30	$+60
Service	8	8	320	320	960	930		−30
Switchboard	6	6	274	274	822	822		
Food								
Dining room	13	14	$ 456	$ 487	$1,368	$1,399	$+31	$+31
Coffee shop	7	6	245	217	735	707	−28	−28
Banquet	11	11	440	440	1,674	1,674		
Beverage								

VARIANCES

In analyzing variances, it may be useful to calculate percentage variances. Percentage variances are calculated by dividing the dollar variance by the budgeted figure for that item. For example, if the budgeted figure were $100, and the variance $10, the percentage variance would be:

$$\frac{\$10}{\$100} \times 100 = 10\%$$

It is unlikely that any sales revenue or controllable expense item will not have a variance because, even with comprehensive information available during the budgeting process, budgeted figures are still estimates. The variances to be analyzed are those that show significant differences from budgeted amounts. *Significance test* What is important in this significance test is the amount of the variance in both dollar and percentage terms, and not just in one of them. If only one is used, it might not provide information that the other provides. For example, using dollar differences alone ignores the base or budgeted figure, and the dollar difference may not be significant when compared to the base figure. To illustrate, if the dollar difference in revenue is $5,000 (which seems significant) and the budgeted revenue is $5,000,000, the percentage variance is:

$$\frac{\$5,000}{\$5,000,000} \times 100 = 0.001\%$$

Effective budgeting

This percentage variance is quite insignificant. In other words, if the actual amount can be this close to the budget in percentage terms, this would indicate remarkably effective budgeting. But this is not disclosed if only the dollar difference is considered.

Similarly, considering the percentage difference alone may not be useful. For example, if a particular expense for this same property were budgeted at $500, and the actual expense were $550, the variance of $50 represents 10% of the budget figure. Ten percent seems a large variance but is insignificant when the dollar figure is also considered. In other words, a variance of $50 is insignificant in a business with revenue of $5,000,000, and investigating it would not be worth anybody's time.

What is significant as a dollar and percentage variance depends entirely on the type and size of establishment. Those responsible for budgets need to establish in advance the variances allowed in both dollar figures and percentages for each sales revenue and expense item. At the end of each budget period, only those variances that exceed what is allowed in both dollar and percentage terms will be further analyzed and investigated.

ZERO-BASED BUDGETING

Most costs (food, beverage, labor, supplies, and others) are usually linked to sales revenue levels in a fairly direct way. That is why they are generally referred to as direct costs, and budgeting for them is relatively easy.

Undistributed expenses

However, there is one category of expenses in the hospitality industry that is not related as directly to sales revenue levels. These indirect expenses, more commonly referred to as undistributed expenses, include:

- Administrative and general
- Marketing
- Property operation and maintenance
- Energy costs

These undistributed costs are not normally charged to the operating departments but are kept separate. There are also other fixed costs that an operation may have, such as property taxes, insurance, interest, and rent, that are also not charged to the operating departments. However, the level of these costs is usually imposed from outside the operation. Since they are not subject to day-to-day control, or even to monthly or annual control, they shall not be of concern here.

Traditionally, these four undistributed costs have been budgeted for, and presumably "controlled," by incremental budgeting. With incremental budgeting, the assumption is made that the level of the last period's cost was correct. For the new period's budget or control period, one only needs to adjust last period's figure upward, or downward, to take care of current conditions. Management monitors only the changes to the budgeted amounts. Whether last period's total cost was justified is not an issue. The amount of cost is just assumed to have been essential to the company's objectives. It is also frequently assumed that, even with no management guidance, the department heads responsible for controlling the undistributed costs are practicing effective cost/benefit analysis, that they are keeping costs in line, and are preventing overspending. No doubt many of the expenses incurred in this category do meet these criteria. But it is likely that the reverse is also true in many establishments that use incremental budgeting.

A technique that might be used by hospitality industry enterprises to control these undistributed expenses is zero-based budgeting (ZBB). As its name implies, with ZBB no expenses can be budgeted for or incurred unless they are justified in advance. Normally, most establishments prepare budgets for undistributed expenses once a year. ZBB basically requires that each department head rejustify, in advance, the entire annual budget from a zero base. ZBB has little value in direct cost budgeting, since the use of other controls should ensure that they are not out of line for any given sales revenue level. But ZBB, properly implemented for undistributed expenses, can not only control these indirect costs, but may lead to costs reduction from previous levels. The main reason for this is that it puts previously unjustified expenses on the same basis as requests for increases to the budget, increases that must also be justified.

DECISION UNITS

One of the key elements in successful implementation of ZBB is the decision unit. The number of decision units will vary with the size of each establishment. For example, a small operation with only one employee in its marketing department would probably have only one decision unit for marketing expenses. A larger organization might have several decision units for marketing. These units might be labeled sales, advertising, merchandising, public relations, and research. A very large organization might further break down these units into decision units covering different activities. For example, advertising might be broken down into a print decision unit and a radio and television decision unit.

Each separate decision unit should contain no more than one or two employees and related costs. Each decision unit should be about the same size insofar as total cost for that unit is concerned. In this way, when all budget requests and justifications are finalized, the general manager can more easily evaluate each of them and rank each of them against all the other units that are, so to speak, competing for the same limited resource dollars.

Once decision units have been established, the next step is for each department head to prepare an analysis of each separate unit that is his or her responsibility. This analysis is carried out each year prior to the start of the new budget period. A properly designed form should be used so that each department head will present the data in a standard format. For each decision unit the department head will document the following:

1. The Unit's Objective

Each decision unit's objective must obviously relate to the organization's overall objectives. For example, the objective of a hotel marketing department's print-advertising decision unit might read as follows:

> To seek out the most appropriate magazines, journals, newspapers, and other periodicals that can be used for advertising in the most effective way at the lowest cost in order to increase the number of guests using the hotel's facilities.

2. The Unit's Present Activities

This would include the number of employees, their positions, a description of how the work is presently carried out, and the resources used. For example, a resource used by the print-advertising decision unit might be an external advertising agency.

The total cost of present activities would be included in this section. Also included would be a statement of how the unit's activities are measured. For example, this might be the number of guests using the hotel's facilities versus column inches or cost of print advertising.

3. Justification for Continuation of Unit's Activities

In the case of our print-advertising unit, this might include a statement to the effect that it would be advantageous for the unit to continue because the employees involved are familiar with the marketing strategy of the hotel, with the various operating departments and their special features, and know what special attractions to promote in the advertisements. The explanation should also include a statement of the disadvantages that would accrue should the decision unit's activities be discontinued.

4. A List of Alternative Ways of Carrying Out the Activities

In the example of the print-advertising decision unit, the alternatives might include taking over some of the work presently given to the advertising agency, having the agency take over more of the unit's activities, having more of the work centralized in the head office (assuming the hotel is one of a chain), doing more head office work at the local level, or combining the print decision unit's activities with those of the radio and television advertising unit. The list should not be overly long, but it should include as many alternatives as would be practical that differ from present activities.

Included with the list would be the advantages and disadvantages of each alternative, and, for each alternative, an estimate of the total annual cost.

5. Selection of Recommended Alternative

Stay with present
activities

The department head responsible must then recommend the alternative that he or she would select for each unit. One alternative would be to stay with the present activities rather than make a change. The selection is based on a consideration of the pros, cons, practicality, and cost of each alternative.

6. Budget Required

The department head's final responsibility is to state the funding required for each decision unit for the next budget based on the alternative recommended. This request starts out with a base, or minimum level. This minimum level may be established at a level below which the unit's activities would no longer exist or be worthwhile. Alternatively, the level may be arbitrarily determined by the general manager at, say, 60% of the present budget. Whatever the minimum level established, each activity above that level is to be shown as an incremental cost. These incremental activities may or may not be subsequently approved.

RANKING PROCESS

Once the decision unit activities have been documented as outlined, it is then the general manager's turn to begin the review process. In order to determine how much money will be spent, and in what areas or departments, the manager must rank all activities in order of importance to the organization. Once this order is established, the activities would be accepted up to the total predetermined budget for all activities.

Ranking difficulty

The major difficulty in ranking is to determine the order of priority for all the operation's activities under review. In a small organization, with the aid of a committee if necessary, this might not be too difficult. Alternatively, each department head might be asked to rank all activities that come within his or her authority. This procedure can then continue through successive levels of mid-management until they reach the general manager.

Another approach might be for the general manager to approve automatically, say, the first 50 or 60% of all activities ranked within each department.

The next 10 or 20% might then be ranked by midmanagement and also be automatically approved. Top management might subsequently review all these rankings, then rank the remainder and decide how many of them will be funded along with any proposed new programs not proposed or adopted at lower levels.

The completed ranking process and approved expenditures constitute the new budgets for those areas or departments. This information can then be incorporated into the regular budget process. Theoretically, as a result of ZBB, the activities of that part of the organization have been examined, evaluated, modified, discontinued, or continued as before. This should produce the most effective possible budget. At the least, it should produce a budget that one can have more confidence in than one produced solely on an incremental basis.

Confidence in budget

ADVANTAGES OF ZBB

Some of the advantages of ZBB are that it:

- Concentrates on the dollar cost of each department's activities and budget and not on broad percentage increases.
- Can reallocate funds to the departments or areas providing the greatest benefit to the organization.
- Provides a quality of information about the organization (because all activities are documented in detail) that would otherwise not be available.
- Involves all levels of management and supervision in the budgeting process and encourages these employees to become familiar with activities that might not normally be under their control.
- Obliges managers to identify inefficient or obsolete functions within their areas of responsibility.
- Can identify areas of overlap or duplication.

DISADVANTAGES OF ZBB

Some of the possible disadvantages of ZBB are that it:

- Implies that the budgeting method presently in use is not adequate. This may or may not be true.
- Requires a great deal more time, effort, paperwork, and cost than traditional budgeting methods.
- May be unfair to some department heads who, even though they may be very cost-effective in managing their departments, are not as capable as others in documentation and defense of their budgets. They might thus find themselves outranked by other more vocal, but less cost-effective, department heads.

VARIANCE ANALYSIS

Once a comparison has been made between budget figures and actual results, it is useful to analyze any difference for each sales revenue and expense item. Let us consider the following situation:

Banquet Revenue, March

Budget	Actual	Difference	
$50,000	$47,250	$2,750	(unfavorable)

The difference is unfavorable because our total sales revenue was less than anticipated. If we analyze the budget and actual figures, we might get the following additional information:

Analysis of budget and actual figures

Budget 5,000 guests × $10.00 average check = $50,000
Actual 4,500 guests × $10.50 average check =   47,250
Variance   (unfavorable) $ 2,750

This variance amount is actually composed of two separate figures: a price variance and a quantity (number of guests) variance. These are calculated as shown in the following subsections.

PRICE VARIANCE

The price variance is $0.50 per customer more than budgeted. This is considered to be favorable.

4,500 guests × $0.50 = $2,250 (favorable)

QUANTITY VARIANCE

The quantity variance is 500 guests, each of whom did not spend the $10.00 we had budgeted for. This would be unfavorable.

500 guests × $10.00 = $5,000 (unfavorable)

If we combine these results, our total variance is made up of:

Combining variances

Price variance	$2,250	(favorable)
Quantity variance	5,000	(unfavorable)
Total variance	$2,750	(unfavorable)

We now have information that tells us the major reason for our difference between budget and actual is a reduction in sales revenue of $5,000 (due to fewer customers served). This has been partly compensated for by $2,250 resulting from the average banquet customers having a more expensive meal. This tells us that our banquet sales department is probably doing an effective job in selling higher priced menus to banquet groups, but is failing to bring in as many banquets or guests as anticipated.

Costs can be analyzed in the same way. Let us examine the following situation for a rooms department in a hotel:

Laundry Expense, June

Budget	Actual	Difference	
$6,000	$6,510	$510	(unfavorable)

Cost higher than budgeted

The difference is unfavorable because we spent more than we budgeted for. With the following additional information we can analyze this variance.

Budget 3,000 rooms sold at $2.00 per room = $6,000
Actual 3,100 rooms sold at $2.10 per room =   6,510
Variance
                              (unfavorable) = $ 510 .

The $510 total variance is made up of two items: a cost variance and a quantity variance.

Cost Variance

The cost variance is $0.10 over budget for each room sold. This is an unfavorable trend.

3,100 rooms × $0.10 = $310.00 (unfavorable)

Quantity Variance

The quantity variance is 100 rooms over budget, at a budgeted cost of $2.00 per room. From a cost point of view, this is considered to be unfavorable.

100 rooms × $2.00 = $200.00 (unfavorable)

If we combine these results our total variance is therefore made up of:

Combining variances

Cost variance	$310.00	(unfavorable)
Quantity variance	200.00	(unfavorable)
Total variance	$510.00	(unfavorable)

This tells us that, although our total variance was $510, or 8.5% over budget ($510 divided by $6,000 × 100), only $310 is of concern to us. The remaining $200 was inevitable. If we sell more rooms, as we did, we would obviously have to pay the extra $200 for laundry. Even though this is considered unfavorable as a cost increase, we would not worry about it since it would be more than offset by the extra revenue obtained from selling the extra rooms. Whether or not the other $310 overspending is serious would depend on the cause. The cause could be a supplier cost increase that we may, or may not, be able to do something about; or it could be that we actually sold more twin rooms than budgeted for (which would mean more sheets to be laundered and therefore cause our average laundry cost per room occupied to go up). In the latter case, the additional cost would be more than offset by the extra charge made for double occupancy of a room.

Let us have a look at another example:

Coffee Shop Variable Ways, for May

Budget 4,350 hours at $4.00/hr. = $17,400

Actual 4,100 hours at $4.10/hr. = 16,810

Variance $ 590 (favorable)

Cost variance:	4,100 hours × $0.10/hr. =	$ 410	(unfavorable)
Quantity variance:	250 hours × $4.00/hr. =	1,000	(favorable)
Variance:		$ 590	(favorable)

Note that the net variance is a $590 favorable amount. Variance analysis shows that there was a $1,000 saving on labor due to a reduced number of hours paid for (perhaps as a result of less business than budgeted for). However, the saving was reduced by $410 because the actual average hourly rate was higher than budgeted for. Was there an increase in the hourly rate paid or was there unanticipated overtime because of poor scheduling (which would tend to increase the average hourly rate paid)? This would need to be verified.

Information helps identify causes

Therefore, as can be seen, variance analysis can provide additional information that is of help in identifying causes of differences between actual and budgeted figures.

The final step in variance analysis is taking corrective action to ensure procedures are in place to prevent undesirable situations reoccurring. For example, investigation of the coffee shop example's increase in actual hourly pay rate may show that it was caused by too much overtime having been paid. To correct this situation, management might initiate new procedures that require the coffee shop manager to have the written approval of her supervisor before any overtime is paid.

Note that in this section differences or variances are labeled as favorable or unfavorable only as a matter of accounting convention. In this context, favorable is used for a variance that is either an increase in sales revenue or a reduction in costs. Unfavorable is used for a variance that is either a reduction in sales revenue or an increase in costs.

The words favorable and unfavorable should not be equated with good and bad, respectively. Indeed, there may be situations in which an unfavorable variance reflects a positive situation, such as cost increase that is labeled as unfavorable even though it is caused entirely by an increase in sales revenue that automatically necessitates an increase in costs. For example, to produce more food sales without changing prices, there will normally have to be an increase in food cost. In such a case, as long as the sales revenue increase is more than the cost increase and the food cost percentage remains as budgeted, the "unfavorable" food cost increase would be perfectly normal and acceptable.

Thus, the word unfavorable should not necessarily be interpreted as having a negative connotation. That judgment cannot be made until the *cause* of the change has been investigated.

FORECASTING

In discussing budgeting earlier in this chapter, the methods demonstrated were somewhat simplistic. However, many hospitality operations use more advanced, quantitatively oriented forecasting techniques, both in budgeting and where other forecasts are required. The ability to accurately forecast is an important aspect of any operation's management. Reliable methods are necessary to help operating department heads forecast sales and plan for use of resources (for example, labor and supplies to meet anticipated demand).

Two common techniques

Two of the more commonly used techniques are moving averages and regression analysis, both of which are sometimes referred to as time-series methods, because they look at the numbers for a series of past periods to see what patterns and/or relationships may be occurring.

Normally, for a hospitality operation, the number of periods considered in the time series is 12 months because over a year's time all of the annual cyclical increases and decreases in demand, month-to-month variances, seasonal variations, and unusual external factors that affect such matters as room occupancy or restaurant volume will be included in the numbers. What has happened during the time series is then assumed to be likely to occur in the future and can thus be the basis of the forecast as long as that forecast is adjusted for the current situation by using good judgment.

MOVING AVERAGES

Daily trends

Most forecasts take into consideration past trends that can be built into the forecast. Some trends can be daily ones used for a weekly projection. For example, most transient hotels have high occupancies early each week, with a trend to reduced occupancies on Friday, Saturday, or Sunday.

Other trends may be seasonal ones (where major changes in demand patterns occur as the climate changes) or cyclical or long-run ones caused by economic events, such as a recession. Cyclical patterns are difficult to determine because historic figures are unreliable in indicating when these events are likely to occur again.

Nevertheless, by observation of past trends, a future trend can usually be built into the forecast figures. However, there may also be random variations that have occurred in historic information for no particular or observable reason and others (for example, sudden and drastic decreases in demand caused by severe and unusual weather conditions) that are difficult and even impossible to include in forecasts because of their unpredictability.

Removing random variations

Moving averages attempt to remove the random variations that can occur from period to period in the operation of the typical hospitality business. Note that the larger the number of periods used, the less likely it is that any random causes will affect the moving average. To take care of those random variations for a monthly forecast, a twelve-month moving average is calculated. The twelve monthly figures for the past year are added together and then divided by 12. For example, suppose for the past year a restaurant's monthly guest counts were as follows:

Month	Guest Count
1	2,406
2	2,502
3	1,986
4	1,829
5	2,312
6	2,587
7	2,804
8	3,009
9	3,102
10	2,748
11	2,406
12	2,312
Total	30,003

The moving average is:

$$\frac{30,003}{12} = 2,500$$

New moving average

This figure can be used (modified for the current situation and other variables) as the forecast for the thirteenth month. At the end of the thirteenth month, a new moving average is calculated for the fourteenth month by deleting from the total the guest count for the first month and including in it the guest count for the immediately past thirteenth month. As a result, the average is constantly recalculated (thus the term moving average) by including in it only the most up-to-date figures for the number of periods used.

Keeping moving average up to date

In calculating the moving average total, it is only necessary to list each of the figures for the number of periods under review when the method is first used. After that, the total figure can be updated by deducting the figure for the earlier period in the series and adding the figure for the most recent period. Therefore, keeping the moving average up to date is a very simple task.

For example, if the actual guest count in the thirteenth month was 2,296, the new 12-month total is:

$$30,003 - 2,406 + 2,296 = 29,893$$

and the forecast for the fourteenth month is:

Moving average equation

$$\frac{29,893}{12} = 2,491$$

In general, the moving average can be expressed by the following equation:

$$\frac{\text{Total for each of the previous } n \text{ periods}}{n}$$

where n is the number of periods being used, in our case 12.

One minor problem with the moving average is that it gives equal weight to each of the periods used in the calculation. For example, in the case of monthly periods each month is treated like any other. This can be risky in forecasting for the month of February, because the average is based on the typical month having 30.42 days (365/12), whereas we know February has only 28 (or 29) days. However, this is where individual adjustments can be made to the raw moving average produced, using the general equation.

Best number of periods

An important question with regard to a moving average is the best number of periods (n) to include. With a large number, the forecast tends to react slowly. On the other hand, a small number provides a forecast that more quickly reflects more recent changes in the time series. One solution is to try moving averages of different lengths to determine which one seems to provide the most accurate forecast.

Also, in using a time series of 12 months, the average is influenced by what happened up to a year ago, and the current operating environment might have changed considerably from that time. Again, this is where personal judgment must be used in refining the raw moving-average figure to adjust it to today's reality.

REGRESSION ANALYSIS

In some large hospitality operations, the forecast for one department may often depend on what happens in another. For example, as the number of guests in a hotel's rooms increases or decreases, there are similar increases and decreases in the restaurants and bars. This is known as a causal relationship (or derived demand) because what happens in the rooms department causes changes in the food and beverage department. Accurate forecasting in the rooms and the food and beverage departments is important because, in many hospitality operations, they provide as much as 80 to 90% of total sales revenue.

Causal relationship

A forecasting technique that allows a restaurant to forecast its sales based on forecast rooms occupancy is regression analysis, which we have already seen used in Chapter 7 for separating fixed and variable costs. In our new situation, regression analysis simply uses the independent variable to forecast the numbers for the dependent variable. In regression analysis, restaurant sales in terms of meals served are the dependent variable Y (because food sales depend on the rooms occupancy) and the room sales in terms of number of guest nights are the independent variable X.

Suppose that the following summarizes the room guests and restaurant meals served each month last year:

	Guests Nights (X)	Meals Served (Y)
January	6,102	7,822
February	6,309	7,544
March	6,384	8,021
April	6,501	8,299
May	6,498	8,344
June	6,382	8,245
July	6,450	8,311
August	6,522	8,274
September	6,608	8,328
October	6,502	8,188
November	6,274	7,985
December	5,811	7,502

Strong relationship

Even though we intuitively know that there is a strong relationship between room occupancy and restaurant meals served, we also know that some people who are not hotel guests eat in the restaurant. Therefore, we must determine these numbers using the following equation:

$$Y = a + bX$$

where

Y = number of restaurant meals
a = meals served to customers not registered in the hotel
b = average number of meals each hotel guest has per day
X = number of guest nights

The values for a and b are calculated using the following two equations:

E = SUM

Equations for a and b

$$b = \frac{n\Sigma XY - \Sigma X \Sigma Y}{n(\Sigma X^2) - (\Sigma X)^2}$$

$$a = \text{average of } Y - (b \times \text{average of } X)$$

n = # of periods

Using information provided from Exhibit 9.6, the solution to b is calculated as follows:

$$\frac{12(616,852,495) - (76,343)(96,863)}{12(486,221,719) - (76,343)(76,343)}$$

$$= \frac{7,402,229,940 - 7,394,812,009}{5,834,660,628 - 5,828,253,649}$$

$$= \frac{7,417,931}{6,406,979} = 1.16$$

To calculate a, we must first calculate the average of Y and the average of X:

$$\text{average of } Y = \frac{96,863}{12} = 8,072$$

Average of X and Y

$$\text{average of } X = \frac{76,343}{12} = 6,362$$

and a is calculated as:

Exhibit 9.6   Calculation of Regression Analysis Data

Month	Guest Nights X	Meals Served Y	XY (X × Y)	X² (X × X)
1	6,102	7,822	47,729,844	37,234,404
2	6,309	7,544	47,595,096	39,803,481
3	6,384	8,021	51,206,064	40,755,456
4	6,501	8,299	53,951,799	42,263,001
5	6,498	8,344	54,219,312	42,224,004
6	6,382	8,245	52,619,590	40,729,924
7	6,450	8,311	53,605,950	41,602,500
8	6,522	8,274	53,963,028	42,536,484
9	6,608	8,328	55,031,424	43,665,664
10	6,502	8,188	53,238,376	42,276,004
11	6,274	7,985	50,097,890	39,363,076
12	5,811	7,502	43,594,122	33,767,721
Total	76,343	96,863	616,852,495	486,221,719

$$8,072 - (1.16 \times 6,362)$$

$$= 8,072 - 7,380 = 692$$

Our result thus shows us that:

$$y = 692 + 1.16 \ (X)$$

This means that there are, on average, 692 customers who are not registered as hotel guests who eat in the restaurant each month and that each registered guest room occupant on average eats 1.16 meals each day in the restaurant. We can use this equation to calculate the restaurant's volume forecast based on the guest night forecast.

Volume forecast

For example, suppose in January the forecast guest night count is 6,200. The restaurant's forecast of meals served will be:

$$692 + (1.16 \times 6,200)$$

$$= 692 + 7,192 = 7,884$$

Finally, note that regression analysis forecasting relies on the assumption that the past relationship between X and Y remains the same during the forecast period.

LIMITATIONS

Observe the following limitations about forecasting techniques, such as those illustrated in this section:

Accuracy of forecast

- Their use provides precise mathematical results that are only as good as the data used. For example, if the guest night forecasts are not very good, then the forecast for restaurant meals served will not be very good.
- Whenever mathematical approaches are used in forecasting, it is emphasized once again that these methods by themselves do not consider variables that can be controlled by management. For example, a forecast of restaurant volume based on historic sales would need to be adjusted for an anticipated increase in demand as a result of a heavier-than-normal advertising campaign that the restaurant manager is planning to implement.

Experience and judgment

- No mathematical forecasting technique can substitute for experience and individual judgment. Indeed, in some cases (such as opening a new property or expanding an existing one) there may be only limited data available on which to base mathematical forecasting techniques, such as moving averages or regression analysis. In such cases judgment and other qualitative considerations have to play a greater role.
- Forecasting involves the future, which is always unpredictable. The longer the time between the date the forecast is made and the period of the forecast, the more likely it is that unpredictable events are going to affect the forecasts. As a result, forecasts are bound to be less accurate than the manager would like. However, forecasts can always be revised as time goes by to adjust them to changed circumstances.
- Because forecasting deals with the future, it also deals with uncertainty. This should not be a problem for most good managers because managers in the hospitality industry typically face many daily uncertainties.
- Most forecasting methods are based on the past and use historic information adjusted for the future. Unfortunately, historic data are often not good indicators of the future. Again, a good manager can adapt to this by using common sense and good judgment to adjust forecasts based solely on historic information.

Deviation from format

- Because of all the above, most operations know that forecasts are likely to deviate from the actual and automatically build in a variance factor of as much as 10%. The actual deviation percentage used can be based on past experience. For example, if an analysis of the past shows that actual results invariably differed by 5% from those forecast, then a 5% variance can be built into future forecasts.

Which Method to Use?

Studies show that the lowest forecasting errors result from the use of trend projections, moving averages, and regression analysis rather than judgmental methods. What is important is not the actual forecasting method used, but how effective the forecasts are and their practical value in the operation.

In a small hospitality operation that can adapt quickly to changing circumstances, most forecasting will be done using simple methods, such as adjusting the sales for the coming month by a certain percentage increase or decrease over last year's or last month's or by using the fairly simple moving average method. Larger enterprises will probably use more complex methods, such as regression analysis.

Requires more work

Even though the regression analysis method requires more work, it does not require tedious manual calculations because most small electronic calculators can be programmed to perform all the arithmetic once each series of X and Y variables have been entered. Indeed, many of the better word processing software programs today contain minispreadsheets that can be used for budgeting and forecasting (and even regression analysis). After the event when actual figures are entered, they can also carry out variance analysis calculations and graphically present the forecast, actual, and variance information.

Once forecasts have been completed, this information could also be used in a food and beverage operation to help determine the quantities of items to be purchased and when they should be purchased.

Computer Applications

Computer software, such as a spreadsheet program, makes the budgeting process much easier. While there are forecasting computer packages available, a good spreadsheet can also perform the necessary moving average and regression analysis calculations.

For example, the calculations required in Exhibit 9.6 and all the subsequent calculations were produced using a spreadsheet capability that is included in the WordPerfect word processing software program.

A spreadsheet can also compare budgeted figures with actual ones and produce the variances.

SUMMARY

Budgeting is part of the planning process. It can involve decisions concerning the day-to-day management of an operation or involve plans for as far ahead as five years.

There are various types of budgets such as capital, operating, departmental, master, and fixed or flexible.

The purposes of budgeting are:

- To provide estimates of future sales revenues and expenses.
- To provide short- and long-term coordinated management policy.
- To provide a control by comparing actual results with budgeted plans and to take corrective action, if necessary.

In a small operation, budgets can be prepared by an individual or by a committee in a large organization. In all cases, whether for a day, a year, or some other time period, budgets should be prepared in advance of the start of the period.

Some of the advantages of budgets are:

- They involve participation of employees in the planning process, thus improving motivation and communication.
- They necessitate, in budget preparation, consideration of alternative courses of action.
- They allow a goal, a standard of performance, to be established, with subsequent comparison of actual results with that standard.
- Flexible budgets permit quick adaptation to unforeseen, changed conditions.
- They require those involved to be forward-looking, rather than looking only at past events.

The budgeting cycle has five segments:

1. Establishing attainable goals (remember the limiting factors).
2. Planning to achieve these goals.
3. Analyzing differences between planned and actual results.
4. Taking any necessary corrective action.
5. Improving the effectiveness of budgeting.

The starting point in budgeting is to predetermine sales revenue levels. In a large organization this forecast would be done by department. In forecasting, one must consider past actual sales revenue and trends, current anticipated trends, and the economic, competitive, and limiting factors.

Once sales revenue has been forecast, direct operating expenses can be calculated based on anticipated sales revenue, and, finally, undistributed expenses can be deducted to arrive at the net income for the operation. Once the departmental and general income statement budgets have been prepared, other required budgets (such as balance sheets and capital budgets) can be made up, if required.

If there is no historic accounting information available, which would be the case in a new venture, then the forecasting of sales revenue and expenses is more difficult. Quite a bit more educated estimating is required.

Zero-based budgeting (ZBB) is a method of controlling certain types of undistributed costs that cannot be related directly to volume or revenue levels. With ZBB each category of cost is broken down into decision units that are then analyzed. The analysis is prepared by the department head responsible for the cost. After each decision unit is analyzed, all decision units are ranked by management and the final budget is allocated according to this ranking.

Variance analysis is a useful technique for isolating the causes of differences between budgeted and actual figures. These differences are broken down into price and quantity variances (when analyzing sales revenue figures) or cost and quantity variances (when analyzing expense figures).

The chapter concluded with a section on forecasting techniques that illustrated the moving average and regression analysis methods and summarized the limitations of using mathematical techniques in forecasting.

DISCUSSION QUESTIONS

1. How would you explain the concept of budgeting?

2. What are some of the purposes of budgeting?

3. List and discuss three advantages of budgeting.

4. Explain the difference between long- and short-term budgeting.

5. Give an example of
   a. A hotel departmental budget.
   b. A capital budget for a restaurant.

6. Explain the difference between a fixed and a flexible budget.

7. Two of the steps in the budgeting cycle are
   a. Establishing attainable goals.
   b. Planning to achieve these goals.

8. What are the other three steps? Discuss three possible limiting factors to consider in preparing a budget for a hotel or restaurant.

9. A cocktail lounge had sales revenue in May of $40,000. Budgeted revenue was $42,000. List three possible questions that could be asked, the answers to which might explain the $2,000 difference.

10. In projecting revenue for the coffee shop breakfast period in a hotel, what factors need to be considered?

11.   What is derived demand?

12.   List the four items that must be multiplied by each other to forecast total annual food revenue for the dinner period of a restaurant.

13.   What is a pro forma income statement?

14.   List three types of cost that are controllable with ZBB.

15.   Give an example of a decision unit in a hotel's accounting office and write a one-sentence objective for that decision unit.

16.   Briefly describe the ranking process under ZBB.

17.   Give two advantages and two disadvantages of ZBB.

18.   Briefly explain how the use of a moving average works as a forecasting method.

ETHICS SITUATION

After the hotel general manager and his department heads have produced the budget for next year, he decides to change some of the figures to produce a $10,000 higher profit. He plans to use this changed budget to convince the hotel's owner that his (the manager's) request for a $5,000 increase in salary is justified. Discuss the ethics of this situation.

EXERCISES

9.1   A restaurant has 100 seats with an average turnover of 2.25, with an average check of $12.00. The restaurant is open 312 days a year. What is the estimated sales revenue for the year?

9.2   A motel operation has 70 rooms, an occupancy of 80%, and an average room rate of $34.00. The owner wants you to give him an estimate of his sales revenue for the month of April. What is the estimated sales revenue?

9.3   A motel had budgeted an occupancy of 6,000 rooms with a selling price of $40 per room and a variable housekeeping cost of $1.85 per room. Actual data indicated a total of 6,240 rooms were sold at an average selling price of $38 per room and the actual cost of housekeeping per room was $2.10 per room. Answer the following regarding a cost variance analysis:

   a. What is the budget variance; is it favorable or unfavorable?

   b. What is the cost variance; is it favorable or unfavorable?

   c. What is the quantity variance; is it favorable or unfavorable?

9.4 Using the same information in Exercise 9.3, answer the following regarding a price variance analysis:

    a. What is the budget variance; is it favorable or unfavorable?

    b. What is the price variance; is it favorable or unfavorable?

    c. What is the quantity variance; is it favorable or unfavorable?

9.5 Assume you had a guest count for the first three months of the year; in January the count was 1,480, in February the count was 1,880, and in March the count was 2,400. What was the moving average guest count for the first quarter of the year?

9.6 You manage a small motel, which has 40 rooms, with an average room rate of $32 on a 70% occupancy rate. Fixed costs of $240,000 and the VC per room sold is $6.00. What do you anticipate your operating income (before tax) to be in the coming year?

9.7 An 80-seat coffee shop is open for all three meals every day of the year. Calculate sales revenue for the coming year. Seat turnover and average check figures are as follows:

	Turnover	Average Check
Breakfast	2.25	$3.80
Lunch	1.75	4.00
Dinner	2.75	5.80

9.8 Calculate the room revenue for a 60-room motel for the first three months of the year. Assume February is not in a leap year and has 28 days. The following formation is given:

	Room Rate	Occupancy
January	$28	60%
February	$32	70%
March	$36	78%

9.9 A 70-room motel's average room rate is $34.00. Its average occupancy is 72%. Fixed cost is $340,000 a year and variable costs are $222,222 a year. Calculate the motel's operating income for the year.

9.10 A restaurant has budgeted sales revenue of $880,000 for the next year. Variable costs are 70% of sales revenue and fixed cost is $244,000. Answer the following questions:

    a. What are total variable costs compared to sales revenue as a percentage?

b. What is the restaurant's gross margin expected to be?

c. What is the amount of operating income (before tax)?

PROBLEMS

9.1 A motel has 30 units. During the month of June its average room rate is expected to be $45.00, and its room occupancy 75%. In July the owner is planning to raise room rates by 10%, and occupancy is expected to be 80%. In August no further room rate raises are contemplated, but occupancy is expected to be up to 90%. For each of the three months of June, July, and August, calculate the budgeted room's revenue.

9.2 As the manager of the 80-room motel, you have the responsibility of preparing next year's budget from the following information:

- Annual occupancy: 70%

- Average room rate: $44.00

- Variable costs per room occupied: $8.00

- Annual fixed costs: $220,000

Prepare the Motorway Motel's budget for next year. Assume a 365-day year.

9.3 A dining room has 75 seats; it is open only for lunch and dinner six days a week (closed Sundays). This particular August has four Sundays. Round your calculations to the dollar. Management has forecast the following:

	Seat Turnover	Average Food Check
Lunch	1½	$10.50
Dinner	2	$15.50

Beverage revenue normally averages 15% of lunch food sales revenue and 30% of dinner food sales revenue. Calculate total budgeted food sales revenue and beverage sales revenue for the month.

9.4 A hotel coffee shop has 130 seats and is open seven days a week for all three-meal periods. During the month of January it anticipates the following seat turnovers and average food checks:

	Turnover	Average Check
Breakfast	1½	$ 4.00
Lunch	1¾	$ 7.50
Dinner	1¼	$12.50

Calculate the budgeted sales revenue for the coffee shop for January.

9.5 The manager of Buff's Buffet is preparing next year's budget. She wants to prepare a flexible budget for three different annual revenue levels using a contribution margin income statement. Three levels of sales revenue are to be used: $800,000, $900,000, $1,000,000. The following information is available to help in preparing the flexible budget.

- Food cost averages 40% of sales revenue.

- Variable labor costs average 25% of sales revenue.

- Fixed labor cost is $60,000 annually, and other fixed costs are $120,000.

- Other variable costs average 12% of sales revenue.

- Income tax rate is estimated to be 30% on operating income (before tax).

From this information, prepare Buff's flexible three-level budget using the contribution margin method. Comment on the results of each budget level with particular reference to the effect of higher sales on net income (after tax).

9.6 A resort hotel has a dining room that has no business from street trade; it is dependent solely on the occupancy of its rooms for its sales revenue. It has 150 rooms. During the month of June it expects 80% occupancy of those rooms. Because the resort caters to the family trade, there are on average three people per occupied room per night. From past experience, management knows that 95% of the people occupying rooms eat breakfast, 25% eat lunch, and 75% eat dinner in the hotel's dining room (some of the units have kitchen facilities, which is why some of the resort's guests do not use the dining room). The dining room is open seven days a week for all three meals. Its average meal prices are:

Breakfast: $ 4.50
Lunch: 7.50
Dinner: 12.60

Calculate the budgeted dining room revenue for the month of June.

9.7 A 120-seat family restaurant is open Mondays to Saturdays only for lunch and dinner. On Sundays and holidays, totaling 60 days annually, the restaurant is open for dinner only. During the coming year, the owner anticipates the following

	Seat Turnover	Average Check
Weekday lunch	1½	$ 5.50
Weekday dinner	1¼	10.70
Sunday and holiday dinner	2	11.00

In addition, it has a small private party room and estimates food sales revenue to be $144,000 next year. Beverage revenue is 12% of lunch food sales revenue and 25% of weekday dinner food sales revenue (no beverages are served Sundays and holidays). In addition, beverage sales revenue for private party room averages 40% of total food sales revenue. Food cost averages 37% of total food revenue, and beverage cost averages 33% of total beverage revenue. Fixed salaries are estimated to be $284,000. The variable wage cost averages 15% of total restaurant revenue. Employee benefits average 12% of total fixed and variable wage cost.

Other operating costs are expressed as percentages of total sales revenue from all food and beverage sales:

Cost	Percentage
China, glass, silver, linen	1.7%
Laundry	1.5
Supplies	3.2
Menus and beverage lists	0.8
Advertising	2.0
Repairs and maintenance	1.5
Miscellaneous expense	1.0
Total variable operating costs	11.7%
Fixed operating overhead costs	
Administration and general	$24,000
Licenses	15,000
Rent	90,000
Equipment depreciation	73,400

Prepare the restaurant's budgeted income statement for next year using the preceding information. (For purposes of this problem, ignore income tax. Also, in this problem, round figures to the nearest whole dollar where necessary.)

9.8   A restaurant's average monthly income statement is as follows:

Sales Revenue:		
Food sales revenue	$40,000	
Beverage sales revenue	10,000	$50,000
Cost of sales:		
Food [45% of food revenue]	$18,000	
Beverage [30% of beverage revenue]	3,000	21,000
Gross Margin		$29,000

Operating expense:

Wages expense	$13,600
Operating supplies expense	4,000
Administration & general expense	2,600
Advertising & promotion expense	1,800
Repairs and maintenance expense	900
Energy expense	1,300
Depreciation expense	700
Interest expense	600

Total Operating Expenses	(25,500)
Operating Income	$ 3,500

The owner is considering two possible alternatives for the coming year:

- By improving purchasing and reducing portions, cutting the food cost from 45% to 40% of food sales revenue. There would be no other changes.
- Cutting the food costs from 45% to 40% of food sales revenue and spending an additional $2,000 a month on advertising. It is estimated that the advertising would bring in extra customers and increase the volume of both food and beverage revenue by 20% over present levels. The extra customers would also incur extra costs over present levels as follows:

Wages	=	$2,000
Supplies	=	800
Administration	=	200
Repairs	=	300
Energy costs	=	100

Prepare budgeted average monthly income statements for both alternatives and advise the owner which alternative you consider the best and why.

9.9   a. Budgeted liquor sales at a banquet were 1,500 drinks at $3.15 each. Actual sales were 1,550 drinks at $2.85 each. Analyze the information for price and volume variances.

b. Banquet food sales for a month were estimated to be 20,000 covers (customers) at $10.80 each. Actual sales were 21,000 at $11.25. Analyze this for price and volume variances.

c. Budgeted banquet food cost for a week was 1,000 covers at $3.00 each. Actual cost was 980 covers at $3.10. Analyze this for cost and volume variances.

d. A snack bar budgets the following: 12,000 customers, average check $5.45, average cost per customer $2.05. Actual results showed: 12,800 customers, average check $5.27, average cost was $2.01. Analyze total cost for cost and volume variances.

e. At a convention buffet 450 customers are expected. It is estimated that one waitress will be required for each 30 anticipated guests (for serving beverages). Basic wage rate is $5.50/hour and a minimum of four hours must be paid each waitress. No overtime is anticipated, but it may occur. Calculate the budgeted payroll cost for this function.

After the event, payroll records indicate that a total of 64 hours work were actually paid for at total labor cost of $371.20. Analyze the total payroll for cost and volume variances.

9.10 An 80-room motel forecasts its average room rate to be $22.00 for next year at 75% occupancy. The rooms department has a fixed wage cost of $85,725. The variable wage cost for housekeeping is $4.50 an hour, and it takes one-half hour to clean a room. Fringe benefits are 15% of total wages. Linen, laundry, supplies, and other direct costs are $2.50 per occupied room per day. The motel also has a 50-seat limited menu snack bar. Breakfast revenue is derived solely from customers staying overnight in the motel. On average, one-third of occupied rooms is occupied by two persons and, on average 80% of overnight guests will eat breakfast. Average breakfast check is $2.00. Luncheon seat turnover is 1 with an average check of $5.50. The snack bar is open 365 days a year for all three meals. Direct operating costs for the snack bar are 75% of total snack bar revenue. Indirect costs for the motel are estimated at $289,400 for next year.

a. Calculate the budgeted net income of the motel for next year.

b. Assume that at the end of next year actual revenue was from 21,700 rooms occupied at an average rate of $22.10 and that actual housekeeping wages (before fringe benefits) were $49,910. Analyze room revenue for quantity and price variance and housekeeping wages for quantity and cost variances, assuming one-half hour to clean each room actually sold.

9.11 You have been asked to help prepare the operating budget for a proposed new 100-room motel, with a 65-seat coffee shop, 75-seat dining room, and 90-seat cocktail lounge. The operating budget for the first will be based on the following information:

Rooms Department

Occupancy is 60% with an average room rate of $63. Fixed wages for bellmen, front office employees, and other personnel attached to the rooms department are estimated at $326,900. In addition, for every 15 rooms occupied each day, one mail will be required for an eight-hour shift at a rate of $6 an hour. Staff fringe benefits will be 12% of total wages. Linen and laundry cost will be 6% of total rooms' revenue. Supplies and other items will be 3% of total rooms' sales revenue.

FOOD DEPARTMENT

The dining room is open 6 days a week, 52 weeks a year for lunch and dinner only. Lunch seat turnover is 1½, with an average food check of $7. Dinner seat turnover is 1, with an average food check of $14.

The coffee shop is open seven days a week for all meal periods. Breakfast seat turnover is 1, with an average food check of $5.50. Lunch turnover is 1½, with an average food check of $8. Dinner seat turnover is ¾, with an average food check of $13. The coffee shop breakfast seat turnover is 6, with an average check of $1.

The cocktail lounge serves an estimated 20 food orders per day, with an average check of $5.50. The lounge is closed on Sundays and certain holidays and only opens for 310 days during the year.

Total payroll cost, including fringe benefits in the food department, will be 45% total food revenue. Other costs, variable as a percentage of total food revenue are:

Food cost	35%
Laundry and linen	2%
Supplies	5%
Other costs	2%

BEVERAGE DEPARTMENT (OPEN 310 DAYS A YEAR)

Each seat in the cocktail lounge is expected to generate $5,250 per year. In addition, the lounge will be credited with any alcoholic beverages served in the coffee shop and dining room. In the coffee shop, beverage revenue is estimated to be 15% of combined lunch and dinner food sales revenue. The beverage department operating costs are:

- Liquor cost is 32% of total beverage sales revenue.
- Payroll and fringe benefits are 25% of total beverage revenue.
- Supplies and other operating costs are 5% total beverage sales revenue.

From the preceding information, you are to prepare income statements for the first year of operating for each of the three departments. Then combine the departmental operating incomes into one figure and deduce the following undistributed, indirect costs to arrive at budgeted income, before depreciation, interest, and income tax. Round all figures to the nearest dollar.

Administrative and general	$156,800
Marketing	147,600
Energy costs	58,900
Property operation & maintenance	52,400
Insurance	15,300
Property taxes	82,100

9.12 You have the following guest-night and meals-served figures for the past 12 months for the Inland Inn.

	Guest Nights	Meals Served
January	5,509	7,301
February	5,811	7,522
March	5,896	7,555
April	6,022	7,732
May	5,999	7,827
June	5,886	7,752
July	5,973	7,866
August	6,001	7,798
September	6,114	7,851
October	6,027	7,658
November	5,798	7,487
December	5,621	7,009

Use regression analysis to solve the hotel's equation $Y = a + bX$.

9.13 The manager of the Hospitality Inn has developed regression analysis equations for forecasting the hotel's dining room sales volume based on the hotel's anticipated guest night count. The monthly equations (where y equals the forecast number of meals to be served, and x equals the number of hotel guests) are:

Breakfast $y = 750 + .82x$
Lunch $y = 900 + .15x$
Dinner $y = 1,200 + .48x$

The hotel has 100 rooms. Its occupancy in November is expected to be 70%, and its double occupancy rate is 1.4 (that is, 40% of all rooms occupied are double occupied).

The average meal checks are:

Breakfast $ 5.25
Lunch   10.24
Dinner   15.78

Calculate the dining room's forecast meal period sales, both in number of guests and revenue dollars, for the month of November.

CASE 9

a. As a step to preparation of the 4C Company's preliminary budget for year 0002, calculate the forecast revenue based on year 0001 actual results adjusted as follows: lunch and dinner seat turnover figures will not change (see Case 6). Note that at lunch the guest count figure will increase as a result of the advertising plan discussed in Case 7. The ratio of food to beverage sales on the average checks will stay the same, but overall the average check for lunch will increase by $0.50 and for dinner by $0.95. No additional seats will be added in the restaurant and days open will remain the same. Calculate the total forecast sales revenue for food and beverages.

b. Complete the budgeted income statement for year 0002 with reference to Case 8 (for fixed and variable cost data) and the following additional information.

   • Food and beverage cost percentages will remain as in year 0001 (see Case 3).

   • Salaries and wages. First deduct Charlie's present salary of $18,000 from the 0001 total. Add the cost of the new employee to be hired as the result of the newspaper advertising (see Case 7). Apply a general across-the-board 10% increase for all employees (except Charlie) for year 0002. Then add on Charlie's salary, which is to be $25,000 next year.

   • Laundry percentage to revenue will remain unchanged.

   • Kitchen fuel. Fixed amount will increase by $400; the variable portion percentage to revenue will remain unchanged.

   • China, glass, etc. percentage to revenue will remain unchanged.

   • Contract cleaning. A $600 increase is anticipated in year 0002.

   • Licenses. No change anticipated.

   • Other operating expense percentage to revenue will be as before.

   • Administrative and general. A 10% increase should be budgeted for.

- Marketing. The only increase will be the $3,000 to be spent on newspaper advertising.
- Energy costs. The fixed cost is expected to rise by $2,000, and the variable portion percentage to revenue will be as before.
- Insurance. A 10% increase is expected.
- Rent. As agreed with the building owner (see Case 2) a 10% increase to be contracted for.
- Interest will decrease to $19,500.
- Depreciation. Calculate on straight-line basis.
- Income tax will be 25% of income before tax.

c. How does your budgeted income statement for year 0002 compare with the actual result for year 0001? Explain why the net income is down despite an increase in revenue.

10

Statement of Cash Flows and Working Capital Analysis

CHAPTER OBJECTIVES

After studying this chapter, the reader should be able to:

1. Define the purpose of the statement of cash flows.
2. Identify the three sections of the statement of cash flows and explain what the nature of each type of transaction is evaluated in each of the named sections.
3. Explain the effect of changes in current asset and current liability accounts have on the adjustment of accrual net income or net loss.
4. Explain how depreciation expense, amortization expense, and gains or losses on the disposal of noncurrent apply in increasing or decreasing the adjustment to net income.
5. Define working capital.
6. List and briefly explain some of the source inflows and use outflows that change working capital.
7. Know how to prepare a change to working capital accounts and identify the net change to working capital.
8. Explain why net income does not infer that cash has increased by an equal amount.
9. Define the term "current ratio" and explain whether the hospitality industry can operate on a relatively low ratio.
10. Explain the common usage of major elements in both the statement of cash flows and the various statements used to analyze working capital.

Historically, profit-oriented businesses use the accrual basis of accounting by which the income statement, balance sheet, statement of ownership equity, and a statement of cash flows are created. Financial statements serve as a basis for measuring operating performance, financial position, ownership status, and an analysis of cash flows over a given accounting period.

Accrual financial statements recognize noncash revenues and noncash expenses, which indicate profitability (the income statement) and solvency (the balance sheet). However, the basic balance sheet and income statement cannot in themselves answer cash-related questions regarding cash inflows and cash outflows that have occurred during a given operating period. The primary purpose of the statement of cash flows (SCF) is to report and identify the effects of cash receipts and cash disbursements regarding three specific areas of business activities. These three specific activity areas are operations, investing, and financing, which will normally occur during a typical period of business operations.

The statement of cash flows provides a foundation to predict future cash flows, which is essential for the effective development of future budgets. The ability to forecast cash needs for the purchase of capital assets, the repayment of noncurrent debt, and other balance sheet noncurrent items, is essential in the development of a capital budget. An income statement that projects sales revenue, cost of sales, and operating expenses is essential for the creation of an operating budget. Also needed and an equally essential document supporting the operating budget is the cash budget that forecasts cash receipts and disbursements. As a current operating period progresses, management should compare actual results to correlating budgets and take necessary corrective action when a cash flow problem is identified. In addition, a statement of cash flows can also serve as a basis for the evaluation of management's performance regarding cash management.

EVALUATING NET CASH FLOWS

Two ways of determining net cash flows

There are two ways of determining net cash flows—the direct and the indirect method. However, the indirect method is generally the easier method and more commonly used by management in hospitality operations and only the indirect method will be discussed in detail in this chapter.

In a hospitality operation, it is possible for the income statement to show positive net income and, at the same time, produce a negative cash flow, or to show a negative net loss and a positive cash flow. The statement of cash flows adjusts and reconciles the net income or net loss for an operating period to a cash basis. It is the change in the cash account which is identified when net cash flow, either positive or negative, is equal to the change in the cash account, and the actual cash on hand at the end of the period is confirmed.

Statement of cash flows adjusts and reconciles

Cash includes cash on hand, cash in the bank, and cash equivalents

Cash includes cash on hand, cash in the bank, and cash equivalents. Cash equivalents typically consist of marketable securities and short-term investments, which can be immediately converted to cash when the need dictates. In this discussion, cash equivalents, marketable securities and short-term investments will be treated as current asset accounts, not actual cash accounts.

There are many questions a statement of cash flows will answer, if management understands the procedures and the necessity to implement effective cash management policies and procedures. A few typical key questions that may be answered are:

- How much did the cash position increase or decrease from operating activities since the last accounting period?
- Which credit card companies offer the best discount fees?
- Which credit card companies have the shortest turnaround regarding the funds owed?
- Did normal operation activities generate the major portion of cash inflows?
- How much was invested in capital assets, such as new furnishings, equipment, or other long-term physical assets?
- How much cash was recovered from the disposal of furnishings, fixtures, equipment, or other long-lived physical assets?
- How much cash was received from the disposal of long-term investments?
- How much cash was obtained by incurring long-term liabilities?
- How much cash was paid to reduce or pay off long-term liabilities?
- How much cash was received through the sale of ownership equity?
- What amount was paid out as dividends?
- What amount of cash did the proprietor or the partners withdraw?

The statement of cash flows allows, by analysis, the identification of cash inflows and cash outflows within operating activities, investing activities, and financing activities. The three sections have the objective of identifying cash flows that occurred from the beginning to the end of a period of operations. The statement of cash flows begins with the reported accrual net income (or loss) that will be converted from an accrual basis to a cash basis by evaluating all balance sheet accounts that have changed during an operating period. The change in the cash account is explained after a conversion of net income (or loss). The final result of the conversion is a positive or negative net cash flow, which is equal to the total change in the cash account.

Each active current asset and current liability account except cash is evaluated to determine the change in the account for the entire reporting period. The change is identified as an increase or decrease, and the type of account being evaluated determines how the change is treated. A positive cash flow is added and a negative cash flow is deducted in the process of converting accrual net income (or net loss) to a cash basis.

Operating activities
evaluate and identify
cash flow changes

SEGMENTING CASH FLOW ANALYSIS

Operating activities evaluate and identify cash flow changes that occur within the major operating accounts, current assets and current liabilities. In addition, specific adjustments are considered which by their nature, are noncash adjustments. The greatest number of transactions affecting cash flows occur within the major operating accounts during actual operations. The investing and financing sections evaluate noncurrent account transactions affecting cash flows, which typically are not considered normal operating transactions, dedicated to the generation of sales revenue. Segmenting the cash flow analysis into three specific levels of activity allows the adjustment accrual net income or loss by adding positive cash flow changes and deducting negative cash flow changes. Each activity is discussed in the sequence it is evaluated in the cash statement.

- *Operating activities* involve the primary objective of business, the production of revenue inflows. Normal operating activities exchange goods, merchandise, and services creating sales revenue inflows for cash or on credit. Credit card and accounts receivables are the primary current asset accounts created by revenue inflows on credit. In addition to cash, other current assets—such as supplies, inventory for resale, and prepaid expenses—are created and consumed to support revenue-generating operations.
- The *generation of sales* revenue creates expense outflows, which are recognized when cash is paid or incurred on credit. Accounts payable is the primary current operating liability account. Current liabilities, when paid, represent expense outflows incurred supporting the generation of sales revenue. Ongoing expense outflows occur for payment of cost-of-sales items, employee costs, insurance costs, facilities support, interest, taxes, and other necessary reoccurring costs of operations.
- *Investing activities* involve transactions that affect noncurrent accounts. The purchase of a long-term asset creates a cash outflow; the sale of a long-term asset creates a cash inflow. The purchase of long-term noncash equivalent investment creates a cash outflow; the sale of a noncash equivalent investment creates cash inflow.
- *Financing activities* involve transactions that cause changes to ownership equity. Investment or withdrawal of equity capital and operating returns of income (or losses) typically affect financing activities of a proprietorship or

partnership. In an incorporated operation, financing activities are affected by the issuance of capital stock, a cash inflow, and the recovery by the corporation's own stock (treasury stock), a cash outflow. The reissue of treasury stock creates a cash inflow. The assumption of long-term debt creates a cash inflow; repayment of long-term debt (principle and interest) creates a cash outflow. The payment of cash dividends to stockholders is a cash outflow.

The accrual income statement reports revenue inflows, expense outflows, and the resulting net income or net loss from operations for an entire operating period. The income statement, however, does not allow management to readily see why or how cash changes occurred.

Net income or loss

Although the amount of net income or net loss may generally affect the cash account, the reported net income or net loss will not normally equal the increase or decrease in the cash account. The reported net income or loss at the end of an accounting period is normally based on accrual accounting. The accrual method includes recognition of noncash expenses,

Based on accrual accounting

losses, and noncash revenue transactions.

Typical noncash accrual items deducted in arriving at net income (or loss) are depreciation and amortization expenses and losses on disposal of long-lived assets. These are noncash expense and loss items not requiring cash outflows, and are added back as adjustments in the operations activities section. Gains on disposal of long-lived assets are noncash revenues not involving a cash inflow. These noncash gains are deducted as adjustments in the operations activities section.

To prepare a statement of cash flows, the following financial statements and information are required to conduct an analysis of balance sheet accounts and essential income and expense items:

- Income statement for the current period.
- Balance sheet for the current period.
- Trial balance of the accounts and balances at the beginning of the period (or the prior period balance sheet and statement of retained earnings).
- Statement of retained earnings for the current period.
- Information relating to noncurrent transactions during the current period.

Trial balance will isolate changes

A trial balance of accounts and balances at the beginning of the period, compared to the ending adjusted trial balance of accounts, will isolate changes in the accounts. If preferred, the comparison of the prior and current year balance sheets and statements of retained earnings will provide the same changes occurring in the accounts.

NET CASH FLOW FROM OPERATING ACTIVITIES

The objective of this section is to discuss and describe the procedure to convert reported accrual net income (or net loss), which is not a cash basis income report, to a cash basis. The accrual nature of reported net income (or net loss) means that sales and expenses are recorded when earned and incurred, not when cash is actually received or paid. The basic format of the accrual income statement is

Sales revenue − Cost of sales = Gross margin − expenses = Operating income (or loss)

Sales are made only two ways, for cash or on credit. Expenses are incurred only two ways, paid when incurred or incurred on credit, which creates an accounts payable. The indirect method of determining cash flows from operations starts with reported net income (or net loss), which is the value being converted. To accomplish conversion of net income (or loss), each current asset and current liability account must be analyzed to find the change that occurred in each account over the operating period. Simply determine the amount of the change and identify the amount as an increase or a decrease.

For example: The current income statement of a motel reported $800,000 of room sales revenue. The current asset accounts receivable increased from $10,000 at the beginning of the period to $14,000 at the end of the period. Considering only the $4,000 increase to accounts receivable, reported room sales revenue will be converted to a cash basis of $796,000. This adjustment using the effect of only one current asset account is determined as follows:

Beginning accounts receivable	−	Ending accounts receivable	=	Increase, accounts receivable
$10,000	−	$14,000	=	$4,000 Increase
Sales revenue	−	Increase, accounts receivable	=	Cash basis sales revenue
$800,000	−	$4,000	=	$796,000

In preparing the operating activities section of the statement of cash flows, the $4,000 increase in accounts receivable, a current asset account, is treated as a negative number and deducted from net income in the conversion of accrual net income to a cash basis. The actual cash inflow was $796,000 due to the increase in accounts receivable during the period of $4,000. An increase in a current asset account represents a decrease to net income when converted to a cash basis. A decrease in a current asset account has the *opposite effect* of causing an increase in the adjustment of net income to a cash basis as it relates to cash sales.

Increase in a current liability is a positive number

An increase in a current liability account represents an increase of expenses incurred on credit over a full operating period. This indicates that actual cash operating expenses were less than the total reported accrual operating expenses. The increase in a current liability account is treated as a positive number and an increase to net income in the conversion to the cash basis. This shows that actual cash outflow paid for operating expenses was less than the expenses reported in the accrual income statement.

For example: Accrual income reports expenses when they are incurred, not when they are paid. Assume that total reported operating expenses were $280,000, and that accounts payable, a current liability account, increased from $10,000 to $12,000 at the end of the period. The $2,000 change in the account is treated as a positive number, and increases the reported net income in the conversion to the cash basis. Considering only the increase of $2,000 to accounts payable, the reported operating expense is converted to $282,000, representing expenses incurred on credit. This adjustment, using only one current liability account, is determined as follows:

Beginning accounts payable	–	Ending accounts payable	=	Increase, Accounts Payable
$10,000	–	$12,000	=	$2,000 Increase
Operating expenses	+	Increase, accounts payable	=	Cash basis expense
$280,000	+	$2,000	=	$282,000

This shows an addition to reported net income of $2,000 indicating that actual cash outflow for operating expenses was $282,000; accounts payable increased by $2,000 indicating $2,000 of operating expenses was recognized on credit, thus not requiring the payment of cash.

The net effect of the two basic adjustments on net income based on the foregoing examples involving a $4,000 increase to a current receivable and a $2,000 increase to a current payable is:

	Accrual Basis	Cash Basis	Effect of Changes	
Sales revenue	= $ 800,000	$ 796,000	Revenue decreased	$4,000
Operating expenses	= $(280,000)	$(282,000)	Expenses increased	$2,000
Net Income	= $ 520,000	$ 514,000	Net Effect	$6,000

Changes to the primary operating accounts

From the foregoing examples, it is evident the changes to the primary operating accounts, current assets and current liabilities, over an accounting period will cause an increase or decrease to the reported accrual income or loss, with the exception of the cash account. Changes in each operating account provide a trail to identify accounts that changed the balance of the cash account over the reported period.

The effect of positive increases or negative decreases in the current operating accounts during the conversion to a cash basis from accrual net income or net loss is shown as follows:

Net Income: Changes added increases net cash flows.
             Changes deducted decreases net cash flows.

Net Loss: Changes added decreases net cash flows.
             Changes deducted increases net cash flows.

Some general rules apply to understanding the effect of a change to current operating accounts within the operations activity section of the cash flow statement. The rules will identify how to treat the change in current operating accounts and specify whether the change is treated as a positive (add) function or a negative (deduct) function in determining the effect on accrual net income (or loss).

Current asset increases = Negative effect = Increase is deducted
Current asset decreases = Positive effect = Decrease is added
Current liability increases = Positive effect = Increase is added
Current liability decreases = Negative effect = Decrease is deducted

The general abbreviation rules are expressed and summarized in a symbolization format that serves to describe the effects of changes that cause increases or decreases to current asset and current liability accounts. Symbols are:

Symbols Identification

Current Asset = CA   Current Liability = CL   Change in Account = ▲

Increase = ↑   Decrease = ↓   Deduct = (−)   Add = (+)

Effects of account changes:
$$CA \uparrow = \blacktriangle\ (-) \quad CA \downarrow = \blacktriangle\ (+)$$
$$CL \uparrow = \blacktriangle\ (+) \quad CL \downarrow = \blacktriangle\ (-)$$

After evaluating and adjusting current assets and current liability accounts, the net income figure has to be further adjusted for noncash items that appear on the income statement that do not involve a cash inflow or cash outflow. As discussed earlier, the major noncash item typically used in most hospitality operations is depreciation. This transaction affects only depreciation expense and accumulated depreciation (a contra asset account). Since depreciation expense is deducted on the accrual income statement (no cash is involved), to arrive at

Major noncash item is depreciation

net income, it must to be added back to net income to adjust for cash from operations.

In addition, if amortization expense were reported on the income statement, it would also be added back to net income like depreciation—no cash is involved. Losses or gains on the disposal of long-term assets are noncash transactions, and when such gains or losses are reported, the accrual income statement will normally involve receipt (or payment) of cash. Such losses or gains are not considered as actual cash losses or gains from operations in the conversion of net income to the cash basis. When reported on the income statement, losses will be added back as positive inflows and gains are deducted as negative outflows to adjust reported income (or loss) to the cash basis. The effects of depreciation, amortization, and losses or gains on the disposal of long-lived assets are summarized as follows:

Depreciation expense = Positive effect = Add back
Amortization expense = Positive effect = Add back
Loss, long-term asset disposal = Positive effect = Add back
Gain, long-term asset disposal = Negative effect = Deduct

FINANCIAL STATEMENTS

Financial statements that report key information necessary to complete an analysis of items affecting the conversion of reported accrual net income (or loss) to a cash basis follow. It is important that you review their structure, components, and sequence as we discuss the conversion process.

Each of the three sections of the statement of cash flows indirect method will be individually discussed, beginning with the net cash flow from operations followed by net cash flow from investing and net cash flow from financing. After each section is individually discussed, a completed statement of cash flows will be illustrated.

Net Cash Flow

Income statement identifies the reported net income (or loss)

Finding the net cash flow from operating activities will focus on the income statement in Exhibit 10.1 and the comparative balance sheets in Exhibit 10.2 for information used in conversion of net income (or loss) to a cash basis. The income statement identifies the reported net income (or loss) depreciation and amortization expenses, losses and gains on disposal of long-lived assets. Comparative balance sheets allow the analysis of current asset and current liability accounts to determine their balance changes and how to treat the change as a positive inflow, add adjustment, or a negative outflow, deduct adjustment. The statement of retained earnings shows the net income (or loss) and cash dividends paid for the operating period being reported.

Exhibit 10.1   Condensed Income Statement, December 31, 0001

Sales revenue		$7,262,400
Cost of sales		(2,495,300)
Gross margin		$4,767,100
Payroll expense	$2,306,500	
Direct operating expenses	1,609,900	
Total direct operating expenses		(3,916,400)
Contributory income		$ 850,700
Operating expenses	$ 144,200	
Depreciation expense	541,200	
Total operating expenses		(685,400)
Operating income		$ 165,300
Income tax		(24,200)
Net income		$ 141,100

Discussion: Cash Flow Conversion, Operating Activities

a. Net income, a positive amount of $141,100 is the first item shown and is the amount being converted to a cash basis through the operations activities section. If a net loss were reported, it would remain the first amount being converted to a cash basis, but would be shown as a negative amount. Net income (or loss) is also reported in the statement of retained earnings.

b. One automatic noncash adjustment, depreciation expense, is identified, which is a positive inflow, add-back adjustment.

c. Each of the three current asset accounts shows a decrease in its balance, each of which is treated as a positive inflow, increase adjustment. If a current asset account shows an increase in its balance, it would be treated as negative outflow, deduction adjustment.

d. Four current liability accounts were identified with changes in their balances. Three had increases in their balances and one had a decrease. The three increased current liability account balances are treated as positive inflows, increase, add-back adjustments; the fourth showing a decrease in its balance is treated as negative outflow, deduction adjustment.

Discussion: Cash Flow Conversion, Investing Activities

To determine cash flow adjustments from investing activities, we turn our attention to the comparative balance sheets in Exhibit 10.2. Now we will review

Exhibit 10.2 Comparative Balance Sheets

Assets	12-31-0001	12-31-0002	▲	Change
Current Assets				
Cash	$ 25,200	$ 29,600	+	4,400
Credit card receivables	4,850	4,300	–	550
Accounts receivable	14,550	12,900	–	1,650
Inventories	9,700	8,000	–	1,700
Prepaid expenses	4,100	4,000	–	100
Total Current Assets	$ 58,400	$ 58,800		400
Property & Equipment				
Land	$ 194,000	$ 194,000		-0-
Building	9,800,000	9,800,000		-0-
Equipment	736,400	753,400	+	17,000
Furnishings	184,000	184,000		-0-
Total property & equipment	$10,914,400	$10,931,400	+	17,000
Total accumulated depreciation	(2,400,000)	(2,544,200)	+	144,200
Property & equipment: net	$ 8,514,400	$ 8,387,200	–	127,200
Other assets	509,000	609,000	+	100,000
Total Assets	$ 9,081,800	$ 9,055,000	–	26,800
Liabilities & Stockholders' Equity				
Current Liabilities				
Accounts payable	$ 14,700	$ 15,600	+	900
Accrued payroll payable	3,200	4,100	+	900
Taxes payable	5,900	4,700	–	1,200
Current mortgage payable	14,300	14,900	+	600
Total current liabilities	$ 38,100	$ 39,300	+	1,200
Long-Term Liabilities				
Mortgage payable	$ 7,724,500	$ 7,710,200	–	14,300
Less: Current mortgage payable	(14,300)	(14,900)	+	600
Total Liabilities	$ 7,710,200	$ 7,734,600	+	24,400
Stockholders' Equity				
Capital stock	$ 950,000	$ 950,000		-0-
Retained earnings	383,500	370,400	–	13,100
Total Stockholders' Equity	$ 1,333,500	$ 1,320,400	–	13,100
Total Liabilities & Stockholders Equity	$ 9,081,800	$ 9,055,000	–	26,800

Exhibit 10.3   Statement of Retained Earnings
Year Ended December 31, 0002

Retained earnings, December 31, 0001	$385,500
Net income for the year, 0002	141,100
Subtotal	$526,600
Cash dividends paid in year 0002	(154,200)
Retained earnings, December 31, 0002	$372,400

the property and equipment (fixed assets) section to isolate the purchase sale of long-lived assets and the purchase or sale of noncurrent investments.

a. No changes occurred in the land or building accounts.

b. The fixed asset section shows equipment has increased $17,000, which is treated as a negative outflow and deducted. However, an analysis of this account shows equipment was sold for $3,000, which is treated as a positive inflow, add-adjustment. In addition, $20,000 of new equipment was purchased during the period, which is treated as a negative outflow and deducted. The only other account in the fixed asset section that changed was accumulated depreciation in the amount of $144,200, which has already been used in the depreciation expense (noncash) adjustment in the operating activities section.

Exhibit 10.4   Net Cash Flow from Operating Activities (Solution)

Adjustments to reconcile net Income to		
Net Cash flow from operating activities		
Net income from operations		$141,100
Depreciation expense	$144,200	
Credit card receivables (decreased)	550	
Accounts receivable (decreased)	1,650	
Inventory (decreased)	1,700	
Prepaid expenses (decreased)	100	
Accounts payable (increased)	900	
Accrued payroll payable (increased)	900	
Taxes payable (decreased)	(1,200)	
Current mortgage payable (increased)	600	
Net Cash Flow Adjustment		149,400
Net Cash Flow from Operating Activities		$290,500

Exhibit 10.5 Net Cash Flow from Investing Activities (Solution)

Cash flow adjustments, investing activities		
Purchase of equipment	$ (20,000)	
Sale of equipment	3,000	
Purchase of investment	(125,000)	
Sale of investment	25,000	
Net Cash Flow from Investing Activities		($117,000)

c. The other assets section shows the investment account increased $100,000, which is treated as a negative outflow and deducted. However, an analysis of this account during this period shows an investment was sold for $25,000, which is treated as a positive inflow and added. In addition, a new investment was purchased for $125,000 during the period that is a negative outflow and deducted.

Discussion: Cash Flow Conversion, Financing Activities

To determine cash flow adjustments from financing activities, we look to the comparative balance sheets in Exhibit 10.2 and the statement of retained earnings, Exhibit 10.3. Our focus now turns to long-term liabilities and stockholders' equity. Determine whether any long-term Liabilities accounts have increased, a positive inflow, or decreased, a negative outflow, during the period. Determine whether any stock equity has been sold, a positive inflow, or repurchased (treasury stock), a negative outflow, and whether cash dividends have been paid, a negative outflow, during the period.

Discussion: Cash Flow Conversion, Financing Section

a. The long-term liability section shows the mortgage payable (on a building) account has been reduced by $14,900 in 0004, which is a negative outflow.

b. The statement of retained earnings reports the payment of cash dividends during 0004 in the amount of $154,200, which also creates a negative cash flow.

Exhibit 10.6 Cash Flow from Financing Activities

Cash flow adjustments, financing activities		
Reduction of long-term mortgage	$(14,900)	
Cash dividends paid	(154,200)	
Net Cash Flow from Financing Activities		$(169,100)

The stockholders' equity sections of the comparative balance sheets show the capital stock account has not changed between December 31, 0001 and December 31, 0002, and no cash flow adjustment to net income (or loss) is required. If capital stock account had changed, an increase would be a positive inflow and a decrease would be a negative outflow.

The last account to be looked at is retained earnings, as illustrated in Exhibit 10.3. This shows a beginning balance of $383,500, which was the ending balance at the end of 0001. Net income was $141,100, and cash dividends of $154,200 were paid during year 0002. The year 0002 ending balance of retained earnings is $370,400.

FINALIZING THE STATEMENT OF CASH FLOWS

Final net cash flow change should be equal to the change in the cash account

Exhibit 10.7 shows a sample statement of cash flows from La Quinta Inns, Inc., and a completed statement of cash flows using the information discussed in the example is shown in Exhibit 10.8. Note in Exhibit 10.8 the net cash flow increase of $4,400 during year 0002 is added to the 0001 cash balance to confirm the cash flow change and the 0002 ending cash balance. As discussed earlier, the final net cash flow change reported in the statement of cash flows should be equal to the change in the cash account that occurred over the reported period. If the change in the cash account is not the same as the final adjusted cash flow, an error has occurred and should be traced and corrected.

Value of Statement of Cash Flows

Value of statement of cash flow

The statement of cash flows is of value to management, as it allows an evaluation of the operation's liquidity and provides a basis for analysis of cash performance. In addition, it guides management in its decisions regarding cash budgeting, and assists in decisions about its financing and investing requirements. It is also of value to creditors (such as suppliers of goods and services needed by the operation) to assess the operation's ability to meet its payment requirements. These creditors generally like to see that sufficient cash is being generated from operating activities to meet these obligations rather than relying on investing or financing activities to provide that cash.

Lenders of short-term as well as long-term funds can also use a statement of cash flows to determine the ability of an organization to continue to meet its debt obligations. Stockholders can use the statement of cash flows to assess the operation's ability to pay dividends, or possibly to increase its dividend payments.

The statement of cash flows is an historic document showing what has happened in a comparative review, and it is an essential document for managers, creditors, lenders, and stockholders for evaluating and forecasting the future.

Exhibit 10.7 Statements of Cash Flows, La Quinta Inns, Inc.*
Year Ended December 31 (in thousands)

	1995	1994	1993
Cash flows from operating activities:			
Net earnings	$ 50,657	$ 37,815	$ 20,301
Adjustments to reconcile net earnings to net cash provided by operating activities:			
Depreciation and amortization of property and equipment and asset retirements	40,951	38,080	24,055
Provision for premature retirement of assets	12,630	—	—
Performance stock options	—	—	4,407
Gain on sale of assets	—	(79)	(616)
Partners' equity in earnings	10,277	11,406	12,965
Cumulative effect on change in accounting	—	—	(1,500)
Changes in operating assets and liabilities:			
Receivables	(537)	(2,013)	(1,832)
Income taxes	2,646	9,291	3,585
Supplies and prepayments	(1,818)	(2,622)	(1,334)
Accounts payable and accrued expenses	9,704	(1,291)	14,774
Deferred charges and other assets	656	1,470	460
Deferred credits and other	3,682	2,176	2,778
Net cash provided by operating activities	$ 128,848	$ 94,233	$ 78,043
Cash flows from investing activities:			
Construction, purchase, and conversion of inns	(77,502)	(34,690)	(38,858)
Other capital expenditures	(39,962)	(75,248)	(32,623)
Proceeds from property transactions	—	2,565	982
Purchase of partners' equity interest	(48,200)	(53,255)	(78,169)
Decrease in notes receivable and investments	6,836	4,136	3,641
Net cash used by investing activities	$(158,828)	$(156,492)	$(145,027)
Cash flows from financing activities:			
Proceeds from line of credit and long-term borrowings	645,723	417,102	223,198
Principal payments on line of credit and long-term borrowings	(601,121)	(369,955)	(178,528)
Capital contributions by partners	—	—	35,908
Capital distributions to partners	(2,495)	(1,144)	(3,414)
Dividends to shareholders	(4,957)	(3,465)	(1,015)
Purchase of treasury stock	(12,346)	(7,013)	—
Net proceeds from stock transactions	5,227	5,475	1,822
Net cash provided by financing activities	$ 30,031	$ 41,000	$ 77,971
Increase (decrease) in cash and cash equivalents	1	(21,259)	10,987
Cash and cash equivalents at beginning of year	2,589	23,848	12,861
Cash and cash equivalents at end of year	$ 2,590	$ 2,589	$ 23,848

*The statement in this exhibit is courtesy of La Quinta Inns, Inc.

Exhibit 10.8   Statement of Cash Flows, for the Year Ending December 31, 0002

Net Income		$141,100
Credit card receivables (decrease)	$ 550	
Accounts receivable (decrease)	1,650	
Inventory (decrease)	1,700	
Prepaid expense (decrease)	100	
Accounts payable (increase)	900	
Accrued payroll (increase)	900	
Tax payable (decrease)	(1,200)	
Mortgage payable (increase)	600	
Depreciation expense	144,200	
Net cash flow adjustments		149,400
Net Cash Flow, Operating Activities		$290,500
Cash flow adjustments investing activities:		
Purchase of equipment	$ (20,000)	
Sale of equipment	3,000	
Purchase of investment	(125,000)	
Sale of investment	25,000	
Net Cash Flow, Investing Activities		(117,000)
Cash flow adjustments financing activities:		
Reduction of mortgage	(14,900)	
Dividends paid	(154,200)	
Net Cash Flow, Financing Activities		(169,100)
Net cash flow increase		$ 4,400
Cash balance, December 31, 1998		25,200
Cash balance, December 31, 1999		$ 29,600

ANALYSIS OF CHANGES TO WORKING CAPITAL

Working capital analysis provides another view

The statement of cash flows provides additional information needed for effective cash management and budget planning. Working capital analysis is closely related to the statement of cash flows and provides another view of information in support of effective management of cash.

Working capital defined

Working capital is defined as the excess of current assets compared to current liabilities, and indicates the amount of excess current assets relative to current liabilities available to conduct of revenue-generating operations. Total current assets minus total current liabilities is the value of working capital (CA – CL). These terms are defined as follows:

- *Current assets* consist of cash, marketable securities, notes receivable, credit card receivables, accounts receivable, inventories (for resale), supplies, and prepaid expenses. Current assets are the resources to be consumed in the production of sales revenue in the next operating period.
- *Current liabilities* consist of accounts payable, accrued expenses (wages and salaries payable, interest payable, taxes payable, etc.), and notes payable. Current liabilities represent operating costs, expenses obligations incurred on credit that will be paid within the next operating period.

The preparation of a statement of changes to working capital is similar in many ways to the preparation of a statement of cash flows. However, the analysis of working capital differs in a number of ways from the cash flow analysis, and serves different purposes.

Working capital analysis evaluates changes to working capital over an operating period for the following purposes:

- To show how working capital increased, by identifying the inflows creating the increase.
- To show how working capital decreased, by identifying the outflow creating the decrease.
- To find the net changes to working capital during the completed operating period.
- To provide management with information related to the effectiveness of working capital controls during the operating period.
- To provide prospective lenders information that will be evaluated regarding their risk in lending funds to the hospitality organizations.

Inflows of Working Capital

The following are the major inflows that will increase working capital (also referred to as sources of working capital):

Accrued income is sales revenue less all expenses incurred

- *Income from operations.* In general terms, accrued income is sales revenue less all expenses incurred (including income tax) to produce the sales revenue inflow. Sales revenue is generated by cash sales or on credit through receivables that eventually become cash. Expenses are incurred by immediate payment of cash or on credit through payables. The payables, accounts payable, and accrued payables will eventually be paid. Net income is expected to increase the organization's cash accounts and increase working capital.
- *Accrual net income.* This is determined after deducting noncash outflow expenses. Such noncash expenses adjust the book or carrying value of assets being capitalized through depreciation and/or amortization

expense recognition. To convert net income to the correct inflow increase in working capital, all capitalized expenses must be added back to net income. This uses the same procedure followed in the operating activities section of the statement of cash flows. Other items that are handled in the same way as depreciation and amortization expenses may consist of prepaid franchise fees or the amortization of other intangible assets such as goodwill.

- *Sale of long-term or other noncurrent assets.* These include land, building, furniture, equipment, or an investment and their sale is treated as an inflow, which increases working capital. The sale will create an increase in a current asset, cash, or a current receivable with no corresponding effect to a current liability.
- *Increase in a long-term liability.* This is achieved by creating or increasing a loan, mortgage, bond, or debenture, is an inflow that increases working capital. The assumption of additional long-term debt will create an increase in a current asset, cash, or a current receivable with no corresponding effect to a current liability.
- *The issuance of stock.* Equity financing creates an inflow that increases working capital. In a proprietorship or partnership (an unincorporated company), stock is not issued; however, any investment by the owner(s) increases their equity capital accounts. The sale of equity or receipt of an owner's investment will create an increase in a current asset, cash, or a current receivable with no corresponding effect on a current liability.

OUTFLOWS OF WORKING CAPITAL

The following are the major outflows that will decrease working capital (also referred to as uses of working capital):

- *Loss from operations:* Just as accrual net income is an increase in working capital, an accrual net loss is a decrease in working capital. When a loss occurs, operating expenses have exceeded sales revenue, which decreases working capital. Just as net income has to be adjusted for noncash expenditures (depreciation, franchise, goodwill, write-downs, or amortization), the net loss is similarly adjusted. The net loss may be reduced by any noncash expense shown on the income statement.
- *Purchase of a long-term or other noncurrent asset* such as land, building, furniture, equipment, or an investment is an outflow, which decreases working capital. The cost of another noncurrent asset, such as the prepayment of a long-term franchise fee, is also an outflow, which decreases working capital.

- *Payment of long-term liabilities.* Any payment reducing the principle amount owed on long-term (noncurrent) liability is an outflow, which decreases in working capital.
- *Redemption of stock.* Any previously issued stock repurchased by the issuing company is called treasury stock, an outflow that decreases working capital.
- *Payment of cash dividends.* Previously declared, these are payable obligations, payment of which is an outflow, which decreases working capital. In a non-incorporated company, a partnership, or proprietorship, any cash or other current asset withdrawals made by the owner(s) are reductions of their capital investment and treated as an outflow, decrease of working capital.

The items discussed that create inflows and outflows and will increase or decrease working capital (WC) are summarized here:

Inflow of WC	=	Net Income	Adjusted ←*Income*→	Net Loss	=	Outflow of WC
Inflow of WC	=	Sold	(or Other Asset) ←*Long-term Assets*→	Purchase	=	Outflow of WC
Inflow of WC	=	Borrowed	←*Long-term Liabilities*→	Payment	=	Outflow of WC
Inflow of WC	=	Sale of	←*Ownership Equity*→	Buy Back	=	Outflow of WC
(No opposite)	=		*Cash Dividends*→	Payment	=	Outflow of WC

STATEMENT USES

A statement of changes to working capital is discussed first, followed by a statement of changes to individual working capital accounts, to be discussed later in this chapter. Let us consider the following three situations presented in Exhibits 10.9, 10.10, and 10.11, concerning three different restaurants. Each restaurant began the operating year with $88,000 of working capital and ended the year with $100,000 of working capital; each restaurant increased working capital by $12,000. Each restaurant wants to borrow $15,000 for three years with interest from the same bank. Information is readily available from their balance sheets, but it does not clearly identify the causes of the increase to working capital without a statement of working capital inflow sources and outflow uses. The statement, when completed, will clearly identify each source inflow and use outflow of working capital. We will assume the banker compiled the same information.

Exhibit 10.9   Restaurant "A" Statement of Changes, Working Capital
Year Ending December 31, 0003

Inflows of Working Capital	
Net income (after tax)	$20,000
Outflows of Working Capital	
Dividends paid to stockholders	(8,000)
Net Change, Increase to Working Capital	$12,000

Exhibit 10.10   Restaurant "B" Statement of Changes, Working Capital
Year Ending December 31, 0003

Inflows of Working Capital		
Net income (after tax)	$20,000	
Loan payable (repayable over 4 years with interest)	20,000	$40,000
Outflows of Working Capital		
Investment in new building	$20,000	
Cash Dividends paid	8,000	(28,000)
Net Change, Increase to Working Capital		$12,000

Exhibit 10.11   Restaurant "C" Statement of Changes, Working Capital
Year Ending December 31, 0003

Inflows of Working Capital		
Net income (after taxes)	$ 4,000	
Loans payable (investor, repayable over 4 years with interest	16,000	$20,000
Outflows of Working Capital		
Dividends paid to stockholders		(8,000)
Net Change, Increase to Working Capital		$12,000

Restaurant "A": Exhibit 10.9

The information regarding restaurant "A" has generated sufficient working capital from operations to pay out $8,000 in dividends. In this situation, assuming the restaurant's business is going to stay relatively healthy over the next three years, it appears there is a low risk to the bank that is lending the restaurant the money. The restaurant should be able to repay $5,000 a year, plus interest, to retire the loan.

Restaurant "B": Exhibit 10.10

Based on this information, the banker would consider the restaurant to be a moderate to high risk. True, this restaurant also paid out cash dividends in the amount of $8,000; however Restaurant "B" already has a loan outstanding, which requires a payment of $5,000 per year plus interest. If a new loan were granted, it might be questionable whether the restaurant could make and sustain yearly payments of $10,000 per year plus interest. A modest decline in net income over the next few years would decrease the working capital and potentially create difficulties for the restaurant in meeting its debt obligations and paying dividends. If this should occur, the risk involved would grow in proportion to the reduction of net income. Thus, there is a high risk involved.

Restaurant "C": Exhibit 10.11

In this last situation, it would be an extremely high risk for the bank to loan this restaurant $15,000. A net income of $4,000 was apparently adequate to meet the current debt payment of $4,000, but not the interest. Payment of the dividend in this situation is in itself questionable. If net income remains at this level, the restaurant will not meet its present debt obligation, let alone pay dividends.

Although the Restaurant "C" illustration is somewhat extreme, it does point out the way in which information provided by the statement of changes to working capital can be of value in decision making.

TRANSACTIONS AFFECTING ONLY CURRENT ACCOUNTS

Note that all the items discussed and listed earlier under inflows or outflows of working capital affected a current asset or current liability account and a noncurrent account. Transactions causing inflows and/or outflows of working capital identify the cause of such changes in net working capital. However, it does not show specific details of changes in individual current asset or current liability accounts. Transactions affecting only current asset or current liability accounts will not appear on the statement of changes to working capital. For example, consider the following partial balance sheet information:

Current Assets		Current Liabilities	
Cash	$12,000	Accounts payable	$10,800
Credit card receivables	800	Interest payable	200
Accounts receivable	2,000	Bank loan payable	4,800
Inventories (for resale)	8,000		
Total	$22,800		$15,800

The working capital, CA − CL = $22,800 − $15,800 = $7,000. If $4,500 cash were paid on accounts payable, only two current accounts would be affected. A new partial balance sheet would be:

Current Assets		Current Liabilities	
Cash	$ 7,500	Accounts payable	$ 6,300
Credit card receivables	800	Interest payable	200
Accounts receivable	2,000	Bank loan payable	4,800
Inventories (for resale)	8,000		
Total	$18,300		$11,300

Since the example transaction affected only two current accounts, current assets and current liabilities, working capital will not change. It is still $7,000 ($18,300 − $11,300). This type of simple transaction affects only two current accounts; both accounts are changed by the same amount. If cash is received in payment of a receivable, a transaction is created that causes an exchange of a current asset for a current asset; no change to total current assets occurs.

Purchase of a current asset on credit affects   The purchase of a current asset on credit affects only two current accounts for the same dollar amount. As a result of the above examples, we will not be concerned with changes between individual current asset and current liability accounts.

The statement of changes to working capital views only the effects of transactions, which will change total current assets and/or total current liabilities. To analyze information necessary to complete a statement of changes to working capital, we require the following:

- A balance sheet at the close of the previous accounting period.
- A balance sheet at the close of the current accounting period.
- An income statement for the current period.
- A statement of retained earnings at the close of the current period or detailed information about retained earnings on the balance sheet at the close of the current period.

- Any other information not fully disclosed in the above documents (for example, information about the purchase or sale of individual long-term assets or details about long-term liabilities or share transactions).

COMPLETION OF A STATEMENT OF CHANGES TO WORKING CAPITAL

To illustrate how a statement of changes to working capital can be developed, we will refer to comparative balance sheets in Exhibit 10.12, including some information regarding retained earnings. As we move through the discussion, we will reference Exhibit 10.13, a Condensed Income Statement and, finally, look at Exhibit 10.14, a statement of retained earnings.

Easiest method is to evaluate

The use of working papers to gather necessary information defining the changes to working capital is the most accurate proof of working capital evaluation, although working papers are not an absolute requirement. The easiest method is to evaluate the comparative balance sheets, the income statement, and the statement of retained earnings to identify relevant items as an inflow, increase, or an outflow, decrease of working capital.

Current Account Information, Comparative Balance Sheets

From Exhibit 10.12, the first step is to find the change in working capital from the previous balance sheet ending date to the current balance sheet ending date (CA − CL = WC):

Year Ending 0004:	Current Assets	−	Current Liabilities	=	Working Capital
	$24,000	−	$17,000	=	$7,000
Year Ending 0003:	Current Assets	−	Current Liabilities	=	Working Capital
	$18,000	−	$15,000	=	$3,000

Working Capital 0004	−	Working Capital 0003	=	Net change to working capital
$7,000	−	$3,000	=	$4,000 Increase

The change in working capital is increased $4,000. This figure must agree with the change in working capital figure that appears as the difference between inflow increases and outflow decreases on the statement of changes to working capital.

Having identified the change in working capital, the current asset and current liability sections of our comparative balance sheets can be ignored. Only information from noncurrent sections of the comparative balance sheets, Exhibit 10.12, the income statement, Exhibit 10.13, and the statement of retained

Exhibit 10.12   Comparative Balance Sheets

Assets	12-31-0003	Change ▲	12-31-0004	Change ▲
Current Assets				
Cash	$ 10,000		$ 12,000	
Credit card receivables	2,000		2,000	
Accounts receivable	3,000		6,000	
Inventories	3,000		4,000	
Total Current Assets		$ 18,000		$ 24,000
Fixed Assets				
Land	$ 30,000		$ 30,000	
Building	250,000		250,000	
Equipment	28,000		32,000	
Furniture	7,000		8,000	
Total	$315,000		$320,000	
Less: Accum. Deprecation	(15,000)		(27,000)	
Total Fixed Assets		300,000		293,000
Total Assets		$318,000		$317,000
Liabilities & Stockholders' Equity				
Current Liabilities				
Accounts payable	$ 4,000		$ 5,000	
Accrued expenses	0		4,000	
Bank loan	11,000		8,000	
Total Current Liabilities		$ 15,000		$ 17,000
Long-term Liability				
Mortgage payable		$185,000		$175,000
Stockholders' Equity				
Capital Stock	$100,000		$105,000	
Retained Earnings	18,000		20,000	
Total Stockholders' Equity		$118,000		$125,000
Total Liabilities & Stockholders' Equity		$318,000		$317,000

earnings, Exhibit 10.14 will be required to complete the changes in working capital.

Noncurrent Balance Sheet Information

As already stated, we need concern ourselves no further with current balance sheet accounts. The second step is to evaluate the noncurrent assets and noncurrent liabilities.

**Exhibit 10.13   Condensed Income Statement
for the Year Ended December 31, 0004**

Revenue	$100,000
Operating expenses	(82,000)
Income before depreciation	$ 18,000
Depreciation	(12,000)
Net income	$ 6,000

Noncurrent Assets

The land account remained unchanged at $30,000 and the building account remained unchanged at $250,000 between 0003 and 0004. The furniture account increased by $1,000, and the equipment account increased $4,000 between year 0003 and year 0004. Since additional furniture and equipment were acquired during the 0004 operating period, the total $5,000 increase was to two noncurrent assets, which was increased by an outflow of current assets, specifically cash.

Outflow, decrease to working capital: purchase of furniture, $1,000, and equipment, $4,000. Total decrease to working capital is $5,000.

In addition, the contra asset account, accumulated depreciation increased by $12,000 during the 0004 operating year, reflecting the recognition of a non-cash, depreciation expense transaction. The effect of increasing accumulated depreciation is the reduction of the book value (carrying value) of related long-lived capital assets, which does not affect working capital and is ignored.

**Exhibit 10.14   Statement of Retained Earnings
for the Year Ended December 31, 0004**

Retained earnings January 1, 0004	$18,000
Add: Net income for year	6,000
	$24,000
Less: Dividends declared and paid	(4,000)
Retained earnings December 31, 0004	$20,000

Noncurrent Liabilities

The long-term liability mortgage payable decreased during the 0004 operating period by $10,000. The reduction of the long-term liability was caused by an outflow of current assets, specifically cash.

Outflow, decrease to working capital: mortgage payable reduction, $10,000

Stockholders' Equity

In the final step, the capital stock account increased during the 0004 operating period from $100,000 to $105,000. The increase to the capital stock account shows that $5,000 of additional capital stock was issued for cash, which is an inflow of a current asset. Always assume stock is issued for cash unless specifically noted in the accounting records or as a footnote to the balance sheet.

Inflow, increase, to working capital: capital stock issued (sold), $5,000

Retained Earnings

Changed from year 0003 to year 0004. However, for details concerning this change, we need to refer to the statement of retained earnings (Exhibit 10.14) which we will do after we have looked at the income statement (Exhibit 10.13).

The income statement reports net income of $6,000, which is treated as an inflow, increase to working capital. In arriving at net income, depreciation was recognized under the accrual method, not requiring a cash expenditure. As discussed earlier, depreciation is a noncash expense and is treated as an inflow, increase to working capital.

Inflow, increase to working capital: Net income, $6,000
Inflow, increase to working capital: Depreciation expense, $12,000

The statement of retained earnings identifies the final item remaining to be evaluated from the statement of retained earnings, Exhibit 10.14. Two of the items appearing in the statement of retained earnings have already been evaluated. The first item was net income, which was treated as inflow, increase to working capital of $6,000. The second item was a noncash expense depreciation, which was treated as an inflow, increase to working capital. The only remaining retained earnings item is cash dividends reported as paid in the amount of $4,000. The $4,000 is treated as an outflow, decrease to working capital.

Outflow, decrease, to working capital, cash dividends, $4,000

Since no other information is given, we have all the data required for compiling our statement of source and use of working capital. The summary of inflows and outflows to working capital as they were discussed is:

Outflow, decrease, to working capital:	Purchase furniture	$ 1,000
Outflow, decrease, to working capital:	Purchase equipment	5,000
Outflow, decrease, to working capital:	Reduction of mortgage payable	10,000
Inflow, increase, to working capital:	Additional capital stock issued	5,000
Inflow, increase, to working capital:	Net Income	18,000
Outflow, decrease, to working capital:	Payment of cash dividends	4,000

This information can now be arranged in an orderly fashion in the form of a statement of changes to working capital, Exhibit 10.15. Note that the net change in working capital shown on this statement, an increase of $4,000, agrees with the amount of the change in working capital previously determined from the years 0003 – 0004 from Exhibit 10.12.

Additional information is often required to clarify specific transactions used in the completion of the statement of changes in working capital than is shown in the financial statements and statement footnotes. For example, see Exhibit 10.15 and the furniture account which increased by $1,000 and the equipment account, which increased by $4,000, for a total of $5,000 from year 0003 to 0004. It was stated earlier that we can assume furniture and equipment had been purchased for a total of $5,000; however, in practice, it is necessary to reference

**Exhibit 10.15   Statement of Changes to Working Capital
for the Year Ending December 31, 0004**

Inflows, Increases:		
Net Income	$18,000	
Capital Stock Issued	5,000	
Total inflows, Increases		$23,000
Outflows, decreases:		
Purchase Furniture	$ 1,000	
Purchase Equipment	4,000	
Reduction, Mortgage Payable	10,000	
Payment Cash Dividends	4,000	
Total Outflows, Increases		(19,000)
Net Working Capital Change, Increase		$ 4,000

the actual ledger accounts in the general ledger, and related invoices. The following situation could have occurred with a missing item not being shown:

Furniture account, December 31, 0003	$ 7,000
Equipment account, December 31, 0003	28,000
Furniture purchased during year 0004	1,000
Equipment purchased during year 0004	4,000
Old furniture sold during year 0004	(2,000)
Furniture & equipment accounts, December 31, 0004	$38,000

A $5,000 increase in the account has occurred, but the change is accounted for by two separate transactions, and these two transactions should be recorded separately on the statement of source and use of working capital.

Inflow, increase, to working capital: furniture sold	$2,000
Outflow, decrease, to working capital: equipment purchased	$7,000

Any other noncurrent accounts where similar working capital inflows and outflows transactions occurred during the operating period would have to be analyzed in detail. Only this procedure can insure the changes to the working capital statement provide complete disclosure of such working capital changes during the period.

The statement of changes to working capital shows only the net change in total working capital from an outflow, decrease and inflow, increase basis occurring from noncurrent account transactions in one complete operating period. It does not show how the individual accounts that are part of working capital have changed. If this information is wanted, or required, it is shown separately in a statement of changes to individual working capital accounts. If we use the current asset and current liability sections of the previously used balance sheet Exhibit 10.12, we could summarize the changes in individual working capital accounts, as in Exhibit 10.16.

Analysis of individual account changes

An analysis of individual account changes can be made as a result of preparing a statement of changes in working capital. Questions could then be asked. For example: Assume the cash account has increased by $2,000, or 20% ($2,000 divided by $10,000); do we need extra cash on hand or should the extra cash be used to pay off some of a bank loan and save interest expense? By reducing interest expense, net income may increase. The receivables have gone up by $3,000, or 60%; has our total revenue increased 60%, or have we changed our credit policies, or are we not following up effectively on the collection of accounts? The information in the statement of changes in working capital accounts raises these and other questions.

Exhibit 10.16   Statement of Changes to Individual Working Capital Accounts
Year Ended December 31, 0004

	Year 0001	Year 0002	Increase	Decrease
			Working Capital	
Current Assets				
Cash	$10,000	$12,000	$2,000	
Accounts receivable	5,000	8,000	3,000	
Inventories (for resale)	3,000	4,000	1,000	
Total Current Assets	$18,000	$24,000	$6,000	
Current Liabilities				
Accounts payable	$ 4,000	$ 5,000		$1,000
Accrued expenses payable	0	4,000		4,000
Bank loan payable	11,000	8,000	3,000	
Total Current Liabilities	$15,000	$17,000		
Working Capital	$ 3,000	$ 7,000		
			$9,000	$5,000
Net Change, Working Capital				$4,000
Totals			$9,000	$9,000

The problem of cash management and the control of individual working capital accounts, such as inventory, accounts receivable, and accounts payable, will be discussed in Chapter 11.

As a point of review, the effects of changes to current assets and current liabilities and their effect on working capital can be summarized using a simple base data set, as follows:

Total Current Assets	–	Total Current Liabilities	=	Working Capital
$1,000	–	$800	=	$200
Total Current Assets	–	Total Current Liabilities	=	Working Capital
$900	–	$800	=	$100
Total Current Assets	–	Total Current Liabilities	=	Working Capital
$1,400	–	$800	=	$600
Total Current Assets	–	Total Current Liabilities	=	Working Capital
$1,000	–	$900	=	$100
Total Current Assets	–	Total Current Liabilities	=	Working Capital
$1,000	–	$400	=	$600

Effects in a symbol format: $\uparrow$ = Increased $\downarrow$ = Decreased   nc = No Change

CA = Current Assets   CL = Current Liabilities   WC = Working Capital

CA, $\uparrow$ – CL, nc = WC, $\uparrow$ CA, $\downarrow$ – CL, nc = WC, $\downarrow$
CA, nc – CL, $\uparrow$ = WC, $\downarrow$ CA, nc – CL, $\downarrow$ = WC, $\uparrow$

HOW MUCH WORKING CAPITAL?

What is the amount of working capital a hotel, motel, restaurant, or bar needs available during an operating period? This question cannot be answered in general terms that identify an absolute dollar amount. For example, suppose it were a rule of thumb that an operation should have working capital of $5,000 available. A small restaurant that maintains small amounts of cash, inventories for resale, credit cards, and accounts receivables, and other items that are current assets, might find itself with the following working capital:

Current assets	$15,000	{Current assets	÷	Current liabilities	=	Current Ratio}
Current liabilities	(10,000)	{$15,000	÷	$10,000	=	1.5 : 1}
Working capital	$ 5,000					

A much larger restaurant would have to have larger amounts of cash, inventories for resale, credit card receivables and accounts receivables, and other items that are current assets. It would also be expected to have larger amounts in its various current liability accounts. Its working capital could look like this:

Current assets	$100,000	{Current assets	÷	Current liabilities	=	Current Ratio}
Current liabilities	(95,000)	{$15,000	÷	$10,000	=	1.5 : 1}
Working capital	$ 5,000					

The smaller restaurant is in much better financial shape than the larger one. The former has $1.50 of current assets for each $1.00 of current liabilities, a comfortable cushion. The latter has just over $1.05 of current assets for each dollar of current liabilities, a not-so-comfortable cushion.

As a general rule, a business would prefer to have a 2:1 current ratio, or at least $2.00 of current assets for each $1.00 of current liabilities. This would mean that its working capital (current assets $2.00, minus $1.00) is equivalent to its current liabilities. However, this rule is primarily for companies that need to carry very large inventories that do not turn over very rapidly. On the other hand, restaurants have inventories of food and beverages that, due in part to their perishable nature and the restaurant's ability to replace its inventories for resale frequently, mean a hospitality business can operate with a current ratio of less than 2:1.

Hotels and motels have an inventory that is primarily made up of rooms that appear under fixed, long-lived assets. Relatively speaking, this allows hotels and motels to frequently operate with a very low ratio of current assets to current liabilities, often as low as 1:1. In other words, for each $1.00 of current assets, there is $1.00 of current liabilities. This means that the hotel, motel in fact has no working capital.

At certain times of the year, seasonal hospitality operations may work in a negative working capital position, where current liabilities are greater than current assets. Such an operation during its peak seasonal operating period would have current assets greatly in excess of current liabilities. The reverse situation will prevail in the off-season. During the preopening period of a hospitality operation, a negative working capital will normally exist.

SUMMARY

Two of the most useful documents to support financial statements are the statement of cash flows and a statement of working capital analysis. These two statements are tied together by the analysis of current assets and current liabilities.

The statement of cash flow will attempt to determine the changes that have occurred in the cash account over a specified operating period. The statement is used to convert accrual net income (or net loss) to a cash basis. The conversion process in itself serves to identify sources of cash inflows and the uses of cash outflows, and is commonly used to evaluate the condition of a business entity.

In general, the statement is broken into three separate areas of business activities in which net cash flows are shown as a positive increase or a negative decrease. The first section conducts an analysis of net cash flows from operations that identifies sources of cash flows as net income and decreases in current asset operating accounts (except cash). An operating net loss and increases in current liability accounts are treated as cash outflows. The operating activities section also recognizes the use of noncash expenses such as depreciation and amortization shown in an accrual net income or net loss statement by adding back such noncash expenses to the reported accrual income or loss. In addition, reported losses on the disposal of long-lived assets added back and gains of the disposal of such items are deducted from the reported accrual income or loss.

The final proof of the correctness of a statement of cash flows is to verify that final net cash flow (positive or negative) is in fact the same amount that occurred and is shown in the cash account over the operating period.

As we have seen, the current assets and current liabilities are also the major accounts viewed during an analysis of working capital, as well as an analysis of working capital sources of inflows and uses outflows. This same type of analysis allows insight as to where cash is coming from and where it is going. From that aspect, the statement of cash flows helps measure the effectiveness of cash management.

The second section reviews investing activities, such as the acquisition or sales of long-lived assets and the acquisition or sale of long-lived investments. The acquisitions of such items are treated as cash *use* outflows, and the sales of such items are treated as cash *source* inflows.

The third section of the statement of cash flows views cash inflows and outflows by reviewing the two primary methods used to acquire capital—the sale of ownership equity and the assumption of long-term debt. If ownership equity (stock) is sold or long-term debt is borrowed, the proceeds are treated as cash inflow source. On the other hand, if ownership equity is repurchased (treasury stock) by the business entity or long-term debt is repaid, they are treated as cash use outflows. If cash dividends are paid during the operating period, the amount of dividends paid are treated as cash use outflows.

A statement of source inflows and use outflows of working capital, also relies heavily on an effective analysis of the major operating accounts, current assets and current liabilities. Working capital is defined as current assets minus current liabilities.

In addition to showing how working capital has changed from one operating period to the next, the statement of source inflows and use outflows, management can gain insight into how effectively working capital is being handled. This statement along with a statement of cash flows will provide creditors insight relative to the use of credit by the business operation.

The major source inflows of working capital are:

- Income for operations, with noncash expense items of depreciation and amortization added back.
- Sales of long-lived or other assets.
- The borrowing of additional long-term debt.
- The sale of stock equity.

The major uses of working capital are:

- Net loss from operations.
- Purchase of long-lived or other assets.
- Payments on the principle of long-term debt.
- Repurchase by the business of its own outstanding stock (treasury stock).
- Payment of cash dividends.

A transaction that affects only two current assets accounts will not affect working capital. For example, if payment of $100 is received on a receivable, the cash account will increase by $100 and the current receivable will decrease by the same amount; no overall change to current assets has occurred, the $100 of a current receivable has simply been reclassified. If a single current asset account changes and in the same transaction a single current liability account changes, no change in working capital will exist. The forms of an exchange of a current asset for a current asset or the creation of a current asset and a current liability in the same amount in a transaction would not appear on a statement of source inflows and use outflows.

To prepare a statement of source inflows and use outflows of working capital, the following are required:

- Balance sheets for the two latest consecutive periods of operations.
- An income statement for the operating period just ended.
- A statement of retained earnings and necessary supporting information for the operating period just ended.
- Other necessary supporting information regarding changes in property plant and equipment (fixed assets) and long–term liability accounts, and other assets not available in the balance sheets.

The statement of source inflows and use outflows of working capital identifies only the change and the cause of the changes that determined net working capital. This statement will not identify changes to individual current asset and current liability working capital accounts. This detail is shown in the statement of cash flows, indirect method, which was discussed in this chapter.

DISCUSSION QUESTIONS

1. What is the purpose of the statement of cash flows, indirect method?
2. What are the major operating accounts by category analyzed in the statement of cash flows, indirect method?
3. If a current asset account increases, how is the increase treated in the statement of cash flows?
4. What is the typical noncash item, by name, that is automatically added back in the operating activities section of the statement of cash flows?
5. The financing section of a statement of cash flows can analyze three different items by category. What are they?
6. What are the primary items by category analyzed in the statement of cash flows, investing section?
7. What is working capital?
8. Of what use is the statement of source inflows and use outflows of working capital?
9. List the three major common source inflows and the three major common use outflows of working capital.
10. Explain why depreciation expense is treated as a source inflow of working capital.
11. What is a statement of source inflows and use outflows of working capital?
12. If a business operation has a current ratio of 1.25:1, what does this mean relative to working capital?

ETHICS SITUATION

A motel owner needs to borrow money from her bank. The bank manager has asked for statements of source and use of working capital for the past three years to support the loan application. In preparing these statements, the motel owner omits to show that dividends of $10,000 a year were paid out in each of the last three years. Discuss the ethics of this situation.

EXERCISES

10.1   The following lists current asset and current liability accounts. Identify each account as a current asset (CA) or a current liability (CL) account. After classifying each account, determine how the change in the account balance is treated in the conversion of accrual net income to the cash basis, indirect method. Use (+) for a positive amount being added back, (−) for a negative amount being deducted.

Account Title	CA-CL	Change in the Account		
		Increase	or	Decrease
Credit card receivables	_____	_____		_____
Accounts payable	_____	_____		_____
Inventory (for resale)	_____	_____		_____
Accounts receivable	_____	_____		_____
Prepaid expenses	_____	_____		_____
Accrued payroll payable	_____	_____		_____
Interest payable	_____	_____		_____
Marketable securities	_____	_____		_____

10.2   A monthly income statement reported net income of $80,000. Inventory for resale increased by $14,000. Accounts payable increased by $16,000. Using only these three items, determine the net cash flow from operations, indirect method.

10.3   Net income is $260,000; Depreciation expense is $42,000; Accounts receivable increased $2,500; Credit card receivables decreased $4,600; Prepaid insurance increased $2,400; Inventory increased by $4,500; Accounts payable decreased $3,000; and accrued payroll payable increased $3,600. Complete net cash flow from operations activities, indirect method.

10.4   Identify how each of the following items would be treated in an analysis of changes to working capital. Answer with word INFLOW to show an increase or OUTFLOW to show a decrease in working capital.

Net income	_____	Sale of equity stock	_____
Net loss	_____	Purchase of equipment	_____

Depreciation	_____	Repayment of long-term debt	_____
Cash dividends	_____	Increasing long-term debt	_____
Sale of equipment	_____		

10.5 The following statements relate to accrual income statement items. Complete each of the statements below, indicating whether the item will be *added* or *deducted* in the net cash flow from operations section, statement of cash flows, indirect method.

Depreciation and amortization expense items are _____.

Losses on the disposal of long term assets are _____.

A current asset account increased, the increase is _____.

A current liability account increased, the increase is _____.

Gains on the disposal of long-term assets are _____.

10.6 Given the following information regarding investing and financing activities of a statement of cash flows, indirect method, evaluate each of the given transactions and identify to which section—Investing (INV) or Financing (FIN)—the transaction belongs. In addition, identify how the amount is handled. Use (+) for a positive add back amount or (–) for a negative, deduct amount, in the adjustment conversion in the Statement of Cash Flows, Indirect method.

INV./FIN.	Increase/Decrease	
_____	_____	Purchased equipment for $18,000.
_____	_____	Sold 8,000 shares of equity stock.
_____	_____	Sold office furniture for $26,000.
_____	_____	Paid $100,000, long-term investment.
_____	_____	Paid $145,000 in cash dividends.
_____	_____	Repurchased equity stock for $84,500.
_____	_____	Paid long-term debt $250,000.

10.7 Assume working capital was $44,000 for a given year. During this year, accounts receivable decreased by $1,400, inventory increased by $8,000, and accounts payable decreased by $2,000. Determine the amount of cash from operations.

10.8 Assume the book value of an item of equipment shows $50,000 in year one and $44,000 in year two. Would the $6,000 difference be treated as an inflow source, outflow use, or not shown at all with regard to its effect on working capital?

10.9 A review of a balance sheet indicated the beginning and ending totals of current assets and current liabilities for a one-year operating period. Determine the working capital at the beginning and the end of the year. Find the change in current assets, current liabilities, and working capital.

	Current Assets	Current Liabilities	Working Capital
January 1, 2002	$178,500	$89,250	$
December 31, 2002	122,400	76,500	_____
Change, current assets	$_____		
Change, current liabilities		$_____	
Change in working capital			$_____

10.10   Assume a business enterprise reports its total current assets as $24,000 and its total current liabilities as $16,000. Answer the following:

a. What is the amount of working capital?

b. What is the current ratio (also called the working capital ratio)?

c. Will the working capital or its ratio change if a transaction collects $2,800 in cash from its credit card receivables?

10.11   A restaurant purchased new kitchen equipment for $35,000. Old kitchen equipment was sold for $800. A long-term investment was sold for $50,000. Equity stock was repurchased $12,000, and a cash dividend was paid in the amount of $40,000. The company increased its long-term debt by $70,000.

a. Determine the net cash flow from investing activities. $_____

b. Determine the net cash flow from financing activities. $_____

10.12   The following are operating transactions that occurred during the current year of operations. Analyze each transaction and determine if the transaction will increase, decrease, or have no effect on working capital.

a. Purchased inventory on account, $5,400; terms 2/5, n/30.

b. Borrowed $40,000 on a long-term note.

c. Sold old equipment with a book value of $1,000 for $650.

d. Sold marketable securities at a gain of $2,400.

e. Paid $1,200 for insurance covering one year from the date of purchase.

PROBLEMS

10.1   The following information is extracted from the financial statements of a small restaurant bar operation. Complete a statement of cash flows, operating activities *only*, indirect method.

a. Net income for the year is $20,000.

b. Accounts receivable increased by $12,000.

c. Inventory decreased by $4,000.

d. Depreciation expense for the year is $8,000.

e. Accounts payable decreased by $6,000.

f. Other current liabilities increased by $2,000.

10.2 Balance sheet information for a resort hotel reflects the changes to current accounts that occurred over the annual operating period ended December 31, 0005. Additional information is also provided to complete a cash flow analysis. Cash account balance at 12-31-0004 was $14,000 and the cash balance at 12-31-0005 is $27,600.

Current Asset Accounts	Change	Amount
Cash	Increased	$13,600
Credit card receivables	Increased	1,680
Accounts receivable	Increased	1,120
Inventories	Increased	800
Prepaid expenses	Decreased	500
Current Liability Accounts		
Accounts payable	Decreased	$ 1,100
Accrued payroll payable	Increased	1,200
Taxes payable	Decreased	800
Current mortgage payable	Decreased	200

Additional information applying to the current year ending 12-31-0005:

a. Net income for the year 0005 was $113,400.

b. Depreciation expense for the year 0005 was $121,500.

c. Furnishings with a book value of $1,400 were sold for $5,400.

d. Equipment with a book value of $2,200 was sold for $1,800.

e. New furnishings were purchased for $14,800.

f. New equipment was purchased for $22,200.

g. A total of $55,600 was paid to reduce long-term debt.

h. Cash dividends were declared and paid in the amount of $128,300.

Using the information provided, complete a statement of cash flows, in good form using the indirect method.

10.3 You have the following comparative balance sheets for a restaurant for the years ending December 31, 0001 and December 31, 0002. Calculate the amount of change in working capital and prepare the restaurant's statement of source and use of working capital for the year ending December 31, 0002.

a. Net income for year $7,000. Annual depreciation of $1,000 was included as an expense to arrive at net income.

b. New equipment costing $4,000 was purchased.

c. Dividends of $6,000 were paid out.

d. New shares (100 at $10 each) were issued.

e. The long-term loan was increased by $2,000.

	0001	0002
ASSETS		
Cash	$14,800	$15,600
Accounts receivable	8,300	7,700
Food and beverage inventories	7,900	9,700
Furniture and equipment	15,500	19,500
Accumulated depreciation	(3,500)	(4,500)
Total	$43,000	$48,000
LIABILITIES & STOCKHOLDERS' EQUITY		
Accounts payable	$ 5,600	$ 7,800
Income tax payable	1,400	200
Long-term loan	25,800	27,800
Common stock	4,200	5,200
Retained earnings	6,000	7,000
Total	$43,000	$48,000

10.4   Refer to information provided in the preceding Problem 10.3 and complete in good form a statement of cash flows using the indirect method.

10.5   A motel has the following comparative balance sheets for two years:

Assets	12-31-01	12-31-02
Current Assets		
Cash	$ 4,100	$ 5,200
Credit card receivables	4,700	5,500
Accounts receivable	1,200	700
Inventory	3,000	3,600
Marketable securities	8,000	7,000
Prepaid expenses	1,200	1,500
Total Current Assets	$ 22,200	$ 23,500
Fixed Assets		
Land	30,000	30,000
Building,	150,000	150,000
Accum. Depreciation, building	(41,900)	(50,200)
Furniture & equipment	22,700	25,400
Accum. Depreciation, furniture & equipment	(15,400)	(19,100)
Total Fixed Assets	$145,400	$136,100
Total Assets	$167,600	$159,600
Liabilities & Stockholders' Equity		
Current Liabilities		
Accounts payable	$ 6,900	$ 6,800
Accrued expenses payable	1,400	1,900
Income taxes payable	2,000	1,500
Current portion of mortgage payable	11,500	10,400

Long Term Liabilities		
Long-term mortgage payable	100,000	89,600
Total Liabilities	$121,800	$110,200
Stockholders Equity		
Capital stock, common	23,000	23,000
Retained earnings	22,800	26,400
Total Stockholders' Equity	$ 45,800	$ 49,400
Total Liabilities & Stockholders' Equity	$167,600	$159,600

From this information, prepare a statement of changes to individual working accounts.

10.6 With the balance sheet information from Problem 10.5, and the additional information from the income statement and statement of retained earnings, prepare the motel's statement of changes to working capital for the year ending December 31, 0002.

Income Statement for Year Ended December 31, 0002

Revenue	$204,900
Operating costs	173,800
Income before depreciation and interest and tax	31,100
Depreciation	(12,000)
Income before interest and tax	$ 19,100
Interest	(10,800)
Income before tax	8,300
Income tax	(1,500)
Net income	$ 6,800

Statement of Retained Earnings for Year Ended December 31, 0002

Retained earnings January 1, 0002	$ 22,800
Add: Net income for year	6,800
Subtotal	$ 29,600
Deduct: Dividends paid	(3,200)
Retained earnings December 31, 0002	$ 26,400

10.7 Referring to the preceding Problems 10.5 and 10.6 that presented a comparative balance sheet, income statement, and a statement of retained earnings, complete a statement of cash flows in good form using the indirect method.

10.8 A catering company reported the following additional financial information to accompany a statement of retained earnings and a comparative balance sheet for two successive years.

Additional financial information:

1. In year 0002, the building that was previously rented was purchased for $150,000. The company paid $10,000 cash and assumed a long-term mortgage for $140,000. Depreciation on the building is $7,500 for year 0002. Note: At the end of year 0002, $7,100 of the mortgage payable was reclassified as a current liability payable in year 0003.

2. New stock was issued for cash, 200 shares at $50.00 each.

Statement of Retained Earnings
for Year Ended December 31, 0002

Retained earnings December 31, 0001	$29,900
Operating loss for year 0002	(8,100)
Retained earnings December 31, 0002	$21,800

The equipment account, and its accumulated depreciation contra account, is shown below:

	Equipment	Accum.
Balance December 31, 0001	$31,700	$5,800
Purchased new equipment	6,300	
Disposed of fully depreciated old equipment	(4,100)	(4,100)
Depreciation expense year 0002		4,500
Balance December 31, 0002	$33,900	$6,200

Comparative Balance Sheet

Current Assets	Dec. 31, 0001	Dec. 31, 0002
Cash	$ 8,600	$ 15,000
Accounts receivable	19,800	15,800
Inventory, food	6,100	6,300
Prepaid expenses	1,200	1,700
Total Current Assets	$35,700	$ 38,800
Non-current, Fixed Assets		
Building	-0-	150,000
Accumulated depreciation, building	-0-	(7,500)
Equipment	31,700	33,900
Accumulated depreciation, equipment	(5,800)	(6,200)
Total Non-current, Fixed Assets	$25,900	$170,200
Total Assets	$61,600	$209,000

Liabilities and Stockholders' Equity
Current Liabilities

Accounts payable	$21,200	$ 25,400
Accrued expenses	7,500	8,800
Current portion of mortgage payable	0	7,100
Total Current Liabilities	$28,700	$ 41,300
Long-Term Liabilities		
Long-term mortgage payable	0	$132,900
Stockholder's Equity		
Common stock	$ 3,000	$ 13,000
Retained earnings	29,900	21,800
Total Stockholders' Equity	$32,900	$ 34,800
Total Liabilities and Stockholders' Equity	$61,600	$209,000

Determine the changes in working capital and prepare the company's statement of sources (inflows) and uses (outflows) for the year ended December 31, 0002.

10.9 A motel has the following balance sheets at the end of each of its most recent two years of operation.

Assets	12-31-0001	12-31-0002
Cash	$ 8,800	$ 0
Accounts receivable	17,200	30,600
Inventory	2,100	5,500
Land	20,000	20,000
Building	50,600	100,600
Accumulated depreciation, building	(30,000)	(40,000)
Total Assets	$68,700	$116,700

Liabilities and Stockholders' Equity		
Accounts payable	$ 6,700	$ 12,800
Bank loan	0	7,900
Long-term mortgage on building	0	30,000
Common stock	2,000	2,000
Retained earnings	60,000	64,000
Total Liabilities and Stockholders' Equity	$68,700	$116,700

The income statements provide the following information:

	Dec. 31, 0001	Dec. 31, 0002
Revenue	$100,000	$110,000
Operating costs	90,000	93,200
Net income	$ 10,000	$ 16,800

The statement of retained earnings for year 0002 shows:

Retained earnings December 31, 0001	$60,000
Net income for year 0002	16,800
Subtotal	76,800
Dividends	(12,800)
Retained earnings December 31, 0002	$64,000

The owner cannot understand why he has $64,000 of retained earnings and if he had net income of $16,800 of profit during the year, he has no money in the bank. Give him any explanations you can, using this information.

CASE 10

a. Given the budgeted income statement prepared in Case 9 and the following additional information, prepare a budgeted balance sheet for 4C Company as of December 31, 0002.

- *Cash.* As a result of carrying out a cash budget for year 0002 (this topic will be discussed in Chapter 11), the forecast of the cash balance at December 31, 0002 is $34,400.
- *Current receivables* of December 31, 0002 are estimated to be $14,742 for credit cards receivable and $5,615 for accounts receivable.
- *Food and beverage inventories* as of December 31, 0002 are estimated to be $7,400 for food inventory and $2,510 for beverage inventory.
- *Prepaid expenses.* These are estimated to be $2,400 at December 31, 0002.
- *Furniture and equipment.* No purchases or sales will be made during year 0002.
- *Accounts payable* are estimated to be $9,200 as of December 31, 0002.
- *Accrued expenses payable* are estimated to be $2,510 as of December 31, 0002.
- *Income taxes payable* from year 0002 will not be paid until year 0003.
- *Current (portion of) loan payable* is estimated to be $42,741 due in year 0003.
- *Common stock.* $10,000 of stock will be bought back (treasury stock) by 4C Company from Charlie for cash early in year 0002.

Note: Round final number values to the nearest dollar.

b. After completing the balance sheet, prepare a statement of changes to working capital accounts for the year 0002. Refer to Case 2 balance sheet for December 31, 0001.

c. Prepare a budgeted statement of inflows (sources) and outflows (uses) of working capital for year 0002.

11

Cash Management

INTRODUCTION

This chapter introduces the reader to the concept of cash flow, explaining how cash flows into and out of a company. The fact that net income shows on an income statement but does not necessarily mean there is an equivalent amount of cash in the bank is discussed and illustrated.

The method of compiling a cash budget from cash receipts and cash disbursements is demonstrated. Negative cash flow may result at times. Various other nonrecurring transactions that could affect the preparation of a cash budget are also discussed.

The subject of cash conservation and working capital management is covered. Included are such items as cash on hand and in the bank, use of bank float, concentration banking, use of two bank accounts, accounts receivable, use of lockboxes, aging of accounts, marketable securities, inventories, and accounts payable.

Finally, the topic of long-range cash flow (as opposed to short-term cash budgeting), including the use of CVP analysis (taking income tax into consideration) to convert required cash flow to a sales revenue figure, is discussed and illustrated.

CHAPTER OBJECTIVES

After studying this chapter, the reader should be able to:

1. Explain why cash planning is necessary and state the two main purposes of cash budgeting.

2. Explain why net income on an income statement is not necessarily indicative of the amount of cash on hand.

3. List items that would appear under cash receipts and cash disbursements on a cash budget and prepare a cash budget given appropriate information.

4. Define bank float and discuss the concept of concentration banking.

5. Explain some of the procedures that can be used to minimize accounts receivable outstanding at any given time, including the use of a lockbox.

6. Prepare a schedule of aging of accounts receivable.

7. Discuss the importance of marketable securities with reference to surplus cash funds.

8. Calculate inventory turnover.

9. Explain long-term cash flow budgeting, and use CVP to calculate the revenue required to provide a desired cash flow amount.

CASH MANAGEMENT

Simply stated, cash management is the management of money so that bills and debts are paid when they are due. Money does not always come into a business at the same rate as it goes out. At times there will be excess cash on hand; at other times there will be shortages of cash. Both these events need to be anticipated so that surpluses can be used to advantage and shortages can be covered. In this way the cash balance will be kept at its optimum level.

While the statement of cash flows discussed in Chapter 2 allows an analysis of inflows and outflows of cash on an annual basis, this chapter mainly discusses inflows and outflows of cash on a monthly basis.

THE CYCLE OF CASH FLOW

The cycle of cash flow through an enterprise is illustrated in Exhibit 11.1. This shows that cash management is not just a problem of making sure that the balance of cash in the bank is correct and that the cashiers have the right amount of money on hand. Rather, it is management of all working capital accounts—cash, inventories, accounts receivable, plus the management of accounts payable and loan payments—and of discretionary spending items, such as purchase of new capital assets and payment of dividends if cash is available

Cash budgets aid in control

Control over all these various items of cash receipts and cash disbursements can be managed by preparing cash budgets. The importance of cash planning, or cash budgets, can best be explained by showing that the net income that a company has on its income statement (the excess of sales revenue over expenditure) is not necessarily indicative of the amount of cash the company has on hand.

Exhibit 11.1   Illustration of the Cash Flow Cycle

```
┌─────────────────┐                              ┌──────────────────────┐
│ Initial invest- │                              │ Most of initial      │
│ ment by stock-  │        ┌────────┐            │ investment will      │
│ holders and     │───────▶│  CASH  │───────────▶│ be required for land,│
│ other investors │        └────────┘            │ building, furniture, │
└─────────────────┘             │                │ & equipment          │
                                │                └──────────────────────┘
                                ▼
                     ┌────────────────────┐
                     │ Balance of initial │
                     │ investment will be │
                     │ for food, beverages│
                     │ supplies, services,│
┌─────────────────┐  │ payroll, and other │
│ Period of cycle │  │ operating expenses,│
│ that, depending │  │ which are necessary│
│ on type of      │  │ to provide revenue.│
│ transaction,    │  └────────────────────┘
│ could vary from │      │            │
│ one day to one  │      ▼            ▼
│ month or more in│  ┌────────┐  ┌────────┐
│ a hotel or food │  │CHARGE  │  │ CASH   │
│ service organi- │  │REVENUE │  │REVENUE │
│ zation.         │  │(Accounts  └────────┘
└─────────────────┘  │Receivable)     │
                     └────────┘        │
                         │             │
                         ▼             ▼
                     ┌────────┐   ┌──────────────────────┐
                     │  CASH  │──▶│ Income tax, repayment │
                     └────────┘   │ of loans, dividends   │
                         │        │ to stockholders,      │
                         ▼        │ re-investment in      │
                 ┌───────────────┐│ building, furniture,  │
                 │ Start of New  ││ & equipment           │
                 │ Cycle         │└──────────────────────┘
                 └───────────────┘
```

NET INCOME IS NOT CASH

Let us consider a simple illustration. An entrepreneur has an opportunity to take over a restaurant, fully equipped and furnished, for a rent of $2,000 a month. He decides that his cash savings of $10,000 should be sufficient working capital to start the business, after which the cash from sales revenue should keep the business going and allow him to take out a salary of $1,500 a month. Prior to opening, his balance sheet would look like this:

Assets		Liabilities and Equity	
Cash	$10,000	Owner's investment	$10,000

Cash required for
inventory

However, before he can sell any food he has to use some of his cash for inventory; let us assume he needs $5,000. The balance sheet is now:

Assets		Liabilities and Equity	
Cash	$ 5,000	Owner's investment	$10,000
Inventory	5,000		
	$10,000	Owner's investment	$10,000

The owner is ready for business. During the first month, he has the operating results shown in Exhibit 11.2: total sales revenue of $20,000, total ex-
penses of $18,000, and a net income of $2,000.

Accounts receivable
outstanding

As a result, one might expect to see the bank account increased by $2,000;
but in our case this is not so. Even though sales revenue is $20,000, in order to
achieve this level of sales the owner decided to permit some customers to sign
their bills, send them invoices at the end of the month, and collect the cash in
month 2. In addition, some customers used national credit cards, which he
agreed to honor. As a result, at the end of the month there were $7,000 of ac-
counts receivable and the cash income was only $13,000.

As far as expenses are concerned, the owner did not have to expend any
cash for the food cost of $5,000. He simply used up the inventory, which had
already been paid for.

The actual cash outlays during the first month were for owner's salary,
other wages, suppliers and other expenses, and rent. None of these items were
obtainable on credit, so the net cash expenditures totaled $13,000. In summary:

Cash receipts	$13,000
Cash disbursements	(13,000)
Net change in bank balance	0

Exhibit 11.2   Illustrative Income Statement

Sales revenue		$20,000
Food cost		5,000
Gross profit		$15,000
Owner's salary	$1,500	
Other wages	6,500	
Supplies and other expenses	3,000	
Rent	2,000	13,000
Net income		$ 2,000

Replacement of
inventory

However, since the food inventory has been used up, it has to be replaced, and this will require $5,000 cash. Therefore, since at the beginning of the month there was a bank balance (see earlier balance sheet) of $5,000, the month-end bank balance will be:

Bank balance beginning of the month	$5,000
Change in bank balance from operations	0
Reduction in bank balance for replacement of inventory	(5,000)
Bank balance end of month	0

The month-end balance sheet will now be:

Assets		Liabilities and Equity	
Cash	$ 0	Owner's investment	$10,000
Accounts receivable	7,000	Net income for month	2,000
Inventory	5,000	(Retained earnings)	
	$12,000	Owner's investment	$12,000

Net income but no cash

The balance sheet shows us that, despite the fact there is a net income for the first month, there is no cash in the bank to pay any other immediate expenses. Although this is an oversimplified illustration, it is not untypical of what happens to new businesses and indicates the danger of assuming that any net income on the income statement is going to be in the form of cash. In this case, the net income of $2,000 and the $5,000 of cash the owner started out with at the beginning of the month are now tied up in the accounts receivable of $7,000.

The same principle applies in an ongoing concern. The income statement net income is not generally synonymous with cash. The timing of the cash coming in from sales revenue may not parallel the timing of cash going out to pay for operating expenses. To prevent this difficulty—to see whether a business is going to have excesses or shortages of cash—a cash budget prepared in advance month by month for a year, or at least every quarter, is a useful management tool.

INCOME AND EXPENSE BUDGETS

The starting point in cash budgeting is the income statement showing the budgeted revenues and expenditures by month for as long a period as is required for cash budget preparation. In our case, a three-month period has been selected, and budgeted income statements for a restaurant for the months of April, May, and June are shown in Exhibit 11.3

Exhibit 11.3   Illustration of Budgeted Income and Expenses

	April		May		June	
Sales revenue		$30,000		$35,000		$40,000
Food cost		(12,000)		(14,000)		(16,000)
Gross profit		$18,000		$21,000		$24,000
Payroll and related expense	$9,000		$10,500		$12,000	
Supplies and other expense	1,500		1,750		2,000	
Utilities	500		750		1,000	
Rent	1,000		1,000		1,000	
Advertising	500	(12,500)	500	(14,500)	500	(16,500)
Income before depreciation		$ 5,500		$ 6,500		$ 7,500
Depreciation		(2,000)		(2,000)		(2,000)
Net income		$ 3,500		$ 4,500		$ 5,500

In order to prepare our cash budget we need the following additional information:

Information required for cash budget

1. Accounting records show that, each month, approximately 60% of the sales revenue is in the form of cash and 40% is charged and collected the following month. (If this were a new business, the breakdown between cash and charge revenue would have to be estimated.)

2. March sales revenue was $28,000. (We need this information so that we can calculate the amount of cash that is going to be collected in April from sales made in March.)

3. Purchases of food (food cost) are paid 25% cash and 75% are on credit. The 75% (accounts payable) is paid the month following purchase.

4. March food purchases were $11,000. (Again, we need this information so that we can calculate the amount to be paid for in cash during April.)

5. Payroll, supplies, utilities, and rent are paid 100% cash during each current month.

6. Advertising has been prepaid in January ($6,000 cash) for the entire year. In order not to show the full $6,000 as an expense in January (since the benefit of the advertising is for a full year), the income statements show $500 each month for this prepaid expense.

7. The bank balance on April 1 is $10,200.

Note that the breakdown between cash and charge revenue and expenses is based on historic experience.

PREPARING THE CASH BUDGET

We can now use the budgeted income statements (Exhibit 11.3) and the above information to calculate the figures for our cash budget. The process is simple. Our first cash budget month is April.

Cash Receipts

Current month sales revenue $30,000 × 60% cash	=	$18,000
Accounts receivable collections, previous month sales revenue $28,000 × 40% charged	=	11,200

Cash Disbursements

Current month food purchases (food costs) $12,000 × 25% paid cash	=	3,000
Accounts payable for food purchases from previous month $11,000 × 75%	=	8,250
Payroll and related expense, 100% cash	=	9,000
Supplies and other expense, 100% cash	=	1,500
Utilities, 100% cash	=	500
Rent, 100% cash	=	1,000
Advertising: already paid in January, the $6,000 would have been shown as cash disbursement for that month	=	0
Depreciation: does not require an outlay of cash, it is simply a write-down of the book value of the related assets	=	0

Our completed cash budget for the month of April would then appear as in Exhibit 11.4.

The closing bank balance each month is calculated as follows:

Opening bank balance

+

Receipts

−

Disbursements

=

Closing bank balance

Closing balance becomes opening balance

Each month, the closing bank balance becomes the opening bank balance of the next month. The completed cash budget for the three-month period would be as in Exhibit 11.5. From Exhibit 11.5 it can be seen that the bank account is expected to increase from $10,200 to $30,150 over the next three

Exhibit 11.4   Illustration of Monthly Cash Budget

Opening bank balance	$10,200
Receipts	
Cash sales revenue	18,000
Collection on accounts receivable	11,200
Total	$39,400
Disbursements	
Cash food purchases	$ 3,000
Accounts payable	8,250
Payroll and related expense	9,000
Supplies and other expense	1,500
Utilities	500
Rent	1,000
Total	$23,250
Closing bank balance	$16,150

Exhibit 11.5   Illustration of Three-Month Cash Budget

	April	May	June
Opening bank balance	$10,200	$16,150	$22,650
Receipts			
Cash sales revenue	18,000	21,000	24,000
Collection on accounts receivable	11,200	12,000	14,000
Total	$39,400	$49,150	$60,650
Disbursements			
Cash food purchases	$ 3,000	$ 3,500	$ 4,000
Accounts payable	8,250	9,000	10,500
Payroll and related expense	9,000	10,500	12,000
Supplies and other expense	1,500	1,750	2,000
Utilities	500	750	1,000
Rent	1,000	1,000	1,000
Total	$23,250	$26,500	$30,500
Closing bank balance	$16,150	$22,650	$30,150

months. Continuing the cash budget over the following quarter would show whether or not the bank balance is going to continue to increase or start to decline.

From Exhibit 11.5 it is obvious that in this operation there is a fairly healthy surplus of cash (as long as budget projections are reasonably accurate) that should not be left to accumulate at no or low interest in a bank account. In this particular case, management might decide to take $20,000 or $25,000 out of the bank and invest it in high-interest, short-term (30-, 60-, or 90-day) securities. Without preparing a cash budget, it would be difficult for management to know that it was going to have surplus funds on hand that could be used to advantage to increase net income (and subsequently cash receipts). If the cash were taken out of the bank account and invested, the cash budget would have to show this (listed under disbursements); when the securities were cashed in, the amount would be recorded on the cash budget under receipts, along with the interest earned.

As the budget period goes by, the cash budget for the remaining months in that period may need to be adjusted to reflect any changed conditions.

Negative Cash Budget

On occasion some companies, particularly seasonal operations, may find that for some months in the year their disbursements exceed receipts to the point that they have negative cash amounts. Exhibit 11.6 illustrates such a situation. As can be seen, the operation will be short of cash by an estimated $1,000 in each of months 4 and 5. However, having prepared a cash budget ahead of time, the company has anticipated the cash shortage and can plan to cover it by means of a short-term bank loan or by stockholder or owner loans.

Other Transactions Affecting Cash Budget

Just as a cash investment (because of surplus cash) must be recorded on the cash budget, so much cash loans (from banks or stockholders, for example, to cover short-term requirements) be shown as receipts. Repayments of such loans are recorded as disbursements.

A number of other possible transactions could occur that must be recorded on the cash budget. For example, if any new long-term loans were negotiated, the cash received during a cash budget period must be shown under receipts, as would be cash received from any new issues of stock. If any fixed assets were sold for cash, this would also affect the receipts section of the cash budget.

On the other hand, any repayments of principal amount of loans, redemption of stock for cash, or purchases of new fixed assets would require entries in the disbursements section of the cash budget.

Use of surplus cash (margin note)

Seasonal negative cash flows (margin note)

Other possibilities (margin note)

Typical disbursements (margin note)

	Month 1	Month 2	Month 3	Month 4	Month 5	Month 6
Opening balance	5,000	7,000	8,000	4,000	(1,000)	(1,000)
Receipts	22,000	24,000	20,000	16,000	16,000	20,000
Total	27,000	31,000	28,000	20,000	15,000	19,000
Disbursements	20,000	23,000	24,000	21,000	16,000	16,000
Closing balance	7,000	8,000	4,000	(1,000)	(1,000)	3,000

Exhibit 11.6   Illustration of Negative Cash Flow

Finally, any dividends paid would further reduce cash on hand and therefore require an entry in the disbursements section.

The cash budget, particularly if prepared for a year ahead, can not only help management in making decisions about investing excess funds and arranging to borrow funds to cover shortages, but also aids in making discretionary decisions concerning such factors as major renovations, replacement of fixed assets, and payment of dividends.

A cash budget, if carefully prepared, permits management to plan ahead to do or not do certain things, depending on cash availability. If decisions are made and plans prepared for major spending items without a cash budget having been prepared, sudden shortages of cash may develop. These shortages may not be able to be covered quickly with loans because no plans had been made to arrange for loans.

CASH CONSERVATION AND WORKING CAPITAL MANAGEMENT

Whether a company feels that a cash budget is advantageous is a matter for that company's management to decide. However, there are certain practices that any hospitality operator should institute as a matter of good business sense in order to conserve cash, earn interest on it (one possibility), and thus maximize net income. Some of these more common practices are discussed.

CASH ON HAND

Surplus cash to earn interest

Cash on hand, as distinguished from cash in the bank, is the amount of money in circulation in an operation. This cash is used by cashiers as "floats" for change-making purposes, petty cash, or just general cash in the organization's safe. The amount of cash on hand should be sufficient for normal day-to-day operations only. Any surplus, idle cash should be deposited in savings accounts so that it can earn interest. Preferably each day's net cash receipts should be deposited in the bank as soon as possible on the following day.

CASH IN BANK

Cash in the bank in the current account should be sufficient to pay only current bills due or current payroll. Any excess funds should be invested in short-term securities (making sure there is a good balance between maximizing the interest rate and security and liquidity of the investment) or in savings or other special accounts that earn interest. The typical hospitality industry enterprise will probably determine an appropriate level of cash to be held after considering the following:

Considerations

- Anticipated cash flows indicated by the cash budget.
- Unanticipated events causing deviations from the cash budget.
- Ability to borrow money for emergencies above the minimal cash requirements plus any precautionary amounts.
- Desire of management to always have more than sufficient cash on hand rather than maintaining a minimum level (this minimum level may aid in increasing net income, but at the same time it will increase risk).
- Efficiency of the cash management system (the more efficient the business's system, the more surplus cash will be available for investment and increased profits).
- Historical evidence and past experience, which can be a guide to establishing satisfactory levels of cash.

USE OF FLOATS

Reason for difference

A float is the difference between the bank balance shown on a company's records and the balance of actual cash in the bank. There is a difference because checks a company writes are deducted from its record of the bank balance at that time. However, there is a delay between that time (due to mailing and the handling of the check by the recipient and then by his bank) and the time that the check is received by the company's bank and deducted from its records. If a company can estimate the amount of this float and the period of time involved, it can then invest the amount for that period and increase its net income.

CONCENTRATION BANKING

Concentration banking (also known as integrated banking) might be appropriate for chain-operated hotels or restaurants. It is a method of accelerating the flow of funds from the individual units in the chain to the company's head office bank account. The individual units will still have accounts at the bank's

Head office makes
disbursements

local branch in the city where the unit is operated, but arrangements will be made with the local bank to transfer any surplus above a pre-determined level in the account to the head office's bank immediately.

Disbursements would be made out of the head office account on behalf of the individual units. Only sufficient cash to take care of normal day-to-day disbursements would be held in the account. Any surplus above this amount would be invested in such items as marketable securities (to be discussed later in this chapter). A concentration banking system results in more effective cash management for the entire chain. For example, there might be a temptation for a local unit manager to pay invoices before their due date to keep local suppliers happy. Also, if an individual unit requires cash, it can be provided by the head office so that the local unit manager does not have to negotiate a loan with his local banker at less favorable terms.

In concentration banking, it is important to minimize the cost of funds' transfers. In certain situations, daily transfers from the individual units to the head office account might not be the most appropriate action. To determine how frequently transfers should be made, the following equation may be used:

Transfer frequency
equation

$$\text{Transfer frequency} = \frac{2 \times \text{Average bank balance}}{\text{Average daily deposit}}$$

For example, if a restaurant unit were to require an average bank balance of $10,000, and if its average daily deposit was $2,000, the transfer frequency would be:

$$\frac{2 \times \$10,000}{\$2,000} = \frac{\$20,000}{\$2,000} = 10 \text{ days}$$

Elimination of transfers

This means that at the beginning of each ten-day period, the balance in the unit's bank account will be zero. At the end of ten days it will have accumulated to $20,000, at which time the full $20,000 is transferred, reducing the balance again to zero. Nine transfers are eliminated, thus minimizing transfer costs. In general, the only time that a daily transfer would be profitable for an operation would be if the average bank balance required were less than half the average daily deposit.

Two Bank Accounts

In addition to concentration banking, large chain operations can also benefit from the float effect by having one bank account on the East Coast and the other on the West Coast. Collections from the Pacific-side operations would be deposited in the West Coast bank; payments on behalf of these operations would be made from the East Coast bank. The reverse situation would exist for Atlantic-side operations.

Accounts Receivable

Mail invoices promptly

Attention to accounts receivable should be focused on two areas: ensuring that invoices are mailed out promptly and following up on delinquent accounts to have them collected. Money tied up in accounts receivable is money not earning a return. Extension of credit to customers is an acknowledged form of business transaction, but it should not be extended to the point of allowing payments to lag two or three months behind the mailing of invoices. In hotels a special situation arises. Accounts receivable in hotels are made up of city ledger accounts and house accounts. City ledger accounts include banquet and convention business, regular credit card charges for individuals using the hotel's food and beverage facilities, and the accounts of people who were staying in the hotel but who have checked out and charged their bills. Normal collection procedures prevail for collecting such accounts. The house accounts are for those registered in the hotel who have not yet checked out. In some cases such accounts can build up to large amounts in a very short time. A good policy is to establish a ceiling to which the dollar amount of an individual account may rise. Once this ceiling is reached, the night auditor can be instructed to advise the credit manager, or general manager in a smaller hotel, who must then decide whether or not any action should be taken to request payment, or partial payment, of the account, or discuss a credit arrangement with the guest. Where guests stay for longer periods without necessarily running up large accounts, a good policy is to give the guest a copy of the bill at least once a week. This serves two purposes. It allows the guest to confirm or question the accuracy of the account, and it suggests that payment should be made or arrangements for credit established.

Establish ceiling on house accounts

Aging of accounts

One of the ways to keep an eye on the accounts receivable is periodically (possibly once a month) to prepare a chart showing the age of the accounts outstanding. Exhibit 11.7 illustrates such a chart.

Exhibit 11.7 shows that the accounts receivable outstanding situation has not improved from March to April. In March, 79.5% of total receivables were less than 30 days old. In April only 74.2% were less than 30 days outstanding. Similarly, the relative percentages in the 31- to 60-day category have worsened from March to April. By contrast, in the 61- to 90-day bracket, 11.3% of receivables are outstanding in April, against only 3.2% in March. This particular aging chart shows that our accounts receivable are getting older. If this trend continued, collection procedures would need to be improved. If, after all

Exhibit 11.7   Analysis (Aging) of Accounts Receivable

Age	March 31		April 30	
0–30 days	$29,500	79.5%	$28,200	74.2%
31–60 days	5,900	15.9	4,400	11.6
61–90 days	1,200	3.2	4,300	11.3
Over 90 days	500	1.4	1,100	2.9
Totals	$37,100	100.0%	$38,000	100.0%

Uncollectible accounts

possible collection procedures have been explored, an account is deemed to be uncollectible (a bad debt), it would then be removed from accounts receivable. The decision on its uncollectibility in a small operation should be made by the manager or owner. In a larger operation, it would be made by the credit manager or comptroller.

LOCKBOXES

The collection of accounts receivable can also be speeded along by the use of a lockbox. Lockboxes are most appropriate for chain operations. When they are used, customers are directed to mail their checks in payment of accounts to a designated post office mailbox. The hospitality establishment's bank picks up the mail and deposits the receivables' payments into the hospitality operation's bank account and subsequently notifies the establishment of the necessary detail for it to record payments in its accounts receivable. The main advantages of the lockbox system are that the individual units in the chain are freed from receiving and depositing payment checks and that the collection process is speeded up by one or more days.

There is a cost attached to using a lockbox. To determine whether the added efficiency is profitable, the cost should be compared with the increased income from the cash released for investment elsewhere. If income exceeds cost, the system is profitable; if the reverse is the case, it is not.

Alternatively, it may be useful to calculate the minimum level of accounts receivable payment that would make a lockbox system profitable. Suppose that the bank charges 20 cents for each payment check handled and that the opportunity cost of alternative investments is 9%. (The opportunity cost is the interest that the hospitality operation could earn by investing freed-up cash in, let us say, marketable securities.) By using a lockbox, the collection of accounts receivable is speeded up by two days. An equation for determining the minimum level of accounts receivable that would make the lockbox system profitable is:

Lockbox equation

$$\frac{\text{Bank charge per item}}{\text{Opportunity cost percentage per day} \times \text{Time savings in days}}$$

Using our figures, the minimum accounts receivable amount is:

$$\frac{\$0.20}{(0.09/365) \times 2} = \frac{\$0.20}{0.00024666 \times 2} = \frac{\$0.20}{0.0004932} = \$405$$

Given these assumptions, this means that with a lockbox system, payments in excess of $405 on accounts receivable would be profitable and payments less than $405 would not be profitable. A decision could be made to use a lockbox if the average payment exceeded $405. Alternatively, a more profitable approach might be to handle accounts receivable according to size. For example, when the accounts are mailed out, those in excess of $405 would carry instructions to use the lockbox mailing address and those less than $405 would be handled in the regular manner.

MARKETABLE SECURITIES

Making investments

Generally, any surplus cash not needed for immediate and precautionary purposes should be invested in some type of security. Investments could be for as short a period as one day, but are usually for longer periods, although seldom more than a year. If surplus cash were available for periods of a year or more, it might then be wise to seek out long-term investments, such as building a new property or expanding an existing one, because the return on those investments over the long run could be expected to be greater than for investment in short-term securities.

Most hospitality industry enterprises, particularly those that rely for much or all of their trade on seasonal tourists, have peaks and valleys in their cash flows. Surplus cash from peak-season flows should be invested in short-term securities until it is necessary to liquidate them to take care of low, or negative, cash flows during the off-season. Sometimes it is necessary to build up surplus cash amounts to take care of periodic lump sum payments, such as quarterly tax or dividend payments. These built-up amounts could well be invested in marketable securities until they were needed for payment of these liabilities.

In times of high interest rates, many companies find it profitable to invest all cash in excess of day-to-day needs in the most liquid of marketable securities: that is, those that can be converted into cash quickly if an unanticipated event requiring cash occurs. In this way, little if any precautionary cash will be carried.

Risk versus liquidity

Two important factors need to be considered when investing in marketable securities: risk and liquidity. A low risk generally goes hand in hand with a low interest rate. A more risky investment would have to offer a higher interest rate in order to attract investors. Government securities have very low risk and usually guarantee that the security can be cashed in at full face value at any time. Their interest rate, however, is also relatively low. On the other hand, investments in long-term corporate bonds, with a distant maturity date, may offer a higher interest rate. This type of security is, however, subject to economic factors that make their buy-sell price more volatile. This volatility increases the risk and can reduce the profitability of investing in them if they have to be liquidated, or converted into cash, at an inappropriate time.

Short-term, liquid marketable securities include such items as government treasury bills, bankers' acceptances, short-term notes, bank deposit receipts, and corporate or finance company paper. Long-term, less liquid investments include corporate bonds, preferred and common stock, equipment trust certificates, and municipal securities.

INVENTORIES

The level at which inventories should be maintained for food and beverages can be established by calculating the inventory turnover rates for each. The turnover rate for food is calculated as follows:

Inventory turnover equation

$$\frac{\text{Food cost for the month}}{\text{Average food inventory during month}}$$

The inventory turnover could be calculated annually, but it is preferable to do it monthly, particularly if monthly income statements are prepared, because, if the turnover rate at the end of any month is out of line, corrective action can be taken then, instead of only at the year-end.

In the preceding equation, food cost is calculated as follows:

Beginning of the month inventory + Purchases during month

− End of month inventory

Average inventory calculation

Average inventory is calculated as follows:

(Beginning of the month inventory + End of the month inventory) ÷ 2

Assuming we had the following figures:

Beginning of the month inventory	$ 7,000
End of the month inventory	8,000
Purchases during month	24,500

our calculation of the inventory turnover rate is:

$$\frac{\$7,000 + \$24,500 - \$8,000}{(\$7,000 + \$8,000) \div 2} = \frac{\$23,500}{\$7,500} = 3.1 \text{ times}$$

Trend of turnover

Traditionally, the food industry food inventory turnover ranges between two and four times a month. At this level the danger of running out of food items is minimal; on the other hand, there is not an overinvestment in inventory tying up money that could otherwise be put to use earning interest income. However, despite this range of two to four times a month, there may be exceptions. Perhaps of more importance to an organization is not what its actual turnover rate is, but whether or not there is a change in this turnover rate over time, and what the cause of the change is. For example, let us assume that the earlier figures—$23,500 for food cost and $7,500 for average inventory, giving a turnover rate of 3.1—were typical of the monthly figures for this operation. If management noticed that the figure for turnover changed to two, this could mean that more money was being invested in inventory and not producing a return.

$$\frac{\$23,500}{\$11,750} = 2 \text{ times}$$

Too little in inventory

Alternatively, a change in the turnover rate to four could mean that too little was invested in inventory and that some customers may not be able to get certain items listed on the menu.

$$\frac{\$23,500}{\$5,875} = 4 \text{ times}$$

In some establishments, the turnover rate may be extremely low (less than two). For example, a resort property in a remote location may only be able to get deliveries once a month and is thus forced to carry a large inventory. On the other hand, a drive-in restaurant that receives daily delivery of its food items from a central commissary and carries little inventory overnight could conceivably have a turnover rate as high as 30 times a month. Each organization should establish its own standards for turnover and then watch for deviations from those standards.

Establish turnover standards

Beverage inventory turnover is calculated using the same formula, but it substitutes beverage inventories and beverage purchases for food. (The word "beverage" here applies to alcoholic beverages only.) The normal monthly turnover rate for beverages is from one-half to one turnover a month. Again, however, there are exceptions to this rule of thumb.

Accounts Payable, Accrued Expenses, and Other Current Liabilities

Consider taking discount

The objective here, to conserve cash in the organization, is to delay payment until payment is required. However, this does not mean delaying payment until it is delinquent! A company with a reputation for delinquency may find it has difficulty obtaining food, beverages, supplies, and services on anything other than a cash basis. If a discount for prompt payments is offered, the advantages of this should be considered. For example, a common discount rate is 2% off the invoice total if paid within ten days, otherwise payable without discount within 60 days. On a $1,000 purchase paid within ten days, this would save $20. This may not seem to be a lot of money, but multiplied many times over on all similar purchases made during a year, it could amount to a large sum. However, in the example cited, the company may have to borrow the money ($980) in order to make the payment within ten days. Let us assume the money was borrowed for 50 days at an 8% interest rate. The interest expense on this borrowed money would be:

$$\frac{\$980 \times 50 \text{ days} \times 8\%}{365 \text{ days}} = \$10.74$$

It would still be advantageous to borrow the money since the difference between the discount saving of $20.00 and the interest expense of $10.74 is still $9.26.

Other Items

There are other methods of operating with the objective of conserving cash in the business. One example is leasing, rather than purchasing, an asset in order to take advantage of a tax saving. This and other more long-range techniques are covered in Chapter 12.

LONG-RANGE CASH FLOW

The long-range cash flow budget differs somewhat from day-to-day cash budgeting. The long-range cash flow projections ignore any changes within working capital and assume that the current asset and liability amounts remain relatively constant over the long run. The long-range cash flow budget is usually prepared for yearly periods for up to five years ahead.

The starting point in preparation of a long-range cash flow budget is the annual net income figure. To this is added back the depreciation to convert the net income to a cash position, and from that amount is deducted the amount of any principal payments on long-term borrowings. A simple cash flow budget for five years appears in Exhibit 11.8.

The long-term cash flow budget serves the following purposes:

Purposes of long-range
cash budget

- Allows the manager to see whether there will be cash available to meet long-term mortgage, bond, or other loan commitments.
- Indicates a possible need to arrange additional long-term borrowings or the need to issue additional stock to raise cash.
- Allows for planning replacement of additions to long-term assets (note that if any long-term assets were bought or sold, the cash disbursed or received would be included in the cash flow projections).
- Permits the planning of a dividend payment policy since it shows whether or not there will be surplus cash available for dividends.

CASH FLOW AND CVP

CVP analysis (discussed in Chapter 8) can also be applied to cash flow. It can answer the question: How much sales revenue is needed to produce various levels of cash flow? For example, suppose the management of the operation illustrated in Exhibit 11.8 wanted a cash flow of $38,000 in year one, rather than the $30,000 illustrated. What would this require in terms of total sales revenue?

First, the desired cash flow has to be converted to an after-tax profit figure by adding to the desired cash flow the long-term loan payments and deducting depreciation as in Exhibit 11.8:

$$\$38,000 + \$60,000 - \$80,000 = \$18,000$$

The after-tax figure then has to be converted to a before-tax amount by the following equation:

Before-tax equation

$$\text{Operating income (before tax)} = \frac{\text{Net income}\left[\text{AT}\right]}{1 - \text{Tax rate}}$$

Exhibit 11.8 Illustration of Long-Range Accumulated Cash Flow

	Year 1	Year 2	Year 3	Year 4	Year 5
Net income after tax	$10,000	$21,500	$30,000	$ 35,500	$ 40,000
Add back depreciation expense	80,000	72,000	65,000	59,000	55,000
Deduct long-term loan payments	(60,000)	(63,000)	(65,000)	(67,000)	(68,000)
Net cash flow	$30,000	$30,500	$30,000	$ 27,500	$ 27,000
Accumulated cash flow		$60,500	$90,500	$118,000	$145,000

If the company's tax rate were 25%, this would be:

$$\frac{\$18,000}{1-0.25} = \frac{\$18,000}{0.75} = \$24,000$$

The following CVP equation can then be used to convert the before-tax profit desired to a revenue figure:

$$\frac{\text{Fixed costs} + \text{Before-tax profit}}{\text{Contribution margin}}$$

If fixed costs (including depreciation) were $180,000, and contribution margin were 60% sales, revenue required would be:

$$\frac{\$180,000 + \$24,000}{0.6} = \frac{\$204,000}{0.6} = \$340,000$$

Proof of calculations

This is proved as follows:

Sales revenue		$340,000
Variable costs 40% × $340,000	$136,000	
Fixed costs	180,000	(316,000)
Income before tax		$ 24,000
Tax 25%		(6,000)
Net income		$ 18,000
Add depreciation		80,000
		$ 98,000
Deduct loan payments		(60,000)
Net cash flow		$ 38,000

COMPUTER APPLICATIONS

If operations budgets are computerized using a spreadsheet, the same spreadsheet can take the budgeted figures and produce a cash budget. This cash budget can be produced so rapidly it can indicate cash needs not only on a monthly basis but also on a weekly or even daily basis. This is particularly true when things like the ratio of cash to charge sales remains relatively constant. Because a computerized budget can be constantly updated, it allows management to readily anticipate cash surpluses so the excess cash can be invested or to allow the surpluses to be used for discretionary expenditures.

A spreadsheet program can also handle all the necessary calculations for preparing a long-range cash flow budget as illustrated in Exhibit 11.8.

SUMMARY

Excesses and deficiencies of cash can occur in any business. This is particularly true of the cyclical hospitality industry. Therefore, cash management becomes most important.

Net income and cash are not synonymous. An organization may have a net income but no cash available to pay bills. Alternatively, the income statement may show a loss, yet there will be cash available to pay dividends.

In order to foresee surpluses and shortages of cash, the preparation of a cash budget for up to a year can be useful. The cash budget converts the budgeted income statements to a cash position. Sales revenue for a particular month is not always received in cash during that month. If some sales are made on a charge basis, that cash may not be received until 30 or more days later. Similarly, expenses recorded on the income statement do not always involve an outlay of cash during that month. Payments can often be deferred. Finally, there are some items of cash revenue (the sale of a fixed asset) or cash outlay (principal payments on a loan) that do not appear on an income statement. These items can be incorporated into the cash budget so that excess funds can be foreseen (and used profitably by, for example, investing) and so that cash shortages can be forecast (and covered by arranging, in advance, for short-term financing).

Cash management involves a process of cash conservation. This simply means that the good manager will control the amount of cash on hand, and in the bank, inventory levels, accounts receivable, and accounts payable so that the most liquid cash position of the business can be maintained at all times.

Cash budgets require careful day-to-day observation of the various current asset and liability accounts in order to maximize the day-to-day cash position of the organization.

Long-range cash flow budgets differ somewhat from day-to-day cash budgets in that they ignore changes in the working capital accounts. Long-term cash flow budgets assume that the net income an enterprise makes will, over the long run, be converted into cash. Long-term cash flow budgets, prepared up to five years ahead, permit management to see whether long-term mortgage and other loan commitments can be met, or whether further mortgages and/or loans need to be arranged. They also allow management to make plans for capital asset purchases and replacements and to plan dividend payment policies.

DISCUSSION QUESTIONS

1. What is the meaning of cash management or cash planning?
2. What two main purposes are served by preparing a cash budget?

3. Why is net income shown on an income statement not necessarily the same as cash?

4. List three items that could appear on a cash budget under the receipts section.

5. List three items that could appear on a cash budget under the disbursements section.

6. Define the term "bank float" and explain how it can be used.

7. Explain concentration banking and give the equation for funds transfer frequency when concentration banking is used.

8. What two procedures will help ensure that the total accounts receivable amount is kept to a minimum?

9. Differentiate between city ledger accounts receivable and house accounts receivable in a hotel.

10. What two procedures can be instituted in a hotel to minimize the dollar amount of house accounts?

11. Explain the procedure of aging accounts receivable.

12. Explain how a lockbox is used to minimize funds outstanding in accounts receivable.

13. Discuss the use of marketable securities with reference to temporary surplus cash.

14. What is the formula for calculating food or beverage inventory turnover?

15. Differentiate between an operating cash budget and a long-term cash flow budget.

ETHICS SITUATION

In reviewing actual cash flows for the past three months and the cash budgets for the next three, a hotel manager notices that the cash sales from the hotel's bar operation have been slowly declining each month. The manager suspects that not all cash sales are being recorded and that bar employees may be pocketing the cash. He has approached a private security firm to have one of their representatives pose as a customer at the bar and observe if his suspicions are in fact true. Discuss the ethics of this situation.

EXERCISES

11.1 The following information is available regarding sales revenue for March and April, year 0004:

	March	April
Sales revenue	$42,484	$43,200
Cash sales	13,595	12,096
Credit card sales	26,340	29,376
Accounts receivable sales	2,549	1,728

What is the percentage of sales revenue by category?

	March	April
Sales revenue	100%	100%
Cash sales	%	%
Credit card sales	%	%
Accounts receivable sales	%	%

11.2 The following information is available regarding sales revenue for March and April, year 0004: Credit card sales are collected on the average of every three days and the amount remaining uncollected at the end of each month represents 8% of the monthly credit card sales revenue. Accounts receivable sales are collected in the month following sale. Using the following information regarding sales, calculate the cash inflow for the months of April and May, year 0004.

	March	April	May
Sales revenue	$42,000	$44,000	$44,800
Cash sales [38% of sales]	15,960	16,720	17,024
Credit card sales [62% of sales]	26,040	27,280	27,776

11.3 A restaurant reported the following information for the months of August, September, and October, year 0005. Of the cost of sales, 75% is paid in the current month and the remainder is paid in the following month. Of the operating expenses, 98% is paid in the current month and the remainder in the following month.

	August	September	October
Sales revenue	$48,000	$48,880	$49,300
Cost of sales	(18,240)	(18,574)	(18,734)
Operating expenses	(24,480)	(24,929)	(25,143)
Operating income	$ 5,280	$ 5,377	$ 5,423

Calculate the cash outflow (cash payments) for the months of September and October, year 0005.

11.4   The following is income statement information of a restaurant for the first two months of operation. Of the sales revenue, 80% is collected in cash with the remainder collected in the following month. Of cost of sales, 75% is paid in the current month and the remainder is paid in the next month. Wages and operating expenses are paid in the month incurred. The beginning cash balance was $4,500.

	January	February
Sales revenue	$38,300	$36,600
Cost of sales	(14,554)	(13,908)
Wages expense	(13,022)	(12,444)
Other operating expenses	(5,477)	(5,294)
Depreciation expense	(800)	(800)
Operating income	$ 4,447	$ 4,154

11.5   A restaurant has provided the following information regarding its food inventories for the month of March.

Beginning food inventories	$18,300
Purchases during the current month	72,600
Ending food inventories, current month	12,200

a. Calculate the food inventory turnover for the month.

b. Calculate the days inventory was available for the month of March.

PROBLEMS

11.1   You have the following information about a restaurant in year 0001:

Actual sales revenue	October	$8,400
	November	8,000
Actual purchases (cost of sales)	October	3,200
	November	3,000

Fifty percent of sales revenue is cash; 50% is credit. Of the credit revenue, half is collected in the month following the sale and the remainder in the month following that. Twenty percent of purchases are cash. The remaining 80% is paid in the month following purchase. The budgeted income statement for December 0001 is

Sales revenue		$7,500
Cost of sales	$3,000	
Wages	2,100	
Operating expenses	1,400	
Rent	550	
Depreciation	250	7,300
Net income		$ 200

Note that the wages and operating expenses included in the income statement will be paid in December 0001. Note also that rent is prepaid in January each year for the entire year. Prepare a cash budget for the month of December 0001. Cash in the bank on December 1, 0001, amounts to $3,300.

11.2 On December 31, 0003, a motel has a bank balance of $7,100. On that same date its balance sheet showed that it had a bank loan payable of $73,900.

The motel's budgeted income statement is as follows for the year 0004:

Sales revenue		$403,900
Operating costs		302,300
		$101,600
Other expenses:		
Management salary	$23,000	
Building rent	18,500	
Insurance	2,400	
Interest on loan	7,600	
Furniture depreciation	9,700	(61,200)
		$ 40,400
Income tax		(10,100)
Net income		$ 30,300

Note that the motel does not accept any credit cards. All sales are on a cash basis. Similarly, it pays its expenses at the time they occur in order not to carry any accounts payable. However, the income tax amount on the year 0004 income will not be paid until March 0005.

The motel owner plans to buy new furniture in May 0004 at an estimated cost of $15,600. By December 31, 0004, the bank loan payable will have been reduced to $49,200.

Calculate the motel's bank balance at December 31, 0004. Collections on credit revenue average 90% in the month following the sales and the remaining 10% in the month following that.

11.3   You have the following information about a restaurant:

	Budgeted Cash Revenue	Budgeted Credit Revenue
August	$30,300	$16,000
September	29,500	14,000
October	27,900	13,000
November	25,100	12,000
December	32,400	15,800

Collections on credit revenue average 90% in the month following the sales and the remaining 10% in the month following that.

Cost of sales (purchases) average 40% of total sales revenue. Forty percent of cost of sales is on a cash basis, and 60% is paid in the month following purchase.

Payroll costs (which are paid on a cash basis) are forecast to be:

October	$13,100
November	12,700
December	12,200

Other budgeted expenses according to the forecast income statements are:

	October	November	December
Rent	$2,500	$2,500	$2,500
–Insurance	300	300	300
Utilities	500	450	550
Other operating costs	1,100	900	1,300
–Depreciation (equipment)	4,600	4,600	4,600
Interest	400	400	400

Note that the rent, utilities, other operating costs, and interest are paid in cash each month as the expense is incurred. The insurance expense is paid in January each year in advance for the whole year ($3,600).

The restaurant financed its equipment and makes monthly payments on the balance owing (principal amount) of $1,000.

In December, the restaurant plans to sell off some old equipment and estimates it will receive $1,500 from the sale. At the same time it must spend $5,400 on new equipment.

If there is sufficient cash on hand, the owner plans to pay a bonus to the staff. This bonus will amount to $3,600 and will be paid in December.

Prepare the restaurant's cash budget for each of the three months: October, November, and December. The opening bank balance October 1 is $2,410.

11.4   You own a new restaurant that is due to open on June 1. The restaurant expects to take in $500 a day in sales revenue and is open seven days a week. Sales revenue is estimated to be 80% cash and 20% credit. The payments on credit sales are not expected to be received until the end of the month following the sale.

Labor and food cost combined will be 70% of sales revenue. Both these expenses will be on a cash basis.

Other operating costs are estimated to be 10% of sales revenue. These costs will not have to be paid until the month following the incurrence of the cost.

Depreciation is $1,000 a month. Rent is $300 a month payable in advance on the first of each month.

Principal payments on a loan you made to get into business are $3,000 a month. The first payment is due on June 15. You have only $500 cash on hand on June 1. You will not be able to borrow any more money, and you have no income of your own other than the money generated by your new restaurant venture.

a.   Produce the budgeted income statement for the restaurant for the month of June.

b.   Prepare the restaurant's cash budget for the month of June.

c.   Comment about the results shown by these two statements, with particular reference to any possible financial difficulties you might have.

11.5   A small hotel provided you with the following information for a three-month period showing, at each month-end, the length of time its accounts receivable were outstanding at that time:

	January	February	March
0–30 days	$21,100	$21,500	$22,100
31–60 days	4,900	7,500	8,500
61–90 days	1,000	900	1,400
over 90 days	500	400	600

During this period, the sales revenue was approximately the same for each of the three months.

Carry out any further calculations necessary so that you can then comment about or discuss the results.

11.6 A motel chain uses a system of concentration banking. Calculate the transfer frequency for each of the following individual motels:

	Average Bank Balance	Average Daily Deposit
Motel A	$3,200	$1,600
Motel B	5,700	1,900
Motel C	6,500	6,500
Model D	2,600	5,800

11.7 For each of the following alternatives, calculate the minimum account receivable payment (to the closest dollar) that would make a lockbox system profitable:

	Bank Charge per Item	Opportunity Cost	Days Saved
a.	$0.20	10%	2
b.	$0.18	8	3
c.	$0.25	8.5	4

11.8 A motel with a small dining room has prepared the following estimates for the year 0005:

Sales revenue	
Rooms	$350,000
Dining room	150,000
Labor cost	
Rooms	25% of rooms revenue
Dining room	40% of dining room revenue
Food cost	35% of dining room revenue
Other operating costs	
Rooms	5% of rooms revenue
Dining room	10% of dining room revenue
Other income	$5,500

Indirect expenses

Administrative and general	$25,600
Marketing	15,400
Property operation and maintenance	16,700
Energy costs	12,500
Land rent	28,300
Interest	11,500

Depreciation

Building	50,200
Furniture and equipment	24,800

In July of year 0005, the owner plans to buy $30,000 of new equipment (for cash), less a $5,400 trade-in of used equipment.

During year 0005, principal payments to be made on a mortgage on the building will amount to $30,300, and principal payments to be made on a bank loan will be $25,300.

The owner, who is also the only shareholder in the company, plans to pay herself dividends of $40,000 during 0005.

a. Prepare a budgeted income statement for 0005.

b. Calculate the motel's cash flow for 0005.

11.9 From the information following for Cato's Catering, prepare a cash budget for the six months commencing April 1:

	Sales		Purchases		Other	
	Food	Beverage	Food	Beverage	Wages	Expenses
February	$30,000	$ 9,000	$12,000	$4,400	$12,000	$10,400
March	31,000	9,600	12,200	4,800	12,400	10,400
April	34,000	10,800	13,600	5,400	13,000	10,800
May	35,600	12,600	14,000	6,400	13,800	11,200
June	46,000	13,800	14,600	6,800	15,000	11,600
July	50,000	16,200	16,600	8,200	14,800	11,400
August	45,000	14,200	14,600	7,200	13,400	10,600
September	40,800	13,000	14,200	6,400	12,200	10,200

- Assume that all sales are cash sales.
- The annual interest of $1,600 on the restaurant's marketable securities will be received in July.

- The time delay in paying suppliers for purchases is two months. For example, February purchases are paid in April.

- Wages are paid without any time delay.

- Other expenses are paid with a one-month delay.

- In May, new kitchen equipment will be purchased for $10,000. Payment for this will be made in the following month.

- The restaurant's bank balance on April 1 is $30,000.

11.10 A new restaurant was incorporated on January 1, year 0001. Forty thousand shares were issued for $6.00 cash per share. The cash received from the sale of shares was used, in part, as follows:

Construction of building, estimated life 20 years	$120,000
Kitchen equipment and restaurant furniture, estimated life 10 years	90,000
China, silverware, etc., estimated life 5 years	18,000
Food and beverage inventories	6,000

The remaining cash was deposited in a bank account.

The following estimates were made about the volume of business and operating expenses for the first three months:

a. Sales revenue:

January	$30,200
February	60,800
March	90,400

b. Sales revenue will be 50% cash and 50% credit; maximum credit to be allowed is 30 days.

c. Food cost and liquor cost will average 40% of revenue. Half this cost each month will be cash; the balance will be paid in the month following purchase.

d. Wages and salaries: the fixed portion of wages will be $5,200 a month; the variable portion will be 30% of any sales revenue in excess of $25,000 a month. (Total wages and salaries is the sum of the fixed and variable portions.)

e. Other operating costs will be $3,800 a month to be paid in the month following incurrence of the cost.

f. Depreciation for building, equipment and furniture, china and silverware is to be calculated on a straight-line basis. The annual depreciation amount must be prorated monthly to the income statements.

Note that, because of increasing sales revenue, a further cash investment in food and beverage inventories of $2,000 will have to be made in February, with another increase of $2,000 in March. This will increase total inventory invest-ment to $10,000 by the end of March.

REQUIRED

1. A cash budget for each of the first months of year 0001.

2. A budgeted income statement for the three months ending March 31, 0001.

3. A balance sheet as of March 31, 0001.

11.11 Stew and Brew have decided to lease a new restaurant. Rent for the building will be $3,000 a month to be paid on the first day of each month. They initially invested $225,000 of their own money, which was used in part to purchase:

Furniture and equipment	$180,000
China, glass, and silverware	25,200
Food inventory	9,000

Furniture and equipment are to be depreciated straight-line over five years. China, glass, and silverware are to be fully depreciated in year one.

Sales are forecast as follows for the first three months after opening:

Month 1	$48,000
Month 2	66,000
Month 3	84,000

Sales will be 80% cash and 20% credit with the maximum credit period allowed 30 days.

Food cost is expected to average 30%. All purchases will be cash.

Wages and salaries will be $15,000 a month. However, in any month when sales exceed $60,000, additional staff will have to be hired and the extra wage cost is estimated to be 20% of any excess sales. All salaries and wages will be paid in the month during which they were earned.

Other operating costs are expected to be 10% of sales and will be paid in the following month.

At the end of month three, Stew and Brew plan to pay themselves back part of their initial investment. This payment will be from any cash in excess of $15,000 at that time. (In other words, they wish to leave only $15,000 in the restaurant's cash account at the end of month 3.)

PREPARE

a. A forecast income statement for each of the three months.

b. A cash budget for each of the three months.

c. The balance sheet for the end of month three.

11.12   Fritz, the owner of the Ritz Cafe, needs an after-tax cash flow of $27,000 next year. Principal payments on loans are $42,000 a year, and depreciation is $21,000. Tax rate for the Ritz Cafe is 25%. Fixed costs (including depreciation) are $55,000, and variable costs are 30% of sales.

   a. What level of sales will provide Fritz with his desired cash flow next year?

   b. Prove your answer.

11.13   Cece Saw, a carpenter who has saved some money, has decided to build and operate, with his wife, a ten-unit highway budget motel. Cece invests $25,000 of his own money in the company ($5,000 by way of common stock and $20,000 as a long-term loan). He also obtains a long-term mortgage on the land and building for $120,000 at a 12% interest rate. Interest is estimated to be $1,200 per month for the first few months of the new business, and principal payments are expected to be $500 per month.

   Cash was paid for land at $20,000, building construction and completion at $90,000 (estimated 30-year life), and furniture and equipment at $24,000 (estimated 10-year life). Linen was also purchased with cash for $6,000. This linen amount will be written off (depreciated) over five years. Cece's company also prepared advertising costs of $1,200 for brochures and other items. This cost will be written off during the first year of business. The first year's insurance premium of $2,400 was also prepared before the business started.

   For the first three months of business, occupancy is forecast to be 60%, 65%, and 70% respectively, and, in order to build up volume, a low average room rate of $18 is to be offered. When calculating sales revenue, use a 30-day month for simplicity, and round monthly sales revenue figures to the nearest $100. All sales revenue will be on a cash basis. Since the motel is relatively small, Cece and his wife will run it themselves but expect to hire some casual help at a cash cost of $100 per month.

   Cece and his wife will each be paid $750 a month by the company for their services. However, for each of the first six months, they will each only take $250 cash out of the business for living expenses, until they are sure the company has sufficient cash resources to pay them the balance.

   Laundry and supplies are estimated to be 10% of monthly revenue (round this expense to the nearest $100). This will be paid in cash. Utility costs are forecast to be $200, $250, and $300 for the first three months, respectively; however, the month-one cost will not be paid until month two, and so on. Office expenses are expected to be $100 per month in cash.

   For each of the first three months of the motel's operation, prepare an income statement and a cash budget. Also, prepare the balance sheet for the end of month three.

CASE 11

In the preceding chapter and case, the compilation of a statement of source and use of working capital was covered. Another useful statement for purposes of cash budgeting is the statement of source and use of cash. The rules for showing an item as a source or use of cash are:

ASSET ACCOUNTS

- Decreases are a source
- Increases are a use

LIABILITY AND EQUITY ACCOUNTS

- Increases are a source
- Decreases are a use

With these rules, the budgeted income statement for year 0002 (Case 9), the December 31, 0001, actual balance sheet (Case 2), and the budgeted December 31, 0002, balance sheet (Case 10), prepare a budgeted statement of source and use of cash for year 0002.

12

The Investment Decision

INTRODUCTION

This chapter begins by discussing some of the problems associated with capital asset decisions, such as the long life of the assets, the initial high cost, and the unknown future costs and benefits.

Two fairly simple methods of measuring proposed investments are then illustrated and explained: the average rate of return and the payback period.

The concept of the time value of money is then discussed, and discounted cash flow is illustrated in conjunction with time value.

Discounted cash flow is then used in conjunction with two other investment measurement methods: net present value and internal rate of return. Net present value and internal rate of return are then contrasted, and capital investment control is discussed.

The chapter concludes by demonstrating how discounted cash flow can be used to help make leasing versus buying decisions.

CHAPTER OBJECTIVES

After studying this chapter, the reader should be able to:

1. Discuss the ways in which long-term asset management differs from day-to-day budgeting.
2. Explain how the average rate of return is calculated, use the equation, and explain the major disadvantage of this method.
3. Give the equation for the payback period, use the equation, and state the pros and cons of this method.

4. Discuss the concept of the time value of money and explain the term "discounted cash flow."

5. Use discounted cash flow tables in conjunction with the net present value method to make investment decisions.

6. Use discounted cash flow tables in conjunction with the internal rate of return method to make investment decisions.

7. Contrast the net present value and internal rate of return methods and explain how they can give conflicting rankings of investment proposals.

8. Solve problems relating to the purchase versus the rental of fixed assets.

THE INVESTMENT DECISION

Decision to invest
or not

This chapter concerns methods of evaluating investments in long-term assets. This is sometimes referred to as capital budgeting. We are not so much concerned here with the budgeting process as we are with the decision about whether or not to make a specific investment, or with the decision about which of two or more investments would be best. The largest investment that a hotel or food service business has to make is in its land and building, which is a one-time investment for each separate property. This chapter is primarily about more frequent investment decisions, for items such as equipment, and furniture purchases and replacements. Investment decision making, or capital budgeting, differs from day-to-day decision making and ongoing budgeting for a number of reasons. Some of these will be discussed.

LONG LIFE OF ASSETS

Decision affects many
years

Capital investment decisions concern assets that have a relatively long life. Day-to-day decisions concerning current assets are decisions about items (such as inventories) that are turning over frequently. A wrong decision about the purchase of a food item does not have a long-term effect. But a wrong decision about a piece of equipment (a long-term asset) can involve a time span stretching over many years. This long life of a capital asset creates another problem—that of estimating the life span of an asset to determine how far into the future the benefits of its purchase are going to be spread. Life span can be affected by both physical wear and tear on the equipment and by obsolescence—the fact that a newer, better, and possibly more profitable piece of equipment is available.

COSTS OF ASSETS

Recovery value of asset

Day-to-day purchasing decisions do not usually involve large amounts of money for any individual purchase. But the purchase of a capital asset or assets normally requires the outlay of large sums of money, and one has to be sure that the initial investment outlay can be recovered over time by the net income generated by the investment.

FUTURE COSTS AND BENEFITS

As will be demonstrated, analysis techniques to aid in investment decision making involve future costs and benefits. The future is always uncertain; on the other hand, if we make a decision based solely on historic costs and net income, we may be no better off, since they may not be representative of future costs and net income. For example, one factor to be considered is the recovery (scrap) value of the asset at the end of its economic life. If two comparable items of equipment were being evaluated and the only difference from all points of view was that one was estimated to have a higher scrap value than the other at the end of their equal economic lives, the decision would probably be made in favor of the item with the highest future trade-in value. However, because of technological change, that decision could eventually be the wrong one in five or more years.

Investment techniques

Such, then, are some of the hazards of making decisions about capital investments. The hazards can seldom be eliminated, but there are techniques available that will allow the manager to reduce some of the guesswork. Although a variety of techniques are available, only four will be discussed in this chapter. They are:

- Average rate of return
- Payback period
- Net present value
- Internal rate of return

To set the scene for the average rate of return and the payback period methods, consider a restaurant that is presently using a manual system of processing guest checks, with a cashier taking care of this function on a part-time basis. The part-time wages of the cashier total $4,000 a year. The restaurant is investigating the value of installing a precheck machine system that will eliminate the need for the cashier, since the servers can operate the machine and look after their own cash until the end of the shift. Two machines are being considered, and we have information about them, as shown in Exhibit 12.1.

Exhibit 12.1   Data Concerning Two Alternative Machines

	Machine A	Machine B
Cash cost, including		
installation	$5,000	$4,700
economic life	5 years	5 years
trade in value	0	0
depreciation	$\dfrac{\$5,000}{5} = \$1,000/\text{year}$	$\dfrac{\$4,700}{5} = \$940/\text{year}$
Saving, wages of cashier	$4,000	$4,000
Expenses		
maintenance	$ 350	$ 300
stationery	650	1,000
depreciation	1,000	940
total	$2,000	$2,240
Net saving before	$2,000	$1,760
income tax 50%	1,000	880
Net annual saving	$1,000	$ 880

AVERAGE RATE OF RETURN

The average rate of return method compares the average annual net income (after taxes) resulting from the investment with the average investment. The formula for the average rate of return (ARR) is:

ARR equation

$$\frac{\text{Net annual saving}}{\text{Average investment}}$$

Using the information from Exhibit 12.1, the ARR for each machine is:

Machine A

Calculation of ARR

$$\frac{\$1,000}{(\$5,000 \div 2)} \times 100 = \frac{\$1,000}{\$2,500} \times 100 = \underline{40.0\%}$$

Machine B

$$\frac{\$880}{(\$4,700 \div 2)} \times 100 = \frac{\$800}{\$2,350} \times 100 = \underline{37.4\%}$$

Note that average investment is initial investment divided by 2. If a machine had a trade-in value at the end of its economic life, average investment would then be:

Average investment calculation with trade-in

$$\frac{(\text{Initial investment} + \text{Trade-in value})}{2}$$

In the example given, the assumption was made that net annual saving is the same for each of the five years. In reality, this may not always be the case. For example, there might be expenses in year one (or in any of the other years) that are nonrecurring—for example, a training cost or a major overhaul. Alternatively, the amount of an expense may change over the period, for example, depreciation computed on a declining balance basis. (Different depreciation methods were fully discussed in Chapter 1.) One way to take care of this is to include such items in the calculations and project total savings and total costs for the entire period under review. The total savings amount less the total costs amount will give us a net saving figure for the entire period. This net saving figure for the entire period can then be divided by the number of years in the period to give an average annual net savings figure to be used in the equation.

Fluctuations in net annual saving figure

Let us illustrate this for Machine A only. Savings and expenses are as in Exhibit 12.1, except that in year three there will be a special overhaul cost of $1,000 and a declining balance method of depreciation (rather than straight line) will be used. Exhibit 12.2 shows the results.

Total net saving over the five-year period will be the sum of the individual years' saving. This amounts to $4,500. The average annual net saving will be $4,500 divided by 5 equals $900. Our ARR will then be:

Recalculation of ARR

$$\frac{\$900}{\$2,500} \times 100 = 36.0\%$$

The same approach should be carried out for Machine B and then a comparison can be made. Note that in Exhibit 12.2 the change of method of depreciation, by itself, did not affect the change in the ARR since average depreciation is still $1,000 per year, and average tax and average net saving are the same. In this particular case, the only factor that caused our ARR to decrease from 40.0% to 36.0% for Machine A was the $1,000 overhaul expense.

Pros and cons of ARR

The advantage of the average rate of return method is its simplicity. It is frequently used to compare the anticipated return from a proposal with a minimum desired return. If the proposal's return is less than desired, it is rejected. If greater than desired, a more in-depth analysis using other investment techniques might then be used. The major disadvantage of the average rate of return method is that it is based on net income rather than on cash flow.

Exhibit 12.2   Net Saving for Machine A
after Special Overhaul and Declining Balance Depreciation

	Machine A				
	Year 1	Year 2	Year 3	Year 4	Year 5
Wage saving	$4,000	$4,000	$4,000	$4,000	$4,000
Maintenance	350	350	350	350	350
Stationery	650	650	650	650	650
Depreciation	1,667	1,333	1,000	667	333
Overall			1,000		
Total	$2,667	$2,333	$3,000	$1,667	$1,333
Net saving (before tax)	1,333	1,667	1,000	2,333	2,667
Tax (50%)	(667)	(834)	(500)	(1,667)	1,334
Net Saving	$ 666	$ 833	$ 500	$1,666	$1,333

PAYBACK PERIOD

The payback period method overcomes the cash flow shortcoming of the average rate of return method. The payback method measures the initial investment with the annual cash inflows. The formula is:

Payback period equation

$$\text{Payback period (years)} = \frac{\text{Initial investment}}{\text{Net annual cash saving}}$$

Since Exhibit 12.1 only gives us net annual saving and not net annual cash saving, we must first convert the figures to a cash basis. This is done by adding back the depreciation (an expense that does not require an outlay of cash). The cash-saving figures are:

Conversion to net annual cash saving

	Machine A	Machine B
Net annual saving	$1,000	$ 880
Add depreciation	1,000	940
Net annual cash saving	$2,000	$1,820

Therefore, our payback period for each machine is:

Calculation of payback periods

Machine A	Machine B
$\dfrac{\$5,000}{\$2,000} = 2.5 \text{ years}$	$\dfrac{\$4,700}{\$1,820} = 2.58 \text{ years}$

ARR considers all
benefit flows

Despite its higher initial cost, Machine A recovers its initial investment in a shorter period of time than does Machine B. This confirms the results of the average rate of return calculation made earlier. However, the ARR calculation takes into account all of the benefit flows from an investment and not just those during the payback period. For this reason, the average rate of return method could be considered more realistic.

Using accelerated
depreciation

Note that, in this illustration, straight-line depreciation was used and it was assumed the net annual cash saving figure was the same for each year. This may not be the case in reality. For example, the use of an accelerated method of depreciation (such as declining balance) will increase the depreciation expense in the early years. This, in turn, will reduce income taxes and increase cash flow in those years, making the calculation of the payback period a little more difficult. To illustrate, consider an initial $5,000 investment with the following annual cash flows:

Year 1	$2,000
Year 2	1,500
Year 3	1,200
Year 4	900
Year 5	700

By the end of year three, $4,700 ($2,000 + $1,500 + $1,200) will have been recovered, with the remaining $300 to be recovered in year four. This remaining amount will be recovered in one-third of a year ($300 divided by $900). Total payback time will therefore be three and one-third years.

Payback method only
considers speed of
investment recovery

The payback period analysis method, although simple, does not really measure the merits of investments, but only the speed with which the investment might be recovered. It has a use in evaluating a number of proposals so that only those that fall within a predetermined payback period will be considered for further evaluation using other investment techniques.

Common fault

However, both the payback period and the average rate of return methods still suffer from a common fault: They both ignore the time value of cash flows, or the concept that money now is worth more than the same amount of money at some time in the future. This concept will be discussed in the next section, after which we will explore the use of the net present value and internal rate of return methods.

DISCOUNTED CASH FLOW

The concept of discounted cash flow can probably best be understood by looking first at an example of compound interest. Exhibit 12.3 shows, year by year,

Exhibit 12.3　Compound Interest, $100 @ 10%

	Jan. 1 0001	Dec. 31 0001	Dec. 31 0002	Dec. 31 0003	Dec. 31 0004
Balance forward	$100.00	$100.00	$110.00	$121.00	$133.10
Interest 10%		10.00	11.00	12.10	13.31
Investment value end of year		$110.00	$121.00	$133.10	$416.41

Discounted cash flow reverse of interest compounding

what happens to $100 invested at a 10% compound interest rate. At the end of four years, the investment would be worth $146.41.

Discounting is simply the reverse of compounding interest. In other words, at a 10% interest rate, what is $146.41 four years from now worth to me today? The solution could be worked out manually using the following equation:

$$P = F \times \frac{1}{(1 + i)^n}$$

where P is the present value, F is the future amount, i is the interest rate, and n is the number of years ahead for the future amount. For example, using the already illustrated figures, we have:

$$P = \$146.41 \times \frac{1}{(1 + 0.10)^4}$$

$$= \$146.41 \times \frac{1}{1.4641}$$

$$= \$146.41 \times 0.683$$

$$= \$100$$

Although a calculation can be made for any amount, any interest rate, and for any number of years into the future with this formula, it is much easier to use a table of discount factors.

Exhibit 12.4 illustrates such a table, and, if we go to the number (called a factor) that is opposite year four and under the 10% column, we will see that it is 0.6830. This factor tells us that $1.00 received at the end of year four is worth only $1.00 × 0.683 = $0.683 right now. In fact, this factor tells us that any amount of money at the end of four years from now at a 10% interest (discount) rate is worth only 68.3% of that amount right now. Let us prove this by taking our $146.41 amount at the end of year 0004 from Exhibit 12.3 and discounting it back to the present.

Exhibit 12.4   Table of Discounted Cash Flow Factors

Period	5%	6%	7%	8%	9%	10%	11%	12%	13%	14%	15%	16%	17%	18%	19%	20%	25%	30%
1	0.9524	0.9434	0.9546	0.9259	0.9174	0.9091	0.9009	0.8929	0.8850	0.8772	0.8696	0.8621	0.8547	0.8475	0.8403	0.8333	0.8000	0.7692
2	0.9070	0.8900	0.8734	0.8573	0.8417	0.8264	0.8116	0.7972	0.7831	0.7695	0.7561	0.7432	0.7305	0.7182	0.7062	0.6944	0.6400	0.5917
3	0.8638	0.8396	0.8163	0.7938	0.7722	0.7513	0.7312	0.7118	0.6951	0.6750	0.6575	0.6407	0.6244	0.6086	0.5934	0.5787	0.5120	0.4552
4	0.8227	0.7921	0.7629	0.7350	0.7084	0.6830	0.6587	0.6355	0.6133	0.5921	0.5718	0.5523	0.5337	0.5158	0.4987	0.4823	0.4096	0.3501
5	0.7835	0.7473	0.7130	0.6806	0.6499	0.6209	0.5935	0.5674	0.5428	0.5194	0.4972	0.4761	0.4561	0.4371	0.4191	0.4019	0.3277	0.2693
6	0.7462	0.7050	0.6663	0.6302	0.5963	0.5645	0.5346	0.5066	0.4803	0.4556	0.4323	0.4104	0.3898	0.3704	0.3521	0.3349	0.2621	0.2072
7	0.7107	0.6651	0.6228	0.5835	0.5470	0.5132	0.4817	0.4524	0.4251	0.3996	0.3759	0.3538	0.3332	0.3139	0.2959	0.2791	0.2097	0.1594
8	0.6768	0.6274	0.5820	0.5403	0.5019	0.4665	0.4339	0.4039	0.3762	0.3506	0.3269	0.3050	0.2848	0.2660	0.2487	0.2326	0.1678	0.1226
9	0.6446	0.5919	0.5439	0.5003	0.4604	0.4241	0.3909	0.3606	0.3329	0.3075	0.2843	0.2630	0.2434	0.2255	0.2090	0.1938	0.1342	0.0943
10	0.6139	0.5584	0.5084	0.4632	0.4224	0.3855	0.3522	0.3220	0.2946	0.2697	0.2472	0.2267	0.2080	0.1911	0.1756	0.1615	0.1074	0.0725
11	0.5847	0.5298	0.4751	0.4289	0.3875	0.3505	0.3173	0.2875	0.2607	0.2366	0.2149	0.1954	0.1778	0.1619	0.1476	0.1346	0.0859	0.0558
12	0.5568	0.4970	0.4440	0.3971	0.3555	0.3186	0.2858	0.2567	0.2307	0.2076	0.1869	0.1685	0.1520	0.1372	0.1240	0.1122	0.0687	0.0429
13	0.5303	0.4688	0.4150	0.3677	0.3262	0.2897	0.2575	0.2292	0.2042	0.1821	0.1625	0.1452	0.1299	0.1163	0.1042	0.0935	0.0550	0.0330
14	0.5051	0.4423	0.3878	0.3405	0.2993	0.2633	0.2320	0.2046	0.1807	0.1597	0.1413	0.1252	0.1110	0.0986	0.0876	0.0779	0.0440	0.0254
15	0.4810	0.4173	0.3625	0.3152	0.2745	0.2394	0.2090	0.1827	0.1599	0.1401	0.1229	0.1079	0.0949	0.0835	0.0736	0.0649	0.0352	0.0195
16	0.4581	0.3937	0.3387	0.2919	0.2519	0.2176	0.1883	0.1631	0.1415	0.1229	0.1069	0.0930	0.0811	0.0708	0.0618	0.0541	0.0281	0.0150
17	0.4363	0.3714	0.3166	0.2703	0.2311	0.1978	0.1696	0.1456	0.1252	0.1078	0.0929	0.0802	0.0693	0.0600	0.0520	0.0451	0.0225	0.0116
18	0.4155	0.3503	0.2959	0.2503	0.2120	0.1799	0.1528	0.1300	0.1108	0.0946	0.0808	0.0691	0.0592	0.0508	0.0437	0.0376	0.0180	0.0089
19	0.3957	0.3305	0.2765	0.2317	0.1945	0.1635	0.1377	0.1161	0.0981	0.0829	0.0703	0.0596	0.0506	0.0431	0.0367	0.0313	0.0144	0.0068
20	0.3769	0.3118	0.2584	0.2146	0.1784	0.1486	0.1240	0.1037	0.0868	0.0728	0.0611	0.0514	0.0433	0.0365	0.0308	0.0261	0.0115	0.0053

Example of discounting

$$\$146.41 \times 0.683 = \$99.99803 \text{ or } \underline{\$100.00}$$

We know $100 is the right answer because it is the amount we started with in our illustration of compounding interest in Exhibit 12.3. To illustrate with another example, assume we have a piece of equipment that a supplier suggests to us will probably have a trade-in value of $1,200 five years from now. At a 12% interest rate, what is the present value of $1,200? The answer is:

$$\$1,200 \times 0.5674 = \underline{\$680.88}$$

Timing of cash flow assumption

The factor (multiplier) of 0.5674 was obtained from Exhibit 12.4 on the year five line under the 12% column. The factors in Exhibit 12.4 are based on the assumption that the money is all received in a lump sum on the last day of the year. This is not normally the case in reality, since outflows of cash expenses relating to an investment (wages, supplies, and maintenance, for example) occur continuously or periodically throughout its life and not just at the end of each year. Although continuous discounting is feasible, for most practical purposes the year-end assumption, using the factors from Exhibit 12.4, will give us solutions that are acceptable for decision making.

For a series of annual cash flows, one simply applies the related annual discount factor for that year to the cash inflow for that year. For example, a cash inflow of $1,000 a year for each of three years using a 10% factor will give us the following total discounted cash flow:

Calculation of series of cash flows

Year	Factor	Amount	Total
1	0.9091	$1,000	$ 909.10
2	0.8264	1,000	826.40
3	0.7513	1,000	751.30
			$2,486.80

In this illustration, the cash flows are the same each year. Alternatively, in the case of equal annual cash flows, one can total the individual discount factors (in our case, this would be 0.9091 + 0.8264 + 0.7513 = 2,4868) and multiply this total by the annual cash flow.

$$2.4868 \times \$1,000 = \underline{\$2,486.80}$$

Factors for equal annual
cash flows

Special tables have been developed from which one can directly read the combined discount factor to be used in the case of equal annual cash flows, but they are not included in this chapter because Exhibit 12.4 will be sufficient for our needs.

NET PRESENT VALUE

The equation for calculating the net present value of an investment is:

$$NPV = A_0 + \frac{A_1}{(1+i)} + \frac{A_2}{(1+i)^2} + \cdots + \frac{A_n}{(1+i)^n}$$

where A_1 through A_n are the individual annual cash flows for the life of the investment, and i is the interest or discount rate being used. Although it is possible with this formula to arrive at an NPV investment decision, it is much easier to use the table of discount factors illustrated in Exhibit 12.4. For example, Exhibit 12.5 gives projections of savings and costs for two machines. Machine A has an investment cost of $5,000; Machine B an investment cost

Estimating future savings
and costs

of $4,700. Estimating the future savings and costs is the most difficult part of the exercise. In our case, we are forecasting for five years. We have to assume the figures are as accurate as they can be. Obviously, the longer the period of time, the less accurate the estimates are likely to be.

Note that depreciation for each machine is calculated as follows:

Calculation of straight-
line depreciation

	Machine A	Machine B
Initial cost	$5,000	$4,700
Trade-in (scrap value)	(1,000)	(200)
	$4,000	$4,500
Depreciation, straight line	$\frac{\$4,000}{5} = \$800 / \text{yr}$	$\frac{\$4,500}{5} = \$900 / \text{yr}$

Depreciation added
back

The scrap value is a partial recovery of our initial investment and is therefore added in as a positive cash flow at the end of year five in Exhibit 12.5. Note that depreciation is deductible as an expense for the calculation of income tax, but this expense does not require an outlay of cash year by year. Therefore, in order to convert our annual additional net income (saving) from the investment to a cash situation, the depreciation is added back each year. Note also that with Machine A there is a negative cash flow in year one.

Exhibit 12.5   Calculation of Annual Net Cash Flows for Each Machine

	Machine A (Investment Cost $5,000)				
	Year 1	Year 2	Year 3	Year 4	Year 5
Saving (wages)	$4,000	$4,000	$4,000	$4,000	$4,000
Expenses					
Initial training cost	$3,500				
Maintenance contract	350	$ 350	$ 350	$ 350	$ 350
Special overhaul			250		
Stationery	650	650	650	650	650
Depreciation	800	800	800	800	800
Total expenses	$5,300	$1,800	$2,050	$1,800	$1,800
Saving less expenses	($1,300)	$2,200	$1,950	$2,200	$2,200
Income tax 50%	0	1,100	975	1,100	1,100
	($1,300)	$1,100	$ 975	$1,100	$1,100
Add back depreciation	800	800	800	800	800
					$1,900
Add scrap value					1,000
Net cash flow	($ 500)	$1,900	$1,775	$1,900	$2,900

	Machine B (Investment Cost $4,700)				
	Year 1	Year 2	Year 3	Year 4	Year 5
Saving (wages)	$4,000	$4,000	$4,000	$4,000	$4,000
Expenses					
Initial training cost	$2,000				
Maintenance contract	300	$ 300	$ 300	$ 300	$ 300
Special overhaul			100		
Stationery	1,000	1,000	1,000	1,000	1,000
Depreciation	900	900	900	900	900
Total expenses	$4,200	$2,200	$2,300	$2,200	$2,200
Saving less expenses	($ 200)	$1,800	$1,700	$1,800	$1,800
Income tax 50%	0	900	850	900	900
	($ 200)	$ 900	$ 850	$ 900	$ 900
Add back depreciation	900	900	900	900	900
					$1,800
Add scrap value					200
Net cash flow	$ 700	$1,800	$1,750	$1,800	$2,000

Exhibit 12.6   Conversion of Annual Cash Flows to Net Present Values

Year	Net Cash Flow	×	Machine A Discount Factor	=	Present Value	Net Cash Flow	×	Machine B Discount Factor	=	Present Value
1	($ 500)		0.9091		($ 455)	$ 700		0.9091		$ 636
2	1,900		0.8264		1,570	1,800		0.8264		1,488
3	1,775		0.7513		1,333	1,750		0.7513		1,315
4	1,900		0.6830		1,298	1,800		0.6830		1,229
5	2,900		0.6209		1,801	2,000		0.6209		1,242
Total present value					$5,547					$5,910
Less: Initial investment					(5,000)					(4,700)
Net present value					$ 547					$1,210

The data we are interested in from Exhibit 12.5 are the initial investment figures and the annual net cash flow figures for each machine. These figures have been transferred to Exhibit 12.6 and, using the relevant 10% discount factors from Exhibit 12.4, have been converted to a net present value basis. Observe how the negative cash flow for Machine A in year one has been handled.

Positive versus negative NPV

As can be seen from Exhibit 12.6, from a purely cash point of view, Machine B is a better investment than Machine A: $1,210 net present value against $547. In this example, both net present value figures were positive. It is possible for a net present value figure to be negative if the initial investment exceeds the sum of the individual years' present value. In this case, the investment should not be undertaken since, assuming the accuracy of the figures, the investment will not produce the rate of return desired.

Finally, the discount rate actually used should be realistic. It is frequently the rate that owners and/or investors expect the company to earn, after taxes, on investments.

INTERNAL RATE OF RETURN

As we have seen, the NPV method uses a specific discount rate to determine if proposals result in a net present value greater than zero. Those that do not are rejected.

Discounted cash flow and IRR

The internal rate of return (IRR) method also uses the discounted cash flow concept. However, this method's approach determines the interest (discount) rate that will equate total discounted cash inflows with the initial investment.

The mathematical formula for the IRR method is:

$$A_0 = \frac{A_1}{(1+i)} + \frac{A_2}{(1+i)^2} + \cdots + \frac{A_n}{(1+i)^n} - IC$$

where A_1 through A_n are the individual annual cash flows for the life of the investment, i is the interest or discount rate being used, and IC is the investment cost. Although it is possible with this formula to arrive at an IRR investment decision, it is usually easier to use the table of discount factors illustrated in Exhibit 12.4.

For example, suppose a motel owner decided to investigate renting a building adjacent to his motel in order to run it as a coffee shop. His investigation showed that it would cost him $100,000 to redecorate, furnish, and equip the building with a guaranteed five-year lease. The projected cash flow (net income after tax, with depreciation added back) for each of the five years is:

Projected cash flows
before discounting

Projected Annual Cash Flow	
Year 1	$ 18,000
Year 2	20,000
Year 3	22,000
Year 4	25,000
Year 5	30,000
	$115,000

In addition to the total of $115,000 cash recovery over the five years, it is estimated the equipment and furnishings could be sold for $10,000 at the end of the lease period. The total cash recovery is therefore $125,000, which is $25,000 more than the initial investment required of $100,000. On the face of it, the motel owner seems to be ahead of the game. If the annual cash flows are discounted back to their net present value, a different picture emerges, as illustrated in Exhibit 12.7.

Projected cash flows
after discounting

Exhibit 12.7 shows that the future stream of cash flows discounted back to today's values using a 12% rate is less than the initial investment by almost $14,000. Thus, we know that if the projections about the motel restaurant are correct, there will not be a 12% cash return on the investment. The IRR method determines the rate to be earned if the investment is made. From Exhibit 12.7, we know that 12% is too high. By moving to a lower rate of interest, we will eventually, by trial and error, arrive at one where the net present value (the difference between total present value and initial investment) is virtually zero. This is illustrated in Exhibit 12.8 with a 7% interest (discount) rate.

Exhibit 12.7   Annual Cash Flows Converted to Net Present Value

Year	Annual Cash Flow	×	Discount Factor 12%	=	Present Value
1	$18,000		0.8929		$ 16,072
2	20,000		0.7972		15,944
3	22,000		0.7118		15,660
4	25,000		0.6355		15,888
5	30,000		0.5674		17,022
Sale of equipment and furniture	10,000		0.5674		5,674
Total present value					$ 86,260
Less: Initial investment					(100,000)
Net present value (negative)					$(13,740)

Exhibit 12.8 tells us that the initial $100,000 investment will return the initial cash outlay except for $157 ($100,000 – $99,843) and earn 7% on the investment. Or, stated slightly differently, the motel operator would recover the full $100,000 but earn slightly less than 7% interest. If the motel owner is satisfied with a 7% cash return on the investment (note this is 7% after income tax), then he could go ahead with the project.

A mathematical technique known as interpolation could be used for determining a more exact rate of interest but, since our cash flow figures are estimates

Exhibit 12.8   Discount Factor Arrived at by Trial and Error

Year	Annual Cash Flow	×	Discount Factor 7%	=	Present Value
1	$18,000		0.9346		$16,823
2	20,000		0.8734		17,468
3	22,000		0.8163		17,959
4	25,000		0.7629		19,073
5	30,000		0.7130		21,390
Sale of equipment and furniture	10,000		0.7130		7,130
Total present value					$99,843

to begin with, the value of this interest rate exactness is questionable. In most practical situations, knowing the expected interest rate to the nearest whole number is probably good enough for decision-making purposes.

NET PRESENT VALUE VERSUS INTERNAL RATE OF RETURN

Mutually exclusive proposals

Despite the difference in approach used by the NPV and IRR methods, they will both always give the same accept or reject decision for any single project. However, if a number of proposals that were mutually exclusive were being evaluated and were being ranked, the rankings from NPV might differ from the rankings from IRR. A mutually exclusive alternative means that, if only one of a number is accepted, the others will be rejected. For example, if a restaurant were assessing a number of different electronic registers and only one was to be selected, it would want to select the most profitable one and reject all others, even if the others were profitable. In this sense "profitable" could mean reduction in costs from present levels.

Capital rationing

Another situation where profitable proposals are rejected is when the company is faced with capital rationing. "Capital rationing" means that there is sufficient capital to handle only a limited number of investments for any budget period. Once the maximum amount of capital budget has been exhausted, all other proposals, even if profitable, are postponed for reconsideration during some future budget period.

Conflicting rankings with NPV versus IRR

Therefore, at times, the ranking of projects in order of potential profitability is important if a company wishes to maximize the profitability from its investment. Unfortunately, the NPV and IRR results can indicate conflicting ranking of profitabilities because of differences in the cost of, and/or differences in the timing of cash flows from, alternative investments.

To illustrate this refer to Exhibit 12.9, which shows two alternative investments, each with the same initial cost, but each of which has different amounts of cash flow, differences in timing of cash flow amounts, and differences in total cash flow amounts. Using the NPV method at 10% and the IRR method, the ranking decision is contradictory. Alternative A is preferable from an NPV point of view ($4,290 to $3,973), whereas Alternative B is preferable using IRR (31% to 25%).

Assumptions under NPV versus IRR

The reason for this is that the NPV method assumes annual cash inflows are reinvested at the rate used, in our case, 10%, for the balance of the life of the project. The IRR method assumes that the cash inflows are reinvested at the rate resulting from IRR analysis (in our case 25% and 31% for Alternatives A and B, respectively) for the balance of the life of the project, an assumption that may not be realistic.

Exhibit 12.9   Two Investments and Their Respective NPV and IRR Ranking Results

	Alternative A			Alternative B		
Net Present Value	Annual Cash Flow	Discount Factor 10%	Present Value	Annual Cash Flow	Discount Factor 10%	Present Value
Year 1	$ 3,000	0.9091	$ 2,727	$7,000	0.9091	$ 6,364
2	3,000	0.8264	2,479	4,000	0.8264	3,306
3	3,000	0.7513	2,254	3,000	0.7513	2,254
4	10,000	0.6830	6,830	3,000	0.6830	2,049
Total present value			$14,290			$13,973
Less: initial cost			(10,000)			(10,000)
Net present value			$ 4,290			$ 3,973

	Annual Cash Flow	Discount Factor 25%	Present Value	Annual Cash Flow	Discount Factor 31%	Present Value
Internal Rate of Return						
Year 1	$ 3,000	0.8000	$ 2,400	$7,000	0.7634	$ 5,344
2	3,000	0.6400	1,920	4,000	0.5827	2,331
3	3,000	0.5120	1,536	3,000	0.3396	1,019
4	10,000	0.4096	4,096	3,000	0.3396	1,019
Total present value			$ 9,952			$10,028
Initial cost			$10,000			$10,000

NPV versus IRR

Theoretically, the NPV method is considered to be the better method since it uses the same discount rate for alternative proposals and that rate would normally represent the minimum rate acceptable for investments to be made by the company. On the other hand, proponents of the IRR method contend that it is easier to interpret, does not require the predetermination of a discount rate, and allows a more meaningful comparison of alternatives.

CAPITAL INVESTMENT CONTROL

Review at end of project life

One of the major difficulties in capital investment decision making is that it is only possible to approximate the investment rate to be achieved. Investment proposals are based on estimated cash flows, and the decisions based on those cash flows can only be judged as good or otherwise after actual cash flows are known. A review of all investment proposals is thus recommended at the end of each project's life. In this way, among other benefits, the process of fore-casting cash flows can be reviewed and refined so that future investment decisions can be based on potentially more accurate figures.

INVESTMENT AND UNCERTAINTY

Risk factor in investments

In this chapter, we ignored the risk factor in investments, or we assumed that the risk of alternative investments was equal and was built into the discount or investment rates used. Risk is defined as the possible deviation of actual cash flows from those forecast. Also, in the illustrations, only short periods were used: five years or less. As the time grows longer for more major investments (for example, hotel or restaurant buildings that may have an economic life of 25 years or more), the risk factor must play a more important role. Forecasting cash flows for periods of five years or less is difficult enough. Forecasting for periods in excess of that is increasingly more difficult, and the risks thus become much greater.

Use of probabilities

Although there are techniques, such as the use of probabilities, that can be used to deal with risk, they are quite theoretical and may be difficult to use in practice, for which reason they are not discussed in this text. However, this does not imply that the business manager should ignore risk, since it does exist. The interested reader wishing to gain more insight into techniques available to encompass risks, or uncertainty, is referred to any of the excellent textbooks available on general managerial finance.

NONQUANTIFIABLE BENEFITS

Consideration of intangible factors

The results obtained using investment decision techniques may not be the only information needed to make decisions. Some information is not easily quantifiable but is still relevant to decision making. One should not ignore such factors as prestige, goodwill, reputation, employee acceptability, and the social or environmental implications. For example, if a hotel invests in a redecoration of its lobby, what are the cash benefits? They may be difficult to quantify but, to retain customer goodwill, the lobby may need to be redecorated. Similarly, how are the relative benefits to be assessed in spending $50,000 on improvements to the staff cafeteria or using the $50,000 for Christmas bonuses? Personal judgment must then come into play in such investment decisions.

TO OWN OR LEASE?

Lease payments are tax deductible

Until this point, the discussion concerning long-term, or fixed, assets has been based on purchasing and owning them. However, there may be situations where renting or leasing may be favorable from a cost point of view. For example, income tax is a consideration. Since lease payments are generally tax deductible, there can be an advantage in leasing. On the other hand, ownership permits deduction for tax purposes of both depreciation and the interest expense on any debt financing of the purchase. What may be advantageous in one situation may be disadvantageous in another. Each case must be investigated on its own merits. Let us look at a method by which a comparison between the two alternatives can be made. Assume that we are considering whether to buy or rent new furnishings for a motel.

Purchase of the furniture will require a $125,000 loan from the bank. Cost of the furniture is $125,000. The bank loan will be repayable in four equal annual installments of principal ($31,250 per year) at 8% interest. The furniture will be depreciated over five years at $25,000 per year. It is assumed to have no trade-in value at the end of that period. The income tax rate is 50%. Alternatively, the furniture can be leased for five years at a rental of $30,000 per year.

Bank repayment schedule

First, with the purchase plan, we must prepare a bank repayment schedule showing principal and interest payments for each of the four years (see Exhibit 12.10). Next, under the purchase plan we must calculate the net cash outflow for each of the five years. This is shown in Exhibit 12.11. In Exhibit 12.11, note that since depreciation and interest expense are tax deductible and since the motel is in a 50% tax bracket, there is an income tax saving equal to 50% of these expenses. Thus, in year one, the expenses of $35,000 are offset by the $17,500 tax saving. The net cost, after tax, is therefore only $17,500. This $17,500 has to be increased by the principal repayment of $31,250 on the bank loan and reduced by the depreciation expense of $25,000, since depreciation does not require an outlay of cash. In year one, the net cash outflow is thus $23,750. Figures for the other years are calculated similarly. Note that in year five, since there is no interest expense and bank loan payment to be made, the cash flow is positive rather than negative.

Income tax saving

No depreciation with rental

Exhibit 12.12 shows the calculation of annual net cash outflows under the rental plan. Note that under the rental option there is no depreciation expense (since the motel does not own the furnishings) and no interest or principal payments since no money is to be borrowed.

Exhibit 12.10   Bank Repayment Schedule for $125,000

Year	Interest at 8%	Principal Amount	Balance
1	$10,000	$31,250	$93,750
2	7,500	31,250	62,500
3	5,000	31,250	31,250
4	2,500	31,250	0

Exhibit 12.11   Annual Net Cash Outflow with Purchase

	Year 1	Year 2	Year 3	Year 4	Year 5
Interest expense (from Exhibit 12.10)	$10,000	$ 7,500	$ 5,000	$ 2,500	0
Depreciation expense	25,000	25,000	25,000	25,000	25,000
Total tax deductible expense	$35,000	$32,500	$30,000	$27,500	$25,500
Income tax saving (50%)	(17,500)	(16,250)	(15,000)	(13,750)	(12,500)
After-tax cost	$17,500	$16,250	$15,000	$13,750	$12,500
Add: principal payments	31,250	31,250	31,250	31,250	0
Deduce: depreciation expense	(25,000)	(25,000)	(25,000)	(25,000)	(25,000)
Net annual cash outflow (inflow)	$23,750	$22,500	$21,250	$20,000	($12,500)

Finally, the net cash flow figures from Exhibits 12.11 and 12.12 have been transferred to Exhibit 12.13 and discounted, using the appropriate discount factor from Exhibit 12.4. The discount rate used is 8%. This rate was selected since it is the current cost of borrowing money from the bank. Exhibit 12.13 shows that from a present value point of view it would be better to rent in this particular case, since total present value of cash outflows is lower by $4,450 ($64,339 – $59,889).

Various alternative possibilities

In any buy-or-lease situation, there could be other factors to be taken into the calculations. For example, in the purchase option, a firm might use some of its own cash as a down payment and borrow less than the full purchase amount required. In such a case, the down payment is an additional cash outflow at the beginning of the first year. Under a purchase plan, there might also be a trade-in value at the end of the period. This trade-in amount would be handled in the calculations as a cash inflow at the end of the period. In a rental

Exhibit 12.12   Annual Cash Outflow with Rental

	Year 1	Year 2	Year 3	Year 4	Year 5
Rental expense	$30,000	$30,000	$30,000	$30,000	$30,000
Income tax saving 50%	(15,000)	(15,000)	(15,000)	(15,000)	(15,000)
Net cash outflow	$15,000	$15,000	$15,000	$15,000	$15,000

Exhibit 12.13   Total Present Value (converted from figures in Exhibits 12.11 and 12.12)

	Purchase				Rental			
Year	Annual Cash Outflow (Inflow)		Discount Factor 8%		Present Value	Annual Cash Outflow		Discount Factor 8%		Present Value
1	$23,750	×	0.9259	=	$21,990	$15,000	×	0.9259	=	$13,888
2	22,500	×	0.8573	=	19,289	15,000	×	0.8573	=	12,860
3	21,250	×	0.7938	=	16,868	15,000	×	0.7938	=	11,907
4	20,000	×	0.7350	=	14,700	15,000	×	0.7350	=	11,025
5	(12,500)	×	0.6806	=	(8,508)	15,000	×	0.6806	=	10,209
Total present value					**$64,339**	*Total present value*				**$59,889**

plan, the annual payment might be required at the beginning of each year, rather than at the end, as was assumed in our illustration. This means that the first rental payment is at time zero, and each of the remaining annual payments is advanced by one year. Under a rental plan, there might also be a purchase option to the lessee at the end of the period. If the purchase is to be exercised, it will create an additional cash outflow.

Changing depreciation method

Furthermore, terms on borrowed money can change from one situation to another, and different depreciation rates and methods can be used. For example, the use of an accelerated depreciation method will give higher depreciation expense in the earlier years, thus reducing income tax and increasing the cash flow in those years.

Each situation different

Because of all these and other possibilities, each buy-or-lease situation must be investigated on its own merits taking all the known variables into consideration in the calculations before a decision is made.

COMPUTER APPLICATIONS

Computers can readily handle the calculations necessary for investment decisions. For example, spreadsheet programs can be used to handle all of the calculations required for the ARR, NPV, and IRR investment methods and can indicate the preferable investment option. Once the spreadsheet has been programmed with the correct formulas, it can be used repeatedly to eliminate the time it takes to perform the calculations manually.

A spreadsheet program can also be used to perform all the calculations necessary in a buy or lease situation.

SUMMARY

Capital asset management concerns decision making about whether or not to make a specific investment or which alternative investments would be best. Capital assets are assets with a long life that have a relatively high cost and about which future costs and benefits are uncertain.

Four methods of analyzing capital asset investments were illustrated: average rate of return (ARR), payback period, net present value (NPV), and internal rate of return (IRR).

The equation for the ARR is:

$$\frac{\text{Net annual saving}}{\text{Average investment}}$$

The disadvantage of this method is that it is based on accounting income rather than on cash flow.

The payback period method is based on cash flow, and the equation is:

$$\frac{\text{Initial investment}}{\text{Net annual cash saving}}$$

The disadvantage of the payback period method is that it ignores what happens beyond the payback period. Both the ARR and the payback period methods also share a common fault. They do not take into consideration the time value of money. Discounted cash flow tables (the reverse of compound interest tables) have been developed so that flows of future cash can be readily discounted back to today's values. The NPV and IRR methods make use of these tables.

With NPV, the initial investment is deducted from the total present value of future cash flows to obtain NPV. If the NPV is positive, the investment is favorable; if negative, the investment should not be made.

With IRR, one simply uses the tables to determine the rate of interest (rate of return) that will equate the total future discounted cash inflows with the initial investment. If the rate of return is higher than the company has established as a minimum desired return, then the investment should proceed; otherwise, it should not.

Both the NPV and IRR methods will always give the same accept or reject decision for any specific investment. However, if a number of alternative projects were being evaluated, the rankings may differ depending on whether NPV or IRR were being used.

Regardless of the investment method used, subsequent to each investment the results should be reviewed so that the investment process can be refined and improved.

Finally, one should not ignore the potential nonquantifiable benefits of each particular investment.

There may be situations where it is preferable to rent or lease rather than purchase long-term assets. Cash flows under both alternatives can be discounted back to their present values to make a comparison. In each situation all the known variables must be taken into consideration so that the final decision can be made on its own merits.

DISCUSSION QUESTIONS

1. Discuss the ways in which long-term asset management differs from day-to-day budgeting.

2. How is the average rate of return calculated? What is the major disadvantage of using this method?

3. What is the equation for calculating the payback period? What are the pros and cons of this method?

4. Under what conditions might a hotel consider buying an item of equipment with a rapid payback rather than one with a high average rate of return?

5. Discuss the concept that money is worth more now than that same amount of money a year from now.

6. How would you explain discounted cash flow to someone who had not heard the term before?

7. In Exhibit 12.4, in the 11% column opposite year five, is the number 0.5935. Explain in your own words what this number or factor means.

8. If an investment requires an outlay today of $10,000 cash and, over the five-year life of the investment, total cash returns were $12,000, and the $12,000 had a present value of $9,500, would you make the investment? Explain.

9. Contrast the NPV and the IRR methods of evaluating investment proposals.

10. Under what circumstances might NPV and IRR give conflicting decisions in the ranking of proposed investments?

11. Landscaping for a resort hotel is an investment for which the benefits might be difficult to quantify. In what ways might you be able to quantify them? Even if investment analysis (for example NPV) proved negative, what other considerations might dictate that the investment be made?

12. What factors other than purely monetary ones might one want to consider in a buy-versus-rent decision?

ETHICS SITUATION

The manager of a hotel has the permission of the owner to have a new swimming pool built. The manager contacts three companies for bids to do this construction work. The highest bidder has told the manager that if his bid is accepted he will also install a swimming pool at her house at a 25% discount. She agrees to accept this offer and justifies her decision by telling herself that the higher swimming pool cost to the hotel will provide a larger depreciation expense amount. This, in turn, will reduce the income tax that the hotel has to pay and therefore provide the hotel with more working capital. Discuss the ethics of this situation.

EXERCISES

12.1   Assume you are given the following information regarding a point-of-sale computer terminal: The net annual saving was calculated to be $2,000 on an average investment cost of $4,500. What is the average rate of return (ARR) on the terminal?

12.2   Information is provided on two machines, which had an original cost of $25,800 for machine X and $24,200 for machine Y.

	Machine X	Machine Y
Net annual saving	$1,440	$1,800
Add: Depreciation	4,500	6,000
Net annual cash saving	$5,940	$7,800

a. Which is the best investment using the payback period method?

b. Will either of the machines provide the cash investment back in less than four years?

12.3   Investment in an item of equipment is $18,000. It has a five-year life and no salvage value and straight-line depreciation is used. The equipment is expected to provide an annual saving of $2,000, which does not include depreciation. What is the payback period?

12.4   What is the net present value of $2,125 for each year of two years with a discount factor of 0.8929 in year 1 and 0.7972 in year 2?

12.5   Assume an item of equipment is purchased at a cost of $22,500 to be paid for over five years, requiring a payment on principle of 20% per year at an annual interest rate of 10%. Complete a repayment schedule for each of the five years.

PROBLEMS

12.1 You have the following information about three electronic sales registers that are on the market. The owner of a restaurant asks for your help in deciding which of the three machines to buy.

	Register A	Register B	Register C
Cash investment required	$6,300	$6,000	$6,700
Machine life	5 years	5 years	5 years
Trade-in value at end of life	$ 500	0	$ 300
Annual operating costs (excluding depreciation)	$ 400	$ 300	$ 300
Annual saving before deduction of costs	$2,000.	$2,000	$2,000

Income tax rate is 50%. Assume straight-line depreciation.

a. Use the ARR method to decide which of the three machines would be the best investment.

b. If the restaurant owner wanted a return on investment of at least 10%, what would you advise?

12.2 Using the information provided in Problem 12.1, which would be the best investment using the payback period method? If the owner wanted her cash back in less than four years, should she invest in any of the machines?

12.3 An investor is planning to open a new fast food restaurant. He has a five-year lease on a property that would require an investment estimated at $205,000 for redecorating and furnishing. He would use his own cash. The present cost of capital (borrowed money) is 13%. Use this figure as the discount rate.

Calculation of net cash flow from the restaurant for the five years of operation shows

Year	Cash Flow
1	$37,500
2	43,800
3	46,300
4	50,000
5	60,000

At the end of the lease, the furniture and equipment would have a cash value of $18,500. Should he make the investment? What IRR comes closest to giving him a complete return on his $205,000 investment?

12.4   Dinah, the operator of Dinah's Diner, wishes to choose between two alternative investments providing the following annual net cash inflows over the five-year investment period:

Year	Alternative 1	Alternative 2
1	$8,000	$ 4,200
2	8,600	5,800
3	8,800	8,500
4	8,200	11,500
5	4,100	12,100

a. Calculate the payback time for each alternative, assuming an initial investment of $33,000 under each alternative.

b. Using NPV at 12%, would either of them be a good investment for Dinah?

12.5   A hotel manager wishes to choose between two alternative investments giving the following annual net cash inflows over a five-year period:

Year	Alternative 1	Alternative 2
1	$ 4,200	$12,100
2	5,800	9,900
3	8,500	8,600
4	11,500	5,400
5	12,000	4,000

The amount of the investment under either alternative will be $35,000.

a. Using the payback period method, in which year, under both alternatives, will she have recovered the initial investment?

b. Using NPV at 10%, would either alternative be a good investment?

12.6   A motel operator wishes to choose between two alternative front office machines. Machine A will cost $9,000 and have a trade-in value at the end of its five-year life of $1,500. Machine B will cost $8,500 and at the end of its five-year life will have a trade-in value of $700. Assume straight-line depreciation.

  Investment in the machine will mean that a part-time night auditor will not be required, and there will be an annual wage saving of $9,600. The following will be the operating costs, excluding depreciation, for each machine, for each of the five years.

Year	Machine A					Machine B				
	1	2	3	4	5	1	2	3	4	5
Training	$800					$700				
Maintenance	750	$750	$750	$750	$750	650	$650	$650	$650	$650
Overhaul			$550					400		
Supplies	300	300	300	300	300	500	500	500	500	500
Electricity	100	100	100	100	100	100	100	100	100	100

Income tax rate is 50%. For each machine, calculate the NPV by using a 12% rate. Ignoring any other considerations, which machine would be the preferable investment?

12.7 Pete's Pizza is planning to purchase a new type of oven that cooks pizza much faster than the conventional oven presently used. The new oven is estimated to cost $20,000 (use straight-line depreciation) and will have a five-year life, after which it will be traded in for $4,000. Pete has calculated that the new oven will allow him to increase his sales by $30,000 a year. His food cost is 30%, labor cost 40%, and other costs 10% of sales. Tax rate is 40%. For any new investment, Pete wants a minimum 12% return. Use IRR to help him decide if he should purchase the new oven.

12.8 You have to make a decision either to buy or to rent the equipment for your restaurant. Purchase cost would be $30,000. Of this amount, $7,500 would be paid cash now, and the balance would be owed to the equipment supplier. The owner agrees to accept $4,500 a year for five years as payment toward the principal, plus interest at 10%. The equipment will have a five-year life, at the end of which it can be sold for $5,000. Calculate depreciation on a straight-line basis over the five years.

Alternatively, the equipment can be rented for the five years at a rental cost of $7,000 a year.

Income tax rate is 50%. Discount rate is 8%.

a. Using discounted cash flow, which would be the better investment?

b. What other factors might you want to consider that would change your decision?

12.9 A delivery service is provided by a pizza restaurant. It is considering purchasing a new compact vehicle or leasing it.

Purchase price would be $6,750 (cash), which the restaurant has. Estimated life is five years. Resale price (trade-in) is $1,250.

Under the purchase plan, the additional net cash income (increased revenue less additional costs such as vehicle maintenance and driver's wages) before deducting depreciation and income tax would be.

Year	Cash Revenue Less Cash Costs
1	$38,000
2	47,000
3	55,000
4	60,000
5	65,000

Depreciation will be straight-line. Income tax rate is 50%. Under the rental plan the cash income will be the same as under the purchase plan, except that vehicle maintenance will not be required (the leasor pays for this). Therefore, the given net cash income figures will have to be increased by the following maintenance amount savings.

Year	Amount
1	$1,000
2	2,500
3	2,500
4	4,000
5	5,000

However, under the rental plan, there is a rental cost based on mileage. Estimated mileage figures are

Year	Mileage
1	30,000
2	45,000
3	50,000
4	55,000
5	60,000

Rental cost is $0.20 per mile. Income tax rate will be 50%.

a. On a net present value basis using a 10% rate, would it be better to rent or buy?

b. Would your answer change if the rental cost were $1,000 a year plus $0.20 a mile? Explain your decision.

12.10 For many years a motor hotel has been providing its room guests with room service of soft drinks and ice, using the services of a part-time bellhop to deliver to the rooms. Typically, the service has been losing money. The average figures for each of the past few years are as follows:

Sales revenue:	soft drinks	$12,500	
	ice	1,200	$13,700
Expenses:	cost of sales	$10,200	
	labor	5,600	15,800
Loss:			($ 2,100)

The motor hotel has an offer from a soft drink vending company to install vending machines at no cost to the motor hotel. The vending company would collect the sales revenue (forecast to be as above for the next several years) from the soft drink machines, paying the motor hotel a commission of 10% on that revenue. Customers would help themselves to both soft drinks (by inserting cash in the machine) and ice (which would be free), thus eliminating the labor cost. An ice machine would have to be purchased by the motor hotel at a cost of $5,500. It would have a five-year life and a trade-in value at the end of that time of $500. Use straight-line depreciation. Annual maintenance and operating costs of the ice machine are estimated to be $100 per year. The motor hotel is in a 50% tax bracket.

a. Calculate the payback period.

b. Calculate the ARR.

c. Calculate the NPV of the investment using a 12% discount factor and state whether or not the investment should be made.

12.11 A motel presently leases out its 1,000-square-foot coffee shop, although it continues to own the equipment. The lease is due for renewal. The motel could continue to rent the space for $4 a square foot per year for the next three years, and then $5 a square foot for the following two years.

Alternatively, the motel could cancel this lease and take over the operation of the restaurant. If this occurs, the motel's management estimates that sales revenue in the first year would be $130,000 and that is would increase by $10,000 per year for each of the following four years. Variable operating costs of running the restaurant (food cost, wages, supplies) would be 90% of sales revenue. The motel would also have to assume certain other costs presently paid by the lessee for such items as supervision, advertising, and utilities. These are estimated to be $8,000 in year one, increasing by $500 per year for each of the following four years, so that by year 5, these costs will be $10,000.

If the motel reassumes operation of the restaurant, it will trade in some of the old equipment, for which it will get $2,000, and buy $10,000 of new equipment (this will not happen if the lease is renewed). The new equipment will have a five-year life and would be depreciated on a straight-line basis with no scrap value.

The motel is in a 25% tax bracket. Use NPV to decide whether the motel should operate the coffee shop itself or continue to lease it out. Use a 10% discount rate.

CASE 12

a. Early in year 0002 the owner of the building made Charlie an offer. The lease contract has four more years to run and, as you will recall from Case 2, the rent is to be increased by 10% a year each year over the preceding year. The rent is payable in equal monthly installments but, for the sake of simplicity, assume it is all paid at the year end. The building owner's offer is that a lump sum payment now (early in January 0002 before the January rent check had been prepared) of $80,000 would be considered as prepaid rent for the remaining four years of the contract. If the offer is accepted Charlie would borrow $80,000 from the bank. The arrangement with the bank is that $20,000 of the principal will be repaid on December 31 of years 0002 through 0005, with interest at 12% on the amount owing at each year end. Use the interest rate as the discount rate. Should the offer be accepted?

b. You will note in part *a* that year-end discount tables were used, even though the annual rent was paid each month. If monthly discount tables were available to you and you recalculated the present value with those monthly tables, do you think your decision would change?

c. Can you suggest a way that an annual discount table might be used to give you a slightly more correct present value in a case where you were dealing with monthly payments?

13

Feasibility Studies— An Introduction

INTRODUCTION

This chapter explains what a feasibility study is designed to do and covers the highlights of the two major parts of such a study.

Part one includes the front matter, general market characteristics, site evaluation, supply and demand information, and supply and demand analysis.

The chapter illustrates a detailed approach to supply and demand analysis for a hotel and covers the four steps involved.

1. Calculate the most recent 12-month average occupancy rate of the most competitive hotels.
2. Calculate the composite growth rate of demand from the various sources.
3. Calculate the additional rooms required year by year.
4. Calculate the future supply of rooms required.

Part two of a feasibility study covers the financial analysis. A financial analysis generally requires four major sections.

1. Calculation of the capital investment required and tentative financing plan.
2. Preparation of pro forma statements.
3. Preparation of cash flow projections from the net income forecasts.
4. Evaluation of the projections.

CHAPTER OBJECTIVES

After studying this chapter, the reader should be able to:

1. Discuss the value of a feasibility study and the facts that would be covered in its nonfinancial sections.
2. List and briefly discuss the four steps in hotel room supply and demand analysis.
3. Calculate forecast rooms required from given demand information.
4. Prepare pro forma income statements for rooms, food, and beverages, from given information.
5. Convert pro forma income statements to cash flow from given information.
6. Evaluate the financial analysis projections of a feasibility study.

FEASIBILITY STUDIES

A feasibility study is an in-depth analysis of the financial feasibility of a property development, rather than a promoter's guess that a new idea will be economically viable. A feasibility study is not designed to prove that a new venture will be profitable. An independent feasibility study that is professionally prepared by an impartial third party could result in either a positive or a negative recommendation. If it is negative, both the borrower and the lender should be happy that the proposal goes no further. However, if it is positive, this should not be taken as a guarantee of success. A feasibility study can only consider what is known at present and what may happen in the future. But, since the future is impossible to forecast accurately, and so many unforeseen factors that cannot be anticipated can come into play, there can be no guarantees. In other words, a feasibility study may reduce the risk of a particular investment but does not eliminate it.

Study may reduce risk   Some feasibility studies seek out the most appropriate location for a new property and continue with the study from there. Others take a given location without considering alternatives.

FEASIBILITY STUDY FORMAT

Although the scope of a feasibility study for a suburban restaurant differs considerably from one for a major downtown hotel complex, the basic format of any feasibility study is the same. Most feasibility studies conclude with a financial analysis of the proposal. This will be covered in more depth later in this chapter. However, the other parts of a feasibility study that precede the financial analysis will be briefly discussed here. In this discussion we will assume that the feasibility study is for a hotel with food and beverage facilities. In a feasibility study for a motel with only rooms, facilities data relevant to only guest rooms would be included. In a study for a restaurant, the rooms data would be irrelevant.

Suggested format

A suggested format for a hotel feasibility study would generally cover each of the following.

FRONT MATTER

This includes an introduction covering the reasons the study was carried out, what property is being evaluated and how this evaluation was conducted, when the study was conducted and by whom, and a summary highlighting the findings, conclusions, and recommendations.

GENERAL MARKET CHARACTERISTICS

This section covers such items as site location and the general area's population growth trends, industrial diversification and growth, building permit activity, employment and economic trends, disposable incomes, housing, transportation, attractions, convention facilities, and special factors (for example, is the area's economy highly dependent on its local university population?). Only those items relevant to the proposed new hotel should be discussed. Both descriptive and statistical data should be included. The information should be concise and primarily related to the demand for rooms (since other services offered by a hotel are generally derived directly from rooms usage).

Include descriptive and statistical data

SITE EVALUATION

If an in-depth section on site location is included in the study, that section should include detailed maps of the location. Wherever possible, those maps should show important subcenters of activity related to the proposal, such as industrial areas, shopping malls, and convention and support center locations. Transportation routes, including, for example, routes to and from the airport, should be shown. If auto access methods are important (as they frequently are), these auto routes should be indicated.

Physical information

Physical information about the site should be included, such as dimensions, existing improvements (buildings) on the site, and adequacy of the site for possible future expansion.

Cost of the site, site preparation costs prior to construction, and property taxes should be covered. Finally, any other important matters such as zoning restrictions, height restrictions, parking space requirements, future traffic flow changes, and availability of utility services should be part of this section.

SUPPLY AND DEMAND INFORMATION

Three possibilities

There are three possible reasons for a new hotel. One is that the present demand for rooms is greater than the present supply; another is that there is a demand from a new market that is not presently served with the existing supply; and the third is that the present supply is inferior in quality to the needs of the present demand or market. It is therefore important that the study analyze the supply/demand situation in order to identify the market for a proposed new property. This is preferably done by looking at the entire local market insofar as the current situation is concerned and then adjusting for anticipated future changes.

Certain basic information should be included, as follows:

- Occupancy trends in the local area for the past five years. This should be broken down by class of hotel (see next item), if possible.
- A list of hotels currently serving the local market. The list should be categorized by class of hotel. Three classes are normally listed: those that would be the most competitive properties, those that would be somewhat competitive, and those that would be less competitive. The list should include each hotel by name, the number of rooms it has, and its current room rates. Any hotels in this list that were built in the past five years should be highlighted with added information, such as the facilities they have other than rooms (for example, number of seats in their restaurants) and the quality of those facilities.

  Highlight newest properties

  In addition, the most competitive hotels should be further highlighted by including additional information (if available) about their rooms occupancy rates, food and beverage facilities usage (for example, seat turnovers and average checks), and the composition of their market for rooms, food, and beverages.
- The principal likely sources of demand should be covered. Generally, for a city hotel, the sources of room demand are from three main types of customer: the traveling businessperson, the convention delegate, and the general tourist or vacationer. For each category, relevant data should be provided that could be indicative of demand for rooms.

High correlation

For the business traveller, relevant data might include growth in local airport traffic, and/or growth in local office space occupancies for the past five years, since there is frequently a high correlation between these items and demand for hotel rooms.

Data concerning the convention or business meeting delegate would include the number of conventions held each year in the area, types of conventions, their size, total number of delegates, average length of delegate stay, and average conventioneer daily spending.

Data concerning vacationer arrivals would include number of tourists, average length of stay, average daily spending on hotel accommodation and meals, and any change in or extension of the tourists season over the past several years.

If there is any significant demand for hotel accommodations from any special source, this should be covered. For example, sporting events can often be a major source of demand for hotel rooms close to the sporting event location.

Much of the information necessary for this section of the study can be obtained from local chambers of commerce, convention and visitor bureaus, hotel and motel associations, airport authorities, government agencies, and, in the case of office space occupancies, the local office building owners' association. Each individual situation will require other possible sources of information to be contacted for relevant information.

Sources of data

SUPPLY AND DEMAND ANALYSIS

Four steps

Once the supply and demand information has been assembled and tabulated, it must then be analyzed to determine if additional hotel rooms in the area can be justified. This requires four steps.

Step 1. Calculate the most recent 12-month average occupancy of the most competitive hotels.

Let us assume there are five competitive hotels and their number of rooms and occupancies are as follows for the most recent year:

Hotel	Rooms in Hotel	Average Occupancy (%)	Average Nightly Demand
#1	320	70%	224
#2	108	75	81
#3	246	85	209
#4	170	70	119
#5	312	85	265
Total	1,156		898

For each hotel the number of rooms has been multiplied by that hotel's average occupancy percentage to arrive at average nightly demand. Total average nightly demand of 898 rooms has then been arrived at.

Average annual occupancy

The average annual occupancy of the most competitive hotels is then calculated by dividing the total average nightly demand by the total rooms available and multiplying the result by 100:

$$\frac{\text{Average Nightly Demand}}{\text{Rooms in Hotel}} \times 100 = \begin{array}{c}\text{Average}\\\text{Annual}\\\text{Occupancy}\end{array} \qquad \frac{898}{1,156} \times 100 = 78\%$$

Step 2.   Calculate the composite growth rate of demand from the various sources.

Let us assume that our demand information gave the breakdown figures in percentages for each source, as well as annual compound growth rates for that source, as follows:

Source	Source of Demand (%)	Annual Compound Growth (%)	Composite Growth (%)
Business travellers	75	8%	6.0
Convention delegates	10	5	0.5
Vacationers	15	10	1.5
Total	100%		8.0%

Estimate from historic information

    Source-of-demand percentages have been multiplied by the annual compound growth rate percentages in the next column to provide the composite growth rate figures in the right-hand column (for example, 75% × 8% = 6.0%). The annual compound growth rate figures can be estimated from historic growth rate figures projected into the future. The total overall composite growth rate figure is 8.0%, indicated above.

Step 3.   Calculate future rooms demand year by year.

This calculation is shown as follows:

Year	Demand	Composite Growth (%)	Future Demand
1	898	108%	970
2	970	108	1,048
3	1,048	108	1,132
4	1,132	108	1,223
5	1,223	108	1,321

    In year 1 the current average nightly demand for rooms figure of 898 (calculated in step 1) is multiplied by the composite growth rate figure of 108% (100% + 8% composite growth rate figure calculated in step 2) to arrive at the future demand figure of 970 rooms in the year 1. The 970 figure is carried forward into year 2 and is itself multiplied by 108%. Similar calculations are made for each of the remaining three years.

Step 4. *Calculate the future supply of rooms required.*

We know from step 1 that the current occupancy rate in the competitive area is 78%. Let us now assume that a 70% occupancy of hotel rooms is "normal" for our competitive area. Normal means that, at that occupancy, a hotel should be profitable. We therefore know that the local market could support additional rooms right now, since current occupancy is averaging 78%. We can calculate the current need for additional rooms at a 70% occupancy rate by dividing current nightly demand by 70%:

"Normal" occupancy

$$\frac{\text{Average Nightly Demand}}{\text{Average Occupancy \%}} \times 100 = \frac{\text{Rooms}}{\text{Required}} \qquad \frac{898}{70\%} \times 100 = 1{,}283$$

From this we can conclude that there is currently a "shortage" of 127 rooms (1,283 that the market could support less the 1,156 that the market presently offers). Stated another way, if a new 127-room hotel were built today, given the current demand for rooms, the new overall average occupancy rate would be 70%.

$$\frac{\text{Average Nightly Demand}}{\text{Rooms Shortage} + \text{Rooms in Hotel}} \times 100 = \frac{\text{Average}}{\text{Occupancy}} \qquad \frac{898}{127 + 1{,}156} \times 100 = 70\%$$

Next, the future demand for additional hotel rooms is projected for the next five years, as follows:

Year	Rooms Demand	÷	Normal Occupancy (%)	=	Supply Required	−	Current Supply	=	New Rooms Required
Current	898		70%		1,283		1,156		127
1	970		70		1,386		1,156		230
2	1,048		70		1,497		1,156		341
3	1,132		70		1,617		1,156		461
4	1,223		70		1,747		1,156		591
5	1,321		70		1,887		1,156		731

In the above tabulation, the future demand figures from step 3 have each been divided by a 70% occupancy rate (as was demonstrated earlier for the current year situation) to arrive at the figures in the supply required column. From each year's supply-required figure, the current supply of rooms (1,156) has been deducted. The end result is a forecast of the number of new rooms that could be supported over each of the next five years, given all these assumptions.

We see that, at the end of five years, 731 additional rooms could be supported at an average occupancy of 70%. Note also that the rooms-required figures in the right-hand column are cumulative year by year.

Figures are cumulative

To reduce risk we might want to assume that a 75%, rather than a 70%, occupancy should be used. In that case, the year-by-year demand figures would be divided by 75%, resulting in a reduced number of additional rooms per year that the market could support.

However, before the supply/demand analysis is finalized, and a recommendation is made about the size of property to be planned, some other factors may need to be considered. For example, if any of the existing competitive facilities are planned for removal from the market (demolished or converted to some other use), the supply figures should be adjusted accordingly. Similarly, if any information is available about other proposed competitive hotels in the area, this should be adjusted for in the future supply figures. Finally, the decision about whether or not to build should not be based on numbers alone. Frequently, two adjacent, competitive hotels, motels, or restaurants will have vastly different demands for their products. There are many nonquantifiable factors that cause this to be so, such as atmosphere, quality of decor, management, and staff training, to name only a few.

Other considerations

SPACE RECOMMENDATIONS

The feasibility study at this point could include information that the architect might require in order to prepare more detailed plans. This should include not only such items as number of rooms and the proportion of rooms of various types (singles, doubles, twins), but also the proportion of space and number of seats recommended for food, beverage, and related facilities, such as meeting rooms and public spaces (lobbies), and possibly even suggested themes for bars and restaurants. Back-of-the-house facilities and space requirements (kitchens, storerooms, offices) should be included, as should parking space requirements. Finally, any recommendations concerning recreation facilities should be covered in this section.

Suggested themes

FINANCIAL ANALYSIS

A major part of any feasibility study is the financial analysis section. This section is normally broken down into a number of subsections, such as the capital investment required and a tentative financing plan, pro forma income statements, projected cash flow, and evaluation of projections.

Subsections of analysis

Each of these subsections will be discussed in relation to the financial feasibility of a hypothetical new 100-room motor hotel that will have a 65-seat coffee shop, 75-seat dining room, and 90-seat cocktail lounge. Any income received other than from these operating departments will be incidental.

CAPITAL INVESTMENT REQUIRED AND TENTATIVE FINANCING PLAN

Estimates based on professional advice from architects, contractors, and other useful sources indicate that the investment required in the proposed property will be:

Breakdown of required investment

Land	$ 300,000
Building (including all professional fees for architects, designers, and lawyers)	2,100,000
Furniture and equipment	600,000
Interest on construction financing	220,000
Preopening operating expenses	100,000
Initial working capital	50,000
Total	$3,370,000

The total estimated investment required of $3,370,000 is tentatively broken down into the following possible financing plan:

	Debt	Equity	Total
Land and building (75% debt/25% equity	$1,800,000	$ 600,000	$2,400,000
Furniture and equipment (80% debt/20% equity)	480,000	120,000	600,000
Interest on construction financing		220,000	220,000
Preopening expenses		100,000	100,000
Initial working capital		50,000	50,000
Totals	$2,280,000	$1,090,000	$3,370,000

Assumptions and other information:

Interim financing

1. Interim, or bridge, financing will be required in the amount of $1,800,000 for partial payment of land and for construction financing. This amount, advanced by the lender month by month as required, will carry a 12% interest rate, or 1% per month. Interest will be paid monthly out of equity funds available. The full amount of the advance ($1,800,000) will be refunded, just prior to opening, out of the proceeds of a permanent first

mortgage to be taken out on the land and building. Total preopening interest cost will be $220,000 as illustrated in Exhibit 13.1. This interest expense is the amount the developer has to pay the lender at the prevailing rate on the total amount of money advanced to that date.

2. The permanent first mortgage of $1,800,000 will be for a 20-year term and will carry a 10% interest rate for the first five years. A schedule showing the breakdown between interest and principal for the first five years, following the hotel opening, is illustrated below.

Mortgage repayment schedule

Year	Annual Payment	Interest	Principal	Balance
				$1,800,000
1	$208,000	$180,000	$28,000	1,772,000
2	208,000	177,000	31,000	1,741,000
3	208,000	174,000	34,000	1,707,000
4	208,000	171,000	37,000	1,670,000
5	208,000	167,000	41,000	1,629,000

In these calculations figures have been rounded to the nearest $1,000. (Note that payments on such a mortgage would normally be made monthly and the schedule of repayments calculated on this basis. However, for the sake of simplicity, annual payments have been assumed.)

3. The financing of equipment and furniture will be by way of a chattel mortgage (the chattels being the equipment and furniture) over five years at a 12% interest rate. Repayment will be made with combined equal annual installments of principal and interest. A schedule showing these repayment amounts broken down into principal and interest is illustrated below. (Again, all figures are rounded to the nearest $1,000.)

Year	Annual Payment	Interest	Principal	Balance
				$480,000
1	$133,000	$58,000	$ 75,000	405,000
2	133,000	48,000	85,000	320,000
3	133,000	38,000	95,000	225,000
4	133,000	27,000	106,000	119,000
5	133,000	14,000	119,000	0

Chattel mortgage schedule

4. The total initial equity investment is forecast to be $1,090,000. It is useful to prepare a schedule showing the timing of this investment, by month,

Exhibit 13.1 Equity Investment Schedule

Months Before Opening	Equity Amount	Land and Building	Furniture and Equipment	Interest on Interim Financing	Prepaid Expenses	Working Capital
19	$ 216,500	$215,000		$ 1,500		
18	15,000	10,000		5,000		
17	15,500	10,000		5,500		
16	16,000	10,000		6,000		
15	32,000	25,000		7,000		
14	33,000	25,000		8,000		
13	34,000	25,000		9,000		
12	35,000	25,000		10,000		
11	36,000	25,000		11,000		
10	37,000	25,000		12,000		
9	38,000	25,000		13,000		
8	39,000	25,000		14,000		
7	40,000	25,000		15,000		
6	41,000	25,000		16,000		
5	61,500	25,000	$ 20,000	16,500		
4	82,000	20,000	20,000	17,000	$ 25,000	
3	102,500	20,000	40,000	17,500	25,000	
2	103,000	20,000	40,000	18,000	25,000	
1	113,000	20,000		18,000	25,000	$50,000
TOTALS	$1,090,000	$600,000	$120,000	$220,000	$100,000	$50,000

prior to opening, so that the equity investors know when they have to put up the money and what it is for. This is illustrated in Exhibit 13.1 for our proposed hotel.

5. The interest expense of $220,000 on interim financing will be recorded as an expense on the income statement in the first year of operation.

6. The preopening expenses of $100,000 (for such items as insurance, property taxes, wages and staff training, advertising, and other operating costs incurred prior to opening) will be amortized (shown as an expense) over the first two years of operation.

7. For building, as well as furniture and equipment, declining balance depreciation will be used. Building depreciation will be 3.75% per year, and furniture and equipment, 20% per year. Depreciation schedules are as follows:

Depreciation schedules

BUILDING

Year	Depreciation Expense	Balance
		$2,100,000
1	3.75% × $2,100,000 = $79,000	2,021,000
2	3.75 × 2,021,000 = 76,000	1,945,000
3	3.75 × 1,945,000 = 73,000	1,872,000
4	3.75 × 1,872,000 = 70,000	1,802,000
5	3.75 × 1,802,000 = 67,000	1,735,000

FURNITURE AND EQUIPMENT

Year	Depreciation Expense	Balance
		$600,000
1	20% × $600,000 = $120,000	480,000
2	20 × 480,000 = 96,000	384,000
3	20 × 384,000 = 77,000	307,000
4	20 × 307,000 = 61,000	246,000
5	20 × 246,000 = 49,000	197,000

PRO FORMA INCOME STATEMENTS

The next step is the preparation of pro forma income statements by two departments (Rooms and Food and Beverage).

Rooms

Rooms revenue calculation

Rooms revenue is based on the assumption that, in the first year, occupancy of the 100 rooms will be 60% and that the average room rate will be $52. This rate would be competitive with what other motor hotels in the area are charging. In year 2, and for the remaining three years of our five-year projections, occupancy is expected to climb to 70%, and average room rate will be increased to $56. Year 1 room revenue is therefore:

$$100 \text{ rooms} \times 60\% \times \$52 \times 365 \text{ nights} = \$1,138,800$$

and for each of the next four years it will be:

$$100 \text{ rooms} \times 70\% \times \$56 \times 365 \text{ nights} = \$1,430,800$$

Rooms department operating costs are estimated as follows for year 1:

Payroll and related expenses	$244,000
Other direct operating costs	54,000
Total	$298,000

Estimated operating costs

These estimated operating costs can generally be based on a percentage of sales, using national averages for that size and type of operation, adjusting for local conditions, if necessary. In year 2 and the remaining years of our forecast, these costs are increased in total by $74,000 a year to take care of the increased occupancy. Our rooms department income statements would now be as follows, with figures rounded to the closest $1,000:

	Year 1	Year 2 to 5
Sales revenue	$1,139,000	$1,431,000
Operating costs	(298,000)	(372,000)
Net department operating income	$ 841,000	$1,059,000

Food and Beverage

Food and beverage, insofar as sales and cost of sales are concerned, should be broken down into two separate components: food and alcoholic beverages. Food sales should in turn be broken down by sales area (coffee shop and dining room) and then in turn by meal period within each sales area. Sales are then calculated by using the basic equation given in Chapter 9.

Food revenue calculation

$$\text{Number of seats} \times \text{Seat turnover rate} \times \text{Average check} \times \text{Days open in year}$$

For example, in our 65-seat coffee shop, assuming it will be open every day of the year, breakfast sales are calculated as follows, assuming one turnover and a $5.25 average check:

$$65 \times 1 \times \$5.25 \times 365 = \text{total sales } \underline{\$124,556}$$

Similar calculations would have to be made for the other meal periods, and, possibly, for coffee break periods if these were expected to generate significant enough amounts of sales revenue. Seat turnover figures and average check amounts normally vary enough from one meal period to another to require these separate calculations. Turnover rates and average checks can often be based on an assessment of what competitive hotel restaurant operations in the local area are doing, combined with an evaluation of the type of clientele the guess rooms will be catering to.

Derived demand

In the calculation of total food revenue, it might be necessary to take into consideration sales generated in areas such as room service. In room service the rooms occupancy figure will give an indication of an estimated average check of the number of guests per day who might require some type of food service. This would give total daily sales, which should then be multiplied by 365.

In addition, the derived demand from nonfood areas may add to total food sales. For example, if food service is offered to customers in the cocktail lounge, an estimate of the number of daily orders that could be expected multiplied by an assumed average check would give a forecast of daily sales. This daily sales figure can then be multiplied by the days in the year that the lounge will be open.

Alcoholic beverage sales

Let us assume that this work has been completed and that total annual food revenue is estimated at $1,570,000. To this food figure must be added the alcoholic beverage sales in the coffee shop and dining room, as well as in the lounge. You are referred to the relevant section in Chapter 9 for forecasting beverage sales. Assume that total annual beverage sales for the proposed hotel have been calculated and are estimated to be $1,038,000. Combined food and beverage sales will be $2,608,000.

From the combined food and beverage sales figures, the direct operating costs must be deducted. As was the case with the rooms department, these costs can be estimated on a percentage of sales basis, using national restaurant industry figures for this size and type of operation, adjusting if necessary for local conditions. The departmental income statement can now be prepared.

	Food	Beverage		Total
Sales revenue	$1,570,000	$1,038,000		$2,608,000
Cost of sales	(628,000)	(261,000)		(889,000)
Gross profit	$ 942,000	$ 777,000		$1,719,000
Payroll and related expenses			$921,000	
Other direct operating expenses			519,000	(1,440,000)
Net departmental operating income				$ 279,000

Deduct undistributed expenses

Once the forecast departmental income statements have been finalized, the total departmental operating income can be calculated. From this can be deducted the undistributed expenses (administrative and general, marketing, property operation and maintenance, and energy costs). These expenses are generally primarily fixed in nature and can usually be estimated with some accuracy. In this case the figure is estimated to be $480,000 annually.

Increasing costs ignored

The forecasted departmental operating income figures, less undistributed expenses, have been transferred to Exhibit 13.2 for each of the first five years of operation. It should be noted that these figures are constant for each of the years (except for rooms departmental income from year two on, due to the anticipated increase in occupancy percentage, room rate, and direct expenses, as explained earlier). In all other cases, the possibility of increasing costs has been ignored on the assumption that any increased costs will be passed on in the form of higher room rates or food and beverage prices; thus, net operating income will not change significantly. Also, for the years two through five, no upward adjustment has been made for any additional sales revenue that the food and beverage areas would derive from the additional rooms occupancy. At this point the sales revenue figures should be kept as conservative as possible.

In Exhibit 13.2, in years 1 and 2, $100,000 preopening operating costs have been deducted: $50,000 in each of the years. Also, the $220,000 interest expense incurred on preopening financing has been deducted in year one. Note that for tax purposes in the United States (as well as some other countries) the interest expense on interim financing of $220,000 cannot be deducted to arrive at income before tax. Instead, the interest has to be capitalized, that is added, to the total cost of building construction. Some of the interest expense is thus included each year as part of the building's depreciation expense.

Exhibit 13.2   Pro Forma Income Statements

	Year 1	Year 2	Year 3	Year 4	Year 5
Departmental contributory income					
Rooms	$ 841,000	$1,059,000	$1,059,000	$1,059,000	$1,059,000
Food and beverage	279,000	279,000	279,000	279,000	279,000
	$1,120,000	$1,338,000	$1,338,000	$1,338,000	$1,338,000
Less: undistributed expenses	(480,000)	(480,000)	(480,000)	(480,000)	(480,000)
Preopening expenses	(50,000)	(50,000)			
Interim financing interest	(220,000)				
Income before interest and depreciation	$ 370,000	$ 808,000	$ 858,000	$ 858,000	$ 858,000
Interest	(238,000)	(225,000)	(212,000)	(198,000)	(181,000)
Depreciation	(199,000)	(172,000)	(150,000)	(131,000)	(116,000)
Income before income tax	($ 67,000)	$ 411,000	$ 496,000	$ 529,000	$ 561,000
Income tax	0	(172,000)	(248,000)	(265,000)	(281,000)
Net income (loss)	($ 67,000)	$ 239,000	$ 248,000	$ 264,000	$ 280,000

Deduct interest and
depreciation

In order to arrive at the proposed hotel's overall net income (or loss), permanent and chattel mortgage interest, as well as building, furniture, and equipment depreciation, have been deducted for each of the five years. Finally income tax has been deducted. There is no income tax in year 1 because of the loss of $67,000. Also, that loss is carried forward into year 2 and deducted from the income before income tax ($411,000 – $67,000 = $344,000) before applying the 50% tax rate on the $344,000 of taxable income.

PROJECTED CASH FLOW

The next step in our financial feasibility is to convert the hotel's annual net income to an annual cash flow. This is illustrated in Exhibit 13.3.

Adjustments required

First, to net income has been added back those expenses, previously deducted to arrive at net income, that did not require an outlay of cash in that year. These include depreciation (which is simply a write-down of the book value of the related assets), interim financing interest (the cash that was paid out prior to opening and is part of the equity investment amount), and the preopening expenses for years one and two (which were also paid out prior to opening from equity investment).

Finally, the principal portions of the permanent and chattel mortgage payments have been deducted, since these require an outlay of cash that is not shown as a deduction to arrive at net income. The resulting figure for each year is the net cash flow. See Exhibit 13.3.

Note that, even though there is an operating loss in year one (due to the heavy burden of the preopening interest expense), the cash flow is still positive. This means that, with the proposed financing plan, there will be no problem in meeting both the interest and principal payments on the debt.

Exhibit 13.3   Cash Flow

	Year 1	Year 2	Year 3	Year 4	Year 5
Net income	($67,000)	$239,000	$248,000	$264,000	$280,000
Add: Depreciation	199,000	172,000	150,000	131,000	116,000
Preopening expenses	50,000	50,000			
Interim financing interest	220,000				
	$402,000	$461,000	$398,000	$395,000	$396,000
Deduct: Principal payments	(103,000)	(116,000)	(129,000)	(143,000)	(160,000)
Net cash flow	$299,000	$345,000	$269,000	$252,000	$236,000

EVALUATION OF PROJECTIONS

Return on investment

At this point in the analysis, it might be useful to determine the return on equity investment that would be achieved with the given estimates of revenue and expenses. Over the first five years the total net income from Exhibit 13.2 is:

Year 1	($67,000)
Year 2	239,000
Year 3	248,000
Year 4	264,000
Year 5	280,000
Total	$964,000

This is an average of slightly less than $193,000 a year ($964,000 divided by 5), or an average return on the initial $1,090,000 equity investment of about 17.7% which, although not high for the risk involved, could be considered reasonable after income tax. However, as seen in Chapter 12, return on investment may not be the best criterion to use in evaluating an investment proposal. The net present value (NPV) and/or internal rate of return (IRR) methods discussed and illustrated in that chapter are frequently more valid measures for project evaluation.

Use NPV or IRR

Also, the forecasts used were based on only one level of occupancy, set of room rates, and food and beverage prices. It is normal in practice to determine estimated net income from a level of sales higher than expected (thus providing a higher return on investment), as well as a level of sales lower than expected.

Try different financing

If a satisfactory return could not be anticipated, the project might be terminated at this point. Alternatively, a different financing arrangement might be attempted, using more or less leverage and/or different terms and interest rates. To do this manually may require considerable work, but today's microcomputers can be easily programmed to handle changes in a number of variables, individually or at the same time, to produce new net income and cash flow figures based on the changes.

If a plan were to be arranged that seemed to produce net income and cash flow figures that were, in the initial years, acceptable, then the cash flow projections should be continued beyond the five-year period to extend them for the entire life of the project. Finally, the lifetime cash flow figures could then be evaluated, using the NPV or IRR investment analysis methods, before a final decision, considering all necessary facts, is made to proceed or not with the development.

FEASIBILITY OF EXPANDING EXISTING OPERATION

Availability of historic records

Although this chapter has discussed a financial feasibility study for a new operation, the same techniques can be applied equally as well to the feasibility of expanding an existing hotel, motel, restaurant, or similar business. In that case only the marginal or incremental revenues and expenses, as well as debt and equity financing costs associated with the expansion, would be considered in the net income and cash flow projections. In fact, these projections are much easier to make for an existing business, since it has its present operation's historic accounting data to use as a basis for forecasting.

COMPUTER APPLICATIONS

A spreadsheet program can be used for all the calculations necessary for a feasibility study forecast income statement and cash flow statement for as many years into the future as desired. It will also allow rapid results to be produced in "what if" situations, for example, by changing forecast room rates and/or occupancy percentages. Finally, it will allow NPV or IRR to be applied to the forecasts to provide a more valid measure of a proposed project's viability.

SUMMARY

A feasibility study is an in-depth analysis of the financial feasibility of a property expansion or a new property development. A feasibility study cannot guarantee financial success, but it does reduce much of the guesswork and risk of a new venture.

A feasibility study for a hotel can usually be broken down into two major parts. The first part includes such items as the front matter (including conclusions and recommendations), general market characteristics (location, population and industrial growth, employment, incomes, economic trends), site evaluation (including maps, transportation routes, and physical information about the site), and supply-and-demand information (market to be served, information about competitive properties, and the likely sources of demand for the facilities to be offered). The next section in the first part of the study would be a supply-and-demand analysis for guest rooms (in a hotel situation). The four steps in this analysis are:

1. Calculate the most recent 12-month average occupancy of the most competitive hotels.
2. Calculate the composite growth rate of demand from the various sources.
3. Calculate the additional rooms required year by year.
4. Calculate the future supply of rooms required.

Once these steps have been completed, the first part of the study can be concluded with recommendations about the number and types of rooms proposed and about other facilities proposed, such as number of seats and themes for food and beverage areas.

The second part of a feasibility study is a financial analysis of the proposal based on the facilities recommended. This part is composed of four major sections:

1. Calculation of the capital investment required and tentative financing plan. The investment required is broken down into such items as land, building, furniture and equipment, construction loan interest, other preopening expenses, and working capital. The financing plan is then broken down into its debt and equity elements.

2. Preparation of pro forma income statements. These are usually initially prepared for a minimum five-year period. Sales revenue for each department is first forecast, and from this are deducted estimated direct expenses (usually based on a percentage of sales revenue). Next are deducted the indirect expenses, construction financing interest, and other preopening expenses. Finally, mortgage interest and depreciation are deducted, as well as income tax, where relevant, to arrive at net income.

3. Preparation of cash flow projections from the net income forecasts. Net income is adjusted for depreciation and principal payments on debt financing to arrive at cash flow.

4. Evaluation of the projections to date is made at this point. If necessary, revenue levels and/or other variables can be changed to see how this might affect the results. Finally, if the proposal appears feasible, a complete evaluation of the project's entire life, using NPV or IRR (see Chapter 12) should be carried out before making the final decision on the investment.

DISCUSSION QUESTIONS

1. Since a feasibility study for a proposed new venture cannot guarantee that the venture will be successful, of what value is such a study?

2. In a feasibility study for a restaurant in a downtown office building, what general market characteristics do you think would be relevant?

3. In preparing a feasibility study for a motor hotel to be located in an area where there are several other motor hotels, what factors would you consider to determine which of the other operations are the most competitive?

4. A resort hotel is to be located in a mountain area near a major highway about 150 miles from the closest town or city. What sources of demand might you consider in a feasibility study for this property?

5. Briefly describe how a composite growth rate of demand for hotel rooms can be calculated.

6. Two similar competitive restaurants have quite different levels of demand (average total number of customers per day). What factors could cause this to be so?

7. In preparing the pro forma income statement for a rooms department, how do you think the average room rate and occupancy figures could be established?

8. In estimating total sales revenue for a coffee shop in a proposed new hotel, why is it important to begin by estimating sales revenue by meal period?

9. What adjustments generally have to be made to the net income figures to convert them to a cash flow basis?

10. In what way might a change in the depreciation method used affect the projected cash flow figures in a feasibility study?

11. If the initial feasibility of a proposed new hotel does not appear good from a financial point of view, what variables might one try to change in order to improve the result?

ETHICS SITUATION

The owner of a proposed new motel has received a feasibility study from a consultant that shows that, at best, the operation would be only marginally profitable. The owner knows that this report will not convince possible investors to advance the funds for this proposed project, so he changes the feasibility study figures to improve the profitability of the operation. Discuss the ethics of this situation.

PROBLEMS

13.1   There are five competitive motels in a resort area with the following number of rooms and current occupancy rates:

Motel	Rooms	Occupancy (%)
A	74	82%
B	45	73
C	58	85
D	48	70
E	52	75

Demand for rooms in the area is broken down into the following sources and growth rates:

Source	Percentage	Growth Rate (%)
Business traveller	10%	5%
Vacation traveller	80	8
Other travellers	10	1

a. Calculate the current average occupancy of the five motels.

b. Calculate the composite rate of growth in demand.

c. Apply the composite growth rate to the demand figures to obtain projected demand for each of the next four years.

d. Assume that a 70% average room occupancy for the motels in this resort would be profitable. Calculate the future supply of rooms that could be supported for each of the next four years.

13.2   Six competitive motor hotels have the following number of rooms and current occupancy rates.

Motor Hotel	Rooms	Occupancy (%)
#1	140	85%
#2	160	80
#3	84	75
#4	90	70
#5	120	80
#6	144	75

Demand for rooms in the area where the motor hotels are located is broken down into the following sources and growth rates:

Source	Percentage	Growth Rate (%)
Business traveller	50%	5%
Vacation traveller	40	6
Other travellers	10	1

a. Calculate the current average occupancy of the six motor hotels.

b. Calculate the composite rate of growth in demand.

c. Apply the composite growth rate to the demand figures to obtain projected demand for each of the next four years.

      d. Assume a 75% average room occupancy for the motor hotels in this area would be profitable. Assume also that motor hotel three is due to be demolished in year two to make way for a new highway. Calculate the future supply of rooms that could be supported for each of the next four years.

13.3   A financial feasibility study is being carried out for a proposed new 120-seat restaurant. It will be open for both lunch and dinner from Monday through Saturday and for dinner only on Sunday. For the sake of simplicity, assume a 52-week year. Seat turnover and average food check figures are estimated as follows:

	Turnover	Average Food Check
Weekday lunch	$1\frac{1}{2}$	$ 5.60
Weekday dinner	$1\frac{1}{4}$	10.50
Sunday dinner	$1\frac{3}{4}$	13.00

In addition, the restaurant has a small banquet room, and food revenue in this area is estimated at $14,000 a month. Alcoholic beverage revenue is estimated to be 12% of lunch food revenue and 30% of dinner food revenue. In the banquet room, alcoholic beverage revenue is forecast to be 40% of food revenue in that area. Food cost is estimated at 40% of total food revenue, and beverage cost 30% of total beverage revenue. Wage cost for salaried personnel (manager, chef, hostess, head waitress, and cashier) is estimated at $300,000 per year. Wages for all other employees will be 15% of total annual restaurant revenue. Employee benefits (vacations, meals, etc.) will be 10% of total annual wages. Other operating costs are estimated at 12% of total annual revenue. Undistributed costs are forecast to be $130,000 per year.

Prepare the restaurant's pro forma income statement for the first year, rounding all figures to the nearest dollar. Ignore income tax.

13.4   A new 50-room budget motel is being planned. Total cost will be $1,450,000, of which land will be $150,000, building $900,000, furniture and equipment $300,000, and the balance for preopening interest and other expenses. The building will be financed 70% by an 8% mortgage. The annual payment to amortize (pay back principal and interest) this mortgage will be $63,000. The furniture and equipment will be financed 75% by a chattel mortgage at 11%, repayable in five equal installments of $61,000 principal and interest. Apart from the mortgage and chattel mortgage amounts, the balance of the total investment required will be from equity.

      a. Calculate the amount of the equity investment.

b. Prepare the building mortgage repayment schedule for the first five years. Round figures to the nearest $1,000.

c. Prepare the chattel mortgage repayment schedule. Round figures to the nearest $1,000.

13.5   Given the facts in problem 13.4, assume the building will be depreciated at 6% declining balance and that furniture and equipment will be depreciated at 25% declining balance. Prepare depreciation schedules for the first five years. Round figures to the nearest $1,000.

13.6   Given the facts in problems 13.4 and 13.5 and the following additional information, prepare the pro forma income statements for each of the first five years:

Year	Average Room Rate	Occupancy (%)
1	$30	70%
2	30	75
3	33	75
4	35	75
5	35	80

Rooms operating costs average 60% of total room revenue. Indirect expenses will be $40,000 in year one and will increase by $4,000 a year for each of the next four years. The preopening interest and other expenses total $100,000 and will be amortized equally over each of the first five years. Income tax, if any, will be 25% of earnings before income tax. Note, however, that if there are any losses, they may be carried forward and deducted from earnings before income tax, before the 25% tax rate is applied. Round all numbers to the nearest $1,000.

13.7   Given the facts in problems 13.4, 13.5, and 13.6, calculate the net annual cash flow figures for each of the five years. What would be your evaluation of the financial feasibility of this proposed motel?

CASE 13

Although he has only been in business for a short time, Charlie is already thinking about opening a second restaurant similar to the present one (a relatively medium-priced operation catering to the local neighborhood's family and small business trade).

Assume that he has asked you to do some preliminary work on a feasibility study for this second restaurant. Select a specific geographic location in your town with which you are familiar and which you think would be suitable for this new operation.

Prepare a two- or three-page report for Charlie describing this location (include a map if you think it will help), explaining why that location might be suitable, and briefly discussing the economic and demographic factors (about which you would eventually need more detailed information) that would support the need for a restaurant in this location.

14

Financial Goals and Information Systems

INTRODUCTION

This chapter has two major parts: the first part is about financial goals and the second is about information systems. The section on financial goals discusses mission statements and the objectives and purposes of financial statements. Two financial management goals are then explored: profit maximization and maximization of return on investment, neither of which is a commonly used goal.

Some time is spent on the most commonly used goal, maximization of stockholder wealth. Subgoals are then discussed, as is management by objectives (MBO). This section of the chapter also includes comments about other goals, such as social goals, and concludes with developing an action plan to achieve goals.

The second section of the chapter covers information systems. The four levels of an information system are introduced: data production, data sorting, information production, and decision making. Most of this section concentrates on the last two of the four levels, since these are the keys for a company to establish an information system that will allow it to meet its financial goals.

This section of the chapter concludes with comments about the effectiveness of a management information system.

CHAPTER OBJECTIVES

After studying this chapter, the reader should be able to:

1. Discuss the role of mission statements with reference to financial goals.

2. Discuss the general concept of financial management and list the types of financial and other goals that a company might have.

3. Discuss the pros and cons of wealth maximization as a financial goal.

4. Define MBO, explain how it is used to measure performance, and define the term "goal congruence."

5. Discuss social goals.

6. Discuss the role of strategies and tactics with reference to developing an action plan to achieve financial goals.

7. List the four levels in the decision-making process.

8. Explain the ways in which information is obtained in an organization, list the main criteria for information to be useful in the decision-making process, and state how an information system should be judged for quality.

9. Define management by exception.

FINANCIAL GOALS

Regardless of the type and size of enterprise in the hospitality industry, financial management will be an ongoing aspect of the overall management of the business. This financial management may be quite unsophisticated in a small, owner-operated establishment and considerably more complex in a large, multi-unit organization. Despite the vast range of sizes and types of establishments in the industry, any operation can benefit from an understanding of the value and importance of financial management. Even nonprofit organizations, such as hospitals, must be able to obtain funds and then invest them to maximize benefits; stated another way, they must be able to provide the most benefits at the least possible cost. The concepts of financial management are, therefore, the same for both profit-oriented and nonprofit organizations; the only difference is how the operating or financial results are measured against the objectives.

Profit versus nonprofit organizations

MISSION STATEMENT

Before developing financial goals, some large hospitality corporations first prepare the organization's mission, or purpose, in a statement. A mission statement is sometimes referred to as a statement of business purpose. This statement should be definable and measurable and should consider customer needs. For example, a mission statement for a resort hotel might read as follows:

Sample mission statement

The Redwood Resort will position itself as the dominant luxury hotel in its area. Its prime weekday market will be corporate meeting and conference groups who will patronize both its guest rooms and food and beverage facilities. The hotel will offer a combination of first-class meeting, guest room, food and beverage, and recreational facilities in a relaxing resort environment. The major sales strategy will be to seek out meeting planners and organizers and use a personal sales approach to obtain their business.

At weekends and during holiday periods, its market will include the upper end of the social scale. To satisfy the entertainment needs of both the corporate and society markets there will be nightly live entertainment.

Its pricing strategy will be to establish high prices that reflect the quality of its facilities and that the market segments selected can afford to pay. Prices will be set to yield an average minimum year-round guest room occupancy of 75% and allow overnight guests free use of all the resort's recreational amenities.

In comparison, the following is the mission statement of a major restaurant chain (Domino's Pizza, Inc.):

To be the leader in delivering off-premise pizzas convenience to customers around the world. As a team united throughout the world, we will accomplish our mission by:

1. Being fanatical about product quality and service consistency.
2. Providing product variety to meet all customer needs.
3. Placing team member and customer safety and security above all other concerns.
4. Operating an environment in which all team members feel valued, because they are.
5. Building and maintaining relationships that reward franchises and other partners for their contributions.

Philosophy of business

As well as being the focus for developing financial goals, the mission statement establishes a sense of direction for an organization by defining what the organization is, what it does, how it does it, and for whom it is being done. In other words, a mission statement is a philosophy for doing business. Mission statements for an organization can:

- Provide a brief statement of its current market position.
- Show which customer groups will be its targets for the marketing plan.
- Provide guidelines for allocation of its resources.
- Indicate where its future growth will occur.

- Give an indication of how its products differ from its competitors' products.
- Focus management's attention on marketing opportunities that conform to its mission.
- Serve as a basis for internal communication.
- Provide a direction to all its employees by alerting them to a common goal.
- Provide a basis for its control and evaluation.

OBJECTIVES OF FINANCIAL MANAGEMENT

Use of funds

Any business, at any particular time, has funds available to it. These funds come from creditors who lend the company money, from owners or stockholders who invest in the company or who own shares in it, and from earnings (profits) retained in the business. These funds may be kept in the business in a very liquid form, such as cash or marketable securities. They can also be tied up in food, beverage, and other inventories or in accounts receivable, or they can be invested in long-term assets, such as land, buildings, and furniture and fixtures.

At any particular point, the balance sheet will give a picture of the business's financial position. At a later date, another balance sheet will probably indicate a different financial position, because the position is never static. Funds are constantly flowing into and out of the business. The mix between the various sources of funds and the various uses of funds is constantly charging. The mix of sources and mix of uses, according to some overall plan, are what financial management is all about.

In large organizations this plan is usually coordinated by a financial manager, who works closely with the general manager. In a smaller operation, the general manager and financial manager are one and the same person.

Generally, the objectives of financial management are:

Three objectives

1. To establish goals, such as how large the company will be, how rapidly it will expand, and how it will measure its success in meeting these goals.

2. To decide on the sources of needed capital and to obtain the funds required by the firm to meet its goals.

3. To allocate these funds effectively to the various assets of the company, again with the company's goals in mind.

Only with clearly stated goals can an organization effectively manage its finances; without them, a business operates without a plan. In a small owner-operated enterprise a goal may be expressed in simple terms, such as that the owner wishes to make enough net income in the first 11 months of the year to

Goals in monetary terms

take a vacation in the twelfth month. In a large, or chain, operation, goals would be established in a much more formal way by the board of directors. Goals are frequently expressed in monetary terms. Some of these financially measurable goals will be discussed.

PROFIT MAXIMIZATION

Profit maximization, or making the most amount of money in the shortest possible time, is one of the commonly considered objectives or goals of a company. It is argued that the total amount of profit or net income is not a realistic measure, since one can always sell more shares and invest the proceeds in marketable securities, thus increasing total net income. Because of this, maximization of earnings per share may be a better way to measure net income. In

Timing of profits

either case, however, the time element is important because of the time value of money. Most people would agree that $100,000 net income in the first year and nothing in each of the following nine years is preferable to $10,000 per year for each of ten years. The reason is that the entire $100,000 could be invested in the first year and continue to accumulate interest until the end of the tenth year, thus maximizing net income.

However, one of the problems with profit maximization as a goal is that it may ignore the possible risks of an investment. An international hotel corporation could open new, profitable hotels in countries with politically unstable governments, ignoring the threat of future government expropriation of the investment. Is the immediate potential net income worth the risk?

Share value dilution through leverage

The profit maximization goal also ignores investment financing risks. A company might become highly levered by borrowing large amounts of debt money at high interest rates in pursuit of some extra net income. Owners of shares, perceiving the risk, might begin selling their shares, thus reducing the market value of the shares. Alternatively, the company might issue new shares to obtain the financing (considerably reducing leverage), thereby diluting the value of present stockholders' shares. In other words, profit maximization as an objective might tend to ignore the company's commitment to its stockholders and create a rift between them and the company's management.

Profit can also be maximized by not paying dividends or by making dividend policy a less important goal. This, too, would probably engender a negative reaction from stockholders.

Finally, if management is being measured by profit maximization, it might tend to emphasize very profitable but short-run investments while ignoring long-run, more consistently profitable investments.

Shortsighted goal

Thus, while a business must have profits, profit maximization as a sole goal is generally shortsighted, particularly if the company has many stockholders.

Maximization of Return on Investment

The maximization of percentage return on investment is a variation of the maximization of profit goal. To meet this goal, the company's management attempts to use its funds so that each dollar invested returns the most dollars of net income, or the higher return on investment.

Obviously, no investment would be made if the return were less than the cost of financing. Frequently, a minimum return on investment will be established for the company as a whole, and no individual investment will be made unless it is expected to yield at least this minimum. The return on investment goal, although it has its place, also has many of the disadvantages of the profit maximization goal.

Maximization of Stockholder Wealth

Generally speaking, most successful larger companies try, over time, to maximize stockholder wealth because this will make stockholders happier than if the wealth were not maximized. One could ask why a company attempts to maximize stockholder wealth and not the wealth of its debt lenders, or the tax department, or employees, or the company's management. The reason is that stockholders are, legally, the owners of the company. All the other groups mentioned must be given their due before the stockholders, as residual claimants, get what is left over.

Maximization of stockholder wealth has as its objective the highest combination of dividend payouts by the company and increase in the market value of the price of the company's shares. With this goal, net income is not as important as earnings per share. The time value of earnings, mentioned earlier, must be a consideration, as must the relative risks of alternative investments and alternative methods of financing those investments. In emphasizing earnings per share, dividend policy and its effect on market price per share must also be considered. Note that maximizing earnings per share may not be the same as maximizing market price per share. The market price shows how well management is doing for stockholders. Dissatisfied stockholders will sell their shares and invest their money elsewhere. If enough of them do this, the market price of the shares will drop.

A company can maximize its earnings per share by never paying dividends, but this would please neither the individual stockholder nor the market for stockholders generally. The market comprises all present and prospective stockholders, who assess the risk of ownership of shares of the company, including potential future earnings, the timing and risk of these earnings, the company's dividend policy, and other factors that are deemed important to establish the price of a share. The individual in the market buys or sells shares according to

Residual claimants

Never paying dividends

Management barometer

his or her perception of the firm. The market price is influenced upward by those wishing to buy shares and downward by those selling. It thus serves as a barometer of how well management is doing on behalf of the stockholders.

Management's policies and plans will therefore be established, under the maximization of stockholder wealth goal, to ensure that wise investments are made, that they are sensibly financed, and that an appropriate dividend policy is established.

One of the disadvantages of this goal is that the price of the company's shares on the market is sometimes influenced by factors beyond the control of the company's management, such as a general recession. Management could also be so concerned with the goal of maximizing stockholder wealth that it forgets about the business's day-to-day operations, and in the interest of its own short-run survival, management might be unwilling to take reasonable risks, even though the investments would be to the stockholders' advantage. Further, where the company is large and share ownership is separate from control of the company, management may not always operate in the best interest

Maximizing
management wealth

of stockholders, although in the long run this is unlikely to occur. Sometimes managers may attempt to maximize their own wealth at the expense of stockholders, but again, in the long run, if management does not appear to maximize stockholder wealth, it can be fired by the board. Note again, however, that the board may be less responsive if stockholders are widely dispersed, and the absence of effective stockholder representation on the board may decrease the pressure on management to maximize stockholder wealth.

Finally, earnings per share in the hospitality industry may not fully reflect the company's true wealth. In the hospitality industry, a company's value can increase considerably through appreciation of its real estate assets, but it may not be reflected in earnings per share. Nor is it apparent on balance sheets that typically show assets at cost less accumulated depreciation (net book value). For a successful hospitality industry enterprise that has been in business for some years, those cost or net book value figures will not be very meaningful.

Subgoals

Even though a favorite goal of many organizations is maximization of stockholder wealth, some consider this goal too broad. For that reason it is often supported with subgoals that will help the overall organization reach its objective, something that department heads can relate to. These subgoals are often translated into such objectives as achieving a certain minimum rooms occupancy or restaurant seat turnover or aiming for a specific minimum level of sales dollars within a budget period, If these subgoals are then reached, this should ensure that the overall corporate financial goal is achieved. In some cases the subgoals

Examples of subgoals

are not even expressed in monetary terms. For example, a restaurant may only emphasize quality, service, cleanliness, and value for money and achieve its overall financial goal by conforming to those subgoals.

Problem of trade-offs

One problem that subgoals create is that there may have to be a trade-off between a decision in one department and a decision in another, or a conflict between short-run and long-run earnings. An example is reducing prices to gain a larger share of the market. This may lower short-run profits. Another example is the reduction in housekeeping quality standards, which may improve short-run profits but may cause occupancies to drop over the long run. The general manager's role is to maintain a balance between short-run subgoals and the long-term financial objectives of the company.

Ranking priorities

It is important to rank objectives and subgoals in order of priority and implement only those from the top of the list that are achievable. If too many objectives and secondary objectives are established and all are tackled, both financial and other resources might be spread too thin for any of them to be achieved.

Management by Objectives

Achievement of goals in an organization has to be carried out by people. Therefore, an important aspect of subgoal setting is to have the employees involved in the whole process of setting those goals. This basic concept is known as management by objectives (MBO). MBO is based on the assumption that employees can be committed to their work and allows for maximum involvement and participation in setting subgoals, personal goals, and performance standards for judging employees' work. The term "goal congruence" is often used in this

Goal congruence

regard. Goal congruence is the alignment of organizational goals with the personal and group goals of subordinates and superiors.

For example, a hotel might establish as an objective increasing total sales by 10% for the coming year. The rooms department manger of that hotel might then set as two of its goals increasing its average room rate by 5% and increasing rooms occupancy by 3% to help achieve the hotel's overall goal. Goal congruence provides direction so that the activities of each department are working toward achievement of the organization's overall objectives and mission.

Four characteristics

There are four important characteristics of MBO:

- The department head, or department manager, participates in establishing the criteria by which he or she will be judged.
- These criteria are known by the person and his or her supervisor before the period begins.
- Criteria are established in absolute or quantitative terms (such as dollars, percentages, or other units), so that results can be measured.

- Goals should also be expressed relative to desired results to be achieved within a specified time frame.

For example, a restaurant manager might state that her objective is to increase sales by adding a special entrée to the menu each day. This is not an objective because no results have been stated in quantitative terms and no time frame has been established. Instead, the restaurant manager has stated how she is going to achieve something. Stating how something is to be achieved is not an objective. The restaurant manager in this situation would not find it difficult to implement what she says the objective is, but there is no way to measure the results. A more comprehensive objective for this restaurant might be to increase sales by increasing customer average check by $1 by the end of a 90-day period.

Research has shown that the more objective a performance measure is, the more likely it is that supervisors and those they supervise will work with effort. Accounting systems play a key role in this because they can provide relatively objective performance evaluations. Research further shows that unless those being measured think that their behavior can influence the performance measure, they are unlikely to invest effort to achieve goals.

Important aspect of MBO

The measurement criteria, or standards, motivate the individuals to perform according to a clear understanding of expectations. An important aspect of MBO is that the department heads are not judged on a personal basis, but rather against the mutually agreed upon standards.

If standards are not achieved, the employee is not penalized, but rather is assisted by the supervisor in locating problem areas and identifying the cause of the problem. This investigation is then used to assist the department head in future performance or, if necessary, in reestablishing performance standards if the standards are the fault.

OTHER GOALS

The financial goals mentioned so far have been discussed under the assumption that an individual company will decide on one or a combination of them, spell out the goal or goals very clearly, and operate toward that objective. This is probably true of very large concerns in the hospitality industry, and particularly of those whose shares are publicly traded and for whom the goal of maximizing shareholder wealth would be most appropriate.

Smaller enterprises

However, many smaller hospitality corporations do not operate with many shareholders. Indeed, they may operate with as few as two. Such companies operate under quite different circumstances. They might find it inappropriate to have as a goal maximization of stockholder wealth as indicated by market price of the shares, since the shares are not publicly traded. The majority of smaller hospitality industry companies would probably find themselves in this category. They may not even have clearly defined financial goals, and such matters as maximization of profit or stockholder wealth are not relevant in their decision making. Internal operating decisions may be made without reference to financial objectives. For example, a hotel sales department might be convinced that sales could be considerably increased by accommodating bus tour groups. The rooms department manager might think this type of business is too disruptive to normal operations and might cause some regular customers to be denied accommodation when the hotel is full with tour groups. If this hotel had as one of its objectives the maximization of sales revenue (and many companies do establish sales targets as goals), then management would side with the sales department. Management could also decide the issue on a compromise basis, however, agreeing to accept a limited number of tours. This would increase sales revenue and net income, but not necessarily maximize them, and keep regular customers—and the two departments involved—happy. Management and the stockholders (who in many cases will be one and the same) will still be satisfied with the net income. In fact, this method of operating a business is frequently known as "satisficing."

"Satisficing"

Even though companies may not have clear-cut financial goals to rely on for decision making, this should not preclude them from operating toward the other two objectives of financial management: deciding on the sources of funds required by the company and allocating those funds effectively to the various assets of the company to provide a satisfactory net income.

SOCIAL GOALS

Even though the goals discussed so far have been of a financial nature, social goals cannot be ignored. Social responsibility embraces such things as protecting the consumer who buys the hotel's or restaurant's goods or services, maintaining equitable hiring practices and paying fair wages, supporting further education and training of employees, and being concerned about environmental factors.

A resort hotel that owns beachfront property would act in a socially mature way by giving access to the beach to persons other than registered hotel guests. A take-out fast food restaurant that uses disposable paper or plastics supplies would be socially responsible if it were to hire someone to ensure that the neighboring streets were kept free of litter discarded by customers. Obviously, since they have a cost, many social goals may conflict with financial goals. On the other hand, some social goals, even with a cost attached, may improve financial results. For example, in the restaurant situation just cited, the restaurant might find that its business improves considerably as a result of its

Cost of social goals

litter-cleaning decision. More customers might patronize the restaurant because they appreciate its socially responsible action or because they want to visit a restaurant that is in a clean neighborhood. To the extent that the increased net income exceeds the cost of clearing litter, a benefit will accrue.

DEVELOP AN ACTION PLAN

After an organization has developed a suitable mission statement and established financial objectives to conform to that, it must prepare an action plan. An organization's overall mission statement and objectives define what the organization wants to achieve. The action plan shows how it is going to get there. Normally, this plan covers all functional areas of an organization, such as managerial, financial, operational, and marketing. It includes matters such as the way the premises are furnished, the theme it wishes to establish, and the types of customers it wishes to attract. At the same time, it requires an understanding of the limitations that any business has. These limitations include the physical size and condition of the property, competition, funding available, economic environment, and many similar factors.

How to get there

Strategies

An action plan first requires the establishment of strategies to achieve objectives. Objectives and strategies should not be confused. Objectives are simply generally fixed statements that, by themselves, cause no changes. Strategies are stated plans of action that will cause changes in order to meet objectives. Strategies can also be flexible, whereas objectives are often not, at least in the short run. For example, a restaurant might have as an objective to increase sales by a certain percentage over the next 12 months. Strategies to achieve this might include increasing menu prices, increasing seat turnover, selling more wine with meals, or using any combination of these and other approaches. If the chosen strategy or strategies do not work, then they can be replaced or combined in some other way.

Strategies cause changes

It is also important to ensure that a strategy is not implemented while ignoring other strategic alternatives. For example, it is possible for a strategy to be based on an inappropriate or biased management style that has too narrow a focus. Note also that strategies have a life cycle, just as products and mission statements have. And even where a mission statement may still be appropriate for a particular organization, strategies that were appropriate to that mission statement in early years may no longer be practical for achieving that mission.

Tactics

Tactics to supplement strategies may need to be developed. Strategies are often long-term (a year or more) in nature, whereas tactics (of which there may be

Short-term tactics

several for each strategy) are short-run because they often have to be adjusted to circumstances that are constantly changing. This does not imply that strategies do not also need to be changed in the short run. Extraordinary, unanticipated events that require both altered strategies and altered tactics may occur.

INFORMATION SYSTEMS

To achieve the objectives established for a company, it is necessary for the manager to make decisions constantly. In order to make rational decisions, it is necessary to have information and a system that provides this information.

For example, consider a hotel that is contemplating offering its room guests a "free" hair shampoo package as a new marketing tactic. This seems like a relatively trivial matter. What information is needed? First of all, the decision maker must have information about the type of guest that is the hotel's market. Is it the vacationer or the businessperson? Predominantly male or female: If the hotel is an international one, is the nationality of the guest important? Is age relevant? What about average length of stay? Obviously, guest registration cards need to be designed to provide these data, and someone must be delegated to sort through these cards to summarize the data into meaningful information.

Example of information need

However, the manager needs further data from suppliers concerning type of shampoo available, types of packages and their sizes, and information about costs as well as availability of any quantity purchase discounts. Finally, the manager must have information about the added costs of storage and distribution of the shampoo through the housekeeping process.

For many day-to-day decisions, much of the necessary information already exists in most hospitality enterprises. Some of it is a requirement of the law (for example, the requirement to keep accounting records for income tax filing purposes). Other information exists as a by-product of carrying out normal business transactions (such as purchasing records and sales invoices). Further information exists as a result of transactions between departments (for example, requisitions given to the storeroom for needed supplies). But quite a lot of information is available that is not even formalized (such as the chef's knowledge about the best way to tackle each day's production of food requirements).

FOUR LEVELS

Four levels can be identified in the decision-making process, and these can be viewed as a pyramid. These four are data production, data sorting, information production, and decision making.

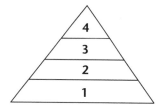

The decision pyramid

Decision making — 4
Information production — 3
Data sorting — 2
Data production — 1

Level 1: Data Production

Data as a by-product

As the base of the pyramid is the production of data. These data are often a by-product of a regular business activity (cash register tapes, sales checks, guest registration cards). It is important to establish what is to be stored and for how long, and what is to be discarded immediately. For example, are dining room sales checks to be kept for a week, a month, a year, or for five years?

Level 2: Data Sorting

A little higher up the pyramid is the second level at which data are sorted, converted, combined, or manipulated into more useful sets of data. In other words, the data need to be classified so that specific items can be recalled or retrieved without processing the entire batch. For example, registration cards can be stored by day and then by month, but has a system been established that segregates registration cards for all VIPs so that they can be accessed without having to go through all registration cards for an entire month?

Level 3: Information Production

Data acquire meaning

These converted sets of data in turn provide the third level in the pyramid, which is the information level. Data are converted into information when they acquire meaning. For example, Exhibit 7.7 in Chapter 7 is a columnar table of two sets of data, one column showing rooms sold month by month and the second showing wage cost month by month. In Exhibit 7.9 these data have been structured in the form of a graph and have taken on a meaning, since the graph indicates information concerning the fixed wage cost.

Normally, the collection and conversion of data to provide information is a routine process that can often be done by mechanical or computerized means. It is not the manager's job to do this. The manager's task is the interpretation of the information and the actual decision making. Nevertheless, it is the manager's task to be involved in establishing the information-gathering system so that it will provide the information that he or she needs to make the kinds of decisions necessary for the company to meet its goals.

As organizations grow, the information system becomes more structured. For example, in a small restaurant, the one and only cook may have the recipes stored in his head, but, in a large restaurant, recipes need to be formalized so that all cooks follow the same food preparation formulas and procedures. In other words, the most desirable system really depends on the specific organization of the business and its needs and, as the organization changes over time, so will the information system. What is good today may not be of value in five years.

Computerized information systems also more readily allow the linking of data from different areas of an operation. For example, a room service department manager could constantly access forecasts of guest room occupancies in order to staff more adequately his department from day to day.

Some sets of data can be compared to provide information (for example, relating last year's sales to this year's, or this year's sales to a budget). At the very elementary level such comparisons are not too helpful, since they do not allow for conditions that have changed between last year and this year, or this year and budget. Also, if, for example, August last year had five Sundays, and this year only four, comparisons can be distorted. Comparisons made on the basis of indices or percentages are an improvement, as is a comparison based on a standard, such as the standard food cost system described in Chapter 5.

Further improvement in information occurs when variances between actual and standard are broken down into differences in quantity and differences in cost or price (see Chapter 9 for a discussion of variance analysis). This breakdown indicates how much of the variance is the fault of poor planning (quantity variances) and how much a failure to achieve standards (for example, cost and price variances in a food cost control system). At this point the information system has reached the stage of providing a guide to solving problems and making decisions.

What prevents many managers from producing more sophisticated information, and in particular with reference to implementing a computerized system, is that costs are often considered, but no price tag is put on the benefits. In fact, some managers consider that there is, and should be, no cost for information gathering; in other words, there is no cost to having a daily food cost or for producing a manager's daily report. These are simply by-products of the accounting and/or control system, and to spend money to provide more and better information makes no sense. For many managers the concept that information is not free creates a dilemma that is difficult to resolve.

An information system should be judged by how well it facilitates the achievement of a given goal or set of goals. The main criterion for judging one system against another is cost benefit. Systems cost money and benefit an organization by helping decision making. If two systems cost the same, that which provides the most desirable operating decisions is preferable. For example, this might be the decision-making factor in judging which of two computerized accounting systems to install, when they both cost approximately the same.

Level 4: Decision Making

It is the information that is provided by the system that is used to identify and help solve problems that are resolved at the top of the pyramid, or the fourth level (which is the decision-making level). The types of decisions that have to be made dictate the information that needs to be collected; the information indicates the data that are needed, and this in turn regulates the data collection system.

Any manager is constantly faced with decisions. These can be routine and simple, often requiring no action, or more complex and important. Most decisions do require the use of information and frequently the use of judgment.

In problem solving, four decision-making steps can be identified:

Four decision-making steps

1. Define the problem. Without doing this, proper analysis of information and identification of alternatives cannot be carried out. If the problem is not defined, or is incorrectly defined, time and effort will be wasted.

2. List alternative solutions. Creativity is a requirement for this, but that creativity should not be subjected to the decision maker's bias or prior experience.

3. Gather all necessary information about the problem and its alternative solutions. The information gathered must be relevant, since that increases knowledge, reduces uncertainty, and minimizes the risk of making the wrong decision. It must also be presented in a format that is understood and must be received in good time to affect any decisions made. Note also that the decision making process is often a matter of judgment based on the best information available.

Obviously, the more accurate the information available, the more value it has for planning, control, and decision making. Speed of information and the risk of incomplete information are also factors to be considered. It is sometimes better to have a rough idea of the daily food cost without taking inventory than to have a more accurate food cost 24 hours after taking inventory. On the other hand, in a feasibility study for expanding the business, risk is so high that the extra time involved in preparing an informative study is well spent. In any decision making situation, the manager, given the constraints of time and data availability, must have enough important information to consider alternative decisions or solutions. Obviously, however, the more time that is spent on collecting data and information, the greater the cost.

Risk versus time

For many decisions, accounting records, forms, and reports are a major source of information. This type of information is verifiable, objective, and quantitative and can provide specific data about an activity, event, or problem. The three most important aspects of accounting information are that it is relevant and appropriate for the problem at hand, that it is current, and that it is accurate within the measurement standards imposed by the needs of the problem.

Relevancy, currency, accuracy

4. Make the decision. Even though the foregoing three steps may be followed, decision making may still be difficult, since important variables of the problem may affect one another.

In some situations, the information can provide its own solution. For example, perpetual inventory cards as an aid to inventory control were described in Chapter 2. These perpetual inventory cards can show, for each storeroom item, the minimum and maximum inventory levels. If the minimum stock level for a specific product is five, and inventory has dropped to that point, and maximum is 15, then 10 more of that item need to be ordered. However, in such a situation, no attempt is made to relate the purchase to current conditions. What if the consumption for that product is no longer as high as it used to be? Perhaps the maximum inventory of 15 should be reduced to 10 and the reorder point to 2 until conditions change again. To make such decisions from manual information might be difficult, but computerized inventory systems can be programmed to provide information concerning such matters as rate of consumption of inventory products as well as quantity discounts and inventory holding costs. In a really intelligent computerized system, the idea of fixed reorder points for any items might be completely abandoned, and the computer will consider all the relevant factors item by item and only print a list of items to be ordered and in what quantities.

Intelligent systems

One type of decision making is known as management by exception. With management by exception, small deviations from normal—which do not require any management action—are not drawn to its attention. For example, the standard food cost is established at 40%. As long as the food cost variance is only 1 percentage point above or below 40% (that is, from 39 to 41%), it is considered acceptable. Only if food cost is below 39% or above 41% is the change drawn to management's attention.

Management by exception

The question of establishing an item's exception level has to be established on a situation-by-situation basis and company by company. There are no rules, or even guidelines, because of the many variables that differ from business to business.

While management by exception has the advantage of relieving higher level management of wasting a lot of time on information when there is no problem, it can also prevent management from noticing worsening trends (for example a cost item that is slowly increasing) until that item of information has reached or exceeded its exception level. In other words, if the manager had been made aware of the worsening trend, some corrective action could have been taken before the exception level was reached.

A further refinement in decision making is to examine the assumptions that were made when earlier plans were formulated and then compare not only actual and planned results, but also actual with possible results. Those possible results are *Opportunity costs* opportunity costs. Earlier in this chapter the possibility of a hotel increasing its sales by accommodating bus tour groups was discussed. If bus tour groups are not accommodated, or only a limited number of them are accepted, the revenue from those not accommodated is an opportunity cost, and this opportunity cost representing lost sales revenue could be built into the information system for management comparison with actual results. One difficulty with building opportunity costs into the information/decision-making system is that some bus tour groups making requests for rooms, who were turned down, may have eventually canceled *Responding to* their reservations anyway, even if they had been accepted. But, if effective deci- *incompleteness* sions are to be made, a well-designed information system must be able to respond to some incompleteness of information and possibly suggest where additional data might be collected to make the information more complete. Obviously, at this level of sophistication, information manipulation would be exceedingly complex without the aid of a computerized system.

The way in which an information system is designed and integrated into a hospitality enterprise is a challenge for any manager. The more appropriately it is designed to support decision making, the more effectively will the enterprise be able to compete in the marketplace and achieve its already established financial objectives.

MIS SYSTEM EFFECTIVENESS

A management information system (MIS) must have stated objectives so that its effectiveness can be measured by how it meets those objectives. Management should also be concerned with whether the system is doing everything it could *Three ways* to be effective. There are three ways of determining this.

One way is to review the reports provided by the system to see if any employees using them have made notations or calculations on them. If any of the information had to be recalculated or redrafted in some way to make it meaningful to the user, or if information has had to be added from some other source, this could indicate that the system is not doing everything it could.

A second method is to use test observations to see whether the information system is used for decision making. If information is required for a decision before the formal MIS can provide it or if the formal MIS has to be supported by information from informal sources, then perhaps the MIS is not doing the job it was designed to do. For example, suppose a hotel has a computerized guest room system that is intended to provide housekeeping and front office personnel with information about the status of each guest room at any time. If the computer system is so slow that housekeeping and front office employees pass this information back and forth by telephone, then the formal computer information system is not performing effectively.

Relevance of reports

The third method is to have those who review system reports list or state which items on a report are relevant and which are irrelevant. If there is consensus that there is a great deal of irrelevant information that is of no use in decision making, then the system is not doing its job. A dramatic test is to temporarily stop producing a report for a period of time. If there is no protest from those who are supposed to use the report, its permanent discontinuance will simplify but not reduce the effectiveness of the information system. However, removal of a report can have unexpected repercussions. For example, department heads may presently be receiving the same report as the general manager, even though they make little direct use of it. If the report is discontinued, department heads may feel they have lost status because they are no longer deemed important enough to receive it.

SYSTEM EFFECTIVENESS VERSUS EFFICIENCY

Terms not synonymous

Management must also be aware of the difference between MIS effectiveness and efficiency. The two terms are not synonymous. With reference to gross profit analysis (see Chapter 6) of menu items, a computerized information system might show that a different set of menu offerings will improve gross profit per guest. However, after the new menu is implemented, total gross profit declines because customers do not like the new menu. The information system was efficient but not effective because it did not consider potential customers' menu preferences.

SUMMARY

Before developing financial goals, some large hospitality operations first prepare a mission statement. Regardless of the type and size of enterprise in the hospitality industry, financial management will be an ongoing part of the business. Generally, the objectives of financial management are:

- To establish certain goals, such as how large the company will be, how rapidly it will expand, and how it will measure its success in meeting these goals.

- To decide on the sources of needed capital and to obtain the funds required by the firm to meet its goals.
- To allocate these funds effectively to the various assets of the company, again with the company's goals in mind.

Profit maximization is one type of goal. This means making the most amount of money in the shortest possible time. Profit maximization emphasizes the short run over the long run and ignores any risks involved.

Maximization of return on investment is a goal that allows no investment that does not yield at least a minimum return on investment. The disadvantages of this goal are similar to those for the profit maximization goal.

The goal most commonly used by business is that of maximization of stockholder wealth. Under this goal, management plans to ensure that wise investments are made, that they are sensibly financed, and that an appropriate dividend policy is established.

Subgoals are also often established. These could be for individual operations within a chain and/or for individual departments within an operation. With subgoals, management by objectives (MBO) is a useful managerial technique. With MBO, managers are involved in establishing their own goals and standards against which their performance is subsequently measured. Goal congruence is an alignment of organizational goals with the personal and group goals of subordinates and superiors.

With any form of goal setting, social goals must not be ignored.

An organization's overall mission statement and objectives define what the organization wants to achieve. The action plan, through strategies and tactics, shows how it is going to get there.

To achieve its financial goals, an organization must have a reliable information system that allows the best decisions to be made. Four levels can be identified in an information system: data production, data sorting, information production, and decision making. The larger the organization, the more structured is this information system.

A well-defined information system is also invaluable in problem solving. Four steps can be identified in problem solving. These are defining the problem, listing the alternative solutions, gathering all necessary relevant information, and making decisions.

Information is a resource that costs money. When comparing different information systems, a cost-benefit analysis is required. An information system should be judged by how well it facilitates the achievement of a given goal or set of goals.

The way an information system is designed and integrated into a hospitality enterprise is a challenge for any manager. The more appropriately it is designed to support decision making, the more effectively will the enterprise be able to compete and achieve its already established financial objectives.

Finally, management also needs to be sure (and determine from time to time) that its information system is effective and also be aware that there is a difference between efficiency and effectiveness.

DISCUSSION QUESTIONS

1. Explain your understanding of a mission statement and state four purposes that it can serve.
2. Briefly describe your understanding of the meaning of financial management.
3. Explain how you think a small restaurant operation can practice good financial management.
4. What is your understanding of the term "satisficing"?
5. In what way might a policy to pay no dividends affect a hotel corporation's market price of shares? If the policy were to pay out all net income in dividends, how might this affect the company's future net income? How might this affect the future share price?
6. Explain why wealth maximization, as indicated by market price of shares, may not be achieved by profit maximization.
7. Would the objective of no net income for a certain period (for example, three years) be consistent with the goal of wealth maximization? Explain.
8. What is a subgoal? Give an example of a subgoal that might be appropriate for the housekeeping department of a hotel.
9. Define MBO and explain how it is used in an organization. What is goal congruence, and how does it fit in with MBO?
10. Explain why a resort hotel that is the only one in the area would or would not be likely to practice social responsibility. Do you think such a resort hotel might act differently if it were only one of a number of competitive hotels in that area? Explain.
11. Discuss the need for an action plan with reference to achieving goals and differentiate between strategies and tactics.
12. What are the four steps in the decision-making process?
13. Discuss how you think an information system should be judged for quality.
14. What are the main criteria for information to be useful in the decision-making process?
15. Define management by exception and give an example of a circumstance where it might be used.
16. Briefly discuss two ways in which the effectiveness of a management information system can be determined.

PROBLEMS

14.1 Some hospitality enterprise entrepreneurs, even with limited education, have been successfully operating their businesses for many years. They have probably never heard of management by objectives (MBO). Their only goal is to work hard and make an adequate profit. In your opinion, and given examples from your own experience and/or observations where this might be helpful, why are they successful? If they are successful, why should they bother using managerial techniques such as MBO?

14.2 The following paragraph appeared in a chain motel's monthly in-house newsletter announcing the creation of a trophy that will be awarded to the motel with the most outstanding performance each year:

> The trophy will be given to the motel with the best combination of sales percentage increase and net income percentage increase. The actual calculation will be to take the sales percentage increase, add the net income percentage increase, and to divide that total by 2, with equal weight given to both sales and net income growth. Only motels achieving a minimum 15% sales increase will be eligible.

What is your evaluation of the way performance is to be measured in this motel chain?

14.3 Following are performance objectives for three different organizations:

a. A restaurant's manager: "To establish a position in the market by providing top-quality menu items created from the freshest locally grown produce."

b. Year-round recreational resort hotel's marketing manager: "To establish an image for the resort as an exclusive one providing a luxurious atmosphere and environment."

c. A hotel's nightclub manager: "To considerably increase visits to the nightclub by residents of the area living within driving distance."

Evaluate each of these objectives. Comment about how each of them does, or does not, satisfy the criteria for a good objective. Rewrite each objective in your own words in such a way that it meets the criteria for a well-stated objective.

14.4 You are the manager of the maintenance department of a hotel. You are paid a basic salary, plus a bonus. The bonus consists of another $1,000 each time your expenses are under budget, plus 2% of the amount you are able to save. For the past six budget periods the following are the results. Note that U stands for unfavorable, or over budget, and F for favorable, or under budget.

Period	Budget	Actual	Variance
1	$80,000	$82,000	$2,000 *U*
2	80,000	79,000	1,000 *F*
3	78,000	74,000	4,000 *F*
4	72,000	74,000	2,000 *U*
5	72,000	73,000	1,000 *U*
6	72,500	72,000	500 *F*

a. Using this information, as a rational person what would you do if you were the department manager running the maintenance department over again from period one?

b. If you were the hotel's general manager, what would you recommend be done, if anything, to this hotel's maintenance department's bonus system?

14.5   A small resort hotel that caters primarily to the family trade set as an objective an increase of 5% in its rooms occupancy over the next 12 months. Its strategy for achieving this was to convert some unused ground-floor storage space into a conference room that could seat about 30 people. It then marketed the resort property to businesses and organizations that agreed to hold two- or three-day meetings and use the guest rooms overnight. During the first conference that the hotel booked, the conference organizer complained severely about noise from children using the outdoor swimming pool and recreation facilities immediately outside the window area of the conference room. Furthermore, the conference room delegates found there was no provision for them to have an evening meal served to them in the meeting room so that they could continue their discussions in private. Conference delegates were obliged to use the resort's regular dining room, where other residents were also seated. When subsequent conference groups arrived they made the same complaints and the resort found that negative word-of-mouth publicity had created difficulties for them in booking further conference groups. As a result, they did not achieve the desired increase in occupancy. Discuss the resort's problem with specific reference to the strategy it used to achieve its objective.

14.6   The bellman's department of a large hotel normally has a bell captain and nine bellmen on duty during the day shift for the peak tourist months. During the past peak month, there have been far more than the normal number of guest complaints about the slow service received, creating a problem for the rooms department manager.

The following are descriptions of several situations or events pertaining to the bell service department. For each separate item, state in which of the four areas of the problem-solving process the item belongs. The four areas are defining the problem, identifying alternatives, gathering information, and making the decision.

a. Several guests have complained to the front office manager that they are experiencing a longer than usual wait for service or that they have been receiving poor service.

b. The bell service department has priorities for jobs. Guest check-out baggage is handled first. Second is guest check-in baggage. Third is delivery of other items to guest rooms. Fourth is the sale of airport limousine, bus tour, and theater tickets. Fifth is other requests for service.

c. One guest complained that his theater ticket was for the wrong night.

d. One guest suggested replacing the bell captain with a better organizer.

e. One guest complained that his request to have flowers purchased and then delivered to another guest's room was never carried out.

f. The paging system that allows the bell captain to signal to bellmen when they are away from the service area has malfunctioned three times in the last month and has taken as long as 24 hours to repair.

g. One of the desk clerks suggests that the sale of theater and bus tour tickets be handled by a new person who will operate strictly on a commission basis.

h. The rooms department manager will consider having a commission arrangement for next summer, since it is too late to do anything about it this year.

i. The bell captain suggests hiring one more bellman.

j. One bellman has been away sick for the past two weeks.

k. While the sick bellman was away, he was replaced by a temporary employee not familiar with the hotel and its operating procedures. His work was marginal.

l. Guests who complain are advised of the bell service desk's order of priorities.

m. During the past month, the hotel's occupancy has been 10 percentage points above normal for that month, creating extra demands by guests for service.

n. The rooms department manager has approved the hiring of one extra temporary bellman for as long as occupancy stays above normal.

o. A new paging system will be purchased with a maintenance contract guaranteeing instant service.

14.7 In late January 026, George Jarvis, president of Restoration Resort Ltd., is concerned about how he could finance the more than $200,000 he estimates he needs to convert, improve, and expand present resort facilities. The resort has very little cash, and George and his wife have only about $20,000 in savings.

The land on which the resort is located has been in the Jarvis family for 40 years. The 12-unit motel was constructed 25 years ago. The motel is open year-round. Occupancy of rooms in the peak summer months (mid-June to mid-September) is 100%, but a lower occupancy during the shoulder and winter months reduces overall annual occupancy to 60%. In the winter months the rooms are rented on a monthly basis.

About 20 years ago, a swimming pool was added along with a change house, snack bar/souvenir shop, and a 20-space trailer park. The trailer park is only open during the summer months (approximately 150 days), and, during that period, spaces are 90% occupied.

Although losses have occurred in earlier years, the resort is now reasonably profitable. However, the resort has not until now been considered the main business of the Jarvis family, since both George (who inherited the resort from his parents ten years ago) and his wife do work at other jobs and look at the resort as a part-time business. However, it has become increasingly apparent to them that, because of the economic times, they will have to make changes to the resort and work at it full time if it is to remain successful.

After considerable thought and discussion, the Jarvises decided that the following changes would have to be made to bring the resort up to a standard acceptable to today's traveling public:

a. Add eight fully furnished 400-square foot cabins with a potential of 32 additional overnight guests.

b. Fill in the present pool, which has become badly corroded from minerals in the water. This pool has been fully depreciated.

c. Construct a new 3,300-square-foot swimming pool.

d. Renovate and modernize the combined frame change house and snack bar.

e. Add an extension to the change house that includes shower rooms for trailer park guests and houses the resort's office.

f. Expand the trailer park area from 20 to 50 stalls and provide electrical and sewer hookup to all stalls.

In addition to the Restoration Resort land, George personally owns land that includes a hill at the back of the property, which has potential for skiing. This piece of land is estimated to be worth about $50,000 at today's prices. However, George feels that the investment required to develop it for skiing would not make the project feasible at the present time, even though it might considerably improve the winter rooms occupancy.

The investment costs for the proposed changes to the present property are estimated as follows:

Construction/renovation of buildings	$128,000
Swimming pool	27,000
Furniture, equipment and fixtures	16,000
Trailer park site improvements	21,000
Contingency	10,000
Total	$202,000

A balance sheet for the year ending December 31, 0025, follows, as do income statements for the years 0024 and 0025.

Restoration Resort Balance Sheet as of December 31, 0025

Assets		
Current assets		
Cash	$ 8,700	
Inventory	3,000	$ 11,700
Fixed assets		
Land	$ 70,200	
Buildings	83,800	
Furniture & equipment	14,600	
Swimming pool	15,400	
Station wagon	5,600	
Total fixed assets	$189,600	
Accumulated depreciation	(64,200)	125,400
Total Net Assets		$137,100

Liabilities and Owner's Equity		
Current liabilities		
Bank loan	$ 4,300	
Accounts payable	2,100	
Current mortgage	12,800	$ 19,200
Long-term liabilities		
Mortgage	$24,600	
Loan from shareholder	8,700	33,300
Owner's equity		
Capital—shares issued	$40,000	
Retained earnings	44,600	84,600
Total Liabilities and Owner's Equity		$137,100

Restoration Resort income statements:

	Year Ending Dec. 31, 0024		Year Ending Dec. 31, 0025	
Sales revenue				
Rooms and trailer rentals	$65,100		$74,400	
Snack bar/souvenir shop	23,900	$89,000	26,700	$101,100
Expenses				
Salaries and wages expense	$36,700		$40,100	
Maintenance and repairs expense	14,100		16,200	
Supplies and other expenses	9,000		9,900	
Interest expense	3,200		2,800	
Depreciation expense	6,900	(69,900)	6,300	75,300
Income operating		$19,100		$ 25,800
Income tax		(4,800)		(6,400)
Net income		$14,300		$ 19,400

Restoration Resort retained earnings statement:

	Year Ending Dec. 31, 0024	Year Ending Dec. 31, 0025
Retained earnings beginning of year	$10,900	$25,200
Add: net income for year	14,300	19,400
Retained earnings, end of year	$25,200	$44,600

Revenue for the year 0026 is estimated to be about 5% above 0025, primarily as a result of a price increase, rather than an increase in occupancy. Expenses are estimated in total to be about 5% higher than in 0025.

a. Given the balance sheet and income statements, calculate whatever financial ratios (see Chapter 4) you feel are appropriate that will indicate the present financial health of the Restoration Resort.

b. List the information that you would like to have that is not shown on the present financial statements, but would make it easier to carry out some financial projections as a preliminary step before going ahead with a complete feasibility study (see Chapter 13) for expansion.

CASE 14

With the possibility of branching out into a second restaurant, Charlie is concerned that he does not have any formal financial objectives, although he does understand that most successful companies do need to have financial, as well as other, objectives. Write a report to Charlie summarizing possible financial objectives that he might wish to consider. Include an explanation of MBO and how it differs from conventional management (where the employee is judged by personal traits such as initiative and integrity) typically used by small businesses. What specific recommendations do you have for Charlie? Support these recommendations with reasons.

APPENDIX

Computers in Hospitality Management

Throughout most of this text, manual systems of financial control have been discussed and demonstrated. The materials within the text are not intended to impart financial accounting expertise, but to make the reader familiar with certain basic accounting procedures and managerial applications to assist management in the decision-making process.

Today, most hospitality businesses in hotels, motels, food service, and beverage operations are using computers to record, report, and analyze the effectiveness of internal operations. One must learn basic accounting concepts to understand not only the necessary information needed as input to a computer system, but also the output of information the computer is capable of providing. Knowing what an average check is for a food service operation is one thing, but knowing how it is determined gives a greater insight as to how it can be changed. This simple analogy rings true for the great majority of developed ratios, percentages, units, and dollar values that can be generated through computer analysis.

In the three decades or so since computers have been commercially available, they have become a major factor in business operations as well as our individual lives. Computers have had a dynamic impact in all forms of business enterprise including the hospitality industry. Initially, computer use was limited due to their high-cost specialized operator technical expertise and rather large requirement for floor space. Computers have evolved to the point that their cost, need of a specially trained operator, and space requirements are no longer major obstacles to their acquisition. Microcomputers are used extensively in all aspects of business operations rather than being limited to only chain operations or very large independent operations.

A majority of hotels now use computers in the areas of reservations, registration, guest history, guest accounting audit, and back office accounting. Similarly, most restaurants are using computerized point-of-sale terminals and registers that control guest checks, kitchen orders, and guest payments. In addition, such a system stores a great amount of data, which can provide a range of averages, and ratios that can be used to evaluate such items as menu-mix analysis, average guest check, seat turnover, cost of sales analysis, and inventory control, to name a few possibilities. Computers have, in effect, successfully removed much of the time-consuming drudgery present in a manual accounting system. The analysis and evaluation of labor productivity, cost control, inventory control, menu costing, budgeting, and so on can be obtained quickly and accurately from a computer, using software designed for a restaurant operation. Needless to say, software programs are available for specific business operations within the hospitality industry, which can assist in the safeguarding of assets, controlling cost, maximizing profit, and providing information to measure the efficiency and productivity of an operation.

Today, small, low-cost, yet powerful microcomputers are available to almost any business operation or an individual. Even a small independent entrepreneur would be remiss by not taking advantage of computer availability. These microcomputers are so low in price that many operations provide a separate computer that can be used cost-effectively by a single department within a large operation. An example of this might be for maintaining storeroom inventory records.

COMPUTER ADVANTAGES

The main advantages of a computerized system over a manual one are speed and accuracy. Computerized systems, however, don't do anything that cannot be done manually, nor do they relieve management of the responsibility of decision making once the information is produced. In reality, computers allow quicker access to all forms of information necessary to allow a quicker managerial response to changes in the business environment.

Computers are no longer expensive, space-consuming units that require a highly skilled technical person to operate them. No longer do they have to be operated by computer departments that are remote from day-to-day operations, producing voluminous reports long after the need for the information they provide is past.

The new, low-cost computers may dictate a change in the way that hospitality managers behave on the job. Competitive survival may require managers to learn how to use computer resources in order to understand and effectively use the wealth of information computers can provide.

TYPES OF COMPUTERS

Generally, computers can be categorized into three types: mainframe computers, minicomputers, and microcomputers.

MAINFRAME COMPUTERS

In the early days, computers were very large, requiring dedicated, air-conditioned rooms, and specialized personnel to operate them. Most often, mainframe computers were often remote from the departments that needed the information that they could provide. In some cases, a terminal located in an individual department could access the mainframe computer, or access could be made by an individual operation that was part of a chain. This type of computer is generally referred to today as a mainframe.

MINICOMPUTERS

With the introduction of minicomputers, this situation changed. A minicomputer was smaller, cheaper, and occupied less space than its mainframe predecessors. A chain organization could now afford to have a minicomputer in each separate operation and still be linked to the head office mainframe. Also, a number of users could be connected through terminals to the minicomputer at the same time. This type of connection is known as computer time-sharing. As a time-share user accesses the minicomputer, the computer locates that user's information, receives instructions from the user to manipulate information or create changes, provide reports, and then becomes a storage host until it is accessed again by a user. For a computer to do this for several users, it needs to be programmed so that information from different users is not mixed up and so that each user is treated in turn as if several were using the computer at the same time.

The result is that time-shared computers—either mainframe or minicomputers—operate at only about 50% efficiency. As the computer gets busier as more users access it, it slows down. Its response time also becomes irregular, and a user may not know, if the computer does not respond promptly, whether the machine has slowed down because of heavy use or because the user has supplied information that the computer does not understand and cannot process.

A minicomputer may also need a complicated set of instructions and an expensive communication system, as well as extra levels of security with passwords and protected security levels, to link it with all its users and prevent unauthorized access to confidential information.

Finally, with a large time-shared mainframe or minicomputer, access plays a valuable and important role in maintaining and sharing common information with a number of different users. This might be the case in a hotel where guest reservation, registration, and accounting information can be accessed not only by front office personnel but also by accounting office, housekeeping, and marketing employees.

MICROCOMPUTERS

The heart of a microcomputer is the microprocessor, sometimes referred to as a microcomputer on a chip. Actually it's a processing and controlling subsystem on an electronic chip (a very small part of the actual microcomputer). Computer chips are so small that 20,000 or more of them can fit into a briefcase. When the microprocessor was introduced, it dramatically changed the accessibility of computer power, and prompted a major reduction in the cost of this power to manipulate, process, report, and store information.

Today, a stand-alone microcomputer or personal computer (or PC, as it is usually referred to) can cost as little as $1,000 (or less) and can be easily placed on a manager's desk or small table. No technical or specialist expertise is required to operate these computers. Indeed, it is no more necessary to know how a computer works internally to use it than it is to know how a car works to drive it. However, it is generally important to understand what it is doing to know what information to give the computer, which is necessary for the software program to return to the user the output requested.

The terms microprocessor and microcomputer are sometimes used interchangeably, even though they do not mean the same thing. A microprocessor is the physical design and structure of a system engraved on the chips that are the "brain cells" that make a microcomputer function. Microcomputers are called so because their systems are miniaturized. A microcomputer could therefore be simply described as a small computer, although that can be misleading because today's microcomputers, as small as they are, are also independently versatile. In fact, it has often become better and in many ways cheaper to buy an additional microcomputer to handle a specific type of job than it is to create a special mainframe or minicomputer time-sharing or networking program that several users can access.

The major disadvantage of microcomputers in their early years was their somewhat limited storage capacity; however, the small microcomputer of today can store more data than many of the older mainframe computers. The average storage capacity of a microcomputer today is approximately 13 gigabytes (GB), and that capacity grows larger each year.

Microcomputers can be operated independently but can also be linked together through a network to access the same information or specific programs that all their users may need from time to time (such as reservation information in a hotel). Networking is the linking of a number of independent computers. Networking capabilities have grown rapidly, and continue to evolve and improve. It is now possible for a hospitality operation to have its purchasing needs transmitted by its microcomputer to a supplier's network to a network of supplier's computers.

This operation is often handled in a new Internet technology-based network solution called an extranet. Such a network allows companies and suppliers to create a secure shared network configuration between the organizations and their suppliers. This network also allows individuals to utilize user-friendly computer applications such as Web browsers, to directly enter and track orders with suppliers. Other technologies, such as intranets, have also entered the computer arena. These intranet configurations also work on Internet-based technologies (Web browsers, Internet protocols). Intranets allow companies to link all of their remote locations to a central secure network of Web pages, which helps to simplify access to personnel, accounting, inventory, and other corporate records, and allows for easier submission of local data to the corporate office. Internet technologies are ever advancing in their capabilities and continually change the work environment.

Also in use today and continuously expanding is the electronic transfer of funds, in which point-of-sale terminals in a hotel or restaurant are connected directly to a computer at a local bank, which is in turn networked to terminals at other banks. If hospitality customers pay their bills by use of a national credit card, a bank credit card, or personal check, the card or check can be verified and approved by the local bank's computer. The bank will then issue instructions that are transmitted to the customer's bank so that the funds are immediately transferred to the hospitality operation's local bank account.

The advantage of this to the hospitality operation is the reduction of the collection period, thereby saving of one or more days and potentially resulting in a near-cash transaction. This procedure significantly decreases potential losses from dishonored credit cards and checks, which would not clear due to insufficient funds (NSF). In addition, with the rapid inflow of cash, interest income on the hospitality operations bank account may increase.

LOCAL AREA NETWORKS

Local area networks (LANs) are systems that connect microcomputers and allow authorized users to share common files. LANs allow computers to be used in ways that previously could be handled only by much larger mini- and mainframe computers.

HARDWARE VERSUS SOFTWARE

The hardware of a computer system is its physical equipment, which follows a predetermined set of instructions in a self-directed fashion. Instructions are developed by programmers. Once a program (or set of instructions) is placed in the hardware, the computer can carry out those instructions without any operator intervention. Any "intelligence" that a computer has must perform a variety of tasks, which must be programmed into it, and any weaknesses in that intelligence are the fault of the program.

SOFTWARE

A computer is able to operate with many different programs for different jobs. Each program is copied from the hard drive to the random access memory (RAM) in a microcomputer when it is needed. When the machine is switched off, any information currently in the RAM is lost. Software is generally stored on hard drives, and when it is loaded into the machine it is not removed from the hard drive but only copied for use into the RAM.

Once stored on the hard drive, information can be used with other computers of the same general type. Information on the hard drive (disk) is read when the computer scans the magnetic surface of the hard drive, copying encoded program data into the computer's temporary RAM memory. Once the data is in the computer, it can be amended, added to, manipulated, or removed if no longer wanted before being stored again on the hard drive or other storage media.

Good hardware is not hard to find, but a good software program is the key to a computer system's performance. Software can be written in a programming language to create industry- or company-specific software. However, many hospitality organizations buy existing software programs from vendors that specialize in industry software.

HARDWARE SYSTEMS

Computer hardware systems normally have a number of components. Even a microcomputer cannot do much without the aid of supporting hardware or peripheral equipment. The main part of the computer, where all the work or manipulation is carried out, is referred to as the central processing unit (CPU). The CPU is often referred to as the "brain" of a hardware system because it controls all other hardware and peripheral equipment or devices.

The CPU has its own set of instructions built in its memory chips that cannot be altered by the user. These instructions are known as read-only memory (ROM), which the user can access and "read" but cannot change. To load user programs or instructions into the CPU, another hardware device is required. For microcomputers, that device is known as a hard disk drive.

Input devices are also needed before the user can interact with the computer. These input devices include such things as a keyboard, mouse, scanner, bar code reader, and a stylus writing device. A monitor, also known as a screen, cathode ray tube (CRT), or video display unit (VDU) is another output device. The monitor displays information and prompts to the user from the CPU; what is input from the keyboard by the user; and the result of the work that is being done.

Another output device is a printer, invariably a separate piece of equipment attached by cable to the computer. When work performed by the user is printed out, the printed material is often referred to as "hard copy" to differentiate it from "soft copy," or work that is viewed only on the monitor and might still have further work needed before a hard copy is output. For example, when a guest is dining in a restaurant that has a computerized sales system, the server can view the soft copy of the guest's check on the monitor during the course of the meal, and add items to it as the meal progresses. The guest check can be reviewed on a monitor before printing a hard copy for presentation to the guest.

Obviously, with all these various pieces of hardware comprising a computer system, there has to be a high degree of compatibility among them. In addition to compatibility of hardware, the software used must be compatible with the hardware.

CANNED SOFTWARE

The question sometimes arises whether it is better to have software specifically written for an individual hospitality operation's needs or to buy an already written software package (known as canned software). Specifically, custom software is far more expensive than canned programs. Also, most hospitality businesses are generally small operations that do not have the resources necessary to carry out a system analysis and undertake the design work necessary to develop their own computer software.

Canned programs normally have been widely tested, and any errors (bugs or glitches) in the program have been detected and corrected. Demonstrations of canned software can usually be viewed before the purchase decision is made since a number of vendors may carry comparable packages. The cost to buy, install, and train employees can also vary between an operation, depending on its needs and the software's capabilities to adjust for those needs.

A successful canned software package represents a proven product that is obtainable at a cost much lower than that for a custom-designed software package. In addition, specialized canned software packages are readily available for a hospitality operation in such areas as food and beverage cost control, payroll, and generation of financial reports and ratio analysis. Obviously, the benefits of using off-the-shelf software have to be considered against the disadvantages. A software package written for broad hospitality requirements may not be as easy to use, or as fast, as one that is custom-designed.

INTERACTIVE PROGRAMS

Software programs can be either interactive or noninteractive. An interactive program prompts the user sequentially step by step and is generally considered "user-friendly." Such a program is normally easier to use because it helps ensure that no information that should be entered by the user is omitted.

A noninteractive program provides no prompts to the user, which means the user must know exactly what information to enter in correct sequence, line by line, following a predetermined sequential format. This requires a higher user skill that also adds to training cost and normally requires a higher employee pay rate; however, the advantage is that the program is a lot faster.

INTEGRATED SOFTWARE SYSTEMS

In a hospitality operation, some information is used for more than one purpose. The name of a guest registering in a hotel is an example of information that might be used for room reservation, registration, guest history, housekeeping, and accounting purposes. Similarly, the name of a food item might be used for receiving, storing, issuing, recipes, production, inventory, and sales control.

With a computer system it is feasible, sensible, and advantageous to use software that is integrated. In integrated software systems, the objective is to record an item of data only once and then to use it in every possible way to provide information for planning and control purposes. If the item of data had to be entered into the computer each time it was wanted, errors could be made. Correcting errors cost time and money.

One could consider a hospitality operation as an entire system and have a completely integrated package of computer software to control and plan every aspect of its operation. However, a completely integrated software package to handle all this would be costly and complex, would probably incur higher training costs because of its complexity, and would create severe maintenance and data security problems. Further, if one part of the system failed, it would create difficulties in all departments or areas. For these reasons, a small operation might find it difficult to justify a completely integrated system financially.

APPLICATION-ORIENTED SOFTWARE SYSTEMS

At the other extreme is a software system that is oriented to a single application. If software is application-oriented, it is generally designed to handle one specific type of job and does not allow much integration. An example is a payroll system that is not integrated with labor cost budgeting or a food inventories control system that is not integrated with purchasing and food costing.

Due to their relative simplicity, application-oriented software systems can be easily evaluated to determine whether they will perform precisely the jobs that they were designed to carry out. These systems are cheaper to buy and install and can be introduced into an operation over time as finances allow. An ideal situation is to move from a piecemeal stand-alone set of application systems to an integrated system over time as long as each part can be made compatible with others. In this type of in-house network, each computer system is capable of operating on a stand-alone basis, but retains the ability to integrate with all others for transmission of certain data.

Obviously, the narrower an application-oriented system is, the easier it is to develop, hence the lower its cost will be. It will also be more efficient and reliable because it controls fewer functions. However, the narrower an application system becomes, the less effective it may be as far as overall control is concerned. For example, if a food inventory control system has to be supported by a separate food cost control system, then two packages of software will be required, two different computer hardware systems may be needed, and two sets of user-operator systems will have to be learned.

Initially, most microcomputer applications in the hospitality industry were stand-alone applications, but as the power and memory capacity of microcomputers increased, available software packages rapidly became more integrated and their use as stand-alone applications is quickly diminished. Three of the common application-oriented software packages are word processing, databases, and spreadsheets.

Word Processing

Word processing refers to software that is programmed to manipulate words (text). Almost all microcomputers have a word processing program installed, as it is quite versatile in the creation of written communications in a business environment.

The purchase of a low-cost microcomputer to be used primarily for word processing is a good way to introduce computers into a business. Word processors can be very useful when a large amount of standard correspondence is handled, as in a hotel reservation department where a form letter is used to confirm reservations, or in a catering operation where a standard banquet contract is used. Only certain information, such as the number of expected guests, the menu selected, and the price of the meal, has to be inserted.

The main purpose of a word processor is to facilitate text creation and editing, and the ease with which this may be done is a major factor in selection of word processing software. One of the major advantages of using computers rather than typewriters for word processing is that documents can be printed more attractively. For example, some computer printers have a variety of type styles that can be used in the same document, as well as allowing text editing; most word processing software contains spelling and grammar checkers.

Database Applications

A database is a collection of records such as addresses of regular customers, a food or beverage inventory listing, personnel data, or a file of recipes. These are all records that form a database. A database application allows quick access to, and ready manipulation of the records that are in that database. In other words, it is much like an office filing system where records (files) can be randomly accessed, used as required, and then restored in the same order or rearranged in some other order before storing. For example, for one query, a database of recipes can be stored in alphabetic sequence according to the main recipe ingredient and only recipes containing that ingredient can be printed out. For another query, all recipes could be stored alphabetically, regardless of ingredients, before printing them.

It may be useful to purchase a software package that includes both word processing and a database. For example, it may be necessary for a hotel to send a standard form letter to all the travel agencies it regularly does business with advising them of a change in room prices or commission rates. The computer can be programmed to take each travel agency's address in turn from the database, type it on the hotel's letterhead, type in the letter from the word processor, then move to the next address and letter on a new page until all addresses have been gone through. All of this can be completed without any user intervention once the process has been started. This process is known as a mail merge. A database application can be particularly useful in yield management (see Chapter 6) because it can be used to store guest history information and reservation patterns.

Spreadsheet Applications

Spreadsheet software is basically a large electronic sheet with rows down the side and columns across the top, much like a worksheet for preparing a budget. Most managers have struggled with budgets using pencils and column pads, and have become frustrated when they wish to see results. For example, if the food cost-to-sales ratio is altered over a 12-month annual budget, the changes that have to be made to food cost, gross margin, and net income require some 36 alterations, considerable erasing and correcting, and a risk that one or more errors will occur.

A properly programmed computerized spreadsheet will allow a manager to answer a what-if question? in seconds and print out the results. Indeed, multiple what-if changes can be made at the same time at rapid speed. Spreadsheets lend themselves not only to budgeting but also to forecasting. For example, a spreadsheet can store in its memory all the various menu items a restaurant offers, including how many of each is sold on average by meal periods and day of the week for each specific month. The availability of information on the basis of past performance could show how many portions of each menu item the kitchen should produce for each meal period each day of the current month. Spreadsheets also lend themselves well to the following applications:

- Scheduling employees for improved labor cost control.
- Preparing depreciation schedules.
- Calculating percentages given the dollar amounts, for common-size vertical financial statement analysis.
- Calculating the sales mix and gross profit figures, given menu items sold and their cost and selling prices.
- Converting budgeted income statements (given appropriate ratios) to cash budgets forecasting cash inflows and outflows.
- Using net present value and internal rate of return analysis for long-term investments.
- Preparing budget variance analyses.
- Using cost-volume-profit analysis for various types of decisions.

As far as planning and control are concerned, word processing, database, and spreadsheet software are closely related. A computer ought to be able to pass data from its database application to a spreadsheet, then in turn pass the results to a word processor for addition of text and final printing of a report. Indeed, for many microcomputers today, single software packages that include all three of these types of programs, such as Microsoft Office®, are available.

Accounting Packages

Another area that lends itself well to an integrated software package, available from a number of different vendors, is general accounting. Most businesses with a manual system of accounting use an integrated approach for their general ledger, sales, accounts receivable, purchases, accounts payable, payroll, and inventory control. Hotel front office system, reservations, registration, and guest accounting can also be integrated into this system. Today, there are integrated software packages available for computerization of this work.

Most hospitality operations have already or will soon computerize their payroll systems. One of the reasons is the time savings computerized payroll software provides. Each time the laws relating to employment change, such as for minimum wage rates, tax deduction rates, and unemployment insurance rates, the software needs only an upgrade to accommodate those changes. In addition, payroll software programs provide, at the user's request, state and federal quarterly reports, W-2s, and transmittal forms. A great number of business operations prepare their payroll and maintain employee records and information using a computerized payroll program within their system.

ECR and POS Systems

For locations where food and beverages are recorded, two types of systems are available—electronic cash register (ECR) and a point-of-sale (POS) system. Basically, the ECR is a stand-alone electronic register, whereas a POS system may link several ECRs to a separate remote host computer, the sales register is primarily a keyboard rather than a separate machine. Customer service terminals respond to creation of customer checks by issuing instructions to the food preparation area for menu items, and print out the customer's bill (customer check). Unfortunately, the acronyms "ECR" and "POS" are often used interchangeably. Technically speaking, a POS system is more sophisticated than a stand-alone ECR, even though today's ECRs can provide a great deal more sales and cost of sales information than their predecessors (mechanical sales registers).

ELECTRONIC CASH REGISTERS (ECR)

The use of ECRs mean cashiers are no longer necessary in most establishments because servers can act as their own cashiers. The machine records, among other things, sales by server so that each knows how much cash to turn in at the end of each shift. Most ECRs have some sort of video display, often just a strip window with space for a limited number of characters. However, increasingly larger video displays are appearing on the equipment so that, for example, the entire bill for a group of people at a table can be seen on the monitor. More sophisticated models can have keys that light up to prompt the operator what to do next, or the monitor displays messages about subsequent steps to make or to explain mistakes.

Most ECRs have automatic pricing that is integrated into the software program, which eliminates pricing errors, change control features (in some cases linked to automatic change dispensers to reduce losses from change-making errors), and automatic tax calculation for jurisdictions where food and/or beverage sales tax applies. Computerized ECRs can summarize sales not only by server (broken down into cash and charge subtotals) but also by categories, such as appetizers, entrees, and desserts. In chain operations, this sales information might be networked to the head office computer for further, more detailed, processing.

Some ECRs can also be programmed to print out the most popular combinations of appetizer, entrée, and dessert that customers choose. This is useful information for menu and sales mix planning. Some ECRs can also provide inventory control for items that can be easily quantified, such as steaks; and if the software program has the capability, complete inventory control is possible. If it were to be used for complete inventory control, however, the system would have to be programmed to remember the recipe of each dish, and that sort of inventory control might be better left to a separate software control system, which will be discussed later. Alternatively, the point-of-entry terminals can be linked to an internal host computer, which receives and stores all information regarding sales. This is not unusual for a software program.

A more sophisticated software program can be used to record servers to clock in and clock out of work on a terminal, which provides hours-worked information for staff planning and payroll purposes. At the end of each shift or day, summary reports of hours worked by employee are recorded and accumulated for each weekly or biweekly payroll period. A built-in time system can also track patterns of sales by time of day or time of guest arrivals and departures. This could be valuable for staff scheduling, labor cost planning, and kitchen food production planning.

Most customer service entry terminals maintain sales check records in detail. In most ECR systems, it is not necessary to have customer sales checks preprinted with sequential numbers. Blank standard sales checks can be purchased at less cost without numbering, and the ECR will print a consecutive number on each when the check is started. If the same check is used for a reorder, the employee must instruct the machine that a previous check number is being used. If the server does not use the previous number when adding items to an active sales check, the machine will assign it a new number since it assumes that it is a brand new check. If a server collects the full amount of a check and turns in only the amount due from a reorder, the first number will show up as a missing check. The server error, made as the result of simple omission or on purpose, will be identified and require correction. The error will be noted since the register prints a report at the end of each shift or day of the "open" checks—that is, those that have not been closed off—and identifies the employee responsible.

INTEGRATED POINT-OF-SALE (POS) SYSTEMS

Generally a point-of-sale (POS) system is a series of individual sales terminals (such as ECRs) linked to a remote computer system. Food and beverage POS systems may be used as stand-alone systems for each separate food and beverage outlet, but may also be linked to other POS systems in other sales outlets. Point-of-sale systems can be linked to other peripheral equipment, such as a printer in the food preparation area that tells the kitchen what is to be prepared, identified by server number or name. Obviously, the server does not walk to the food preparation area until the order is ready to be served. Some software systems enable the kitchen staff to send a message prompt to a server entry monitor to pick up prepared food orders.

The most recent POS device is an electronic server pad (ESP). With an ESP, servers no longer have to write out orders at the customer's table and then go to a terminal to enter them. They simply punch them on to a hand-held computer and the information is beamed to a central computer through low-frequency modulated (FM) waves. The central computer then relays the information to a printer in the kitchen and/or bar.

Hotel POS systems in food and beverage areas may also be linked to the front office accounting system so that hotel guests charging food and beverage items in the restaurant or bar can have the amounts automatically added to their front office accounts. In other words, a POS system has a much greater capability than an ECR and can produce a much larger variety of management reports by sales outlet and in total. It is generally a totally programmable system that can be easily modified within the business to accommodate changes in menu prices and many other items.

A point-of-sale terminal can also be linked to a chain head office where data can be analyzed by the mainframe computer; results compared from unit to unit; and data consolidated by region and for the chain as a whole. In some systems, analysis reports for each individual unit can be sent back to the unit in a process known as downloading. Downloading can also be used to provide each unit's computer with new menu pricing and recipe costing information.

The major disadvantage of a POS system is that, if the central host computer fails, all the POS terminals in the entire system fail. POS terminals cannot operate independently of the central host computer unless the system is backed up with disk memory or the individual terminals have some memory and storage capability to produce reports independently of the central computer.

INVENTORY CONTROL

Computers can be very valuable as a tool in inventory control. Computers can:

- Prepare purchase orders for suppliers. It is now also possible for the computer, through networking, to place orders automatically with approved suppliers who submit the best price for the items and quantities needed.
- Prepare lists of items to be received from each supplier so that receiving employees can compare what is delivered with what should be delivered.
- Compare information as produce is received and product information is recorded in the computer from invoice information against purchase order specifications for those items received.
- Issue appropriate credit memoranda for goods short-shipped or returned to suppliers.
- Prepare food and beverage receiving reports for products delivered.
- Maintain a record of all storeroom purchases from information entered from invoices and update the perpetual inventory of each storeroom item.
- Record all issues from the storeroom from information entered from requisitions. This information is used to adjust the perpetual inventory by item, to calculate total cost of all items issued each day, and to assist in the calculation of daily food and beverage cost.
- Calculate the cost of items requisitioned by any individual department for any period of time.
- Compare requisitions signature (using a scanner) with a record of those signatures stored in the computer to ensure they are authentic.
- Compare at any time quality information of actual inventory for any specific item with the computer-maintained perpetual inventory record, and print out variance reports.
- Alert both management and the food buyer when quantities purchased exceed prescribed limits for storeroom stock.
- Provide monthly a list of all items that were short-stocked during that period.
- Issue monthly dead-stock reports showing items that have not moved in a stipulated period, such as 30, 60, or 90 days.
- List the number of each item purchased from any one supplier and state whether that purchase was made at the best-quoted price.
- List the number of each item used during each month and compare this with what should have been used according to actual food and/or beverage sales based on standard recipes and portion sizes.

- Verify supplier month-end statements against receiving invoices and/or receiving reports, and issue checks in payment of those statements.

A sophisticated inventory control computer program can also adjust the volume of storeroom inventory required according to the level of business. Thus, instead of leaving it to management to establish a fixed minimum and maximum level of stock for each storeroom item, the computer can adjust the recorder point and the order quantity to the actual usage or sales, which can vary over time or by season for that item. Each day, the computer prints out a list of items to be ordered, the quantities needed, and the economic order quantity, if this capability is in the software program. In cases where particular suppliers are under contract to provide specific storeroom items at contracted prices, the actual purchase orders can be prepared for those suppliers.

BAR CODES

One of the more recent advances in inventory control is the use of bar codes on product containers. The bar code is a series of parallel black bars of varying width on a white background. The scanner that reads the code can be a counter-level model such as those found at check-out stands in supermarkets, or a hand-held wand, which is the type most useful in hospitality industry receiving so that heavy cases do not have to be lifted to pass over the scanner.

A common bar code is the ten-digit Universal Product Code (UPC) system, in which the first five digits identify the manufacturer or processor and the second five digits provide information about the product. It is not necessary for the product to be in a sealed container such as a carton or box. Even open crates of fresh produce such as apples and lettuce can be bar coded. The bar code information read and recorded by the computer can include the product's name, package size, and item quantity, from which inventory records can be adjusted. For example, part of the bar code can represent specifications for each product.

The UPC also has known advantages to suppliers who may have dozens of different qualities and container sizes of a particular product, each of which can be quickly identified by reading its bar code and matching it with the purchaser's purchase order specification.

Where bar coding is used by a hospitality operation, it offers the following advantages:

- Fast order processing.
- Reduction in purchasing time.
- Reduction in specification misunderstandings between purchaser and seller.

- More accurate purchasing, ordering, receiving, and inventory records.
- Improved food, beverage, and supplies cost control.
- Improved supplier delivery schedules and performance.
- Simplification of receiving procedures.
- Improved inventory and issuing control. As items are issued, they can again be passed over the scanner so that perpetual inventory count will be adjusted and proper cost information can be recorded on requisitions.

Note that bar codes do not contain price information; they are placed on products by the manufacturer, who usually does not know what the end price of the product will be after it has gone through various distribution levels. Thus, pricing information has to be entered into the hospitality operation's computer from invoices received from suppliers.

FOOD CONTROL SYSTEMS

Many restaurants use a method of food cost control based on accurate costing of standard recipes. Unfortunately, because of the constant daily changes in food purchase costs, a restaurant with an extensive menu may find that manually revising recipe costs is a prohibitively time-consuming task. Even a restaurant with a limited menu may find the job too time-consuming and not worth the effort.

Recipes as Basis for Control

Computers, however, can considerably simplify this work by using a database software system that operates from a computerized file of standard recipes and their ingredients. As new purchases are made, the inventory (ingredient) quantity and cost information are entered into the computer from invoices. Alternatively, terminals can be equipped with a wand reader at the receiving area to read the UPC codes on containers. If items do not have the UPC codes, the information has to be entered manually into the computer. As new ingredient price information is entered, the computer automatically updates all total recipe costs using current portion costs or a weighted average (depending on which method management chooses) for any recipes containing any of these ingredients. A report can be printed to show which recipes are affected and what the new food cost is in dollars and percentages for that recipe; the need to change the menu selling price can also be flagged.

Food Production Control

Each day before production is started, it is only necessary to enter into the computer the name of each recipe item and the number of portions to be produced that day from forecast sales. The computer prints the standard cost of all those recipe items and the total, and prints a requisition listing the ingredients and the quantities required from the storeroom. If more than a required quantity is needed for a particular day (for example a #10 can of an item when only half a can is required for production), the computer makes a note of this excess and takes it into account when future requisitions are prepared. A computerized system can also calculate a food cost for the day, based on food produced according to forecast sales.

INVENTORY CONTROL

As requisitions are printed, the computer adjusts the storeroom inventory count for period-end stocking and can provide a value for items requisitioned but not yet used in production, for example, the half #10 can just mentioned. From time to time, normal storeroom inventory reconciliation must be carried out; that is, comparing the physical count of items actually in stock with the computer listing of what should be there according to production usage.

If bar-coded products are used, inventory count and verification is further simplified, and a manual count of bar coded items is not required. A hand-held bar code reader can be passed over the bar code to count all containers or products, and compile the actual inventory, including pricing and total valuation. The computer can also issue a report showing how the actual inventory, either in total or product-by-product, differs from the computer's perpetual inventory record, which was compiled from invoices and requisitions of what should be in stock.

Taking a physical, or actual, inventory is also easier with a computer even if products are not bar coded. There are programs that print an inventory form, complete with current item costs, leaving only the count quantity to be inserted manually. After the count, figures can be entered into the computer, and a final inventory report showing extensions of item count times price for each item and total inventory value can be produced.

MANAGEMENT REPORTS

Finally, management reports showing planning errors, such as overproduction of menu items because of poor forecasting, can be prepared. A comprehensive food cost control system would have to be built in by a computer linking it to POS terminals. The actual sales histories of various menu items, in combination with other menu items, provide the kitchen with daily food production requirements to minimize such problems as overproduction planning errors.

Other management reports might show operational errors, such as spoilage and waste because standard recipes were not followed, as well as causing errors.

This situation indicates a loss of potential sales revenue in comparison with actual sales revenue because selling prices have not kept up with increasing food costs. Another report might show trends for major purchases, to assist in forward menu pricing planning.

FRONT OFFICE SYSTEMS

The main objective of a front office system for a hotel or motel is maximization of sales revenue. For this reason, most front office computer systems are sales-revenue-oriented rather than cost-control-oriented, and are based on the reservation, registration, and guest accounting needs of the property. They can also be linked to food and beverage POS system terminals. However, front office systems can provide cost control in certain areas. Front office computers can be linked to the telephone system to monitor and bill guests' accounts for charges of local and long distance calls to preclude the hotel from paying for telephone costs not recovered through charges on guest accounts.

The front office system can also provide constantly updated information to other departments such as housekeeping, food, and beverage areas relating to room occupancy and guest counts, so that adequate staffing can be arranged, thereby precluding departments from being overstaffed.

Finally, front office computers can prepare and print room department operating ratios such as occupancy and double occupancy percentages, average daily rates, and the daily yield statistic. In this latter regard, front office computer systems can be immensely useful in maximizing yield by providing information to form a database of guest history and reservation patterns by type of guest for yield management.

SECURITY CONTROL

More recently, front office systems have been keyed to security control. A computer can be programmed to allow certain keys to open doors during limited periods each day. This may mean that housekeeping staff will have access to rooms only during the room makeup period. The system can also issue "keys" to guests, which are simply plastic cards a little smaller than a credit card that have data encoded on them on magnetic strips or have a series of holes punched through them. The guest room door has a device that reads the card and allows the door to be opened.

As guests register, the computer issues new guests a "key card" with a unique code on it for each guest and for each specific room. At the same time, the computer erases the old code for that room in the device on the guest room door. This procedure insures a departed guest's card will not function, and creates a new code corresponding to the arriving guest's card. Departing guests do not have to turn in their "keys"; on checkout, they can be discarded. In cases of emergency, a conventional key may be used by authorized hotel personnel to override a card reader device. The key cards can also be used as internal credit identification cards so that guests can charge to their room account food or beverages consumed in the hotel's dining room and bar areas.

For small hotels and motels, computerized equipment is now available that can be located at the front office to be operated by an arriving guest. The computer accepts specified credit cards and automatically charges the rate for a specific room to the credit card, prints a "paid" invoice for the guest, and issues a key card coded to the door of the assigned room. An all-night employee no longer is required to register late-arriving or early-checkout-guests.

Glossary

The technical words and terms used in this text are briefly explained in this glossary. For more expanded definitions and discussions, the reader should refer to the text itself.

Accelerated depreciation: a method of depreciation that gives greater amounts of depreciation expenses in the earlier years of an asset's life. See also *Depreciation.*

Account: a record in which the current status (or balance) of each type of asset, liability, owners' equity, sales revenue, and expense is kept.

Accounting cycle: a recurring series of steps that occurs during each accounting period.

Accounting equation: assets = liabilities + owners' equity.

Accounting period: the time period covered by the financial statements.

Accounts payable: amounts due to suppliers (creditors); a debt or a liability.

Accounts receivable: amounts due from customers or guests (debtors); an asset.

Accounts receivable aging: preparing a schedule classifying receivables in terms of time left unpaid.

Accounts receivable average collection period: the number of days the average receivable remains unpaid.

Accounts receivable turnover: annual sales revenue divided by average accounts receivable.

Accrual accounting: as opposed to cash accounting, a method of accounting whereby transactions are recorded as they occur and not when cash is exchanged; the matching of sales revenue and expenses on periodic income statements regardless of when cash is received or disbursed.

Accrued expenses: expenses that have been incurred but not paid at balance sheet date; a liability.

Accumulated depreciation: the total depreciation that has been shown as an expense on the income statements since the related assets were purchased. See also *Depreciation.*

Acid test ratio: see *Quick ratios.*

Activity ratios: see *Turnover ratios.*

Adjusted trial balance: a trial balance of accounts after period-end adjustments have been made. See also *Trial balance.*

Adjustments: entries made at the end of each accounting period in journals and then in the accounts so that the accounts have correct balances under the accrual accounting method.

Allowance for bad debts: an amount established to cover the likelihood that not all accounts receivable outstanding at balance sheet date will be collected.

Amortization: a method of writing down the cost of certain intangible assets (such as franchises or goodwill) in the same way that depreciation is used to write down the cost of tangible fixed, or long-term assets.

Asset: a property or resource owned by a business.

Asset shrinkage: the decline in value of assets during bankruptcy.

Audit: a verification of accounting procedures and records.

Audit tape: a continuous chronological record of each transaction recorded in a cash or sales register. The tape can usually only be removed at the end of each day by authorized accounting office personnel.

Audit trail: an internal control method that allows each business transaction to be traced back from its initial source document through each step of the recording process.

Average checks: sales revenue divided by number of people served during a certain period of time. Sometimes called average cover or average spending.

Average cover: see *Average check.*

Average rate of return (ARR): a method of measuring the value of a long-term investment. The equation is net annual saving divided by average investment.

Average room rate: room revenue divided by number of rooms used during a certain period of time.

Average spending: see *Average check.*

Bad debt: an account receivable considered or known to be uncollectible.

Bad debts allowance: see *Allowance for bad debts.*

Balance: the amount of an account at a point in time.

Balance sheet: a statement showing that assets = liabilities + owners' equity. A balance sheet shows the financial position of a company at a point in time.

Bank: see *Float.*

Bank float: the difference between the bank balance shown on a company's records and the actual balance of cash in the bank.

Bank reconciliation: a monthly or periodic procedure to ensure that the company's bank account balance amount agrees with the bank's statement figure.

Beverage cost: see *Cost of sales.*

Bond: a form of financing by a company. A bond is a debt or long-term liability to be repaid with interest over time.

Book value: initial cost of an asset or assets less related accumulated depreciation.

Break-even equation or formula: an equation useful in making business decisions concerning sales levels and fixed and variable costs.

Break-even point: the level of sales at which a company will make neither an income nor a loss.

Bridge financing: see *Interim financing.*

Budget: a business plan, usually expressed in monetary terms. See also *Incremental budgeting* and *Zero-based budgeting.*

Budget analysis: see *Variance analysis.*

Budget cycle: the sequence of events covered by a budget period from initial budget preparation through comparison of actual results with budgeted estimates.

Business entity: the concept that a business, and business transactions, should be kept separate from personal transactions of the business's owners.

Capital asset: see *Fixed asset.*

Capital budget: a budget concerning long-term, or fixed, assets.

Capital rationing: occurs when only a limited amount of funds is available for long-term investments during a budget period, and even profitable investment proposals are deferred to future budget periods.

Capital stock: the amount of money raised by a company from issuing shares.

Capital surplus: the amount of money raised by a company in excess of any par or stated value of the shares.

Cash accounting: a method of accounting (as opposed to accrual accounting) whereby transactions are only recorded at the time cash is received or disbursed.

Cash budget: a budget concerned with cash inflows and cash outflows.

Cash disbursements: money paid by cash or by check for the purchase of goods or services.

Cash flow from operating activities margin ratio: cash flow from operating activities divided by sales revenue.

Cash flow from operating activities to current liabilities ratio: cash flow from operating activities divided by average current liabilities.

Cash flow from operating activities to interest ratio: cash flow from operating activities plus interest divided by interest.

Cash flow from operating activities to total liabilities ratio: cash flow from operating activities divided by average total liabilities.

Cash management: cash conservation and the management of other working capital accounts to maximize effectiveness of the company's use of cash.

Cash receipts: cash or checks received in payment for sale of merchandise or services.

Chattel mortgage: a long-term debt or mortgage secured by the chattels (for example,

equipment and furniture) of the business. See also *Mortgage.*

City ledger: in a hotel, the accounts receivable for guests who have charge privileges in food and beverage areas, and the accounts of room occupants who have left and have charged their accounts.

Collateral: assets pledged by a company as security for a loan.

Collusion: two or more people working together for fraudulent purposes.

Common stock: a form of stock or shares issued by a company to raise money.

Comparative/common-size statements: two or more financial statements presented with all data in both dollar and percentage figures.

Comparative statements: financial statements for two or more periods presented so that the change in each account balance from one period to the next is shown in both dollar and percentage terms.

Concentration banking: a method of accelerating the flow of funds from individual units in a chain operation to the company's head office bank account.

Conservation: a principle of accounting to help ensure sales revenue and assets are not overstated or expenses and liabilities understated.

Consistency: a principle of accounting to help ensure that financial statements are comparable from one period to the next.

Contra-account: accounts with a balance that is shown on the "wrong" side of the balance sheet as a reduction of a related account, for example, allowance for bad debts shown as a reduction of accounts receivable.

Contribution margin: the difference between sales revenue and variable costs or expenses.

Contribution statement: a form of income statement presentation whereby variable costs are deduced from sales revenue to show contribution margin, and then fixed costs are deducted from contribution margin to arrive at net income.

Contributory income: see *Departmental income.*

Controllable cost or expense: a cost that is controllable by an individual (such as a department head) in a company.

Cost: the price paid to purchase an asset or to pay for the purchase of goods or services. Also frequently used as a synonym for expense.

Cost center: a department (such as maintenance) in a hospitality operation that generates no sales revenue.

Cost management: an awareness of the various types of cost and the effect that the relevant ones have on individual business decisions.

Cost of sales: generally referred to simply as food cost or beverage cost. Calculated by adding beginning of the accounting period inventory to purchases during the period, and deducting end of the period inventory, adjusting where necessary for items such as employee meals and/or interdepartmental transfers.

Cost variance: the difference between budgeted cost and actual cost.

Cost-volume-profit analysis: an analysis of fixed and variable costs in relation to sales as an aid in decision making. See also *Break-even equation.*

Credit: 1. an entry on the right-hand side of an account; 2. to extend credit or to allow a person to consume goods or services and pay at a later date.

Credit invoice: an invoice prepared by a supplier showing, for example, that goods delivered to a company have been returned as unacceptable.

Credit memorandum: a dummy credit invoice made out by a company prior to receipt of a credit invoice from the supplier.

Creditor: a person, or company, to whom a firm owes money.

Current assets: cash or other assets likely to be turned into cash within a year.

Current dollars: historic (previous periods') dollars converted to terms of today's dollars for purposes of comparison.

Current liabilities: debts that are due to be paid within one year.

Current liquidity ratios: ratios that indicate a company's ability to meet its short-term debts.

Current ratio: the ratio of current assets to current liabilities.

Day rate: the rate charged by a hotel or motel for the use of a room for a portion of the day and not overnight.

Debenture: a form of financing by a company. A debenture is a debt or long-term liability to be repaid with interest over time.

Debit: an entry in the left-hand side of an account.

Debt: money owed to a person or organization; an obligation.

Debt to equity ratio: the amount of debt (liabilities) expressed as a ratio of stockholders' equity.

Declining balance depreciation: a method of accelerated depreciation whereby higher amounts of depreciation expense are recorded in the earlier years of an asset's life.

Deferred expense: an expense that has been incurred that is gong to be written off over a period of time greater than one year.

Deficit: a deficit situation exists when losses accumulated since a business began exceed accumulated net incomes.

Demand, elasticity of: see *Elasticity of demand.*

Department budget: an operating budget prepared for an individual department in a multidepartment organization.

Departmental income: the income of an individual operating department after direct expenses have been deducted from sales revenue; sometimes referred to as a contributory income.

Dependent variable: an item that is affected by what happens to another item. For example, labor cost is affected by level of sales; labor is the dependent variable.

Depreciation: a method of allocating the cost of a fixed asset over the anticipated life of the asset, showing a portion of the cost, for each accounting period of the life, as an expense on the income statement.

Derived demand: the business that one department has as a result of business in another department, for example, cocktail lounge revenue resulting from customers having drinks while eating in the dining room.

Direct cost or expense: an expense that can be distributed directly to an operating department and generally controllable by that department.

Discount: a reduction of the amount paid on a purchase because of prompt payment.

Discounted cash flow: a method of converting future inflows and/or outflows of cash to terms of today's dollars.

Discount grid: a table that shows the additional hotel room occupancy required to compensate when rack rates are discounted at various percentages.

Discretionary cost or expense: one that could be incurred but does not have to be at the present time.

Dividend: an amount paid out of net income, after tax, to stockholders as a return on their investment in the company.

Double-entry accounting: an accounting procedure that requires equal debit and credit entries in the accounts for every business transaction. This ensures the accounting equation is kept in balance.

Double occupancy percentage: the percentage of rooms occupied in a hotel or motel that are occupied by more than one person.

Drawings: see *Withdrawals.*

Earnings per share: net income for the year divided by average shares outstanding during the year.

Elasticity of demand: the effect that a change in price has on demand for a product or service.

Expenditure: payment in cash for purchase of a good or service, or incurrence of a liability for purchase of a good or service.

Expense: goods or services consumed or used in operating a business.

Feasibility study: a study prepared prior to starting a new business or expanding an existing one, to indicate whether or not the proposal seems feasible and will provide an adequate return on the investment.

First-in, first-out (FIFO) inventory costing: a method of inventory costing where the earliest items purchased are assumed to be the first ones used.

Financial position: the financial condition of a business as indicated by its balance sheet.

Financial statements: a balance sheet and an income statement and, where appropriate, a statement of retained earnings, a statement of source and use of working capital, and other supporting information.

Financing: raising money by debt (liability) or equity (owners).

Financing, interim: see *Interim financing.*

Fiscal period: an annual accounting period that may not coincide with the calendar year.

Fixed asset: asset of a long-term or capital nature that will be depreciated over a number of years.

Fixed asset turnover: annual sales revenue divided by average fixed assets.

Fixed budget: one that is not flexible or variable; one that is not adjusted to compensate for various possible levels of sales or revenue.

Fixed charges: indirect costs such as property taxes, insurance, interest, and depreciation. Sometimes referred to as indirect costs. See also *Direct cost* and *Undistributed operating cost.*

Fixed cost or expense: a cost that does not change, in the short run, with changes in volume of business.

Flexible budget: a budget based on more than one level of possible sales revenue.

Float (or bank): an amount of money advanced to an employee for change-making purposes. See also *Bank float.*

Folio: the account of a guest staying in a hotel or motel. Usually kept in the front office until paid.

Food cost: see *Cost of sales.*

Franchise cost: the cost to purchase the right to use the name and/or services of another organization.

Full disclosure: a principle of accounting whereby financial statements provide all the relevant information that a reader of them should have.

General ledger: a book of accounts holding those accounts from which the financial statements are prepared.

Goal congruence: the alignment of organizational goals with the personal and group goals of subordinates and superiors.

Going concern: an accounting assumption that a business entity is to remain in business indefinitely.

Goodwill: the value of an established business, based on its name or reputation, above the value of its tangible assets.

Graph: a method of illustrating accounting information in pictorial form.

Gross profit: sales revenue less cost of sales.

Gross return on assets: see *Return on assets.*

Guest account: see *Folio.*

Historic cost: the cost of something at the same time it was paid for, not adjusted to current cost.

House accounts: the accounts of guests staying in a hotel. See also *City ledger.*

Hubbart formula: a method of calculating required average room rate so that at a particular level of occupancy all costs will be covered and a desired return on investment achieved.

Income statement: a financial statement showing money earned from sales of goods and services, less expenses incurred to earn that income, for a period of time; sometimes referred to as the profit and loss statement.

Incremental budgeting: a method of budgeting whereby an increase, generally on a percentage basis, is automatically applied to last year's budget. See also *Zero-based budgeting.*

Independent variable: an item that is not affected by what happens to another item. For example, guest rooms sales are not affected by the number of maids on duty; rooms sales are the independent variable.

Indirect cost or expense: a cost not allocated directly to an operating department. See also *Direct cost, Fixed charges,* and *Undistributed operating cost.*

Integrated banking: see *Concentration banking.*

Integrated pricing: a method of reviewing prices in two or more departments to ensure products are not priced independently of each other.

Interim financing: financing that is required for a new project from the time that construction is started until the project is completed. Sometimes referred to as bridge financing.

Internal audit: an appraisal of the operating and accounting controls of an establishment to ensure that internal control and procedures are being followed and assets adequately safeguarded.

Internal control: a system of procedures and forms established in a business to safeguard its assets and help ensure the accuracy of the information provided by its accounting system.

Internal rate of return (IRR): a method of measuring the value of a long-term investment using discounted cash flow. See also *Discounted cash flow.*

Inventory: merchandise (generally food and beverages) purchased but not yet used to generate sales revenue. See also *Physical inventory.*

Inventory turnover: cost of sales for a period of time divided by the average inventory for that period.

Investment: money loaned to a company either by way of a debt (liability) or equity (stock).

Invoice: document prepared to record the sale of goods or services and giving details about the transaction and total value of the sale.

Invoice approval form: a form or stamp showing that all necessary control steps have been carried out to ensure that an invoice is correct and can be paid.

Joint cost or expense: one that is shared by more than one department.

Journal: accounting record summarizing business transactions as they occur prior to posting the information to the individual accounts.

Journal entry: the recording of a business transaction in a journal.

Kiting: writing a check on one bank, failing to record it as a disbursement, and depositing it in another bank for fraudulent purposes.

Lapping: a method of fraud that can occur when an employee has complete control of accounts receivable and payments received on these accounts.

Last-in, first-out (LIFO) inventory costing: a method of inventory costing where the most recently purchased items are assumed to be the first ones used.

Lease: the renting of a building and/or equipment, usually in lieu of a purchase.

Leasehold improvements: architectural and interior design changes made to rented (leased) premises.

Ledger: a book of accounts in which business transactions are entered after having been recorded in journals.

Leverage: a method of financing whereby the amount of debt (liabilities) is increased in proportion to equity (owners' investment).

Liability: a debt; an obligation.

Liquidation: the closing of a business by selling its assets and paying off the liabilities.

Liquidity: the financial strength of a business in terms of its ability to pay off its short-term or current liabilities without difficulty; a healthy working capital position; a good current ratio.

Loan: an amount borrowed; a debt; a liability.

Loan principal: the repayment of the initial amount borrowed on a loan is a principal payment as distinct from interest that is in addition to principal payments.

Lockboxes: a special bank service to speed up the collection of accounts receivable.

Long-range cash flow: a cash flow budget for periods of time generally in excess of one year.

Long-term asset: see *Fixed asset*.

Long-term budget: a budget for a period of time generally in excess of one year.

Long-term liability: a debt or obligation to be paid off more than one year hence.

Long-term solvency ratio: ratio that indicates a company's ability to meet its long-term liabilities as they fall due; an example is the debt to equity ratio.

Loss: an excess of expenses over sales revenue.

Management by objectives (MBO):   a concept based on the assumption that employees can be committed to their work, allowing for maximum involvement and participation in setting subgoals, personal goals, and performance standards for judging employees' work.

Manager's daily report: a report prepared daily, generally by the accounting office, to indicate each day's key business operating statistics, such as rooms occupancy percentage and average food check by meal period.

Marginal cost or expense: see *Variable cost or expense*.

Marketable securities: investments in notes or similar securities that can be readily converted into cash.

Market segment: a type of customer (such as business travelers) with whom an operation does business.

Market segment profit analysis (MSPA):   a method of analyzing both sales and expenses (including indirect expenses) by market segment to determine the most profitable segments.

Market value: the current value of an asset, sometimes known as replacement value.

Markup: the difference between the cost of an item and its selling price.

Master budget: the overall budget for an establishment embracing all other budgets.

Matching: a principle of accrual accounting relating expenses to the sales revenue earned during a period regardless of when the cash was received or the expenses paid.

Materiality: the significance of an item in relation to the total business. If an item is not significant, other accounting principles may be ignored for reasons of practicality.

Memorandum invoice: a temporary, dummy invoice prepared in the absence of a proper invoice.

Menu engineering: a method of menu analysis that combines each menu item's contribution margin (gross profit) with its popularity, or the demand for that item by the restaurant's customers.

Mission statement: a statement detailing the purpose of a business.

Mortgage: a long-term debt or liability generally secured by using long-term assets (such as land and/or building) as collateral. See also *Chattel mortgage*.

Moving average: a method of forecasting that takes an average of the previous *n* periods of business and uses that average as the basis for the next period's forecast.

Mutual exclusivity: a mutually exclusive alternative requires that if only one of a number of proposals (such as a long-term investment) is accepted, all others will be rejected.

Net assets: see *Net worth*.

Net book value: see *Book value*.

Net income: total sales revenue from sales and other income less total expenses.

Net income to revenue ratio: net income divided by sales revenue and multiplied by 100.

Net present value (NPV):   a method of measuring the value of a long-term investment using discounted cash flow. See also *Discounted cash flow.*

Net return on assets: net income after income taxes divided by total average assets for the period.

Net worth: total assets less total liabilities; owners' equity.

Noncontrollable costs or expenses: costs or expenses that are generally fixed in nature in the short run, such as rent or interest.

Notes payable: a liability documented by a written promise to pay at a specified time.

Note receivable: an asset documented by a written promise from the borrower to pay it.

Objectivity: a principle of accounting requiring all business transactions to be documented in writing.

Obligation: see *Debt.*

Occupancy percentage: the ratio of rooms occupied to rooms available expressed in percentage terms.

Operating budget: a budget concerned with sales revenue and/or expenses.

Operating cost: see *Expense.*

Operating department: a department concerned with a particular segment of a business such as rooms or food.

Operating leverage: the relationship between fixed and variable expenses; high fixed expenses compared to variable expenses indicate high operating leverage.

Operating ratios: key business ratios (such as restaurant seat turnover and guest room occupancy percentage) that are often calculated daily.

Opportunity cost: the cost of not doing something. If a company does not invest surplus cash, the interest income not gained by this is the opportunity cost.

Organization chart: a document showing levels of responsibility and authority, and lines of communication for an establishment.

Outstanding check: a check issued in payment of a debt that has not yet been cashed by the payee or that has been cashed in but has not yet been deducted from the payer's bank account.

Owners' equity: total assets minus total liabilities; net worth.

Partnership: an unincorporated business owned by two or more persons.

Payback period: the time it takes to recover an investment; initial investment divided by net annual cash saving.

Periodic inventory: a method of inventory control where the quantity of each item in stock is not known until an actual physical count of storeroom quantities is taken, usually at each month-end.

Periodicity: an accounting principle that states that the operating results of a business should be monitored by preparing financial statements for periods of time.

Perpetual inventory: a method of inventory control where a continuous record is maintained for each item in stock on a perpetual inventory card of items received and items issued and a running balance of the quantity of each item in stock is constantly updated.

Perpetual inventory card: a form that is used to record the movement of all items in and out of storage rooms. One card is used for each item.

Petty cash: a fund of money controlled by an individual from which minor purchases of goods or services can be paid.

Physical inventory: the actual counting, recording, and pricing of assets.

Posting: recording of business transactions in accounts, or from journals to accounts.

Preferred stock or shares: a form of stock or share issued by a company to raise money, generally ranking before common stock with reference to dividends.

Prepaid expense: an expense paid for and shown as an asset until it is matched up with related sales revenue and shown as an expense. See *Matching*.

Present value: see *Discounted cash flow*.

Price earnings ratio: for a company whose shares are publicly traded, market price per share divided by earnings per share.

Price variance: difference between budgeted price and actual price.

Product differentiation: a method of presenting a product or service in a different way from competitors, for example by creating a unique ambience or providing superior service.

Profit: see *Net income*.

Profit and loss statement: see *Income statement*.

Profit center: a department (such as the rooms department) that generates sales revenue.

Profit margin: see *Net income to revenue ratio*.

Profit to sales ratio: see *Net income to revenue ratio*.

Profitability: the net income of a company related to the value of its assets, to the owners' equity, and to sales revenue.

Profitability ratios: ratios that measure profitability such as return on assets, return on investment, and net income to sales revenue.

Pro forma: forecast or tentative figures; a budgeted income statement is a pro forma statement.

Proprietorship: an unincorporated business owned by a single individual.

Prorate: to allocate an amount on a logical basis; for example, to allocate overall company rent expenses to the operating departments on a basis of square footage occupied by each department.

Purchase order: a form prepared by the purchasing department authorizing a supplier to deliver needed goods and services to the establishment.

Purchase requisition: a form, usually prepared by a department head, requesting the purchasing department to buy required goods or services. See also *Requisition*.

Purchasing department: the department responsible for ensuring that supplies, equipment, and services are available to the establishment as required.

Quantity variance: the difference between budgeted and actual quantity.

Quick assets: cash and readily convertible securities and/or receivables.

Quick ratio: the ratio of quick assets to current liabilities.

Rack rate: the normal maximum rate charged for a hotel guest room.

Ratio: the relationship of one item to another. For example, $2,000 of current assets to $1,000 of current liabilities would be a 2:1 ratio.

Ratio analysis: the use of various ratios to monitor the ongoing progress of a business.

Receiving report: a form, completed daily, listing all goods received for the day.

Regression analysis: a statistical method that can be used in such areas as breaking down semifixed or semivariable expenses into their fixed and variable components and that can also be used in forecasting the sales revenue in one department (such as food) based on the sales revenue in another (such as rooms).

Relevant cost or expense: one that is important and to be considered in a particular business decision.

Replacement value: see *Market value.*

Requisition: a form, completed by an authorized person, requesting that needed items be issued from the storeroom.

Resort hotel: generally one that has extensive recreational facilities.

Responsibility accounting: a method of accounting in which department heads or managers are made responsible for the departmental profit achieved.

Retained earnings: accumulated net income less accumulated losses less any dividends paid since the business began.

Return on assets: income before interest and income tax divided by total average assets for the period.

Return on investment: net income after income tax divided by average owners' equity for the period.

Revenue: money earned from sales and/or income received in exchange for goods or services.

Revenue management: a flexible pricing policy for rooms that adjusts quickly to supply and demand, with the objective of selling all rooms at all times.

Revenue mix: the ratio of sales revenue among various departments in a multidepartment establishment. See also *Sales mix.*

Revenue per available room (REVPAR): calculated by dividing total room revenue by available rooms or by multiplying occupancy percentage by average room rate.

Room rate: the price charged for a guest room in a hotel or motel.

Room rate ratio: a hotel's actual average room rate for a period of time expressed as a percentage of the potential or maximum average room rate.

Sales: see *Revenue.*

Sales check: a document used in food and/or beverage operations to record the sales of goods.

Sales mix: the ratio of what people select from various menu items offered. See also *Revenue mix.*

Scrap value: see *Trade-in value.*

Seat turnover: number of seats available in a food and/or beverage operation divided into the number of seats used or occupied during a particular period.

Semifixed or semivariable cost or expense: one that has both fixed and variable elements and is neither entirely fixed nor entirely variable in relation to sales.

Share: see *Common stock* and *Preferred stock.*

Short-term budget: a budget prepared for a period of time generally less than a year.

Skip: a person who has consumed goods or services in an establishment and has left without paying the bill.

Social goals: goals that are generally nonfinancial in nature but that may have an effect, positive or negative, on financial results.

Solvency: the ability of a company to meet its debts as they become due.

Standard cost or expense: what the cost should be for a particular level of sales or revenue.

Statement of business purpose: see *Mission statement.*

Statement of cash flows: a financial statement, produced at least annually, that uses the income statement, beginning and end of the year balance sheets, the statement of retained earnings, and other information to show all sources and uses of cash for the year.

Statement of changes in working capital: a statement showing in dollars the amount of change from one period to the next in each individual current asset and current liability account.

Statement of retained earnings: a statement showing previous balance sheet figures, plus net income for the period, less any dividends paid during the period, to arrive at current period-end retained earnings.

Statement of source and use of working capital: a statement showing previous period working capital balance plus funds received during the period (sources) less funds paid out during the period (uses) to arrive at current period-end working capital.

Stock: see *Common stock* and *Preferred stock*.

Stockholder: an investor who owns shares in a company by way of common and/or preferred stock.

Stockholders' equity: see *Owners' equity*.

Stock redemption: the purchase by a company of shares that it had originally sold to investors or stockholders.

Straight-line depreciation: a method of depreciation whereby equal portions of the amount paid for an asset are shown as an expense during each accounting period of the life of the asset.

Strategic budget: a long-term budget for periods of time generally in excess of one year.

Sum-of-the-years-digits depreciation: a method of accelerated depreciation that allocates larger amounts of depreciation as an expense during the earlier years of the life of an asset.

Sunk cost or expense: a cost incurred that is no longer relevant and cannot affect any future decisions.

"T" account: a simplified form of account in the shape of a T, with account title on top, debit on the left, and credit on the right.

Trade-in value: the scrap or cash value of an asset at the time its useful life is over or when it is exchanged with cash for a new asset.

Transaction: a business event requiring an entry in the accounting records.

Trend index: in a series of periods of operating results, the result for the first (base) period is given the value of one hundred. Subsequent period results are then given a number higher or lower than one hundred to better reflect each period's change relative to the base year.

Trend results: business operating results compared for a number of sequential periods.

Trial balance: a totaling of all debit balances and credit balances in accounts to ensure that total debits equal total credits.

Turnover ratios: ratios that measure the activity of an asset during an accounting period, such as inventory turnover.

Undistributed operating cost or expense: one that is not normally controlled by or the responsibility of an operating department. See also *Direct cost* and *Fixed charges*.

Uniform system of accounts: a method of presenting financial statement information so that comparison is made easier between establishments or with hospitality industry averages.

Units of production depreciation: method of depreciation basing expense on number of units used or produced by the asset during an accounting period to total estimated units to be used or produced during the life of the asset.

Variable budget: see *Flexible budget*.

Variable cost or expense: one that increases or decreases in direct, or linear, fashion with increases or decreases in related sales or revenue.

Variance analysis: a method of comparing budgeted figures with actual results breaking differences down into quantity variance and price or cost variance.

Volume: level of sales expressed in dollars or units.

Voucher: a document supporting a business transaction

Voucher system: a method of preparing special documents (vouchers) to support each purchase transaction to help control disbursements.

Weighted average inventory cost: a method of inventory costing where the average cost of each item in stock is recalculated each time more of that item is purchased and received.

Window dressing: a method of adjusting current asset and current liability accounts to improve the current ratio.

Withdrawals: monies taken out of a business by individual owners in a proprietorship or partnership (similar to dividends in an incorporated company).

Working capital: current assets less current liabilities.

Working capital management: see *Cash management*.

Working capital turnover: sales revenue divided by average working capital for the period.

Working papers: informal accounting records prepared as an aid to completion of the formal accounting records.

Yield management: a method in a hotel of matching customers' rooms purchase patterns and their demand for rooms to derive more precise occupancy forecasts and develop appropriate room rates to maximize revenue.

Yield statistics: actual total room revenue for a period of time divided by potential sales revenue for that period and multiplied by 100.

Zero-based budgeting: a method of budgeting that starts from a zero base and requires budget managers to justify each element of the present budget as well as any requested additions to it. See also *Incremental budgeting*.

Index